MOLECULAR
BIOLOGY
OF
AGING

BASIC LIFE SCIENCES

Alexander Hollaender, General Editor

Council for Research Planning in Biological Sciences, Inc., Washington, D.C.

A Continuation Order Plan is available for this series. A continuation order will bring delivery of each new volume immediately upon publication. Volumes are billed only upon actual shipment. For further information please contact the publisher.

MOLECULAR
BIOLOGY
OF
AGING

Edited by
AVRIL D. WOODHEAD
Brookhaven National Laboratory
Upton, New York

ANTHONY D. BLACKETT
University of Manchester Institute of Science and Technology
Manchester, United Kingdom

and

ALEXANDER HOLLAENDER
Council for Research Planning in Biological Sciences, Inc.
Washington,D.C.

PLENUM PRESS • NEW YORK AND LONDON

Library of Congress Cataloging in Publication Data

Symposium on Molecular Basis of Aging (1984: Brookhaven National Laboratory)
  Molecular biology of aging.

  (Basic life sciences; v. 35)
    1. Aging—Physiological aspects—Congresses. 2. Molecular biology—Congresses. I.
Woodhead, Avril, D. II. Blackett, A. D. (Anthony D.) III. Hollaender, Alexander, date. IV. Ti-
tle. V. Series.
QP86.S86 1984   599′.0372   85-16978
ISBN 0-306-42084-8

Proceedings of a symposium on Molecular Basis of Aging,
held September 30–October 3, 1984, at Brookhaven National Laboratory,
Upton, New York

© 1985 Plenum Press, New York
A Division of Plenum Publishing Corporation
233 Spring Street, New York, N.Y. 10013

Printed in the United States of America

DEDICATION: TO DR. ALEX COMFORT

   Scientific fields are often founded in the morass of speculation and conjecture surrounding a topic of interest. Only after a
great deal of effort, largely unproductive, is sufficient factual
material gleaned and packed down to form a firm foundation for
future endeavors. Subsequent work of a more specialized nature
must always rest heavily on these foundations, but as information
accumulates and the depth of understanding increases, so the
structure becomes more stable and takes on a tangible form.

   Such an evolutionary process has been taking place in gerontology
over recent years. From ill-conceived and ill-received speculation
has grown an increasingly respected area of hard science. For the first
time we are now in the position of being able to reach down through
higher organizational levels to grasp at the Molecular Basis of Aging.
Recent developments in molecular biology, complementing more established biochemical techniques, are on the verge of opening up gerontology at this most fundamental level. As a result we can expect an
explosion both of interest and of understanding.

   Whilst current work is fascinating and the future potential in-
triguing, we must not lose sight of the foundations upon which modern
gerontology is built. Men of vision labored against pervasive skep-
ticism to provide us with our current research possibilities. Their
inspiration won the day then, and they remain our inspiration now.

   Of these founding fathers, none did more to establish the
respectability of our field than did Alex Comfort. His breadth of
interest, combining caring geriatrics with incisive research, was
instrumental in establishing gerontology as legitimate in the eyes
of the wider scientific community. It is appropriate that now we
are on the point of glimpsing the Promised Land, we should remember
those who showed us the way.

   We therefore take great pleasure in dedicating this volume to
Alex Comfort.

                                        Anthony D. Blackett

Alex Comfort

FOREWORD

It is delightful but humbling to find my face at the start of these Proceedings--there are innumerable other faces which could equally well stand there, from among the band who have fore-gathered at every gerontology conference since the subject was launched in its present form; but I deeply appreciate being there.

Gerontology did not grow by accident. Its present standing is the fruit of careful planning, undertaken by European and American scientists back in the 1950's. In those days it was still a "fringe" science, and the conspirators had much the standing of the 1920's Interplanetary Society. The United States itself is the offspring of conspiracy, for when the results of conspiracy are beneficent, the conspirators become Founding Fathers. This has been the case with gerontology. The present meeting is especially gratifying because the papers have been recitals of normal, hard-science investigation. We had to get through the rigors of a long period of semantic argument and a long period of one-shot general theories before this kind of meeting, normal in all other research fields, could take place. It was also necesssary to breed in the menagerie a generation of excellent investigators aware of the theoretical background but unintimidated by it, who share our conviction that human aging is comprehensible and probably controllable, and who go into the laboratory to attack specifics. One can trace this process back to the annual National Institute of Child Health and Human Development seminars of the early '70's, which have borne rich fruit, and for which we should be grateful to Leroy Duncan, Jr., and many others. We had to write gerontological questions into the agenda of the areas - molecular and radiobiology, chemical genetics, electron microscopy - where the hi-tech resources are concentrated.

Gerontology is not a technology subject, however, and did not have its Hahn-Strassmann point in a particular observation--but rather in the arrival of psychological readiness among researchers to tackle the aging problem. If the early stages with their simplistic models which required demolition were tedious, the prospects, now that it is out of the way, seem excellent for progress.

A lot is going for us. The early gerontological evangelists targeted America because of its technical and manpower resources and the openness of its science, but throughout--since nobody is politically threatened by gerontology, and it cannot be fired at anyone or dropped on them, international exchange has been exemplary. What we now have incorporates European and American researches, Soviet experimental physiology, and multiple observations from every country which has one or more people in the field. I do not recall the original conspirators running into any political or national obstacles, even when gerontology and radiobiology briefly crossed paths and radiobiology was a sensitive issue. The same holds true today.

Jobbing backwards, we could have done better--we have been contemplating key findings, such as the dietary restriction experiments of McCay, for nearly half a century without making a fundamental effort to elucidate them, and history may blame us for it (one could have run a human or a primate series in the time which has been wasted). Probably research, like psychotherapy, has a top speed at which it can move. New topics, too, come on the agenda: Alzheimer's disease is not an "aging process", and the realization that it is not constitutes a breakthrough in itself, but the problem is so urgent, and the human consequences of the condition so serious, that it merits intensive special effort. This is welcome in any case because it bridges the gap between gerontology and geriatrics. At the fundamental level, gerontological immunology is about to go clinical. In the long run, since gerontology is a special purpose science, aimed at one problem, a task-force subject, it should blend into general medicine and biology and vanish. When aging is elucidated the task force can rejoin its regiments. By the same token, the last edition of the textbook of biological gerontology should be of pamphlet size.

That objective, of course, is some ways off. We often miss the fact that science forecasting tends to overrate the ten-year but underrate the twenty-year prospects. In that event, the growth of a subject, diligently pursued by competent teams, is ideally exponential--one can be over-depressed by the initial low slope of the curve. How rapidly it will become precipitous depends on the doubling time. The quality of this symposium is a good augury, however. If I am to preface it, I see considerable hope that I and my fellow conspirators still present in force may share the experience of Simeon rather than of Moses.

Alex Comfort M.D., D.Sc.

PREFACE

Aging research has long been characterized by plethora of theories and a dearth of experimental data. The situation is now changing, and one reassuring sign has been the enthusiastic incursion of molecular biologists into aging research. Their findings have augmented some long-standing theories of aging and challenged others. The Brookhaven Symposium in Biology, Number 33, brought together investigators working at molecular and cellular levels with clinicians and with researchers working with aging animals. Our interchanges highlighted the exciting progress that is being made and identified gaps in our knowledge that must be filled before the practical applications of our researchers follow.

The Committee wishes to express its appreciation to the sponsors of the Symposium. We were particularly pleased to have the financial support that enabled young scientists to participate in this symposium. Our thanks to: National Institute on Aging; U.S. Department of Energy; The Procter and Gamble Company; Estée Lauder, Inc.; American Cyanamid Company; American Federation for Aging Research; Associated Universities, Inc.; The Hartford Group of Insurance Companies; and Squibb Corporation.

It is a pleasure to acknowledge the tremendous efforts of Ms. Helen Kondratuk, the Symposium coordinator, who assured the success of our meeting. Changes in the typescript, often from the obscure notes of the editors, were made by Ms. Kathy Kissel, Ms. Gloria Jackson and Ms. Nancy Siemon, whose help we gratefully acknowledge.

Finally, we would like to thank all our Symposium speakers and chairpersons for their participation. We would especially

like to thank Drs. Edward Schneider, Alex Comfort and Lewis
Thomas, who graciously agreed to present their lectures to a public audience and further allowed us to videotape these presentations so that their talks would be available to our senior citizens.

Symposium Committee:

A.D. Woodhead, Chairperson
A.D. Blackett
R.B. Setlow
L. Sokoloff
B.M. Sutherland
R.R. Tice

H.Z. Kondratuk, Coordinator

CONTENTS

AGING IN CELLULAR PROTEINS

SYMPOSIUM LECTURE – II

CHANGES IN DNA WITH AGE – I

CHANGES IN DNA WITH AGE - II

SYMPOSIUM LECTURE - III

DISEASES FEATURING ALTERED RATES OF AGING

FUTURE DIRECTIONS IN AGING RESEARCH

Rapporteurs:

AGING RESEARCH: CHALLENGE OF THE TWENTY-FIRST CENTURY

E.L. Schneider

National Institute on Aging, NIH
9000 Rockville Pike
Bethesda, Maryland 20205

Despite the fact that people have been investigating aging for
thousands of years, only in the last decade or two has the research
effort intensified. Substantial funding for aging research has been
made available only in the last five to ten years.

Aging has become a very popular issue. Why has there been
such intense interest recently in aging research? This has partially been the result of a demographic revolution. At the turn of
the century, in the year 1900, there were three million Americans
aged 65 or above. Today in 1984, there are 27 million Americans
over the age of 65, or 11 percent of the population. If current
trends continue, by the year 2030, as many as 50 or even 65 million
Americans will be age 65 or older, between 15 and 20 percent of the
population. These are projections for the next century, and their
accuracy remains to be determined.

Are these trends going to continue? This year, on the average, a male at birth can expect to live 72 years and a female, 78
years. This is an enormous increase since the turn of the century
when average life expectancy at birth was only 45 years. There are
several views on what will happen to life expectancy in the next
century. To predict what will happen, it is essential to examine
what has happened to survival since 1900. Why are we now living
longer than in 1900? In 1900, there was substantial infant mortality, and many people died in their first years of life. Many individuals died in the middle years of life from fatal infectious diseases. In 1980, few individuals die in the first years of life or
in the middle years of life. This has resulted in a rectangularization of the survival curves. It has been suggested that there is
a biological limit of approximately 85 years to the lifespan, and

1

that, as we live longer and longer, we come up against this barrier. Furthermore, it has been proposed that if we wipe out most
of the diseases that afflict people today, we will die of natural
causes (of natural aging), and that most deaths will be compressed
into a short period of time around age 85. Unfortunately, it is
unlikely that this wonderful dream will occur in the near future.
A careful review of actuarial data on mortality reveals a very different perspective. If you look at the survival of an individual
cohort—for example, a group born in 1860 or 1870, 1890, or 1910—
you do see some trend towards rectangularization, but the survival
curves have long tails, suggesting derectangularization in the last
decades of life. If you look at death rates, they decline at all
ages, not just in the 50s, 60s and 70s but also in the 80s and 90s.

People are living longer at all ages. That is one component
of the health care equation. The most important component is the
health status of those living into their 70s, 80s and 90s. I am
sure no one wants longer life if it is accompanied by disease. How
can we find out what has happened to the quality of health in the
last decades of life? To understand whether we are changing our
spectrum of health with aging, we need to compare a medical snap-
shot taken 20 years ago and another today. This comparison is very
difficult since medical technology has changed enormously in the
last 20 years. However, we can approach this problem by examining
health surveys. Health surveys conducted in 1969 and in 1979 which
examine limitations of major activities due to arthritis, heart
conditions, hypertension, back problems, hip problems and knee
problems reveal no significant difference in the group aged 65 and
above. People appear to be as healthy (or just as ill) over this
10-year period. Therefore, while we are living longer at each age,
there appears to be the same burden of disease and disability. To
meet the challenge of increasing numbers of older Americans, we
must attempt to improve health through research on aging and age-
related diseases.

I am most concerned about the group 85 and above. All too
often, the elderly in this country are described as those ages 65
and above. There is an enormous difference between people in their
60s and people in their 80s. Individuals in their 60s comprise a
relatively healthy group. The diseases of aging have their greatest impact in the 70s and 80s. The group aged 85 and above is the
most rapidly growing group in America. While there are only two
million Americans currently in this group, by the year 2050, there
will be close to sixteen million Americans in this age cohort. The
age group 85 and older have the largest requirements for long-term
care. While they represent only eight-tenths of one percent of the
population, they occupy 21 percent of nursing home beds. For every
individual in a nursing home in this country, there is one at home
who is equally ill, has equal health care needs, but has support
mechanisms and social networks able to take care of them.

Why do we age? What is the nature of aging processes? There are two types of aging theories: stochastic theories based on the accumulation of random events and nonstochastic theories or programmed theories of aging. The error-catastrophe theory is one of the simpler stochastic theories of aging. Dr. Leslie Orgel proposed that during aging, we accumulate errors in transcription and translation resulting in the production of defective proteins. Since some of these proteins may be the enzymes involved in translation and transcription, further errors would accumulate until an "error catastrophe" occurs. When sufficient abnormal proteins are produced, vital cell populations would be affected and aging would ensue. The theory has been tested by a number of researchers, and most of the evidence indicates that defective proteins do not accumulate with aging.

A second theory involves DNA repair. The genetic material is continually exposed to many different types of damage. Fortunately, there are many enzymes that can repair DNA damage. Proponents of a DNA damage theory suggest that these repair enzymes are not totally efficient and that DNA damage accumulates to the point that cell function becomes impaired. The importance of DNA repair in aging is supported by the work of Drs. Richard Setlow and Ronald Hart, who showed that the ability of an animal to repair its DNA was proportional to its lifespan. In a comparative study involving various organisms with different lifespans, they showed that humans were the most efficient organism in repairing DNA and mice, with only a two-year lifespan, were the least efficient.

Another theory of aging is the programmed theory of aging. One of the principal proponents of that theory, Dr. Leonard Hayflick, demonstrated that human cells in tissue culture had finite replicative abilities, that they had a programmed limit. How do cells express this programmed limit to replication? Recently, there has been some exciting insight offered by Drs. James and Olivia Smith. They have created hybrids of young and old cells as well as the obvious controls: young-young and old-old. As would be expected, if you hybridize a young cell with a young cell, it will divide like a young cell--forty or fifty times. The hybrid formed from an old cell with an old cell will divide only four or five times. However, when a young cell was hybridized to an old cell, it behaved like an old/old hybrid. The old cell was suppressing the program in the young cell.

Malignant cells, in contrast to non-malignant cells, will divide forever; they are immortal. Thus the alternative to senescence is malignancy; cells have a choice of two pathways, one of aging, the other, malignancy. When a malignant cell was hybridized to an old cell, the resultant cell had a finite lifespan (that is, it underwent a limited number of replications) that was similar to that of the old cell. A young cell fused to a malignant cell behaved like a young/young hybrid. Therefore, there appears to be a factor made by the old cell which suppresses the replication capabilities of both the young cell and the malignant cell. The Drs. Smith propose that this factor is a protein, a senescence factor.

Now let's consider the whole organism. Some functions decline with aging while others do not. It is very important to separate those functions that decline due to the normal aging process from those due to treatable diseases. All too often, when a patient is in the seventies, eighties and nineties, a doctor will dismiss the symptoms as reflecting old age. What does decline with aging and what does not? An example of a well-known age-related decline is visual acuity. As you grow older, your ability to read the letters on a Snellen chart declines. Other visual and auditory tests also show significant declines with aging. But there are important diseases of the eyes, such as glaucoma and cataracts, which are treatable and reversible and which must be separated from the normal decline with aging.

The relationship between aging and exercise cardiac output demonstrates that one must separate aging from diseases to examine what functions are affected by aging. It was thought that all cardiac functions decline with aging. However, Dr. Edward Lakatta has reexamined exercise cardiac output, eliminating from the patient population those individuals with significant coronary artery disease and found that there is no change with aging. The changes that were previously reported to occur with aging were most likely due to the presence of individuals in the older age groups with arteriosclerosis, the most common, age-dependent disease.

A myth that is frequently reiterated is that we experience generalized intellectual declines with aging. We retire people at 60, 65 and other older ages because we believe they can no longer function intellectually. If at 65, you play Pac-man with your teenage grandson, you will lose, because eye-hand coordination does decline with advancing age. But many important intellectual abilities do not change significantly with aging. This has been demonstrated with PET (Positron Emission Tomography), a very exciting technique that was first pioneered at Brookhaven. With PET scanning, we can examine the effect of aging on glucose metabolism, which represents brain activity. Dr. Stanley Rapoport of the National Institute on Aging examined normal subjects, aged 21-83, and found no significant change with aging.

Let us now turn our attention to the diseases of aging. In 1900, the top three "killers" were pneumonia, tuberculosis, infectious diarrhea. Today, the top three are heart diseases, strokes and cancer. I believe that the top three in the year 2060 will be significantly different. For the last 40 years, we have seen a steady decline in deaths from heart disease and stroke. We are turning the tide on cancer; as many people now are cured as die from cancer. So what will be the top three killers of the 21st century? There is only one that I am sure of, Alzheimer's disease--unless we develop successful interventions. Alzheimer's disease is a terrible, tragic condition that strikes two to three million Americans. To many of them, it is far more malignant than many cancers, often with a five- to ten-year downhill course of intellectual deterioration, until finally the person needs total care. Today the estimated cost of Alzheimer's disease in America is $30 billion, an enormous figure for any one disease. If death certificates were filled out properly, Alzheimer's would rank as killer No. 4 today.

What are we doing about Alzheimer's disease? Five years ago, the situation was dismal. With two million afflicted people, there was less than $5 million spent per year on research on Alzheimer's disease. Today, there is approximately $50 million spent on research. The National Institute on Aging has funded five national Alzheimer's Centers to coordinate research on this disease.

One of the problems with Alzheimer's disease is the difficulty of making the diagnosis during life; it is a diagnosis by exclusion. Ten years ago, Alzheimer's disease was thought to be a rare disorder and senile dementia was thought to be a normal part of the aging process. Alzheimer's disease is now known to be a common disease with a specific pathology, not a normal part of aging. Our emphasis is on developing new ways of diagnosing Alzheimer's disease during life. One approach is by PET scans. With PET scans, Dr. Stanley Rapoport has found that there is an obvious decrease in generalized brain activity reflected by decreased glucose metabolism during the course of Alzheimer's disease.

What clues do we have to the nature of Alzheimer's disease? There is increasing evidence that the levels of certain neurotransmitters are decreased in the brains of Alzheimer's patients. This presents the possibility that, if we can find out which neurotransmitters are missing, we might formulate an effective therapy. An example of such an approach occurred here at Brookhaven in the 1960s, when Dr. George Cotzias found a decrease in dopamine in the substantia nigra in patients with Parkinson's disease. He was then able to administer the precursor to dopamine, L-DOPA. This therapy has been quite successful; it has not cured Parkinson's disease, but certainly has made the course of the disease less tragic. We are hoping that the same sort of approach eventually will occur in Alzheimer's disease, but the path is more difficult because the lesions of Alzheimer's disease are more diffuse, and moreover, several neurotransmitters appear to be involved.

Another important area is the increased susceptibility of the elderly to infectious diseases. Among the chief killers of older

Americans are pneumonia and influenza. Today, we have witnessed a
spectacular drop in deaths from infectious diseases in infancy and
in middle life thanks to the use of antibiotics. However, over the
age of 65, we have not observed as dramatic a change. We need to
learn more about why we become more susceptible to specific infectious diseases as we grow older. We cannot just accept influenza
and pneumonia as killers. Many older people do not take advantage
of the effective influenza vaccine. Only twenty percent of people
over the age of 65 are vaccinated. We must persuade more individuals who are susceptible to infectious diseases like influenza to
take appropriate vaccines.

I want to emphasize that we can no longer accept the diseases
of old age as inevitable. The diseases of old age are diseases and
must be treated as such, and vigorous attempts must be made to find
out the nature of these diseases so that we can come up with effective preventive strategies. One condition that is extremely tragic
is the hip fractures that occur in individuals in their fifties,
sixties, seventies and eighties, particularly in older women. It
is estimated that there are 200,000 hip fractures a year, and if a
functioning older woman enters a nursing home with a hip fracture,
her chances of leaving that nursing home are one in two. The incidence and prevalence of hip fractures are related to the loss of
bone with aging, osteoporosis. This condition may be delayed by
therapy with estrogen, calcium and vitamin D.

What about the stories that we hear about enclaves of longevity in Russia, in Ecuador, in Pakistan, where individuals are
purported to live to 140 or 150? Their reputation for longevity
appears to be based on several factors: hard work, simple food,
lack of stress and, most importantly, the inability to count correctly! Careful examination of these groups has revealed the importance of this last factor. In Russia, in World War I, there was
universal conscription; that is, everyone aged 18 to 65 was eligi-
ble for the draft. So, many individuals rapidly aged. They are
now supposedly in their 110s, 120s, 130s. A research team went to
a village in Ecuador where people were supposed to live to be 130
and 140 on two consecutive years and found a very interesting phenomenon. Some individuals had four, five and even six birthdays,
so that in consecutive years, they were 103 and then 107 or 108.
Therefore, there are no special people, no Shangri-La for aging.

There have been many books advising readers to consume a number of vitamins, nutrients and minerals to live longer. The state
of the art in gerontologic research has not yet revealed sufficient
evidence for any nutritional supplements, except perhaps calcium
and vitamin D to prevent osteoporosis. Before taking large
amounts of various minerals, nutrients, and other dietary supplements, you are advised to consult your physician since there is the
potential of toxicity from some of these products.

While I have not discussed social or behavioral factors related to aging, they clearly are important and need attention. In his book, George Burns suggests that you can never live to be 100 if you stop living at 65. One of the prelavent myths we have is that as people grow older, they become crotchety. In fact, personality is quite stable during life, and if you are crotchety when you are old, you undoubtedly were crotchety when you were young. Alex Comfort, the emminent gerontologist and great expert in this field, will be discussing sexuality in another chapter. I would only comment that the myth that older people lose their sexual functioning simply is not true. Evidence suggests, at least for men, that if you function well in your 20s, you will function well in your 60s, and 70s and 80s.

In summary, aging research is a new and energetic discipline. We have some exciting clues into the nature of aging, and we are beginning to obtain an understanding of the nature of age-dependent diseases. Undoubtedly, this research will significantly impact on the health and welfare of older Americans, today and tomorrow.

DISCUSSION

Question: From your projection based upon more recent epidemiological data, what do you think is going to happen to the maximum lifespan?

Schneider: I can tell you what is going to happen to average longevity if present trends continue. In the 21st century, women on the average will live into their nineties and men into the late eighties. It is more difficult to speculate about maximum lifespan; that is a hard question because it is so difficult to document. We have one or two individuals who have reached 114 or 115 so we are able to estimate maximum lifespan. But I think that it is going to be difficult to broach that maximum unless we have a major breakthrough in our understanding of aging.

Question: Has the arterial bypass made any inroads in regards to longevity?

Schneider: Everyone in the heart field wants to claim responsibility for this tremendous drop in number of deaths due to heart disease and to heart attacks. The cardiac surgeons, of course, will claim it is due to the bypass surgery; the cardiologists will say it is the result of intensive care units; the preventive health people will talk about the changes in diet, such as giving up high cholesterol and polysaturated fat foods; the physiotherapists will tell you that it is because more people are jogging, running and exercizing. But the interesting thing is that this drop in deaths from heart attacks and strokes started before any of these proce-

dures were introduced, and so the bottom line is that we really do
not know the cause. We really do not know how much all of these
factors have contributed to the reduction of heart conditions, if
at all.

Question: My grandmother died about 14 years ago at the age
of 72. She was senile for about 11 of her last years. Are there
other causes of dementia besides Alzheimer's?

Schneider: This is a very important question because until
five or ten years ago people like your grandmother were dismissed
as being senile. Senility is a constellation of symptoms: disori-
entation, confusion, loss of memory, and many things are happening
at once. These individuals should be brought to the attention of
physicians because, first of all, there are treatable, reversible
conditions that may cause this apparent dementia. There are neurological diseases that are treatable and curable (for example, there
is a vitamin deficiency that can cause dementia). Once you remove
the treatable and curable diseases, then there are two main causes
of dementia: one is due to very small strokes, but the other and
more common type--probably fifty or even sixty percent of what we
call senility--is Alzheimer's disease.

Question: Would you say something about teaching nursing
homes?

Schneider: As I indicated tonight, there has been a dramatic
shift in this country from acute diseases to chronic diseases;
acute diseases are those ailments brought on by infections that
strike you down for a week or so, and the chronic diseases are the
ones that persist such as heart disease, Alzheimer's disease, and
arthritis. This shift has not been accompanied by a shift in the
attention of our health professional schools, so that, until about
a year ago, the vast majority of medical and nursing students never
set foot in a nursing home despite the fact that there are now more
nursing home beds than there are hospital beds. Today, hospitals
are changing; a lot of them now have "swing floors" that can become
chronic disease floors, almost nursing home floors. Yet the medical community is not responding to this change. The National Institute on Aging launched the Teaching Nursing Home Initiative to
stimulate medical and other health professional schools to pay
attention to the problems of nursing homes and to bring their edu-
cational and research talents to the problems of long-term care.
For example, one of the reasons Alzheimer's disease did not attract
very much attention was that it was located in the nursing homes.
At present, almost forty to fifty percent of nursing home beds are
occupied by patients with Alzheimer's disease. We set up a program
where medical schools and nursing schools across the country could
go into nursing homes and other long-term care settings to conduct
teaching and research programs. We now have seven National Teach-

ing Nursing Home Centers, but, even more encouraging, thirty institutions applied. Now 75 other places across the country have followed that lead, and have affiliations with nursing homes. Three years ago, there were maybe a handful. One of the pioneer teaching nursing homes in the United States is here on Long Island. Its program was pioneered by Leslie Lebau at the Long Island Jewish Chronic Disease Hospital, where he established a teaching program located in a chronic disease hospital setting.

Question: Could you give us an update as to the status of thymosin as it relates to chronic debilitative diseases and the immune system?

Schneider: I will give you my unqualified view (because I am not an immunologist). We have just finished a five-year study in which we administered to mice a number of thymic hormones. With aging, there is a decline in the immune system which is the system in the body that combats external agents like bacteria and viruses, and abnormal cells such as cancer cells. When the system goes astray, a variety of diseases can occur. With aging, immune system function declines and the thymus gland, which plays a major role in the immune response, almost disappears in old age. So our thought was that maybe we could inject the crucial secretions of the thymus gland called thymic hormones (one of which is thymosin) and thereby restore immune function. This kind of approach is one that I like as I do not accept all aging phenomenon as inevitable. The first attempt has just been concluded in which we gave animals a variety of thymic hormones over a five-year period to see if these animals would show rejuvenation or stimulation of their immune system. The results are negative, but that does not mean that administering hormones will not work. Rather, it means that our knowledge of thymic hormones may be too primitive to know exactly which factors are involved in the aging process. I think this experiment should be repeated in a few years when we know more about thymic hormones and thymic factors.

Question: Is there a relationship between aging and diabetes?

Schneider: Absolutely. The National Institute on Aging has a Gerontology Research Center in Baltimore where we examined healthy, normal individuals over a period of years and gained some very good insight into the question of diabetes. With aging, our response to glucose changes significantly. So if you give the same glucose tolerance test to a 15- to 20-year-old and an 85-year-old, what might be abnormal for a 20-year-old may be normal for an 80-year-old. This whole subject is very important to me because some 20 years ago, this problem of diabetes and old age launched me on my career of aging research. What happened was that my grandmother went to see a physician who gave her a glucose tolerance test and reported that she was diabetic. He started treatment for this condition by prescribing some very strong drugs. But fortunately, before she took them, she called me up at medical school and I talked with some of my teachers about her problem. The result was that I learned that the ability to metabolize glucose changes significantly with aging. She was advised to dump the medicine and she lived to the ripe old age of 89, which she might not have done if she had taken that medicine. So it is very clear that the results of tests for diabetes in an older individual compared with those in a young individual differ greatly. However, your chance of developing diabetes does increase as you grow older so it is very important that the diagnosis be made correctly, and it should be based, most of all, on the fasting level of sugar in your blood--that is the key criterion.

Question: Some years ago, there was a lot of publicity given to research that seemed to show that undernourished mice were longer lived. There are a lot of people who are malnourished in the world today. Is there any evidence that this finding with mice applies to humans as well?

Schneider: There is a big difference between being undernourished and malnourished. In the experiments with mice and rats where calories were reduced by diminishing food intake, the animals were provided with minerals, vitamins and other supplements so that they were not malnourished, just undernourished. Although these experimental animals lived longer, I do not think we can make any comparisons since their conditions were quite different from those of individuals who have been through famines and who are malnourished. There is a one-man experiment going on today; Dr. Roy Walford, who is one of the great proponents of the dietary restriction theory, is eating only five days a week. However, he is also taking dietary supplements, so he is undernourished but not malnourished. Unfortunately, I do not think we will be able to cull conclusive data from a one-man experiment, but I do wish Roy well.

Question: A recent publication suggested that a characteristic of Alzheimer's patients was that they were unable to produce RNA. You did not mention this, and I wonder what the prospects for replacement therapy would be?

Schneider: I did not mention a lot of the promising leads because of the time factor; I could talk about Alzheimer's disease alone for an hour. But what you are asking about is some recent work that has come out of Dr. Charles Marotta's laboratory at the Massachusetts General Hospital. In the brains of patients with Alzheimer's disease, there is less messenger RNA and, therefore, less protein is being made. Marotta showed that this diminution is due to increased levels of an enzyme called ribonuclease that chews up RNA. The increased activity of ribonuclease is the result of a decrease in the level of its inhibitor. So it is a complex story, and the data are preliminary and have been shown, I think, in only five or six individuals. I think we need a lot more information before we can really confirm these findings. The reported changes in RNA levels may not be the cause of Alzheimer's disease but might be the result of Alzheimer's; it is very important to separate cause and effect.

INTRODUCTORY REMARKS, SESSION II

J. R. Totter

Institute for Energy Analysis
Oak Ridge Associated Universities
P. O. Box 117
Oak Ridge, TN 37831

This morning's topics are related to the "wear and tear" hypothesis of aging. The name most commonly associated with early studies involving this hypothesis is that of Max Rubner, who around the turn of the century published a book whose subject is the relationship of duration of life to growth and nourishment. The first two papers to be presented are concerned chiefly and rather directly with effects of oxygen which is considered by many to be the prime agent that produces much of the "wear and tear" in question through its univalent reduction which results in the production of free radicals.

My own introduction to what eventually became a strong interest in the subject of aging came about because of an early and long continued fascination with antioxidants, chain reactions and chemi- and bioluminescence. This interest was stimulated more than 50 years ago by progress in determining the function of vitamin E which was then being studied for its protective action against oxidative destruction of vitamin A and other nutrients. There were needs for cheap natural antioxidants at that time that could be used as food or drug additives. Similarly, the rubber industry was searching for natural products that would protect rubber products from deterioration owing to oxidation. At the same time there was a continuing interest in trying to understand the chemistry of the hardening of certain vegetable oils used in varnishes and paints as well as the autöoxidation of animal fats and oils, both in vivo and in vitro.

Each of the subjects mentioned have given rise to avenues of research the results of which have contributed something to our understanding of the processes involved in aging. More recently

13

the impetus to research on the effects of ionizing radiation given
by the discovery of fission and of artificially induced radioactivity has added a new dimension to research in this field.
Similarly, new methods of detection of free radicals, such as the
use of electron spin resonance developed from wartime radar,
appeared and have greatly stimulated work on these evanescent
compounds in tissue.

Progress in these various lines of research has, I believe,
reached the point at which it is possible to offer a rather
complete physiological explanation of the nature of the
interactions between metabolism, reproduction, temperature
maintenance and longevity. This hypothesis may be most succinctly
stated in ecological terms by making use of the concept of "r" and
"K" selection. "K" and "r" are parameters of the logistic equation
for population growth:

$$dN/dt = rN(K - N)/K$$

where N = the population number; K is the carrying capacity of the
environment and r the intrinsic rate of increase of the population.

Animals appear to respond to a reduction from an abundant to a
barely adequate food supply (if the temperature regime remains
unchanged) by switching from a population poised for "r" type
selection to one poised for "K" type selection. Small size, rapid
reproduction and short life are associated with "r" type animals
(good colonizers) while large size, slow reproduction and long life
are associated with "K" type animals (poor colonizers). The
switching may be accomplished by a neuroendocrine mechanism which
acts in part by changing the slope of the survival curve (hence the
longevity of the animals) and perhaps by changing the reproductive
rate and period.

The molecular basis of these changes are relevant to the
central subject of this symposium, and are by no means fully
understood. Advances in this aspect of aging will be detailed
throughout the next few days.

ANTIOXIDANTS AND LONGEVITY OF MAMMALIAN SPECIES

Richard G. Cutler

Gerontology Research Center
National Institute on Aging
Francis Scott Key Medical Center
Baltimore, Maryland 21224

INTRODUCTION

Humans have the longest maximum lifespan potential of any
mammalian species and also appear to consume more energy over
this lifespan on a per-weight basis than any other species
(Cutler, 1984a). These two unique biological characteristics of
humans are the result of an unusually slow aging rate.

Very little research has been undertaken towards obtaining an
understanding of the biological basis of human longevity. Today,
essentially nothing definite is known about the unique biological
characteristics of human biology that might explain why human aging
processes are so extraordinarily slow as compared to other
mammalian species. One reason why there has been so little interest
in studying the mechanisms governing aging rate is the general lack
of awareness that such an area of scientific inquiry even exists.
That is, a separation of those processes governing aging from those
processes governing longevity has received little recognition as a
theoretical possibility.

However, there is considerable data supporting the possibility
that the processes causing aging are indeed separate from those
determining aging rate. The review of some of this data is the
subject of this chapter, where evidence is presented supporting the
existence of longevity determinant mechanisms. The demonstration
of such longevity determinant mechanisms could play an important
role in identifying the genetic/biochemical basis of a number of
human hereditary diseases and age-related dysfunctions as well as to
offer new possibilities for their treatment.

15

Sacher was one of the first to extensively study the biological basis of species' differences in longevity (Sacher, 1959, 1965, 1970, 1977). His work emphasized the importance of homeostatic mechanisms; in this regard he stressed the importance of superior brain functions in longer-lived mammalian species (Sacher, 1962, 1968, 1978). More recently, Cutler has suggested that small biochemical differences, such as in protective and repair processes, might also play an important role in determining species differences in longevity (Cutler, 1972, 1974, 1975, 1976a,b, 1982a, 1984a).

Our research program on investigating the biological basis of human longevity is based on the Longevity Determinant Gene Hypothesis. For more details on this hypothesis, its supporting data and predictions, the reader is referred to the following papers (Cutler, 1972, 1974, 1975, 1976a,b, 1978, 1979, 1980a,b, 1981, 1982a,b,1983, 1984a,b,c,d). The key observations underlying this hypothesis are as follows:

1. A significant prolongation of the healthy years of human lifespan requires a uniform decrease of all aging processes of the organism. Reduction in the incidence of only a few specific diseases such as cardiovascular-renal disease, heart disease or cancer has a surprisingly small impact on increasing mean lifespan of the population (less than ten years) and even less impact on prolonging the healthy years of lifespan. Because a significant increase in the healthy years of lifespan appears only possible by decreasing the rate of aging uniformly, then one means that may help in achieving this objective is an investigation of the natural processes governing human longevity.

2. The vast complexity of the physiological aspects of aging makes progress in understanding the biological basis of human aging very difficult, particularly when we do not yet understand even the normal non-aging biological characteristics of the human. Moreover, a gain in knowledge limited only to how aging occurs could very well lead to little insight as to what actually can be done about aging or how effective methods of treatment of the elderly could be developed. In contrast to this long-time dilemma of aging research, a new argument has emerged suggesting that a study of the biological basis governing human longevity rather than human aging may involve considerably less complex biology and lead more directly to possible useful methods of intervention of the aging process.

3. Comparative and population genetic studies have indicated that the cause of aging is pleiotropic in nature, being the result of the side effects of normal metabolic and developmental processes. Aging does not appear to be the result of a genetic program that has

evolved specifically to generate this phenomena nor is aging the result of specific genes or death hormones that exist solely for this purpose. Instead, aging is the by-product of the living process and longevity differences among species appear to be the result of a separate genetic program that has evolved for this purpose. Thus, there are specific longevity determinant genes but not aging genes. Longevity determinants may operate by governing the level of defense, protective and DNA repair processes against the aging side effects of normal developmental and metabolic processes.

4. Comparative and evolutionary evidence indicate that the genetic processes governing the aging rate in different species appear to be remarkably less complex than the aging process itself. It has been estimated that perhaps less than 0.5% of the total number of genes in the genome may be involved if point mutations are the genetic mechanism of variation. These small genetic differences exist within the regulatory gene class. Moreover, the structural genes that actively govern aging rate (the longevity determinant genes) are likely to be similar in the different mammalian species. Thus, their longevity would be determined only by the extent these genes are expressed, not by the presence of new genes. These results imply the revolutionary concept that the genetic potential may already exist in humans to gain substantially more healthy and productive years of lifespan if the means could be devised to exploit this potential and that relatively few genetic alterations may be necessary to carry this out. It is important, however, to emphasize that if the evolution of differences in regulatory gene action occurs largely by translocation/recombination types of events instead of by point mutations, then we have yet no information as to what fraction of the genome (gene complexity) is involved in governing human longevity.

5. Comparative and population genetic studies indicate that aging is the result of the effects of development and energy metabolism. The aging effects of developmental processes appear difficult to counter and may have been dealt with by a simple decrease in developmental rate. Thus, the correlation we observe is aging rate with developmental rate. However, much more is known about the possible aging effects of energy metabolism and how evolutionary processes dealt with it. Here, it is found that, for most mammalian species, aging rate is proportional to metabolic rate. This finding led to the concept of Lifespan Energy Potential (LEP), which strongly suggests that oxygen radicals may play a role in causing aging. In turn, this result suggests that antioxidants may be important in determining the length of lifespan of different species. This possibility has been tested by comparing the concentrations of antioxidants in the tissues of mammalian species

as a function of their maximum lifespan potential (MLSP) and
lifespan energy potential. Most of these results will be
illustrated in this chapter.

6.   The primary aging process in humans may be the result of
cells gradually losing their proper state of differentiation. This
idea, which is known as the Dysdifferentiation Hypothesis of Aging,
contrasts sharply with the older Wear and Tear Hypothesis of Aging.
Evidence that dysdifferentiation does occur with aging has been the
appearance of improper gene expression such as the increased
expression of hemoglobin genes or endogenous viral genes in brain
and liver tissues with increased age. Much indirect biochemical and
morphological evidence also supports the Dysdifferentiation
Hypothesis of Aging. Because this hypothesis proposes that aging
results from a natural instability of gene expression in highly
differentiated cells, it naturally follows that longevity is the
result of unknown processes acting to stabilize proper gene
expression. Here, it is of considerable interest that active oxygen
species at extremely low concentrations are found to alter the
proper state of differentiation of cells and that antioxidants can
protect against these effects. Thus, by-products of oxygen
metabolism could act to destabilize proper gene expression and
antioxidants might represent an important class of gene
expression-stabilizing agents.

The above results have led to the formulation of a general
working hypothesis of aging and longevity called the Longevity
Determinant Gene Hypothesis. The major postulates of this
hypothesis are as follows.

1. Aging is the result of the side effects of normal
developmental and metabolic processes. All mammalian species have
essentially the same spectrum of these aging processes, and
therefore age qualitatively in a similar manner, although frequently
at different rates.

2. Longevity of a species (MLSP) is determined by the extent
the aging effects of normal developmental and metabolic processes
have been reduced. All mammalian species have evolved essentially
the same spectrum of methods to reduce these causes of aging. The
longevity of a species is consequently determined largely by
quantitative differences in the expression of a common set of
anti-aging genes acting against a common set of aging processes.

The most novel and far-reaching postulates of the longevity
determinant gene hypothesis are (1) the prediction of specific
longevity determinant processes, which are identical in most
mammalian species, (2) few genetic modifications required in
regulatory genes to uniformly reduce the aging rate of the entire

organism, and (3) that aging is largely a result of a
dysdifferentiative process, where the primary role of longevity
determinant genes are to counteract this dysdifferentiation by
prolonging the time the proper differentiated state of the cell is
maintained.

The above predictions of this hypothesis concerning the
dysdifferentiative nature of aging has been tested by searching for
(1) age-dependent changes in the physico-chemical structure of
chromatin and for related abnormal gene expression and (2) in
identifying potential biochemical stabilizers of differentiation
(longevity determinants) and by determining if they are more
effective and/or at higher concentrations in longer-lived species.

The principal methods used to test for the existence of
longevity determinants have been a biochemical comparison of
mammalian species having different maximum lifespan potentials. The
question asked in these studies is how do these species differ in
quantitative biochemical aspects (although qualitative differences
are not ruled out) that could reasonably explain their maximum
lifespan potential differences. Also, because human appears to be
the longest-lived of all mammalian species and is the species we
are most interested in, we are particularly interested in
determining how the biology of humans differs from closely-related
shorter-lived species such as the great apes and then examining if
these differences could possibly be anti-aging mechanisms.

The Longevity Determinant Gene Hypothesis is based on a broad
base of data, ranging from the evolutionary origin of life,
evolution of different species, population genetics, comparative
biology and the biochemistry of aging. Consequently, it offers
specific answers to some basic questions for mammalian species.
Some of these are as follows.

What causes aging? Aging is caused by the side-effects of
normal developmental and metabolic processes and the natural
instability of the genetic apparatus of cells to maintain their
proper differentiated state.

What is the aging process? The aging process begins with the
loss of the proper differentiated state of cells, a process called
dysdifferentiation. Aging is the slow loss of proper self and the
aging of the organism represents the complex affects and response
of the organism to these primary changes.

What governs aging rate? Aging rate of an organism is
governed by how well the organism maintains the proper
differentiated state of its cells as a function of time. Thus, the
structural and/or metabolic processes that stabilize the proper

state of cell differentiation are predicted to be the antiaging mechanisms we are searching to identify. Antioxidants may play an important role in this regard and, if so, dysdifferentiation would result in part by mechanisms involving oxygen radicals, and antioxidants would then be considered as important stabilizers of differentiation.

Why does aging exist? There is always a high probability that metabolic and developmental processes will have some degree of disadvantage. Thus, all organisms existing today are a result of a long history of tradeoffs between benefits (life prolongation) and disadvantages (life-shortening events).

Why do different species have different aging rates? Longevity has evolved in all species to the point that aging does not play a significant role in determining their lifespan in the wild. Thus, natural environmental hazards are the major determinant of aging rate which evolved. The large extent of aging now seen in human populations is a recent artifact of our culture, reducing environmental hazards much below their normal level.

ANTIOXIDANTS AS POTENTIAL LONGEVITY DETERMINANTS

Our recent studies have concentrated on evaluating the possible role DNA repair and antioxidants may have in determining human longevity (Cutler, 1982a, 1983, 1984a,b,c,d,e). Previous studies have indicated that the hypothetical longevity determinant processes are likely to be similar in different mammalian species and that differences in longevity would be based largely on differences in their expression. There is now much evidence indicating (1) a possible causal role of oxygen radicals in aging, (2) the dysdifferentiative nature of aging, (3) that oxygen radicals can cause dysdifferentiation, and (4) antioxidants protect against oxygen radicals. There is therefore a good theoretical basis for expecting a positive correlation in the concentration of a given type of antioxidant with a species' lifespan energy potential (Cutler, 1982b, 1984b; Cerutti, 1985).

THE COMPARATIVE BIOGERONTOLOGICAL RESEARCH APPROACH

The present objective of the comparative approach is to identify quantitative differences between long-lived and short-lived species of common biochemical characteristics that theoretically could lay a role as longevity determinants. The studies to be described in this chapter are concerned with investigating a number of different antioxidants and two detoxification enzymes.

Maximum Lifespan Potential

        Central to the comparative approach is the concept of Maximum
Lifespan Potential (MLSP): the use of MLSP in these studies needs to
be defined clearly.

        In the experiments to be described, tissue concentrations of
antioxidants and detoxification enzymes are measured as a function
of the aging rate of different mammalian species. The aging rate
of a species is defined as the average rate of decline of a large
number of different physiological functions: this rate has been
shown to be roughly proportional to a species' maximum lifespan
potential (MLSP). It would be best to know the mean physiological
rate for the various mammalian species used in comparative work;
this data does not exist. Instead, we have estimates of MLSP for a
much larger number of species, so this parameter of longevity is
used instead to indirectly estimate their mean physiological aging
rate.

        The term MLSP originally arose from human survival data, where
although a mean lifespan can vary considerably, the maximum
lifespan potential is remarkably constant, being about 100 years.
These data suggest that MLSP reflects the innate biological
potential of a species for longevity. Thus, a comparison of
species' MLSP is believed to represent roughly a comparison of
their respective innate biological aging rates. A few studies in
mice, primates and human of physiological aging rate of specific
functions (such as immune function and the rate of accumulation of
age pigments) support the correlation of MSLP with the aging rate of
specific functions. It should be clear that the term MLSP does not
imply, as is sometimes thought, that some theoretical maximum
lifespan potential actually exists for each species. Such a limit
would be extremely difficult to determine because further
improvement in medical care and/or reduced environmental hazards
may further extend a species' lifespan. Thus, the use of MLSP in
our comparative studies is as a relative estimate of the mean
physiological aging rate of each species. We are really not
interested in determining the absolute length a species could
possibly live but only on estimating their relative innate
abilities to maintain good health and vigor.

        Because we are interested in obtaining the best relative MLSP
estimate possible, other data besides death in populations have been
used. These are (1) the use of a calculated MLSP based on the brain
and body weights of young adult species. This equation is derived
from over 100 different species ranging from mouse to human and is
remarkably successful in predicting MLSP (Sacher, 1959), and (2) the
use of a calculated developmental rate of the species, where, for
example, the age of sexual development has been found to be linearly

related to MLSP for the primate species and non-primate mammalian
species (Cutler, 1976a). Thus, whenever possible, both calculated
MLSP and rate of development are used as well as actual maximum
observed lifespan to estimate the MLSP used in the comparative
studies.

Specific Metabolic Rate

To evaluate whether antioxidants play a role in determining
longevity of different species, a theoretical basis is necessary to
establish what mathematical correlations of antioxidant
concentration with MLSP is to be expected. No such theoretical
basis could be found for a direct correlation of antioxidant
concentration with MLSP. However, both a theoretical and an
experimental basis was found to predict that the concentration of
an antioxidant per specific metabolic rate would be proportional to
MLSP. Part of the experimental evidence is that SMR of an organism
is related to the oxygen utilization rate of its tissues. In turn,
the rate of production of various toxic oxygen radicals is
proportional to the rate of oxygen utilization of the tissue. Thus,
the ratio of antioxidant concentration per SMR represents the
degree of protection a tissue has per amount of oxygen radical
production that exists in that tissue. This ratio would then be
expected to be positively correlated with MLSP if that antioxidant
was having an effect in governing MLSP by reducing the toxic
effects of oxygen metabolism.

Another obvious reason to predict that the ratio of antioxidant
concentration per specific metabolic rate (SMR) is proportional to
species' MLSP is that various species have widely different SMR's,
and one possible important strategy during the evolution of
mammalian species to increase longevity may have been a decrease in
SMR. In many cases, this is accomplished by simply being larger in
size, thus requiring less oxygen utilization per gram body weight
to maintain a given body temperature. An increase in the ratio of
antioxidant concentration to SMR could have occurred then by either
an increase of antioxidant concentration and/or by a decrease in
SMR.

One must be careful, however, because of the possibility that,
although some species may have the same SMR, they may also have
different innate production rates of free radicals or other toxic
by-products of metabolism because of different metabolic pathways.
In this case, their SMRs would not reflect, in a direct proportion,
the innate production of toxic products as compared to other
species. This possibility should always be kept in mind in these
comparative studies.

Lifespan Energy Potential

The concept that aging rate is roughly proportional to a species' metabolic rate originated from the finding that, for many species, the product of MLSP and SMR was a constant. Typical results of this correlation are shown in Figure 1. Thus, for many species, if antioxidant concentration remained unchanged, a decrease in their SMR would have nevertheless resulted in an increase in the amount of protection their tissues would have against oxygen radicals. However, it is evident in this figure that the human and capuchin points are above the curve, indicating that those species utilize much more calories per gram of weight over their lifespan. This observation has led to the definition of a new parameter of longevity called Lifespan Energy Potential (LEP), which is the product of MLSP and SMR, or:

LEP (kc/g) = 2.70 (MLSP, yrs)(SMR, c/g/d)

For mouse species, LEP is about 200-300 kc/g, and for many primates LEP is about twice as great, or 400-600 kc/g. However, the outstanding exceptions are human and capuchin, with LEP values of about 800-900 kc/g. Thus, mammalian species not only have different biological capacities for longevity in terms of chronological time but also differences in the total amount of energy they utilize over their lifespan or in metabolic time. True long-lived animals would have both a high MLSP and a LEP value, as found for the human.

Estimates of MLSP and LEP

Table 1 shows how remarkably well MLSP can be calculated on the basis of the brain/body weight equation as compared to the observed values of MLSP. Tables 2 through 6 represent our most recent estimates of MLSP and LEP values for a number of primate and non-primate mammalian species as based on the considerations previously discussed. It is emphasized, however, that there is still a large range of reliability in these estimates, with some being much better than others. As a consequence, the estimates of MLSP for some species will still likely be subject to significant revision in the future. Table 5 represents some of the most confident MLSP and LEP value estimates for the primates. For example, we are most confident that humans age at a rate about one-half that of the great apes and that the great apes age at about one half the rate of the marmoset, tamarin and squirrel monkey.

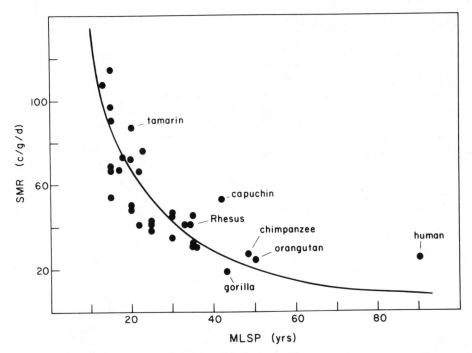

Fig. 1. Maximum lifespan potential (MLSP)of mammalian species in relation to their specific metabolic rate (SMR). Taken from (Cutler, 1984a).

Table 1. Prediction of MLSP on the basis of body and brain weight for some mammalian species.

Species (common name)	Cranial capacity (cm^3)	Body wt (g)	MLSP (yrs) Observed	MLSP (yrs) Predicted
pygmy shrew	0.11	5.3	1.5	1.8
field mouse	0.45	22.6	3.5	3.2
opossum	7.65	5000	7.0	5.8
Mongolian horse	587	260,000	46	38
camel	570	450,000	30	33
cow	423	465,000	30	27
giraffe	680	529,000	34	35
elephant (India)	5045	2,347,000	70	89
mountain lion	154	54,000	19	23
domestic dog	79	13,400	20	21

Compiled from Cutler (1978, 1979).

Table 2. Estimates of maximum lifespan potential and lifespan energy potential for Hominoidea Primate species.

Genus and species (common name)	Sex	Body wt (kg)	Brain wt (g)	MLSP (yrs) Predicted	MLSP (yrs) Obs.	MLSP (yrs) Best Est.	Maturity age (yrs) Predicted	Maturity age (yrs) Obs.	SMR (c/g/d)	LEP (kc/g)
Homo sapiens (human)	♂ ♀	65 58	1450 1330	92 89	92-117	95 ± 10	17	17-18	24.6	853
Pan troglodytes (chimpanzee)	♂ ♀	49 41	410 380	44 33	48- 52 (11)	50 ± 5	8	8- 9	26.4	481
Pan t. paniscus	♂ ♀	38.5 32	356 329	42 42	22- 26 (4)	50 ± 5	8	8- 9	28.0	511
Gorilla gorilla	♂ ♀	140 70	550 460	42 43	37- 52 (8)	50 ± 5	8	8- 9	20.3	370
Pongo pygmaeus (orangutan)	♂ ♀	69 37	415 370	41 44	35- 54 (8)	50 ± 5	8	9-10	24.2	441
Hylobates lar (gibbon)	♂ ♀	5.5 5.3	100 101	30 30	30- 44 (6)	40 ± 5	7	6- 7	45.6	665
S. syndactylus (siamang)	♂ ♀	11.1 10.2	126 123	29 29	20	25 ± 5	6	-	68.0	744

See footnote, Table 6.

Table 3. Estimates of lifespan potential and lifespan energy potential for Old World monkeys.

Genus and species (common name)	Body wt (kg)	Brain wt (g)	MLSP (yrs)			Maturity age		SMR (c/g/d)	LEP (kc/g)
			Predicted	Obs.	Best est.	Pred.	Obs.		
Papio hamadryas	16	179	33	27–38 (20)	40 ± 4	6	5–6	34.9	509
Papio cynocephalus (western baboon)	22	200	35	27–38 (20)	40 ± 4	5	6–7	32.2	470
Papio anubis (olive baboon)	26	205	32.5	27–38 (20)	40 ± 4	5	6–7	30.9	451
Macaca mulatta (Rhesus)	8	110	28.4	29–38 (20)	38 ± 4	5	4–5	41.5	575
Cercopithecus aethiops (African green monkey)	3.9	73	25.8	25–31 (87)	31 ± 4	5	4–5	49.7	562
Presbytis entellus (langur)	21	120	24	24	25 ± 4	4	4–5	32.6	297
Cercocebus albigena (mangabey)	7.9	104	27.5	33	33 ± 4	4	4–5	41.6	379
Colobus polykomos (guereza)	9.4	90	24.1	24	25 ± 4	–	–	39.9	364

See footnote, Table 6.

Table 4. Estimates of maximum lifespan potential and lifespan energy potential for New World monkeys.

Genus and species	Body wt (kg)	Brain wt (g)	MLSP (yrs) Predicted	MLSP (yrs) Obs.	MLSP (yrs) Best est.	SMR	LEP
Cebus capucinus (capuchin)	3	80	29	37–42 (15)	42 ± 5	53.1	814
Ateles geoffroyi (spider monkey)	8	108	28.1	20–34 (20)	34 ± 5	41.5	454
Lagothrix (woolly monkey)	5.2	101	29.7	25	30 ± 4	46.2	421
Alouatta (howler monkey)	6.4	51	18.3	8–15 (8)	20 ± 4	43.9	320
Saguinus oedipus (tamarin)	0.405	10	12	14–20 (35)	20 ± 2	87.6	639
Callithrix jacchus (marmoset)	0.260	7.6	11.2	10–16 (15)	18 ± 3	97.8	642
Aotus trivirgatus (night monkey)	0.850	16	13.8	15–18 (5)	20 ± 3	72.7	530
Saimiri (squirrel monkey)	0.680	22	20	19–22 (12)	20 ± 3	76.9	561

See footnote, Table 6.

Table 5. Most confident relative maximum lifespan potential and lifespan energy potential estimates for primates.

Species (common name)	MLSP (yrs)	LEP (kc/g)
human	100	850
Great Apes chimp, orangutan, gorilla	50	450
Macaca, baboon	40	500
capuchin	40	800
marmoset, tamarin, squirrel monkey	20	600
tree shrew	15	500

Rounded-off estimates of MLSP and LEP, showing relative MLSP and LEP values for species where this data is most reliable. There appears to be a 5-fold difference in MLSP and a 10-fold difference in LEP among the primate species.

Table 6.   Estimates of maximum lifespan potential and lifespan
           energy potential for Prosimii and Tupaiidae.

Genus and species	Body wt (kg)	Brain wt (g)	Predicted	MLSP (yrs) Obs.	Best est.	SMR (c/g/d)	LEP (kc/g)
Lemur macaca fulvus (ring-tailed lemur)	1.4	23.3	16	27-40	40 ± 5	30.7	448
Hapalemur griseus (gentle lemur)	1.3	9.53	9	13	15 ± 2	65.4	358
Microcebus (mouse lemur)	0.054	1.78	6.4	10-11 (9)	13 ± 2	144	683*
Cheirogaleus (dwarf lemur)	0.174	3.14	7	10-15 (7)	13 ± 2	108	512
Propithecus (sifaka)	3.48	26.7	13.9	18	20 ± 2	51.1	373
Daubentonia (aye-aye)	2.80	45.1	20.4	7-28 (5)	30 ± 5	54.0	591
Nycticebus (slow loris)	0.8	12.5	11.9	12-14 (9)	15 ± 3	73.8	430
Perodicticus potto (potto)	1.15	14	12	22	22 ± 3	67.4	393
Galago crassi-caudatus (galago)	0.85	10.3	11	14-17 (27)	17 ± 2	72.7	398
Tarsius syrichta	0.0875	3.68	9	7-15 (5)	15 ± 2	128	700*
Tupaia glis (tree shrew)	0.150	3.15	8	8-14 (11)	14 ± 2	112	572
Urogale everetti (Mindanao tree shrew)	0.278	4.28	8	8-14 (11)	14 ± 2	96.2	491

All data in Tbs. 1-4 are taken from sources cited in the papers (Cutler 1975;
1976a; 1979; Tolmasoff et al., 1980). Recent new estimates of MLSP come from
personal communication with Marvin Jones at the San Diego Zoo and Bowden &
Williams (1985). Best estimate of MLSP is based on predicted MLSP, observed
range of MLSP among the five oldest individuals of a given species, where
number in parentheses is number of individuals these five were chosen from, and
age of maturity. SMR was calculated based on young adult body weight of the
male using the equation:
    SMR (c/g/d) = 393 (body wt., g)$^{-0.25}$
MLSP was calculated using the equation:

    MLSP (yrs) = 10.83 (body wt., g)$^{-0.225}$(brain wt., g)$^{0.636}$
*SMR and LEP values may be overestimated by as much as 40% if these species are
similar to Lemur macaca fulvus, where actual SMR is 40% lower than estimates
based on body weight.

One advantage in doing comparative work with primate species is that substantial detail is known both of their evolutionary and genetic relationships to one another. Another advantage of course is that, of all aniamls, primates are most closely related to human. This is shown in Figure 2 where the primate phylogenic-evolutionary relationships of the living primate species are given with reference to our best estimates of their individual MLSP and LEP values.

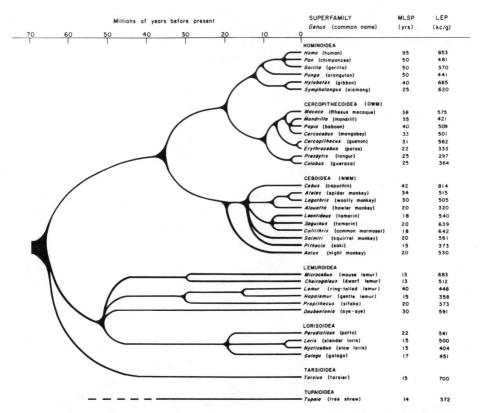

Fig. 2. Phylogenetic relationship of maximum lifespan potential (MLSP) and lifespan energy potential (LEP) estimates for the primate species. Data taken from (Cutler, 1976a, 1980a, 1984a,b).

BODY TEMPERATURE

Body temperature is not necessarily positively correlated to SMR in all animals, but it is for most mammals. Temperature (or thermal energy) is generally considered to be detrimental to the maintenance of complex biological structures. Thus, the constituents of cells are likely to be less prone to random thermal degradation at lower body temperatures. Differences in the longevity of species might then be expected to result in part by differences in their body temperature.

A search to determine if a correlation exists between deep body temperature and longevity is summarized in Table 7 and illustrated in Figure 3. Here, it is seen that body temperature does decrease with increased MLSP for the shorter-lived primate species but, most importantly, the great apes and human appear to be similar. Thus, in the recent evolution of longevity in the hominids leading to human, it appears unlikely that decreased body temperature played an important role.

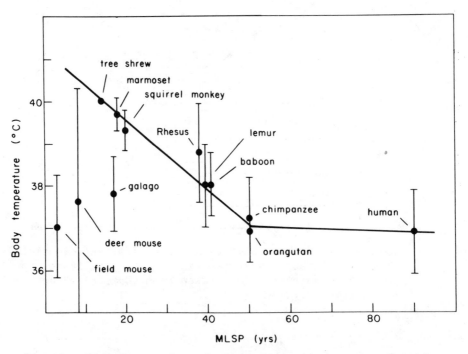

Fig. 3.   Body temperature in mammalian species as a function
of their maximum lifespan potential (MLSP).

Table 7.   Body temperature as a function of maximum lifespan
potential in primates.

Species (common name)	MLSP (yrs)	Body temperature ($^{\circ}$C)
Homo sapiens (human)	95 ± 10	36.9 ± 0.98
Pan troglodytes (chimpanzee)	50 ± 5	37.2 ± 1.06
Pongo pygmaeus (orangutan)	50 ± 5	36.9 ± 0.709
Papio dogura (baboon)	40 ± 5	38.0 ± 0.781
Macaca (Rhesus)	38 ± 4	38.8 ± 1.17
Saimirii sciureus (squirrel monkey)	20 ± 3	39.3 ± 0.427
Saguinus mystax (marmoset)	18 ± 3	39.7 ± 0.38
Lemur fulvus (lemur)	40 ± 5	38.0 ± 1.2
Galago crassicaudatus (bush baby)	17 ± 2	37.8 ± 0.877
Tupai glis (tree shrew)	14 ± 2	40.0
Peromyscus (deer mouse)	8 ± 1	37.6 ± 2.79
Mus musculus	3 ± 1	37.0 ± 1.24

Body temperature data taken from Altman & Dittmer (1968),
Spector (1956); Morrison and Ryser (1952); Wislocki (1933);
Melby and Altman (1976); Yousef et al. (1971).

BIOCHEMICAL CONTROLS FOR COMPARATIVE STUDIES

According to our working hypothesis, identification of a
potential longevity determinant such as an antioxidant can be made
by finding a positive correlation in its concentration per specific
metabolic rate with MLSP. However, for this approach to be
meaningful, one must be reasonably sure that the concentration per
specific metabolic rate of most enzymes or other substances in a
cell that are clearly not longevity determinants do not also
correlate positively with MLSP. It is well known for example that
body size, specific metabolic rate (SMR), and rate of development
are related to MLSP in mammals and other species (Kunkel et al.,
1956; Stahl, 1962; Emmitt and Hochachka, 1981; Lindstedt and
Calder, 1981). Thus, we expect the enzyme concentrations involved
in determining these functions would also correlate with MLSP and
that these functions might be involved with determining MLSP. But
many other enzymes and body constituents that are clearly not
involved in determining longevity could nevertheless also correlate
positively with MLSP. Thus, a positive correlation by itself is
not sufficient evidence that a given substance is a longevity
determinant. This is why such positive correlations we find are
called "potential" longevity determinants.

To evaluate how special the case is when a correlation is found
with MLSP or LEP, a number of enzymes and other factors that were
thought not to be potential longevity determinants were tested for
a possible correlation of their tissue concentrations with MLSP and
LEP. Most of the data used in these studies were taken from the
following cited literature (Albritten, 1952; Altman and Dittmer,
1961, 1962, 1972, 1974; Dixon and Webb, 1964; Mattenheimer, 1971;
Bernirschke et al, 1978; Mitruka and Rawnsley, 1981). The results
showed no significant correlation (negative or positive) in the
concentration of the following substances with MLSP or LEP.

1. Tissue enzymes: random assortment of 57 were analyzed.
2. Vitamins (whole blood): thiamine, riboflavin, pyridine
   cyanocobalamine, nicotinic acid, pantothenic acid, retinol
   (vitamin A).
3. Blood chemistries: albumin, alpha and beta globulins,
   cholesterol, glucose, blood urea nitrogen, minerals
   (Na, K, Ca, Mg), dehydroepiandrosterone (DHEA).

A survey of 50 other enzymes not expected to be longevity
determinants was also made, and no significant correlation was
found with MLSP or LEP (Cutler, 1984b). Recent studies by Ono and
Okada (1984) on lactate dehydrogenase, glucose-6-phosphate
dehydrogenase, superoxide dismutase, glutamic oxalacetic
transaminase, creatin phosphokinase and choline esterase in
non-primate species found no positive correlation in the
concentration of these enzymes with MLSP. In summary, these data

indicate that few biochemical constituents of a mammalian species correlate positively with MLSP or LEP for mammalian species and imply that negative or positive correlations are probably special cases.

SUPEROXIDE DISMUTASE

Superoxide dismutase (SOD) is considered to be one of the most important defensive enzymes against the toxic effects of oxygen metabolism (Fridovich, 1979) This enzyme removes the superoxide free radicals O_2^-. Most organisms that use oxygen (aerobic respiration) cannot live without this enzyme or an equivalent type of protective mechanism.

Tissue concentrations of SOD have been measured in brain, liver and heart tissues of primates and non-primate species. Tables 8 and 9 show the data for liver for primate species and non-primate mammalian species, respectively. Figure 4 illustrates the correlation of SOD per MLSP for primate livers, where a positive correlation is found (linear, r = 0.727, P ≤ 0.01). However, when the correlation of SOD per SMR vs MLSP is evaluated, as shown in Figure 5, a much higher linear correlation coefficient is found (r = 0.961, P ≤ 0.001).

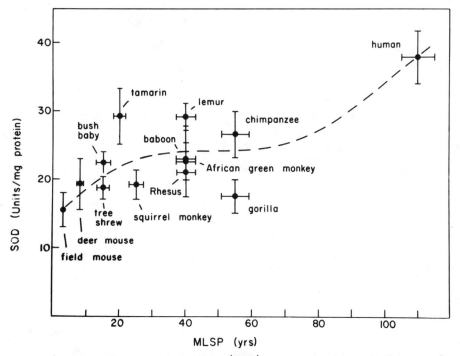

Fig. 4.   Superoxide dismutase (SOD) concentration in liver of mammals as a function of maximum lifespan potential (MLSP).

Table 8. Liver superoxide dismutase concentration in primate
species as a function of maximum lifespan potential
and specific metabolic rate.

Species (common name)	MLSP (yr)	SMR (c/g/d)	SOD U/mgP	SOD/SMR
1 field mouse	3.5 ± 0.5	189 ± 11.7	15.4 ± 2.24	0.0814 ± 0.0127
2 deer mouse	8 ± 1	151 ± 14.1	19.3 ± 3.67	0.131 ± 0.0282
3 tree shrew	15 ± 2	100 ± 2.3	18.7 ± 1.52	0.173 ± 0.146
4 squirrel monkey	25 ± 3	73.9 ± 2.67	19.3 ± 2.26	0.267 ± 0.319
5 bush baby	15 ± 2	68.4 ± 3.34	22.4 ± 1.64	0.327 ± 0.0287
6 tamarin	20 ± 3	88.4 ± 2.85	29.2 ± 4.39	0.330 ± 0.0507
7 lemur	40 ± 5	(30.7)	29.2 ± 2.12	(0.951)
8 green monkey	40 ± 5	43.4 ± 5.39	22.7 ± 3.11	0.523 ± 0.967
9 Rhesus monkey	40 ± 5	37.0 ± 1.2	21.0 ± 3.6	0.567 ± 0.987
10 baboon	40 ± 5	43.2 ± 1.74	22.9 ± 2.32	0.741 ± 0.829
11 gorilla	55 ± 5	19.7 ± 0.352	17.5 ± 2.49	0.888 ± 0.0127
12 chimpanzee	55 ± 5	26.8 ± 0.809	26.6 ± 3.58	0.953 ± 0.137
13 human	110 ± 5	24.8 ± 0.716	38.0 ± 3.87	1.61 ± 0.167

MLSP vs SOD   MLSP vs SOD/SMR
  n = 13   n = 13
  r = 0.721   r = 0.961
  P ≤ 0.010   P ≤ 0.001
SOD data taken from Tolmasoff et al. (1980).

Table 9. Brain sod concentration per specific metabolic rate in non-primate species.

Species and genus (common name)	Body wt (kg)	Brain wt (g)	MLSP (yrs) Predicted	MLSP (yrs) Obser.	MLSP (yrs) Best est.	SMR	LEP (kc/g)	SOD (Units/mg protein)	SOD/SMR
Equus caballus (domestic horse)	461	618	34.2	46	40 ± 5	15.1	220	14.10 ± 1.71	0.933 ± 0.113
Bos taurus (domestic cow)	413	408	26.9	30	30 ± 5	15.5	169	21.63 ± 1.74	1.39 ± 0.111
Felis catus (domestic cat)	3.77	28	14.1	28	25 ± 4	50.1	457	16.72 ± 2.19	0.333 ± 0.436
Sus scrofa (domestic pig)	113	123	16.8	27	25 ± 4	21.4	195	20.28 ± 1.83	0.947 ± 0.854
Ovis aires (domestic sheep)	2.72	53.8	22.9	20	20 ± 4	54.4	397	17.91 ± 0.96	0.329 ± 0.176
Canis familiaris (domestic dog)	14.5	79.9	20.2	20	20 ± 4	35.8	261	13.2 ± 2.19	0.368 ± 0.0610
Ory. cuniculus (domestic rabbit)	0.439	4.5	7.15	13	12 ± 2	85.8	375	13.98 ± 1.83	0.162 ± 0.0212
Cavia porcellus (domestic guinea pig)	0.351	3.63	6.55	7.5	7 ± 2	90.7	231	12.12 ± 0.72	0.133 ± 0.0079
Rattus rattus (domestic rat)	0.197	1.61	4.45	4.7	4.5 ± 0.5	104	170	11.49 ± 1.32	0.11 ± 0.0126
Mesocricetus auratus (golden hamster)	0.120	1.05	3.79	4.0	4.0 ± 0.5	118	172	11.01 ± 0.45	0.0933 ± 0.00381
Mus musculus (domestic mouse)	0.025	0.50	3.30	3.5	3.0 ± 0.5	175	191	8.94 ± 0.78	0.0568 ± 0.00495

Lifespan data taken from Altman & Dittmer (1962, 1972).
Specific metabolic rate (SMR) calculated as
  SMR (o/g/d) = 393 (Body wt, g)$^{-0.25}$
Maximum lifespan potential (MLSP) calculated as
  MLSP (yrs) = 10.8 (Body wt, g)$^{-0.225}$ (Brain wt, g)$^{0.636}$
Lifespan energy potential (LEP) calculated as
  LEP (kc/g) = 2.73 (SMR, o/g/d)(MLSP, yrs)
Superoxide dismutase (SOD) data taken from Ono & Okada (1984).
SMR for horse, cow and pig may be underestimated because of high percent body fat and/or non-correlation with Klieber equation.

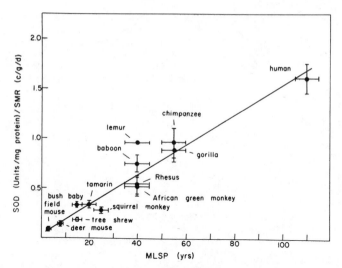

Fig. 5.   Superoxide dismutase (SOD) concentration per specific
metabolic rate (SMR) in liver of mammals as a function of
maximum lifespan potential (MLSP).   Linear correlation
coefficient: r = 0.961, P ≤ 0.001, where n = 13.

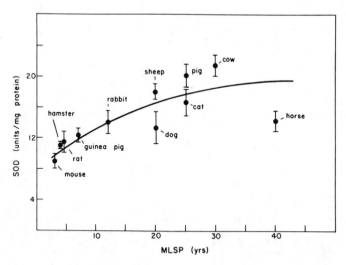

Fig. 6.   Superoxide dismutase (SOD) concentration in brain of
non-primate mammals as a function of maximum lifespan
potential (MLSP).   Linear correlation coefficient
r = 0.698, P ≤ 0.02, where n = 11.

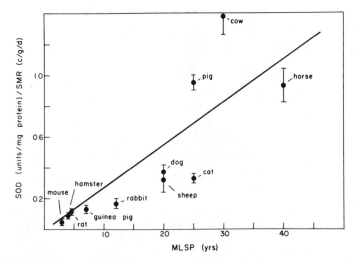

Fig. 7.   Superoxide dismutase (SOD) concentration per specific
          metabolic rate (SMR) in brain of non-primate mammals as a
          function of maximum lifespan potential (MLSP).   Linear
          correlation coefficient r = 0.825, P ≤ 0.001, where
          n = 11.

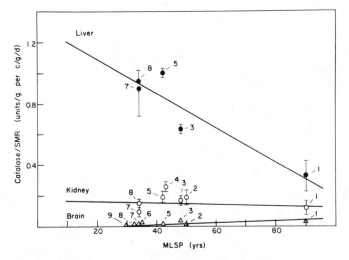

Fig. 8.   Catalase activity in liver, kidney and brain of primate
          species per specific metabolic rate (SMR) as a function of
          maximum lifespan potential (MLSP).

Table 10. Catalase activity in primate species.

Species (common name)	MLSP (yrs)	Activity (units/g wet weight tissue)		
		Liver	Kidney	Brain
human	90	8.07 ± 2.47 n = 6	2.96 ± 1.12 n = 5	0.466 ± 0.0278 n = 10
orangutan	50	-	4.58 ± 1.02 n = 5	0.372 n = 1
chimpanzee	48	16.9 ± 0.556 n = 5	4.29 ± 0.375 n = 6	0.652 ± 0.0268 n = 2
gorilla	43	-	5.09 n = 1	-
baboon	42	31.3 ± 0.395 n = 3	5.94 ± 1.67 n = 4	0.179 ± 0.0517 n = 3
lemur	35	-	-	0.647 + 0.523 n = 2
Rhesus	34	37.2 ± 7.89 n = 5	3.58 ± 0.738 n = 3	0.265 ± 0.00565 n = 7
pig tailed macaque	34	39.5 ± 2.49 n = 3	5.94 ± 0.675 n = 3	0.201 ± 0.117 n = 4
African green monkey	30	-	-	0.194 ± 0.0346 n = 2

MLSP vs catalase concentration in:
  liver :   r = -0.895,   P ≤ 0.001
  kidney: r = -0.644,   P ≤ 0.001
  brain :   r = 0.296,   P not significant
Assayed by both permanganate (Cohen et al., 1970) and ultraviolet detection
of hydrogen peroxide (Beers & Sizer, 1952).

Similarly, when the data of Ono and Okada (1984) for non-primate species is replotted as SOD vs MLSP, as shown in Figure 6, a positive linear correlation is found of $r = 0.698$, $P \leqslant 0.02$. However, on plotting SOD per SMR vs MLSP, as shown in Figure 7, it is found that $r = 0.825$, $P \leqslant 0.001$. This result disagrees with that of Ono and Okada (1984), who concluded that their calculations indicated their correlation was not significant.

Thus, although a positive correlation is found in the tissue concentration of SOD per MLSP, a much stronger positive correlation is found when SOD is normalized per SMR. Moreover, there is a reasonable theoretical justification to expect the SMR normalized data to be biologically significant, as has been previously described. Finally, these data suggest that the LEP value of an animal may be determined in part by the antioxidant concentration in its cells.

CATALASE

Catalase is considered a key antioxidant enzyme important in the removal of hydrogen peroxide (Chance et al., 1979). Measurement of catalase activity in liver, kidney and brain in primates is shown in Table 10 and illustrated in Figure 8. As shown in Figure 8, a significant negative correlation of catalase activity per SMR in liver was found as a function of MSLP.

This data indicates that, at least for these tissues, the unusual extent of human longevity does not appear likely to be the result of higher tissue concentrations of catalase. Indeed, the negative correlations found for liver catalase suggest that (1) hydrogen peroxide generation may have been reduced, thus reducing the requirements of catalase and/or (2) the presence of catalase itself may have a serious toxic effect.

Catalase has iron as its hematic prosthetic group, which might be toxic in terms of the catalytic effect of iron on the rate of lipid peroxidation. Mice with lower catalase appear to be more radiation resistant, and in many cases drugs which inactivate catalase are radioprotective. It is also of interest that, in the evolution of longer-lived species, the concentration of peroxisomes in cells has steadily decreased. Peroxisomes contain urate oxidase and catalase, both of which appear to have decreased with increased MLSP. Thus, it is of interest if other constituents of peroxisomes such as D-amino acid oxidase, xanthine oxidase, cytochrome oxidase and alpha-hydroxyl acid oxidase are also less concentrated in longer-lived mammalian species (Cutler, 1982a).

GLUTATHIONE PEROXIDASE

Glutathione peroxidase has long been considered a major protective enzyme against the accumulation of peroxides. Thus, it is of particular importance to determine if higher levels of this enzyme exist in longer-lived species. To our surprise, like catalase, glutathione peroxidase activity also appears to be lower in longer-lived species, even on a per SMR basis. This is illustrated in typical data shown in Table 11 for liver, Table 12 for liver and brain, and Table 13 for whole blood.

The explanation for this inverse correlation of MLSP vs glutathione per SMR may be similar to that for catalase. That is, the original production of peroxides is lower in longer-lived species, thus reducing in proportion the requirement for the protective enzyme. Also, like iron in catalase, selenium is a necessary co-factor for this enzyme and is highly toxic at higher than normal physiological concentrations. However, reduction of glutathione peroxidase to lower selenium requirement does not seem likely to be the explanation of why the inverse correlation with MLSP appears to exist, although this possibility needs to be considered.

GLUTATHIONE

Glutathione is thought to be one of the most important tissue antioxidants but, unlike other antioxidants, it is used in a number of other biochemical pathways not necessarily associated with its antioxidant protective properties. On measuring the concentration of glutathione in different species as a function of MLSP, we were again surprised to discover that glutathione concentration in all tissues we investigated was lower in the longer-lived animals.

Typical data are illustrated in Table 14 for whole blood, Table 15 for brain and Table 16 for liver. In these tables it is seen that MLSP vs glutathione concentration is negatively correlated for blood, brain and liver. However, for MLSP vs glutathione per SMR, a positive but non-significant correlation is found for blood and brain, but a strong negative correlation is found for liver.

Clearly, much more work needs to be done using better assays and including a larger variety of tissues and species before a conclusion can be arrived at as to what role glutathione may have in accounting for the lifespan differences found in mammalian species. However, the data so far strongly suggests that glutathione has little role as an important longevity determinant for human. This may be related to the toxicity of glutathione, forming the glutathione free radical (thio free radical) in the

Table 11. Glutathione peroxidase activity in liver.

Species (common name)	MLSP (yrs)	SMR (c/g/d)	LEP (kc/g)	GPX [*]	GPX/SMR
hamster	3	107	118	26.0 ± 2.8 n = 3	0.242
rat	4	78.4	115	19.6 ± 4.5 n = 3	0.250
guinea pig	8	69.6	204	0 n = 3	-
sheep	20	25.3	186	3.8 ± 0.9 n = 3	0.150
pig	30	19.9	219	2.5 ± 0.5	0.125
human	110	24.7	991	1.3 ± 0.32	0.0526

[*]One unit of activity is 1 μmol NADPH oxidized per minute.
MLSP vs GPX   MLSP vs GPX/SMR
  n = 5   n = 5
  r = -0.658   r = -0.890
Non-lifespan data taken from Lawrence and Burk (1978).

Table 12. Glutathione peroxidase activity in liver and brain of mammalian species.

Species (common name)	MLSP (yrs)	SMR (c/g/d)	LEP (kc/g)	Liver[*]	L/SMR	Brain[*]	B/SMR
mouse	3.5	180	232	1140 n = 5	6.33	23 ± 3 n = 5	0.127
rat	4.0	78.4	115	153 ± 23 n = 5	1.95	5 n = 5	0.637
guinea pig	8.0	69.6	204	57 n = 5	0.818	14 ± 4 n = 5	0.201
rabbit	12.0	58.4	257	381 n = 5	6.52	20 ± 5 n = 5	0.342
dog	20	34.8	255	ND	-	3 n = 2	0.862
cow	30	14.9	164	ND	-	5 ± 1 n = 5	0.335

n = number of animals used for determination.
[*]Activity cytosol fraction: mean ± SD. Nanomoles glutathione oxidized per minute x milligram protein.
MLSP vs Liver   MLSP vs Brain   MLSP vs Liver/SMR   MLSP vs Brain/SMR
  n = 4   n = 6   n = 4   n = 6
  r = -0.388   r = -0.545   r = 0.209   r = 0.516
                                      $P \leqslant 0.1$ $P \leqslant 0.1$
Non-lifespan data taken from De Marchena et al. (1974).

Table 13. Glutathione peroxidase activity in whole blood.

Species (common name)	MLSP (yrs)	SMR (c/g/d)	LEP (kc/g)	GPX[*]	GPX/SMR
rat	4.0	78.4	115	120 ± 100 n = 4	1.53
sheep	20	25.3	186	152 ± 143 n = 6	6.00
Rhesus	40	41.5	517	19.8 ± 18 n = 5	0.477
human	110	24.7	991	19.0 n = 10	0.769

[*]Glutathione peroxidase activity expressed as nanomoles NADPH oxidized per minute x milligram hemoglobin.

MLSP vs GPX   MLSP vs GPX/SMR
  n = 4   n = 4
  r = -0.740   r = -0.420
  P ≤ 0.1   P ≤ 0.1
[*]Data from Butler et al. (1982).

Table 14. Whole blood concentration of glutathione in mammalian species.

Species	MLSP (yrs)	SMR (c/g/d)	LEP (kc/g)	Glutathione (mg/100 ml)	Glutathione/SMR (mg/100 ml per c/g/d)
human	90	24.7	815	36.8	1.48
horse	49	13.9	152	60	4.31
baboon	35	30.7	394	49	1.59
cow	30	14.9	153	46	3.08
pig	30	19.9	219	36	1.80
sheep	25	25.3	186	26	1.02
dog	20	36.5	268	31	0.849
rabbit	12	58.4	257	45	0.770
guinea pig	8	69.6	204	127	1.82
rat	4	78.4	152	120	1.53
mouse	3.5	180	232	102	0.566

MLSP vs GLU   MLSP vs GLU/SMR
  n = 11   n = 11
  r = -0.468   r = 0.260
Non-lifespan data from Altman & Dittmer (1961, 1962, 1974).

Table 15. Glutathione concentration in brain.

Species (common name)	MLSP (yrs)	SMR (c/g/d)	LEP (kc/g)	BRAIN	BRAIN/SMR
human	110	24.7	991	12.8 ± 3.45 n = 5	0.518
baboon	40	30.7	448	17.4 ± 2.68 n = 4	0.566
pig-tailed macaque	40	41.5	517	17.5 ± 1.41 n = 2	0.421
deer mouse	8	150	440	54.5 ± 2.1 n = 2	0.363
field mouse	3.5	180	232	49.0 ± 1.4 n = 2	0.272

MLSP vs Brain   MLSP vs Brain/SMR
  n = 5   n = 5
  r = -0.794   r = 0.699
Taken from Cutler (1985, in press).

Table 16. Glutathione concentration in liver.

Species (common name)	MLSP (yrs)	SMR (c/g/d)	LEP (kc/g)	LIVER[a]	LIVER/SMR	LIVER/ Total Body Wt[b]
human	110	24.7	991	13.0 ± 9.41 n = 4	0.526	117
baboon	40	30.7	448	36.8 ± 13.0 n = 4	1.19	294
pig-tailed macaque	40	41.5	517	42.6 ± 2.46 n = 3	1.02	298

Data taken from Cutler (1985, in press)
a Relative glutathione concentration
b Relative total liver glutathione concentration per total body
   utilization of calories per day.

presence of oxygen and on metal chelators like iron. Furthermore,
because glutathione is involved in detoxification reactions (which
have been found to be lower in longer-lived species), and
detoxification reactions frequently produce a wide array of free
radical by-products, then perhaps the reasons why catalase,
glutathione peroxidase and glutathione are lower in liver in
longer-lived species is because of a reduced detoxification
capacity.

ALPHA TOCOPHEROL

Alpha-tocopherol or vitamin E is a well known antioxidant and,
being lipid-soluble, the membranes of the cell are likely to be
most protected. Very little data exists in the literature on
vitamin E concentrations in different species in tissues other than
blood. There is, however, some data for plasma, and typical data
are shown in Table 17 and Figure 9. Here, it is evident that,
although a weak positive correlation of MLSP vs vitamin E exists, a
highly significant correlation is found when MLSP vs vitamin E per
SMR is plotted. Thus, it does appear that vitamin E may play some
role as an antioxidant longevity determinant. However, it is
clearly evident that many more tissues and different species need to
be included in these studies before a general conclusion can be
made.

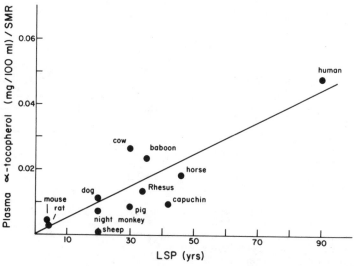

Fig. 9.   Plasma levels of vitamin E per specific metabolic rate
(SMR) as a function of maximum lifespan potential (MLSP) in
mammalian species. Correlation coefficient r = 0.864,
P ⩽ 0.001. Non-lifespan data from Altman and Dittmer (1961)
and Bernischke et al. (1978).

Table 17. Plasma levels of Alpha-Tocopherol in different species.

Species (common name)	MLSP (yrs)	SMR (c/g/d)	LEP (kcal/g)	Alpha-tocopherol (mg/100 ml)	Alpha-tocopherol/SMR
Homo (human)	90	24.8	815	1.2	0.0483
Equus (horse)	46	13.9	233	0.25	0.0179
Cebus (capuchin)	42	52.2	804	0.50	0.00957
Papio (baboon)	35	30.9	394	0.73	0.0236
Macaque (Rhesus)	34	41.3	512	0.56	0.0135
Bos (cow)	30	15	164	0.40	0.0266
Sus (pig)	30	20	219	0.16	0.008
Aotus (night monkey)	20	72.7	530	0.53	0.00729
Ovis (sheep)	20	25.6	186	0.020	0.000781
Canis (dog)	20	35	255	0.41	0.0117
Rattus (rat)	4	104	152	0.31	0.00298
Mus (mouse)	3.5	182	232	0.75	0.00412

MLSP vs a-tocopherol   LEP vs a-tocopherol   MLSP vs a-tocopherol/SMR
    r = 0.554   r = 0.661   r = 0.864
Non-lifespan data taken from Cutler (1984b).

ASCORBATE

Ascorbate or vitamin C is an essential for collagen synthesis and a few other metabolic processes. Its biological role as an anti-viral factor or anti-cancer factor has remained highly controversial, and most data does not support its alleged benefits in these diseases. Ascorbate is also an antioxidant, and it may therefore also have an important biological role in this capacity. Thus, to evaluate its potential role as an antioxidant longevity determinant, tissue concentrations of ascorbate were analyzed as a function of MLSP and SMR (Cutler, 1985).

Typical data are shown in Table 18 for brain, Table 19 for liver, Table 20 for the levels of the eye, and in Figures 10 and 11 for brain and eye, respectively. For the brain, it is seen that there is essentially no correlation of MLSP vs ascorbate for either young or adult individuals. However, it is interesting that ascorbate concentration decreases with age and in such a way that the correlation of MLSP vs ascorbate per SMR is found to become increasingly positive as the animals grow older (see Figure 10). This type of calculation of course assumes that relative SMR for the different species remains constant as the animals grow older, which might not be the case.

For liver, ascorbate concentration is clearly higher in the shorter-lived species, and MLSP vs ascorbate per SMR correlation is

Table 18. Ascorbate concentration in brain of mammalian species.

Species (common name)	MLSP (yrs)	SMR (c/g/d)	LEP (kc/g)	Ascorbate (mg % wet wt)		Ascorbate/SMR	
				Y	A	Y	A
human	90	24.7	815	18	27	0.728	1.09
cow	30	14.9	164	40	8	2.68	0.536
rabbit	12	58.4	257	39	6	0.667	0.102
guinea pig	8	69.6	204	15	20	0.215	0.287
rat	4	103	151	12	20	0.116	0.194
mouse	3.5	118	232	41	10	0.230	0.056

Ascorbate data taken from Kirk (1962).
Data are for young (Y) and adult (A).
MLSP vs ascorbate   MLSP vs ascorbate/SMR
(Y) r = -0.197   (Y) r = 0.264
(A) r = 0.557   (A) r = 0.968

Table 19. Ascorbate concentration in liver of mammalian species.

Species (common name)	MLSP (yrs)	SMR (c/g/d)	LEP (kc/g)	Ascorbate (mg/100 g)	Ascorbate/SMR
human	90	24.7	815	13.5	0.546
Rhesus	35	39.9	512	14.9	0.373
cow	30	14.9	164	26.1	1.73
pig	30	19.9	219	11.2	0.562
rabbit	12	58.4	257	27.0	0.462
guinea pig	8	69.6	204	16.6	0.238
rat	4	103	151	32.9	0.319

MLSP vs ascorbate   MLSP vs ascorbate/SMR
  n = 7   n = 7
  r = -0.554   r = 0.149
Ascorbate data from Altman and Dittmer (1961, 1962, 1974).

Table 20. Ascorbate concentration in eye lens of mammalian species.

Species	MLSP (yrs)	SMR (c/g/d)	LEP (kc/g)	Ascorbate* (mg/100 ml)	Ascorbate/SMR (mg/100 ml per c/g/d)
human	90	24.7	815	30	1.21
cow	30	14.9	164	35	2.34
rabbit	12	58.4	278	20	0.342
rat	4	103	151	22	0.213

*young adults
Ascorbate data taken from Altman & Dittmer, 1961, 1962, 1974.

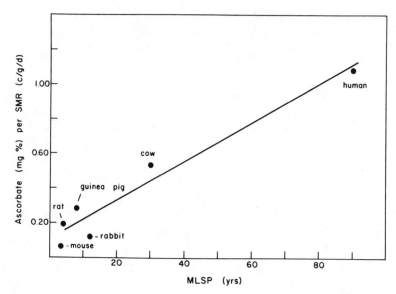

Fig. 10.   Ascorbate concentration per specific metabolic rate
           (SMR) in brain of mammalian species as a function of
           maximum lifespan potential (MLSP).

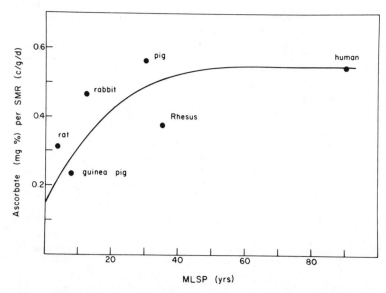

Fig. 11.   Ascorbate concentration per specific metabolic rate
           (SMR) in liver of mammalian species as a function of
           maximum lifespan potential (MLSP).

not significant (see Figure 11). Finally, for the eye lens, it does appear here that MLSP vs ascorbate per SMR is positively correlated. However, cow lens has a higher ascorbate per SMR ratio than human, yet the cow has a MLSP 1/3 that of human. Thus, these data do not strongly support ascorbate as being an important human antioxidant longevity determinant but, as in most of the other antioxidants examined, much more data is required to make this evaluation complete. It is also of interest to note that, in light of this analysis, the inability of humans to synthesize ascorbate may not necessarily be considered a genetic defect, as has frequently been proposed. Indeed, ascorbate can be converted to the free radical form in the presence of iron and oxygen, and so it may have serious limitations as an effective antioxidant under these conditions.

URATE

Uric acid is a product of purine metabolism and has usually been thought to be a waste by-product with no biological function (Wyngaarden & Kelley, 1979; Seegmiller, 1979). Recently it has been found that uric acid or its sodium salt urate is an excellent antioxidant, capable of protecting membranes from lipid peroxidation (Ames et al., 1981). Uric acid was evaluated as a potential longevity determinant by calculating the MLSP vs urate and the MLSP vs urate per SMR correlations (Cutler, 1985).

Typical data for plasma are shown in Figure 12. A significant positive correlation exists for MLSP vs urate, and this correlation is not noticeably improved when MLSP vs urate per SMR is plotted. Similar results were found for other tissues such as for brain.

These data strongly suggest that urate may be a longevity determinant, but the data is not strongly supportive in regards to urate having an antioxidant effect. Indeed urate may be most important as a neural stimulant, where MLSP is positively correlated with learned vs instinctive behavior in mammalian species (Ames et al., 1981; Cutler, 1982a, 1984a, 1985).

CERULOPLASMIN

Ceruloplasmin may be the dominant antioxidant in blood plasma, yet it is not known if its antioxidant properties have any biological significance. For example, the major biological role of ceruloplasmin that has been put forth is as a carrier protein for copper.

Tables 21 and 22 present typical data on the concentrations of ceruloplasmin in the plasma of primates and non-primate mammalian species. These data are illustrated in Figures 13 and 14. In

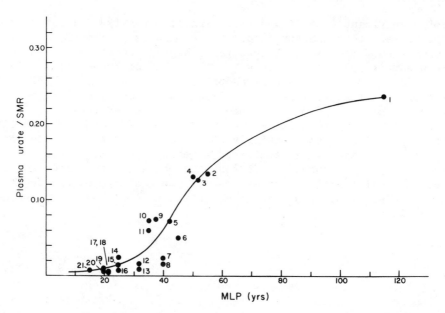

Fig. 12.   Plasma urate levels and urate level per SMR in primates
           as a function of MSLP. Values taken from the literature.
           Correlation coefficient for Fig. 15a is r = 0.82,
           P ≤ 0.001. Species' identification are 1 human,
           2 chimpanzee, 3 orangutan, 4 gorilla, 5 gibbon, 6 capuchin,
           7 macaque, 8 baboon, 9 spider monkey, 10 Siamang gibbon,
           11 wooly monkey, 12 langur, 13 grivet, 14 tamarin,
           15 squirrel monkey, 16 night monkey, 17 potto, 18 patas,
           19 galago, 20 howler monkey, 21 tree shrew (Cutler,
           1985).

Figure 13 for the primates, the results indicate that, although
longer-lived species do not have a significantly higher plasma
concentration of ceruloplasmin, on a per SMR basis there is a
significantly positive correlation. On the other hand, in Figure
14, which includes both primates and non-primate species, human
ceruloplasmin concentration per SMR is not significantly higher
than pig, cow or sheep.

    These results indicate that, during primate evolution,
ceruloplasmin may have had a role as an antioxidant longevity
determinant, particularly in the evolution of MLSP in the
shorter-lived species. These interesting results need to be
expanded using more species and a biochemical assay that is more
specific and quantitative.

Table 21. Plasma ceruloplasmin concentration in primates.

Species (common name)	MLSP (yrs)	SMR (c/g/d)	LEP (kc/d)	CP/mg protein x 10^{-2}	CP/SMR x 10^{-3}
human	90	24.7	815	7.85	3.17
capuchin	42	52.2	804	6.71	1.28
spider monkey	30	47.6	524	7.50	1.57
night monkey	20	72.3	530	8.75	1.21
howler monkey	20	50.6	371	4.05	0.800
squirrel monkey	18	73.5	485	1.89	0.257

MLSP vs CP
  n = 6
  r = 0.430

MLSP vs CP/SMR
  n = 6
  r = 0.931
  $P \leqslant 0.010$

Non-lifespan data taken from Seal (1964), where concentration was measured as p-phenylenediamine oxidase activity.

Table 22. Plasma ceruloplasmin in mammalian species.

Species (common name)	MLSP (yrs)	SMR (c/g/d)	LEP (kc/g)	CP (mg/100 ml)	CP/SMR
human	90	24.7	815	35.6	1.44
cow	30	14.9	153	20.3	1.36
sheep	25	25.3	186	26.5	1.04
pig	25	19.9	219	35.3	1.77
dog	20	36.5	268	17.4	0.476
rat	4	78.4	152	35.9	0.457

MLSP vs CP
  n = 6
  r = 0.260

MLSP vs CP/SMR
  n = 6
  r = 0.508

Non-lifespan data from Evans & Wiederanders (1967).

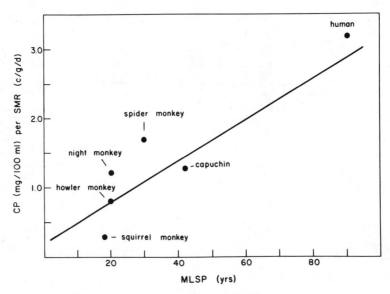

Fig. 13.   Ceruloplasmin (CP) concentration per specific metabolic
rate (SMR) in plasma of primate species as a function of
maximum lifespan potential (MLSP).

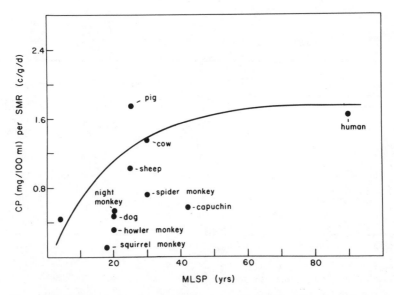

Fig. 14.   Ceruloplasmin concentration per specific metabolic rate
(SMR) in plasma of mammalian species as a function of
maximum lifespan potential (MLSP).

CAROTENOIDS

We have recently completed a study of carotenoids as possible longevity determinants and so will go into more detail in the background of this work. Considerable epidemiological and laboratory evidence exists suggesting that the carotenoids and retinol may be natural protective agents against cancer development (Peto et al., 1981; Calabrese, 1980; Hill & Grubbs, 1982; Ames, 1983; Hicks, 1983). However, little is known about which is most active in this protective role (Peto et al., 1981; Peto, 1983; Kolata, 1984). Since retinol is known to have a wide range of biological effects, particularly on cell growth and differentiation (Lotan, 1980; Newberne & Rogers, 1981; Zile & Cullum, 1983) and also as an antioxidant (Kartha & Krishnamurthy, 1977, 1978), its' protective nature against cancer may be related to these same properties.

There has been much speculation as to the possible biological effects of carotenoids, and most evidence suggests a protective role for a wide variety of plants and microorganisms (Krinsky, 1971, 1982; Simpson & Chichester, 1981). The biological role of the carotenoids in mammals has been less clear (Krinsky, 1971; Goodwin, 1954, 1962; Isler et al. 1971). A role has been suggested for beta carotene as a singlet-oxygen scavenger against photosensitized oxidation (Foote et al., 1970; Mathews-Roth, 1982; Santamaria et al., 1983), but this protection does not explain the presence of carotenoids in tissues never exposed to light radiation. However, more recently, singlet-oxygen has been shown to initiate peroxidation of fatty acids (Frankel, 1980) and beta carotene has been shown to protect against free-radical-induced lipid peroxidation (Krinsky & Deneke, 1982; Kanner & Kinsella, 1983). Thus, in mammalian species, carotenoids could be important as natural protective agents against the oxygen radicals that are produced in all tissues as normal by-products of metabolism (Totter, 1980).

The probability of cancer development is known to be strongly age-dependent (Dix & Cohen, 1980). However, it is not generally appreciated that longer-lived mammalian species also appear to have, in proportion to their innate lifespan potential, a lower time-dependant probability of developing the same types of cancer as shorter-lived species (Ratcliffe, 1933; Lombard & Witte, 1959; Kent, 1960; Lapin & Yakovleva, 1963; McClure, 1973; Siebold & Wolf, 1973; Montagna, 1975). An estimate of the different sensitivities to cancer development of species having different size and lifespan potentials has been made by Peto (1979). He compared mice and human with lifespan potentials of about 3 and 90 years, respectively. Considering that for both species, the onset frequency of transformation is proportional to the fourth power of

their age and that human has about 1000 times more epithelial cells
at risk, it was estimated that human epithelial cells have a risk
factor 10^{-9} times smaller to develop cancer than do equivalent
mouse epithelial cells. Using the same procedure to compare human
to chimpanzee, I estimate the risk factor in human to be about 1.6
x 10^{-5} times smaller than equivalent chimpanzee epithelial cells.
This surprisingly large magnitude of different innate potentials to
develop cancer exists in spite of the remarkable similarities in
the basic biological makeup of the epithelial cells making up these
species. Thus, comparative experiments with animals of different
lifespan potentials and sizes have the potential of uncovering
rather simple biochemical differences accounting for these
extraordinarily large differences in natural susceptibility to
cancer (Cutler, 1975, 1982a, 1984a).

As already noted, nothing is yet known about the biological
basis determining longevity in mammalian species, but a possibility
is that some of the processes determining species' longevity may be
the same as those determining age-dependent cancer frequency. This
is based in part on evidence indicating that both cancer (Weinhouse,
1980) and aging (Cutler, 1982a,b; Ono & Cutler, 1978) appear to
represent a loss in proper gene control, so processes protecting
the differentiated state of cells would affect both aging rate and
sensitivity of cells to spontaneous transformation. In addition,
cancer, accelerated aging, and many other dysfunctions are known to
be induced by radiation, chemical mutagens, or free-radical
generating agents (Kimball, 1979; Pryor, 1978; Walton & Packer,
1980; Williams & Dearfield, 1981). Furthermore, cancer development
can be reduced by antioxidants (Harman, 1981; Ames, 1983) and
differentiated state of cells stabilized (Hornsby & Gill, 1981). In
turn, longer-lived species have been found to have a higher
concentration of some types of antioxidants in their tissues
(Cutler, 1982a, 1984b,e; Tolmasoff et al., 1980). Cancer has also
been correlated with inadequate DNA repair (Kimball 1979; Setlow
1978), and longer-lived species have been found to have higher
levels of DNA repair (Hart & Setlow, 1974; Hart et al., 1979;
Frances et al., 1981; Treton & Courtois, 1982). Finally,
longer-lived species are more resistant to the induction of cancer
by mutagenic agents (Schwartz & Moore, 1979; Pashko & Schwartz,
1982).

The carotenoids represent a widespread group of pigments
synthesized only in plants (Goodwin, 1954, 1962; Isler et al.,
1971; Simpson & Chichester, 1981). Their biological function in
plants and microorganisms is not fully established, but in many
cases they appear to be protective in nature (Calabrese, 1980;
Krinsky, 1971, 1982). The carotenoids are divided into two major
classes, the carotenes and the xanthrophylls (Goodwin 1954, 1962).
For mammalian species, the only biological role of the carotenes

that is generally recognized is as a precursor to the synthesis of vitamin A or retinol. Beta carotene is the major carotene for retinol synthesis and is metabolized to retinol in the intestine and then transported in the blood bound by a retinol-binding protein (RBP) (Goodman, 1979). The amount of retinol in the serum has been found to be more dependent on RBP concentration in the blood than on the amount of carotenoid or retinol intake in the diet. Retinol is transported and stored in the liver, where most retinol resides in the organism. No biological role for the xanthrophylls or their metabolic products in mammals has been found (Goodwin, 1962; Isler et al., 1971; Simpson & Chichester, 1981).

Although a biological function for the carotenes or xanthrophylls themselves is not known in mammalian species, these pigments are absorbed directly into the tissues of some animals. Mammalian species can roughly be divided into three categories according to the types of carotenoids that are absorbed into their tissues (Goodwin 1954; 1962; Isler et al., 1971). The first consists of these animals which absorb all the carotenoids (carotene plus the xanthrophylls) unselectively. Human is the dominant species in this group, and the major carotenoids found in the serum are beta carotein, lycopene and lutein (Krinsky et al., 1958). Whether other primates also unselectively absorb the carotenes has not been determined. The second group absorbs only the carotenes, and examples of these species are horse, cow sheep and elephant. The third and largest group of animals does not absorb any carotenoids in their tissues. Examples are mouse, rat and rabbit.

What is most interesting in these three groups of animals is the uniqueness of human, being the longest-lived of all mammalian species and absorbing unselectively all the carotenoids. The second group of species appears to consist largely of species having intermediate MLSPs of about 20 to 50 years, and those of the third group are largely the shortest-lived of mammalian species, having MLSPs of about 3 to 20 years.

It is not understood what determines the qualitative and quantitative aspects of carotenoid tissue absorption, but it is likely to be based in part on the activity of an enzyme found predominantly in the intestinal mucosa cells, beta carotene 15,15'-dioxygenase (Olson & Hayaishi, 1965). This enzyme is responsible for initiating the conversion of all the carotene to retinol, so animals with low intestinal activity of this enzyme would be expected to have more carotenoids available for tissue absorption. The amount of carotenoids eaten in the diet of course also plays an important role in determining the amount of carotenoids that are absorbed, but not the qualitative aspects.

Thus, both genetic and dietary factors are involved in determining final tissue concentrations.

Because carotenoids and retinoids are known to have antioxidant properties and to stabilize the differentiated state of cells, it was of interest to simply determine if the tissues of longer-lived species naturally had higher concentrations of these substances (Cutler, 1984e).

The concentrations of carotenoids and retinol in serum and brain in different mammalian species are tabulated in Tables 23 and 24, respectively. Although there is a rough positive correlation of MLSP vs carotenoid concentration in serum and brain, this correlation is clearly more significant where correlation per SMR is calculated. This is illustrated in Figure 15. On the other hand, retinol concentration appears to be almost constant in both serum and brain as a function of MLSP or SMR. Thus, as shown in Figures 16 and 17, MLSP vs retinoids per SMR is not positively correlated for animals having MLSPs over 40 years.

These data strongly suggest that the carotenoids but not retinol may have played an important role in the evolution of human longevity as an antioxidant longevity determinant. Further experiments measuring carotenoids (particularly measuring the relative amounts of the various carotenoids, carotenes and xanthrophylls) in other tissues now need to be done to further establish the possible biological importance of carotenoids to human health and longevity.

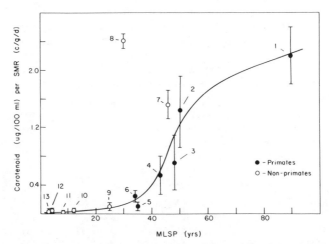

Fig. 15. Carotenoid concentration per specific metabolic rate (SMR) in plasma of mammalian species as a function of maximum lifespan potential (MLSP). See Table 23 for identification of species.

Table 23.   Serum carotenoid and retinol concentration as a function of lifespan potential and specific metabolic rate.

Species (common name)	MLSP (yrs)	SMR (o/g/d)	LEP (kcal/g)	Carotenoids (ug/100 ml)	Caro./SMR	Retinol (ug/100 ml)	Retinol/SMR
				Primates			
1 human	90 ± 5	24.8 ± 0.716	815 ± 51	54.8 ± 10.5 n = 10	2.20 ± 0.424	24.0 ± 3.68 n = 10	0.967 ± 0.150
2 orangutan	50 ± 8	24.5 ± 1.81	447 ± 79	34.8 ± 13.5 n = 4	1.42 ± 0.560	30.2 ± 4.25 n = 4	1.23 ± 0.195
3 chimpanzee	48 ± 5	26.8 ± 0.809	469 ± 51	17.8 ± 11.3 n = 15	0.664 ± 0.422	24.6 ± 4.78 n = 16	0.917 ± 0.180
4 gorilla	43 ± 5	19.7 ± 0.352	309 ± 36	10.6 ± 2.4 n = 3	0.538 ± 0.122	18.7 ± 5.71 n = 16	0.949 ± 0.290
5 gibbon	35 ± 8	42	536 ± 42	4.4 ± 2.1 n = 3	0.104 ± 0.0496	31.3 ± 3.02 n = 3	0.745 ± 0.0718
6 Rhesus	34 ± 5	41.3 + 0.836	512 ± 76	9.9 ± 3.26 n = 4	0.239 ± 0.0788	11.6 ± 1.25 n = 4	0.280 ± 0.0307
				Non-Primate Mammals			
7 horse	46 ± 8	13.9	235 ± 20	21.4 ± 3.07 p = 3	1.53 ± 0.219	9.39 ± 4.18 p = 3	0.675 ± 0.300
8 cow	30 ± 5	15.0	164 ± 15	36.0 ± 2.03 p = 2	2.4 ± 0.135	14.5 ± 0.494 F = 2	0.966 ± 0.0329
9 goat	25 ± 5	30.4	277 ± 30	3.3 ± 1.27 p = 2	0.108 ± 0.0415	18.2 ± 1.31 p = 2	0.598 ± 0.0430
10 rabbit	12 ± 2	58.7	257 ± 30	2.4 ± 1.69 n = 2	0.0408 ± 0.0287	20.6 ± 0.919 n = 2	0.350 ± 0.0156
11 deer mouse	8 ± 1	151 ± 14.1	440 ± 68	1.32 ± 1.76 n = 5	0.00874 ± 0.0116	16.9 ± 7.48 n = 5	0.111 ± 0.0491
12 rat	4 ± 0.5	104	152 ± 30	1.65 ± 2.91 p = 4	0.0158 ± 0.0278	16.2 ± 4.54 p = 4	0.155 ± 0.0434
13 field mouse	3.5 ± 0.5	182 ± 14.2	232 ± 15	1.65 ± 1.13 n = 4	0.00906 ± 0.0112	14.9 ± 4.21 n = 4	0.0818 ± 0.0282

n = number of individuals used
p = number of different serum batches used.

Table 24. Brain concentrations of carotenoids and retinol.

Species (common name)	MLSP (yrs)	SMR (c/g/d)	LEP (kc/g)	Carotenoid (μg/g lipid)	Caro./SMR	Retinol (μg/g lipid)	Retinol/SMR
human	90	24.7	815	4.85 ± 0.64 n = 4	0.196 ± 0.0259	1.79 ± 0.177 n = 4	0.724 ± 0.00716
baboon	35	30.7	394	2.50 ± 0.501 n = 6	0.814 ± 0.0163	1.85 ± 0.200 n = 6	0.0602 ± 0.00651
Rhesus	34	41.1	512	3.74 ± 0.575 n = 4	0.909 ±0.0139	1.77 ± 0.374 n = 4	0.0430 ± 0.00909
stump-tailed macaque	34	41.1	512	3.29 ± 0.896 n = 4	0.800 ± 0.218	1.68 ± 0.166 n = 4	0.0408 ± 0.00403
crab-eating macaque	34	41.1	512	2.73 n = 1	0.664	2.14 n = 1	0.0520
squirrel monkey	18	73.5	485	2.76 ± 0.113 n = 2	0.375 ± 0.00153	2.24 ± 0.737 n = 2	0.0304 ± 0.01002

MLSP vs C/SMR
r = 0.988
n = 6
Data taken from Cutler (1984e)

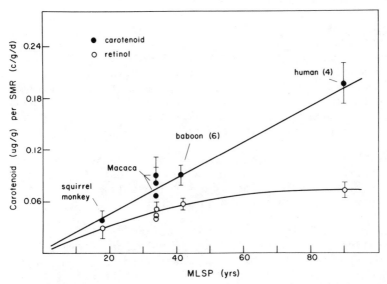

Fig. 16.   Retinol concentration per specific metabolic rate (SMR)
in plasma of mammalian species as a function of maximum
lifespan potential (MLSP).   See Table 23 for identification
of species.

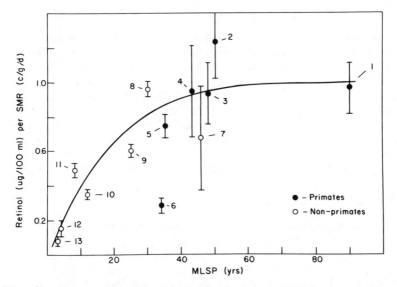

Fig. 17.   Brain carotenoid and retinol concentrations per gram
lipid per specific metabolic rate (SMR) as a function of
maximum lifespan potential (MSLP).

DETOXIFICATION ENZYMES

P-450 Cytochrome

P-450 cytochromes represent a well known class of enzymes involved in detoxification processes which mainly reside in the liver. These enzymes are considered to be protective against toxins found in the foods animals normally eat. It is therefore of interest to determine if longer-lived species have higher concentrations of these detoxification enzymes.

Table 25 presents typical data on the concentration of liver P-450 cytochrome in different mammalian species. As seen in liver, P-450 cytochrome was found to have a remarkably significant negative correlation as a function of MLSP.

However, we are interested in evaluating the total detoxification capacity of the body in relation to the amount of toxins entering the body that need detoxifying. Clearly this amount is not necessarily proportional to concentration of P-450 cytochrome on a per protein weight basis. This fact is illustrated in Table 25, indicating that longer-lived species have proportionally less liver weight per total body weight. However, large body weight species also have lower specific metabolic rates and thus consume less food per body weight. Thus, the amount of P-450 enzyme needed for equivalent detoxification across different species is not immediately obvious.

To make the appropriate comparison we need to calculate the total liver P-450 content per total body food intake which need detoxification. The results of this calculation are shown in Table 25 and illustrated in Figure 18. Here, it is seen that for shorter-lived species with MLSP from 3 to about 25 years, there is a steady increase of P-450 detoxification capacity. However, in species with MSLPs from 25 to 95 years, there is a steady decrease in this capacity. Thus, in the recent evolution of longevity leading to human, there appears to be a steady decrease in actual detoxification capacity of the liver relative to this enzyme.

Glutathione S-transferase

Glutathione S-transferase is another key enzyme used in detoxification reactions. Concentration of glutathione S-transferase in the liver was determined in different mammalian species and tabulated as a function of their MLSP. In addition, the detoxification capacity of the liver, was also calculated as for P-450. These results are shown in Tables 26, 27 and 28 and are illustrated in Figure 19. Here it is clear that either on a concentration basis or on a total liver content per total calorie

consumption per day basis, longer-lived species have less
detoxification capacity relative to this enzyme. Moreover, as
shown in Table 29, even the induced rate of increased
detoxification capacity is lower for longer-lived species. Thus,
both basal level and inducibility becomes lower as MLSP increases.

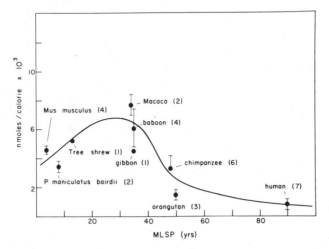

Fig. 18.   Total liver cytochrome P-450 concentration per total
           calorie utilization as a function of maximum lifespan
           potential (MLSP) in mammalian species.

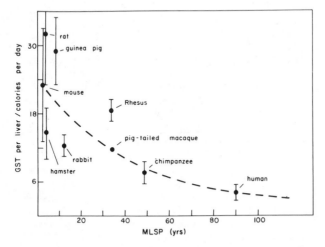

Fig. 19.   Total liver glutathione S-transferase content per total
           body calorie utilization as a function of maximum lifespan
           potential (MLSP) in mammalian species. Substrate used is
           dichloro-4-nitrobenzene.

Table 25.   P-450 cytochrome concentration in liver of primates.

Species	MLSP (yrs)	Body wt. (kg)	Cal/d x 10^3	Liver wt (g)	Liver/ body wt	P-450 conc. nmoles/mg protein	P-450/liver cal/d x 10^{-3}
human	90	63.5	1574	1311	0.0206	0.209 ± 0.0608 n = 7	0.839 ± 0.251 n = 7
orangutan	50	68.9	1671	1405	0.204	0.245 ± 0.107 n = 3	1.53 ± 0.349 n = 3
chimpanzee	48	46.7	1276	1028	0.0220	0.626 ± 0.214 n = 6	3.39 ± 1.39 n = 6
gibbon	35	5.5	335	156	0.0283	0.631 n = 1	4.54 n = 1
baboon	35	26.8	823	619	0.0231	0.799 ± 0.135 n = 4	6.10 ± 1.33 n = 4
Rhesus	34	8.18	339	220	0.0269	0.689 p = 2	8.14 p = 2
pig-tailed macaque	34	8.1	339	220	0.0269	0.947 p = 2	7.2 p = 2
squirrel monkey	18	0.795	58.8	29.0	0.0365	0.572 p = 2	1.66 p = 2
tree shrew	13	0.173	18.7	7.7	0.0445	1.07 p = 2	5.19 p = 2
deer mouse	8	0.021	3.85	1.2	0.0571	1.22 ± 0.197 n = 2	3.58 ± 0.28 n = 2
field mouse	3.5	0.023	4.12	1.3	0.0565	1.10 ± 0.0212 n = 2	4.66 ± 0.190 n = 2
inbred mouse C57BL/6J	3.5	0.025	4.39	1.4	0.0572	1.33 p = 2	5.57 p = 2

MLSP vs P-450 conc.   MLSP vs P-450 liver/total body calories
  n = 12   n = 12
  r = -0.853   r = -0.410
  P ≤ 0.001
n = number of different individuals used in determination.
p = number of different individuals pooled in determination.
Data taken from Cutler (1985, in press).

Table 26. Glutathione S-transferase activity in liver of adult
mammalian species.

Species (common name)	MLSP (yrs)	Total cal/day x 10	Liver wt (g)	Liver GS-T* (nmoles/min/mg P)	GS-T/Liver/ total cal/day
human	90	1574	1311	4.6 ± 1.7	3.83 ± 1.41
chimpanzee	48	1276	1028	9.2 ± 2.6	7.41 ± 2.09
pig-tailed macaque	34	339	220	18.0	11.6
Rhesus	34	339	220	28.8 ± 3.3	18.6 ± 2.17
rabbit	12	120	66.6	21.9 ± 4.3	12.1 ± 2.38
guinea pig	8	71.2	36.1	57.0 ± 13.0	29.1 ± 6.6
hamster	4	19.3	8.08	35.0 ± 11.1	14.6 ± 4.64
rat	4	21.9	9.23	76.4 ± 28.9	32.1 ± 12.1
mouse	3.5	4.1	1.32	74.1 ± 31.1	23.9 ± 10.0

*1.2 dichloro-4-nitrobenzene is substrate for GST determination.
(Chasseaud, 1979)

Table 27. Liver glutathione S-transferase concentration.

Species	MLSP (yrs)	SMR (c/g/d)	LEP (kc/g)	GS-T (nmoles/min/mg)	GS-T per liver cal per day
human	90	24.7	815	1800	1.58
chimpanzee	45	26.6	469	3000	2.53
Rhesus	34	41.5	5.7	6250	4.16

Non-lifespan data taken from Summer and Greim (1981).

Table 28.   Induced rate of increase of glutathione S-transferase in
            liver of mammalian species.

Species	MLSP (yrs)	Substrate	Control activity		Induced activity		Percent increase
Rat	4.0	DCNB	492	± 104	695	± 140	41.2
		DEM	6.4 ±	1.4	7.3 ±	1.0	14.0
		BA	2.7 ±	1.1	2.6 ±	0.5	-3.7
Rhesus	34	DCNB	129	± 33	189	± 25	46.5
		DEM	2.5 ±	0.4	2.6 ±	0.4	4.0
		BA	0.4 ±	0.3	0.4 ±	0.3	0
Baboon	42	DCNB	64	± 3.3	74	± 14	15.6
		DEM	1.6 ±	0.7	1.9 ±	1.4	18.7

Oral dosage of induced phenobarbital 15 mg/kg.
Substrates: DCNB : 1,2 dichloro-4-nitrobenzene
            DEM : diethyl maleate
            BA   : benzylidene acetone
Activity: μmoles GSH/hr mg protein
Data taken from Chasseaud (1979).

These inverse correlation results for P-450 cytochrome and
glutathione S-transferase are supported in part by work published
by Schwartz' group (Schwartz and Moore, 1979; Pashka and Schwartz,
1982).   They showed that skin fibroblast cells taken from
longer-lived species and grown in vitro have less P-448
concentration.   However, they found no significant correlation
with P-450.   In contrast to this result, our in vivo studies found
no correlation with P-448 but an inverse correlation with P-450 for
whole liver tissue in primate species.   Thus, primates and/or liver
tissues may be different from skin fibroblasts or such cells grown
under in vitro conditions.   However, we do agree that detoxification
capacity relative to the P-448/P-450 cytochrome group of enzymes is
decreasing with increased MLSP.

The inverse correlation results of catalase, glutathione
peroxidase, glutathione, P-450 cytochrome and glutathione
S-transferase in liver may be explained in part by the toxic side
effects of the detoxification reactions, which in many cases is
known to produce a number of free radicals as well as hydrogen

peroxide and activated polyhydrocarbon mutagens. Moreover, the detoxification process is known to produce a number of mutagens. Thus, longer-lived species may have evolved means to minimize these toxic side effects of detoxification by restricting the types of food eaten and/or evolving less toxic detoxification processes which we are not yet aware of. Thus, in addition to further increasing the concentration of antioxidants during the evolution of increased MLSP, another strategy might have been to simply decrease the need for antioxidants to counter the toxic side effects of detoxification. This type of change could be brought about by changes in regulatory genes governing the cellular levels of the detoxifying enzymes.

SUMMARY AND CONCLUSION

This paper summarizes recent results evaluating the possible role a number of antioxidants and detoxification enzymes may have in accounting for the longevity differences existing in the mammalian species. In this study, the major objective was to identify unique biological characteristics in human that could help explain the extraordinary longevity and disease-free lifespan that characterize the human species. Our studies are clearly of a preliminary nature, and so all results are inconclusive. Nevertheless, there are some interesting trends which can be summarized as follows.

Significant Positive Correlation of MLSP vs Antioxidant per SMR (with human having highest concentration):

SOD (both CuZn and Mn types)
Urate
Carotenoids
Alpha tocopherol
Ceruloplasmin

No Significant Correlation of MLSP vs Antioxidant per SMR:

Ascorbate

Significant Negative Correlation of MSLP vs Antioxidant per SMR (with human having lowest concentration):

Catalase
Glutathione
Glutathione peroxidase

Significant Negative Correlation of MLSP vs Detoxification Capacity (with human having lowest concentration):

P-450 cytochrome (liver)
Glutathione S-transferase (liver)

These experimental results strongly support the general prediction of the Longevity Determinant Gene hypothesis, where (1) longevity of mammalian species is governed in part by the expression of a common set of antioxidant protection processes and (2) aging is caused in part by toxic side effects of normal oxygen metabolic and detoxification processes. Furthermore, it is becoming clear that several strategies may be involved in increasing the amount of protection, such as an absolute increase of antioxidant concentration, a decrease in specific metabolic rate or a decrease in the extent toxic metabolic reactions exist in tissues. Moreover, all of these changes appear to be of a quantitative nature, which could evolve relatively quickly by few genetic alterations occurring in regulatory gene sequences, which is consistant with what has been predicted.

ACKNOWLEDGEMENTS

This paper is dedicated to the late Dr. Howard Curtis, who as my post-doctoral supervisor at Brookhaven National Laboratory, provided me the inspiration, guidance and the necessary scientific freedom to develop the Longevity Determinant Gene hypothesis (Cutler, 1972). Appreciation is expressed to Edith Cutler for laboratory assistance, drawing of the figures and typing of the manuscript. Her assistance was made possible by support received from the Paul Glenn Foundation for Medical Research.

REFERENCES

Albritten, E.C., ed., 1952, "Standard Values in Blood", Federation of American Societies of Experimental Biology, Bethesda, Md.

Altman, P., and Dittmer, D., eds., 1961, "Blood and Other Body Fluids," Federation of American Societies of Experimental Biology, Bethesda, Md.

Altman, P., and Dittmer, D., eds., 1962, "Biological Handbook, Growth," Federation of American Society of Experimental Biology, Bethesda, Md.

Altman, P., and Dittmer, D., eds., 1968, "Biological Handbook. Metabolism," Federation of American Society of Experimental Biology, Bethesda, Md.

Altman, P., and Dittmer, D., eds., 1972, "Biology Data Book, " Federation of American Society of Experimental Biology, Bethesda, Md.

Altman, P., and Dittmer, D., eds., 1974, "Biology Data Book, 2nd ed.," Federation of American Society of Experimental Biology, Bethesda, Md.

Ames, B.N., 1983, Dietary carcinogens and anticarcinogens, Science, 221:1256.

Ames, B.N., Cathcart, R., Schwiers, E., and Hochstein, P., 1981, Uric acid: An antioxidant defense in humans against oxidant- and radical-caused aging and cancer. A hypothesis, Proc. Natl. Acad. Sci. USA, 78:6858.

Beers, R.F., and Sizer, I.W., 1952, A spectrophotometric method for measuring the breakdown of hydrogen peroxide by catalase, J. Biol. Chem., 195:133.

Bernirschke, K., Garner, F.M., and Jones, T.C., 1978, "Pathology of Laboratory Animals," Springer-Verlag, Basel.

Bowden, D., and Jones, M.L., 1979, Aging research in nonhuman primates, in: Aging in Non-human Primates," D.M. Bowden, ed., p. 1, Van Nostrand Reinhold, New York.

Bowden, D.M., and Williams, D.D., 1985, Aging, Adv. Vetern. Sci. Comp. Med., 21: 305.

Butler, J.A., Whanger, P.D., and Tripp, M.J., 1982, Blood selenium and glutathione peroxidase activity in pregnant women: Comparative assays in primates and other animals. Am. J. Comp. Nutr., 36: 15.

Calabrese, E.J., 1980, "Nutrition and Environmental Health", J. Wiley and Sons, New York.

Cerutti, P.A., 1985, Prooxidant states and tumor promotion. Science, 227:375.

Chance, B., Sies, H., and Boveris, A., 1979, Hydroperoxide metabolism in mammalian organs, Physiol. Rev. 59: 527.

Chasseaud, L.F., 1979, The role of glutathione and glutathione S-transferase in the metabolism of chemical carcinogens and other electrophilic agents, Adv. Cancer Res. 29:175.

Cohen, G., Dembiec, D., and Marcus, J., 1970, Measure of catalase activity in tissue extracts, Anal. Biochem. 34:30.

Comfort, A., 1964, "The Biology of Senescence", Elsevier, New York.

Cutler, R.G., 1972, Transcription of reinterated DNA sequence classes throughout the life-span of the mouse, "Advances Gerontological Research," Vol. 4, p. 219, B.L. Strehler, ed., Academic Press, New York.

Cutler, R.G., 1974, Redundancy of information content in the genome of
    mammalian species as a protective mechanism determining aging rate,
    Mech. Ageing Develop., 2:381.
Cutler, R.G., 1975, Evolution of human longevity and the genetic
    complexity governing aging rate, Proc. Natl. Acad. Sci. USA, 72:4664.
Cutler, R.G., 1976a, Evolution of longevity in primates, J. Human
    Evolution, 5:169.
Cutler, R.G., 1976b, Nature of aging and life maintenance processes, in:
    "Interdisciplinary Topics Gerontology," Vol. 9, p. 83, R.G. Cutler,
    ed., Karger, Basel.
Cutler, R.G., 1978, Evolutionary biology of senescence, in: "The Biology
    of Aging", p. 311, J.A. Behnke, C.E. Finch, and G.B. Moment, eds.,
    Plenum Press, New York.
Cutler, R.G., 1979, Evolution of longevity in ungulates and carnivores,
    Gerontology, 25:69.
Cutler, R.G., 1980a, Evolution of human longevity, in: "Advances in
    Pathobiology 7. Aging, Cancer and Cell Membranes," p. 43, C. Borek,
    C.M. Fenoglio, and D.W. King, eds., Thieme-Stratton, Inc.,
    New York.
Cutler, R.G., 1980b, Central vs peripheral aging, in: "Aging Phenomena.
    Relationships Among Different Levels of Organization," p. 261,
    K. Oota, T. Makinodan, M. Iriki, and L.S. Baker, eds., Plenum Press,
    New York.
Cutler, R.G., 1982a, Longevity is determined by specific genes: Testing
    the hypothesis, in: "Testing the Theories of Aging," p. 25, R. Adelman
    and G. Roth, eds., CRC Press, Boca Raton, FL.
Cutler, R.G., 1982b, The dysdifferentiative hypothesis of mammalian aging
    and longevity, in: "The Aging Brain. Aging," Vol. 20, p. 1, E.
    Giacobini, G. Giacobini, G. Filogamo and A. Vernadakis, eds., Raven
    Press, New York.
Cutler, R.G., 1983, Species probes, longevity and aging, in: "Intervention
    in the Aging Process: Basic Research, Pre-clinical Screening and
    Clinical Progress," p. 69, V. Cristofalo, J. Roberts and G. Baker,
    eds., A.R. Liss, New York.
Cutler, R.G., 1984a, Evolutionary biology of aging and longevity in
    mammalian species, in: "Aging and Cell Function," p. 1, J.E. Johnson,
    ed., Academic Press, New York.
Cutler, R.G., 1984b, Antioxidants, aging and longevity, in: "Free
    Radicals in Biology," Vol. 6, p. 371, W.A. Pryor, ed., Academic
    Press, New York.
Cutler, R.G., 1984c, Free radicals and aging, in: "Molecular Basis of
    Aging," p. 263, A.K. Roy and B. Chatterjee, eds., Academic Press,
    New York.
Cutler, R.G., 1984d, Antioxidants and longevity, in: "Free Radicals in
    Molecular Biology, Aging and Disease. Aging," Vol. 27, p. 235,
    D. Armstrong, R.S. Sohal, R.G. Cutler and T.F. Slater, eds.,
    Academic Press, New York.
Cutler, R.G., 1984e, Carotenoids and retinol. Their possible importance in
    determining longevity of primate species. Proc. Natl. Acad. Sci. USA,
    81:7627.

Cutler, R.G., 1985, Urate and ascorbate: Their possible role as antioxidants in determining longevity of mammalian species, in press, Arch. Gerontol. Geriatrics.

Dix, D., and Cohen, P., 1980, On the role of aging in cancer incidence, J. Theor. Biol., 83:163.

Dixon, M., and Webb, E.C., 1964, "Enzymes," Academic Press, New York.

Emmett, B., and Hochachka, P.W., 1981, Scaling of oxidative and glycolytic enzymes in mammals, Respir. Physiol., 45:273.

Evans, G.W., and Wiederanders, R.E., 1967, Blood copper variation among species, Amer. J. Physiol., 213:1183.

Foote, C.S., Chang, Y.C., and Denny, R.W., 1970, Chemistry of singlet oxygen X. Carotenoid quenching parallels biological protection, J. Amer. Chem. Soc., 92:5216.

Frances, A.A., Lee, W.H., and Regan, J.D., 1981, The relationship of DNA excision repair of ultraviolet-induced lesions to the maximum lifespan of mammals, Mech. Ageing Develop., 16:181.

Frankel, E.N., 1980, Analytical methods used in the study of autoxidation processes, in: "Autoxidation in Food and Biological Systems," p. 141, M.G. Simic and M. Karel, eds., Plenum Press, New York.

Fridovich, I., 1979, Superoxide dismutases: Defence against endogenous superoxide radical, in: "Oxygen Free Radicals and Tissue Damage, Ciba Found. Symp. 65," p. 77, Excerpta Medica, Amsterdam.

Goodman, D.S., 1979, Vitamin A and retinoids: Recent advances, Fed. Proc. 38:2501.

Goodwin, T.W., 1954, "Carotenoids. Their Comparative Biochemistry," Chem. Pub. Co., Inc., New York.

Goodwin, T.W., 1962, Carotenoids: Structure, distribution, and function, in: "Comparative Biochemistry," Vol. IV, p. 643, M. Florkes and H.S. Mason, eds., Academic Press, New York.

Harman, D., 1981, The aging process, Proc. Natl. Acad. Sci. USA, 78:7128.

Hart, R.W., Sacher, G.A., and Hoskins, T.L., 1979, DNA repair in a short- and a long-lived rodent species, J. Gerontol., 34:808.

Hart, R.W., and Setlow, R.B., 1974, Correlation between deoxyribonucleic acid excision repair and lifespan in a number of mammalian species. Proc. Natl. Acad. Sci. USA, 71:2169.

Hicks, R.M., 1983, The scientifc basis for regarding vitamin A and its analogues as anti-carcinogenic agents, Proc. Nutr. Soc., 42:83.

Hill, D.L., and Grubbs, C.J., 1982, Retinoids as chemopreventive and anticancer agents in intact animals, Anticancer Res., 2:111.

Hornsby, P.J., and Gill, G.N., 1981, Regulation of glutamine and pyruvate oxidation in cultured adrenocortical cells by cortisol, antioxidants, and oxygen: Effects on cell proliferation, J. Cell Physiol., 109:111.

Isler, O., Gutmann, H., and Solms, U., eds., 1971, "Carotenoids," Birkhauser, Basel.

Kanner, J., and Kinsella, J.E., 1983, Initiation of lipid peroxidation by a peroxidase-hydrogen peroxide/halide system, Lipids, 18:204.

Kartha, V.N.R., and Krishnamurthy, S., 1977, Antioxidant function of vitamin A, Intern. J. Vit. Nutr. Res. 47:394.

Kartha, V.N.R., and Krishnamurthy, S., 1978, Effects of vitamins, antioxidants and sulfhydryl compounds on in vitro rat brain lipid peroxidation, Intern. J. Vit. Nutr. Res., 48:38.

Kent, S.P., 1960, Spontaneous and induced malignant neoplasms in monkeys, Ann. New York Acad. Sci., 83:819.

Kimball, R.F., 1979, DNA repair and its relationship to mutagenesis, carcinogenesis, and cell death, in: "Cell Biology. A Comprehensive Treatise," Vol. 2, p. 439, D.M. Prescott and L. Goldstein, eds., Academic Press, New York.

Kirk, J.E., 1962, Variations in tissue content of vitamins and hormones, Vit. Horm., 20:82

Kolata, G., 1984, Does vitamin A prevent cancer? Science, 223:1161.

Krinsky, N.I., Cornwall, D.G., and Oncley, J.L., 1958, The transport of vitamin A and carotenoids in human plasma, Arch. Biochem. Biophys., 73:233.

Krinsky, N.I., 1971, IX. Function, in: "Carotenoids," p. 669, O. Isler, ed., Birkhauser Verlag, Basel.

Krinsky, N.I., 1982, Photobiology of carotenoid protection, in: "The Science of Photomedicine," p. 397, J.D. Regan and J.A. Parrish, eds., Plenum Press, New York.

Krinsky, N.I., and Deneke, S.M., 1982, Interaction of oxygen and oxy-radicals with carotenoids, J. Natl. Cancer Inst., 69:205.

Kunkel, H.O. Spalding, J.D. de Franciscis, G., and Futress, M.F., 1956, Cytochrome oxidase activity and body weight in rats and in three species of large animals, Amer. J. Physiol., 86:203.

Lapin, B.A., and Yakovleva, L.A., 1963, "Comparative Pathology in Monkeys," C.C. Thomas, Pub., Springfield, Ill.

Lawrence, R.A., and Burk, R.F., 1978, Species, tissue and subcellular distribution of non Se-dependent glutathione peroxidase activity, J. Nutr., 108:211.

Lindstedt, S.L., and Calder, W.A., 1981, Body size, physiological time, and longevity of homeothermic animals, Quart. Rev. Biol., 56:1.

Lombard, L.S., and Witte, E.J., 1959, Frequency and types of tumors in mammals and birds of the Philadelphia zoological garden, Cancer Res., 19:127.

Lotan, R., 1980, Effects of vitamin A and its analogs (retinoids) on normal and neoplastic cells, Biochim. Biophys. Acta, 605:33.

McClure, H.M., 1973, Tumors in nonhuman primates: Observations during a six-year period in the Yerkes Primate Center colony, Amer. J. Phys. Anthrop., 38:425.

De Marchena, O., Guarnieri, M., and McKhann, G., 1974, Glutathione peroxidase levels in brain, J. Neurochem., 22:773.

Mathews-Roth, M.M., 1982, Photosensitization by porphyrins and prevention of photosensitization by carotenoids, J. Natl. Cancer Inst., 69:279.

Mattenheimer, H., 1971, "Mattenheimer's Clinical Enzymology. Principles and Applications," Ann Arbor Science Pub., Ann Arbor, Mi.

Melby, E.C., and Altman, N.H., eds., 1976, "Handbook of Laboratory Animal Science," Vol. III., p. 57, CRC Press, Boca Raton, FL.

Mitruka, B.M., and Rawnsley, H.M., 1981, "Clinical, Biochemical and

Hematological Reference Values in Normal Experimental Animals and Normal Humans," Masson Pub., New York.

Montagna, W., 1975, "Nonhuman Primates in Biomedical Research," Univ. of Minnesota Press, Minneapolis.

Morrison, P.R., and Ryser, F.A., 1952, Weight and body temperature in mammals, Science, 116: 231.

Newberne, P.M., and Rogers, A.E., 1981, Vitamin A, retinoids, and cancer, in: "Nutrition and Cancer: Etiology and Treatment," p. 217, G.R. Newell and N.M. Ellison, eds., Raven Press, New York.

Olson, J.A., and Hayaishi, O., 1965, The enzymatic cleavage of β-carotene into vitamin A by soluble enzymes of rat liver and intestine, Proc. Natl. Acad. Sci. USA, 54:1364.

Ono, T., and Cutler, R.G. (1978) Age-dependent relaxation of gene repression: Increase of endogenous murine leukemia virus-related and globin-related RNA in brain and liver of mice, Proc. Natl. Acad. Sci. USA, 75:4431.

Ono, T., and Okada, S., 1984, Unique increase of superoxide dismutase level in brains of long living mammals, Exp. Gerontol., 19:349.

Pashko, L.L., and Schwartz, A.G., 1982, Inverse correlation between species' lifespan and species' cytochrome P-488 content of cultured fibroblasts, J. Gerontol., 37:38.

Peto, R., 1979, Detection of risk of cancer to man. Proc. Royal Soc. London B, 205:111.

Peto, R., 1983, Differences between carotene and retinol, Proc. Nutr. Soc., 42:81.

Peto, R., Doll, R., Buckley, J.D., and Sporn, M.B., 1981, Can dietary β-carotene materially reduce cancer rates? Nature, 290:201.

Pryor, W.A., 1978, The formation of free radicals and the consequences of their reactions in vivo, Photochem. Photobiol., 28:787.

Ratcliffe, H.L., 1933, Incidence and nature of tumors in captive wild mammals and birds, Amer. J. Cancer, 17:116.

Sacher, G.A., 1959, Relation of lifespan to brain and body weight, in: "Ciba Foundation Colloquia on Ageing, The Lifespan of Animals," Vol. 5, p. 115, G.E.W. Wolstenholme and C.M. O'Connor, eds., Churchill, London.

Sacher, G.A., 1962, The stochastic theory of mortality, Ann. N.Y. Acad. Sci., 96:985.

Sacher, G.A., 1965, On longevity regarded as an organized behavior: The role of brain structure, in: "Contributions to the Psychobiology of Aging," p. 99, R. Kastenbaum, ed., Springer Pub., New York.

Sacher, G.A., 1968, Molecular versus systemic theories on the genesis of ageing, Exp. Geront., 3:265.

Sacher, G.A., 1970, Allometric and factorial analysis of brain structure in insectivores and primates, in: "The Primate Brain," p. 245, C.R. Noback and W. Montagna, eds., Appleton-Century-Crofts, New York.

Sacher, G.A., 1977, Life table modification and life prolongation, in: "Handbook of the Biology of Aging," p. 582, C.E. Finch and L. Hayflick, eds., Van Nostrand Reinhold, New York.

Sacher, G.A., 1978, Age changes in rhythms of energy metabolism, activity, and body temperature in Mus and Peromyscus, in: "Aging and Biological Rhythms," p. 105, H.V. Samis and S. Capobianco, eds., Plenum Pub. Corp, New York.

Santamaria, L., Bianchi, A., Arnaboldi, A., Andreoni, L., and Bermond, P., 1983, Dietary carotenoids block photocarcinogenic enhancement by benzo(A)pyrene and inhibit its carcinogenesis in the dark, Experientia, 39:1043.

Schwartz, A.G., and Moore, C.J., 1979, Inverse correlation between species life span and capacity of cultured fibroblasts to metabolize polycyclic hydrocarbon carcinogens, Fed. Proc., 38:1989.

Seal, U.S., 1964, Vertebrate distribution of serum ceruloplasmin and sialic acid and the effects of pregnancy, Comp. Biochem. Physiol., 13: 143.

Seegmiller, J.E., 1979, Disorders of purine and pyrimidine metabolism, in: "Contemporary Metabolism," Vol. 1, p. 1, N. Frienkel, ed., Plenum Press, New York.

Setlow, R.B., 1978, Repair deficient human disorders and cancer, Nature, 271:713.

Siebold, H.R., and Wolf, R.H., 1973, Neoplasms and proliferative lesions in 1065 nonhuman primate necropsies, Lab Animal Sci., 23:533.

Simpson, K.L., and Chichester, C.O., 1981, Metabolism and nutritional significance of carotenoids, Ann. Rev. Nutr., 1:351.

Spector, W.S., ed., 1956, "Handbook of Biological Data", Div. of Biol. and Agr., Natl. Acad. Sci., Natl. Res. Council.

Stahl, W.R., 1962, Similarity and dimensional methods in biology, Science, 137:205.

Summer, K.-H., and Greim, H., 1981, Hepatic glutathione S-transferases: Activities and cellular localization in rat, Rhesus monkey, chimpanzee and man, Biochem. Pharm., 30:1719.

Tolmasoff, J.M., Ono, T., and Cutler, R.G., 1980, Superoxide dismutase: correlation with lifespan and specific metabolic rate in primate species, Proc. Natl. Acad. Sci. USA, 77:2777.

Totter, J.R., 1980, Spontaneous cancer and its possible relationship to oxygen metabolism, Proc. Natl. Acad. Sci., USA, 77:1763.

Treton, J.A., and Courtois, Y., 1982, Correlations between DNA excision repair and mammalian lifespan in lens epithelial cells, Cell Biol. Intern., 6:253.

Walton, J.R., and Packer, L., 1980, Free radical damage and protection: Relationship to cellular and cancer, in: "Vitamin E: A Comprehensive Treatise," p. 495, L. J. Machlin, ed., M. Dekker, New York.

Weinhouse, S., 1980, New dimensions in the biology of cancer, Cancer, 45:2975.

Williams, J.R., and Dearfield, K.L., 1981, DNA damage and repair in aging mammals, in: "Biochemistry of Aging," p. 25, J.R. Florini, ed., CRC Press, Boca Raton, FL.

Wislocki, G.B., 1933, Location of the testes and body temperature in mammals, Quart. Rev. Biol., 8:385.

Wyngaarden, J.B., and Kelley, W.N., 1976, "Gout and Hyperuricemia", Grun & Stratton, New York.

Yousef, M.K., Chaffee, R.R.J., and Johnson, H.D., 1971, Oxygen consumption of tree shrews: Effects of ambient temperatures, Comp. Biochem. Physiol., 38A:709.

Zile, M.H., and Cullum, M.E., 1983, The function of vitamin A: Current concepts, Proc. Soc. Exp. Biol. Med., 172:139.

RELATIONSHIP BETWEEN METABOLIC RATE, FREE RADICALS, DIFFERENTIATION

AND AGING: A UNIFIED THEORY

R.S. Sohal and R.G. Allen

Department of Biology
Southern Methodist University
Dallas, Texas 75275

INTRODUCTION

There is presently no single, widely accepted, unifying theory of aging that is applicable to a wide spectrum of organisms. This fact has led many gerontologists to believe that mechanisms of aging may differ in various phylogenetic groups, albeit no compelling evidence or a priori reason has been forwarded to support this view. Given the basic similarity of molecular and cellular processes in living systems, it is indeed more probable that the contrary may be true, and that the underlying causal mechanisms of aging are essentially similar in all organisms. Conceptually, theories of aging can be assigned to two fundamentally different schools. One view regards aging as a continuation of the process of differentiation involving a programmed "shutdown" of genomic activity or a sequential activation of specific genes whose products have deleterious effects on cellular functions. Alternatively, aging is postulated to be a direct or indirect product of metabolic damage arising from the inadequacy of protective and reparative mechanisms.

Variations in the life spans of hybrids, strains and species strongly support the concept that, to a considerable extent, the rate of aging is under genetic control. The major difficulty in demonstrating a purported underlying genetic program of aging is that no gene products or molecular events have been found which can be used as specific indicators of aging. Nevertheless, from another perspective, genetic control of the aging process can be envisioned to involve a generalized deterioration of genetic control, or dysdifferentiation, rather than an activation of deleterious aging genes (Cutler, 1984). Conceptually, a fully differentiated state

75

is associated with the maximal level of mechanistic efficiency,
whereas dysdifferentiation is reflected by functional inefficiency.

Theories of aging which consider the accumulation of unrepaired
damage as the cause of aging and death are often referred to as
"wear and tear" theories. In the past, these theories have been
criticized not only for their imprecision but also for equating
living organisms, which are capable of self-renewal and self-
maintenance, with inanimate objects. However, a deeper analysis,
which we provide here, indicates that molecular damage beyond the
reparative capacity of cells may be a cause of genomic modification
cellular dysdifferentiation and aging. There is strong evidence
that the rate of organismic aging is a function of a genetically
determined metabolic potential and of metabolic rate.

We present evidence and a rationale supporting a unified
hypothesis of aging which encompasses elements of "wear and tear"
theories--that is, the rate of living and free radical theories--
and which does not necessarily conflict with programmatic theories
of aging. We propose that metabolic rate is a major factor governing the aging process. By-products of oxygen metabolism induce
molecular damage which destabilizes the optimal state of cellular
differentiation and ultimately results in functional and regulatory
insufficiency associated with the aging process.

METABOLIC RATE AND AGING

A general survey of longevities in different phyla indicates
that the concept of species-specific life span is strictly applicable only to homeothermic mammals, which have a stable basal
metabolic rate. Life spans of poikilothermic species in general
are highly variable and are determined by environmental conditions.
Those environmental factors which reduce metabolic rate extend
life span, and those which increase metabolic rate shorten life
span. For example, the adult life span of a common housefly in
the summer is about 3 weeks whereas, at the end of summer, flies
retreat to relatively dark, cool areas, restrict their physical
activity and live six months or longer until the next summer (Hewitt,
1914). Thus, the answer to the question, "What is the average life
span of a housefly?" is "At what metabolic rate?"

There is a large body of evidence that indicates a relationship
between metabolic rate and aging in both poikilotherms and homeotherms (Sohal, 1976; 1981a). The existence of such a relationship
was first noted by Rubner (1908), who calculated that the total
amount of energy consumed by five different domesticated mammalian
species was relatively constant, around 200 kcal/g/life span. The
implication of this observation was later encapsulated by Pearl
(1928) in the "rate of living theory," which postulated that life

span was dependent on two factors: (i) a genetically determined
metabolic potential, and (ii) the rate at which this potential is
expended. However, more recent studies have indicated that
metabolic potential tends to vary in different mammalian species.
For example, Cutler (1984) has shown that non-primate mammals
expend about 200 kcal/g/life span as first reported by Rubner, but
non-human primates have a metabolic potential of about 400 kcal/
g/life span while in humans it is about 800 kcal/g/life span. In
the housefly, the total amount of energy consumed/life span
(metabolic potential) is only about 25 kcal (Sohal, 1982).
Together these comparative data indicate that the fixed metabolic
potential is not a rigid characteristic. Metabolic potential at
different ambient temperatures is fairly constant in milkweed bugs
(McArthur and Sohal, 1982) and fruitflies (Miquel et al., 1976),
whereas, in the housefly, metabolic potential was about 15% greater
at 18°C than at 25°C, but nearly equal under conditions of relatively high and low physical activity (Sohal, 1982). Metabolic
potential seems to be a general rather than a precisely fixed sum.
It can vary in different genotypes and under different environmental
conditions and would be expected to be lower under suboptimal
conditions.

In poikilotherms, a variety of physical, environmental and
behavioral factors, among them temperature, light, ionizing
radiations, sex ratios, mating activity, and physical activity, can
affect life span. A common denominator of their effects of life
span is an alteration in the rate of metabolism. It would, therefore, seem germane to this discussion to consider some of the
exogenous factors which influence metabolic rate and longevity.
Only those environmental regimes which prolong the maximum rather
than the average life span can be considered to have an effect on
the underlying rate of aging, because extension of the average
life span can be due to mere optimization of environmental
conditions.

Ambient Temperature

A large number of reports document the inverse relationship
between life span and ambient temperature in poikilotherms (Sohal,
1976, 1981a). We have studied the effects of different ambient
temperatures on the life spans of houseflies and milkweed bugs.
At 20°C, the average life span of houseflies was 44% and 190%
longer than at 25° and 30°C, respectively (Fig. 1). In the milkweed bug, longevity was 70% and 200% longer at 18°C than at 25°
and 30°C, respectively (McArthur and Sohal, 1982). The beginning
of the "dying phase", defined here as the age at which 20%
mortality has taken place, occurred earlier in populations maintained at 25° and 30°C than those kept at 18°C. In both insects,
slopes of age-specific death rate plots (Gompertz plots) were

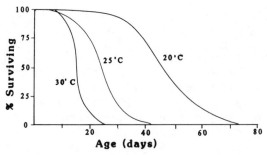

Fig. 1. Survivorship curve of
adult male houseflies
(200 flies/1 cubic/foot
cage) kept at 20°, 25°, and
30°C throughout life.
Average life spans were
46 ± 11, 23 ± 7 and
16 ± 3 days, respectiv-
ely. Dead flies were
counted daily

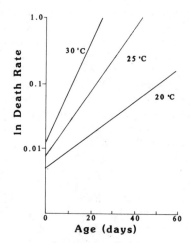

Fig. 2. Gompertz plots of
housefly populations
depicted in Fig. 1.

steeper and intercepts higher at the relatively warmer temperatures
(Fig. 2). According to Sacher (1977), slopes of Gompertz plots
indicate aging rates of populations, and intercepts reflect their
vulnerability to age-independent causes of death. Hence in these
studies, both aging rates and age-independent vulnerability to
death were inversely influenced by ambient temperature.

The effects of temperature on the longevity of poikilotherms
have generally been interpreted to support the "rate of living"
theory. However, on the basis of studies on Drosophila subobscura,
involving transfers from high to low ambient temperature and vice
versa, Maynard Smith (1963) proposed the "threshold theory of
aging" which postulated that aging is independent of ambient
temperature, with the implication that metabolic rate has no effect
on the aging process. Subsequent studies and numerous observations
have failed to confirm many of his observations thereby casting
doubt on the validity of the threshold theory (for review see
Sohal, 1976; Sohal, 1981a). It can now be safely inferred that
the threshold theory is invalid.

Within the species-specific viable range, ambient temperature
affects metabolic rate by stimulating both basal metabolic rate and
the level of physical activity. In dipteran insects, the basal
metabolic rate approximately doubles with each 10°C rise in
temperature (Tribe and Bowler, 1968), but the most significant
effect of temperature on metabolic rate is due to an increase in
walking and flying activity (Buchan and Sohal, 1981a). Using a
radar-Doppler device which measured walking and flying activity

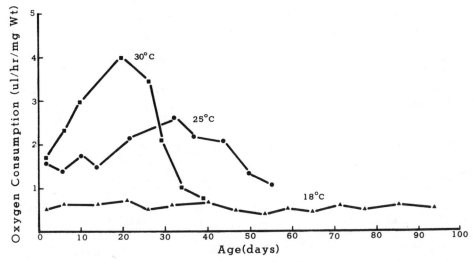

Fig. 3. Rate of oxygen consumption of milkweed bugs maintained at 18°, 25° and 30°C.

separately, we found that between 17 and 26°C, walking activity of houseflies increased about 15-fold and flying activity increased about 10 times. The rate of oxygen consumption in dipterans increases about 100 times during flight (Davis and Fraenkel, 1940). Nevertheless, metabolic rate of poikilotherms cannot be automatically assumed to correspond to the ambient temperature under all circumstances. For example, the rate of oxygen consumption of the milkweed bug is higher at 30°C than at 25°C during the first 2/3 of life but lower during the last trimester of life (Fig. 3; McArthur and Sohal, 1982).

Evidence also exists that poikilotherms possess temperature acclimation and metabolic compensative abilities and can maintain a relatively stable metabolic rate when transferred from one temperature to another (Bullock, 1955; Prosser, 1973). For example, in Culex larvae the rate of oxygen consumption remains relatively stable between 15° and 25°C (Buffington, 1969). Spiders (Anderson, 1970) and cockroaches (Dehnel and Segal, 1956) transferred from one temperature to another exhibit metabolic rates unlike those kept continuously at one temperature. It is quite evident that variations in ambient temperature cannot be assuredly related to the resultant changes in specific metabolic rate (Prosser, 1973). Experimental regimes, using ambient temperature as a means to affect aging rate, are further complicated by the fact that at different ambient temperatures poikilotherms show varying adaptive responses. Several important biological functions such as rates of enzyme synthesis and degradation, proportions of isozymes, membrane composition and permeability and the balance between various metabolic pathways differ at various temperatures (see Prosser, 1973). Furthermore, the overall efficiency of a

variety of different biological functions at different temperatures
is affected by the temperature preferendum of the species.

Physical Activity

In order to avoid the secondary effects associated with
variations in temperature, we used variations in physical activity
as an experimental regime to alter the metabolic rate in houseflies
(Ragland and Sohal, 1973). The physical activity of houseflies can
be altered by methods such as varying the size of housing containers
(Ragland and Sohal, 1973), removal of wings (Sohal and Buchan,
1981a), changing population density, and varying sex ratios
(Ragland and Sohal, 1973). Because the metabolic rate of flies
increases up to 100-fold during flight (Kammer and Heinrich, 1978),
large differences in metabolic rate can be obtained by the modulation of flying activity. To facilitate an understanding of our
experimental design, certain aspects of the sexual behavior of
houseflies are outlined. Female houseflies generally mate only
once in life; thereafter, they become unreceptive to further
copulations, while males remain sexually active and attempt to mate
repeatedly (Ragland and Sohal, 1973). In a sexually mixed
population with relatively few females, all the females are mated
rather quickly, rendering them resistant to further copulatory
attempts. The flight activity of males then increases, apparently
due to an enhanced search for sexually receptive females. Using
radar-Doppler to measure the physical activity of flies, we found
that flying activity is relatively greater and life spans are
shorter in populations with a high male-to-female ratio (Sohal
and Buchan, 1981a). In populations consisting of males only,
sex-related physical activity does not cease because males make
persistent homosexual copulatory attempts on each other.

Ragland and Sohal (1973) manipulated physical activity in
houseflies by using differently sized housing containers and
varying sex ratios. To enhance physical activity, populations of
flies (4 males:1 female) were placed in 1-cubic-foot cages where
flight was possible (HA populations); physical activity was
minimized by confining single flies in a small bottle partitioned
with a cardboard maze, where they were able to walk but were
unable to fly (LA populations). The average and maximum life
spans of the LA flies were about 2.5 times longer than in the HA
populations (Fig. 4).

Excision of wings increases the life span of male houseflies
about 25%, which is significantly less than the life extension
caused by individual confinement (Sohal and Buchan, 1981a).
Solitary confinement of flies is essential for reducing physical
activity because males make persistent, homosexual, copulatory
attempts on each other. Actual measurements of physical activity
with radar-Doppler indicated that grouping of flies in one cage

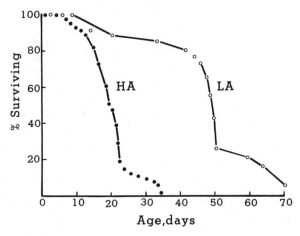

Fig. 4.   Survivorship curves of houseflies kept under conditions
of high activity (HA;100 flies/1-cubic-foot cage; 4 males:
1 female) and low physical activity (LA;one fly/250 ml
glass bottle).

increases flying and walking activity more than 4-fold, as compared
to the aggregate activity of the same flies confined singly in
cages of the same size. Furthermore, life spans of flies singly
confined in 1-cubic-foot cages were longer than those kept as a
group in a similar sized cage, suggesting that solitary confinement
of flies prolongs life span. De-winged flies, individually confined in vials, lived 70-80% longer than de-winged flies kept as
groups (Sohal and Buchan, 1981a). One of the major questions
concerning the relationship between metabolic rate and life span
is whether the individual differences in life spans, observed among
cohorts, are related to differences in their physical activity.
The flying and walking activity of individual flies was measured
and it appeared to be inversely related to the achieved life spans
(Sohal and Buchan, 1981a). Altogether, our results indicated that
the life span of houseflies is longer under conditions which reduce
the level of physical activity and metabolic rate.

The life span of worker honeybees is modulated by physical
activity related to foraging. The average total distance flown by
foraging bees was reported to be fixed at around 240 km. Life
span of the bees primarily depended upon the time spent in the
hive when they were inactive. Longer life spans in honeybees were
associated with longer periods of inactivity (Neukirch, 1982).

Trout and Kaplan (1970) investigated the relationship between
physical activity, metabolic rate and longevity in "shaker" mutants
of Drosophila melanogaster. This condition results from a sex-

linked, semidominant, neurological mutation caused by ethyl
methanesulphonate treatment of normal Canton-S males. In general,
mutants which exhibit decreased life spans as well as metabolic
potentials cannot validly be employed for aging studies or identification of longevity determinants because other inherited
deleterious effects, rather than accelerated aging, may be responsible for the shortened life span. The total amount of oxygen
consumed by the shaker mutants and the normal control was similar
at approximately 6 ml/mg wet wt/life span. The increased physical
activity of the shaker mutants directly corresponded to an increased
rate of metabolism and decreased life span, while the average life
span of mutants and the control was inversely proportional to the
average metabolic rate. The authors inferred that total metabolic
rate (basal and activity-related) is a major variable determining
longevity in Drosophila.

Physical Activity in Homeotherms

    There appears to be a fundamental difference in the response
of poikilotherms and homeotherms to variation in physical activity.
Physical activity in mammals is well known to stimulate anabolic
processes and a lack of activity results in muscular and glandular
atrophy. A certain level of physical activity is essential for
the maintenance of physiological fitness (Brunner and Jokl, 1970).
On the other hand, in poikilotherms atrophy from disuse does not
seem to occur. For example, flight muscles in wingless Drosophila
mutants (Deak, 1976) or in de-winged Drosophila (Sohal, 1975) do
not exhibit degenerative changes. We examined the relationship
between physical activity and subsequent flight ability (Ragland
and Sohal, 1975). Older houseflies exhibiting little wing damage
tend to lose flight ability one to three days prior to death. The
flight ability of sedentary flies, confined for life in small vials,
was compared with those kept in 1-cubic-foot cages. Flight loss
occurred earlier and with greater frequency in active flies as
compared with the sedentary flies. Thus, high levels of physical
activity were associated with an early physiological decline.

    Several studies have shown that voluntary exercise prolongs
the life of laboratory rodents (Goodrick, 1980); however, there is
no report documenting the effects of various levels of mild to
strenuous chronic exercise on life span. A fundamental flaw in
the design of mammalian studies dealing with physical activity and
life span is that comparisons of experimental animals are made
with sedentary controls. Such studies can only demonstrate that
lack of muscular activity is detrimental. It is possible that
physical activity beyond a certain level may be deleterious, as
indicated by the work of Davies et al. (1982).

Ionizing Radiations

Exposure to ionizing radiation induces two completely opposite effects on the life span of organisms. Whereas large doses decrease longevity, low doses tend to increase life span (for review, see Ducoff, 1972; Sacher, 1977). Interestingly, decreased physical activity has been frequently observed following irradiation (Allen and Sohal, 1982). We examined the relationship between radiation exposure, metabolic rate and life span by exposing adult male houseflies to 0, 20, 40 and 66 kR γ-radiation under conditions of either high or low physical activity (Allen and Sohal, 1982). The mean longevity of high-activity males exposed to 20 and 40 kR significantly increased, but lifespan decreased in high-activity males exposed to 66 kR, and in low-activity males at all doses. Metabolic rate as well as metabolic potential decreased in all groups in proportion to dose. Decreased metabolic potential in irradiated animals clearly indicates that there was irreversible damage; however, the reduction in metabolic rate was apparently sufficient to compensate for the life-shortening effects of radiation. Thus, no reduction in longevity was observed in high-activity flies at lower doses of radiation exposure. When placed under low activity conditions, metabolic rate was nearly equal in all groups, and the decreased metabolic potential was reflected by a decrease in life span proportional to dose. On the basis of these results, we rejected previous suggestions that radiation increases life span because it induces conservation of energy, kills harmful bacteria, or induces over-compensatory repair mechanisms (Ducoff, 1972; Sacher, 1977). Instead, our results indicated that the life-lengthening effects of low doses of radiation were a consequence of reduced metabolic rate.

Hibernation in Mammals

Mammalian hibernators can be considered to constitute a physiological link between poikilotherms and homeotherms in their ability to maintain a stable metabolic rate. Lyman et al. (1980) examined the relationship between hibernation and longevity in Turkish hamsters that hibernated for 0 to 33% of their lives. Metabolic rate was lower in hibernators kept at 5°C, than in controls maintained at 22°C. In general, maximum life span of hibernators was longer than non-hibernators, and animals that hibernated longer also lived longer.

METABOLIC RATE AND FREE RADICALS

Although the existence of a relationship between metabolic rate and life span has been known for a long time and originally formed the basis of the "rate of living" theory, until recently its significance remained rather obscure. A relationship between oxygen utilization and free radicals was first suggested by Gerschman et al.

(1954), and a large body of evidence now exists to indicate that, under normal physiological conditions, oxygen consumption generates potentially deleterious free radicals and hydroperoxides. In the current view, the potentially toxic effects of oxygen are primarily due to the univalent reduction of oxygen (Fridovich, 1976). Whereas most of the oxygen consumed by cells is reduced tetravalently in mitochondria by the activity of cytochrome oxidase, a small amount is apparently reduced by single electron additions (Chance et al., 1979; Halliwell, 1981). The latter type of respiration can be recognized by its resistance to cyanide. Univalent reduction of oxygen results, first, in the generation of the superoxide radical (O_2^-), which is then dismutated to hydrogen peroxide (H_2O_2) by the enzyme superoxide dismutase (SOD). H_2O_2 is normally eliminated by the activities of catalase and peroxidases. Although O_2^- and H_2O_2 are cytotoxic, the main agent of damage is believed to be the hydroxyl radical (OH·), which is apparently produced by the interaction between O_2^- and H_2O_2, catalysed by transition metals ($O_2^- + H_2O_2 \longrightarrow O_2 + OH^- + OH·$). In addition to enzymes superoxide dismutase, catalase and peroxidases, whose combined functions tend to decrease the risk of OH· generation, cells also possess non-enzymatic defenses against free radicals. Glutathione, β-carotene, α-tocopherol and ascorbate are the best known endogenous antioxidants (Forman and Fischer, 1981).

Free radicals and hydroperoxides are produced within cells under normal physiological conditions. Despite the presence of enzymic and non-enzymic defenses against these intermediates of oxygen reduction, a small proportion is believed to escape quenching. This is indicated by the presence of small quantities of partially reduced oxygen species in cells under steady-state conditions (Britton et al., 1978; Chance et al., 1979). There is ample evidence that the intermediates of oxygen reduction can cause damage to cellular constituents. For example, fluxes of experimentally generated O_2^- have been shown to cause lipid peroxidation, inactivation of enzymes, lysis of membranes and cleavage of DNA (Brawn and Fridovich, 1980).

There is some evidence that enhanced metabolic rate increases the intracellular concentration of free radicals which cause damage to biological organelles. Such free radical-induced damage may be a source of the gradual physiological attrition occurring with age, as originally suggested by Harman (1956). Davies et al. (1982) have reported a two- to three-fold increase in free radical (R·) concentration in homogenates of muscle and liver of rats exercised until exhaustion at submaximal work load intensity. A similar R· signal (g = 2.004) was detected in homogenates from vitamin E-deficient animals. Mitochondrial respiratory control values were lower in exhausted rats and in vitamin E-deficient rats than in controls. State 4 respiration was increased in exercised and vitamin E-deficient rats, while state 3 respiration appeared to be unaffected, suggesting leakiness of mitochondria to protons. Concentrations of conjugated dienes and TBA-reactants were greatly increased in both vitamin E-deficient and exercised animals, indicating enhanced lipid peroxidation.

METABOLIC RATE, LIPID PEROXIDATION AND AGING

Lipofuscin

One of the most ubiquitous, age-related changes in a variety of post-mitotic and slowly dividing cells is the cytoplasmic accumulation of fluorescent, granular structures, usually referred to as lipofuscin (Sohal, 1981b). In the current view, lipofuscin is believed to arise by a variety of processes such as autophago-cytosis, oxidation of lipids and co-polymerization of organic molecules. Areas of cytoplasm, segregated in autophagic vacuoles, fuse with primary lysosomes resulting in the degradation of the enclosed cellular components (DeDuve and Wattiaux, 1966). Membrane lipids are believed to undergo progressive autoxidative changes resulting in the formation of pleiomorphic lipoidal structures (Elleder, 1981). Morphologically, lipofuscin granules can be considered to be secondary lysosomes containing peroxidated lipids and polymers of phospholipids. One of their main attributes is the emittance of orange-yellow fluorescence under UV light. The excitation maxima of the in situ and isolated lipofuscin granules ranges from 340 to 395 nm; however, several different emission maxima have also been reported, such as 450 nm, 540–580 nm and 620 nm (see Elleder, 1981).

Biochemical investigations of lipofuscin have centered on the nature and formation of the fluorescent material in lipofuscin granules (Mead, 1976; Tappel, 1975; 1980). Tappel has inferred that lipofuscin fluorophores form as an end-product of free radical-induced lipid peroxidation, so providing a link between oxygen consumption, free radicals, lipofuscin and aging. A highly attractive feature of Tappel's hypothesis is that the chloroform-soluble fluorescent material (SFM) provides a marker for studying the involvement of free radicals and oxidative damage in the aging process. Indeed, SFM accumulates with age in a variety of tissues and organisms (Donato and Sohal, 1981). For the sake of clarity, the term "lipofuscin" will be applied here to the in situ, morphologically detectable, autofluorescent granules and the term "soluble fluorescent material (SFM)" will refer to the substance present in tissue extracts.

Relationship Between Lipofuscin, Metabolic Rate and Aging

Paradoxically, the ubiquity of lipofuscin originally led many gerontologists to dismiss it as being non-specific and irrelevant to the study of aging. However, a considerable body of evidence suggests that lipofuscin accumulation may be a by-product of

reactions which play a causal role in the aging process (Sohal,
1981a). Short-lived mammalian species with high metabolic rate
tend to accumulate lipofuscin at a faster rate than longer-lived
species with lower metabolic rate. For example, lipofuscin
accumulates in the hearts of dogs approximately 5.5 times faster
than in humans, which roughly corresponds to the differences in
their life spans (Munnel and Getty, 1968). Friede (1962) compared
the distribution of oxidative enzymes with the relative amount of
lipofuscin in 66 different nuclei in the aged human brain. Nerve
cells exhibiting high oxidative enzyme activity contained more
lipofuscin than nerve cells characterized by low activity of
oxidative enzymes. A fortuitous insight into the relationship
between functional activity, oxidative enzyme activity and the
amount of lipofuscin was provided by studies on two persons who
had lost an eye. Alternate layers of the lateral geniculate
showed a marked decrease in DNP-diaphorase activity and in the
amount of lipofuscin. According to the author, the presence of
"wear and tear" pigment appeared to be related to the functional
"wear and tear" of a given region, as reflected by the intensity
of oxidative metabolism.

The relationship between oxidative activity and deposition of
lipofuscin is not universal. For example, the flight muscles of
dipteran insects have an extremely high rate of oxygen consumption
but contain no lipofuscin granules. Further, deposition of lipofuscin depends on dietary as well as innate factors (Wolman, 1981).

The relationship between metabolic rate and lipofuscin
accumulation was first experimentally demonstrated in our laboratory
(Sohal and Donato, 1979; Sohal, 1981c). Average, as well as maximum,
life spans of adult houseflies were prolonged approximately 2.5
times by elimination of flying activity. The rate of lipofuscin
deposition, measured in three different tissues by quantitative
electron microscopy, was faster in the short-lived, high-activity
flies as compared to the long-lived, low-activity flies. However,
the maximum level of lipofuscin reached in the two groups was
nearly equal.

Further evidence supporting this relationship was reported by
Papafrangos and Lyman (1982) in Turkish hamsters. As discussed
before, Lyman et al. (1981) found that Turkish hamsters that spend
part of their lives in the depressed metabolic state of hibernation
have 23% longer average life spans than non-hibernators. A comparison of lipofuscin content in the brain and heart of hamsters
that hibernated for 11-23% of their lives showed a slower rate of
lipofuscin accumulation than in those which hibernated only 0-7%
of their lives. These differences between the hibernators and the
non-hibernators became more marked with age, especially in the
heart. Although the rate of lipofuscin deposition was not directly
proportional to the alteration in life spans, the total volume of

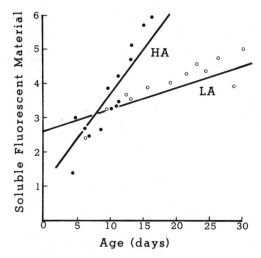

Fig. 5. Effects of physical activity on the age-associated
         accumulation of soluble fluorescent material (SFM) in
         houseflies. HA, high activity; LA; low activity.

lipofuscin reached at the end of life was similar in the two groups.
Thus, studies in both poikilotherms and hibernating mammals show
that in certain tissues, lipofuscin deposition corresponds to
alterations in metabolic rate and life span. However, this relationship should not be interpreted to imply that the two are
causally related.

Soluble Fluorescent Material (SFM)

     The concentration of fluorescent material in chloroform-
methanol extracts of tissues exhibiting Schiff-base, fluorescent
characteristics has been shown to increase with age in a variety
of organisms (Donato and Sohal, 1981). Environmental conditions
such as ambient temperature and physical activity, which enhance
metabolic rate, tend to increase the rate of SFM accumulation. In
milkweed bugs (McArthur and Sohal, 1982) and fruitflies (Sheldahl
and Tappel, 1974), rates of SFM accumulation are faster at higher
than at lower ambient temperatures, and the maximum levels reached
earlier in flies kept at higher temperatures. A comparison of
houseflies kept under conditions of high and low levels of physical
activity indicated that SFM accumulation was faster in the former
than in the latter group, but the maximal level reached was similar
in both (Fig. 5; Sohal and Donato, 1978). Individual flies which
exhibited a greater tendency for spontaneous flight activity tended
to have a shorter life span and contained more SFM than the relatively inactive flies (Sohal and Buchan, 1981b). Basson and
co-workers (1982) also reported that the rate of SFM accumulation

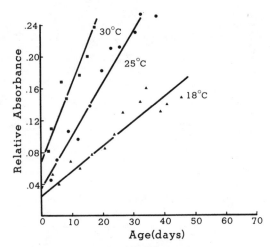

Fig. 6. Age-associated changes in the concentration of TBA-reactants
in whole body homogenates of milkweed bugs kept at 18°,
28° and 30°C throughout life.

is faster in rats undergoing treadmill physical training than in
sedentary controls.

Thiobarbituric Acid (TBA) Reactants

One of the consequences of free radical interactions with
cellular structures can be the peroxidation of polyunsaturated
lipids, detectable by the evolution of alkanes, such as ethane and
n-pentane, from the animal and by the production of TBA-reactive
material (Tappel, 1980). However, Gutteridge (1982) has reported
that in addition to lipid peroxidation, TBA-reactants or malon-
dialdehyde-like substances can be produced as a result of free
radical damage to organic molecules, such as amino acids, DNA and
carbohydrates. In milkweed bugs (McArthur and Sohal, 1982) and
houseflies (Sohal et al., 1981), the concentration of TBA-reactants
increased with age at significantly faster rates in organisms
raised at higher ambient temperatures (Fig. 6). Similarly,
houseflies kept under conditions of high physical activity tended
to contain a higher concentration of TBA-reactants than those kept
under low activity conditions (Sohal et al., 1981). Increased
metabolic rate may increase the susceptibility of tissues to
peroxidative changes in vitro and may reflect in vivo damage.

Effects of Age and Metabolic Rate on Alkane Production

Alkane exhalation by organisms has been proposed as a sensitive
indicator of in vivo lipid peroxidation (Riley et al., 1974).
Ethane and n-pentane, which are scission products of ω-3 and ω-6

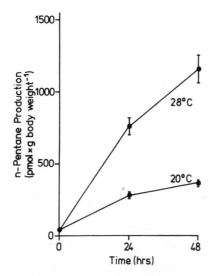

Fig. 7. In vivo n-pentane production by adult male houseflies
         kept at 20°C and 28°C for 48 hours.

polyunsaturated fatty acids respectively, have been the most common
indicators. An increase in alkane production has been reported in
rats with age (Sagai and Ishinose, 1980), as well as in response to
vitamin E deficiency (Tappel, 1980). Dillard et al. (1978) reported
increased levels of pentane exhalation by humans during physical
exertion. In the housefly n-pentane production increases 1.7-fold
during the average life span (Sohal et al., in press). The amount
of n-pentane generated by the flies in vivo was 2.7 times greater
at 28°C than at 20°C (Figs. 7 and 8), which clearly demonstrates
that an increase in metabolic rate causes an increase in the in vivo
rate of lipid peroxidation. Furthermore, homogenates of houseflies
aged at higher temperatures exhibit a greater susceptibility to
undergo lipid peroxidation in response to t-butyl hydroperoxide-
induced oxidative stress than those aged at a lower ambient
temperature. Age-associated increases in the in vivo evolution
of n-pentane and in response to t-butyl hydroperoxide in vitro
are suggestive of the increased vulnerability of flies to free
radical-induced damage, probably resulting from a decrease in the
efficiency of endogenous antioxidants. Levels of antioxidants such
as SOD, catalase, glutathione and vitamin E decline with age in the
housefly (Fig. 9; Sohal et al., 1984a). Levels of H_2O_2, a precursor
of the hydroxyl radical OH·, increase with age as well as in
response to an increase in the level of physical activity (Fig. 8;
Sohal et al., 1984b).

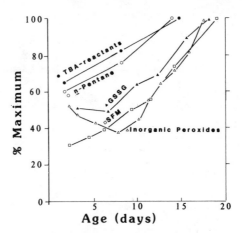

Fig. 8.   Pattern of age-associated changes in the concentration of
various products of free radical reactions. Inorganic
peroxides primarily consist of H_2O_2; GSSG, oxidized
glutathione; n-pentane, TBA-reactants and chloroform-
soluble fluorescent material (SFM) are indicators of
lipid peroxidation.

ANTIOXIDANT DEFENSES AND AGING

There are at least two lines of evidence suggesting that
antioxidant defenses may be related to aging and to variation in
species-specific longevity. We made a comprehensive analysis of
age-related changes in antioxidant defenses of a single species
(Fig. 9; Sohal et al., 1984a). In the housefly, superoxide
dismutase activity decreased during the last one-third of life;
catalase activity steadily declined with age to approximately half
the former level. Glutathione (GSH) level sharply declined in
older flies, whereas oxidized glutathione increased steadily with
age. The concentration of chloroform-soluble antioxidants sharply
declined during the first part of life. The concentration of
inorganic peroxides (H_2O_2) increased about 3-fold during the later
part of life. In toto, results of this study indicated that
enzymatic and non-enzymatic defenses against free radicals and
hydroperoxides in the adult housefly tend to deteriorate with age.

Cutler (1984) made comparative studies of life span potential
(LSP, or age of oldest survivor), life span energy potential

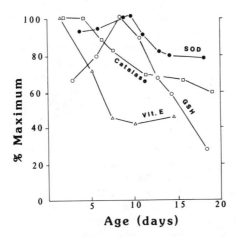

Fig. 9. Age-associated pattern of antioxidant levels in male
houseflies. SOD, superoxide dismutase; GSH, reduced
glutathione.

(LEP, or metabolic potential) and antioxidant defenses in various
mammalian species. There was a 30-fold difference in LSP, whereas
only 3 distinct classes of LEP were evident. Non-primate mammals
had an LEP of about 200 kcal/g/life span; non-human primates had
an LEP of 458 kcal/g/life span, and humans, capuchin monkeys
and lemurs had an LEP of 781 kcal/g/life span. He hypothesized
that rate of oxygen utilization was related to aging, and animals
with higher LEP values would be more resistant to the deleterious
effects of oxygen utilization. Antioxidants such as SOD, uric acid,
carotenoids and tocopherols were positively correlated with LEP
while ascorbate, glutathione, glutathione peroxidase and S-transferases were negatively correlated with LEP. Brain homogenates of
organisms with a high LEP were more resistant to autoxidation than
homogenates of organisms with a low LEP. Serum levels of TBA-
reactants were inversely correlated with LEP. These results
suggested that antioxidant defenses are correlated with LSP and
LEP; nevertheless, such correlations cannot demonstrate a cause-
and-effect relationship.

Experimental studies on the relationship between antioxidants,
oxidative stress and life span were made in the housefly in our
laboratory (reviewed by Sohal, 1984b). Oxidative stress was
induced by a variety of methods and putative levels of free radicals

increased by the administration of diamide, an -SH oxidizer.
Antioxidant defenses were inhibited with diethyldithiocarbamate
(DDC; an SOD inhibitor) and 3-amino-1,2,4-triazole (3-AT; an
inhibitor of catalase). In addition, antioxidant defenses were
augmented by the administration to the flies of ascorbate, α-
tocopherol or β-carotene. DDC administration caused a significant
decrease in SOD activity but failed to decrease longevity (Sohal
et al., 1984b). Metabolic rate was decreased and the concentration
of GSH was significantly elevated in DDC-treated flies. Total
inhibition of catalase with 3-AT had no effect on the longevity of
houseflies (Allen et al., 1983); again, the rate of oxygen utilization was greatly decreased and levels of GSH were augmented in
treated flies. Diamide administration also induced a decrease in
the rate of oxygen consumption and in SOD activity whereas catalase
and GSH levels were increased (Allen et al., 1984). Ascorbate
intake decreased GSH concentration, vitamin E slightly decreased
SOD activity while intake of β-carotene had no effect on any
parameter. Life spans and metabolic rates were unaffected by
vitamin E and β-carotene; ascorbate did not appreciably affect
the rate of oxygen utilization but caused a significant decrease
in longevity. Administration of a relatively low concentration
of the above oxidants did not increase the rates of age-associated
changes such as accumulations of SFM and TBA-reactive material.
Exposure to higher concentrations of oxidants caused rapid mortality. Long-term vitamin E deficiency also enhances the activities
of SOD, glutathione peroxidase and glutathione reductase in the
rat, apparently as a compensatory response to oxidative stress
(Cutler, 1984). In general, the results of these studies indicate
that: (i) a complex balance exists between the products of oxygen
metabolism and antioxidant defenses, (ii) experimentally induced
imbalances in antioxidant defenses provoke compensatory responses,
(iii) houseflies adapt to mild oxidative stress by decreasing
their metabolic rate and increasing GSH content, (iv) oxidative
stress decreases metabolic potential even though life span may
remain unaffected, and (v) augmentation of antioxidant defenses
results in a compensatory decrease in a related or overlapping
antioxidant mechanism.

Attempts to determine if age-related changes occur in antioxidant efficiency have produced varied results. Kellogg and
Fridovich (1976) measured total SOD activity in Sprague-Dawley
rats at various ages and detected a slight age-dependent decrease
in the liver but not in the brain. Conversely, Massie et al.
(1979) reported a 36% decline in total SOD activity in the brain
of C57BL/6J mice between 50 and 900 days of age. Vanella et al.,
(1982) found that in the brain of male albino Wistar rats,
cytosolic SOD activity declined during the first 30 months of life,
however, mitochondrial SOD activity increased at a proportional
rate, so that the total SOD activity remained relatively stable.
Catalase activity decreases in aging Drosophila (Nicolosi et al.,

1973; Massie and Baird, 1976) and the housefly (Sohal et al., 1984c). With few exceptions (Sohal et al., 1984a), no attempts have been made to determine whether the overall antioxidant protection in cells declines with age. In order to determine whether or not a decrement occurs in the overall antioxidant efficiency of cells, it is imperative to obtain comprehensive information concerning the various overlapping defense mechanisms. In summary, it seems that a net balance exists between various antioxidant defenses implying that steady state concentrations of free radicals are maintained at an optimal constant level. According to Cutler (1984) this steady-state concentration of active oxygen species is inversely related to the maximal life span of organisms. Decrease in the level of antioxidant defenses accompanied by manifestation of increased free radical-induced reactions (as indicated by n-pentane production and the amount of TBA-reactants) in the house-fly leads us to hypothesize that aging is associated with relatively high concentrations of oxygen-free radicals and hydroperoxides.

FREE RADICALS, CELLULAR DIFFERENTIATION, DYSDIFFERENTIATION AND AGING

Although free radicals are constantly generated in cells and can cause molecular damage, it is unlikely that aging is solely due to the accumulation of physical damage. No single cellular alter-ation of sufficient magnitude so as to be incompatible with the continuation of life has been found. A survey of age-associated changes clearly suggests that aging is not entirely due to wear and tear of the structural components of cells.

Cutler (1984) suggested that aging may be due to free radical-induced changes in the differentiated state of cells, whereby normally repressed genes become derepressed with increasing age. In his view, the optimal state of differentiation gradually degenerates into a state of dysdifferentiation as a result of long-term exposure to free radicals. It appears to us that the fundamental question regarding the relationship between differ-entiation and aging, concerns the nature of the factors which control repression and derepression of genes during developmental and in post-developmental states. We suggest that free radicals may be involved in the maintenance of differentiated state, and that alteration in the balance between free radical generation and antioxidant defenses may be a causal factor in dysdifferentiation. Our model concurs with that proposed by Cutler in that free radical-induced dysdifferentiation rather than molecular damage is a causal factor in the aging process. However, our model further proposes that free radicals also play a role in the main-tenance of differentiated state and that dysdifferentiation is due to an alteration in the free radical generation/antioxidant balance. On the basis of several lines of evidence, outlined below, we postulate that free radicals, resulting from a decline in anti-oxidant defenses, lead to genic modifications responsible for the deleterious events occurring during aging.

Free Radicals and Differentiation

A variety of fields and gradients are known to affect developmental processes in multicellular organisms (Child, 1915;
MacCabe and Parker, 1976). Many of the changes during embryonic
development appear to correspond directly or indirectly to alterations in oxygen metabolism (Frieden, 1981). Child (1915)
postulated that in regenerating organisms the regions of higher
metabolic activity influenced the development of regions with
lower metabolic activity. Differential vascularization, which
presumably would lead to unequal oxygenation of tissues, is
believed to influence developmental patterns in higher organisms
(MacCabe and Parker, 1976; Osdoby and Caplan, 1979; Jariegiello
and Caplan, 1983). Furthermore, phenotypic expression in cultured
embryonic chick cells can be experimentally controlled by variations
in oxygen tensions (Caplan and Koutroupas, 1973).

Several lines of evidence indicate that free radicals may be
involved in the process of cellular differentiation and derepression
of genes. Polytene chromosomes of salivary glands in insects
exhibit characteristic puffing patterns during development (reviewed
by Zegarelli-Schmidt and Goodman, 1981). Uncouplers of mitochondrial
respiration, such as dinitrophenol, menadione, oligomycin and anti-
mycin A have been observed to induce chromosomal puffing (Leeders
and Berendes, 1972; Rensing, 1973).

Alterations in differentiated state are invariably accompanied
by changes in the level of cellular free radical defenses. Most
notably, cancer cells appear to exhibit a reduction in the activity
of mitochondrial SOD (mangano-isozyme) (Dionisi et al., 1975; Bize
et al., 1980; Oberley, 1983). In many cases, the activity of
cytosolic SOD (Cu/Zn isozyme) is also greatly reduced (Sykes et al.,
1978). The rate of cell division, which is indicative of the
extent of dedifferentiation, has been found to vary inversely with
SOD activity; that is, the highest rates of cell division occur
in cells with the lowest SOD activity (Barotoli et al., 1980;
Bize et al., 1980). Other antioxidant enzymes in cancer cells also
exhibit decreased activity (Sun and Cederbaum, 1980). Conversely,
SOD activity increases during metamorphosis in insects (Fernandez-
Souza and Michelson, 1976) and during differentiation of the
cellular slime mold, Didymium iridius (Lott et al., 1981).

We have observed an up to 46-fold increase in SOD activity
during differentiation of the syncytial slime mold Physarum
polycephalum. Treatments which alter the rate of differentiation
have a corresponding effect on SOD activity (Fig. 10 and 11;
Nations et al., 1984; Nations and Allen, 1984). Under identical
culture conditions, strains of Physarum which do not differentiate,
fail to exhibit an increase in SOD activity (Fig. 10; Nations and
Allen, 1984). These data suggest that antioxidant defenses and

Fig. 10.
   Time course differentiation in the
   slime mold, <u>Physarum</u> <u>polycephalum</u>,
   after transfer to a medum which induces dormancy. BUS is the Y-strain
   treated with 4mM buthione sulfoximine, an inhibitor of glutathione
   synthesis. Y and FY are differentiating strain; H is a heterokaryon
   formed by fusion of Fy and W. W
   is not depicted because it did not
   differentiate.

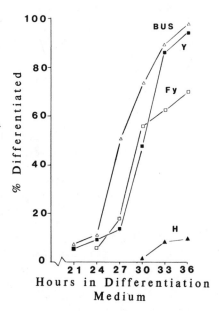

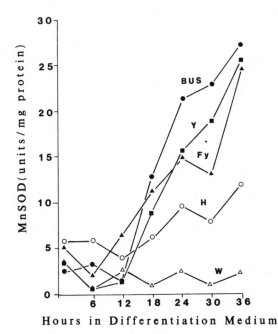

Hours in Differentiation Medium

Fig. 11.
   Changes in cyanide-insen-
   sitive superoxide dismutase activity in differentiation medium. The
   rate of increase in SOD
   activity corresponds to
   the differentiation.

the level of free radicals are associated with the process of
cellular differentiation.

   It is notable that rates of H_2O_2 generation and lipid peroxidation are lower in cancer cells than in normal cells; the former
is believed to be due to low SOD activity (Dionisi et al., 1975)
and the latter to result from alterations in membrane composition
of tumor cells (Bartoli and Galeotti, 1979; Bartoli et al., 1980).
The rate of tumor growth has also been reported to be inversely
related to lipid peroxidation (Bartoli and Galeotti, 1979), which
is consistent with the observation that lipid peroxides inhibit

mitosis (Wilber et al., 1957). Lipid peroxidation and H_2O_2 increase
during differentiation of Physarum. In regenerating rat liver, the
level of lipid peroxides decreases during the mitotic phase of
regeneration and increases during redifferentiation (Wolfson et al.,
1956). Results of these studies suggest that differentiation is
associated with relatively high levels of free radicals and
hydroperoxides.

Increases in nuclear concentration of ions, such as K+, Na+
and Mg++, cause chromosomal puffing in insects (Kroeger and Muller,
1973). Variations in GSH concentration can greatly affect the ion
distribution in cells (Jewell et al., 1982). GSH is also a modulator
of cell redox state (Chance et al., 1982). A large change in intracellular GSH concentration may thus affect the distribution of
charges in the cell, and will markedly affect the ratio of reducing
to oxidizing equivalents. GSH concentration is frequently high in
tumor cells (Meister and Griffith, 1979); addition of GSH to tissue
extracts gives a positive response to the Ames mutagenicity test
(Glatt et al., 1983). GSH concentration decreases about 70% during
differentiation in Physarum (Nations et al., 1984). The cause of
this decrease is unknown but increased free radical production during
differentiation may result in GSH oxidation and extrusion from
cells. GSH is also known to affect enzyme activities by breaking
disulfide bonds and by binding with proteins (Kosower and Kosower,
1976). A comparison of GSH in larval and adult insects reveals a
significantly lower GSH concentration in adults (Allen, unpublished).
In vertebrates, GSH concentration has been observed to vary greatly
during regeneration; GSH level is increased during the mitotic
phase but declines during redifferentiation (see Balinsky, 1970
for review). On the basis of the above-cited evidence, we hypothesize that differentiation is associated with high SOD activity
and low GSH concentration. Further, differentiation and aging are
characterized by relatively high levels of oxygen-derived free
radicals and peroxides.

Although free radical defenses may increase longevity by
decreasing free radical damage, a more immediate function of cellular
antioxidants is probably the maintenance of cellular redox state.
The redox state of the cell is dependent on the ratio of oxidizing
to reducing equivalents (Chance et al., 1979). In light of the
involvement of DNA morphology in the expression of genes (DiBerardino
et al., 1984), it would seem probable that gene expression is
influenced by the redox state of the cell, as well as by the net
ion balance in the cell, which is a function of the redox state
(Jewell et al., 1982). The influence of metabolic rate on life span,
and the changes which occur in the free radical defenses during
differentiation raise the possibility that a dynamic equilibrium

exists between the rate of free radical generation, antioxidant defenses, cellular charge distribution and the expression of genes. We propose the hypothesis that differentiation, in part, results from the establishment of this equilibrium and that dysdifferentiation is due to the loss or modification of this equilibrium. According to our model, antioxidant defenses modulate nuclearcytoplasmic interaction. High concentrations of oxygen-free radicals and peroxides are associated with differentiation and a decline in the level of antioxidants leads to genomic modifications responsible for aging.

SUMMARY

i. Metabolic rate is a major factor governing the rate of aging in both homeotherms and poikilotherms and is inversely related to life span.
ii. Homeotherms exhibit stable basal metabolic rates and species-specific life spans. Conversely, in poikilotherms, both basal methabolic rate and life span vary greatly.
iii. Metabolic potential (total energy consumed/g/life span) is a species-specific characteristic in Homoetherms and poikilotherms. Length of life is dependent upon the rate at which this fixed metabolic potential is expended, that is, metabolic rate.
iv. Oxygen-free radicals produced by metabolism can cause molecular damage. Accumulation of lipofuscin granules, Schiff-base-like, fluorescent material and thiobarbituric acid-reactants, as well as increased exhalation of pentane with age are indicative of free, radical-induced molecular damage.
v. Metabolic rate influences the rate of age-related changes.
vi. There is an overlapping compensatory balance between various components of the antioxidant defense system.
vii. The total antioxidant capacity of cells tends to decline with age.
viii. A dynamic equilibrium may exist between the rate of free radical generation and antioxidant levels. The establishment of theis equilibrium is associated with differentiation. It is hypothesized that loss of the equilibrium between free radical generation and antioxidant defenses results in dysdifferentiation, aging and cancer.

ACKNOWLEDGMENTS

Research work of the authors has been supported by grants from the National Institutes of Health, National Institute on Aging, and the Glenn Foundation for Medical Research. R.G.A. is a postdoctoral fellow of the Glenn Foundation.

REFERENCES

Allen, R.G., Farmer, K.J., and Sohal, R.S., 1983, Effect of catalase inactivation on levels of inorganic peroxides, superoxide dismutase, glutathione, oxygen consumption and life span in adult houseflies (Musca domestica), Biochem. J., 216:503.

Allen, R.G., Farmer, K.J., and Sohal, R.S., 1984, Effect of diamide administration on longevity, oxygen consumption, superoxide dismutase, catalase, inorganic peroxides and glutathione in the adult housefly, Musca domestica, Comp. Biochem. Physiol, 78C:31.

Allen, R.G., and Sohal, R.S., 1982, Life-lengthening effect of γ-radiation in the housefly, Musca domestica, Mech. Ageing Dev., 20:369.

Anderson, J.F., 1970, Metabolic rate of spiders, Comp. Biochem. Physiol., 33:51.

Balinsky, B.I., 1970, "Embryology," 3rd ed., Saunders, Philadelphia.

Bartoli, G.M., Bartoli, S., Galeotti, T., and Bertoli, E., 1980, Superoxide dismutase content and microsomal lipid composition of tumors with different growth rates, Biochim. Biophys. Acta, 620:205.

Bartoli, G.M., and Galeotti, T., 1979, Growth-related lipid peroxidation in tumor microsomal membranes and mitochondria. Biochim. Biophys. Acta, 574:537.

Basson, A.B.K., Treblanche, S.E., and Oelofsen, W., 1982, A comparative study on the effects of ageing and training on the levels of lipofuscin in various tissues of the rat, Comp. Biochem. Physiol., 71A:369.

Bize, I.B., Oberley, L.W., and Morris, H.P., 1980, Superoxide dismutase and superoxide radical in Morris hepatomas, Cancer Res., 40:3686.

Brawn, K., and Fridovich, I., 1980, Superoxide radical and superoxide dismutases: threat and defense, Acta Physiol. Scand. Suppl., 492:9.

Britton, L., Malinowski, D.P., and Fridovich, I., 1978, Superoxide dismutase and oxygen metabolism in Streptococcus faecalis and comparisons with other organisms, J. Bacteriol., 134:229.

Brunner, D., and Jokl, E., 1970, "Physical Activity and Aging," University Park Press, Baltimore.

Buchan, P.B., and Sohal, R.S., 1981, Effect of temperature and different sex ratios on physical activity and life span in the adult housefly, Musca domestica, Exp. Geront., 16:223.

Buffington, J.D., 1969, Temperature acclimation of respiration in Culex pipens pipens (Dipteria:Culicidae) and the influence of seasonal selection, Comp. Biochem. Physiol., 30:865.

Bullock, T.H., 1955, Compensation for temperature in the metabolism and activity of poikilotherms, Biol. Rev., 30:311.

Caplan, A.I., and Koutroupas, S., 1973, The control of muscle and cartilage development in the chick limb: the role of differential vascularization, J. Embryol. Exp. Morph., 29:571.

Chance, B., Seis, H., and Boveris, A., 1979, Hydroperoxide metabolism in mammalian organs, Physiol. Rev., 59:527.

Child, C.M., 1915, Individuation and reproduction in organisms, in: "Senescence and Rejuvenescence," page 199, editor(s) University of Chicago Press, Chicago, Illinois.

Cutler, R.G., 1984, Antioxidants, aging and longevity, in: "Free Radicals in Biology," Vol. 6, page 371, W.A. Pryor, ed., Academic Press, New York.

Davies, K.J.A., Quintanilha, A.T., Brooks, G.A., and Packer, L., 1982, Free radicals and tissue damage during exercise, Biochem. Biophys. Res. Comm. 107:1198.

Davis, R.A., and Fraenkel, G., 1940, The oxygen consumption of flies during flight, J. Exp. Biol., 17:402.

Deak, I.I., 1976, Use of Drosophila mutants to investigate the effects of disuse on the maintenance of muscle, J. Insect Physiol., 22:1159.

DeDuve, G., and Wattiaux, R., 1966, Functions of lysosomes, Ann. Rev. Physiol., 28:435.

Dehnel, P.A., and Segal, E., 1956, Acclimation of oxygen consumption to temperature in the American cockroach (Periplaneta americana), Biol. Bull., 111:53.

DiBerardino, M.A., Hoffner, N.J., and Etkin, L.D., 1984, Activation of dormant genes in specialized cells, Science, 224:946.

Dillard, C.J., Litov, R.E., Savin, W.M., Dumelin, E.E., and Tappel, A.L., 1978, Effects of exercise, vitamin E, and ozone on pulmonary function and lipid peroxidation, J. Appl. Physiol., 45:927.

Dionisi, O., Galeotti, T., Terranova, T., and Azzi, A., 1975, Superoxide radicals and hydrogen peroxide formation in mitochondria from normal and neoplastic tissues, Biochim. Biophys. Acta., 403:293.

Donato, H., and Sohal, R.S., 1981, Lipofuscin, in: "Handbook of Biochemistry in Aging," page 221, J. Florini, ed., CRC Press, Cleveland.

Ducoff, H.S., 1972, Cause of death in irradiated adult insects, Biol. Rev., 47:211.

Elleder, M., 1981, Chemical characterization of age pigments, in: "Age Pigments," page 204, R.S. Sohal, ed., Elsevier/North Holland, Amsterdam.

Fernandez-Souza, J.M., and Michelson, A.M., 1976, Variation of superoxide dismutases during the development of the fruitfly, Ceratitis capitata, Biochem. Biophys. Res. Commun. 73:217.

Frieden, E., 1981, The dual role of thyroid hormones in vertebrate development and calorigenesis, in: "Metamorphosis," 2nd ed., page 545, L.I. Gilbert and E. Frieden, ed., Plenum Press, NY.

Forman, H.J., and Fischer, A.B., 1981, Antioxidant Defenses, in: "Oxygen and Living Processes," D.L. Gilbert, ed., page 235, Springer-Verlag, New York.

Fridovich, I., 1976, Oxygen radicals, hydrogen peroxide, and oxygen toxicity, in: "Free Radicals in Biology," Vol. 1, page 239, W.A. Pryor, ed., Academic Press, New York.

Friede, R.L., 1962, The relationship of formation of lipofuscin to the distribution of oxidative enzymes in the human brain, Acta Neuropath (Berl.), 2:113.

Gerschman, R., Gilbert, D.L., Nye, S.W., Dwyer, P., and Fenn, W.O., 1954, Oxygen poisoning and X-radiation: a mechanism in common, Science, 119:623.

Glatt, H., Protic-Sabljic, M., and Oesh, F., 1983, Mutagenicity of glutathione and cysteine in the Ames test, Science, 220:961.

Goodrick, C.L., 1980, Effects of long-term voluntary wheel exercise on male and female rats, Gerontology, 26:22.

Gutteridge, J.M.C., 1982, Free radical damage to lipids, amino acids, carbohydrates and nucleic acids determined by thiobarbituric acid reactivity, Int. J. Biochem. 14:649.

Halliwell, B., 1981, Oxygen toxicity, free radicals and aging, in: "Age Pigments," R.S. Sohal, ed., page 1, Elsevier/North Holland, Amsterdam.

Harman, D., 1956, Aging: A theory based on free radical and radiation chemistry, J. Geront., 11:298.

Hewitt, C.G., 1914, "The House-fly," Cambridge University Press, Cambridge.

Jargiello, D.M., and Caplan, A.I., 1983, The establishment of vascular-derived microenvironments in the developing chick wing, Dev. Biol. 97:364.

Jewell, S.A., Bellomo, G., Thor, H., and Orrenius, S., 1982, Bleb formation in hepatocytes during drug metabolism is caused by disturbances in thiol and calcium ion homeostasis, Science, 217:1257.

Kammer, A.E., and Heinrich, B., 1978, Insect flight metabolism, in: "Advances in Insect Physiology," Vol. 13, page 133, J.E. Treberne, M.J. Berridge, and V.B. Wigglesworth, eds., Academic Press, New York.

Kellogg, E.W., and Fridovich, I., 1976, Superoxide dismutase in the rat and mouse as a function of age and longevity, J. Geront., 31:405.

Kosower, N.S., and Kosower, E.M., 1976, Functional aspects of glutathione disulfide and hidden forms of glutathione, in: "Glutathione," page 159, I.M. Arias and W.B. Jakoby, eds., Raven Press, New York.

Kroeger, H., and Muller, G., 1973, Control of puffing activity in three chromosomal segments of explanted salivary gland cells of Chironomus thummi by variation in extracellular Na+, K+ and Mg2+, Exp. Cell Res., 82:89.

Leenders, H.J., and Berendes, H.D., 1972, The effect of changes in the respiratory metabolism upon genome activity in

Drosophila, Chromosoma, 37:433.

Lott, T., Gorman, S., and Clark, J., 1981, Superoxide dismutase in Didymium iridis: characterization and changes in activity during senescence and sporulation, Mech. Ageing Dev., 17:119.

Lyman, C.P., O'Brian, R.C., Greene, G.C., and Papafrangos, E.D., 1981, Hibernation and longevity in the Turkish hamster Mesocricetus brandti, Science, 212:668.

MacCabe, J.A., and Parker, B.W., 1976, Evidence for a gradient of morphogenetic substance in the developing limb, Dev. Biol., 54:297.

Massie, H.R., Baird, M.C., 1976, Catalase levels in Drosophila and the lack of induction by hypolipidemic compounds. A brief note, Mech. Ageing Dev., 5:39.

Maynard Smith, J., 1963, Temperature and the rate of aging in poikilotherms, Nature, London, 199:400.

McArthur, M.C., and Sohal, R.S., 1982, Relationship between metabolic rate, aging, lipid peroxidation and fluorescent age pigment in milkweed bug, Oncopeltus fasciatus (Hemiptera), J. Geront., 37:268.

Mead, J.F., 1976, Free radical mechanisms of lipid damage and consequences for cellular membranes, in: "Free Radicals in Biology," W.A. Pryor, ed., Vol. 1, page 51, Academic Press, New York.

Meister, A., and Griffith, O.W., 1979, Effects of methionine sulfoximine analogs on the synthesis of glutamine and glutathione: possible chemotherapeutic implications, Cancer Treat. Rep., 63:1115.

Miquel, J., Lundgren, P.R., Bensch, K.G., and Atlan, H., 1976, Effect of temperature on the life span, vitality and fine structure of Drosophila melanogaster, Mech. Ageing Dev., 5:347.

Munnel, J.F., and Getty, R., 1968, Rate of accumulation of cardiac lipofuscin in the aging canine, J. Geront., 23:154.

Nations, C., and Allen, R.G., 1984, Free radical defenses and accelerated differentiation in Physarum polycephalum, J. Cell Biol.,99:242a (abstr.).

Nations, C., Allen, R.G., and McCarthy, J.L., 1984, Nonhistone proteins, free radical defenses and acceleration of spherulation in Physarum, in: "Growth, Cancer and Cell Cycle," P. Skehan and S.J. Friedman, eds., page 71, Humana Press Inc., Clifton, NJ.

Neukirch, A., 1982, Dependence of the life span of the honeybee (Apis mellifera) upon flight performance and energy consumption, J. Comp. Physiol., 146:35.

Nicolosi, R.J., Baird, M.B., Massie, H.R., and Samis, H.V., 1973, Senescence in Drosophila II. Renewal of catalase activity in flies of different ages, Exp. Geront., 8:101.

Oberley, L.W., 1983, Superoxide dismutase and cancer, in: "Superoxide Dismutase," L.W. Oberley, ed., Vol. 2, page 127, CRC Press, Boca Raton, Florida.

Osdoby, P., and Caplan, A.M., 1979, Osteogenesis in cultures of limb mesenchymal cells, Dev. Biol., 73:84.

Papafrangos, E.D., and Lyman, C.P., 1982, Lipofuscin accumulation and hibernation in Turkish hamster Mesocricetus brandti, J. Geront., 3:417.

Pearl, R., 1928, "The Rate of Living," Knopf, New York.

Prosser, C.L., 1973, "Comparative Animal Physiology," 3rd ed., Sanders, Philadelphia.

Ragland, S.S., and Sohal, R.S., 1973, Mating behavior, physical activity and aging in the housefly, Musca domestica, Exp. Geront., 8:135.

Ragland, S.S., and Sohal, R.S., 1975, Ambient temperature, physical activity and aging in the housefly, Musca domestica, Exp. Geront., 10:279.

Rensing, L., 1973, Effects of 2,4-dinitrophenol and dinactin on heat-sensitive and ecdysone-specific puffs of Drosophila salivary gland chromosomes in vitro, Cell Differ., 2:221.

Rieley, C., Cohen, G., and Lieberman, M., 1974, Ethane evolution: a new index of lipid peroxidation, Science, 183:208.

Rubner, M., 1908, "Das Problem der Lebensdauer," Berlin.

Sacher, G.A., 1977, Life table modification and life prolongation, in: "The Biology of Aging," page 582, C.E. Finch and L. Hayflick, eds., Van Nostrand Reinhold, New York.

Sagai, M., and Ishinose, T., 1980, Age-related changes in peroxidation as measured by ethane, ethylene, butane and pentane in respired gases of rats, Life Sci., 27:731.

Sheldahl, J.A., and Tappel, A.L., 1974, Fluorescent products from aging Drosophila melanogaster: an indicator of free radical lipid peroxidation, Exp. Geront., 9:33.

Sohal, R.S., 1975, Mitochondrial changes in the flight muscles of normal and flightless Drosophila melanogaster with age, J. Morph., 145:337.

Sohal, R.S., 1976, Metabolic rate and life span, in: "Interdisciplinary Topics in Gerontology," Vol. 9, page 25, H.P. von Hahn, ed., S. Karger, Basel.

Sohal, R.S., 1981a, Metabolic rate, aging and lipofuscin accumulation, in: "Age Pigments," page 303, R.S. Sohal, ed., Elsevier/North Holland, Amsterdam.

Sohal, R.S., 1981b, (Editor) "Age Pigments,", Elsevier/North Holland, Amsterdam.

Sohal, R.S., 1981c, Relationship between metabolic rate, lipofuscin accumulation and lysosomal enzyme activity during aging in the adult housefly, Musca domestica, Exp. Geront., 16:347.

Sohal, R.S., 1982, Oxygen consumption and life span in the adult male housefly, Musca domestica, Age, 5:21.

Sohal, R.S., 1984a, Assay of lipofuscin/ceroid pigment in vitro during aging, in: "Methods in Enzymology," Vol. 105, page 484, L. Packer, ed., Academic Press, New York.

Sohal, R.S., 1984b, Metabolic rate, free radicals and aging, in: "Free Radicals in Molecular Biology, Aging and Disease," Vol. 27, page 119, D. Armstrong, R.S. Sohal, R.G. Cutler, and T.F. Slater, eds., Raven Press, New York.

Sohal, R.S., and Buchan, P.B., 1981a, Relationship between physical activity and life span in the adult housefly, Musca domestica, Exp. Geront. 15:137.

Sohal, R.S., and Buchan, P.B., 1981b, Relationship between fluorescent age pigment, physiological age and physical activity in the housefly, Musca domestica, Mech. Ageing Dev., 15:243.

Sohal, R.S., and Donato, H., 1978, Effects of experimentally altered life spans on the accumulation of fluorescent age pigment in the housefly, Musca domestica, Exp. Geront., 13:335.

Sohal, R.S., and Donato, H., 1979, Effect of experimental prolongation of life span on lipofuscin content and lysosomal enzyme activity in the brain of the housefly, Musca domestica, J. Geront., 34:489.

Sohal, R.S., Donato, H., and Biehl, E.R., 1981, Effect of age and metabolic rate on lipid peroxidation in the housefly, Musca domestica, Mech. Ageing Dev., 16:159.

Sohal, R.S., Farmer, K.J., Allen, R.G., and Cohen, N.R., 1984a, Effect of age on oxygen consumption, superoxide dismutase, catalase, glutathione, inorganic peroxides, and chloroform-soluble antioxidants in the adult male housefly, Musca domestica, Mech. Ageing Dev., 24:185.

Sohal, R.S., Farmer, K.J., Allen, R.G., and Ragland, S.S., 1984b, Effects of diethyldithiocarbamate on life span, metabolic rate, superoxide dismutase catalase, inorganic peroxides and glutathione activity in the adult male housefly, Musca domestica, Mech. Ageing Dev., 24:175.

Sohal, R.S., Allen, R.G., Farmer, K.J., and Procter, J., 1984c, Effect of physical activity on superoxide dismutase, catalase, inorganic peroxide and glutathione in the adult male housefly, Musca domestica, Mech. Ageing Dev., 26:75.

Sohal, R.S., Muller, A., Koletzko, B., and Sies, H., 1985, Effect of age and ambient temperature on n-pentane production in adult housefly, Musca domestica, Mech. Ageing Dev., (in press).

Sun, A.S., and Cederbaum, A.I., 1980, Oxidoreductase activities in normal rat liver, tumor-bearing rat liver, and hepatoma HC-252, Cancer Res., 40:4677.

Sykes, J.A., McCormack, F.X., and O'Brian, T.J., 1978, A preliminary study of the superoxide dismutase content of some human tumors, Cancer Res., 38:2759.

Tappel, A.L., 1975, Lipid peroxidation and fluorescent molecular damage to membranes, in: "Pathobiology of Cell Membranes," Vol. 1, page 145, Academic Press, New York.

Tappel, A.L., 1980, Measurement of and protection from in vivo
        lipid peroxidation, in: "Free Radicals in Biology," Vol. 4,
        page 1, W.A. Pryor, ed., Academic Press, New York.
Tribe, M.A., and Bowler, K., 1968, Temperature dependence of
        "standard metabolic rate" in a poikilotherm, Comp. Biochem.
        Physiol., 25:427.
Trout, W.E., and Kaplan, W.D., 1970, A relationship between
        longevity, metabolic rate and activity in shaker mutants
        of Drosophila melanogaster, Exp. Geront., 5:83.
Vanella, A., Geremia, E., D'Urso, G., Tiriolo, P., Di Silvestro,
        I., Germaldi, R., and Pinturo, R., 1982, Superoxide
        dismutase activities in ageing rat brain, Gerontology, 28:108.
Wilber, K.M., Wolfson, N., Kenaston, C.B., Ottolengi, A., Gaulden,
        M.E., and Bernheim, F., 1957, Inhibition of cell division
        by ultraviolet irradiated unsaturated fatty acid, Exp. Cell
        Res., 13:503.
Wolfson, N., Wilber, K.M., and Bernheim, F., 1956, Lipid peroxide
        formation in regenerating rat liver, Exp. Cell Res., 10:556.
Wolman, M., 1981, Factors affecting lipid pigment formation, in:
        "Age Pigments," page 265, Elsevier/North Holland, Amsterdam.
Zegarelli-Schmidt, E.C., and Goodman, R., 1981, The dipteran as a
        model system in cell and molecular biology, Intern. Rev.
        Cytol., 71:245.

STATE OF KNOWLEDGE ON ACTION OF FOOD RESTRICTION AND AGING

Edward Masoro

Department of Physiology
University of Texas Health Science Center
San Antonio, Texas 78284

INTRODUCTION

Approximately 50 years have passed since McCay and Crowell
(1934) published their findings that restriction of the amount of
food consumed by rats resulted in some individuals reaching an
extremely old age and a population of rats with a greater mean age
at death than was the case for rats fed ad libitum. This finding
has often been repeated in mice and rats as well as in lower
vertebrates and invertebrates (Barrows and Kokkonen, 1977).
Although McCay and Crowell (1934) used severe food restriction
which markedly slowed skeletal growth and delayed sexual maturation, Berg and Simms (1960) subsequently showed that moderate
levels of restriction, not markedly influencing skeletal growth or
sexual maturation, were also effective. However, severe restriction increases life span more than moderate restriction (Masoro,
1984b). Of all experimental manipulations so far studied, food
restriction is by far the most effective in extending the life
span of mammalian species (Sacher, 1977).

In recent years, evidence has accumulated indicating that
food restriction not only extends life but must also retard one or
more basic aging processes. The reasons for such a view are: 1)
food restriction extends life span; 2) food restriction retards a
spectrum of age-related deteriorations of the physiologic systems;
and 3) food restriction delays the onset and/or slows the progression of age-related diseases. The data in regard to each of
these will be briefly reviewed before focusing on possible mechanisms by which food restriction retards basic aging processes.

105

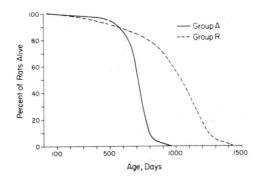

Fig. 1.   Survival curve for ad libitum fed (group A) and restricted
           (group R) rats.   The solid line refers to group A rats
           (n=115) and the broken line to group R rats (n=115).   For
           group A, the mean length of life ± SE is 701 ± 10 days,
           the median length of life is 714 days and the maximum
           length of life is 963 days.   For group R, the mean length
           of life ± SE is 986 ± 25 days, the median length of life
           is 1047 days and the maximum length of life is 1435 days.
           (From Yu et al., 1982)

LONGEVITY

     Typical of the effects of food restriction on longevity are
the findings obtained with male Fischer 344 rats by Yu et al.
(1982), depicted in the survival curves shown in Fig. 1.   Each of
the curves was generated from the survival characteristics of 115
rats.   The rats in group A were ad libitum fed and those in group R
were restricted to 60% of the mean food intake of the rats in group
A from 6 weeks of age on.   The survival curve of the rats in group
A was rather rectangular with few deaths occurring before 600 days
of age and most dying between 600 and 800 days of age.   The shape
of this curve is what would be expected for rats maintained in a
barrier facility free of pathogenic organisms and other environmental insults.   The survival curve of the rats in group R was less
rectangular than, and shifted to the right of, the curve of the
rats in group A.   Clearly, food restriction markedly increased
mean, median, and maximum length of life.   Indeed, when the one
hundred and fifteenth rat in group A died, approximately 70% of the
rats in group R were still alive.   This should be contrasted to the
influence of technology and medicine on longevity of Americans
during the past 100 years in which the survival curve has become
more rectangular, resulting in an increase in mean length of life
(life expectancy) but no change in maximum length of life (life
span).

     Early studies (Barrows and Roeder, 1965) indicated that food
restriction was only effective if initiated at or soon after weaning.

Recently, however, several laboratories (Ross, 1972; Stuchlikova et al., 1975; Weindruch and Walford, 1982; Cheney et al., 1983; Goodrick et al., 1983) have shown that food restriction initiated in adult life can increase the length of life. In a recent study by Yu et al. (1984), the effects of food restriction initiated soon after weaning were compared to restriction initiated in young adult life (6 months of age), and restriction limited to early life (6 weeks to 6 months of age). The mean and median length of life were markedly increased by food restriction started soon after weaning, less markedly increased by restriction initiated in adult life, and increased to a small but significant extent by restriction limited to early life. Strikingly, food restriction initiated in young adult life was as effective as that initiated soon after weaning in extending the life span (maximum length of life) and the age of tenth percentile survivors. In contrast, the life span and the age of the tenth percentile survivors were only increased to a small extent by food restriction limited to early life.

There have been some studies which indicate that protein restriction is at least in part responsible for the effects of food restriction (Leto et al., 1976; Goodrick, 1978) while other studies disagree with this (Ross and Bras, 1973; Nakagawa and Masano, 1971; Davis et al., 1983). This discrepancy may relate to differences in food intake, since in the above studies either food intake was not measured, was not fully reported, or was reduced. Yu et al. (1984) carried out a study in which caloric intake of ad libitum fed rats was not reduced but protein intake was restricted. They found that protein restriction significantly increased longevity but that the effect was small compared to that obtained with the comparable level of protein restriction occurring in food restriction regimens.

PHYSIOLOGICAL DETERIORATION

Many changes occur in physiological systems with advancing age (Masoro, 1976) and most of these changes appear to be of a deteriorating nature. Many of these changes are either slowed in progression or prevented by food restriction (Masoro, 1984b). Moreover, food restriction started in adult life is as effective as restriction started soon after weaning in modulating age-related physiologic changes.

An example of this is the findings of Masoro et al. (1983) shown in Fig. 2, concerning the effects of food restriction and protein restriction in rats on age changes in serum cholesterol concentration. In the rats of group 1, fed a 21% protein-containing but cholesterol-free diet, ad libitum, there was a marked rise in serum cholesterol concentration with age. A 60% restriction of food intake from 6 weeks to 6 months of age (group 3) had little effect on the age-related rise in serum cholesterol concentration.

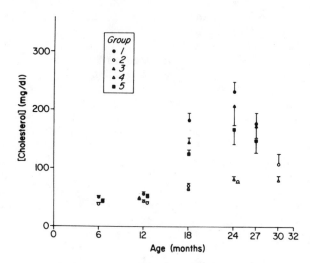

Fig. 2.   Influence of diet and age on total serum cholesterol con-
           centration. Each data point represents the mean value
           and SE for 10 rats, except for the 30 month old group 2
           rats, where there were 9. Measurements were made at 6,
           12, 18, 24, 27 and 30 months of age. Some data are
           displaced from these ages to maximize legibility. (From
           Masoro et al., 1983)

However, food restriction started soon after weaning (group 2) or
in young adult life (group 4), and continued throughout life
almost totally prevented this age-related increase. Restriction
of protein intake without restriction of caloric intake (group 5)
had only a small effect on the age-related increase in serum
cholesterol.

      Another example is the effect on serum calcitonin concentra-
tion obtained on the same rats (Kalu et al., 1983). Again, in the
ad libitum fed rats (groups 1 and 5), there was a marked age-
related increase in serum calcitonin concentration (Fig. 3).
Restriction of food intake from 6 weeks to 6 months of age (group
3) had little effect on this. However, lifelong food restriction
starting soon after weaning (group 2) or in young adult life (group
4) markedly reduced this increase with advancing age.

      These are not isolated examples. Food restriction has been
shown to retard or prevent the following age-related changes: the
loss of responsiveness of target cells to hormones (Bertrand et
al., 1980b; Yu et al., 1980); alterations in skeletal muscle
structure and function (McCarter et al., 1982); alterations in

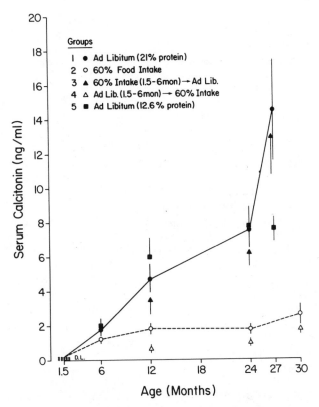

Fig. 3.   Effects of aging and dietary manipulation on serum calcitonin in male Fischer 344 rats.   Each point is the mean
of data from 7-10 animals and the vertical bars are SE's.
(From Kalu et al., 1983)

vascular smooth muscle function (Herlihy and Yu, 1980); loss of
corpus striatal dopamine receptors (Levin et al., 1981); altered
immune function (Weindruch et al., 1979; Fernandes et al., 1978);
loss of bone mass (Kalu et al., 1984).

Clearly, the spectrum of age changes in physiological activity
influenced by food restriction is broad. Such breadth implies that
basic aging processes are the site of action of food restriction.

AGE-RELATED DISEASE

Food restriction either delays the onset or slows the progression of most of the age-related diseases of rodents (Ross, 1976; Saxton and Kimball, 1941; Berg and Simms, 1961; Bras and Ross, 1964; Yu et al., 1982). Recently, Yu et al. (1984) compared food restriction initiated after weaning with: 1) restriction limited to early life, 2) restriction initiated in young adult life, and 3) restriction of protein but not calories, on the onset and progression of age-related disease in male Fischer 344 rats. Chronic nephropathy is a major age-related disease process in this strain of rat. Food restriction initiated soon after weaning, and restriction initiated in young adult life, so markedly slowed the progression of this disease process that almost none (less than 3%) of the rats had a severity of lesion at death which causes clinical expression of this disease. This is to be compared to the group of rats allowed to eat ad libitum throughout life, in which 72% of the rats at death exhibited lesions causing clinical expression of renal disease. Food restriction limited to early life had little effect on the progression of chronic nephropathy. However, the restriction of protein but not calories did significantly slow the progression of chronic nephropathy, with only 37% of the rats at death exhibiting lesions causing clinical expression of this disease process. Another significant age-related disease process in male Fischer 344 rats is cardiomyopathy. The dietary manipulations of Yu et al. (1984) modulated the progression of cardiomyopathy in a fashion similar to that observed with chronic nephropathy. Food restriction initiated soon after weaning, and that started in young adult life significantly delayed the occurrence of neoplastic disease, but food restriction limited to early life, and protein restriction without caloric restriction had no effect on the age of occurrence of tumors.

Age-related disease is clearly another example of how broadly food restriction modulates age-associated events. This again points to the likelihood that food restriction is retarding a primary aging process or processes.

MECHANISM BY WHICH FOOD RESTRICTION RETARDS AGING

Several serious proposals have been made in regard to the mechanism by which food restriction retards the aging process and prolongs life. It is of value to critically review these at this point in the discussion. However, one of these, the modulation of hypothalamic-pituitary function as the primary action of food restriction, will not be reviewed because it represents a major aspect of the paper in this volume by Merry and Holehan.

One of the first proposals on the mechanism of action of food restriction was that it prolongs life by delaying maturation and by slowing and prolonging growth. This view was based on the concept that aging is a post-maturational and post-growth event. McCay and his colleagues (McCay et al., 1935) subscribed to this concept and felt that their findings supported it. Further support came from the study of Barrows and Roeder (1965) in which food restriction of rats was found not be effective when initiated in adult life. Other data that were in support of this hypothesis were the findings that in mice and rats the rate of growth correlates inversely (Goodrick, 1977; Goodrick, 1980) and the duration of growth correlates directly (Goodrick, 1980; Everett and Webb, 1957; Ross et al., 1976) with the length of life. However, the recent studies (Ross, 1972; Stuchlikova et al., 1975; Weindruch and Walford, 1982; Cheney et al., 1983) showing that food restriction initiated in adult life increased life span do not support such a view. Probably the strongest data against this hypothesis are the findings of Yu et al. (1984) showing that food restriction started in adult life was as effective as when started soon after weaning in regard to increasing life span, delaying physiological deterioration and modulating age-related disease. In contrast, food restriction limited to early life had much less effect on these characteristics of aging.

The publication of the Society of Actuaries (1960) showing a direct relationship between adiposity and mortality in humans led to the hypothesis that food restriction increased longevity by decreasing body fat content. However, no experimental data have been reported in support of this view, and several studies (Lesser et al., 1973; Stuchlikova et al., 1975; Bertrand et al., 1980a; Harrison et al., 1984) have yielded data contrary to it. Harrison et al. (1984) showed that dietary restriction of obese (ob/ob) mice resulted in an increase in longevity, with the length of life being greater than that of the ad libitum fed lean mice, even though the fat content of the restricted obese mice was much greater than that of the ad libitum fed lean mice. Bertrand et al. (1980a) reported no correlation between fat mass and longevity with ad libitum fed rats, and found a positive correlation in the case of rats on a life-prolonging food restriction regimen.

Sacher (1977) postulated that the marked extension in longevity and retardation of the aging process by food restriction in laboratory rodents resulted from the reduction in metabolic rate per unit of body mass. This concept was embraced by many and is in agreement with the general belief in medical circles that reducing diets lower the metabolic rate. Sacher supported this hypothesis by calculations based on the published data of Ross (1969). In that study, five different dietary regimens were used, resulting in a spectrum of longevity characteristics. Sacher calculated that all groups, whatever the longevity, consumed close to 102 Kcal per gram body weight per lifetime. Thus, the long lived groups must have had a lower daily metabolic rate per gram body weight than those with shorter lives. Data obtained in our laboratory (Masoro et al., 1982) are not in agreement with this. In our study, rats fed a life-prolonging food restriction regimen had a greater daily consumption of calories than rats fed ad libitum. Moreover, the calories consumed per gram body weight per lifetime increased as the mean length of life was increased by the various food restriction regimens (Yu et al., 1984). However, food intake is a rather crude index of metabolic rate. We have, therefore, initiated a study in which oxygen consumption is being measured for 24-hour periods under housing and environmental conditions nearly identical to those encountered during the daily life of the rat. As of this time, the metabolic rate has been measured in 6-month-old ad libitum fed rats, and in rats of the same age restricted to 60% of the food intake from 6 weeks of age (i.e., a duration of 4½ months on the restricted diet). The metabolic rate of the ad libitum fed rats was found to be 136.4 ± 6.8 Kcal per Kg lean body mass per day, and that of the rats fed the restricted diet to be 142.5 ± 2.9 Kcal per Kg lean body mass per day. Thus, it seems unlikely that food restriction prolongs life by reducing the metabolic rate per unit of body mass.

Although all of the hypotheses that have been seriously proposed appear to be wanting, the data amassed to this date do provide a solid basis for developing a framework for future research. A general scheme (Fig. 4) for the action of food restriction, recently described by Masoro (1984a), provides such a framework. This scheme proposes that the coupling of food restriction to the slowing of the aging process involves a specific metabolic mechanism or mechanisms. The retardation of physiological and immune deterioration, and of age-related diseases are viewed as secondary events inevitably resulting from the slowing of the aging process. The increase in life span is viewed as a tertiary event, a consequence of the retardation of the deterioration of the physiologic and immune systems and of age-related disease. Although the coupling of food restriction to the aging process by a metabolic mechanism is logically satisfying, the specific nature of the coupling mechanism is totally unknown. The slowing of the cellular metabolic rate is an obvious possibility but data from our laboratory make it unlikely. Other possibilities, based on current theories of aging, are that food restriction influences either the rate of production or destruction of free radicals, modifies the rate of turnover of macromolecules and related biological structures, or influences the homeostatic control of the concentrations of hormones and/or metabolites. This list could go on, but what is really needed at this time is further experimental work aimed at providing clues to the nature of the metabolic mechanism.

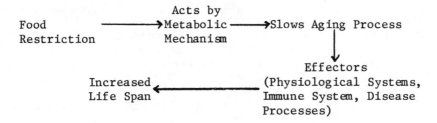

Fig. 4.   A general scheme for the action of food restriction.
          (From Masoro, 1984a)

CONCLUSIONS

     Food restriction extends the life span of rodents and delays
or prevents a broad spectrum of age-related deteriorations of the
physiological systems and of age-related disease.   Thus, it is
reasonable to conclude that food restriction retards basic aging
processes.   However, the mechanisms by which food restriction
retards aging are not known.   Available data and logic point to one
or more specific metabolic processes as the means of coupling food
restriction to the basic aging processes.   Attention of the cellular
and molecular biologists should be focused on uncovering the nature
of this coupling, since knowledge in this area not only will provide
an understanding of how food restriction influences the aging process but also should yield insight on the basic nature of aging
itself.   Moreover, knowledge in this area has a high probability of
yielding practical interventions for the modulation of human aging.

REFERENCES

Barrows, C. H. and Kokkonen, G. C., 1977, Relationship between
     nutrition and aging, Adv. Nutr. Res., 1:253-298.
Barrows, C. H., Jr. and Roeder, L. M., 1965, The effect of reduced
     food intake on enzymatic activities and life span of rats,
     J. Gerontol., 20:69-71.
Berg, B. H. and Simms, H. S., 1960, Nutrition and longevity.   II.
     Longevity and onset of disease with different levels of food
     intake, J. Nutr., 71:251-263.
Berg, B. H. and Simms, H. S., 1961, Nutrition and longevity.   III.
     Food restriction beyond 800 days, J. Nutr., 74:23-32.
Bertrand, H. A., Lynd, F. T., Masoro, E. J. and Yu, B. P., 1980a,
     Changes in adipose mass and cellularity through adult life of
     rats fed ad libitum or a life-promoting restricted diet.
     J. Gerontol., 35:827-835.
Bertrand, H. A., Masoro, E. J. and Yu, B. P., 1980b, Maintenance of
     glucagon-promoted lipolysis in adipocytes by food restriction,
     Endocrinology, 107:591-595.

Bras, G. and Ross, M. H., 1964, Kidney disease and nutrition in the
    rat. Toxicol. Appl. Pharmacol., 6:246-262.
Cheney, R. L., Liu, R. K., Smith, G. S., Meredith, P. J., Mickey,
    M. R. and Walford, R. L., 1983, The effect of dietary restric-
    tions of varying duration on survival, tumor patterns, immune
    function, and body temperature in B103F$_1$ female mice, J.
    Gerontol., 38:420-430.
Davis, T. A., Bales, C. W. and Beauchene, R. E., 1983, Differential
    effects of dietary caloric and protein restriction in the
    aging rat, Exp. Gerontol., 18:427-435.
Everett, A. V. and Webb, C., 1957, The relation between body weight
    change and life duration in rats, J. Gerontol., 12:128-135.
Fernandes, G., Friend, P., Yunis, E. J. and Good, R. A., 1978,
    Influence of dietary restriction on immunologic function and
    renal disease in (NZB x NZW)F$_1$ mice, Proc. Natl. Acad. Sci. USA,
    75:1500-1504.
Goodrick, C. L., 1977, Body weight change over the life span and
    longevity for C57Bl/6J mice and mutations which differ in
    maximal body weight, Gerontology, 23:405-413.
Goodrick, C. L., 1978, Body weight-increment and length of life:
    The effect of genetic constitution and dietary protein,
    J. Gerontol., 33:184-190.
Goodrick, C. L., 1980, Effects of long-term voluntary wheel exercise
    on male and female Wistar rats. I. Longevity, Gerontology,
    26:22-23.
Goodrick, C. L., Ingram, D. K., Reynolds, M. A., Freeman, J. R. and
    Cider, N. L., 1983, Differential effects of intermittent
    feeding and voluntary exercise on body weight and life span in
    adult rats, J. Gerontol., 38:36-45.
Harrison, D. E., Archer, J. R. and Astle, C. M., 1984, Effects of
    food restriction on aging: separation of food intake and adi-
    posity, Proc. Natl. Acad. Sci. USA, 81:1835-1838.
Herlihy, J. T. and Yu, B. P., 1980, Dietary manipulation of age-
    related decline in vascular smooth muscle function, Am. J.
    Physiol., 238:H652-H655.
Kalu, D. N., Cockerham, R., Yu, B. P. and Roos, B. A., 1983, Life-
    long dietary modulation of calcitonin levels in rats, Endo-
    crinology, 113:2010-2016.
Kalu, D. N., Hardin, R. R., Cockerham, R., Yu, B. P., Norling, B.
    K., and Egan, J. W., 1984, Lifelong food restriction prevents
    senile osteopenia and hyperparathyroidism in F344 rats,
    Mech. Ageing Dev., 26:103-112.
Lesser, G. T., Deutsch, S. and Markofsky, J., 1973, Aging in the
    rat: Longitudinal and cross-sectional studies of body compo-
    sition, Am. J. Physiol., 225:1472-1478.
Leto, S., Kokkonen, G. and Barrows, C., 1976, Dietary protein, life
    spans and biochemical variables in female mice, J. Gerontol.,
    31:144-148.
Levin, P., Janda, J. K., Joseph, J. A., Ingram, D. K. and Roth, G.
    S., 1981, Dietary restriction retards the age-associated loss

of rat striatal dopaminergic receptors, Science, 214:561-562.

Masoro, E. J., 1976, Physiologic changes with aging, in "Nutrition and Aging," p. 61-76, M. Winick, ed., Wiley, New York.

Masoro, E. J., 1984a, Food restriction and the aging process, J. Am. Geriat. Soc., 32:296-300.

Masoro, E. J., 1984b, Nutrition as a modulator of the aging process, Physiologist, 27:98-101.

Masoro, E. J., Compton, C., Yu, B. P. and Bertrand, H., 1983, Temporal and compositional dietary restrictions modulate age-related changes in serum lipids, J. Nutr., 113:880-892.

Masoro, E. J., Yu, B. P., and Bertrand, H. A., 1982, Action of food restriction in delaying the aging process. Proc. Natl. Acad. Sci., USA, 79:4239-4241.

McCarter, R. J. M., Masoro, E. J. and Yu, B. P., 1982, Rat muscle structure and metabolism in relation to age and food intake, Am. J. Physiol., 242:R89-R93.

McCay, C. M. and Crowell, M. F., 1934, Prolonging the life span, Sci. Monthly, 39:405-414.

McCay, C. M., Crowell, M. F. and Maynard, L. M., 1935, The effect of retarded growth upon the length of life span and upon ultimate body size, J. Nutr., 10:63-79.

Nagagawa, I. and Masano, Y., 1971, Effect of protein nutrition on growth and life span in the rat, J. Nutr., 101:613-620.

Ross, M. H., 1969, Aging, nutrition and hepatic enzyme activity patterns in the rat, J. Nutr., 97:Suppl. Part II:563-602.

Ross, M. H., 1972, Length of life and caloric intake, Am. J. Clin. Nutr., 25:834-838.

Ross, M. H., 1976, Nutrition and longevity in experimental animals in "Nutrition and Aging," p. 43-57, M. Winick, ed., Wiley, New York.

Ross, M. H. and Bras, G., 1973, Influence of protein under- and overnutrition on spontaneous tumor prevalence in the rat, J. Nutr., 103:944-963.

Ross, M. H., Lustbader, E. and Bras, G., 1976, Dietary practices and growth responses as predictors of longevity, Nature, 262:548-553.

Sacher, G. A., 1977, Life table modification and life prolongation, in "Handbook of Biology of Aging," p. 582-638, C. Finch and L. Hayflick, eds., Van Nostrand Reinhold, New York.

Saxton, J. A., Jr. and Kimball, G. C., 1941, Relation of nephrosis and other diseases of albino rats to age and to modifications of diet, Arch. Pathol., 32:951-965.

Society of Actuaries, 1960, "Build and blood pressure study", Society of Actuaries, Chicago.

Stuchlikova, E., Juricova-Horakova, J. and Deyl, Z., 1975, New aspects of the dietary effects of life prolongation in rodents. What is the role of obesity in aging?, Exp. Gerontol., 10:141-144.

Weindruch, R., Kristie, J. A., Cheney, K. E. and Walford, R. L., 1979, Influence of controlled dietary restriction on immunologic function, Fed. Proc., 38:2007–2016.

Weindruch, R. and Walford, R. L., 1982, Dietary restriction in mice beginning at 1 year of age: Effect on life-span and spontaneous cancer incidence, Science, 215:1415–1418.

Yu, B. P., Bertrand, H. A. and Masoro, E. J., 1980, Nutrition-aging influence of catecholamine-promoted lipolysis, Metabolism, 29:438–444.

Yu, B. P., Maeda, H., Murata, I. and Masoro, E. J., 1984, Nutritional modulation of longevity and age-related disease, Fed. Proc., 43:85.

Yu, B. P., Masoro, E. J., Murata, I., Bertrand, H. A. and Lynd, F. T., 1982, Life span study of SPF Fischer 344 male rats fed ad libitum or restricted diets: Longevity, growth, lean body mass and disease, J. Gerontol., 37:130–141.

THE ENDOCRINE RESPONSE TO DIETARY RESTRICTION IN THE RAT

B.J. Merry and Anne M. Holehan

Wolfson Institute
University of Hull
Hull. HU6 7RX U.K.

INTRODUCTION (GENERAL CONCEPTS)

Subsequent to the slow historical development of the use of controlled feeding to extend maximum lifespan in rodents, interest is now focussed on exploring the potential of this animal model to understand more fully the mechanisms of aging and the biochemical etiology of chronic age-related pathologies. The use of diet to extend lifespan has so far been restricted to rodent species within the Mammals, but confirmation of the reproducibility of this effect has been reported in spite of widely differing experimental designs (Merry and Holehan, 1985a, 1985b). Controlled underfeeding such as to limit access to the normal diet so that the body weight of experimental animals is maintained at 50% of age-matched ad libitum fed rats is one of the simplest and most effective designs to delay the age at which the rate of mortality increases and results in a 36-66% extension of the maximum lifespan (Masoro et al., 1980; Merry and Holehan, 1979, 1981). Although the immediate postweaning period is not the only phase of the lifespan susceptible to the effects of underfeeding, treatments which are continued for a longer fraction of the postweaning lifespan generally have a greater effect on extending longevity. It is uncertain if the immediate postweaning period is more sensitive to the effects of underfeeding in terms of lifespan extension, but it is clear that nutrition intervention restricted to 49 days postweaning substantially reduces tumor incidence in later life (Ross and Bras, 1971). Refeeding previously dietary restricted rodents, particularly during the first year of life, tends to negate the advantages accrued by underfeeding in terms of lifespan extension, (Merry and Holehan, 1985b). It is recognised that undernutrition instigated within a few days of birth by forming large litters is detrimental to subsequent growth and development while

117

life expectancy and maximum lifespan are not increased (Widdowson
and Kennedy, 1962). The authors are not aware of any study which
systematically investigated the earliest age before weaning at which
rodents will respond to undernutrition with extended lifespans.

OPERATIVE EFFECT OF DIETARY RESTRICTION

     A study of a number of physiological and biochemical variables
demonstrating significant age-related changes suggests that animals
maintained on restricted feeding are retained in a physiologically
younger condition than age-matched fully fed control rats and that
the extension of lifespan is far greater than can be explained by
delaying the onset of age-related pathologies (Moment, 1982; Bertrand, 1983). The mechanism or operative effect of dietary restriction is unknown but the early work of McCay et al. (1939) showed
that retarding maturation for as long as 1000 days by underfeeding
would extend lifespan. An inverse correlation existed between the
length of retarded growth and the period of life remaining after
maturation subsequent to accelerated growth following addition of
carbohydrate and fat to the calorie deficient diet. Thus the period
of life remaining after maturation became progressively less as the
length of the retarded development increased. The retention of the
immature state for prolonged periods and the study of Mulinos and
Pomerantz (1940) in which they induced a pseudo-hypophysectomy condition by chronic malnutrition has led several authors to suggest
that restricted feeding operates through the pituitary as a dietary
hypophysectomy (Samuels, 1946; Comfort, 1979; Moment, 1982).

     It is possible to mimic certain aspects of the dietary restrict-
ed rat by hypophysectomy linked to hormone replacement therapy during
early postweaning life (Everitt, 1976, 1982). Hypophysectomised rats
show reduced incidence of pathological lesions, retarded collagen
cross-linkage, depressed heart rate, haemoglobin, white cell count
and creatinine excretion. When compared with intact animals hypophysectomised rats have a shortened lifespan. Cortisone replacement
therapy will significantly improve survival so that mean life duration
does not differ significantly from intact controls and Everitt (1976)
has suggested that the retarded aging in the food restricted animal
may be due to the diminished secretion of pituitary hormones.

     A number of authors have reviewed the role of hormones in both
development and aging (Everitt, 1976; Cole et al., 1982; Vernadakis
and Timiras, 1982) while Denckla (1981) and Regelson (1983) have
suggested that hypophysectomy linked with hormonal maintenance will
result in a significant reversal of age-related pathology and induce
a broad base physiological rejuvenation in aged mice and rats. Evidence for the delay or reversal of aging by hypophysectomy has been
reviewed by Everitt (1976), Denckla (1981), Cutler (1981), Cole et
al., (1982), Regelson (1983). While the rate of change of many bio-

markers of aging can be reduced by hypophysectomy (see Regelson, 1983) the effect of hypophysectomy on survival rates is much more controversial. Everitt (1976, 1980, 1981) does not find increased survival of hypophysectomised rats with hormone support and Harrison et al. (1982) reported shortened survival times for hypophysectomised mice despite an apparent increase in motor activity and youthful appearance. It is still to be resolved what role the reduced food intake has in delaying aging in hypophysectomised rats. Everitt (1976) has shown that hypophysectomy decreases body weight in rats through appetite depression and this may well represent an alternative means of chronic dietary restriction with the hormonal changes being secondary to the reduced food intake.

ENDOCRINE RESPONSES TO CHRONIC UNDERNUTRITION

Reproduction in the Male

Reduced food intake in adult male rats has been reported to result in decreased secretion of anterior pituitary hormones accompanied by a reduction in weight and function of target organs (Campbell et al., 1977). Such studies have employed severe food restriction with complete food withdrawal for 7 days followed by 25% of ad libitum consumption. The detrimental effect of underfeeding on reproductive function in adult male rats is well documented (Grewal et al., 1971).

The effect of moderate food restriction implemented immediately at weaning on sexual maturation, fertility and serum hormone profiles in male rats was reported by Merry and Holehan (1981). Growth rate was restricted from 21 days to 50% that recorded for ad libitum fed animals. Maximum lifespan was increased from 1056 days in fully fed rats to 1500 days in rats on restricted feeding. There was a significant delay (p<0.005) in sexual maturation with 30% of underfed animals siring litters between 63 and 84 days compared to 90% in the control group. At all other ages assessed no significant difference in fertility was evident between groups with fertility reaching 90% in the dietary restricted animals by 107 days. At two years fertility had declined to 30-50% in both groups of animals. Growth of the testis was not retarded to the same degree as other organs and by one year of age no difference in testis weight could be demonstrated between groups (Fig. 1), although the ratio of testis weight to body mass was significantly higher throughout life in underfed rats.

Rats dietary restricted from 21 days showed both a delay of 20 days in the timing of the pubertal peak of serum testosterone and a marked suppression of the peak height (Fig. 2). At 100 days a marked fall in serum testosterone levels was recorded both in fully fed and dietary restricted rats but in contrast to ad libitum fed animals no age-related fall in testosterone levels was observed in the restricted

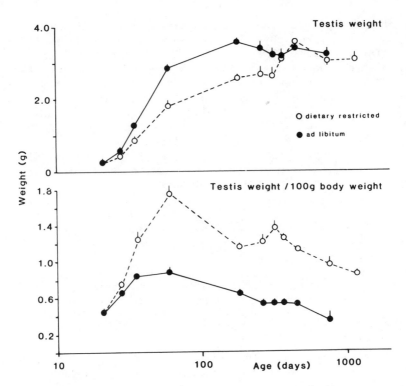

Fig. 1.   Testis weight with age in fully fed and dietary restricted
          (DR) rats.

group.   In contrast to the report of Howland (1975) on adult rats
restricted to 50% feed, such restriction in prepubertal postweaning
rats results in a precipitous fall in FSH levels by 30-40 days
(Fig. 3).   Stewart et al. (1975) found that immature rats on a 50%
restricted diet had decreased serum FSH levels which they presumed
was the result of a depletion of FSH-RH (Negro-Vilar et al., 1971).

      There is considerable disagreement between published data of
serum LH values during development in the rat.   The profile reported
by Merry and Holehan (1981) is in agreement with the report of
Piacsek and Goodspeed (1978) and Saksena and Lau (1979), (Fig. 3).
The wide fluctuations in serum LH observed during development which
were reported by Piacsek and Goodspeed (1978) and Mackinnon et al.
(1978) were not observed in ad libitum fed male rats housed 4 to a
cage, (Fig. 3).   Restricted feeding results in very high and unstable
prepubertal LH values and these may result from the severe stress
imposed by underfeeding (Fig. 3) (Döhler et al., 1977).   The slightly
delayed puberty observed in the dietary restricted male rat would
appear to result from the lowered serum FSH and an inability of the
testes to respond to the elevated serum LH.   This would appear to be

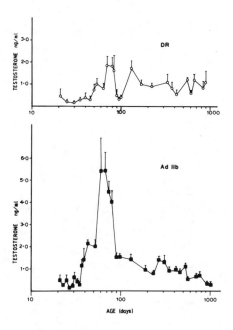

Fig. 2.   Serum profiles of testosterone with age in fully fed and
          dietary restricted male rats.

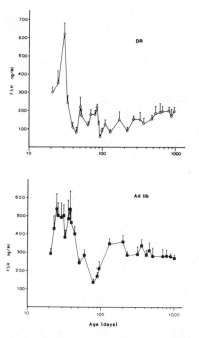

Fig. 3.   Serum profiles of FSH and LH with age in fully fed and
          dietary restricted male rats.

in agreement with the hypothesis expressed by Odell et al. (1974)
that sexual maturation is, at least partly, the result of FSH induced testicular sensitivity to LH.

Reproduction in the Female

Carr et al. (1949) studied the increase in both total and reproductive lifespan in chronic calorie-restricted mice. On a diet containing half the calories of a standard mouse diet, C3H females,
which are normally sterile at 11-12 months of age, were still fertile
at 21 months when returned to ad libitum feeding but were unable to
maintain their litters to weaning. Similar results were recorded
for the A strain of mice by Ball et al. (1947) while Berg and Simms
(1960) assessed fertility between 730 and 790 days in 24 rats returned to ad libitum feeding after restriction to 67% normal food
intake. In this study 67% of the animals were fertile but the
litters were small and the weaning quotient was low. Long-Evans
rats in which growth had been suspended for 2 years by maintenance
on a tryptophan-deficient diet were able to reproduce at 17-33 months
of age when growth was resumed after returning to ad libitum feeding
(Segall and Timiras, 1975; Segall et al. 1983). In female Sprague-
Dawley rats fed a restricted diet from weaning to maintain growth
rate at 50% that of fully fed controls, longevity was increased by
36% (Merry and Holehan, 1979). Vaginal opening and first estrus
were observed in 75% of the control animals between the ages of 38
and 42 days while restricted feeding extended and delayed the age
range for sexual maturation from 63 to as late as 227 days. After
the first estrus greater than 70% of the control and experimental
animals demonstrated a normal five day estrous cycle. In fully fed
rats there was a significant increase in cycle length with increasing age but no such increase in length of the cycle was observed in
dietary restricted rats even though normal estrous cycles were maintained to a much greater age (Table 1). Underfeeding resulted in a
much later onset of the age related irregularities of the estrous
cycle. After 200 days estrous cycles in fully fed rats became
irregular, the most common abnormality being an extension of the
period of cornification (persistent estrus or stage 1) with an increased frequency of recurrent pseudopregnancy (stage 2) occurring
in the second year of life (Table 1). It is clear that the observations of vaginal cytology indicate a slowing down in the rate of
reproductive ageing in the dietary restricted rat. As the irregularities in estrous cyclicity have been attributed to changes in
ovarian endocrine secretion and reduced capacity of the hypothalamic-
pituitary system to respond to gonadal hormone feedback it would
appear that these factors remain undisturbed in restricted rats for
a longer period (Lu, 1983).

In the studies reported by Merry and Holehan (1979); Merry,
Holehan and Phillips (1985), and Holehan (1984) rats retained on a
restricted diet throughout postweaning life were fertile, bearing

Table 1. Effect of diet on age-related changes in vaginal cytology

Age (days)	No. Rats	Cycle Length ± S.E.(days)	% females			
			Cycling	Stage 1	Stage 2	Stage 3
Fully fed						
100 - 120	50	4.7 ± 0.1	94	4	2	0
148 - 168	50	4.8 ± 0.1	78	18	4	0
180 - 200	176	5.0 ± 0.1	74	25	1	0
320 - 340	38	5.1 ± 0.2	55	32	13	0
390 - 410	122	5.8 ± 0.2	38	46	16	0
540 - 560	90	*	13	17	27	43
Dietary restricted						
180 - 200	150	5.1 ± 0.1	76	0	0	0
240 - 260	150	4.8 ± 0.1	69	21	10	0
500 - 520	60	5.0 ± 0.1	67	23	10	0
650 - 670	60	4.9 ± 0.1	65	20	15	0
730 - 750	39	5.1 ± 0.1	61	13	18	8

* Cycles too irregular to determine

multiple live litters to an age far exceeding that of the fully fed
control females (Fig. 4). Control animals show a rapid decline in
fertility from 270 days and were infertile by 500 days while in the
dietary restricted females maximum fertility was achieved by 500 days.
Fully fed animals on repeated breeding showed a decline in litter
size with age which was not apparent in the multiple litters recorded
for dietary restricted rats. However, returning the restricted
mothers to full feeding reinitiated the age-related decline in litter
size in subsequent pregnancies while cessation of breeding occurred
at an earlier age in dietary restricted rats returned to full feeding.

A comparison of the serum hormone profiles for LH, FSH, progesterone and estradiol-17β from weaning to puberty was made in fully
fed and dietary restricted rats (Holehan, 1984). No significant
effect of diet on prepubertal serum LH levels was observed, however
in agreement with the findings of Merry and Holehan (1981) for the
male dietary restricted rat FSH levels were significantly decreased.
Underfeeding resulted in a 2-3 fold elevation of circulating
estradiol-17β and a decrease in serum progesterone. Due to the
presence of an estrogen binding protein (α-fetoprotein) not all

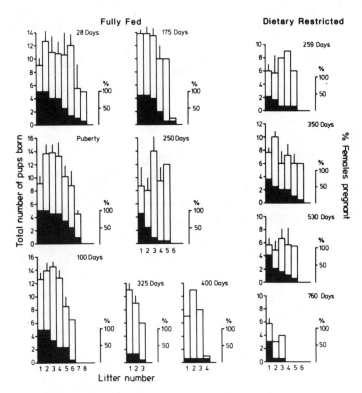

Fig. 4.   Breeding performance in control and dietary restricted
          female rats.

circulating estradiol-17β is biologically active.   The biological
activity of estradiol-17β increases prior to puberty as that fraction bound by α-fetoprotein falls and it has been suggested by
Andrews and Ojeda (1977) that this probably accounts for the decrease
in serum FSH at this time as a result of the feedback action on the
hypothalamus.   It is unclear at present whether the decreased circulating levels of FSH result from a negative feedback induced by the
elevated estradiol-17β or a direct result of underfeeding on gonado-
trophin release.

     Recent work from this Institute (Holehan and Ocana Gil, 1985)
has investigated the ability of the prepubertal ovary from the
dietary restricted rat to respond to hormonal regimes designed to
induce superovulation and elevated progesterone in fully fed animals.
This study was designed to resolve whether the lowered serum progesterone recorded in prepubertal dietary restricted rats was the result
of underfeeding limiting precursor availability or whether there was
a lack of pituitary hormone stimulation.   Circulating progesterone
was elevated in dietary restricted animals in response to PMSG/HCG
(pregnant mare serum gonadotropin/human choriogonadotropin) priming

at all ages tested, and from 25-35 days, where a comparison could be
made with the prepubertal fully fed animals, there was no significant
difference between dietary groups. When the elevation in serum
progesterone is expressed as a percentage increase over basal levels,
maximum response occurred at 28 days in fully fed animals and 35 days
in underfed females (Fig. 5) after which age there was a significant
decline in the superovulatory response of dietary restricted rats.
In contrast to the observations on serum progesterone there were
significantly fewer ova recovered from the fallopian tubes in superovulated dietary restricted rats compared to their fully fed counterparts.

     In a study to investigate hormonal profiles of the estrous
cycle, restricted animals were chosen at an age when more than 95%
had reached puberty. At this age (180-200 days) 74-78% of rats in
both groups were demonstrating normal estrous cycles of a regular
duration, as assessed by vaginal cytology, but in the fully fed group
17-25% of females demonstrated constant estrus vaginal smears and
1-5% recurrent pseudopregnancy. The hormonal profile for LH, FSH,
progesterone and estradiol-17β was assessed across the five day
cycle at 3 hourly intervals. Significantly higher levels of serum
FSH were observed in dietary restricted rats associated with an
early release of the preovulatory peak of LH which occurred approximately 6½ hours earlier on the afternoon of proestrus (Fig. 6).
The overall profile of estradiol-17β across the estrous cycle was
similar to that observed in fully fed animals (Fig. 6) but the total
amount of the hormone released in dietary restricted females was only

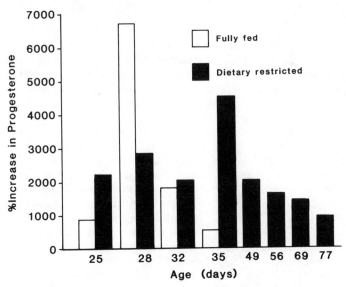

Fig. 5. Percentage increase in serum progesterone in superovulated
         rats compared to controls.

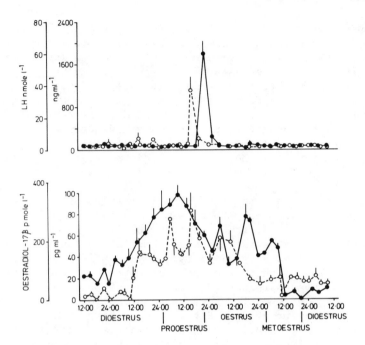

Fig. 6.   Serum profiles of LH and estradiol-17β in the 5-day estrous
cycle of ad libitum fed and dietary restricted rats,
(●) ad libitum fed   (O) dietary restricted.

46% of that observed in the control animals with the rise in estra-
diol-17β occurring 6 hours later in the cycle.

A study was initiated to investigate the altered steroidogenic
pathways in the ovary which resulted in the decreased circulating
progesterone and estradiol-17β seen in the dietary restricted rats.
Individual follicles were removed from mature cycling control and
underfed females and were incubated in 0.5ml medium 199 for 4 hours
at 37°C under an atmosphere of 95% O_2 / 5% CO_2 to measure release of
estradiol-17β and progesterone. Follicles were also incubated with
50ng/ml testosterone or 20μg/ml ovine LH according to the method of
Uilenbroek et al. (1981) to enhance steroid synthesis. In ovarian
follicles from both dietary restricted and fully fed rats incubation
with testosterone significantly increased the release of estradiol-
17β throughout all stages of the cycle. Maximum sensitivity to enhanced estradiol-17β release was observed in fully fed and dietary
restricted rats during proestrus. While no significant difference
was observed in individual follicular response from dietary groups
to enhanced estradiol-17β release in response to testosterone stimulation a significantly greater release of estradiol-17β was observed
in response to LH from follicles of underfed rats. No significant
difference was observed between fully fed and dietary restricted

rats in the response of proestrus follicles to release elevated
amounts of progesterone in response to LH. It is unclear as to why
follicles from dietary restricted animals at proestrus should show
greater sensitivity to LH in terms of estradiol-17β release.

Parathyroid Hormone

Maintaining rats on 60% of the average food intake of fully fed
animals, which increased mean lifespan from 701 to 1057 days, was
associated with delayed skeletal maturation as indicated by the
longer time taken to reach plateau levels for bone length, weight,
density and calcium content (Kalu et al., 1984). The food restriction
completely prevented the senile bone loss that occurred in ad libitum
fed rats. The marked terminal increase in immunoreactive serum PTH
was completely suppressed by food restriction indicating that the
bone loss experienced by the ad libitum fed rats at advanced age was
most likely due to increased bone resorbtion secondary to terminal
hyperparathyroidism and that food restriction attenuated the increase
in circulating PTH. Although the mechanism by which food restriction
prevented hyperparathyroidism in aged F344 rats is unknown, Kalu et
al. (1984) suggest an association with the depressed incidence of
renal lesions resulting from chronic underfeeding.

Calcitonin

A dramatic decrease in the age-associated increase in circulating and thyroid calcitonin levels was reported by Kalu et al. (1983)
for male rats restricted to 60% normal food intake levels from 6
weeks of life. The thyroid concentration of calcitonin appeared to
determine the basal level of circulating calcitonin, demonstrating
a positive correlation with serum calcitonin levels. Only a weak
correlation between serum calcium and serum calcitonin could be demonstrated. Whilst again the mechanism of action of food restriction
to decrease calcitonin levels is unknown, Kalu et al.(1983) propose
that in F344 rats the decrease in serum calcitonin is most likely
related to the simultaneous decrease in the thyroidal pool of calcitonin and that their findings are in accord with other observations
that food restriction maintains physiological processes at more youthful levels.

ACTH and Corticosterone

Everitt (1976) and Nikitin (1979) have reported elevated serum
ACTH and corticosterone in underfed rats, at least during the early
stages of undernutrition. Several workers report hypertrophy of the
adrenal cortex during caloric restriction (Chowers et al., 1969;
Bouille and Assenmacher, 1970) with elevated plasma corticosterone
(Boulouard, 1963) associated with a significant rise in the corti-
cotropin releasing factor content of the median eminence (Chowers
et al., 1969). Prolonged starvation may be associated with depressed

adrenocortical function (Bouille and Assenmacher, 1970).

Adrenocortical function was reinvestigated in rats maintained on a dietary regimen known to significantly increase lifespan. Underfeeding reduced total adrenal size and the rapid increase in adrenal mass observed in the second year of life in fully fed animals was not observed (Fig. 7). When adrenal weight is expressed per unit body mass (Fig. 7) a significantly higher ratio is observed in the dietary restricted rat indicating that as recorded for the testis, growth of the adrenal was less affected by underfeeding than skeletal and muscle growth.

Fully fed, dietary restricted and dietary restricted rats returned to full feeding seven days prior to killing were exposed to an environmental stress known to elevate corticosterone (removal from the animal house to the laboratory environment). Plasma corticosterone was measured in groups of animals ranging from 28 to 756 days of age (Fig. 8). Seven days of restricted feeding did not significantly impede the stress response of male rats as shown by the ability to elevate circulating corticosterone but by 35 days (14 days of restricted feeding), animals failed to respond to the stress with elevated plasma corticosterone. Refeeding seven days prior to killing at 35 days partly returned the ability to elevate plasma corticosterone. During the first year of life the response of fully fed

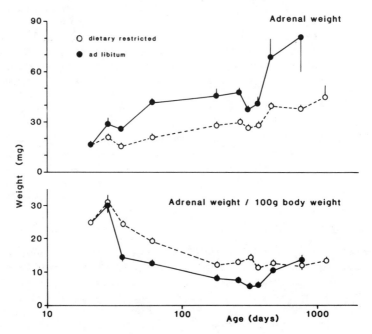

Fig. 7.   Adrenal weight with age in fully fed and dietary restricted
          male rats.

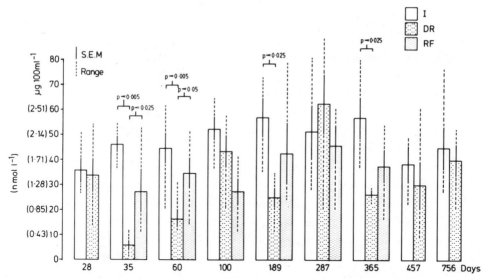

Fig. 8. Stress levels of plasma corticosterone with age in ad libi-
         tum fed (I), dietary restricted (DR), or dietary restricted
         male rats returned to ad libitum feeding for seven days (RF).

rats to the stress increased, as shown by the rise in plasma corticosterone, but after one year of life no effect of diet on depress-
ing the stress response of corticosterone could be observed. During
the first year of life refeeding for seven days prior to measuring
circulating corticosterone enhanced the plasma levels of this steroid
(Fig. 8). These observations would support the view that chronic
underfeeding from weaning at 21 days will initially inhibit the elevation of corticosterone in response to stress but this facility is
gradually recovered during the first year of life. The failure to
respond to stress in young dietary restricted rats may originate at
the hypothalamic/pituitary level. Pituitary and circulating ACTH
(and hypothalamic releasing factors) have not been measured in dietary restricted rats, however it is possible to demonstrate an elevation in plasma corticosterone in response to ACTH in young conscious free-moving animals with indwelling cannulae (Fig. 9). This
observation would indicate that it is a failure to elevate plasma
ACTH rather than end-organ insensitivity induced by underfeeding
that is the cause of the lack of response to the environmental stress.

Thyroxine and Triiodothyronine

Inanition or low protein diets have been observed to markedly

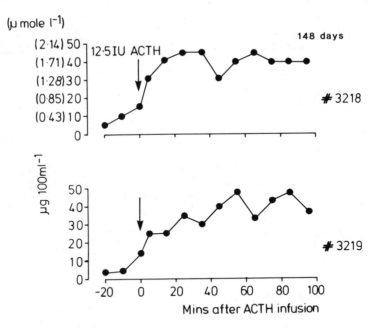

Fig. 9.   Plasma corticosterone response to infusion of synthetic
          ACTH, in two young, conscious free-moving dietary restricted
          male rats.

depress pituitary-thyroid activity in adult rats.   In the study of
Campbell et al. (1977) with acutely starved adult male rats, serum
LH and TSH were more severely depressed than other anterior pituitary
hormones suggesting a greater sensitivity to underfeeding.   Total
caloric restriction can significantly reduce circulating levels of
thyroxine and triiodothyronine in a matter of a few days.   Less
severe dietary restriction implemented at 21 days which is known to
extend maximum longevity in male Sprague-Dawley rats (Merry and
Holehan, 1981) is associated with depressed levels of circulating T4
(Fig. 10) although individual animal response is variable.   Depressed
T4 levels are observed within the first 7 days of restricted feeding
and as late as 457 days significantly lower circulating T4 levels are
recorded in dietary restricted rats.   Seven days of refeeding was
sufficient to restore T4 circulating levels to or above control
values (Fig. 10).

     Within 3 to 4 days of restricted feeding, circulating T3 levels
were severely depressed to approximately 40% of values in ad libitum
fed rats.   The peak of plasma T3 recorded at puberty in fully fed
rats was still observed in the dietary restricted animals (Fig. 11)
although a delay of 10-20 days was observed in the timing of the peak
in agreement with the data for serum testosterone.   During the first

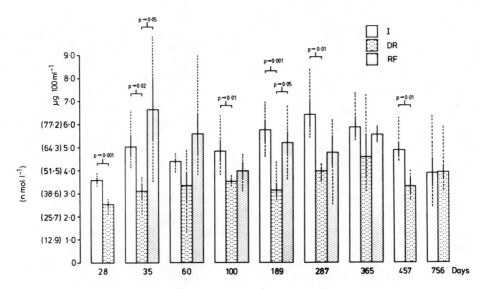

Fig. 10.   Plasma T4 levels with age in male fully fed (I), dietary
restricted (DR) and dietary restricted rats returned to
ad libitum feeding for seven days (RF).

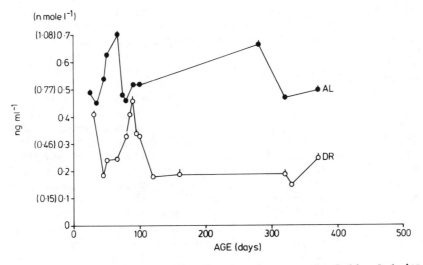

Fig. 11.   Plasma T3 levels during development in fully fed (AL) and
dietary restricted (DR) male rats.

year of life the circulating T3 levels continued to be depressed
(Fig. 11). Despite the fact that under most circumstances T4 appears
to be the principal secretory product of the thyroid gland, current
evidence suggests that T4 derives most of its hormonal potency from
its conversion to T3 in the peripheral tissues. Thyroxine does exert
thyroid hormone effects independent of its conversion to T3, but the
intrinsic hormonal effects of T4 probably contribute only a small
proportion (10-15%) of the overall thyroidal status of the target
tissues (Oppenheimer and Dillman, 1978). It would therefore appear
that a chronic dietary restriction regimen effective in prolonging
lifespan has a greater effect on the peripheral conversion of T4 to
T3 than at the central neuroendocrine level to moderate the release
of TSH and T4.

Growth Hormone

Everitt and Porter (1976) have commented that the effects of
food restriction on GH secretion in the rat depend on the duration
of restriction. Starvation for 2 to 5 days in the rat elevates
circulating GH levels which is similar to the human response to fasting (Pimstone et al., 1968), but chronic undernutrition continued
for 7 days or longer results in a depression of both pituitary and
plasma GH levels (Sorrentino et al., 1971). In the rat, growth hormone is characterised by an endogenous ultradian rhythm with major
episodes of GH secretion occurring at approximately 3.3 hr. intervals throughout a 24 hr. period with GH concentrations reaching 400-
800 ng/ml during a secretory burst and a fall to undetectable levels
(<1 ng/ml) during the nadir (Tannenbaum et al., 1978).

Central nervous system control of growth hormone secretion is
achieved by the interaction of hypothalamic growth hormone releasing
factor, GRF and a GH release inhibiting factor, somatostatin. In
response to prolonged food deprivation Tannenbaum et al. (1977) reported a marked suppression in the growth hormone secretory episodes
which they subsequently attributed to somatostatin inhibition of
growth hormone release. Growth hormone levels were re-examined in
the dietary restricted rat model described earlier (Merry and Holehan, 1981). Free-moving conscious rats with indwelling atrial cannulae were monitored every 20 minutes for immunoreactive rGH (Fig.
12). Considerable individual animal variation was evident in both
fully fed and dietary restricted rats of 120-148 days of age in both
the timing of rGH peaks and the absolute frequency of their release.
Preliminary data would suggest that the frequency of release of rGH
is unaffected at 120-148 days by chronic underfeeding but a restriction in peak duration is apparent. Further studies are required over
a wide age range to verify this point. The individual ultradian
rhythms of GH release in rats calls into question conclusions drawn
from single estimations of growth hormone, the values of which are
then presented as a mean with a variance estimate.

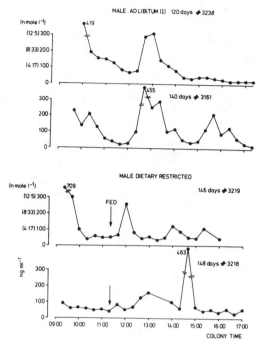

Fig. 12.   Plasma GH in free-moving conscious rats with indwelling atrial cannulae.

Hrůza and Fábry (1957) adapted rats to 6 weeks intermittent feeding to reduce growth rate. It was possible to prolong the period of growth subsequent to refeeding by the administration of growth hormone and without exogenous growth hormone realimented rats failed to achieve the maximum body weight observed in control animals. This failure to recover to full weight after only 6 weeks underfeeding is in contrast to the findings reported from other studies on the effect of refeeding (Stuchliková et al., 1975).

Decreased circulating levels of GH have been shown not to be primarily the cause of restricted growth in underfed rats. The growth rate of 140 day old fully fed and dietary restricted male rats was monitored over a three week period in animals injected with 500μg ovine GH per day or with saline vehicle. The mean difference in growth rate over this period for animals receiving ovine GH compared to saline is shown for the two dietary groups (Fig. 13). A steady and enhanced gain in body mass was evident in GH injected fully fed rats but no such accelerated growth was observed in underfed animals during 18 days of GH administration. Subsequent to this time a marginal increase in growth rate was seen over the saline injected animals.

It has been postulated that many of the growth promoting actions

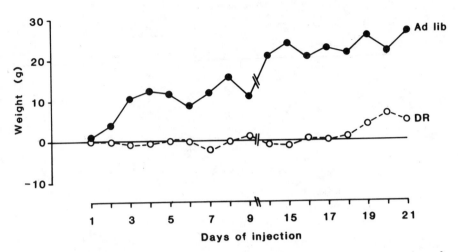

Fig. 13.   Growth rates for male fully fed and dietary restricted
(DR) rats injected with 500µg ovine GH/day compared with
saline injected controls as baseline.

of GH are mediated by the family of peptides known under the generic
title of somatomedin.   Several somatomedins have been identified as
insulin-like growth factors and there appears to be a relation between insulin-like growth factors and nutritional status.   Tannenbaum et al. (1983) suggest that this family of peptides which are
depressed in undernutrition play a role in the maintenance of body
weight and nutritional homeostasis at the CNS level.

The control of synthesis and release of pituitary growth hormone
in underfed rats is further complicated by the synergistic induction
of growth hormone biosynthesis by glucocorticoids and thyroid hormones, operating by hormonal stimulation of growth hormone mRNA
levels in the pituitary (Rosenfeld et al., 1983).   The induction of
both mRNA and nuclear precursors suggests that glucocorticoids act
by increasing the rate of transcription of the growth hormone gene.

Insulin and Glucagon

The age-related increase in serum insulin is eliminated by dietary restriction.   However only at one year of age was serum glucose
concentration reduced in food restricted rats in the study of Reaven
and Reaven (1981).   In an in vitro investigation of isolated pancreatic

islets it was shown that the ability of islets to respond to glucose by secreting insulin declined with age and this loss of glucose responsiveness was not affected by food restriction. Examination of islet morphology revealed a histological appearance characteristic of a chronologically younger animal in the dietary restricted rats. One explanation for the apparent contradiction in these data was proposed by Reaven and Reaven (1981) who suggested that food restriction reduced the functional demand on the islets and this delayed the morphological deterioration in comparison with ad libitum fed animals.

Bertrand et al. (1980) and Voss (1982) have investigated the mechanism underlying the effect of age and food restriction on the lipolytic response of adipocytes to glucagon. Adenylate cyclase and phosphodiesterase activities of cell fractions and the glucagon binding by adipocytes between 6 and 15 weeks of age were studied in fully fed and dietary restricted rats (Voss, 1982). It was concluded that the loss in the glucagon promoted lipolytic response of adipocytes that occurs with age but is prevented by food restriction (Bertrand et al., 1980) is primarily the result of a loss of hormone binding or a dissociation of this event from adenylate cyclase activation.

DiGirolamo et al. (1984) attempted to dissect the influence of age versus adiposity on fat cell metabolism and responsiveness to insulin and epinephrine in rats subjected to variable degrees of chronic food restriction. Male Wistar rats were fed at 3 months of age either ad libitum or restricted amounts (75 or 50% ad libitum) and were killed at 3,6,12,18,24 months of age. It was observed that the basal glucose conversion in fat cells to fatty acids declined rapidly with age and remained low in both ad libitum and restricted rats. Underfeeding reduced basal glyceride synthesis but preserved the relative response to insulin which slowly declined with age, however chronic dietary restriction totally prevented the decline in lipolytic response observed with age in fully fed animals. In contrast the age related effect of insulin on fat cells was not affected by nutritional status.

CONCLUSIONS

The complex events required for development and for the maintenance of homeostasis in mammals require an intricate control of specific gene expression. This function is largely subserved by the neuroendocrine system and it has been proposed by Segall (1979) that the process of senescence, similar to development, growth and maturation, may be under neural and endocrine control. Basic to this argument is the postulate that the neuroendocrine axis which is central to other ontogenetic processes, also plays a basic role in induction of senescent changes.

The maintenance of Long-Evans female rats on a diet deficient
in tryptophan has been reported to postpone the age at which tumors
appear and to delay the aging of some homeostatic processes (Segall,
1979; Segall and Timiras, 1976). The use of tryptophan deficient
diets has been shown to mimic many of the features observed in the
caloric restriction studies. It has been found that both tryptophan
deficient and the caloric restricted diets can alter the concentration
of cerebral monoamines (Segall, 1979). The ability of certain neurons to synthesise and release neurotransmitters is dependent on the
concentration of serum amines and on the composition of the diet.
It has been reported by Fernstrom (1977) that brain serotonin is
subject not only to the concentration of unbound tryptophan in serum,
but also to the concentration of several other large neutral amino
acids that share the same transport system at the blood-brain barrier.
Similarly the synthesis of acetylcholine is accelerated by increasing
the level in the brain of its precursor choline and the synthesis
and release of dopamine and norepinephrine are also influenced by
the levels of their dietary precursor, the amino acid tyrosine.

Everitt (1976), Segall (1979) and Moment (1982) have suggested
that restricted feeding may operate through a dietary hypophysectomy
whereby the pituitary gland remains dormant for long periods of time.
The interpretation of the data presented above as indicative of a
hypophysectomised state is in the authors' view too simplistic.
The concept that decrements in nervous and endocrine function are
implicated in the aging process has led to the development of several
neuroendocrine theories of aging (for review see Timiras, 1983).
The operative effect of dietary restriction may well be a complex
central neuroendocrine response mediated by monoamine neurotransmitters in the hypothalamus but it is still unclear how central
are the endocrine changes reported to the effect on longevity.
Chronic underfeeding significantly reduces protein and nucleic acid
synthesis and it is still to be resolved whether such tissue responses are dependent on the hormonal status of the dietary restricted rat.

REFERENCES

Andrews, W.W., and Ojeda, S.R., 1977, On the feedback actions of
        estrogen on gonadotropin and prolactin release in infantile
        female rats, Endocrinology, 101:1517-1523.
Ball, Z.B., Barnes, R.H., and Visscher, M.B., 1947, The effects of
        dietary caloric restriction on maturity and senescence, with
        particular reference to fertility and longevity, Am. J.
        Physiol., 150:511-519.
Berg, B.N., and Simms, H.S., 1960, Nutrition and longevity in the
        rat. 1. Food intake in relation to size, health and fertility,
        J. Nutr., 71:242-254.

Bertrand, H.A., 1983, Nutrition-Aging interactions: life prolonging action of food restriction, Rev. Biol. Res. Aging, 1:359-378.

Bertrand, H.A., Lynd, F.T., Masoro, E.J., and Yu, B.P., 1980, Changes in adipose mass and cellularity through the adult life of rats fed ad libitum or a life-prolonging restricted diet, J. Geront., 35:827-835.

Bouille, C., and Assenmacher, I., 1970, Effects of starvation on adrenal cortical function in the rabbit, Endocrinology, 87:1390-1394.

Boulouard, R., 1963, Effects of cold and starvation on adrenocortical activity of rats, Fed. Proc., 22:750.

Campbell, G.A., Kurcz, M., Marshall, S., and Meites, J., 1977, Effects of starvation in rats on serum levels of follicle stimulating hormone, luteinising hormone, thyrotropin, growth hormone and prolactin: response to LH releasing hormone and thyrotropin releasing hormone, Endocrinology, 100:580-587.

Carr, C.J., King, J.T., and Visscher, M.B., 1949, Delay of senescence infertility by dietary restriction, Fed. Proc., 8:22.

Chowers, I., Einat, R., and Feldman, S., 1969, Effects of starvation on levels of corticotrophin releasing factor, corticotrophin and plasma corticosterone in rats, Acta Endocrinol, 61:687.

Cole, G.M., Segall, P.E., and Timiras, P.S., 1982, Hormones during aging, in: "Hormones in Development and Aging," page 477-550, A. Vernadakis and P.S. Timiras, eds., Spectrum Publ., New York.

Comfort, A., 1979, "The Biology of Senescence," 3rd edition, Churchill Livingstone, New York.

Cutler, R.G., 1981, Life span extension, in: "Aging, Biology and Behaviour," page 31-76, J.L. McGaugh and S.B. Kiesler, eds., Academic Press, New York.

Denckla, W.D., 1981, Aging, dying and the pituitary, in: "Biological Mechanisms of Aging," page 673, R.T. Schimke, ed., NIH Publ. 81-2194, Baltimore.

DiGirolamo, M., Crandall, D., Fried, S.K., Nickel, M., and Hill, J.O., 1984, Effects of chronic food restriction (CFR) and aging on rat adipocyte metabolic activities and hormonal responsiveness, Proc. 7th Int. Congr. Endocr., Quebec, 547 (abstr).

Döhler, K.D., von zur Mühlen, A., and Döhler, U., 1977, Pituitary luteinizing hormone (LH), follicle stimulating hormone (FSH) and prolactin from birth to puberty in female and male rats, Acta Endocrinol, 85:718-728.

Everitt, A.V., 1976, The Nature and Measurement of Aging, in: "Hypothalamus, Pituitary and Aging," page 5-42, A.V. Everitt and J.A. Burgess, eds., Ch. C. Thomas, Springfield, IL.

Everitt, A.V., 1980, The neuroendocrine system and aging, Gerontology, 26:108-119.

Everitt, A.V., 1981, Pituitary function and aging, in: "Aging: A Challenge to Society VI," page 249, D. Danon, N.W. Shock and M. Marois, eds., Oxford Univ. Press, New York.

Everitt, A.V., 1982, Nutrition and the hypothalamic-pituitary
    influence on aging, in: "Nutritional Approaches to Aging
    Research," page 245-256, G.B. Moment, ed., CRC Press,
    Boca Raton, FL.
Everitt, A.V., and Porter, B., 1976, Nutrition and Aging, in:
    "Hypothalamus, Pituitary and Aging," page 570-613, A.V. Ever-
    itt and J.A. Burgess, eds., Ch. C. Thomas, Springfield, IL.
Fernstrom, J.D., 1977, Effects of the diet on brain neurotransmitters,
    Metabolism, 26:207-223.
Grewal, T., Mickelson, O., and Hafs, H.D., 1971, Androgen secretion
    and spermatogenesis in rats following semistarvation, Proc.
    Soc. Exp. Biol. Med., 138:723-727.
Harrison, D.E., Archer, J.R., and Astle, C.M., 1982, The effect of
    hypophysectomy on thymic aging in mice, J. Immunol, 129:
    2673-2677.
Holehan, A.M., 1984, The effect of ageing and dietary restriction
    upon reproduction in the female CFY Sprague-Dawley rat,
    Ph.D. Thesis, University of Hull, U.K.
Holehan, A.M., and Ocana Gil, M.L., 1985, The effect of chronic food
    restriction on the ability of immature rats to superovulate,
    in preparation.
Howland, B.E., 1975, The influence of feed restriction and subsequent
    re-feeding on gonadotrophin secretion and serum testosterone
    levels in male rats, J. Reprod. Fertil., 44:429-436.
Hrůza, A., and Fábry, P., 1957, Some metabolic and endocrine changes
    due to long-lasting caloric under-nutrition, Gerontologia,
    1:279-287.
Kalu, D.N., Cockerham, R., Yu, B.P., and Roos, B.A., 1983, Lifelong
    dietary modulation of calcitonin levels in rats, Endocrinology,
    113:2010-2016.
Kalu, D.N., Hardin, R.R., Cockerham, R., Yu, B.P., Norling, B.K.,
    and Egan, J.W., 1984, Lifelong food restriction prevents
    senile osteopenia and hyperparathyroidism in F344 rats,
    Mech. Ageing Dev., 26:103-112.
Lu, J.K.H., 1983, Changes in ovarian function and gonadotropin and
    prolactin secretion in aging female rats, in: "Neuroendo-
    crinology of Aging," page 103-122, J. Meites, ed., Plenum
    Press, New York.
Mackinnon, P.C.B., Puig-Duran, E., and Laynes, R., 1978, Reflections
    on the attainment of puberty in the rat: have circadian
    rhythms a role to play in its onset?, Symposium Report no. 11,
    Puberty, J. Reprod. Fertil., 52:401-412.
Masoro, E.J., Yu, B.P., Bertrand, H.A., and Lynd, F.T., 1980,
    Nutritional probe of the aging process, Fed. Proc., 39:3178-
    3182.
McCay, C.M., Maynard, L.A., Sperling, G., and Barnes, L.L., 1939,
    Retarded growth, lifespan, and ultimate body size and age
    changes in the albino rat after feeding diets restricted in
    calories, J. Nutr., 18:1-13.

Merry, B.J., and Holehan, A.M., 1979, Onset of puberty and duration of fertility in rats fed a restricted diet, J. Reprod. Fertil., 57:253-259.

Merry, B.J., and Holehan, A.M., 1981, Serum profiles of LH, FSH, testosterone and 5α-DHT from 21 days to 1000 days of age in ad libitum fed and dietary restricted rats, Exp. Geront., 16:431-444.

Merry, B.J., and Holehan, A.M., 1985a, In vivo DNA synthesis in the dietary restricted long-lived rat, Exp. Gerontol., in press.

Merry, B.J., and Holehan, A.M., 1985b, The effect of refeeding on subsequent survival and DNA synthesis in the dietary restricted long-lived rat, in preparation.

Merry, B.J., Holehan, A.M., and Phillips, J.G., 1985, Modification of reproductive decline and lifespan by dietary manipulation in female CFY Sprague-Dawley rats, Proc. 9th Int. Symp. Comp. Endocr., Hong Kong, December, 1981.

Moment, G.B., 1982, Theories of aging : An overview, in: "Testing the Theories of Aging," page 1-23, R.C. Adelman and G.S. Roth, eds., CRC Press, Boca Raton, FL.

Moment, G.B., Adelman, R.C., and Roth, G.S., 1982, "Nutritional Approaches to Aging Research," CRC Press, Boca Raton, FL.

Mulinos, M.G., and Pomerantz, L., 1940, Pseudo-hypophysectomy, a condition resembling hypophysectomy produced by malnutrition, J. Nutr., 19:493-504.

Negro-Vilar, A., Dickerman, E., and Meites, J., 1971, Effects of starvation on hypothalamic FSH-RF and pituitary FSH in male rats, Endocrinology, 88:1246-1249.

Nikitin, V.N., 1979, Biochemistry and endocrine status of laboratory animals during experimentally prolonged life under growth-restricting nutrition, Gerontol. Geriatr., 127-134.

Odell, W.D., Swerdloff, R.S., Bain, J., Wollesen, F., and Grover, P.K., 1974, The effect of sexual maturation on testicular response to LH stimulation of testosterone secretion in the intact rat. Endocrinology, 95:1380-1384.

Oppenheimer, J.H., and Dillman, W.H., 1978, Nuclear Receptors for triiodothyronine : A physiological perspective, in: "Receptors and Hormone Action, vol III," page 1-33, L. Birnbaumer and B.W. O'Malley, eds., Academic Press, New York.

Piacsek, B.E., and Goodspeed, M.P., 1978, Maturation of the pituitary gonadal system in the male rat, J. Reprod. Fertil., 52:29-35.

Pimstone, B.L., Barbezat, G., Hansen, J.D.L., and Murray, P., 1968, Studies on growth hormone secretion in protein-calorie mal-nutrition, Am. J. Clin. Nutr, 21:482.

Reaven, E, and Reaven, G.M., 1981, Structure and function changes in the endocrine pancreas of aging rats with reference to the modulating effects of exercise and caloric restriction, J. Clin. Invest, 68:75-84.

Regelson, W., 1983, The evidence for pituitary and thyroid control of aging : Is age reversal a myth or reality?! The search for a "Death Hormone", in: "Intervention in the Aging Process,

Part B : Research and Preclinical Screening," page 3-52,
W. Regelson and M. Sinex, eds., Alan R. Liss, New York.

Rosenfeld, M.G., Amara, S.G., Birnberg, N.C., Mermod, J-J., Murdoch,
G.H. and Evans, R.M., 1983, Calcitonin, Prolactin, and Growth
Hormone Gene Expression as Model Systems for the Characterization of Neuroendocrine Regulation, Recent Prog. Horm. Res.,
39:305-351.

Ross, M.H., and Bras, G., 1971, Lasting influence of early caloric
restriction on prevalence of neoplasms in the rat, J. Natn.
Cancer Inst., 47:1095-1113.

Saksena, S.K., and Lau, I.F., 1979, Variations in serum androgens,
progestins, gonadotropins and prolactin levels in male rats
from prepubertal to advanced age, Exp. Aging Res., 5:179-194.

Samuels, L.T., 1946, The relation of the anterior pituitary hormones
to nutrition, Recent Prog. Horm. Res., 1:147.

Segall, P.E., 1979, Interrelations of dietary and hormonal effects
in aging, Mech. Ageing Dev., 9:515-525.

Segall, P.E., and Timiras, P.S., 1975, Age-related changes in thermo-
regulatory capacity of tryptophan deficient rats, Fed. Proc.
34:83-85.

Segall, P.E., and Timiras, P.S., 1976, Patho-physiologic findings
after chronic tryptophan deficiency in rats : a model for
delayed growth and aging, Mech. Ageing Dev., 5:109-114.

Segall, P.E., Timiras, P.S., and Walton, J.R., 1983, Low tryptophan
diets delay reproductive aging, Mech. Ageing Dev., 23:245-252.

Sorrentino, S., Jr., Reiter, R.J., and Schalch, D.S., 1971. Interactions of the pineal gland, blinding and underfeeding on
reproductive organ size and radioimmunoassayable growth hormone.
Neuroendocrinology, 7:105-115.

Stewart, S.F., Kopia, S., and Gawlak, D.L., 1975, Effect of underfeeding, hemigonadectomy, sex and cyproterone acetate on
serum FSH levels in immature rats, J. Reprod. Fertil., 45:
173-176.

Stuchlikova, E., Juricova-Horakova, M., and Deyl, Z, 1975, New aspects
of the dietary effect of life prolongation in rodents. What
is the role of obesity in ageing? Exp. Gerontol., 10:141-144.

Tannenbaum, G.S., Epelbaum, J., and Brazeau, P., 1977, Ultradian
growth hormone (GH) rhythm in the rat : effects of prolonged
food deprivation, Fed. Proc, 36:323.

Tannenbaum, G.S., Epelbaum, J., Colle, E., Brazeau, P., and Martin,
J.B., 1978, Antiserum to somatostatin reverses starvation-
induced inhibition of growth hormone but not insulin secretion,
Endocrinology, 102:1909-1914.

Tannenbaum, G.S., Guyda, H.J., and Posner, B.I., 1983, Insulin-like
growth factors : A role in growth hormone negative feedback
and body weight regulation via brain, Science, 220:77-79.

Timiras, P.S., 1983, Neuroendocrinology of Aging : Retrospective,
Current, and Prospective Views, in: "Neuroendocrinology of
Aging," page 5-30, J. Meites, ed., Plenum Press, New York.

Uilenbroek, J. Th. J., van der Schoot, P., and Woutersen, P.J.A.,
    1981, Changes in steroidogenic activity of preovulatory rat
    follicles after blockage of ovulation with nembutal, in:
    "Dynamics of Ovarian Function," page 44-46, N.B. Schwartz and
    M. Hunzicker-Dunn, eds., Raven Press, New York.
Vernadakis, A., and Timiras, P.S., 1982, "Hormones in Development
    and Aging," MTP Press, Lancaster, England.
Voss, K.H., Masoro, E.J., and Anderson, W., 1982, Modulation of age-
    related loss of glucagon-promoted lipolysis by food restriction,
    Mech. Ageing Dev., 18:135-149.
Widdowson, E.M., and Kennedy, G.C., 1962, Rate of growth, mature
    weight and life-span, Proc. R. Soc., Lond (Biol)., 156:96-108.

AGE DEPENDENT CHANGES IN MITOCHONDRIA

J.E. Fleming, J. Miquel and K.G. Bensch

Linus Pauling Institute of Science and Medicine
Palo Alto, CA 94306

Recent work from our laboratory has provided evidence which
suggests that mitochondrial disorganization may be an important
aspect of age related changes of fixed postmitotic cells such as
those found in the adult insect Drosophila melanogaster (Miguel
et al., 1979; Fleming et al., 1982). For example, increased
mitochondrial respiration in insects exposed to moderately high
temperature results in both higher rates of lipopigment
accumulation and life shortening (Miquel et al., 1976). Moreover,
adult Drosophila showing lower respiration rates because of exposure to the mitochondrial DNA-intercalating dye ethidium bromide
in their diet during development live longer than controls raised
on normal medium (Fleming et al., 1981). Also, there is an inverse
correlation between oxygen consumption and life span in flies
treated with high levels of dietary antioxidants (Miquel et al.,
1982). More recently, we have confirmed this inverse relationship
for several strains of Drosophila raised under identical conditions (Miquel et al., 1983). Collectively, the above results
which are shown in Fig. 1 provide strong support for the concept
that respiration rate is a critical determinant of the lifespan in
this organism. It is remarkable that a statistically significant
correlation exists for experiments performed at different times
with flies raised under various conditions.

We have previously suggested that the mitochondria of post-
mitotic cells, both from insects and mammals, may be the "Achilles
heel" of the aging cell because of damage induced by free radicals
originating in the organelles as a byproduct of the reduction of
oxygen during respiration (Miquel et al., 1980; Fleming et al.,
1982). The logic behind this concept stems from the above
observations relating respiration rate with lifespan and the fact

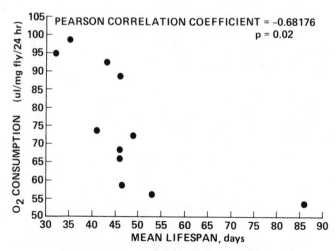

Fig. 1. Relationship between oxygen consumption and mean
lifespan in populations of <u>Drosophila</u> <u>melanogaster</u> (Ore
R strain). Data have been combined from references
(Miquel et al., 1976; Fleming et al., 1981; Miquel et
al., 1982; Miquel et al., 1983).

that most of the oxygen consumed by an aerobic eukaryotic cell is
reduced in the mitochondrial electron transport chain (Miquel et
al., 1980; Harman, 1972). Furthermore, damaging free radials have
been demonstrated to arise as metabolites of O_2 during this
process (Nohl and Hegner, 1978). In view of this, it is tempting
to implicate the mitochondria as the primary target of free
radical-mediated damage in aging cells (Harman, 1972). Fig. 2
provides a schematic view illustrating the central role of
mitochondria in the metabolism of a typical eukaryotic cell.
Unrepaired damage to mitochondria could be expected to jeopardize
cell survival by lowering the available pool of ATP necessary for
energy-dependent reactions.

Support for the involvement of mitochondria in senescence
starts with the finding that normal aging is accompanied by
mitochondrial alteration and loss, and by lipid peroxidation of
mitochondrial membranes (Miquel et al., 1978; Miquel et al.,
1979). Several studies have shown that aging in insects results in
a decrease in the number of flight muscle mitochondria and in an
enlargement of the senescent organelles (Miquel et al., 1980).
Moreover, morphometric techniques have shown that significant
changes occur in the size and structure of mitochondria from aging
Drosophila (Anton-Erxleban et al., 1983). This observation is also

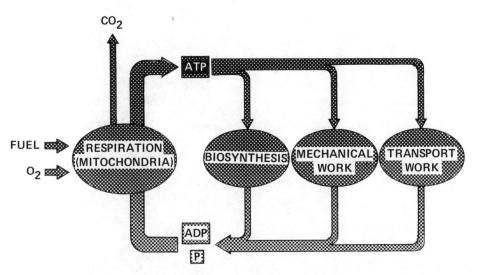

Fig. 2.   Schematic diagram illustrating the central role played
by the mitochondria in cellular metabolism. ATP,
adenosine triphosphate; ADP, adenosine diphosphate; P,
inorganic phosphate. Redrawn from Lehninger (1965).

supported by the work of Turturro and Shafiq (1979) who have
investigated the effects of aging on house fly flight muscle using
quantitative electron microscopy. Their analysis showed a loss of
about 50% of the stacked arrays of mitochondrial cristae and a
disruption of cristal packing with expansion of the intracristal
space. We have also observed similar structural changes in the
flight muscle mitochondria from old fruit flies (Miquel et al.,
1980; Fleming et al., 1981),(see Fig. 3).

The accumulation of age pigment (lipofuscin) has been
observed in the oenocytes, digestive apparatus and brain of aging
Drosophilia (Herman et al., 1971; Miquel, 1971; Miquel et al.,
1972). Similar increases in age pigment have also been noted in
house flies (Sohal, 1970). The role of age pigment is of
particular interest since several reports link the origin of this
fluorescent compound to a process of mitochondrial degeneration
both in insects and mammals (Miquel et al., 1980; Miquel et al.,
1978; Miquel et al., 1979; Anton--Erxleban et al., 1983; Glees et
al., 1974). Moreover, the rate of increase in lipofuscin is reduced in aging flies fed dietary antioxidants (unpublished
observations).

That aging results in a loss of mitochondria is also
supported by biochemical studies showing a decrease in the total
amount of mitochondrial DNA present in whole lysates of old fruit
flies (Massie et al., 1975) and livers of senecent rats (Stocco

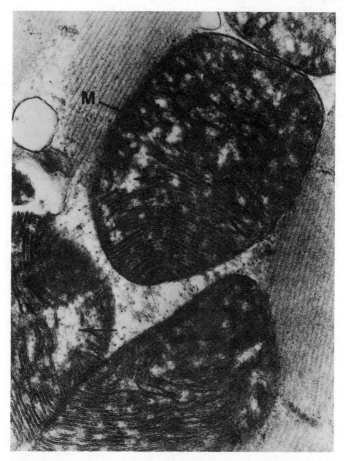

Fig. 3. High magnification of the flight muscle of an 84 day
         old fruit fly reared at 21 °C. Arrows show the slight
         disruption in the packing of the cristae. (From Miquel
         et al, 1980)

and Hutson, 1978). Further, numerous studies have revealed an
age-related decline in the activity of key enzymes involved with
respiration and energy production in insect flight muscle,
(Rockstein and Miquel, 1973; Baker, 1976; Sohal, 1976; Stoffolano,
1976).

     It is interesting that we have found that certain
mitochondrial enzymes such as NADH cytochrome c reductase do not
show significant differences with age when measured per mg
mitochondrial (mt) protein. However, when assayed on a per fly
basis, significant differences become apparent. On the other

hand, some enzymes, e.g. cytochrome oxidase, actually decrease
per mitochondria with age (Fig 4). Apparently, such data indicate
that mitochondria from old cells work as well as those from young
cells in some respects and that decreases in many enzymes merely
reflect the numerical loss of mitochondria as a function of age.
Our recent data on protein synthesis in mitochondria isolated from
old flies suggests that they are deficient in this capacity, a
finding which correlates with the loss of efficiency of old
mitochondria in synthesizing ATP (Vann and Webster, 1977). This
observation has been supported by data from several studies in
both mammals and insects (Baily and Webster, 1984; Marcus et al.,
1982; Marcus et al., 1982).

   Overall, these results imply that mitochondria from aged
cells sustain signficant disruption in only a few key functions
and that much of their activity is preserved. In view of this, we

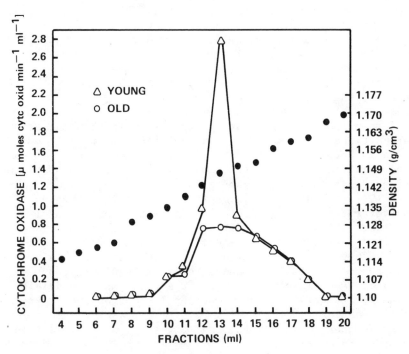

Fig. 4. Cytochrome oxidase activity of isolated mitochondria
         from two age groups of adult Drosophila melanogaster
         raised at 24°C. Young and senescent flies were 7 days
         old and 45 days old respectively. Mitochondria were
         isolated on a linear metrizamide gradient.

have addressed the question of differential changes in aged
mitochondria by quantitative two-dimensional gel electrophoresis.
This approach was designed to provide information on age-dependent
changes in individual proteins.

Previously, aging studies involving mt-proteins have either
utilized assays of specific enzymes or have employed radioactive
tracer techniques to study synthesis or turnover of mt-polypeptides (Marcus et al., 1982; Marcus et al., 1982; Menzies and Gold,
1971). Unfortunately, enzyme assays cannot determine whether
altered activity is the result of damaged molecules, fewer
molecules, or changes in the amount of "inhibitors" present in old
tissue. Also, synthesis and turnover studies do not provide
information relating to changes in individual proteins.
Furthermore, isolation procedures usually result in the loss of
more fragile mitochondria in old preparations.

In view of these methodological limitations, we have
developed a novel technique for identifying and analyzing
mitochondrial proteins of whole cells on two-dimensional gels
without the need of isolating the organelle (Fleming et al.,
1984). This method reduces the chance that loss of damaged
mitochondria from senescent cells in the isolation process will
distort the final results. Furthermore, we can quantify the
individual mitochondrial proteins by computer-assisted
microdensitometry of the gel pattern, thus obtaining data on the
turnover of individual polypeptides.

Another problem with many aging studies is that the examined
system contained both dividing and non-dividing cells or cells
grown in culture. The observation that true senescence may only
proceed in differentiated, fixed post-mitotic cells probably makes
the tissue culture model inappropriate for aging research (Miquel
et al., 1979; Bozcuck, 1972). We therefore employed Drosophila
melanogaster for this particular analysis because the adult insect
is comprised entirely of nondividing somatic cells (Bozcuck,
1972). It can be assumed that senescence at the molecular level in
Drosophila closely resembles that in mammalian post-mitotic cells
such as neurons or cardiac muscle cells. Essentially, our
analysis of age-related changes in Drosophila mitochondrial
proteins by quantitative two-dimensional electrophoresis yielded
three interesting findings (Fig. 5). First, we found no
qualitative changes in mt-proteins between young and old flies (no
differences in isoelectric point or molecular weight). Second,
the total amount of label incorporated into mitochondria from
senescent flies was only 65% of that occuring in young organisms.
Finally, we found that two proteins were upregulated in the old
flies relative to the young flies.

The autoradiograms reveal that no changes in molecular weight

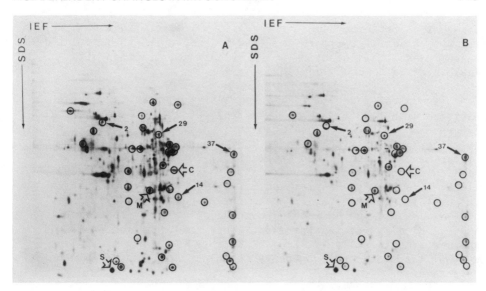

Fig. 5. Representative two-dimensional autoradiograms of whole
cell proteins from adult male Drosophila melanogaster
(Ore R strain) raised at 25°C. A, 6-day old and B,
38-day old adult at beginning of labeling period. The
mean lifespan for this population was 32.5 days.
Circles indicate the positions of the mitochondrial
proteins (Fleming et al., 1984). Spots # 29 and # 37 are
the two proteins which are upregulated in the old group.
Proteins designated # 2 and # 14 contained the least
radioactivity in the old group. C, cytochrome oxidase;
S, superoxide dismutase; M, protein synthesized by the
mitochondrial genome (Fleming et al., 1984). Flies were
labeled continuously for 6 days with ^{35}S-methionine
(New England Nuclear NEG 009H, 1057 Ci/nmole) and
homogenized according to Parker et al.(1975). The
two-dimensional gel electrophoretic technique was
performed as described by O'Farrell (1975) with the aid
of the Anderson Iso Dalt System (Anderson and Anderson,
1978). The isolelectric focusing dimension was carried
out with the method employed by Stephensen et al.
(1980). Ten gels were prepared for each group.

or in electric charge of any singular mitochondrial protein exist
between young and old flies (Fig. 5). This observation suggests
that the fidelity of synthesis of mt-proteins is conserved
throughout the cell's lifetime. Analyses utilizing isoelectric
focusing, which is capable of distinguishing a single charge

change in a protein, have not revealed any alterations with age in any mitochondrial polypeptides (Fig 5). However, this technique is not capable of detecting an amino acid substitution with another amino acid of equal charge.

In contrast, we did find quantitative changes in the gel patterns with respect to age. Previous studies have shown that the rate of protein synthesis declines with age in Drosophila melanogaster (Baily and Webster, 1984; Webster et al., 1979; Richardson, Birchenall and Sparks 1983; Rothstein, 1983). Our studies extend these observations to the turnover of mt-polypeptides. Previously, Menzies and Gold (1971), had shown that the turnover rate of mt-proteins does not change with age in rats. However, studies using labeled compounds can only provide an average of all proteins involved. Thus, the question as to whether a decreased rate might be uniform for all polypeptides or whether there is a heterogeneity in this process has not been addressed.

Our data indicate that individual proteins vary in the extent of decreased incorporation of (^{35}S)-methionine. To test for quantitative differences in the label content of individual mt-polypeptides from young and old flies, we analyzed the same 43 polypeptides in ten gels from both age groups. Computer-assisted microdensitometry was used to determine how much of each polypeptide was present in each gel. We then applied Student's t-test to the resulting two distributions (young vs. old) for each of the 43 mitochondrial polypeptides.

These results indicate that all but two mt-polypeptides are significantly reduced in turnover rate in old flies (see Fig. 5). It is important to point out that this study cannot distinguish between decreased synthesis rates and increased degradation rates. However, the suggestion that decreased label content in the old group results from increased degradation rates is not likely because several studies suggest that both synthesis and degradation (turnover rates) are slowed with age (Rothstein, 1981).

Because labeling was carried out continuously for six days the autoradiograms generated were representative of the turnover of these proteins. Our data showing a decreased label content of most of the mt-proteins in senescent flies can therefore best be explained by a general decrease in the turnover of these polypeptides.

The mean uptake of label into mitochondria from old organisms is 65% of that in young as determined by measuring total radioactivity in isolated preparations. However, our initial quantitative data suggest that this reduction may be distributed heterogenously among the subset of mitochondrial polypeptides. Thus, one mt-protein from old insects may be reduced to 10%, another to 80% of the same protein in a young fly. Further work with a larger number of gels and several age groups will be required in order to confirm these observations.

These findings imply that the age-related changes in the turnover apply to certain enzymes whilst others do not change. Such results support the previously discussed findings which suggest that old mitochondria may be deficient in certain functions and not in others. Thus, the two polypeptides which show highly significant decreases (to less than 20% of their counterpart in young flies) may be enzymes which play a critical role in the demise of aged mitochondria. Fig. 5 shows the results of this experiment and the location of the two polypeptides which are dramatically decreased in senescence. The protein labeled C indicates the position of cytochrome oxidase as determined by comigration analysis. Its turnover also appears to be reduced significantly more than that of most of the remaining mt-proteins.

The consequences of an age-related decrease in protein turnover rates have been addressed by Rothstein and coworkers (1983). They argue that if the total number of polypeptides remains constant with age, then an enzyme which has a reduced turnover would remain longer in the cell before it is replaced. Furthermore, if such an enzyme were susceptible to subtle alterations that would render it less efficient, e.g. denaturation, the functional capacity of the mitochondria would be reduced because of a greater proportion of "old" enzymes. This would explain the decrease in enzyme activity observed with cytochrome oxidase (Fig. 4). Also noted in Fig.5 is a polypeptide synthesized by the mitochondrial genome (see Fleming et al., 1984). It is interesting that the turnover of this particular protein is conserved with age. In this regard, we also noted that superoxide dismutase shows no change in turnover in old flies. In addition, we found two polypeptides (# 29 & # 37) that are upregulated to levels greater than twice their conterparts in young Drosophila. Possibly, these polypeptides are upregulated in response to deficiences in other mt-enzymes, or through the decrease in the synthesis of key regulator proteins involved in the control of expression of # 29 and # 37.

Previous work from our laboratory has already shown that # 29 is most likely to be an outer membrane polypeptide (Fleming et al., 1984). The likelihood that this protein participates in the transfer of components into the mitochondria prompted us to determine whether old mitochondria are altered in their ability to transport cytoplasmically synthesized precursor proteins. Fig. 6 shows the results of such an experiment. Basically, we have taken advantage of the fact that mt-protein transport, which is energy

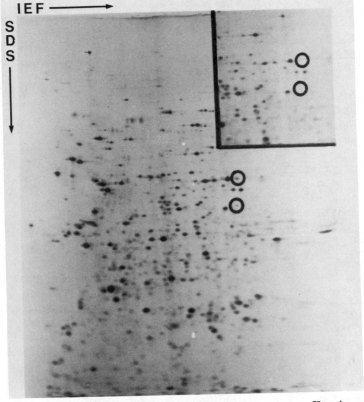

Fig. 6.   Two dimensional autoradiogram of a young fly treated
           with nonactin prior to labeling with (^{35}S) methionine.
           Circles indicate the positions of the two
           cytoplasmically synthesized mitochondrial precursors
           that are absent on similar patterns from old flies
           (insert). The two dimensional gel technique was
           performed as described in figure 5 except the
           isoelectric focusing dimension was carried out with a
           narrower pH range.

dependent, can effectively be blocked by various inhibitors
(Tzagoloff, 1982). In effect inhibitors such as nonactin collapse
the vectorial translocation of mt-precursors of cytoplasmic origin
(Fleming et al., 1984). Thus, when a cell is radio-labeled in the
presence of nonactin, the precursor(s) which is translated on
cytoplasmic ribosomes appears as a "new" polypeptide on the 2D gel
pattern since many of such precursors are orignally synthesized as
higher MW proteins (Fleming et al., 1984; Tzagoloff, 1982; Schatz
and Butow, 1983; Parker et al., 1981). It is quite remarkable that
the two precursor proteins noted in Fig. 6 appear on autoradiograms from young flies treated with nonactin, but that they do not
appear on similar patterns from old flies. Possibly, these

precursors are not being synthesized or synthesized in very low
amounts in old flies. However, this does not seem likely, since
we have not observed the absence of any mature mitochondrial
proteins in old organisms. A more attractive explanation for
these missing precursors is that they are rapidly degraded by
aspecific proteases in the cytoplasm. Such a mechanism implies
the lack of a mitochondrially-controlled feedback mechanism that
prevents the degradation of the precursors in old flies (Fleming
et al., 1984). Finally, these results may reflect the increase in
rate of transport of these precursors. Such data are consistent
with our finding of an increase in the turnover rate of certain
outer membrane proteins.

Taken as a whole, these recently obtained data suggest that
specific molecular changes in mitochondria may contribute to the
finite lifespan of fixed postmitotic cells. We suspect that there
could be specific mitochondrial enzymes whose activity are
especially critical for the maintenance of cell viability.
Further characterization and identification of such proteins is
expected to provide a better understanding of the mitochondrial
role in senescence.

ACKNOWLEDGEMENTS

This work was supported in part by The Japan Shipbuilding Industry
and the Glenn Foundation for Medical Research.

REFERENCES

Anderson, L., 1981, Identification of mitochondrial proteins
        and some of their precursors in two dimensional
        electrophoretic maps of human cells, Proc. Natl.
        Acad. Sci., USA., 78:2407.
Anderson, N. G. and Anderson, N. L., 1978, Analytical
        techniques for cell fractions, XXI Two dimensional
        analyses of serum and tissue proteins, Multiple
        isoelectric focusing, Anal. Biochem., 85:331.
Anton-Erxleban, F., Miquel, J., and Philpott, D. E., 1983,
        Fine structural changes in the midgut of old
        Drosophila melanogaster. Mech. Ageing. Dev.,
        23:265.
Baily, P. J., and Webster, 1984, Lowered rates of protein
        synthesis by mitochondria isolated from organisms of
        increasing age, Mech. Age. Dev., 24:233.
Baker, G. T., 1976, Insect flight muscle maturation and
        senescence: A review, Gerontology., 22:334.
Bozcuck, A. N., 1972, DNA Synthesis in the absence of
        somatic cell division associated with aging in
        Drosophila Subobscura, Exp. Gerontol., 7:147.
Fleming, J. E., Leon, H. A. and Miquel J., 1981, Effects of

ethidium bromide on development and aging of
Drosophilia: Implications for the free radical
theory of aging, Exp. Gerontol., 16:287.

Fleming, J. E., Miquel, J., Cottrell, S. F., Yengoyan, L. S.
and Economos, A. C., 1982, Is cell aging caused by
respiration-dependent injury to the
mitochondrialgenome? Gerontology., 28:44.

Fleming, J. E., Melnikoff, P. S. and Bensch, K. G., 1984,
Identification of mitochondrial proteins on two
dimensional electrophoretic gels of Adult Drosophila
melanogaster. Biochim. Biophys. Acta., 802:340.

Glees, P., Hassan, M. and Spoerri, P. E., 1974,
Mitochondrial genesis of lipofuscin: evidence based
on electron microscopic studies of brain, heart and
neural tissue culture, J. Physiol., 239:87.

Harman, D., 1972, The biologic clock: The mitochondria?
J. Am. Geriatr. Soc., 20:145.

Herman, M. M. Miquel, J. and Johnson, M., 1971, Insect brain as a
model for the study of aging. Age related changes in
Drosophila melanogaster. Acta Neuropath., Berlin, 19:167.

Lehninger, A. L., 1965, "Bioenergetics," W. A. Benjamin,
Menlo Park.

Marcus, D. L., Ibrahim, N. G. and Freedman, M. L., 1982,
Age-Related decline in the biosynthesis of
mitochondrial inner membrane proteins, Exp. Gerontol.,
17:333.

Marcus, D. L. Lew, G., Gruenspecht-Faham, N. and Freedman, M. L.,
1982, Effect of inhibitors and stimulators on isolated
liver cell mitochondrial protein synthesis from young and
old rats, Exp. Gerontol., 17:429.

Massie, H. R., Baird, M. B., and McMahon, M. M., 1975, Loss
of mitochondrial DNA with aging, Gerontology.,
21:231.

Menzies, R. A. and Gold, P. H., 1971, The turnover of mitochondria
in a variety of tissues of young adult and aged rats,
J. Biol. Chem. 246 (8):2425.

Miquel, J., 1971, Adv. Gerontol. Res., 3:39.

Miquel, J., Lundgren, P. R., and Binnard, R., 1972,
Drosophila Information Service., 48:60.

Miquel, J., Lundgren, P. R., Bensch, K. G., and Atlan, H., 1976,
Effects of temperature on the life span, vitality and
fine structure of Drosophila melanogaster. Mech. Aging Dev.,
5:370.

Miquel, J., Lundgren, P. R. , and Johnson, J. E., Jr., 1978,
Spectrophotofluorometric and electron microscopic study
of lipofuscin accumulation in the testis of aging mice,
J. Gerontol., 33:5.

Miquel, J., Economos, A. C. Bensch, K. G., Atlan, H. and Johnson,
J. E. Jr., 1979, Review of cell aging in

Drosophila and mouse, Age., 2: 78.

Miquel, J., Economos, A. C., Fleming, J. and Johnson, J. E.
    Jr., 1980, Mitochondrial role in cell aging, Exp.
    Gerontol., 15: 575.

Miquel, J., Fleming, J. E. and Economos, A. C., 1982,
    Antioxidants, metabolic rate and aging in
    Drosophila, Arch. Gerontol. Geriat., 1: 159.

Miquel, J., Binnard, R. and Fleming, J. E., 1983, Role of
    metabolic rate and DNA repair in Drosophila aging:
    Implications for the mitochondrial mutation theory
    of aging, Exp. Gerontol., 18:167.

Nohl, H. and Hegner, D., 1978, Do mitochondria produce
    oxygen radicals in vitro? Eur. J. Biochem, 82 563.

O'Farrell, P. H ., 1975, High resolution two dimensional
    electrophoresis of proteins, J. Biol, Chem.,
    250:4007.

Parker, J., Flanagan, J., Murphy, J. and Gallant, J., 1981,
    On the accuracy of protein synthesis in Drosophila
    melanogaster, Mech. Ageing. Dev, 16: 127.

Richardson, A. and Birchenall-Sparks, M. C., 1983,
    Age-related changes in protein synthesis, Rev. Biol.
    Res. Ageing, 1: 255.

Rockstein, M. and Miquel, J., 1973, in "The Physiology of
    Insecta," M. Rockstein, ed., Academic Press, New
    York.

Rothstein, M.,1983, Enzymes, enzyme alteration, and protein
    turnover, Rev. Biol. Res. Ageing, 1: 305.

Schatz, G. and Butow, R. A., 1983, How are proteins imported
    into mitochondria? Cell, 32: 316.

Sohal, R. S., 1970, Mitochondrial changes in Drosophila
    repleta Wollaston with age. Exp. Geront., 5:213.

Sohal, R. S.,1976, Aging changes in insect flight muscle,
    Gerontology, 22: 317.

Stephensen, G., Marzuki, S. and Linnane, A. W., 1980,
    Biogenesis of mitochondria. Two dimensional
    electrophoretic analysis of mitochondrial
    translation products in yeast, Biochim. Biophys.
    Acta, 609: 329.

Stocco, D. M. and Hutson, J. C., 1978, Quantitation of
    mitochondrial DNA and protein in the liver of
    Fischer 344 rats during aging, J. Gerontol.,
    33:802.

Stoffolano, J. G., 1976, in "Experimental Aging Research" M.
    F. Elias, B. E. Eleftheriou and P. K. Elias eds.,
    EAR inc., Bar Harbor. Maine.

Turturro, A. and Shafiq, S. A., 1979, Quantitative
    morphological analysis of age-related changes in
    flight muscle of Musca Domestica L. J. Gerontol.,
    34:823.

Tzagoloff, A., 1982, "Mitochondria", Plenum Press, New York.

Vann, A. C. and Webster, G. C., 1977, Age-Related
        changes in mitochondrial function in Drosophila
        melanogaster, Exp. Gerontol., 12:1.
Webster, G. C. and Webster, S. L., 1979, Decreased protein
        synthesis by microsomes from aging Drosophila
        melanogaster, Exp. Gerontol., 14: 343.
Webster, G. C., Webster, S. L. and Landis, W. A., 1979, The
        Effect of Age on the initiation of protein synthesis
        in Drosophila melanogaster, Mech. Ageing. Dev.,
        16:71.

INTRODUCTORY REMARKS--WITH CONSIDERATION OF A T-CELL

MODEL FOR AGING IN CELLULAR PROTEINS

Takashi Makinodan, Timothy C. Fong, Tsutomu Inamizu, and Mei-Ping Chang

Geriatric Research, Education and Clinical Center
VA Medical Center West Los Angeles, CA 90073, and
Department of Medicine, UCLA, Los Angeles, CA 90024

In 1947, Henshaw, Riley, and Stapleton first proposed that aging can be caused by alterations in DNA. Unfortunately, they were a decade ahead of their time, for it was not until the early 60's that attempts were made to resolve the extent to which cellular proteins are vulnerable to aging, and the genetic bases for the changes. One of the driving forces behind this surge of activity was Orgel (1963), who proposed that errors in transcription and translation can bring about senescence through a progressive accumulation of errors in the protein-synthesizing machinery. Although most investigators focused their efforts at the transcriptional and translational levels, a few also considered the effects of aging at the post-translational level, especially after Robinson et al. (1970) observed that deamidation of asparagine and glutamine can cause conformational changes in proteins. Suffice to say, the efforts of the 60's and 70's clearly documented that aging at the cellular protein level is complex and heterogenous, and therefore could be polymorphic at the genetic level.

With recent advances in DNA and peptide technologies, coinciding with an increase in financial support for research on aging, there appears to be a new surge of interest in the influence of age on cellular proteins. Thus, the four model systems on aging in cellular proteins to be discussed at this session are very timely. The first speaker, Dr. A.S. Sun of the Mt. Sinai Medical Center of New York, will discuss how an enzyme, 5'nucleotidase, could play a major modulating role in the proliferation of normal cells as individuals age. The second speaker, Dr. A. Schwartz of Temple University, will discuss how dehydroepiandrosterone, an adrenal steroid and inhibitor of NADPH, could modulate the rate of aging and

Table 1. Effect of thiols (5×10^{-5}M) on the production of
IL-2 by human peripheral lymphocytes (1×10^6/ml)[a]

Thiols	Relative levels of IL-2 (%)
Rat IL-2 (Reference)	100
2-Mercaptoethanol	94
α-Thioglycercol	97
2-Mercaptoethylamine	71
Dithiothreitol	32
Glutathione (reduced)	30
None	30

[a]Cultures were stimulated with PHA (2.5 µg/ml) in the presence of
the indicated thiol for 24 hr at 37°C in humidified 5% CO_2
incubator. The supernatants were collected and assayed for IL-2
using an IL-2 dependent indicator CTLL-2 cell line. The reference
rat IL-2 was produced in the presence of 2-mercaptoethanol. After
Fong and.Makinodan (1985, in press).

cancer development in various tissues. The third speaker, Dr. M.
Rothstein of the State University of New York at Buffalo, will
discuss the molecular basis of age-related changes in rat enzymes
with emphasis on changes which occur post-translationally. The
fourth and final speaker, Dr. J.R. Williams of Johns Hopkins, will
discuss the use of DNA-damaging agents as probes to assess how aging
affects the template function of DNA, which can lead to alterations
in cellular proteins.

    Before introducing the speakers, we wish to comment on the T
cell model for aging of cellular proteins. The T cell model is
attractive because T cell-dependent immunologic activities are
vulnerable to aging both in vivo and in vitro and because age-
related altered immunologic activities of T cells are associated
with altered metabolic activities and morphological properties
(Makinodan, 1983). Moreover, recent advances in T cell culture and
cloning techniques allow us to analyze their metabolic and genetic
properties (Albertini et al., 1982). We decided, therefore, to
focus our effort on resolving the molecular/genetic basis for the
inability of regulatory T cells of old individuals to produce
adequate amounts of interleukin(IL)-2 (Gillis et al., 1981; Miller
and Stutman, 1981; Thoman and Weigle, 1981; Chang et al., 1982a;
Gilman et al., 1982; Joncourt et al., 1982), a growth factor
essential for antigen/mitogen stimulated T cells to expand clonally
(Morgan and Ruscetti, 1976; Gillis and Smith, 1977).

    In one series of studies, a variety of sulfhydryl compounds
(thiols) were screened in an attempt to understand why thiols, such

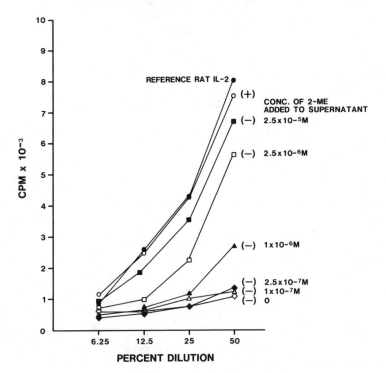

(+) IL-2 PRODUCED WITH 5x10⁻⁵M 2-ME

(−) IL-2 PRODUCED WITHOUT 2-ME

Fig. 1.   Effect of various concentrations of 2-mercaptoethanol on
          the IL-2 activity of the supernatant of cultures in which
          human peripheral mononuclear cells (1 x 10^6/ml) were
          stimulated with PHA (2.5 µg/ml) in the absence of a thiol.

as 2-mercaptoethanol, potentiate the production of biologically
active IL-2 in vitro by mouse T cells (Chang et al., 1982) and by
human T cells at low cell densities ($\leq$ 1 x 10^6 cells/ml) in the
absence of feeder cells (Fong and Makinodan, 1985). The results of
one representative experiment are summarized in Table 1. It would
appear that, at a concentration of 5 x 10^{-5}M, thiols with the
ability to rapidly penetrate cells are effective potentiators and
that the mechanism of action may not be related to their reducing
potentials. Of course, further studies are required to identify the
specific intracellular target(s) of the thiols. To determine
whether 2-mercaptoethanol is also effective at the post-secretion
protein product level, supernatants of cultures (1 x 10^6 cells/ml)
stimulated in the absence of 2-mercaptoethanol were treated with
varying concentrations of 2-mercaptoethanol and assessed for IL-2
activity (Fong and Makinodan, 1985, in press). Fig. 1, which

summarizes the results of one experiment, shows that increasing
levels of IL-2 are detected in supernatants treated with increasing
amounts of 2-mercaptoethanol (2×10^{-7} to 2×10^{-5}M). This would
suggest that the IL-2 molecule itself is also a target of
2-mercaptoethanol.

These preliminary findings are encouraging, for they indicate
that 2-mercaptoethanol and related compounds can be used as
effective probes to identify the specific site(s) of the IL-2
synthesizing machinery of T cells which are vulnerable to aging.

The focus of another series of studies has been on the influence of age on DNA stability in T cells as it relates to their immunologic activities. We began by assessing the influence of age on
the frequency of 6-thioguanine resistant cells (6-TG^r) in clones of T
cells that are deficient in hypoxanthine guanosine phosphoribosyl
transferase in mice. Our preliminary results indicate that the
frequency of 6-TG^r T cells increases with age at a rate of 0.2 cells
per 10^6 T cells per month, or about 20 cells per mouse per month
(Inamizu and Makinodan, 1984). Interestingly, the rate of increase
in the frequency of 6-TG^r T cells with age in mice is of the same
order of magnitude as that in humans (Vijayalaxmi and Evans, 1984)
when the rate is normalized to mean life span units; that is, 30
months equal one mean life span for mice and 70 years equal one mean
life span for humans. Thus, the rate was 2 cells per 10^6 T cells
per one mean life span in mice and 7 cells per 10^6 T cells per one
mean life span in humans. This would suggest that the increase in
the frequency of 6-TG^r T cells with age is related to the metabolic
rate rather than to chronological age. Studies are in progress to
determine whether the frequency of 6-TG^r T cells is related to the
ability of T cells to produce IL-2 or proliferation in response to
mitogenic stimulation (Inamizu and Makinodan, 1985; Chang and
Makinodan, 1985). Finally, having received the IL-2 gene from Dr.
Tadatsugu Taniguchi of Japan, we are now in the process of preparing
the necessary probes, to assess the possible age-related changes in
the IL-2 producing machinery of the regulatory T cells.

Based on our preliminary findings and on the availability of
appropriate genetic and chemical probes, we are cautiously
optimistic that the T cell model will play a prominent role in
obtaining new information on aging in cellular proteins--comparable
to the other model systems to be discussed in this session.

REFERENCES

Albertini, R. J., Castle, K. L., and Borcherding, W. R., 1982,
    T-cell cloning to detect the mutant 6-thioguanine-resistant
    lymphocytes present in human peripheral blood, Proc. Natl. Acad.
    Sci. USA, 79:6617.

Chang, M-P., Makinodan, T., Peterson, W. J., and Strehler, B. L.,
    1982a, Role of T cells and adherent cells in age-related decline
    in murine interleukin 2 production, J. Immunol., 129:2426.
Chang, M-P., Strehler, B. L., and Makinodan, T., 1982b, Requirement
    of 2-mercaptoethanol for in vitro growth factor production by T
    cells and vulnerability of the responses to age, Mech. Ageing
    Dev., 20:65.
Chang, M-P., and Makinodan, T., 1985, Age-associated increase in
    specific locus somatic mutation in murine T cells stimulated
    with N-ethyl-N-nitrosourea (ENU), Proceedings of XIIIth Congress
    of the International Association of Gerontology, July 12-17 (in
    press).
Fong, T. C., and Makinodan, T., 1985, Nature of action of immuno-
    potentiating thiols on interleukin(IL)-2 production.
    Proceedings of the XIIIth Congress of the International
    Association of Gerontology, July 12-17 (in press).
Gillis, S., Kozak, R., Durante, M., and Weksler, M. E., 1981,
    Immunological studies of aging. Decreased production of and
    response to T cell growth factor by lymphocytes from aged
    humans, J. Clin. Invest., 67:937.
Gillis, S., and Smith, K. A., 1977, Long term culture of tumor-
    specific cytolytic T cells, Nature, London, 268:154.
Gilman, S. C., Rosenberg, J. S., and Feldman, J. D., 1982, T
    lymphocytes of young and aged rats, J. Immunol., 129:644.
Henshaw, P. S., Riley, E. R., and Stapleton, G. E., 1947, The
    biological effects of pile radiation, Radiology, 49:349.
Inamizu, T., and Makinodan, T., 1984, Influence of age on the fre-
    quency of 6-thioguanine (6-TG) resistant murine T cells. Fed.
    Proc., 43:1822.
Inamizu, T., and Makinodan, T., 1985, Influence of age on the
    frequency of specific locus mutation in T cells in relation to
    their immunologic activities, Proceedings of XIIIth Congress of
    the International Association of Gerontology, July 12-17 (in
    press).
Joncourt, F., Wang, Y., Kristensen, F., and De Weck, A. L., 1982,
    Aging and immunity: decrease in interleukin-2 production and
    interleukin-2-dependent RNA synthesis in lectin-stimulated
    murine spleen cells, Immunobiology, 163:521.
Makinodan, T., 1983, Age-related alterations in cell-mediated
    immunity: qualitative changes in the parenchymal and stromal
    cells, in: "Progress in Immunology V," pp. 1539-1547, Y.
    Yamamura and T. Tada, eds., Academic Press, Inc., Tokyo.
Miller, R. A., and Stutman, O., 1981, Decline, in aging mice, of the
    anti-2,4,6-trinitrophenyl (TNP) cytotoxic T cell response
    attributable to loss of Lyt 2⁻, interleukin 2-producing helper
    cell function, Eur. J. Immunol., 11:751.
Morgan, D. A., and Ruscetti, F. W., 1976, Selective in vitro growth
    of T lymphocytes from normal human bone marrow, Science,
    193:1007.
Orgel, L. E., 1963, The maintenance of the accuracy of protein

synthesis and its relevance to aging, Proc. Natl. Acad. Sci USA, 49:517.

Robinson, A. B., McKerrow, J. H., and Cary, J., 1970, Controlled deamidation of peptides and proteins: an experimental hazard and a possible biological timer, Proc. Natl. Acad. Sci. USA, 66:885.

Thoman, M. L., and Weigle, W. O., 1981, Lymphocytes and aging. Interleukin-2 production and activity in aged animals, J. Immunol., 127:2102.

Vijayalaxmi and Evans, H. J., 1984, Measurement of spontaneous and x-irradiated induced 6-thioguanine-resistant human blood lymphocytes using a T-cell cloning technique, Mutation Res., 125:87.

IMPLICATIONS OF 5'-NUCLEOTIDASE AND ITS INHIBITOR FOR CELLULAR

AGING AND CANCER

Alexander S. Sun and James F. Holland

Mount Sinai School of Medicine
City University of New York, New York, N.Y.   10029

INTRODUCTION

   The concept of using neoplastic cells as a control to study
cellular aging has been generally accepted and become very popular
in recent years. Using this approach to study the change of
5'-nucleotidase during the aging of normal cells in vitro has led
us to a number of consistent findings, including the discovery of
an inhibitor for 5'-nucleotidase (Sun et al., 1975; Sun, et al.,
1979; Sun, et al., 1982; Sun, et al., 1983, Lee, et al., 1985).
In this article we review our study of using neoplastic cells as a
control to study 5'-nucleotidase and its inhibitor in cellular
aging and the previous work of others on 5'-nucleotidase related
to cancer and cell proliferation. The criteria for using cancer
cells as a control to study cellular aging are defined.   A
hypothesis is proposed on the biochemical role of 5'-nucleotidase
and its inhibitor in the control of the proliferation and aging of
normal cells and the lack of this control in neoplastic cells.

AGING AND CANCER

   Aging and cancer are two extremely complicated problems.
Different types of cells and organs may age at different rates and
even through different mechanisms.   The word cancer actually
denotes many different diseases.   Moreover, many properties of
normal cells overlap those of cancer cells.   Thus the characteristics of neoplastic cells that can be used as a control to
study cellular aging must be defined specifically to avoid
confusion. For our study of 5'-nucleotidase in cellular aging the
characteristic used is the unlimited lifespan of the neoplastic
cells versus the limited lifespan of normal cells in the identical
environment.

One apparent aging phenomenon is the atrophy of various organs as we get old. Atrophy is due to the loss (because of death) of functional cells in these organs, together with an inability to regenerate new cells for their replacement. Many age-related diseases are caused by cellular death and sublethal changes in the remaining functional cells of these organs. Similar phenomena have also been observed when normal cells are cultured in vitro. Young normal cells can regenerate rapidly in vitro but their rate of proliferation gradually slows down and finally they lose their ability to proliferate (Hayflick & Moorhead, 1961). Thus cellular aging is defined as a gradual loss of the cell's ability to proliferate. Normal cells have a limited lifespan in vitro, but they can be transformed by exogenous viruses and chemicals from a normal diploid karyotype to cancer-like heteroploid cells (Weinberg, 1983; Pitot, 1979). In an environment identical to that when normal cells have a finite lifespan these transformed cells as well as cells originating from malignant cancers can proliferate indefinitely, and thus they are considered immortal. Although the environment of cells in vivo is more complicated than in vitro, the gradual death of normal functional cells in vivo increases with the age of the animal. In the identical animal, however, cancer cells, such as transplantable malignant tumors, can proliferate indefinitely. Therefore, the mechanisms that control the aging of normal cells in vivo and in vitro should be absent in immortal neoplastic cells.

CRITERIA FOR USING NEOPLASTIC CELLS AS A CONTROL TO STUDY CELLULAR AGING

There are many different kinds of cancers. Thus cancer cells cannot be indiscriminately used as a control to study cellular aging. For example, many cancer-like transformed cells, such as Rous sarcoma virus-transformed chick embryo fibroblasts, have a finite lifespan in vitro*. Although these cells can produce Rous sarcoma virus and are morphologically distinguished from normal chick embryo fibroblasts (Ponten, 1970), they cannot be used as a control to study cellular aging. On the other hand, many transformed cells possess some of the characteristics of normal cells but nonetheless, have an unlimited lifespan. For example, Swiss albino mouse embryo fibroblasts have a predominantly diploid karyotype at first but, after a crisis period with very little cell proliferation, change to an immortal heteroploid cell line

---

* RATZ-1 is the only Rous sarcoma virus-transformed cell line that has an unlimited lifespan in vitro (Dinowitz, 1977). These cells maintain the chromosomal characteristics of chick cells and produce Rous sarcoma virus. It is speculated that Rous sarcoma virus used to infect the cells might also contain Rous sarcoma-associated viruses (Dinowitz, 1984).

without exogenous virus infection, known as the 3T3 cell line
(Todaro and Green, 1963).   These heteroploid 3T3 cells maintain
some characteristics of normal cells, such as contact inhibition,
but also have an unlimited lifespan; thus they have been used as
a control to study cellular aging (Sun, et al., 1979).

Normal organs and tissues are drastically different from each
other physiologically. Neoplastic cells originating from different
tissues must therefore be compared with their normal counterpart.
However, when a biochemical parameter is evaluated as a function
of the age of normal cells, we originally compare mother with
daughter cells, the only difference among these cells being their
in vitro age.   When neoplastic cells are used as a control to
study cellular aging, the biochemical parameter should be examined
in the same manner.   The change of a biochemical parameter as a
function of the in vitro age of neoplastic cells could thus be
compared with that of normal cells even though they are of
different origins.   A biochemical parameter in neoplastic cells
that is not evaluated in the same mother-daughter cells as a
function of in vitro age, cannot be used as a control to study
cellular aging.

A LARGE INCREASE IN 5'-NUCLEOTIDASE ACTIVITY WITH AGING IN VITRO

5'-Nucleotidase is an ectoenzyme found both in plasma membranes
(the enzyme faces extracellularly) and in the membranes (the
enzyme faces the cytoplasm) of many subcellular organelles of normal cells (Edelson and Cohn, 1976; Edwards, et al. 1982; Farquhar,
et al., 1974; Little and Widnell, 1975; Stanley and Luzio, 1979a;
Stanley, et al., 1979b; Stanley, et at., 1980; Trams and Lauter,
1974; Widnell and Little, 1977; Widnell, et al., 1982).   It is
specific for hydrolyzing 5'-nucleoside monophosphates. In 1975 we
found that 5'-nucleotidase in normal human embryonic lung fibroblasts, WI-38, increased 10-fold from rapidly proliferating young
stage to nonproliferating senescent stage (Sun, et al. 1975; Table
I).   If a phenomenon is closely associated with cellular aging in
vitro, it should be present in all cell lines having a limited
lifespan in vitro but absent in all cell lines having an unlimited
lifespan.   Thus we explored this hypothesis further using two
additional normal cell lines and three immortal transformed cell
lines.   In another line of human embryonic lung fibroblasts,
IMR-90 cells, and in chick embryo fibroblasts 5'-nucleotidase
specific activity increased 6-fold and 20-fold respectively with
increasing age of the cells in vitro (increasing   accumulated
population doubling) (Sun, et al. 1975 and 1979; Table I).   In
SV-40 virus-transformed WI-38 cells, VA-13 cells, which have an
unlimited lifespan in vitro (Girardi, et al., 1966), 5'-nucleoti-
dase did not increase with increasing in vitro age (Sun et al.,
1979; Table I).   No activity was detectable in the two transformed
immortal mouse embryo fibroblast cell lines,   3T3 and SV-3T3 cells

(Sun, et al., 1979; Table I). The validity of these observations
had thus been tested with three normal and three transformed cell
lines, including three species (human, mouse, and chick).

A LARGE INCREASE IN 5'-NUCLEOTIDASE ACTIVITY WITH AGING IN VIVO

Aging of normal cells in vitro has not been tested vigorously to
show whether it truly represents aging of normal cells in vivo.
It is generally assumed, however, that if a phenomenon is truly
associated with cellular aging, it should be observed with aging
of normal cells both in vitro and in vivo. In an unrelated study,
Rodan et al. observed that 5'-nucleotidase activity increased
5-fold from a proliferative (young) to a hypertrophying (old and
non-proliferative) state during the maturation of chick epiphyseal
cartilage (Rodan, et al., 1977). Goldberg and Belfield (1974) have
also shown that 5'-nucleotidase in human ribs and shaft of femur
increases 4-fold from children to adults. Thus the increase of
5'-nucleotidase activity in normal cells in vivo was observed in
two different tissues of two different species. Although we have
not tested whether the large increase in 5'-nucleotidase specific
activity with aging in vitro is also associated with aging in
vivo, these data suggest that such an increase in 5'-nucleotidase
activity may also be a characteristic of aging of normal cells in
vivo.

THE INVERSE RELATION BETWEEN 5'-NUCLEOTIDASE ACTIVITY AND THE RATE OF CELL PROLIFERATION, POSSIBLY A NORMAL CELLULAR FUNCTION

Cellular aging in vitro could also be considered as a phenomenon manifested by a gradual loss of the cell's ability to proliferate. Therefore, our finding of a gradual but large increase in
5'-nucleotidase activity from young to senescent normal cells
could also be interpreted as an inverse relation between the
5'-nucleotidase activity and proliferative ability. In a study of
rat liver regeneration, Fritzson reported that cytoplasmic
5'-nucleotidase activity showed cyclic variations, that were
inversely related to the rate of cell proliferation (Fritzson,
1967). This observation was independently confirmed by Arima et
al. (1972). Furthermore, many reports indicate that 5'-nucleoti-
dase is markedly reduced in proliferating normal and tumor cells,
such as proliferating liver tissue (Fritzon, 1967; Arima, et al.,
1972), leukemic cells (Kramers, et al., 1976; Lopes, et al., 1973;
Reaman, et al., 1979), rat liver and various hepatomas (Arima, et
al., 1972; Bukovsky and Roth, 1964; de Lamirande, et al., 1958;
Fiala, et al., 1959; Fiala et al., 1962; Fritzson, 1967; Goodlad,
et al., 1982; Hardonk and Koudstaal, 1968). Therefore, this
inverse relation observed by us with aging of normal cells in
vitro also occurs in various types of cells both in vitro and in
vivo. These data also suggest that the inverse relation between
5'-nucleotidase activity and the rate of cell proliferation could

be a normal biochemical function related to the regulation of cell
proliferation.

UNDETECTABLE 5'-NUCLEOTIDASE ACTIVITY IN LEUKEMIC CELLS IN VITRO AND IN VIVO

Although we have observed that the large increase in specific
activity of 5'-nucleotidase was absent in immortal cancer-like
transformed cells, VA-13, 3T3 and SV3T3, these cells were not
truly cancer cells (Sun, et al. 1979). Furthermore, 5'-nucleoti-
dase activity was not even detectable in 3T3 and SV3T3 cells (Sun,
et al., 1979). It was of interest to know whether these observations could also be found in cancer cells. Subsequently
5'-nucleotidase activity was found also to be undetectable in four
cell lines subcultivated from human acute lymphoblastic leukemia
(MOLT 3, B85, RPMI 8402, and RPMI 8422), four from human Burkitt's
lymphoma (DAUDI, B46B, HRIK, and DND 39A), one from cells of
blastic crisis of chronic myelocytic leukemia (NALM-1), and two
from virus-transformed lymphoid cells from normal donors (B411-4
and RPMI 1788). These data are shown in Table I. All these cell
lines have been subcultivated continuously for more than five
years in our laboratory. Since no decline in their rate of proliferation has been observed they are considered permanent cell
lines having an infinite lifespan in vitro (Ohnuma, et al., 1977;
Sun, et al., 1983; Lee, et al., 1985). Our findings are consistent with the finding of Lopez et al. (1973), Kramers et al.
(1976), and Reaman et al. (1979), who reported that 5'-nucleoti-
dase activity in lymphocytes freshly isolated from leukemic
patients was undetectable or much lower than that from normal
donors. 5'-Nucleotidase activity was undetectable in two other
permanent cell lines, L929 and Chinese hamster embryo fibroblasts
(Trams and Lauter, 1974; Peterson and Biedler, 1978). Thus our
observation of the undetectable 5'-nucleotidase activity in
rapidly proliferating neoplastic cells has been independently
found by others (Kramers, et al., 1976; Lopes, et al., 1973;
Peterson and Biedler, 1978; Reaman, et al., 1979; Trams and
Lauter, 1974).

A NEWLY IDENTIFIED PROTEIN MOLECULE IN HUMAN LEUKEMIC CELLS THAT INHIBITS 5'-NUCLEOTIDASE

The undetectability of 5'-nucleotidase in leukemic cells could
be due to the absence of the enzyme, the presence of an inhibitor
that prevents 5'-nucleotidase from working, or the rate of
anabolism of 5'-nucleoside monophosphates exceeding the rate of
catabolism by 5'-nucleotidase. These possibilities can be distinguished by mixing the homogenate of normal cells, which contains
5'-nucleotidase activity, with that of neoplastic cells, which has
no detectable 5'-nucleotidase activity. If the 5'-nucleotidase
activity in the homogenate of normal cells is undetectable in this

Table 1 5'-Nucleotidase Activity During Cellular Aging in vitro
and the Undetectable Activity in Human Leukemic Cells*

Cell Strain	Life- span(P)	5'-Nucleotidase Activity (nmoles per min per mg protein)					Above
		P1	P20	P30	P60	P280	P350
CEF	28 ± 5	1.5-2.0		30-35 (senescent)			
WI-38	50 ± 10		[a]50-100		[a]450-550 (senescent)		
IMR-90	50 ± 10		[b]100-200		[b]900-1,000 (senescent)		
VA-13	Unlimited					[a]90-200	[a]90-200
3T3	Unlimited						Undetectable
SV3T3	Unlimited						Undetectable
RPMI 8422	Unlimited						Undetectable
RPMI 8402	Unlimited						Undetectable
Molt 3	Unlimited						Undetectable
B85	Unlimited						Undetectable
NALM-1	Unlimited						Undetectable
DND39A	Unlimited						Undetectable
B46M	Unlimited						Undetectable
DAUDI	Unlimited						Undetectable
HRIK	Unlimited						Undetectable
B411-4	Unlimited						Undetectable
RPMI 1788	Unlimited						Undetectable

*The data are summarized from Sun et al. (1975, 1979, and 1982).
Lifespan(P): accumulated population doubling.   a) measured with
Tris-HCl, 50 mM at pH 7.4.   b) measured with Tris-Maleate, 50 mM
at pH 8.5.

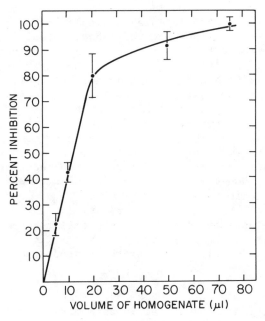

Fig. 1.   Inhibition of 5'-nucleotidase activity by the homogenate
          of RPMI 8402 cells

          The control contains IMR-90 cell homogenate, 0.032 mg
          protein/ml having a 5'-nucleotidase specific activity of
          106.2 + 3.5/nmoles/min/mg protein.   Except for the
          controls, all samples contained RPMI 8402 cell homogenate
          (0.13 mg protein/ml) in various volumes, as indicated on
          the abscissa. The 5'-nucleotidase activity of the control
          and of the samples containing the admixed homogenates was
          defined as 5NT(IMR-90) and 5NT(IMR-90 + RPMI 8402)
          respectively.   The percent inhibition shown on the
          ordinate was defined as:

          [1 - 5NT(IMR-90 + RPMI 8402) $\div$ 5NT(IMR-90)] x 100%

mixed homogenate, the latter two explanations become possible.

    As shown in Figure 1, 5'-nucleotidase activity in the homoge-
nate of IMR-90 cells is inhibited by increasing the amounts of
human leukemic RPMI 8402 cell homogenate in the sample;   more than
90% of the 5'-nucleotidase activity can be inhibited.   One unit
of inhibition is defined as the 50% inhibition of 5'-nucleotidase
activity under the same experimental conditions.   The specific
inhibiting activity is defined as units of inhibition per mg of

leukemic protein.   Further studies showed that homogenates of
various leukemic cell lines and of fresh leukemic cells all
inhibited 5'-nucleotidase activity (Table 2).   Approximately 97%
of the inhibiting activity was found in the supernatant fraction
of RPMI 8402 cells (Table 3).   The inhibiting activity increased
slightly after the supernatant was heated at 56°C for 30 min or
treated with RNase and DNase (Table 4).   However, it was inactivated after digestion by papain or heating at 100°C (Table 4).
These data suggest that the inhibiting activity could be due to a
protein in the leukemic cells.   This protein could be a non-
specific protease that could inactivate 5'-nucleotidase and other
enzymes as well.   However, the heated (56°C) supernatant fraction
(containing the inhibitor) of RPMI 8402 cells did not inactivate
alkaline,   neutral, and acid phosphatases, cytochrome c oxidase,
and N-acetyl-β-glucosaminidase in IMR-90 cell homogenate (Table 5
and 6).   Neither did prolonged preincubation increase the percent
of inhibition of 5'-nucleotidase by the heated supernatant (Table

Table 2   Inhibition of 5'-Nucleotidase Activity in the Homogenate
           of Normal Cells by the Homogenate of Leukemic Cells

Source of Inhibitory Extract		Specific Inhibiting
Cell Line	Origin	Activity (Units/mg)
RPMI 8402	Lymphoblastic leukemia	664.0 + 33.1
MOLT 3	Lymphoblastic leukemia	720.0 + 35.6
RPMI 8422	Lymphoblastic leukemia	11.5 + 1.0
NALM-1	Blastic phase of chronic myelocytic leukemia	36.1 + 3.9
DAUDI	Burkitt lymphoma	16.4 + 1.3
HRIK	Burkitt lymphoma	53.8 + 2.1
DND-39	Burkitt lymphoma	24.0 + 0.7
Lymphocytes	Sezary circulating T-cell lymphoma	53.1 + 5.7

Table 3   Distribution of Inhibiting Activity for 5'-Nucleotidase
           in Subcellular Fractions of RPMI 8402 Cells

Subcellular Fraction	Specific Inhibiting Activity (Units/mg protein)	Recovery (Percent)
Homogenate	858.3 + 44.3	100.0
Nuclear	148.8 + 12.6	0.45 + 0.58
Plasma Membranes	135.3 + 11.8	1.14 + 0.06
Microsomal	110.8 + 10.7	1.55 + 0.45
Supernatant	2,573.8 + 256.0	96.63 + 1.54

Table 4   Treatment of Supernatant Fraction of RPMI 8402 With
           Various Conditions

Treatment	Time of treatment (hours)	Specific Inhibiting Activity (Units/mg protein)	
		Control	Treated
Heat at 56°C	0.5	458.9 + 31.3	563.2 + 69.5
Heat at 100°C	0.5	387.8 + 9.0	0
RNase A	5	364.1 + 32.3	487.6 + 38.9
	17	461.6 + 26.6	507.5 + 24.1
DNase II	5	366.3 + 17.7	652.6 + 67.6
	17	295.1 + 15.6	438.3 + 51.0
Papain	1	248.0 + 5.0	37.1 + 0.9
	4	277.7 + 3.1	29.5 + 2.7

Table 5   Effect of Supernatant of RPMI 8402 Cells on Alkaline
           Phosphatase Activity

Rate of Reaction (nmoles/minute)			Ratio
IMR-90 Cell Homogenate (A)	Supernatant of RPMI 8402 (B)	Admixture (C)	$\dfrac{(C)}{(A)+(B)}$
0.101 + 0.007	0.026 + 0.003	0.128 + 0.008	1.008
same as above	0.051 + 0.003	0.148 + 0.002	0.974
same as above	0.102 + 0.001	0.183 + 0.001	0.902
same as above	0.271 + 0.014	0.345 + 0.015	0.928
same as above	0.545 + 0.013	0.624 + 0.009	0.966
same as above	1.161 + 0.007	1.182 + 0.001	0.936
		Average:	0.952
			+ 0.038

The sample containing IMR-90 cell homogenate alone (0.036 mg
protein per sample) had a rate of reaction of 0.101 + 0.007 nmoles
per min (Column A).   Values in column (B) are rate of reaction of
sample containing only supernatant of RPMI 8402 cells at 5.5, 11,
22, 55, 110, and 220 mg of protein per sample respectively.
Values in column (C) are the rate of the reaction of the •samples
containing the admixture of the IMR-90 cell homogenate and supernatant of RPMI 8402 cells of the same protein concentrations.

Table 6   Effect of Heated Supernatant of RPMI 8402 Cells on
            Activities of Various Enzymes

Enzyme	(Experimental Rate of the Admixture) (Sum of Respective Rates) Preincubation Time (minutes)		
	1	20	40
5'-Nucleotidase	0.398 + 0.032	0.406 + 0.042	0.371 + 0.030
Alkaline Phosphatase	1.037 + 0.005	0.967 + 0.037	0.985 + 0.028
Acid Phosphatase	0.998 + 0.010	0.973 + 0.034	0.994 + 0.048
Neutral Phosphatase	1.061 + 0.025	1.033 + 0.011	1.123 + 0.014
N-Acetyl-β-glucosaminidase	1.056 + 0.017	1.022 + 0.022	1.040 + 0.030
Cytochrome C Oxidase	1.047 + 0.042	1.076 + 0.016	1.100 + 0.141

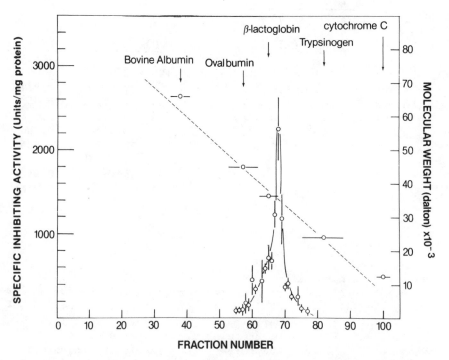

Fig 2. Determination of Molecular Weight of the Inhibitor for
        5'-Nucleotidase with Sephadex G-100 Chromatography

6).   Using a Sephadex G-100 gel filtration and sedimentation centrifugation in a sucrose gradient, the molecular weight of this
inhibitor of 5'-nucleotidase was found to be 35,000 as compared
with other proteins of known molecular weight (Fig 2).

5'-NUCLEOTIDASE INHIBITOR IN NON-HEMATOPOIETIC MOUSE EHRLICH ASCITES CARCINOMA CELLS

The inhibiting activity for 5'-nucleotidase was found in all
the human leukemic cells tested (Table 2) and the inhibitor for
5'-nucleotidase was identified in one of these leukemic cell
lines, RPMI 8402 cells (Sun, et al., 1983). Whether the inhibitor
was specifically associated with hematopoietic neoplasms or could
also be found in other types of cancers was of major interest.
Therefore, a different type of neoplastic cell from a different
species was studied, namely, mouse Ehrlich ascites carcinoma
cells.   Subsequently an inhibitor for 5'-nucleotidase was
identified in this non-hematopoietic cell line (Lee, et al.,
1985). Similiar to the findings for human 5'-nucleotidase inhibitor, 95% of the mouse inhibitor was in the supernatant fraction
with a molecular weight of 35,000.   The inhibitor was also relatively heat-stable (56°C for 30 min), insensitive to digestion by
RNase and DNase, but destroyed by heating at 90°C and digestion by
proteinase K.   It was also found that the mouse inhibitor could
inhibit human 5'-nucleotidase and that it was not a nonspecific
protease.

In a study of a 6-mercaptopurine resistant subline of Ehrlich
ascites carcinoma cells, Paterson and Hori found that the activity
of 5'-nucleotidase of the admixture of nuclear, mitochondrial, and
supernatant fractions was only 50% of the sum of the 5'-nucleoti-
dase activities of the fractions measured separately (Paterson and
Hori, 1962). Similarly the 5'-nucleotidase activity of the admixture of mitochondrial and supernatant fractions as well as of the
nuclear and supernatant fractions was much lower than the sum of
their individual activities.   However, when the nuclear and mitochondrial fractions were mixed, the 5'-nucleotidase activity of
the admixture was equivalent to the sum of the activities of these
fractions.   Therefore, these authors suggested that an inhibitor
for 5'-nucleotidase could be present in the supernatant fraction
of these cells.   They measured 5'-nucleotidase activity by estimating the inorganic phosphate hydrolyzed from 5'-AMP. However,
in our study (Lee, et al., 1985) 5'-nucleotidase activity was
measured by estimating the (^{3}H)-labelled adenosine released from
the substrate.   Although the inhibitor was not extensively identified in the study of Paterson and Hori, the presence of an
inhibitor for 5'-nucleotidase in the supernatant fraction of
Ehrlich ascites carcinoma cells was independently established by
their work and by ours.

PRESENCE OF BOTH 5'-NUCLEOTIDASE AND ITS INHIBITOR IN THE SAME
NEOPLASTIC CELLS: A MODIFICATION OF THE PREVIOUS CONCEPT ON THE
CATABOLISM OF THE INTRACELLULAR 5'-NUCLEOSIDE MONOPHOSPHATES

Prior to the knowledge of the inhibitor for 5'-nucleotidase,
the catabolism of 5'-nucleoside monophosphates to 5'-nucleosides
was thought to be controlled primarily by the enzyme. Since the
inhibitor prevents 5'-nucleotidase from working, this concept
should be modified if both 5'-nucleotidase and its inhibitor or
just one of them is present in the same cells. In our study of
Ehrlich ascites carcinoma cells, 5'-nucleotidase was low and
sometimes negligible (small mean $\pm$ large standard deviations).
The subcellular distribution of 5'-nucleotidase was 1,667 $\pm$ 36% in
plasma membranes and 405 $\pm$ 25% in microsomal fraction, assuming
the total but small 5'-nucleotidase activity detected in the homogenate to be 100% (Table 7).

Table 7   Distribution of 5'-Nucleotidase and Its Inhibiting
             Activity In Mouse Ehrlich Ascites Carcinoma Cells

Subcellular Fraction	5'-Nucleotidase Activity		Inhibiting Activity	
	Specific Activity (nmoles/min/mg)	Recovery (Percent)	Specific Activity (Units/mg)	Recovery (Percent)
Homogenate	0.11 $\pm$ 0.04	100	49 $\pm$ 4	100.0
Nuclear	0	0	11 $\pm$ 1	6.0 $\pm$ 0.2
Plasma membranes	19.64 $\pm$ 0.43	1,667 $\pm$ 36	0	0
Microsomal	3.98 $\pm$ 0.74	405 $\pm$ 25	0	0
Supernatant	0	0	139 $\pm$ 17	122.3 $\pm$ 7.0

5'-Nucleotidase is active intracellularly and extracellularly
and has been considered to be the major enzyme controlling the
catabolism of 5'-nucleotides. Our study shows that both the
enzyme and its inhibitor are present in the same neoplastic cells.
This modifies the previous concept on the catabolism of 5'-nucleo-
tides. It is possible that both 5'-nucleotidase and its inhibitor
work in a cooperative way to control the intracellular level of

5'-nucleotide pools. Further study is needed to define how and to what degree the enzyme and its inhibitor interact to determine the level of intracellular 5'-nucleoside monophosphates.

INTRACELLULAR AND EXTRACELLULAR 5'-NUCLEOTIDASE ACTIVITY

5'-nucleotidase is active both intracellularly and extracellularly. Using ɤ,β-methylene adenosine diphosphate to inhibit ecto-5'-nucleotidase, Edwards et al. concluded that intracellular purine metabolism is most likely regulated by cytoplasmic 5'-nucleotidase (Edwards, et al., 1982). Widnell and Little (1977) and Stanley et al. (1979b) showed that in rat hepatocytes 30% of the enzyme activity was distributed in the cytoplasm on the cytoplasmic side of the Golgi apparatus, endoplasmic reticulum, lysosomes, microsomes and mitochondria. Farquhar et al. (1974) observed 5'-nucleotidase on the inside of secretion vacuoles from the Golgi apparatus; this was independently confirmed (Widnell and Little, 1977). Edelson and Cohen (1976), Stanley et al. (1979a, 1979b, and 1980), and Widnell et al. (1982) demonstrated that up to 60% of 5'-nucleotidase activity took place intracellularly, and that there was a continual and rapid exchange of 5'-nucleotidase between the cell surface and cytoplasmic side of the membranes of subcellular organelles. Thus there is a general consensus that 5'-nucleotidase plays an active role in the intracellular catabolism of 5'-nucleotides.

THE EFFECT OF 5'-NUCLEOTIDASE AND ITS INHIBITOR ON INTRACELLULAR NUCLEOTIDES, RNA, DNA AND CELL PROLIFERATION: A HYPOTHESIS TO BE TESTED

5'-Nucleotidase has been considered to be the major enzyme controlling the catabolism of 5'-nucleotides (Fritzson, 1978; Henderson and Paterson, 1973). Using histochemical methods and autoradiography, Hardonk and Koudstaal found no incorporation of (^{3}H)-thymidine into normal and tumorous cells that showed high 5'-nucleotidase activity. However, abundant incorporation was detected when 5'-nucleotidase was absent or low (Hardonk and Koudstaal, 1968). Thus they suggested that this enzyme was mainly involved in the catabolism of nucleotides, which can affect the rate of DNA synthesis indirectly. In a study of regenerating liver, Fritzson (1967) found that the dephosphorylation of ribonucleotides was largely due to cytoplasmic 5'-nucleotidase, which showed a cyclic variation inversely proportional to the rate of cell proliferation; this view was further elucidated (Fritzson, 1978). Similar conclusions were also reached by Arima, et al. who observed that the incorporation of nucleosides into 5'-nucleoside monophosphates was inversely related to the 5'-nucleotidase activity (Arima, et al., 1972). Our study further suggests that both 5'-nucleotidase and its inhibitor may work in a cooperative way in the control of their common proximate substrates, namely,

intracellular 5'-nucleoside monophosphates. In the presence of
its inhibitor in cancer cells 5'-nucleotidase may not bring about
the catabolism of 5'-nucleoside monophosphate, thus facilitating
the anabolism of nucleosides into nucleotides, RNA, and DNA, a
necessary event for cell proliferation.

HYPOTHESIS THAT THE INHIBITOR FOR 5'-NUCLEOTIDASE IS AN ONCOGENE
PRODUCT

Many oncogenes, proteins coded from these oncogenes, and the
biochemical functions of these proteins have been identified
(Bishop, 1982; Erikson and Erikson, 1980; Padhy, et al., 1982;
Weinberg, 1983).   Although the biochemical role of many of the
oncogene proteins has not been well understood, it has been
thought to concern the continuous and indefinite proliferation of
cancer cells (Erikson and Erikson, 1980; Padhy, et al., 1982).

In our previous studies an inhibitor for 5'-nucleotidase was
identified in both hematopoeitic and non-hematopoeitic neoplastic
cells (Sun, et al., 1983). The inhibiting activity for 5'-nucleo-
tidase was also detected in all eight different leukemic cell
lines tested thus far (Table 2), suggesting the possible presence
of the inhibitor in all immortal neoplastic cells. Thus we proposed that this inhibitor may also play a role in the continuous
and indefinite proliferation of cancer cells (Sun et al., 1983).
Since the inhibitor is produced predominantly in cancer cells, it
could also be one of the oncogene proteins-- a hypothesis to be
tested.

THE EFFECT OF ADENOSINE DEAMINASE

Recently Dornand et al. (1984) reported that they were able to
reproduce all our data on 5'-nucleotidase inhibitor. They further
found that adenosine deaminase interferes with the method of
Avruch and Wallach (1970) for assaying 5'-nucleotidase and thus
challenged the presence of 5'-nucleotidase inhibitor. However,
using two different colorimetric methods and one isotope labelled
method (5'-AMP^{32} as the substrate), which are not influenced by
adenosine deaminase, we again demonstrated the presence of the
5'-nucleotidase inhibitor in both fresh and cultured leukemic
cells (Sun and Holland, 1985). The inability of Dornand et al. to
detect the 5'-nucleotidase inhibitor was found to be due to a
methodological flaw in their experiments (Sun and Holland, 1985).

THE RELATION OF OUR STUDY TO OTHER ASPECTS OF AGING AND CANCER

No one expects that one mechanism can explain every aspect of
the complicated phenomena of both cancer and cellular aging. It is
known that many nucleotide anabolic enzymes, such as UDP kinase,
adenylosuccinate synthetase, and adenylosuccinase, increase, while

many other enzymes, including xanthine oxidase, dihydrouridine
dehydrogenase, monoamine oxidase, cytochrome c oxidase, catalase,
urate oxidase, L-α-hydroxy oxidase, decrease in cancer cells as
compared with their normal counterparts (Sun, et al., 1980; Sun,
et al., 1981; Weber, 1978).   It is also known that many anabolic
reactions, such as the rate of protein synthesis, are lower in
senescent than in young tissues (Coniglio, et al., 1979;
Blazejowski and Webster, 1983; Hardwick, et al., 1981).   These
changes might all be important for explaining one of the many
specific aspects of cancer and aging.   The implications of our
study of 5'-nucleotidase and its inhibitor may shed light on one
specific aspect of the complicated phenomena of aging and cancer.

ACKNOWLEDGEMENT

We are indebted to Ms. Suzanne Noguere for her editing work.

REFERENCES

Arima, T., Shirasaka, T., Okuda, H., & Fujii, S., 1972, Studies on
      a reciprocal relationship between nucleoside kinases and
      5'-nucleotidase, Biochim. Biophys. Acta, 277, 15.
Avruch, J. and Wallach, D.F.H., 1970, Preparation and properties
      of plasma membrane and endoplasmic reticulum fragments from
      isolated rat fat cells, Bioch. Biophys. Acta, 233, 334.
Bishop, M. J., 1982, Oncogenes, Scientific American, 246, 80.
Blazejowski, C. A. and Webster, G. C., 1983,   Decreased rates of
      protein synthesis by cell-free preparations from different
      organs of aging mice, Mech. Aging Develop.,   21, 345.
Bukovsky, J. and Roth, J.S., 1964, Some factors affecting thymidy-
      late kinase activities in normal rat liver and some hepa-
      tomas, Fed. Proc., 23, 278.

Coniglio, J.J., Liu, D.S.H., and Richardson, A., 1979, A comparison of protein synthesis by liver parenchymal cells isolated from Fischer F344 rats of various ages, Mech. Aging Develop. 11, 77.

de Lamirande, G., Allard, C., and Cantero, A., 1958, Purine metabolizing enzymes in normal rat liver and Novikoff hepatoma, Can. Res., 18, 952.

Dinowitz, M., 1977, A continuous line of Rous Sarcoma virus-transformed chick embryo cells, J. Natl. Cancer Inst., 58, 307.

Dinowitz, M., 1984, Personal communication.

Dornand, J., Bonnafous, J., Favero, J., Gartner, A., Mani, J., 1984, The proposed 5'-nucleotidase inhibitor in human leukemic cells is an artefact, Bioch. Biophys. Acta, 804, 398.

Edwards, N.L., Recker, D., Manfredi, J., Rembecki, R., and Fox, I. H., 1982, Regulation of purine metabolism by plasma membrane and cytoplasmic 5'-nucleotidase, Amer. J. Physiol., 243, C270.

Edelson, P.J. and Cohn, Z.A., 1976, 5'-Nucleotidase activity in mouse peritoneal macrophages. I. Synthesis and degradation in resident and inflammatory population, J. Expt. Med., 144, 1581.

Erikson, E. and Erikson, R. L., 1980, Identification of a cellular protein substrate phosphorylated by the Avian Sarcoma Virus-transforming gene products, Cell, 21, 829.

Farquhar, M.G., Bergeron, J.J.M., and Palade, G.E., 1974, Cytochemistry of Golgi fractions prepared from rat liver, J. Cell Biol., 66, 8.

Fiala, S., Glinsmann, W., and Fiala, A., 1959, Deoxyribonucleotidase activity during carcinogenesis in rat liver, Naturwissenschafter, 46, 653.

Fiala, S., Fiala, A., Tobar, G., and McQuilla, H., 1962, Deoxyribonucleotidase activity in rat liver and certain tumor, J. Nat. Cancer Inst., 28, 1269.

Fritzson, P., 1967, Dephosphorylation of pyrimidine nucleotides in the soluble fraction of homogenates from normal regenerating rat liver, Europ. J. Biochem., 1, 12.

Fritzson, P., 1978, Regulation of nucleotidase activities in animal tissues, Adv. Enzy. Regul., 16, 43.

Girardi, A.J., Weinstein, D., and Moorhead, P.S., 1966, SV40 virus transformation of human diploid cells, Ann. Med. Exp. Biol. Fenn., 44, 242.

Goldberg, D.M. and Belfield, A., 1974, Reciprocal relationship of alkaline phosphatase and 5'-nucleotidase in human bone, Nature, 247, 286.

Goodlad, G. A. J. and Clark, C. M., 1982, Alterations in hepatic 5'-nucleotidase in tumor-bearing rat, Enzyme, 27, 119.

Hardonk, M.J. and Koudstaal, J., 1968, 5'-Nucleotidase II. The significance of 5'-nucleotidase in the metabolism of nucleotides studied by histochemical and biochemical methods, Histochemie, 12, 18.

Hardwick, J., Hsieh, W., Liu, D. S .H., and Richardson, A., 1981, Cell-free protein synthesis by kidney from the aging female Fischer F344 rat, Biochim. Biophys. Acta, 652, 204.

Hayflick, L. and Moorhead, P.S., 1961, The serial cultivation of human diploid cell strains, Exp. Cell Res., 25, 585.

Henderson, J.F. and Paterson, A. R. P., 1973, "Nucleotide Metabolism" Academic Press, New York.

Kramers, M. T. C., Catovsky, D., Foa, R., Cherchi, M., and Galton, D. A. G., 1976, 5'-Nucleotidase activity in leukemic lymphocytes, Biomed., 25, 363.

Lee, Y., Sun, A. S., Holland, J. F., and Mowshowitz, S. L., 1985, Implications of 5'-nucleotidase and its inhibitor in mouse Ehrlich Ascites carcinoma cells for cellular aging and cancer, submitted.

Little, J. S. and Widnell, C., 1975, Evidence for the translocation of 5'-nucleotidase across hepatic membranes in vivo, Proc. Natl. Acad. Sci., 72, 4013.

Lopes, J., Zucker-Franklin, E., and Silber, R., 1973, Heterogeneity of 5'-nucleotidase activity in lymphocytes in chronic lymphocytic leukemia, J. Clin. Invest., 52, 1297.

Ohnuma, T., Holland, J. F., Arkin, H., and Minowada, J., 1977, L-Asparagine requirements of human T-lymphocytes in culture, J. Nat'l Cancer Inst., 59, 1061.

Padhy, L. C., Shih, C., Cowing, D., Finkelstein, R., and Weinberg, R. A., 1982, Identification of a phosphoprotein specifically induced by the transforming DNA of rat neuroblastomas, Cell, 28, 865.

Paterson, A. R. P. and Hori, A., 1962, Resistance to 6-mercaptopurine: Deletion of a 5'-nucleotidase in a 6-mercaptopurine resistant subline of the Ehrlich Ascites Carcinoma, Can. J. Biochem. Physiol., 41, 1339.

Peterson, R.H.F. and Biedler, J.L., 1978, Plasma membrane proteins and glycoproteins from chinese hamster cells sensitive and resistant to actinomycin D, J. Supramol. Struct., 9, 289.

Pitot, H.C., 1979, Biological and enzymatic events in chemical carcinogenesis, Ann. Rev. Med., 30, 25.

Ponten, J., 1970, The growth capacity of normal and Rous virus-transformed chicken fibroblasts in vitro, Int. J. Cancer, 6, 323.

Reaman, G.H., Levin, N., Muchmore, A., Holiman, B.J., and Poplack, D.G., 1979, Diminished lymphoblast 5'-nucleotidase activity in acute lymphoblastic leukemia with T-Cell characteristic, New England J. Med., 300, 1374.

Rodan, G.A., Bourett, A., and Culter, L.S., 1977, Membrane changes during cartilage maturation, J. Cell Biology, 72, 493.

Stanley, K.K., Edwards, M.R., and Luzio, J.P., 1979a, Rapid internalization of plasma-membrane 5'-nucleotidase in rat spleen lymphocytes in response to rabbit anti-(rat liver 5'-nucleotidase) serum, Biochem. Soc. Trans., 7, 1023.

Stanley, K. K. and Luzio, J. P., 1979b, The Subcellular distribu-
    tion of 5'-nucleotidase in isolated fat cells and liver
    cells from rat, Biochem. Soc. Trans., 7, 1023.
Stanley, K.K., Edwards, M.R., and Luzio, J.P., 1980, Subcellu-
    lar distribution and movement of 5'-nucleotidase in rat
    cells, Biochem. J., 186, 59.
Sun, A.S., Aggarwal, B.B., and Packer, L., 1975, Enzyme levels of
    normal human cells: Aging in culture, Arch. Biochem.
    Biophys., 170, 1.
Sun, A. S., Alvarez, L. J., Reinach, P. S., and Rubin, E., 1979,
    5'-Nucleotidase levels in normal and virus-transformed
    cells: Implications for Cellular Aging in vitro, Lab.
    Invest., 41, 1.
Sun, A. S. and Cederbaum, A., 1980, Oxidoreductase activities in
    normal rat liver, tumor-bearing rat liver, and hepatoma
    HC-252, Cancer Res., 40, 4677.
Sun, A. S., Sepkowitz, K., and Geller, S., 1981, A comparison of
    some mitochondrial and peroxisomal enzyme activities in
    normal mucosa and carcinoma of human colon, Lab. Invest.,
    44, 13.
Sun, A.S., Holland, J.F., Slankard-Chahinian, M., and Ohnuma, T.,
    1982, 5'-Nucleotidase activity in permanent human lymphoid
    cell lines: Implication for cell proliferation and aging in
    vitro, Biochim. Biophys. Acta, 714, 530.
Sun, A. S., Holland, J. F., Lin, K. and Ohnuma, T., 1983, Impli-
    cations of a 5'-nucleotidase inhibitor in human leukemic
    cells for cellular aging and cancer, Biochim. Biophys. Acta,
    762, 577.
Sun, A. S. and Holland, J. F., 1985, in preparation.
Todaro, G. J. and Green, H., 1963, Quantitative studies of the
    growth of mouse embryo cells in culture and their develop-
    ment into established lines, J. Cell Biology, 17, 299.
Trams, E. G. and Lauter, C. J., 1974, On the sidedness of plasma
    membrane enzymes, Biochim. Biophys. Acta, 345, 180.
Weber, G., 1978, Biochemical strategy of the genome as expressed
    in regulation of pyrimidine metabolism, Adv. Enzyme Regul.,
    16, 3.
Weinberg, R.A., 1983, Alteration of the genomes of tumor cells,
    Cancer, 52, 1971 (1983)
Widnell, C. and Little, J. S., 1977, Membranes involved in exo-
    cytosis and endocytosis: A cytochemical approach, in:
    "Membraneous Elements and Movement of Molecules," p. 149,
    E. Reid, ed., John Wiley and Sons Inc. N.Y.
Widnell, C., Schneider, Y. J., Pierre, B., Baudhuin, P., and
    Trouet, A., 1982, Evidence for a continual exchange of
    5'-nucleotidase between the cell surface and cytoplasmic
    membranes in cultured rat fibroblasts, Cell, 28, 61.

THE EFFECTS OF DEHYDROEPIANDROSTERONE ON THE RATE OF DEVELOPMENT

OF CANCER AND AUTOIMMUNE PROCESSES IN LABORATORY RODENTS

Arthur Schwartz

Fels Research Institute and Department of
Microbiology, Temple University Medical
School, Philadelphia, PA   19140

INTRODUCTION

Mammalian species vary tremendously in their rates of aging.
The maximal life-span of the smaller rodents (mouse, rat, and
hamster) is about 3.5 years, whereas for the human it is over 110
years (Altman and Dittmer, 1964). It is probable that the biological processes responsible for aging are fundamentally similar in
different mammalian species, but that they occur at different
rates.

One of the classical theories to account for aging is that
this biological process results from the progressive accumulation
of somatic mutations (Szilard, 1959; Failla, 1960; Hart et al.,
1975). If the rate of development of mutations among different
mammalian species correlated with the potential life-span of each
species, this would indeed strengthen a mutational hypothesis.

One source of mutagenic activity results from specific metabolic oxidative reactions in mammalian cells requiring the enzyme
co-factor nicotinamide adenine dinucleotide phosphate, reduced
form (NADPH). Two enzyme systems carrying out such reactions are
the microsomal mixed-function oxidase, which metabolizes many
different types of chemical carcinogens into reactive mutagens
(Miller, 1970), and a superoxide anion (O_2^-)-generating oxidase
found in high levels in stimulated granulocytes (Lew et al., 1981;
Babior, 1982). The metabolic products of both of these enzymes
play an important role in chemically induced tumors: the interaction of the reactive products of the mixed-function oxidase with
specific macromolecules is critical to the process of initiation
(Miller, 1978), and the O_2^- and subsequent oxygen metabolites

produced by the granulocyte oxidase are believed to contribute to
the 12-0-tetradecanoylphorbol-13-acetate (TPA) promotion of tumor
development (Goldstein et al., 1981; Emerit and Cerutti, 1983;
Weitberg et al., 1983). In addition O_2^- and subsequent oxygen
metabolites generated by the granulocyte oxidase may also be a
source of immune complex-mediated tissue damage in various autoimmune diseases (Johnson and Ward, 1981; McCormick et al., 1981;
Shingu et al., 1983).

The hypothesis is presented here that mutagenic metabolites
formed from NADPH-dependent oxidases contribute to spontaneous
cancer development and aging, and that the adrenal steroid,
dehydroepiandrosterone (DHEA), retards cancer development and
delays aging by inhibiting these oxidases through a lowering of
the NADPH cellular pool. Caloric restriction may also retard
cancer development and the rate of aging through an alteration
of the NADPH cellular pool.

MAXIMAL LIFE-SPAN AND METABOLISM OF CHEMICAL CARCINOGENS INTO REACTIVE MUTAGENS

The microsomal mixed-function oxidase system is a multi-
component, membrane-bound electron transport system which catalyzes
the oxidative metabolism of a variety of endogenous and exogenous
substances, including fatty acids, steroids, drugs, and chemical
carcinogens (Gillette, 1966; Lu and Coon, 1968; Miller, 1970).
This system is composed of NADPH cytochrome c reductase,
cytochrome P-450, and phosphatidyl choline (Lu et al., 1969;
Stroebel et al., 1970).

Most chemical carcinogens require metabolic transformation
to chemically reactive molecules in the tissues of animals to
which they are administered (Miller, 1970). The majority of these
transformation products are inactive, water-soluble substances
which are excreted by the organism, but a small percentage are
chemically reactive mutagens which produce changes leading to
neoplasia.

Using a cell-mediated assay to measure the metabolism of
7,12-dimethylbenz(a)anthracene (DMBA) into a mutagenic product,
Huberman and Sachs (1974) found that mouse, rat, and hamster
diploid fibroblasts actively converted DMBA into a mutagen,
whereas human diploid fibroblasts were inactive. Employing this
cell-mediated assay with cultured fibroblasts from six mammalian
species of widely differing life-spans, we found an inverse
correlation between maximal life-span and capacity to convert
DMBA into a mutagenic metabolite (Schwartz, 1975) (Fig. 1).
Further studies demonstrated an inverse correlation between potential life-span and the rate at which cultured fibroblasts bound

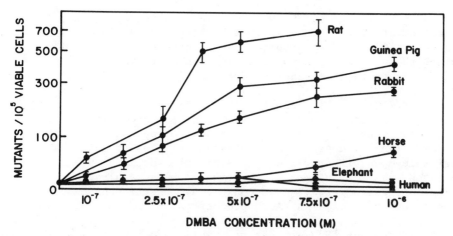

Fig. 1. Capacity of cultured fibroblasts from various mammalian
species to metabolize DMBA into a mutagenic product.
X-irradiated feeder fibroblasts from different species were
co-cultivated with V79 cells and incubated with varying
molar concentrations of DMBA for 24 hours. Following
this the V79 cells were collected and the number of
8-azaguanine resistant mutant cells per 10^5 viable cells
was determined. (By permission (Schwartz, 1975).)

^{3}H-DMBA to their DNA (Schwartz and Moore, 1977) and metabolized
the polycyclic hydrocarbon into water-soluble metabolites (Moore
and Schwartz, 1978).

The above studies demonstrating an inverse correlation
between potential life-span and capacity to convert one class of
pre-mutagen into mutagenic and carcinogenic metabolites suggest
that the enzymatic formation of such reactive substances may
contribute to spontaneous cancer development and to aging.

DEHYDROEPIANDROSTERONE

Dehydroepiandrosterone and DHEA-sulfate are abundantly produced adrenal steroids in the human with no apparent biological
function (Vande Wiele and Lieberman, 1960). DHEA is a potent
non-competitive inhibitor of mammalian glucose-6-phosphate
dehydrogenase (G6PDH), the first enzyme in the pentose-phosphate
shunt, which is the main generator of extra-mitochondrial NADPH
(Marks and Banks, 1960; Oertel and Rebelein, 1969).

DHEA protects cultured rat liver epithelial-like cells and
hamster embryonic fibroblasts against DMBA- and aflatoxin B_1-

induced cytotoxicity and transformation, and inhibits the rate of
metabolism of ^{3}H-DMBA into water-soluble products (Schwartz and
Perantoni, 1975). Very probably DHEA protects cultured cells
against these carcinogens by reducing NADPH production, that, in
turn, inhibits their metabolic activation.

In 1977 Yen et al. reported that long-term treatment of A^{vy}/a
(obese) or a/a (non-obese) mice with DHEA reduced weight gain
without suppressing appetite. There was no apparent toxicity
following long-term treatment, and the anti-obesity action was
reversible upon withdrawal of the drug. Yen et al. (1977)
suggested that the anti-obesity action of DHEA resulted from an
inhibition of lipogenesis as a consequence of the DHEA inhibition
of G6PDH and reduction in NADPH production.

My laboratory (Schwartz et al., 1981) and others (Tagliaferro
and Davis, 1983; Cleary et al., 1984b) have confirmed the anti-
obesity action of DHEA in other strains of mice and rats. The
steroid has also been reported to have anti-diabetic action in
both the streptozotocin induced insulin-dependent and the genetically determined non-insulin dependent diabetes in the mouse
(Coleman et al., 1982). Although treatment of some strains of
mice and rats with DHEA does reduce food intake, pair-feeding
experiments indicate that the reduction in food consumption alone
cannot account for the anti-obesity effect of the steroid (Nyce et
al., 1984; Weindruch et al., 1984).

The precise mechanism by which DHEA treatment inhibits weight
gain is not clear. Recent evidence suggests that the anti-
obesity effect is not simply due to a reduction in the rate of
lipogenesis as a result of G6PDH inhibition (Coleman et al., 1982;
Cleary et al., 1984b). Treatment with the steroid decreases the
efficiency of food utilization, possibly by enhancing energy
expenditure through the stimulation of futile cycles, metabolic
cycles which produce a net dephosphorylation of ATP (Cleary et
al., 1984a; Cleary et al., 1984b).

FOOD RESTRICTION AND DHEA

Reducing the food intake of laboratory rodents is the only
regimen that extends the mean and maximal life-span and delays the
rate of development of biomarkers of aging (McCay et al., 1935;
Harrison et al., 1978; Yu et al., 1982; Weindruch and Walford,
1983). Underfeeding also inhibits the development of both spontaneous and chemically induced tumors in many different organs
(Tannenbaum and Silverstone, 1953).

Both the anti-obesity action of DHEA as well as its capacity
to protect cultured cells against chemical carcinogens led us to

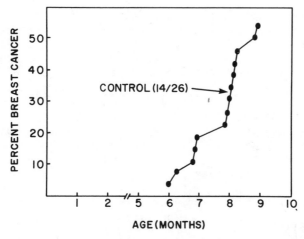

Fig. 2.   Inhibition of spontaneous breast cancer development in
C3H-A^{vy}/A mice by long-term treatment with DHEA. C3H-
A^{vy}/A mice were intubated p.o. thrice weekly with 450
mg/kg of DHEA in sesame oil or with sesame oil alone.
Mice were palpated weekly for the presence of breast
tumors, and each tumor was recorded at the time of first
palpation. The cumulative breast cancer incidence over a
9-month period is shown, with each point representing a
single mouse with a tumor. By 9 months of age, 14/26
control mice and 0/24 DHEA-treated mice had developed
tumors. However, after one year some of the DHEA-treated
mice developed tumors. (By permission (Schwartz, 1979).)

undertake experiments to determine if treatment with the steroid
would inhibit tumor development in vivo. We did indeed find that
long-term treatment of C3H-A^{vy}/A (obese) and C3H-A/A (non-obese)
mice with DHEA inhibited the rate of appearance of spontaneous
breast cancer (Fig. 2) (Schwartz, 1979; Schwartz et al., 1981).
Subsequently we found that DHEA treatment inhibited the development of DMBA- and urethan-induced lung adenomas in the A/J mouse
(Schwartz and Tannen, 1981) and 1,2-dimethylhydrazine-induced
colon adenomas and adenocarcinomas in the Balb/c mouse (Nyce et
al., 1984).

Topical application of DHEA retards the rate of development
of DMBA-initiated and TPA-promoted skin papillomas at both the
initiation and promotion stages (Pashko et al., 1984b) and also
inhibits DMBA-induced skin papillomas and carcinomas in the
complete model for carcinogenesis (Pashko et al., 1984a). Application of DHEA topically at doses which retard skin tumor formation
does not inhibit weight gain and indicates that the prophylactic
effect of DHEA may be mediated by both a direct action of the
steroid on cells as well as by its anti-obesity effect.

The anti-tumor-initiating and anti-promoting-activity of DHEA
may result from an inhibition of G6PDH and consequent depression
of NADPH-dependent oxidase activity. Topical skin application
(Pashko et al., 1984b) or oral treatment (Pashko and Schwartz,
1983) of mice with DHEA inhibits the rate of binding of ^{3}H-DMBA to
skin DNA, very probably by decreasing the NADPH cellular pool and
diminishing the activity of the mixed-function oxidase. Likewise,
DHEA treatment blocks the TPA stimulation of O_2^- by human granulocytes in vitro (Whitcomb and Schwartz, 1985). 16αBr-epiandrosterone,
a more active inhibitor of G6PDH than DHEA, is also more active in
reducing O_2^- production, again suggesting that a reduction in the
NADPH cellular pool by these steroids reduces oxidase activity.

Food restriction depresses G6PDH activity in liver and adipose tissue in the rat and human (Freedland, 1967; Timmers and
Knittle, 1982). Underfeeding the mouse resulted in a reduced
capacity to bind ^{3}H-DMBA to skin DNA, mimicking the effect of DHEA
treatment (Pashko and Schwartz, 1983).

G6PDH DEFICIENCY

G6PDH deficiency is a sex-linked hereditary defect occurring
with high frequency in certain populations. Among the most preva-
lent deficiency mutants are the Mediterranean variant, found primarily among Sephardic Jews, Greeks, and Sardinians, and G6PDH A-,
common in Negro populations. Another variant, G6PDH A, with
abnormal electrophoretic properties but near normal enzyme activity, is also common in Negroes (Beutler, 1971).

Feo et al. (1984) recently reported that cultured fibroblasts
from individuals with the Mediterranean variant of G6PDH deficiency are less sensitive to the cytotoxic and transforming
effects of benzo(a)pyrene (BP) and are less efficient in metabolizing ^{3}H-BP to water-soluble products than are fibroblasts from
normal individuals. Treatment of normal fibroblasts with DHEA
mimicked the effect of the G6PDH deficiency. The authors also
reported a marked deficiency in pentose-phosphate shunt activity
and a lowering of the NADPH/NADP ratio in the G6PDH deficient
fibroblasts.

Beaconsfield et al. (1965) first proposed that the lowered
cancer rates in Israelis of North African or Asian origin compared
to those of Western European or American origin might be due to
the higher frequency of G6PDH deficiency in the former populations. Three retrospective epidemiologic studies have found a
lowered frequency of G6PDH deficiency in cancer patients than
in control populations in both Negroes (Naik and Anderson,
1970; Mbensa et al., 1978) and in Sardinians (Sulis, 1972).
Interestingly Long et al. (1967) reported a lowered incidence of

coronary artery disease in American Negroes with the A- and A
variants of G6PDH compared to a group with normal G6PDH. While
additional work is clearly needed to establish a causal relationship between the incidence of G6PDH deficiency and tumor
development, the above studies suggest an inverse correlation and
are consistent with the hypothesis that a reduction in the NADPH
pool size may protect against cancer development.

AUTOIMMUNE DEVELOPMENT

     Studies in my laboratory have shown that DHEA treatment inhi-
bits the rate of development of a Coomb's positive hemolytic
anemia in the NZB mouse (Tannen and Schwartz, 1982), and Lucas et
al. (1984) have found that DHEA treatment significantly extends
the life-span of the NZB/NZW F_1 hybrid, which is prone to a lupus
erythematosus-like disease. Recent evidence suggests that O_2^- and
subsequent oxygen metabolites produced by stimulated white blood
cells may be a source of immune complex mediated tissue damage in
various autoimmune diseases (Johnson and Ward, 1981; McCormick et
al., 1981; Shingu et al., 1983). The DHEA inhibition of O_2^-
formation by TPA stimulated granulocytes (Whitcomb and Schwartz,
1985) may in part explain the ability of this steroid to ame-
liorate the development of autoimmune processes in the NZB and
NZB/NZW F_1 mouse.

     Although DHEA treatment inhibited the rate of development of
the Coomb's positive anemia in the NZB strain, it did not significantly prolong life-span. Autopsy data revealed a high incidence
of pituitary tumors in the DHEA treated mice. Pituitary tumors
are produced in many strains of female rodents by chronic estrogen
treatment. DHEA is readily metabolized into estrogens and is
uterotrophic (stimulates uterine growth) in the sexually immature
rat (Knudsen and Mahesh, 1975). This estrogenic effect of DHEA
could seriously limit its potential use as a drug in humans. In
collaboration with John Williams of the Chemistry Department,
Temple University, we have prepared the synthetic steroid
3 β-methylandrost-5-en-17-one (DE-7) (Pashko et al., 1984b). The
replacement of the 3β-hydroxy group with the 3β-methyl group in
DE-7 should prevent conversion to androstenedione, an intermediate
on the pathway to estrone. DE-7 was indeed without activity in
the rat uterotrophic test at dosages at which DHEA was highly
active (Pashko et al., 1984b). On oral administration, the
synthetic steroid is about three times as active as DHEA as an
anti-obesity and anti-diabetic agent in the mouse and is also more
active in inhibiting skin papilloma (Pashko et al., 1984b) and
carcinoma (Pashko et al., 1984a) formation when applied topically.
Steroids such as DE-7, which lack the estrogenic side-effect of
DHEA but which retain its other biological activities, may find
application as an anti-obesity, anti-diabetic, and cancer

preventive drug in humans. It is not improbable that such a drug
will also inhibit the development of autoimmune processes and
retard the appearance of biomarkers of aging.

REFERENCES

Altman, P.L., and Dittmer, D., 1964, "Biology Data Book," Fed.
     Am. Soc. Exp. Biol., Bethesda, MD.
Babior, B.M., 1982, The enzymatic basis for O_2^- production by
     human neutrophils, Can. J. Physiol. Pharmacol., 60:1353.
Beaconsfield, P., Rainsbury, R., and Kalton, G., 1965, Glucose-6-
     phosphate dehydrogenase deficiency and the incidence of
     cancer, Oncologia, 19:11.
Beutler, E., 1971, Abnormalities of the hexose monophosphate
     shunt, Seminars in Hematology, 8:311.
Cleary, M.P., Billheimer, J., Finan, A., Sartin, J.L., and
     Schwartz, A.G., 1984a, Metabolic consequences of
     dehydroepiandrosterone in lean and obese adult Zucker rats,
     Horm. Metab. Res., 16:in press.
Cleary, M.P., Shepherd, A., and Jenks, B., 1984b, Effect of
     dehydroepiandrosterone on growth in lean and obese Zucker
     rats, J. Nutr., 114:1242.
Coleman, D.L., Leiter, E.H., and Schwizer, R.W., 1982,
     Therapeutic effects of dehydroepiandrosterone (DHEA) in
     diabetic mice, Diabetes, 31:830.
Emerit, I., and Cerutti, P., 1983, Clastogenic action of tumor
     promoter phorbol-12-myristate-13-acetate in mixed human
     leukocyte cultures, Carcinogenesis, 4:1313.
Failla, G., 1960, The aging process and somatic mutations, in:
     "AIBS Symposium, The Biology of Aging," 170, AIBS,
     Washington, D.C.
Feo, F., Pirisi, L., Pascale, R., Daino, L., Frassetto, S.,
     Garcea, R., and Gaspa, L., 1984, Modulatory effect of
     glucose-6-phosphate dehydrogenase deficiency on
     benzo(a)pyrene toxicity and transforming activity for in
     vitro cultured human fibroblasts, Cancer Res., 44:3419.
Freedland, R.A., 1967, Effect of progressive starvation on rat
     liver enzyme activation, J. Nutr., 91:489.
Gillette, J.R., 1966, Biochemistry of drug oxidation and
     reduction of enzymes in hepatic endoplasmic reticulum,
     Adv. in Pharmacol., 4:216.
Goldstein, B.D., Witz, G., Amoruso, M., Stone, D.S., and
     Troll, W., 1981, Stimulation of human polymorphonuclear
     leukocyte superoxide anion radical production by tumor
     promoters, Cancer Lett., 11:257.
Harrison, D.E., Archer, J.R., Sacher, G.A., and Boyce, F.M.,
     1978, Tail collagen aging in mice of thirteen genotypes
     and two species: Relationship to biological age. Exp.
     Gerontol., 13:63.

Hart, R.W., Setlow, R.B., Gibson, R.E., and Hoskins, T.L., 1975, DNA repair: one possible control mechanism in cellular aging, Int. Congr. Gerontol., 1:22.

Huberman, E., and Sachs, L., 1974, Cell-mediated mutagenesis of mammalian cells with chemical carcinogens, Int. J. Cancer, 13:326.

Johnson, K.J., and Ward, P., 1981, Role of oxygen metabolites in immune complex injury of lung, J. Immunol., 126:2365.

Knudsen, T.T., and Mahesh, V.B., 1975, Initiation of precocious sexual maturation in the immature rat treated with dehydroepiandrosterone, Endocrinol., 97:458.

Lew, P.D., Southwick, F.S., Stossel, T.P., Whitin, J.C., Simons, E., and Cohen, H.J., 1981, A variant of chronic granulomatous disease: deficient oxidative metabolism due to a low affinity NADPH oxidase, New Engl. J. Med., 305:1329.

Long, W.K., Wilson, S.W., and Frenkel, E.P., 1967, Association between red cell glucose-6-phosphate dehydrogenase variants and vascular disease, Am. J. Human Genetics, 19:35.

Lu, A.Y.H., and Coon, M.J., 1968, Role of hemeprotein P-450 in fatty acid ω-hydroxylation in a soluble enzyme system from liver microsomes, J. Biol. Chem., 243:1331.

Lu, A.Y.H., Junk, K.W., and Coon, M.J., 1969, Resolution of the cytochrome P-450 containing ω-hydroxylation system of liver microsomes into three components, J. Biol. Chem., 244:3714.

Lucas, J., McDonald, P.C., and Casey, M.L., 1984, Prevention or delay in onset of lupus erythematosus (LE) in NZB/NZW F_1 mice by dehydroepiandrosterone, 7th Int. Congr. Endocrinol., in press. Abstract.

Marks, P.H., and Banks, J., 1960, Inhibition of mammalian glucose-6-phosphate dehydrogenase by steroids, Proc. Natl. Acad. Sci. USA, 46:447.

Mbensa, M., Rwakunda, C., and Verwilghen, R.L., 1978, Glucose-6-phosphate dehydrogenase deficiency and malignant hepatoma in a Bantu population, East African Med. J., 55:16.

McCay, C.M., Crowell, M.F., and Maynard, L.M., 1935, The effect of retarded growth upon the length of life-span and upon the ultimate body size, J. Nutr., 10:63.

McCormick, J.R., Harkin, M.M., Johnson, K.J., and Ward, P.A., 1981, Suppression of superoxide dismutase of immune complex-induced pulmonary alveolitis and dermal inflamation, Am. J. Pathol., 102:55.

Miller, E.C., 1978, Some current perspectives on chemical carcinogenesis in human and experimental animals: Presidential address, Cancer Res., 38:1479.

Miller, J.A., 1970, Carcinogenesis by chemicals: an overview, Cancer Res., 30:559.

Moore, C.J., and Schwartz, A.G., 1978, Inverse correlation between species life-span and capacity of cultured fibroblasts to convert benzo(a)pyrene to water-soluble metabolites, Exp. Cell Res., 116:359.

Naik, S.N., and Anderson, D.E., G.-6-P.D. deficiency and cancer,
     Lancet, 1970, i:1060.
Nyce, J.W., Magee, P.N., Hard, G.C., and Schwartz, A.G., 1984,
     Inhibition of 1,2-dimethylhydrazine-induced colon
     tumorigenesis in Balb/c mice by dehydroepiandrosterone,
     Carcinogenesis, 5:57.
Oertel, G.W., and Rebelein, I., 1969, Effects of dehydro-
     epiandrosterone and its conjugates upon the activity of
     glucose-6-phosphate dehydrogenase in human erythrocytes,
     Biochim. Biophys. Acta, 184:459.
Pashko, L.L., Hard, G.C., Rovito, R.J., Williams, J.R., Sobel,
     E.L., and Schwartz, A.G., 1984a, Dehydroepiandrosterone and
     3β-methylandrost-5-en-17-one inhibit 7,12-dimethylbenz(a)-
     anthracene-induced skin papillomas and carcinomas in mice,
     Cancer Res., in press.
Pashko, L.L., Rovito, R.J., Williams, J.R., Sobel, E.L., and
     Schwartz, A.G., 1984b, Dehydroepiandrosterone (DHEA)
     and 3β-methylandrost-5-en-17-one: inhibitors of
     7,12-dimethylbenz(a)anthracene (DMBA)-initiated and
     12-0-tetradecanoyl-phorbol-13-acetate (TPA)-promoted
     skin papilloma formation in the mouse, Carcinogenesis,
     5:463.
Pashko, L.L., and Schwartz, A.G., 1983, Effect of food restric-
     tion, dehydroepiandrosterone, or obesity on the binding
     of ^{3}H-7,12-dimethylbenz(a)anthracene to mouse skin DNA,
     J. Gerontol., 38:8.
Schwartz, A.G., 1975, Correlation between species life span and
     capacity to activate 7,12-dimethylbenz(a)anthracene to a
     form mutagenic to a mammalian cell, Exp. Cell Res., 94:445.
Schwartz, A.G., 1979, Inhibition of spontaneous breast cancer
     formation in female C3H-A^{vy}/A mice by long-term treatment
     with dehydroepiandrosterone, Cancer Res., 39:1129.
Schwartz, A., Hard, G., Pashko, L., Abou-Gharbia, M., and
     Swern, D., 1981, Dehydroepiandrosterone: an anti-obesity
     and anti-carcinogenic agent, Nutr. Cancer, 3:46.
Schwartz, A.G., and Moore, C.J., 1977, Inverse correlation
     between species life-span and capacity of cultured fibro-
     blasts to bind 7,12-dimethylbenz(a)anthracene to DNA,
     Exp. Cell Res., 109:448.
Schwartz, A.G., and Perantoni, A., 1975, Protective effect of
     dehydroepiandrosterone against aflatoxin B$_1$- and
     7,12-dimethylbenz(a)anthracene-induced cytotoxicity and
     transformation in cultured cells, Cancer Res., 35:2482.
Schwartz, A.G., and Tannen, R.H., 1981, Inhibition of
     7,12-dimethylbenz(a)anthracene- and urethane-induced lung
     tumor formation in A/J mice by long-term treatment with
     dehydroepiandrosterone, Carcinogenesis, 2:1335.
Shingu, M., Oribe, M., Todoroki, T., Tatsukawa, K., Tomo-oka, K.,
     Yasuda, M., and Nobunaga, M., 1983, Serum factors from
     patients with systemic lupus erythematosus enhancing

superoxide generation by normal neutrophils, J. Invest. Dermatol., 81:212.

Stroebel, H.W., Lu, A.Y.H., Heidema, J., and Coon, M.J., 1970, Phosphatidylcholine requirement in the enzymatic reduction of hemeprotein P-450 and in fatty acid, hydrocarbon and drug hydroxylations, J. Biol. Chem., 245:4851.

Sulis, E., G.-6-P.D. deficiency and cancer, Lancet, 1972, i: 1185.

Szilard, L., 1959, On the nature of the aging process, Proc. Natl. Acad. Sci. USA, 45:30.

Tagliaferro, A.R., and Davis, J.R., 1983, The effect of dehydro-epiandrosterone (DHEA) on caloric intake, body weight, and resting metabolism, Fed. Proc., 42:326. Abstract.

Tannen, R.H., and Schwartz, A.G., 1982, Reduced weight gain and delay of Coomb's positive hemolytic anemia in NZB mice treated with dehydroepiandrosterone (DHEA), Fed. Proc., 41: 463. Abstract.

Tannenbaum, A., and Silverstone, H., 1953, Nutrition in relation to cancer, Ad. Cancer Res., 1:451.

Timmers, K.I., and Knittle, J.L., 1982, Regulation of glucose-6 phosphate dehydrogenase activity during caloric restriction in human adipose tissue, Enzyme, 28:66.

Vande Wiele, R., and Lieberman, S., 1960, The metabolism of dehydroepiandrosterone, in: "Biological Activities of Steroids in Relation to Cancer," 93, G. Pincus and E. Vollmer, eds., Academic Press, New York.

Weindruch, R., and Walford, R.L., 1983, Dietary restriction in mice beginning at 1 year of age: effect on life-span and spontaneous cancer incidence, Science, 215:1415.

Weindruch, R., McFeeters, G., and Walford, R.L., 1984, Food intake and immune function in mice fed dehydroepiandrosterone, submitted.

Weitburg, A.G., Weitzman, S.A., Destrempes, M., Lath, S.A., and Stossel, T.P., 1983, Stimulated human phagocytes produce cytogenetic changes in cultured mammalian cells, New Engl. J. Med., 308:26.

Whitcomb, J.M., and Schwartz, A.G., 1985, Inhibition of 12-0-tetradecanoylphorbol-13-acetate stimulation of superoxide production in human polymorphonuclear leukocytes by dehydroepiandrosterone and related steroids, Carcinogenesis, in press.

Yen, T.T., Allan, J.W., Pearson, D.V., Acton, J.M., and Greenberg, M., 1977, Prevention of obesity in A^{vy}/a mice by dehydroepiandrosterone, Lipids, 12:409.

Yu, B.P., Masoro, E.J., Murata, I., Bertrand, H.A., and Lynd, F.T., 1982, Life-span study of SPF Fischer 344 male rats fed ad libitum or restricted diets: longevity, growth, lean body mass and disease, J. Gerontol. 37:130.

THE ALTERATION OF ENZYMES IN AGING ANIMALS

Morton Rothstein

State University of New York at Buffalo
Biological Sciences
Buffalo, New York 14260

The earliest experiments dealing with the effect of aging on
enzymes consisted of simple comparisons of activity in crude homogenates from various young and old tissues. In general, the
results from different laboratories through the 1950's and 1960's
could not profitably be compared because they were carried out
with crude preparations, a variety of assays and undoubtedly
there were differences between the old animals raised in different
laboratories. Most of the reported changes in activity were
relatively small, few being more than 30%. Some results were
even contradictory - a few enzyme activities were reported both
to increase and decrease. However, even if the early work had
been carried out in more sophisticated fashion, it is doubtful
that any insight into aging phenomena would have resulted. In
fact, more recent work with carefully matched animals which
measured a spectrum of enzymes from various tissues failed to
show any consistent behavior which could be interpreted as
being a mark of the aging process (Lindena et al, 1980). There
does appear to be a generalized decline in the enzymes involved
in fatty acid oxidation and the tricarboxylic acid cycle in
soleus muscle and diaphragm in 24 compared with 6 month old
rats and a decline in the former parameter in heart (Hansford and
Castro, 1982)

The Error Catastrophe hypothesis, first proposed in 1963
(Orgel, 1963) and modified in 1970 (Orgel, 1970), generated
considerable research which sought to demonstrate age-related
alterations in protein structure. The hypothesis proposed that
errors in the protein synthesizing machinery would result in
errors in proteins. If these proteins, in turn, became part of
the protein synthesizing system, even more errors would be

generated. Above a certain level, errors would thus be amplified until a "catastrophe" occurred. It was in search of such error-laden proteins that Gershon and Gershon (1970), found evidence that in homogenates of aged Turbatrix aceti, a small free-living nematode, isocitrate lyase had altered properties. This conclusion was subsequently confirmed by studies with the pure enzyme isolated from young and old T. aceti (Reiss and Rothstein, 1975; Reiss and Rothstein, 1974). In the next ten years, evidence for the existence of additional altered enzymes was reported in rats, mice and human embryo-derived late-passage cells in culture as well as in nematodes.

Three alterations in enzymes from old organisms were generally tested for: a change in sensitivity to heat, a loss of specific activity and an altered response to antiserum prepared to young enzyme. Whereas all of these criteria are appropriate for pure enzymes, the first two procedures are questionable when used with crude homogenates. For example, differing amounts of protein in the young and old samples or the presence of proteases could affect heat-sensitivity. Indeed, one can see examples in which the same enzyme in different crude preparations of the same tissue or in different tissues does not yield the same loss of activity over time when heated at a given temperature. Specific activity is likewise an inadequate criterion, as the amount of protein in old homogenates may differ. Moreover, there may be less, though perfectly normal enzyme present in old homogenates, thus making it appear that the old enzyme in question has a lower specific activity. For these reasons, Table I lists only altered enzymes which have been obtained in the pure state. Except as noted, the old enzymes were tested by all three procedures - specific activity, heat-sensitivity and immunological response. The lower specific activity of old enzymes, where it occurred, was observed even in crude homogenates. Only nematode phosphoglycerate kinase (PGK) showed no difference in heat-sensitivity. Immunotitration, even in crude homogenates, gives the same titer (μl of antiserum/unit of activity) whether the enzyme in question is pure or not (Sharma et al., 1976; Sharma et al., 1980).

In general, there are a number of differences between young and old enzymes which appear to be common. There is typically an altered sensitivity to heat, the old enzyme usually, but not always, being more sensitive; there is usually a loss of specific activity in the old enzyme; there are spectral differences and an altered response to immunotitration. On the other hand, there is no significant change in Michaelis constant (Km), response to inhibitors, molecular weight or C-terminal residues - that is, there are no cuts in the old proteins.

As various altered enzymes were being identified, it became clear that many enzymes do not become altered with age. Pure triosephosphate isomerase in nematodes (Gupta and Rothstein, (1976a), enolase in rat muscle and liver (Rothstein, et al., 1980), tyrosine aminotransferase in rat liver (Szajnert and Schapira, 1983), and aldolase in mouse liver (Burrows and Davison, 1980; Petell and Lebherz, 1979) were purified and found to be unchanged with age. Moreover, a considerable number of other enzymes in various tissues and organelles were shown by immunotitration, not to become altered with age (Rubinson et al., 1976).

Table I. Pure Altered Enzymes

Enzyme	Source	Specific Activity of old enzyme % of young value	Reference
Phosphoglycerate kinase[a]	T. aceti	50	Gupta & Rothstein, 1976b
Isocitrate lyase	" "	25	Reiss & Rothstein, 1975
Aldolase	" "	53	Reznick & Gershon, 1977
Enolase	" "	58	Sharma et al., 1976
Superoxide dismutase[b]	rat liver	41	Reiss & Gershon, 1976
Phosphoglycerate kinase	rat muscle	100	Sharma et al., 1980
Phosphoglycerate kinase	rat liver	100	Hiremath & Rothstein, 1982a
Phosphoglycerate kinase	rat brain	100	Sharma & Rothstein, 1984
Maltase[c]	rat kidney	70	Reiss & Sacktor, 1982
3-Phosphoglycerate dehydrogenase[a]	rat muscle	61	Gafni, 1981
NADPH-Cyt c (P-450) reductase	rat liver	56	Schmucker & Wang, 1983

a Immunotitration not performed.
b Reported by others not to be altered with age.
c Heat-sensitivity not determined.

Two enzymes have been the subject of conflicting reports as to whether or not they become altered in old animals. Aldolase was first reported to be altered in homogenates of old mouse liver (Gershon and Gershon, 1973). Subsequently, Reznick et al., (1981) reconfirmed the original claim that the enzyme was

altered. The authors attributed the differences to the presence
of proteolytic enzymes in the preparations used by Petell and
Lebherz (1979). Indeed, in rabbit liver, the enzyme can be
inactivated by removal of C-terminal residues by a lysosomal
enzyme (Pontremoli et al., 1982). The modified molecule cross-
reacts with antiserum prepared to the normal enzyme. Moreover,
the modified enzyme does not bind to phosphocellulose which may
perhaps account for the putative loss of "altered" enzyme
referred to above. It is not clear whether these recent reports
account fully for the contradictory findings concerning aldolase
in old rodents. Another enzyme for which there is contradictory
evidence is superoxide dismutase which was reported to be
altered in old rat liver (Reiss and Gershon, 1976). However,
other investigators have found no age-related differences
(Burrows and Davison, 1980). The discrepant results have not
been resolved.

The search for altered enzymes obtained its impetus from
the Error Catastrophe hypothesis. However, it soon became
apparent that multiple errors (sequence changes) were an
unsatisfactory explanation for the existence of such enzymes.
The major lines of evidence are that isoelectric focusing has
demonstrated that there is no change of charge in old enzymes
such as nematode enolase (Sharma et al., 1976) and aldolase
(Goren et al., 1977), rat muscle PGK (Sharma et al., 1980), rat
liver PGK (Hiremath and Rothstein, 1982a), and rat liver superoxide dismutase (Goren et al., 1977). The technique can readily
show the loss or addition of a single amide group and indeed,
has been so used for PGK itself. A human mutant of the enzyme
substitutes Asp → Asn and the two proteins are clearly
separable (Fujii et al., 1980). Thus, any sequence change
(errors) in altered enzymes would have to involve an exchange of
equally charged amino acids, basic for basic, acidic for acidic
and neutral for neutral, or some equivalent combination. It is
hard to believe that catastrophic errors could fall within such
a limitation. A further problem is that if the protein
synthesizing machinery caused faulty transcription or translation, all proteins produced would incorporate errors. Yet,
as indicated above, many (probably most) proteins remain
unaltered with age. One might argue that error-laden proteins
are present in old tissues, but are lost during purification of
old enzymes. However, this is highly unlikely as immunotitration
of old rat muscle PGK in crude homogenates and in the pure
state was shown to yield the same value per unit of activity.
The same was true of nematode enolase. Therefore there are
either no altered molecules present (cross-reacting material) in
old crude homogenates, or if they exist, they are altered so
much so as not to react with the antiserum. If there were a
spectrum of error-laden proteins present, surely some of them
would react with the polyclonal antibodies present in the test

antiserum, thus lowering the specific activity (units of activity/ μl of serum) of the enzyme being tested. It is of interest that there is one example of an old enzyme which is not detected by young antiserum. Aldolase in aged rat lens contains an inactive form of the enzyme which can be detected only with an antiserum prepared against aldolase which has been denatured by boiling in the presence of SDS and mercaptoethanol (Dovrat and Gershon, 1983). One should bear in mind that the aged lens does not synthesize new protein, so that there can be no "errors." In the case of old rat kidney maltase, an inactive form of the enzyme was differentiated from the active form by use of mono- clonal antibodies (Reiss and Sacktor, 1983). In old animals, the maltase consists of active (normal) and inactive forms which co-purify to yield "old" enzyme. The inactive molecules, in this case, cross-react with antiserum prepared to young enzyme, thus lowering the specific activity.

It is quite clear that an error catastrophe does not apply to altered enzymes. The likelihood of even small errors in sequence is also small. The above arguments vis-a-vis change in charge or errors in transcription or translation apply not only to an error catastrophe, but equally to single errors. In fact, it is highly unlikely that _any_ covalent modification occurs. For example, if there is no change in ionic charge, then deamidation, phosphorylation, acetylation and sulfation are ruled out. Methyl- ation, SH oxidation and sulfoxide formation have also been excluded. On the basis of the information available, Rothstein and co- workers proposed that old enzymes re sult from conformational modification without covalent changes (Reiss and Rothstein, 1974; Rothstein, 1975; Rothstein, 1977). Unequivocal evidence for this thesis was provided when it was shown that young and old nematode enolase, respectively, after unfolding in solutions of guanidine HCl, refolded to an identical product as determined by spectral, immunological and kinetic tests (Sharma and Rothstein, 1980). The refolded enolase was similar but not identical in these respects to the native old enzyme. Identical structures would not be obtained from refolded young and old enzymes if the original difference in the two forms was due to a difference in sequence or to a covalent modification.

If altered enzymes are indeed conformational isozymes, how are they formed? It was proposed that if protein turnover slows with age, then the "dwell time" of enzyme molecules in the cell would be increased and they would have time to become subtly denatured (altered) (Reiss and Rothstein, 1974; Rothstein, 1975; Rothstein, 1977). Moreover, under such conditions, the altered molecules would accumulate rather than be replaced. Of course, certain enzymes might become altered in such a manner that they had no activity and could not be recognized by the antiserum

prepared to the normal (young) enzyme. This situation would
perhaps apply to triosephosphate isomerase in old nematodes
(Gupta and Rothstein, 1976a) in which there is only half as much
enzyme as in young organisms, but that half is perfectly normal.
It may also apply to old human aldolase which is normal but
present in lowered amounts (Steinhagen-Thiessen and Hilz, 1976).
The idea that slowed protein synthesis is involved in the
formation of altered enzymes is supported by the fact that it
slows dramatically with age in T. aceti: proteins have a half-
life of 10 hours at two days of age, increasing to over 10 days
at 28 days of age (Sharma et al., 1979). The results are
similar whether for total soluble proteins or the single protein,
enolase. In mammals, the case is less well detailed, but what
information is available indicates a slowed turnover in aged
rat heart (Crie et al., 1981) and mouse liver (Lavie et al., 1981).
Turnover of aldolase is also reported to slow in old mice
(Reznick et al., 1981).

Whatever the mechanism, an important question is whether or
not altered enzymes in mammals follow the pattern of change
demonstrated for nematode enolase. Are they simply conformational
isozymes or are covalent changes involved in their formation?

To answer this question, studies of muscle PGK in young and
old rats were undertaken (Sharma et al., 1980). After purification to homogeneity, the old enzyme showed an altered heat
sensitivity (it was more stable), an altered response to young
antiserum, greater stability to storage, and altered spectral
properties. One difference from the usual characteristics of
old enzymes was that specific activity was unchanged. As
expected, there was no difference in Km or in the C-terminal amino
acid. Young and old forms of PGK were also obtained from rat
liver (Hiremath and Rothstein, 1982a). Surprisingly, both liver
enzymes differed from their muscle counterparts in several
characteristics. The liver enzymes had a higher specific
activity, a lower isoelectric point, greater heat lability and
differing immune response. The C-terminal residue, leucine,
was the same as for the muscle enzyme, but the experimental
results indicate that there may be differences three or four
amino acids into the chain. Nonetheless the fact that PGK
consists of a single chain and thus has no isozymes in the usual
sense, would suggest that in liver, it is synthesized as muscle
enzyme and then modified - say by a deamidation, to the liver
form. In fact, recent results have failed to show differences in
sequence (Hardt and Rothstein, unpublished). Sets of peptides
generated by treatment of the liver and muscle enzymes with various
proteases (trypsin, chymotrypsin and Staphylococcus aureus protease)
showed no discernable differences after high pressure liquid
chromatography (HPLC). Thus, it appears that liver and muscle
PGK differ rather subtly as one might predict from the fact

that they are close enough in structure to respond to antisera produced to either enzyme. If liver and muscle PGK indeed come from separate genes, it is particularly interesting that both tissues generate young and old forms of the enzyme. Pure PGK from brain is muscle type and also has young and old forms (Sharma and Rothstein, 1984).

The finding that altered PGK is present in old liver, muscle and brain was presaged by titration of crude homogenates of these tissues with "young" muscle antiserum (Sharma et al., 1980). The results from heart and lung preparations were not clear in this respect; the titer of the old tissues was increased, but only slightly.

In order to ascertain whether or not old muscle PGK was simply altered in conformation, unfolding-refolding experiments were carried out in analogy to the work with nematode enolase. Surprisingly, the refolding kinetics for the two forms of PGK were quite different. Moreover, the refolded young and old enzymes were not identical to each other nor to their respective native forms (Sharma and Rothstein, unpublished). It thus appeared that the enzyme differed either by a sequence change or because of some covalent modification. The latter process seemed an unlikely one, based upon the lack of change observed after isoelectric focusing and the fact that common covalent changes such as methylation, SH oxidation or sulfoxide formation do not occur in old PGK. The evidence, then, suggested that there is an altered sequence in old muscle PGK.

In an attempt to detect such a sequence change, young and old PGK were carboxymethylated and digested with three proteolytic enzymes - trypsin, chymotrypsin and protease from S. aureus. The resulting young vs. old sets of peptides derived from digestion with each protease were analysed by HPLC. No qualitative or quantitative differences were found in the respective young-old pairs. In fact, the traces from young and old digests were literally superimposable (Hardt and Rothstein, unpublished). Thus, insofar as could be determined by these experiments, there are no sequence changes in old muscle PGK. If these results are correct, why did young and old PGK show differences in the refolding experiments? One may postulate that the enzymes were not completely unfolded in 2M guanidine and the degree of structure remaining in one or the other mandated a different refolding pathway. The only other reasonable explanation for the anomalous results would be that there is a change in sequence undetectable by the HPLC procedures, but which nonetheless changes enzyme properties and refolding characteristics.

The idea that the age-related alteration of rat muscle PGK is due to conformational change without covalent modification, finds support from other investigations, though none of the evidence really proves the case. For example, experiments which may be interpreted as showing that conformational changes occur were carried out by isolating pure PGK from regenerating liver in old rats (Hiremath and Rothstein, 1982b). For the first three days, the newly regenerated tissue produced young PGK. Between four and five days, the enzyme showed some characteristics of old PGK. By nine days, the enzyme had become old as judged by all three criteria utilized (heat sensitivity, stability, immunotitration). These results may be interpreted to mean that the newly formed liver produces young PGK which, because turnover is reportedly slowed in regenerating liver (Scornik, 1972) remains in the tissue without being replaced. The enzyme would thus gradually change in conformation and become "old." This situation represents the slowed turnover model presented above. The same rationale would hold if liver PGK is first produced as muscle type and subsequently modified to liver type by a process such as deamidation. On the other hand, one could argue that the new liver cells start producing young PGK but eventually recognize that they are really "old" cells and begin producing old enzyme. Thus, these experiments do not truly distinguish between the idea of a post-synthetic conformational change and the expression of a separate gene for old PGK.

There is other support for the idea of conformationally altered enzymes in rodents. For example, when rat muscle 3-phosphogly-ceraldehyde dehydrogenase is treated with iodine, one of the cysteine residues, cysteine - 149, is oxidized. Subsequent reduction with mercaptoethanol leads to recovery of a form of the enzyme with properties similar to those of old 3-phosphoglyceral-dehyde dehydrogenase (Gafni, 1983). Thus, the change must be due to conformational changes. The fact that old rat kidney maltase consists of normal and inactive molecules also supports the idea that the latter are conformationally altered; peptide maps show no differences in sequence between young, old and inactive maltase.

It should be noted that there are other mechanisms besides conformational modification by which altered enzymes may arise. For example, certain proteins undergo deamidation in old lens (Cramps et al., 1978) and triosephosphate isomerase, in particular, loses amide groups from asparagine residues in several human tissues (Yuan et al., 1981). In tissues such as lens and red cells, enzymes must exist for periods of relatively long duration without resynthesis; in other tissues, deamidation may reflect the marking of certain enzymes for subsequent proteolysis. In any case, the altered enzymes in senescent animals are not deamidation products.

The recent discovery of an oxidase system in liver microsomes (Fucci et al., 1983; Levine, 1983) which inactivates a
number of enzymes suggests that this process may play a role in
the formation of altered enzymes. It is possible that such a
system differentially attacks certain enzymes (for example,
PGK) in old animals, thus changing their conformation. In such
a case, damaged old PGK would not refold to the same product as
undamaged young PGK. On the other hand, one may speculate that
it is the change of conformation in certain old enzymes which
makes them subject to attack by the oxidase. It is yet to be
ascertained how this system works and if it is truly involved
in the formation of altered enzymes.

It is not unreasonable to believe that most altered mammalian
enzymes result from conformational modification, whereas PGK,
which has a single peptide chain is an exception, being altered
in old animals because of a change in gene expression. Supporting
this idea is the report of Michelson et al. (1983) which provides
evidence from cloning experiments that in humans, PGK is
represented by a small family of genes. At the present time, one
cannot choose with certainty the mechanism by which this enzyme
is altered in old animals - by conformational change or by a
change in gene expression. By weight of evidence and by anology,
the former concept would seem to be heavily favored.

REFERENCES

Burrows, R.B., and Davison, P.F., 1980, Comparison of specific
    activities of enzymes from young and old dogs and mice, Mech.
    Ageing Dev. 13:307.
Cramps, J.A., DeJong, W.W., Wollensak, J., and Hoenders, N.J.,
    1978. The polypeptide chains of α-crystallin from old human
    eye lens, Biochim. Biophys. Acta 533:487.
Crie, J.S., Millward, D.J., Bates, P.C., Griffin, E.E., and
    Wildenthal, K., 1981, Age-related alterations in cardiac
    protein turnover, J. Mol. Cell. Cardiol. 13:589.
Dovrat, A., and Gershon, D., 1983, Studies on the fate of aldo-
    lase molecules in the aging rat lens, Biochim. Biophys.
    Acta 757:164.
Fucci, L., Oliver, C.N., Coon, M.J., and Stadtman, E.R., 1983,
    Inactivation of key metabolic proteins by mixed-function
    oxidation reactions: possible implication in protein turn-
    over and ageing, Proc. Natl. Acad. Sci. USA 80:1521.
Fujii, H., Krietsch, W.K.G., and Yoshida, A., 1980, A single
    amino acid substitution (Asp→ Asn) in a phosphoglycerate
    kinase variant (PGK Munchen) associated with enzyme deficiency,
    J. Biol. Chem. 255:6421.
Gafni, A., 1981, Purification and comparative study of
    glyceraldehyde-3-phosphate dehydrogenase from the muscles of
    young and old rats, Biochemistry 20:6035.

Gafni, A., 1983, Molecular origin of the ageing effects in glyceraldehyde-3-phosphate dehydrogenase, Biochim. Biophys. Acta 742:91.

Gershon, H., and Gershon, D., 1970, Detection of inactive enzyme molecules in ageing organisms, Nature London 227:1214.

Gershon, H., and Gershon, D., 1973, Inactive enzyme molecules in aging mice: Liver aldolase, Proc. Natl. Acad. Sci. USA 70:909.

Goren, P., Reznick, A.Z., Reiss, U., and Gershon, D., 1977, Isoelectric properties of nematode aldolase and rat liver superoxide dismutase from young and old animals, FEBS Lett. 84:83.

Gupta, S.K., and Rothstein, M., 1976a, Triosephosphate isomerase from young and old Turbatrix aceti, Arch. Biochem. Biophys. 174:333.

Gupta, S.K., and Rothstein, M., 1976b, Phosphoglycerate kinase from young and old Turbatrix aceti, Arch. Biochem. Biophys. 445:632.

Hansford, R., and Castro, F., 1982, Age-linked changes in the activity of enzymes of the tricarboxylate cycle and lipid oxidation, and of carnitine content, in muscles of the rat, Mech. Ageing Dev. 19:191.

Hiremath, L.S., and Rothstein, M., 1982a, The effect of aging on rat liver phosphoglycerate kinase and comparison with the muscle enzyme, Biochim. Biophys. Acta 705:200.

Hiremath, L.S., and Rothstein, M. 1982b, Regenerating liver in aged rats produces unaltered phosphoglycerate kinase, J. Gerontol. 37:680.

Lavie, L., Reznick, A.Z., and Gershon, D., 1981, Decreased protein and puromycinylpeptide degradation in livers of senescent mice, Biochem. J. 202:47.

Levine, R.L., 1983, Oxidative modification of glutamine synthetase, J. Biol. Chem. 258:11832.

Lindena, J., Friedel, R., Rapp, K., Sommerfeld, U., Trautschold, I, and Deerberg, F., 1980, Long-term observation of plasma and tissue enzyme activities in the rat, Mech. Ageing Dev. 14:379.

Michelson, A.M., Markham, A.F., and Orkin, S.H., 1983, Isolation and DNA sequence of a full-length cDNA clone for human X chromosome-encoded phosphoglycerate kinase, Proc. Natl. Acad. Sci. USA 80:472.

Orgel, L.E., 1963, The maintenance of the accuracy of protein synthesis and its relevance to ageing, Proc. Natl. Acad. Sci. USA 49:517.

Orgel, L.E., 1970, The maintenance and accuracy of protein synthesis and its relevance to ageing; a correction, Proc. Natl. Acad. Sci. USA 67:1476.

Petell, J.K., and Lebherz, G.L., 1979, Properties and metabolism of fructose disphosphate aldolase in livers of "old" and "young" mice, J. Biol. Chem. 254:8179.

Pontremoli, S., Melloni, E., Salamino, F., Sparatore, B., Michetti, M., and Horecker, B., 1982, Cathepsin M: A lysosomal proteinase with aldolase-inactivating activity, Arch. Biochem. Biophys. 214:376.

Reiss, U., and Gershon, D., 1976, Rat liver superoxide dismutase: purification and age-related modifications, Eur. J. Biochem. 63:617.

Reiss, U., and Rothstein, M., 1974, Heat-labile isozymes of isocitrate lyase from aging Turbatrix aceti, Biochem. Biophys. Res. Commun. 61:1012.

Reiss, U., and Rothstein, 1975, Age-related changes in isocitrate lyase from the free-living nematode, Turbatrix aceti, J. Biol. Chem. 250:826.

Reiss, U., and Sacktor, B., 1982, Alteration of kidney brush border membrane maltase in aging rats, Biochim. Biophys. Acta 704:422.

Reiss, U., and Sacktor, B., 1983, Monoclonal antibodies to renal brush border membrane maltase: age-associated antigenic alterations, Proc. Natl. Acad. Sci. USA 80:3255.

Reznick, A.Z., and Gershon, D., 1977, Age related alterations in purified fructose-1,6-diphosphate aldolase in the nematode Turbatrix aceti, Mech. Ageing Dev. 6:345.

Reznick, A.Z., Lavie, L., Gershon, H.E., and Gershon, D., 1981, Age-associated accumulation of altered FDP aldolase B in mice, FEBS Lett. 128:221.

Rothstein, M., 1975, Aging and the alteration of enzymes: a review, Mech. Ageing Dev. 4:325.

Rothstein, M., 1977, Recent developments in the age-related alteration of enzymes: a review, Mech. Ageing Dev. 6:241.

Rothstein, M., Coppens, M., and Sharma, H.K., 1980, Effect of aging on enolase from rat muscle, liver and heart, Biochim. Biophys. Acta 614:591.

Rubinson, H., Kahn, A., Boivin, P., Schapira, F., Gregori, C., and Dreyfus, J.C., 1976, Aging and accuracy of protein synthesis in man: search for inactive enzymatic cross-reacting material in granulocytes of aged people, Gerontology 22:438.

Schmucker, D.L., and Wang, R.K., 1983, Age-dependent alterations in rat liver microsomal NADPH-cytochrome c (P-450) reductase: a qualitative and quantitative analysis, Mech. Ageing Dev. 21:137.

Scornik, O.A., 1972, Decreased in vivo disappearance of labelled liver proteins after partial hepatectomy, Biochem. Biophys. Res. Commun. 47:1063.

Sharma, H.K., Gupta, S.K., and Rothstein, M., 1976, Age-related alteration of enolase in the free-living nematode, Turbatrix aceti, Arch. Biochem. Biophys. 174:324.

Sharma, H.K., Prasanna, H.R., Lane, R.S., and Rothstein, M., 1979, The effect of age on enolase turnover in the free-living nematode, Turbatrix aceti, Arch. Biochem. Biophys. 194:275.

Sharma, H.K., Prasanna, H.R., and Rothstein, M., 1980, Altered
    phosphoglycerate kinase in aging rats, J. Biol. Chem. 255:5043.
Sharma, H.K., and Rothstein, M., 1980, Altered enolase in aged
    Turbatrix aceti results from conformational changes in the
    enzyme, Proc. Natl. Acad. Sci. USA 77:5865.
Sharma, H.K., and Rothstein, M., 1984, Altered brain phosphogly-
    cerate kinase from aging rats, Mech. Ageing Dev. 25:285.
Steinhagen-Thiessen, E., and Hilz, H., 1976, The age-dependent
    decrease in creatine kinase and aldolase activities in human
    striated muscle is not caused by an accumulation of faulty
    proteins, Mech. Ageing Dev. 5:447.
Szajnert, M.F., and Schapire, F., 1983, Properties of purified
    tyrosine aminotransferase from adult and senescent rat liver,
    Gerontology 29:311.
Yuan, P.M., Talent, J.M., and Gracy, B.W., 1981, Molecular basis
    for the accumulation of acidic isozymes of triosephosphate
    isomerase on aging, Mech. Ageing Dev. 17:151.

DIFFERENTIAL AND SIMILAR RESPONSES BETWEEN RODENT AND HUMAN CELLS

TO DNA-DAMAGING AGENTS: POSSIBLE IMPLICATIONS FOR CELLULAR AGING

Jerry R. Williams, Peter D'Arpa, John Opishinski, Larry
Dillehay and David Jacobson-Kram

Radiobiology Laboratory
The John Hopkins Oncology Center
600 North Wolfe St., Baltimore, MD 21205

INTRODUCTION

Deterioration in the fidelity of the informational content of
cells in the aging animal has remained an attractive hypothesis
for the mechanism of somatic aging. It is attractive to the
degree that it offers a plausible, single etiology for a
multifaceted process; a process that is expressed in different
ways in several tissues of an aged individual. Conceptually,
there is no question that a deterioration in DNA informational
fidelity could cause a global deterioration in cellular function,
independent of the specific differentiated state of a particular
cell type. We have reviewed the deterioration of chromatin/DNA
structure in aging mammals (Williams and Dearfield, 1981;1982)
and have reported that there is considerable evidence that
several aspects of deterioration do occur. The question remains
whether such changes are precedents, concomitants or sequelae of
the aging process.

To answer this question or to seek another possible etiology
of aging, scientists have adopted several strategies:

1) Identification of agents that accelerate the aging
process. The rationale for such studies lies in the possible
similarity of molecular damage produced by such agents compared
to the damage produced by the aging process. X-irradiation is
the best studied example of such agents.

2)   Identification of agents that extend the lifespan, using the inverse of the above rationale. Dietary restriction is the best example of successful studies of this sort.

3)   Identification of differences in the molecular state in cells of young and old animals in order to deduce the etiology based on observed differences, or to apply the same rationale studying individual animals throughout their lifespan.

4)   Comparison of molecular states between animal variants in the same species that age at rates different than normal members of the species. This has included the study of human syndromes such as Progeria and Werner's syndrome.

5)   Study of the differences between multiple species of mammals that produce a spectrum of mammalian lifespans.

Our laboratory has studied aging through several of these approaches, concentrating on the comparison of the response to DNA-damaging agents of short-lived species (rodents) and longer-lived species (human beings). This approach proves partially successful. We have expanded the description of the kinetics of DNA repair in rodents and in human beings, and have documented an accumulation of unrepaired lesions at higher rates in the chromatin-masked regions of the genome in short-lived rodents (Williams, 1983). It seems clear, based on our studies and the literature, that until now there has been no DNA-damaging agent that elicits a qualitatively different response in rodent cells than in human cells as general classes of cells. Certainly there are numerous examples of cell lines and strains that possess genetic deficiencies occurring naturally or by induction, but these have been demonstrated in both rodent and in human cells. We are now investigating another biological response that differs between human and rodent cells: the toxic response of cells to the photoaddition of 8-methoxypsoralen by irradiation with near ultraviolet light (UVA, 365 nm). This treatment is now by convention referred to as PUVA treatment. We suggest that the unique nature of the molecular events involved in this response may yield some insight into the differences in cells that produce differential responses to PUVA treatment.

RESULTS AND DISCUSSION

The Response of Cells to PUVA Treatment

8-methoxypsoralen is one of a group of furocoumerins that intercalate into the DNA and upon excitation by photons of the near ultraviolet spectrum, de-excite by the formation of monoadducts and diadducts to nitrogen bases of the DNA. Fig. 1 presents a schema for some of the possible types of adducts formed.

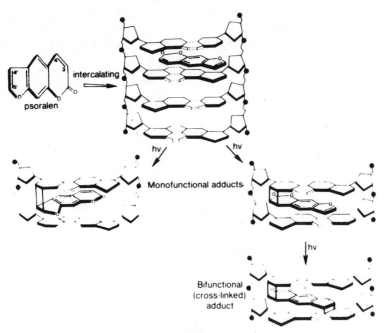

Fig. 1. Photoreaction of psoralen in the formation of DNA
        monoadducts and cross-strand links.

The initial step in the formation of the DNA adducts is the
intercalation of the psoralen molecule between adjacent base
pairs of the DNA helix.   This initial step for intercalating
agents is dependent on the extent of supercoiling of the DNA
helix.   Thus   it   seems logical, though not conclusively
demonstrated, that the number of photoadditions induced into a
region of DNA by PUVA is dependent on supercoiling, as may be the
toxic response of cells that results from such photoaddition.
Although other information that relates to the possible role of
supercoiling in the toxic response will be dealt with
subsequently, we propose that the difference in response between
rodent and human cells is based on chromatin conformation.

It seems now to be well established that the number of
photoadditions that occur when cells are incubated in 8-MOP and
then irradiated with graded doses of UVA is a linear function of
UVA dose over a wide range of exposure. The cytotoxic response
of cells to this treatment, however, is extremely "shouldered."
That is, there is a range of exposure that produces little
cytotoxicity, followed by a relatively rapid increase in toxicity
occurring over a limited dose range. Based on target theory,
such a curve would suggest that a relatively large number of

separate targets would require lethal events before the cell
would be killed. When the incubation temperatures are precisely
regulated, we observe that the amount of cell killing as a
function of dose, represented by the killing portion of the
curve, becomes exponential.

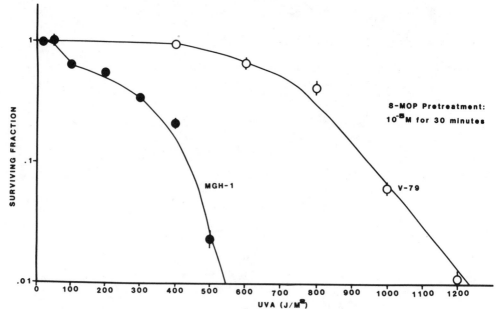

Fig. 2.   Representative responses of a human diploid fibroblast
          line (MGH-1) and a rodent cell (Chinese hamster cells,
          V-79).

     Fig. 2   illustrates the differences between human and rodent
cell responses.   Cells were plated at appropriate densities,
allowed to reach exponential growth, and incubated for 30 minutes
in 10 mM solutions of 8-methoxypsoralen in phosphate buffered
saline.   Without rinsing, plates were immediately irradiated with
graded doses of near ultraviolet light (365 nm). Subsequent to
exposure cells were rinsed and were incubated in complete medium
to assay for colony formation.   Error bars represent the standard
error of the mean for replicate platings.

Comparative Responses to PUVA in Rodent and Human Cells

     We have measured the patterns of PUVA cytotoxicity in a large
number of cell lines and strains that were initially derived from
several species of mammals.   Generally, we have compared the
response of cells from several rodents: the mouse, the rat and
the hamster, to those derived from human beings. This comparison
reflects our interest in using rodent models for aging and
carcinogenesis studies.   Our use of multiple rodent lines and

multiple human lines makes it extremely likely that our results represent a general phenomenon rather than an idiosyncratic response of particular cell types.

When the D37 dose, as derived from data similar to those represented in Fig. 2, is compared between cells derived from different species, there is a significant difference. This difference is shown in Table 1.

Table 1. D37 for PUVA Cytotoxicity in Human and Rodent
          Cell Lines

Cell Line	D37
Human Cell Lines:	
MGH-1 diploid fibroblast	290
MGH-2 diploid fibroblast	220
IMR-90 diploid fibroblast	220
Ag3513 (progeria) diploid fibroblast	155
HeLa	330
Rodent Cell Lines:	
REF-9 (rat)	350
H4 (rat)	650
3T3 (mouse)	700
CHO (hamster)	1300
V-79 (hamster)	930

It is important to point out that these large differences may not reflect cellular characteristics present in the somatic cells of young rodents or humans, but rather may reflect the state of the cells in culture. Using data to be published elsewhere, we demonstrate that a major portion of characteristic PUVA resistance is acquired during extended serial propagation in culture. The difference in the rodent cell and the human cell, we suggest, is the rate at which this resistance is acquired.

Whether these hypotheses prove true, the differential responses of rodent and human cells as classes seem remarkable when placed in the overall context of cellular responses to other DNA-damaging agents. Two important questions must be addressed: first, what is the nature of the possible differences in DNA structure or function between the two classes of cells that determines the difference in response to PUVA; second, what type of difference in DNA structure or function might predispose rodent cells to be more susceptible to the changes that confer PUVA resistance? Solutions to these two related questions can be approached indirectly by considering the nature of the PUVA response itself.

The Toxic Response of Cells to PUVA may be Dependent upon the State of the DNA Supercoiling

We have made several observations that suggest that the cellular response to PUVA may reflect the state of DNA supercoiling in some regions of the DNA. First, we have observed that altering chromatin structure by inducing single strand DNA breaks with x-rays enhances PUVA-induced toxicity. Second, we have observed that novobiocin, a known inhibitor of topoisomerase II mitigates PUVA-induced toxicity. Third, we have observed that PUVA resistance in rodent cells, and to a lesser extent in human cells, is a cold-sensitive process; this suggests that acquired PUVA resistance is an enzyme-mediated process. These observations, together with the knowledge that psoralen intercalation, as with the intercalation of other planar molecules, depends upon the state of supercoiling of the DNA, lead to our previous hypothesis that PUVA response may reflect the state of DNA supercoiling.

If this hypothesis is true, then the molecular events in rodent cells that confer PUVA resistance may reflect changes in chromatin structure which in turn permits, to different extent, supercoiling of DNA regions. It is thus possible to conjecture that an event as simple as the freeing of a region of DNA from the nuclear matrix could produce such a change in the extent of supercoiling.

SUMMARY AND CONCLUSIONS

We have outlined a model in which aging may be associated with changes in chromatin structure that produce alterations in the extent of DNA supercoiling. Our model would suggest that the major difference in a short-lived rodent and a long-lived human being would be reflected as the rate at which such changes occur. In support of this model we have presented data that rodent cells as a class are more resistant to PUVA than are human cells. Further, we have outlined corroborating data that would suggest that such resistance may reflect a difference in the extent of psoralen intercalation that in turn is dependent on DNA supercoiling. Since it is known that changes in DNA supercoiling can alter both the expression of genes and the repair of DNA, it is feasible that changes in supercoiling could lead to a deterioration both in gene regulation and in DNA fidelity.

Our model relates to multistage carcinogenesis in a straightforward manner, predicting that cancer initiators produce a heritable change in chromatin structure, while cancer promoters induce transient changes in chromatin structure. We propose that this model is consistent with the developing molecular model of cancer as caused by the inappropriate expression of dominant transforming oncogene(s). Indeed, our model would predict that aging and carcinogen exposure would share a common capacity to alter chromatin structure within regions of the genome, with carcinogens perhaps more random than aging in their induction of such alterations.

In summary, our data demonstrate for the first time a systematic difference in the responses of rodent and human cells to an agent whose mechanism of action may depend on DNA supercoiling. These data, considered in the context of current knowledge of the role of chromatin structure in DNA function, lead us to postulate that changes in chromatin structure underlie aging in somatic tissue. Such changes may occur incrementally in domains within the genome--one characteristic of such change is an alteration in the state of supercoiling of DNA in the affected domain. In short, such changes alter the inherent stability of chromatin structure. Changes of this nature may alter transcription, replication and repair of the gene sequences contained within the affected regions, leading to inappropriate and perhaps aberrant expression of such sequences. This instability of gene expression could produce the multifacted deterioration observed in somatic cells of the aging mammal.

Supported by NIH grants: CA-39654; ES-03644; CA-39531; CA-39543

REFERENCES

Williams, J.R., 1983, Alteration in DNA/chromatin structure during aging, in: "Intervention in the Aging Process, Part B: Basic and Preclinical Screening," page 145, Alan R. Liss, Inc., New York.

Williams, J.R. and Dearfield, K.L., 1981, Induction and repair of DNA/chromatin alterations, in: "Biological Mechanisms in Aging," page 245, R.T. Schimke, ed., NIH Publications, Bethesda, MD.

Williams, J.R. and Dearfield, K.L., 1982, DNA damage and repair in aging mammals, in: "Handbook Series in Aging, Section D: Biological Sciences," Volume 1, Biochemistry, page 25, J.R. Florini and R.C. Adelman, eds., CRC Press, Boca Raton, Florida.

LIVING ALL YOUR LIFE

Alex Comfort

Neuropsychiatric Institute

University of California at Los Angeles

Los Angeles, CA 90024

When I came to the United States ten years ago, I expected to
work in gerontology, a field in which I had been working for some
20 years. I was delighted to find that gerontology was alive and
well, that there are a lot of people involved in it, and that
progress is being made in a great many different areas. I should
perhaps explain that gerontology is a word which is sometimes
corrupted to mean teaching old people to do macrame work.
Gerontology is in fact the biological study of the processes of
aging. Geriatrics is the branch of medicine which deals with the
medical care and health needs of the old, and social gerontology
is the branch of sociology which concerns itself with the old.
But I found that what was missing in the United States compared
with Europe was the awareness of geriatric medicine, which
generally was absent from the curricula of medical schools; it is
in teaching geriatrics I have been working for the last few years.

Aging concerns us all because it is the process which causes
us to become more likely to die the older we get. There are two
kinds of aging. One of these is the physical change with which we
are all familiar: skin wrinkling, hair graying, and a growing
liability to system failure, which, in plain language, means ill
health. We get some weakening of muscles; there is also a real,
but practically unimportant, slowing in some of the mind-body
reactions, but the older person compensates for this by the years
of experience. In view of our myth that the old cannot learn, one
of the most interesting things I have encountered recently has
been the number of people in their 70s and 80s who suddenly decide
that they would like to take out an amateur radio license. In
order to do this, they have to learn Morse code, which is a pretty
abstract task (some of you may remember learning it in the service

213

and taking quite a time to do it). These old people learn their
Morse code just as well as the young, but they take rather longer
over it; whereas the young people will learn the code in a couple
of weeks and sometimes will be able to copy seven words a minute
after two or three weeks, the old may take two or three months to
achieve this. But they get there, and this difference is very
typical of the mental change with age. In the absence of ill
health, and of conditions such as untreated high blood pressure,
aging does not have an adverse effect on intelligence and learning
power. Working capacity remains, provided that the person is not
time-stressed. Very often, when an old person asks for a light
job, they mean a heavier job which is not time-stressed.
Sexuality, which is one of the things which people often fear they
will lose with age, changes very little in character. The changes
of age would not be very conspicuous if they were not accompanied
by the rise in the force of mortality and the fact that because of
this we have a limited lifespan. Our chances of surviving longer
decrease steadily as we pass our eighties and enter our nineties.
A few of us, by reason of strength, as the Bible says, exceed four
score years or live on to be a hundred, but such people are
relatively few in the population at large.

We do not yet know the cause of physical aging in mammals
including humans. We know that there is probably more than one
"clock" process to consider. There are probably timing processes
which occur at the hypothalamic level--the level in the brain
where puberty is turned on and the menopause turns off and where
various other hormones are controlled. But underlying those
processes may be basic cellular changes which, in turn, act as a
timekeeper; there also may be other independent clocks running. I
remember a study of the effects of background levels of radiation
on collagen in kangaroo tails, and the conclusion was reached that
kangaroos would fall to pieces through the effects of this
radiation after about 200 years. But of course, since no kangaroo
lives that long, it is largely irrelevant to speculate in this
way. Be that as it may, the mortality curve is remarkably
stable. It steepens as we grow older, and there is a peak in the
number of people dying around the age of 75. Beyond this peak,
there is a tail which contains, finally, the few people who live
on to a hundred. That portion of the curve is not disturbed by
very many things. There are a few conditions in which aging could
be said to be premature, such as the rare disease progeria. One
must question, however, whether that disease is truly a reflection
of premature aging or whether it is an enzyme deficiency that is
genetically determined. The pathological change which is
characteristic of aging is, in fact, an increase in the number of
pathological changes. If you do a postmortem on a man who dies at
forty, you usually find he has one predominant cause of death, but
a man who dies at ninety will have thirteen to fifteen potential
causes of death. It is a little like the Wonderful One-horse

Shay: if it had not fallen to pieces for one reason, it would
have done so for another. At present, the length of life is
manifestly changing: over the last hundred years, the mean length
of life has vastly increased. But, in fact, the lifespan has not
altered. What has happened is that more people are living to
reach old age. We get old at the same age that Moses and Pharaoh
got old, but the difference is that more of us reach old age
because we do not die prematurely from other causes.

Now advanced societies are approaching the practical limits
of those public health measures that prolong life by this process
of "squaring up" of the survival curve. While the expectation of
life at birth has gone up over the last century, the expectation
at 65 has changed remarkably little; it has changed by two years
since 1901. It has been computed that the cure of the three
leading causes of natural death, which are cardiovascular disease,
cerebrovascular disease, and cancer, while highly desirable for
the people who suffer from these conditions, would only increase
the mean expectation of life at 65 by about 2.5 years. One can
envision a situation in which we lived until we ran out of kidney
units or some other vital support function, which under present
conditions, last us out, because other things kill us first. Many
studies indicate that when the heart disease rate is reduced by
diet or by some other manipulation, the cancer rate appears to
increase; if you do not die of the commonest disease, you will die
of the second commonest. It looks very much as if all piecemeal
therapeutic supportive medical and social measures can only bring
about a state of affairs in which the lifespan remains much the
same, but the age at death has a far narrower scatter. There is
the possibility that biological interference could alter the
actual rate of aging. This sort of experiment has already been
done in rats and mice by the relatively simple expedient of
caloric restriction. I think something similar could quite
possibly be done in humans, but there are serious problems in
actually performing this research. Nobody is going to live on
lettuce for eighty years to see if they live longer. One of the
troubles in aging research is that it is very hard to find an
animal which is less long-lived than a Ph.D. student; if you set
up an experiment on human beings, you are in for an eighty-year
experiment that you will not see finished, and that you will have
to leave to your children as a sacred task. So whenever you read
in the newspapers that somebody has a medicine that slows down
aging or prolongs life, you want to ask how it has been tested,
because they would have had to run a very, very long experiment in
order to be able to establish the case. I think it is very
probable, in fact certain, that eventually we shall have a system
of rate-modification medicine which will enable us to change the
rate of aging, but I do not expect that we shall enable patients
to live to the exorbitant ages that some people have predicted.
What we should most likely see initially is a state of affairs in

which it takes us eighty years to reach seventy and sixty years to reach fifty--a gain of ten years. Even that would be very hard on the insurance industry, because once you have effected a shift in the firm foundation of mortality experience underlying actuarial statistics by a quarter or a half percent increase, there is nothing to ensure that there may not be future development of a ten, twenty, thirty, forty or even one hundred percent increase. I should think that is a great worry for demographers and for actuaries. I do not think that if we are able to alter the rate of aging, it will be done primarily to increase longevity, but rather as a means of postponing specific age-related diseases. Tumors and illnesses could be made to occur at a later age by rate-control medicine, and even pedestrian road deaths would peak at a later age. We shall probably use such methods initially to postpone the date of onset of diseases that we are not yet able to control. Obviously, if you knew that somebody was liable to get cancer when he was fifty, it would be a great benefit to postpone the disease until he was sixty, because by that time, we might have gotten a treatment for it. Quite apart from anything else, he would get another ten years of life. That, I think, is the first form in which experimental gerontology will probably be applied. We can expect that in the lifetime of some of us, physical aging in humans will be susceptible to some postponement, not just through removing individual diseases but by actually putting a screwdriver into the clock and resetting the timing mechanism. I am afraid some of us will be Moses rather than Joshua, however, in regard to this prediction at the present rate of funding.

Physical aging, however, accounts for only about 25% of the ills of aging that we see in American society and similar societies. Some seventy-five percent is accounted for by another kind of aging, which we may properly call sociogenic aging. Sociogenic aging is, quite simply, the sum of the folklore, the prejudices, and the misconceptions about age which are imposed on the old. It does not require any scientific discovery to alter this aspect of aging, merely public education and a change of attitude. We tend to forget that when you reach old age, you will not feel any different, and you will be surprised that other people treat you as if you were different. When you go into a restaurant with your son and the waiter points at you and says, "Does he have cream in his coffee?", you begin to realize that somehow you have been expelled from the club and that you are no longer a citizen in good standing. It is precisely on that sort of aging, imaginary or imposed, that I want to concentrate here.

If you insist that there is a group of people who, on a fixed calendar basis, cease to be people in good standing and become unintelligent, asexual, unemployable, sickly, or crazy without reason, then the people so designated are under some pressure to

be like that, just as much as oppressed ethnic minorities have
been kept below their full potential because other people spook
them out of it. The fact that no person who is not sick becomes
any one of those things by virtue of age is quite beside the
point, and the fact that most older people obstinately fail to "be
like that" is beside the point. It is amazing how the stereotypes
get built in. As older people are known to be unemployable, we do
not let them work. As they are known to be asexual (and it is
very embarrassing when they are not), we tend to herd them into
institutions which deny even elementary privacy. As they are
known to be liable to go crazy without reason--symptoms which are
due, in fact, to infection, to overmedication, to simple
exasperation with society or to specific diseases, such as
Alzheimer's Disease that are missed--the elderly sick are regarded
as "senile." The greatest advance in the field of Alzheimer's has
already been made; we now recognize it as a disease and not a
natural consequence of aging. As a consequence, a large research
investment is now being focused on finding out whether it is a
genetic, an infectious, or an autoimmune condition. In actual
fact, rather few old people go crazy compared with people at
earlier ages. Only about nine persons per thousand over age 65
need psychiatric hospitalization (if you exclude those who suffer
from the various forms of dementia, one of which is caused by
multiple emboli in the brain, and another of which is Alzheimer's
disease). Usually, old people become crazy for only three
reasons: because they always were crazy, because they have an
illness, or because we drive them crazy.

Prejudice has a bad effect on its victims, and it tends to
corrupt people, as we have seen in the case of racial and
religious prejudice. Prejudice against the aged is particularly
stupid because we all become old. Do you think Archie Bunker
would go on being rude to immigrants if he knew that he was going
to turn into a Puerto Rican on his 65th birthday? Recently,
people seem to have mended their manners in regard to minorities,
and there is less bandying of ethnic insults. I would like to see
the day when such slurs as "dirty old men", "old ladies in tennis
shoes", "old buffers", "old gomers", and so forth, go exactly the
same way as the ethnic insult--as being words that are left unsaid
or you face the risk of having your head punched if you use
them.

When we get wise to it, we realize that aging is as
irrelevant as race. The old have some earned entitlements--the
right to a pension for which they have subscribed and the right to
benefit from certain programs which meet their particular needs.
Administratively, the right way to handle the old is to stop
treating them as a problem and begin treating them as a
resource. I am glad to say that we are beginning to see a little
more movement in that direction. The only really relevant

administrative feature of oldness is the increased risk of illness
and decreased mobility, but neither ill health nor lack of mobility are confined to the old. The person who needs a wheelchair at
any age needs a wheelchair. The person who needs medical care at
any age needs medical care, and the age of the person concerned or
the reason which causes them to have those needs is largely
irrelevant. I think it is quite scientifically and politically
sound to start striking age out of the reckoning, but this will be
difficult to do until the elderly operate as a political pressure
group in order to get some of their share of the goodies.

   To remain in optimal health, old people need what other
people need: they need work to do, money to live on, a place to
live in, and other people who have some concern whether they live
or die. The old today run the risk of being prematurely buried
and not getting those things. I am inclined to think that work is
the greatest preservative of all. What we call retirement is
often compulsory unemployment. Thomas Jefferson said that a man
should not too long occupy the same ground. He made this
statement when he was arguing against a life presidency (and I
think one would agree), but he did not say that a man or woman,
when no longer president or whatever, should be excluded from
society and obliged to be idle. Compulsory idleness is as onerous
to the rich as it is to the poor, and it also is something that
the country can ill afford, because, among the older people, there
are many who have top skills. I know that there are problems
here. I had to update my medicine very rapidly when I came back
to clinical practice after having been out of the field for a few
years. Any of us who were brought up on vacuum tube radio would
find ourselves in the Dark Ages when it came to dealing with solid
state circuitry, and the people who were brought up on germanium
transistors will find that they have been left behind by modern
chips and integrated circuits. Technology advances very fast
indeed. When I was a medical student, medical botany was in the
curriculum but radiation biology was not. It is increasingly hard
to keep up, but even the fact that you have not kept up with the
state of the art does not mean that you are not good for anything;
you do have experience. As a consequence, an old doctor who is
not au fait with the latest drug can still retain his clinical
experience and be a very valuable member of the firm, and he may
sometimes offer Trousseau's advice to his pupils, "Use the new
drug, gentlemen, while it retains its efficacy." All projects and
professions benefit from a balance between experience and
innovation.

   If we persist in the fiction that the old can be of no use to
society except as volunteers, we are going to have twenty percent
of the population of some states permanently unemployed. That
situation may be difficult to address at a time when vast numbers
of the young are unemployed, but room still needs to be found for

the old as well as for the teenagers. Their skills and potentials
are different. The old need something to do and, preferably,
something that does not displace other people. Still, as one old
lady said to me, "What every firm wants is a person of 20 or 25
with 40 years of experience, and they just do not come that
way." One of the difficult problems of society is how to allocate
work fairly among different age groups so that nobody is being
exploited. It is interesting that in two world wars, the old went
back to work with excellent results. You must remember that at
the same time, women started doing things they never did before.
Barriers against blacks and other minorities were dropped and they
too started doing new things, and they did them extremely well.
But there is a big difference between the old and the other
minorities: while minorities and women who had gained new
recognition as citizens, kept it to some extent, despite a certain
amount of ground lost after the wars, the old underwent turnover,
and a new generation of older people had to fight again for their
rights. If you are a woman or if you are a member of a minority,
you will have been subjected to some degree of prejudice and will
have had to fight for your rights all your life. This experience
is something which only comes to the old when they get to be old,
making it rather difficult for them to retain political and social
gains from generation to generation.

I do not like the emphasis placed on the beauties of leisure,
because leisure as stressed by this society is a fraud. Leisure
is a great thing to occupy an occasional afternoon or even an
occasional two weeks, but not twenty years. I know it is very
easy for elderly academics who never will retire as long as they
can talk, write or even make intelligible noises, to say this when
other people who perform heavy or demeaning manual labor may be
very glad to retire. But the opposite of drudgery is not
idleness. I am horrified that we not only talk of leisure
centers but we even have courses in organizing the leisure of
others, when we should be talking about occupation. Obviously,
that does not mean that occupation until death should be
compulsory. The old in India may choose to become contemplatives
when they are old, and anyone who wants to be a yogi rather than
remain in employment has a perfect right to do that. I think,
however, that this is one of the areas in which we have failed,
perhaps because it is such a socially difficult area. But as we
age, we near the end of our lives, and our toleration for
triviality, which is what leisure tends to mean in this culture,
declines.

Among the other important needs of the old is the ability to
stay in their homes. Institutionalization has been a very great
evil and still confronts us with insoluble problems. Although
only something like four percent of the old live in nursing homes,

those who do sometimes live under very bad or at least unrewarding
conditions. We are launching a drive in several states to remedy
this state of affairs. The State of Maine, for example, has
recently switched a lot of its Medicare funding from nursing homes
to ambulatory care, so that quite a few people can remain at home,
provided certain facilities are available. It is very much
cheaper to the community, it is very much better for older
people. Some of them will always need to live in institutions,
and we have to ride shotgun on those institutions to see that they
conduct themselves properly. In the best centers, we have been
incorporating nursing homes into teaching medical hospitals so
that there are medical residents in attendance and the patients
are not left to molder; instead, they receive active supervision,
treatment, and encouragement to be engaged.

These comments bring me to the question of geriatrics.
Geriatric medicine has been a specialty in European medical
schools, and it has always been practiced in Jewish hospitals,
although they do not separate it from the general idea of
excellent medicine. It has spread from there and has begun to
achieve recognition throughout medicine. Some doctors ignorant of
geriatric medicine do not believe it is a "real" discipline. Yet
it is, in fact, very real because the treatment of the old differs
as much from the treatment of the young and middle aged as
standard medicine differs from the treatment of babies. The doses
and the modalities of treatment which are appropriate for young
babies are not appropriate for persons in their twenties and
thirties, and in the same way, treatments appropriate in midlife
are not always appropriate for people in old age. For a start, as
life continues, tolerance of drugs decreases for a variety of
reasons, and doses that are appropriate at a younger age can
produce serious disturbances in the elderly. Furthermore, as one
grows older, the symptoms of disease tend to become blurred and,
indeed, a characteristic feature of geriatric medicine is the
nonspecific presentation of specific disease. With an
overwhelming infection, a baby will have a convulsion, a young
adult will experience a rigor and perhaps delirium, and an old
person may show no symptoms except confusion. If you assume that
all old people are confused anyway by virtue of age, you will miss
the infection. One highly important measure in geriatrics is the
so-called plastic bag test, whereby you produce a plastic bag--and
I do not mean a little sandwich bag, I mean a great big bag like a
garment bag--and you tell the patient to put all the medication
they are taking in there. In my experience, the record was 41
medications! Now and then you see people who have a sort of
buffet bar of medications which they sample from time to time. I
met one old lady who used to put all her pills in one box and take
them at random. Nobody had bothered to explain the correct
regimen to her, until she took three Digoxin in a row and landed
in the hospital. Others will lend pills. A lady who was taking

the anticoagulant Coumadin for thrombosis of her legs was a very good patient. She came in every week to have her clotting time recorded and took her medicine religiously. Unfortunately, her landlady also developed a bad leg, so our patient gave Coumadin tablets to her landlady. The landlady duly took them and bled from every orifice much to the mystification of her physician, who was unable to make out what was the matter! I have seen an apparently demented patient whose dementia was due to eating Vitamin D tablets by the handful because somebody had told her they were not medicine, but were "good for her". There is a great deal of patient education to be done here. One sees literal echoes of the celebrated case of the man who was given a suppository for his hemorrhoids and ate it. The doctor said, "Well, you idiot, I told you what to do with it". The man said, "Yes, but you will have your little joke, doctor". It is easy to blame the patient but we also should blame ourselves as physicians for not cultivating a better attitude towards medication in the old and in the young as well. Hidden away in cupboards all over the country are bottles of dangerous drugs that have been withdrawn or outdated. They are at the back of the medicine cabinet labelled "headache pills," or the like, and waiting to wreak havoc when somebody takes them. The trouble in modern medicine is that all our operations are conducted with live ammunition, and we have to be careful that the troops to whom we issue it know how to handle it.

Geriatric medicine is a marvelous occupation. However, you have to cure medical students of the idea that it is a branch of embalming, and therefore not interesting. When students see older people who appear to be demented, or decrepit or depressed put on their feet again and restored to vigorous life, they come to realize that it really is a worthwhile occupation. This is an area where role models are important, which is why we set out to train people to become full-time geriatricians. The time will come when they can re-merge with mainstream medicine, physicians who also know how to treat the old. But to start with, we have to have centers of excellence to provide role models. This field is a growth stock in medical practice. Sixty percent of prescriptions are written for people over 65. In some areas of the country, the elderly will soon comprise up to twenty percent of the population, and that twenty percent is going to make up eighty percent of patient visits, because a lot of illness is concentrated towards the end of life. People in a doctor's office now very often have degenerative and age-dependent diseases, whereas a century ago, they were patients with infections. The diseases include myocardial and cardiovascular disease, arthritis, malignancies—they are diseases of late middle life but are carried over into old age. As I have said, geriatrics differs in the same way from general medicine as does pediatrics. It requires specialized knowledge.

The name geriatrics was invented in America, but the
discipline is something which we can claim for England and
Scotland through the work of people like Sheldon, Howell,
Ferguson, Anderson, Elizabeth Williams, and Lord Amulree. I was
interested, however, to find that many of these people were, in
turn, resident physicians under a certain Noah Morris, who, I
believe, came over to Scotland from the Yeshiva Hospital. Thus, a
subject is developed by role modeling. I want to say something
about present conditions here in contrast with Europe. There is
one problem in Europe that does not exist in California but which
you may have here outside the Sun Belt, namely, hypothermia. A
lot of old people in England still live in houses where the toilet
is outside the house, and they have great difficulty in not
freezing to their seats. The old are very susceptible to cold,
and hypothermia is a dangerous and insidious condition. Even in
California houses and wards are kept cool with air conditioning.
The temperature only has to go down to about 60°, and some old
people begin to get problems. Another difference between America
and Europe that is sometimes not realized is that the per capita
cost of medical treatment to seniors out of pocket has actually
increased in dollars since Medicare was introduced because of the
increased cost of services. One great advantage in England is
that with a health service, not a "sickness industry," you cannot
be put out on the pavement because you cannot produce cash down
for medical services. In other words, you have got a floor under
you as you age. Another feature that makes geriatrics here very
different from Europe is the general lack of family physicians in
America. The family physician in England sees the patient and
everything goes through him including the specialist's opinions.
If the specialist recommends unnecessary surgery, it is up to the
family physician to be gatekeeper and see that common sense
prevails. The family doctor does not have hospital privileges,
but the hospital reports to him when the patient is discharged.
At the moment, I am engaged in a program of training family
physicians for the rather different American scene. We have an
excellent program in Ventura County Hospital, where we are
training people in family practice, and we are likely to see an
expansion of this branch of medical teaching. Geriatrics is an
important skill in family practice. You also need geriatricians
in hospitals. In fact, in England, a geriatrician is in the
emergency room so that he will be there when the patient is
admitted and avoid the harm done by delays over what is called
"disposal."

Finally, the biggest problem here is that geriatric work
depends largely on social services, and the multitier structure in
America, with its federal, state, county, local, and voluntary
services, makes it very difficult to integrate them, whereas in
England, one telephone call will usually turn on all the social
services. The problem does not even stem entirely from the

Neanderthal interpretation of <u>laissez faire</u>--that social services should be provided as grudgingly as possible. The real trouble has been that America has indeed been spending huge sums on social services, large amounts of which never reach the people for which they are intended. The Neanderthal view has failed in the clinical trial, and one may have to take another look at how it operates. People are very kind, and, if some old lady goes on television and says her roof has fallen in and she is unable to pay for it, dozens of people will volunteer to fix it for her. But strangely, if you try to put a penny on the sales tax to pay for social services, it is vigorously resisted and even categorized as "Communistic."

I think that an American medical service has to be American; it cannot be patterned after the English, Swedish, Soviet, Chinese or other systems you may name. The old are going to play a very big part in determining how those medical services are delivered and perhaps a deciding role in the future pattern of American medicine. The elderly are going to be the big consumers, and they pack much more punch than most of them realize. For a start, they have this devil's gift of leisure, which enables them to go around stomping the country, holding registration drives and exerting pressure. They include a lot of retired judges, congressmen, senators, and business executives with a lot of political clout and a lot of political experience. Congress is beginning to feel the heat from the senior lobby, not just because of the Grey Panthers but also because it is a lobby with a lot of experience and skill. One sometimes forgets that if Benjamin Franklin had retired at 65, we would not have the American Constitution in its present form, because nearly all his best work in that area and his great political influence on the growth of the new country was done after he was 65. As a gerontologist, I am often asked whether the president ought to run again when he is in his seventies. It always seems to me that his age is quite irrelevant. If a man is well and fit and in his right mind, there might be many other reasons for voting against him but his age is not one of them, and this applies to all our politicians. Of course, it is true over history that some figures have stayed on when they were not in a fit state of mental or physical health, but that applies to some younger politicians, too. We are at last coming to recognize that the old have a role to play, and the only thing I find disappointing is that so many old politicians tend to forget their constituency, or not realize that they have it. With the creditable exception of people like Sen. Claude Pepper, it is certainly true that there are a lot of old politicians who do not do much for the old. But the people who can change this are the electorate, because they can lobby their representatives. I think that we are going to see the old adopting a very major activist role in this society, far more so than they have done in the past. And those of us who are not yet old may find that by the

time we are, we will have moved into a situation where the options
are very different.

I would not like to see an old-young conflict set up. It is
very easy to create group antagonisms and is the way that
conventional politics very often operates, by playing groups up
against each other. The old have to guard against it. They will
have to decide whether to join an organization which is
specifically for the old, in the way that the NAACP is
specifically for blacks or minorities, or whether to work through
existing parties and lobby the party of your choice. Both forms
of pressure are effective in changing the attitudes of society.
But I think that this is one revolution which is almost bound to
come about, simply because of the change in demographics. And, in
a sense, the art of being old is to learn to play an effective
game and not an end game and to cultivate, among other things, a
characteristic which is not describable by an Americanism--it is
what the British army calls bloody-mindedness. The expression
means a combination of cussedness, feistiness, and general refusal
to budge. It may range from being deliberately obstructive to
standing up for one's rights. More and more people are coming to
recognize the need to be "bloodyminded," and I am always very
pleased when I see an audience containing older people, because I
know they are much less willing to be spooked by stereotypes, in
exactly the same way as black or Hispanic Americans are not
prepared to put up with the traditional racist images. Groups are
no longer prepared to put up with traditional stereotyping when it
is insulting or a hindrance to them, and the old are joining that
movement. America will be a rather good place for the old if they
are able to keep up this behavior. This is why I chose as my
title, "Living All of Your Life," to suggest the task which lies
ahead of the older citizen.

I have to return to England soon, and my next job will be to
try to organize the teaching of geriatric medicine, not to a
public such as ourselves which has doctors, hospitals and the
problem of the cost of Medicare, but to such Third World countries
as India. There, medical services will have to be based on the
village concept. It will be of no use sending doctors to Britain
and America to learn geriatrics as practiced in teaching hospitals
and with the type of social services that exist there if, when
they go home, they will have to think in terms of the village and
the extended family. And so the job goes on, and those of us who
are interested in working with the elderly see that there are many
areas of research involved. They range from the study of fruit
flies, mice, molecular biology, and biochemistry, about which we
are hearing in this Symposium, to the study of how to deliver the
best health care to the old, and how to improve social attitudes
so that unnecessary burdens are not placed on the old. This
three-fold task involves some gerontology and geriatrics, and is

the key to insuring that people do get an opportunity to live all of their lives.

DISCUSSION

Question: Are you as optimistic now about the future of aging research as you were thirty years ago?

Comfort: Yes, I am, although I was a bit too optimistic about how fast the research would get funded; I thought then that because so many politicians were old, and so many rich men who were growing older were worried about their aging, there would be a gathering rush to fund experimental gerontology. There has not been because those people when they did fund anything tended to fund quacks and not people who have been doing the serious research. But I am still optimistic that the research can be done. What we have to learn here is that we tend to take an over-optimistic view of the ten-year outlook, and an underoptimistic view of the twenty-year outlook; that just about fits. I did expect to see rather more investment in gerontology, but I am also quite pleased with the solid progress that is been made. You can say, ten years ago we were talking about the need to do experiments to see whether caloric restriction works in humans, and we are still saying that today. There are major difficulties in doing such experiments, and it is probably more economical to find out what exactly caloric restriction does so that we can short-circuit the need of doing it. So the answer is yes, I am optimistic about the future, and I think we have actually made a lot more progress than appears to the public. The reason lies in what Winston Churchill said about supplies and logistics in wartime. The first year, nothing; the second year, a little; the third year, all you want. These things do take very long time to brew, and I think a lot of the good work has been done. You cannot put your finger on which of it will pay off at the moment, so we have to continue along numerous lines.

Question: So are you saying that the National Institute on Aging has not been funding research properly?

Comfort: Oh, it has; the National Institute has been doing a good job, but one could use yet more funding than we have had. Funding for research in this country depends on two sources: federal money, like the national institutes, and large-scale voluntary money. Sometimes this method works easily and well. The best example was the polio immunization campaign where the money came partly from federal and partly from voluntary sources. I think we shall see this same cooperation with Alzheimer research. As soon as it becomes clear that we are beginning to get a handle on this problem, I am sure that there probably will be as vigorous fundraising as there was for polio.

I am not sure funding alone will resolve the problem any more than throwing money at cancer has produced a cure. So I think we have to reach the point in our research where the funding will be correctly applied.

Question: How would you compare caloric restriction in mice and rats with fasting in humans?

Comfort: In mice, the reduction of the caloric intake to sixty percent produces a large change in lifespan, and the ladies who say their prayers every day to the Goddess Diameter and live on lettuce should do alright on this diet. But what I was saying was that it is very difficult to conduct this sort of program with human subjects, simply because it must be kept up consistently for a very long time before you have any results. I think we are beginning to make a dent in heart disease alone by altering dietary habits; that seems the most logical explanation of the decline in the incidence of myocardial infarction. Probably the reduction in the consumption of saturated fats is responsible.

Question: Is there an age at which caloric restriction is more appropriate?

Comfort: We have not worked that out. We heard in this Symposium about experiments in which caloric restriction was started at early adolescence of mice that showed quite a considerable effect. I think we would have to do a lot of figuring out for humans. The real problem is that mice and rats in the wild are annuals, and they may have a special device which enables them to overwinter by postponing their aging when their food supply is low, whereas humans already have a long period of latency introduced in their childhood. The first stage both of physical growth and psychosexual development occurs early in humans, and then there is a long plateau, followed by another spurt of development of both at adolescence. So probably the whole life cycle in primates, with this long latency period, is different in its control mechanism from what it would be in other mammals. We may have some surprises in store over this. And that is why I would rather analyze the nature of the caloric restriction effect--find out whether it is operating at the cellular level or on a hypotholamic clock--and then see whether we can simulate it by some means other than just cutting down in calories.

Question: Do you still hold with the spacecraft analogy for aging?

Comfort: I will have to explain that analogy. The idea is that in a sense the organism is like a spacecraft that has been designed to go and photograph Mars. It has to be overengineered

to the extent that all the tolerances will carry it at least that
far. With the Pioneer and Voyager spacecraft, they have been
overengineered to the point at which they are going tootling off
into far space and look like they will last for a very long time
and produce far more results than anybody expected. Now, if an
organism has been "designed" by evolution to live a certain length
of time, various things can happen to it when it reaches the end
of that period. It can run out of the program so that the
organism tends from then on not to maintain homeostatis because it
is no longer programmed for a further course. Alternatively, the
organism can actively self-destruct or it can simply not recharge
its batteries. We really do not know whether organisms follow one
of those processes or whether it is a process of "wearing out".
In general, the body seems to have backup systems. Russian
physiologists have done a lot of work on the change in homeostatic
mechanisms with age, and it seems that there is a computer on
board which produces backup systems, but those systems change in
character, and in their view, when one reaches the end of the
lifespan, one has run out of backups. All of these possibilities
have to be investigated by analyzing what actually goes on when
organisms age.

Question: If you had unlimited funds, what would you be
working on in the field of aging research?

Comfort: If I had unlimited funds to devote to research,
leaving aside the question of applying money for the training of
physicians, I would press on more quickly with existing
projects. With more staff, we could get more experiments done,
and I think the direction of aging research at the moment is
extremely satisfactory. I would like to see slightly more federal
investment in the immunobiology of aging because the people in
that area could do more with bigger staffs.

Question: In regard to your comment about elderly
politicians, the problem is not were they picked well, the problem
is surely that their ideas all must have been formulated several
decades earlier. Would you like to comment on that?

Comfort: When you see all those boys standing up on top of
Lenin's tomb and looking rather forbidding, I mean, you do feel
that way. If you sometimes look at the British establishment or
the American establishment, you feel, "My God, what a shower".
But then, there are plenty of young members of the establishment
who are a shower, too. So it is much more the selection of
shower-worthy people by politics than it is the age of the person
concerned. And it is just not true that old people do not
change. It is very obvious that in field of sexual mores, a lot
of old people stay with the mores they learned many years ago.
Others are quite prepared to start living together unmarried

because the young are doing and it pays off from the point of view of social security. So some people update and go with the times, others do not and they say the times are corrupt and they do not want to go with them. So it is rather this fallacy of treating all old people as if they were identical twins. They are not. There are old Conservatives and old Liberals. There are old Progressives and old Reactionaries. There are just as many different kinds of old people as there are young people. So it does not follow that all old people are irrevocably conservative and incapable of changing their attitudes. Some are.

Question: Does exercise have any impact on aging?

Comfort: It probably does, but I think that the trouble with exercise is that some people do well on it and others do not. It is quite good where day-to-day living involves exercise, like the Swiss who, whenever he goes out his front door, has to walk either up or downhill, and return in the opposite direction or the nomadic herdsmen who have to follow their flocks on foot or the old-time cowboys who followed their herds on horseback. But the exercise you do at the spa to work off the extra calories you have eaten is not. There is a tendency for exercise to be what you do as a penance for all the guzzling and slurping that you have done in the interval. It does not work terribly well that way.

Question: In the context of exercise in your most famous book, do you have any comments?

Comfort: I always thought that sex ought to be good for you, as it does involve an acceleration of the heart rate, but the physiologists tell me it is not really sustained enough. The exercise physiologist also says that you have to reassure people that that type of exertion is no more hazardous to patients who have suffered a heart attack than walking up a flight of stairs. And since people have this concern regarding sexuality, they are very easily spooked out of it, and that is too bad. The actual amount of calories you burn off in the course of sexual intercourse is probably fairly low, so I do not think you can, as it were, screw your way out of overweight. Sorry if I have disappointed anybody.

Question: The centers for Alzheimer's research are in the United States. What are the Europeans doing along that line?

Comfort: There are a number of places in Europe where work is being done. In England, for example, the Medical Research Council has a research group. It depends on which theory you adopt, because the people who think that Alzheimer's disease is caused by an infection by an unconventional agent are working in infectious diseases institutes. Others are working on immune or

genetic factors. So there is a lot of work scattered over the
whole area, with a certain amount of coordination now that we are
aware of the subject. I think that the project is going well. I
am not sure whether setting up another Manhattan project and
trying to have a crash program to deal with Alzheimer's would be
beneficial--it would not have been if you started such a program
prematurely. I think we must go on a little bit longer before we
can embark on a crash program, but when we reach the point at
which we know that the project is feasible, then we can begin to
put more resources into it. At that point, it will be very
important to act as quickly as possible because Alzheimer's is the
most expensive disease in the country. Apart from an incredible
amount of suffering, it leads to an enormous amount of prolonged
ill health and institutional time and cost in services. It is
what the majority of people fear most about growing old. It is
bad enough if you become bedridden, but if your intellect is okay,
you can still do things from your bed, but if your "marbles" go,
that is it.

ENVIRONMENTAL AND GENETIC FACTORS THAT INFLUENCE IMMUNITY AND LONGEVITY IN MICE

D.J. Anderson*,**, A.L.M. Watson*,+, E.J. Yunis*,**,+

*Division of Immunogenetics, Dana-Farber Cancer Inst.
**Department of Pathology, Harvard Medical School
+Center for Blood Research, Boston, MA   02115

INTRODUCTION

The potential lifespan of a species, defined as the duration of life of the longest survivors, is determined by genetic factors which control the rate of cellular and organ development and involution. However, the incidence of disease increases exponentially with age (Simms, 1946), and longevity of individuals within a species is also determined by an absence of genetic susceptibility to disease and the maintenance of a vigorous and well-balanced immune system which continues to cope with environmental stimuli and internal degenerative changes. The thymus, a principal lymphoid organ, is governed by a genetic "time clock" which programs its involution with age. Environmental influences can accelerate or delay this natural process. Concomitant with thymic involution is a progressive decline in immune function. The incidence of autoimmune, neoplastic and infectious diseases increases dramatically as immune and immunoregulatory functions decline, and such diseases are hallmarks of the aging process. In this report we will present theories and experimental findings from our laboratory and others on the subject of the interaction between genetic and environmental factors affecting longevity, focusing on the immune system as a major interface between genetic aging programs and the environment.

THE IMMUNOLOGIC THEORY OF AGING

The Thymic Time Clock and Age-Associated Decline in Immunologic Function

The thymus begins to involute shortly after puberty. Age of onset and rate of involution are affected by as yet undefined genetic factors (Yunis et al., 1972; Good and Yunis, 1974) as well as by gonadal and pituitary hormonal levels (Dumont et al., 1982; Harrison et al., 1982) and environmental influences. Progressive morphologic changes include a decrease in the cortical mass and number of cortical thymocytes (Tosi et al., 1982) and infiltration of plasma cells (Farr and Sidman, 1984). Levels of thymic hormones decline, and systemic thymic-dependent (T) lymphocyte functions progressively lose their vigor (reviewed by Kay, 1979). In addition, Ia expression by thymic epithelial cells diminishes with age (Farr and Sidman, 1984) and could affect intercellular communication (differentiation and programming) within the thymus. The thymic time clock theory of aging postulates that a genetic program controls the decline in function of the thymus, which, in turn, affects immune competence (ability to cope with environmental factors and internal degenerative changes) and immunoregulatory mechanisms. Declining immune competence and an imbalance in immunoregulatory mechanisms promote infectious, neoplastic and autoimmune diseases which curtail lifespan.

The Role of Products of the Major Histocompatibility Complex (MHC) in Immune Functions which Influence Longevity

Immune response (Ir) genes which have been mapped to the Ia (Class II) region of the MHC in mice encode molecules which clearly regulate immune responses. The expression of certain Ia phenotypes is predictive of whether an individual can respond to a given antigenic stimulus. The responder/nonresponder genetic phenomenon was first described in inbred guinea pig strains immunized with synthetic antigens. The mechanisms underlying MHC control of immune responses are still incompletely understood. Benacerraf (1981) hypothesized that Ir gene products are antigen-presenting molecules on the surface of macrophages. It is possible that other Ia-expressing cells such as the thymic epithelium and vascular endothelium also have an antigen-presenting role and drive lymphocyte differentiation and activation (Farr and Sidman, 1984; Pober et al., 1983). Sasazuki et al., (1983) found evidence linking Ir genes with suppressor cell functions. They showed that individuals who fail to respond to a particular antigen have preferentially activated suppressor cells which block the reactivity of other T and B lymphocyte populations. It is clear that individuals inheriting Ir phenotypes associated with immunoregulatory imbalances or an inability to respond to certain infectious organisms could develop autoimmune or other diseases early in life which could significantly decrease their lifespan.

Class I MHC antigens (H-2D and K in mouse) are found on the surface of virtually all somatic cells in the body and are important signals in self-recognition. Cytotoxic and helper T-cells, with few exceptions, must recognize antigens in the context of self HLA Class I markers to respond to antigen (Zinkernagel and Doherty, 1979). In addition, it has been shown that antigen-specific soluble intercellular signaling molecules secreted by regulatory T lymphocytes have considerable homology with MHC products (Germain, 1981). Many diseases are also associated with Class I MHC phenotypes and may be attributable to inefficient or false signals given to the immune system by Class I antigens.

GENES THAT AFFECT LONGEVITY

An Association Between MHC and Aging

Numerous studies have shown that mice of different inbred strains differ in survival rate. For example, the studies of Russell (1975) clearly demonstrated that C57Bl/6 mice lived longer than DBA/2 mice. The F_1 hybrid outlived parents of either sex, and females lived longer than males. Since genes of the H-2 region govern the immune system, it was anticipated that longevity may be associated with expression of certain H-2 phenotypes (Katz and Benacerraf, 1976; Meredith and Walford, 1977; Greenberg and Yunis, 1975, 1978). Several investigators (Smith and Walford, 1977; Popp, 1978; Williams et al., 1981) have addressed this question by using congenic strains of mice differing only in the H-2 region. The study performed by Smith and Walford (1977) using congenic mice demonstrated that median survival time does correlate with certain H-2 haplotypes and immune responsiveness. Their study showed considerable survival differences between congenic strains differing only at the H-2 region. In another study, it was shown that longevity in H-2 congenic mice was associated with immune responsiveness as measured by phytohemagglutinin (PHA) mitogen assay. B10.RIII ($H-2^r$), the longest-lived congenic strain, displayed the highest response to PHA, whereas B10.AKM ($H-2^m$), the shortest-lived strain was least responsive (Meredith and Walford, 1977). These data support the concept that there is a genetic influence on longevity controlled by genes in the MHC, and that the MHC effect may be mediated by the immune system.

The Role of Other Genes and Genetic Interactions in Longevity

We recently performed aging studies on $(C57BL/6 \times DBA/2)F_1 \times DBA/2$

backcross mice to determine the influence of other genetic
regions and genetic interactions on lifespan. In this study we
looked at the determinants of coat color (brown locus of
Chromosome 4 and dilute locus of Chromosome 9), the
serologically determined H-2 antigens (Chromosome 17), and sex as
genetic markers. Our results suggest that the genes in the brown
locus (b) segment of Chromosome 4, genes in a segment of the sex
Chromosome and genes in the segment of Chromosome 17 containing
the H-2 haplotype significantly influence life span in the
backcross combinations of the C57BL/6 and DBA/2 strains. Two
important findings were: 1) effects of a segment of genes in
Chromosome 4 (b locus), as studied by coat color, which was more
significant in females than in males; and 2) an influence of the
simultaneous presence of certain alleles of the sex Chromosome,
of Chromosome 17 (H-2) and Chromosome 4 (b locus) on life span.
For example, among 8 different genotypes: B/b;H-2^b/H-2^d,
B/b;H-2^d/H-2^d, b/b;H-2^b/H-2^d and b/b;H-2^d/H-2^d males and females,
we found the longest-lived group to be the females B/b;H-2^b/H-2^d
(median 30.5 months) and the shortest-lived group to be the males
b/b;H-2^d/H-2^d (median 24.1 months). Within these 8 genotypes,
the observed spread of 6 months represents a 25% increase in mean
survival rate (Yunis et al., in press).

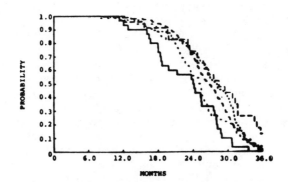

Fig. 1. Length of survival is influenced by the degree of genetic
        heterozygosity at the four loci examined in this study.
        The heterozygosity score was determined by adding the
        number of heterozygous loci. A score of 0 indicates
        homozygosity at all four loci, a score of 4 indicates
        heterozygosity at all four loci (H-2, brown locus, dilute
        locus and sex).

	HETEROZYGOSITY SCORE	NUMBER	MEDIAN
————	0	30	24.1
- - -	1	68	25.1
— — --	2	162	26.8
- - - -	3	105	28.1
— — -	4	23	28.4

We also found that increased heterozygosity directly correlated with longer life span (Fig. 1). This effect may represent a case of hybrid vigor (heterosis), associated either with dominance of favorable alleles not held in common by the parental strains (Roderick and Schlager, 1975) or with avoidance of the deleterious effects of recessive genes which limit life span (Russell, 1975). These findings suggest that interaction between a number of genes and the environment is more important in conferring longer life span than the presence of specific individual genes (Yunis et al., in press).

ENVIRONMENTAL FACTORS AFFECTING THE AGE-ASSOCIATED DECLINE IN IMMUNE FUNCTION AND LONGEVITY

Although the regulation of immune response is predominantly under genetic control, non-lymphoid factors, such as nutrition, hormone levels and drugs are also influential. Earlier studies have demonstrated that in the autoimmune-prone NZB mouse strain diets low in fat and high in protein and fiber content lead to delayed development of autoimmunity and are associated with prolonged life span in both males and females. However, restriction of protein intake alone, while conferring beneficial influences on T-cell functions, did not significantly suppress the occurrence of autoimmune disease or prolong the life span of NZB mice. In contrast, B/W mice fed a normal diet in restricted amount (12 cal/day) lived at least twice as long as mice fed a normal diet (24 cal/day) (Fernandes et al., 1981) (Fig. 2). This

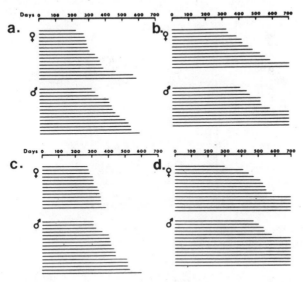

Fig. 2. Survival of B/W mice on diets of different composition (Each line represents the life span of a single mouse) a) 24 calories, 22% protein; b) 12 calories, 22% protein; c) 24 calories, 6% protein; d) 12 calories, 6% protein.

dramatic influence of nutrition was accompanied by prolonged
maintenance of T-cell-mediated functions, inhibition of the
development of spontaneously active suppressor cells, and
maintenance of inducible suppressor cells. Dietary restriction
also inhibited immunocomplex-dependent renal injury and anti-DNA
antibody production in B/W mice as well as preventing the
development of circulating immune complexes.

Extensive nutritional studies revealed that the total food
intake alone was responsible for inhibiting the development of
autoimmune disease in B/W mice. Manipulation of the proportion
of dietary components--for example, protein, carbohydrates, or
fats--without reduction of calories produced no such influence.
Restricted dietary intake from weaning as well as beginning in
adult life led to significant extension of life and reduced
severity of the disease. Biochemical analysis of individual sera
from 7-month-old B/W females fed the normal 24 cal/day diet from
weaning showed elevations in serum cholesterol levels, decreased
hematocrit, total protein and albumin content, as compared to
mice given the 12 cal/day diet. When a high-calorie, high-fat
diet was given, the autoimmune diseases were more severe and the
animals also developed high levels of serum cholesterol,
arteriosclerosis, and coronary and myocardial lesions. In mice
fed low-calorie and low-fat diet, all of the cardiovascular
lesions as well as the kidney disease were prevented (Fernandes
et al., 1983; Fernandes et al., 1981; Lane and Yunis, 1981).

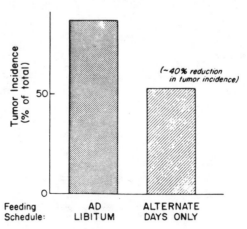

Fig. 3   Reduction of breast tumor incidence by
           alternate-day feeding of female C_3H mice.

	AD LIBITUM	ALTERNATE DAYS ONLY
Total N	47	49
N with Tumor	41	26
$\chi^2 = 13.28$		
$p = <0.005$		

In C$_3$H mice, which develop spontaneous breast tumors, two
methods, alternate-day feeding and daily caloric restriction,
have been successful in the prevention or delay of tumor
development (Fig. 3). Alternate-day feeding influences both
tumor incidence and survival in these mice. Control mice fed ad
libitum and experimental mice fed on alternate days showed mean
survival times of 545 + 24 and 619 + 28 days, respectively
(p<0.05). The control mice had a tumor incidence of 83%, whereas
the experimental mice had only a 53% incidence of mammary tumors
(p<0.005) (Yunis et al., 1981).

In another study using the same alternate-day feeding
schedule versus the ad libitum feeding in CBA/H (a long-lived
strain of mice), we have seen 70% survival of the experimental
mice and only 42% survival of the control mice at 960 days of
age. The difference in survival continues to be observed at
1,080 days of age: 40% and 5%, respectively, for the experimental
and control mice (Fig. 4).

SUMMARY

Many different theoretical approaches may be taken toward
understanding the association between aging and immunologic
malfunction. The leading theory is based on the natural

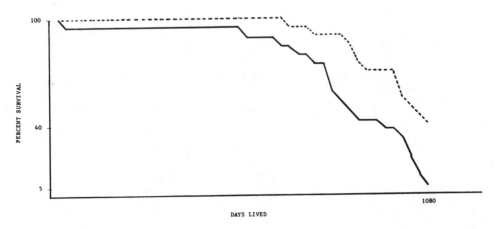

Fig. 4. Alternate-day feeding schedule increases longevity in the
CBA/H long-lived strain of mouse.

    — — — —   Fed On ALTERNATE DAYS ONLY (20 mice)
    ————————   Fed AD LIBITUM (20 mice)

phenomenon of thymic involution and argues that the T-dependent
lymphoid system is genetically programmed to decline in
effectiveness, possibly through altered endocrine and central
nervous system controls. The "thymic time clock" theory of aging
is strongly supported by the consistent finding of defective
cellular immunity functions in aged humans and animals and an
associated development of the age-related diseases.

In several animal models, including autoimmune-prone strains,
high spontaneous tumor incidence strains, and normal long-lived
strains, it has been possible to forestall the development of the
major diseases of aging and extend longevity by restricting diet.
The predominant effect of dietary restriction is prolongation of
immunologic vigor and retardation of the immunologic dysfunction
that normally occurs with age. Studies on environmental factors
affecting longevity such as these and others which demonstrate a
complex interaction between genes influencing longevity
underscore the complexity and challenge of aging research.

ACKNOWLEDGMENT

The work described in this report was supported by NIH grants
AGO 2329 and CA 06516. The authors wish to thank Ms. Linda
Williams for typing assistance.

REFERENCES

Benacerraf, B., 1981, A hypothesis to relate the specificity of T
    lymphocytes and the activity of I-region-specific Ir genes in
    macrophages and B lymphocytes, J. Immunol., 120:1809.
Dumont, F., Barrois, R., and Habberset, R.C., 1982, Prepubertal
    orchidectomy induces thymic abnormalities in aging
    (NZBxSJL)F1 male mice, J. Immunol., 129:1642.
Farr, A.G., and Sidman, C.L., 1984, Reduced expression of Ia
    antigens by thymic epithelial cells of aged mice, J. Immunol.,
    133:98.
Fernandes, G., Good, R.A., and Yunis, E.J., 1981, Responses of
    autoimmune diseases and diseases of aging to dietary
    restriction, in: "Immunological Aspects of Aging," p. 207, D.
    Segre and L. Smith, eds., Marcel Dekker, Inc., New York.
Fernandes, G., Alonso, D.R., Tanaka, T., Thaler, H.T., Yunis,
    E.J., and Good, R.A., 1983, Influence of diet on vascular
    lesions in autoimmune-prone B/W mice, Proc. Natl. Acad. Sci.
    USA, 80:874.
Germain, R.N., 1981, Specific T cell factors with MHC
    determinants, in: "The Role of the Major Histocompatibility
    Complex in Immunobiology," p. 303, M.E. Dorf, ed., Garland
    STPM Press, New York.

Good, R.A., and Yunis, E.J., 1974, Association of autoimmunity, immunodeficiency and aging in man, rabbits and mice, Fed. Proc., 33:2040.

Greenberg, L.J., and Yunis, E.J., 1975, Immunopathology of aging, Hum. Pathol., 5:122.

Greenberg, L.J., and Yunis, E.J., 1978, Genetic control of autoimmune disease and immune responsiveness and the relationship to aging, in: "Genetic Effects of Aging," p. 249, D. Bergsma and D. Harrison, eds., Alan R. Liss, Pub., New York.

Harrison, D.E., Archer, J.R., and Astle, C.M., 1982, The effect of hypophysectomy on thymic aging in mice, J. Immunol., 129:2673.

Katz, D.H., and Benacerraf, B., eds., 1976, "The Role of the Products of the Histocompatibility Gene Complex in Immune Responses," Academic Press, New York.

Kay, M.B., 1979, An overview of immune again, Mech. Ageing Dev., 9:39.

Lane, M.A., and Yunis, E.J., 1981, Nutritional alteration in aging and immune reactivity: Application of the rate-limit concept, in: "Integrated Medicine: Volume II of A Companion to the Life Sciences," p. 238, S.B. Day, ed., Van Nostrand Reinhold Company, New York.

Meredith, P.J., and Walford, R.L., 1977, Effect of age on response to T- and B-cell mitogens in mice congenic at the H-2 locus, Immunogenetics, 5:109.

Pober, J.S., Gimbrone, M.A., Cotrani, R.S., Reiss, C.S., Burakoff, S.J., Fiers, W., and Ault, K.A., 1983, Ia expression by vascular endothelium is inducible by activated T cells and by human interferon, J. Exp. Med., 157:1339.

Popp, D., 1978, Use of congenic mice to study the genetic basis of degenerative disease, in: "Genetic Effects of Aging," p. 261, D. Bergsma and D. Harrison, eds., Alan R. Liss, Pub., New York.

Roderick, T.H., and Schlager, G., 1975, Multiple factor inheritance, in: "Biology of the Laboratory Mouse," 2nd Revised Edition, p. 151, The Staff of The Jackson Laboratory, eds., Dover Publications, Inc., New York.

Russell, E.S., 1975, Lifespan and aging patterns, in: "Biology of the Laboratory Mouse," 2nd Revised Edition, p. 511, The Staff of The Jackson Laboratory, eds., Dover Publications, Inc., New York.

Sasazuki, T., Nishimura, Y., Muto, M., and Ohta, N., 1983, HLA-linked genes controlling immune response and disease susceptibility, Immunol. Rev., 70:51.

Simms, H.S., 1946, Logarithmic increase in mortality as a manifestation of aging, J. Gerontol., 1:13.

Smith G.W., and Walford, R.L., 1977, Influence of the main histocompatibility complex on aging in mice, Nature, 270:727

Tosi, P., Kraft, R., Luzi, P., Cintroino, M., Fankhauser, G.,

Hess, M.W., and Cottier, H., 1982, Involution patterns of the human thymus. I. Size of the cortical area as a function of age, Clin. Exp. Immunol., 47:497.

Williams, R.M., Kraus, L.J., Lavin, P.T., Steele, L.L., and Yunis, E.J., 1981, Genetics of survival in mice: Localization of dominant effects to subregions of the major histocompatibility complex, in "Immunological Aspects of Aging," p. 247, D. Segre and L. Smith, eds., Marcel Dekker, Inc., Pub., New York.

Yunis, E.J., Fernandes, G., Teague, P.O., Stutman, O., and Good, R.A., 1972, The thymus, autoimmunity and the involution of the lymphoid system, in: "Tolerance, Autoimmunity and Aging," p. 62, M. Siegel and R.A. Good, eds., Thomas, Springfield, IL.

Yunis, E., Shankariah, K., Watson, A.L.M., Derr, L.K., and Halberg, F., 1981, Longevity and delayed mammary carcinogenesis compatible with competing (24-hour) lighting and (48-hour) feeding schedules: internal circadian-circaduodian murine desynchronization, Int. J. Chronobiol., 7(4):154.

Yunis, E.J., Watson, A.L.M., Gelman, R.S., Sylvia, S.J., Bronson, R., and Dorf, M.E., in press, Traits that influence longevity in mice, Genetics.

Zinkernagel, R.M. and Doherty, P.C., 1979, MHC-restricted cytotoxic T cells: Studies on the biologic role of polymorphic restriction-specificity, functional and responsiveness, Adv. Immunol., 27:51.

CELLULAR SENESCENCE: FACTORS MODULATING CELL PROLIFERATION

IN VITRO

Vincent J. Cristofalo, Paul D. Phillips and
Katherine M. Brooks

The Wistar Institute of Anatomy and Biology
36th Street at Spruce
Philadelphia, Pennsylvania 19104, USA

INTRODUCTION

The characteristics of normal diploid cell proliferation are
widely used to describe in vitro models of cellular aging. In
fact, it is the predictable loss in proliferative capacity that
was first used to argue that normal human fibroblast cultures
could serve as a model system for the study of cellular aging.
Although there are many other physiological changes that occur
during the lifespan of cells in culture, the regulation of cell
proliferation remains a primary target of research in this area
of cell biology. There have been two general approaches taken in
studying the regulation and eventual loss of proliferative capacity in normal human cells in culture. They can be broadly
characterized as genetic and hormonal approaches.

GENETIC APPROACHES USED TO STUDY THE REGULATION OF CELL
PROLIFERATION

Stein and Yanishevsky (1981) have shown that entry into DNA
synthesis may be negatively controlled in both quiescent and
senescent human diploid fibroblasts. They fused either quiescent
or senescent cells to replicating cells and found that the initiation of DNA synthesis was temporarily inhibited while ongoing
DNA synthesis was unaffected. Their results suggest that both
quiescent and senescent cells possess an inhibitor to the initiation of DNA synthesis. In these studies, however, it is not
possible to determine if the quiescent and senescent cells are

blocked at the same point in the cell cycle with the quiescent
cells able to exit following an appropriate signal while the
senescent cells remain blocked.

Earlier studies involving the fusion of normal and transformed cells have contained reports of the isolation of indefinitely proliferating hybrid clones (Goldstein and Linn, 1972;
Croce and Koprowski, 1974; Stanbridge, 1976). However, Bunn and
Tarrant (1980) and Muggleton-Harris and De Simone (1980) have
shown that the majority of these isolated hybrid clones displayed
a finite proliferative capacity. In these latter studies, the
finite lifespan of most hybrid clones may have been due to the
loss of specific HeLa cell chromosomes or viral SV40 DNA. This
question was addressed directly by Pereira-Smith and Smith
(1981). They studied the proliferative potential of hybrid
clones formed from the fusion of presenescent or senescent human
cells with SV40-transformed human cells. Of the hybrid clones
isolated, 85% showed finite in vitro lifespans while 15%
displayed indefinite lifespans. Most significantly, though, all
of the hybrid clones expressed the viral T antigen. Therefore,
even though the viral genome was being expressed in all of the
hybrid clones, often the senescent phenotype was eventually
dominant.

Human cells transformed by the DNA tumor viruses SV40 and
adenovirus were able to initiate DNA synthesis in senescent
fibroblast nuclei in heterodikaryons. However, in contrast, car-
cinogen-transformed cells were unable to stimulate entry into S
phase in the senescent nuclei and, in fact, were themselves inhibited from synthesizing DNA in heterodikaryons (Stein et al.,
1982). Fusing HeLa cells (Stein, 1983) or L cells (Nette et al.,
1982) leads to DNA synthesis in the senescent nuclei of the
hybrids, heterodikaryons or cybrid fusion products.

Several groups have focused their studies on various fusions
between young and senescent cells, and the general observation is
that the young cell nuclei are inhibited from entering S phase in
such heterodikaryons. This work has now been extended to include
the inhibition of DNA synthesis in young cells fused with
cytoplasts formed from senescent cells (Drescher-Lincoln and
Smith, 1983). Furthermore, this senescent cell-dependent inhibition is sensitive to either cycloheximide or puromycin (Burmer et
al., 1982) and can be optimally blocked by cycloheximide treatment during the first 3 hr after fusion; this implies a late G1
block in senescent cells.

Several lines of evidence from our own laboratory also support a late G_1 block in senescent cells. First, we found that

the level of thymidine kinase activity in old, slowly proliferating cultures of WI-38 cells was similar to that of young, rapidly
dividing populations (Cristofalo, 1973). This anomaly raised the
possibility that senescent cells retain the ability to phosphorylate thymidine and thus are arrested in late G_1. Recently, we
found that thymidine triphosphate (TTP) synthesis is not impaired
in senescent cells (Olashaw et al., 1983). The addition of serum
to density-arrested populations of young and old cells induced
TTP synthesis to a similar extent after 12 hours in both populations. However, a far greater percentage of young cells subsequently initiated DNA synthesis as compared to old cells.
Because induction of thymidine kinase activity and TTP synthesis
are cell cycle-dependent events that normally occur in late G_1,
senescent cells might not be blocked in G_0 as are quiescent
cells. Finally, additional support for a late G_1 block comes
from examining nuclear fluorescence following staining with
quinacrine dihydrochloride (Gorman and Cristofalo, 1984). As
serum-stimulated cells traverse G_1 and reach S, the staining pattern changes from bright and homogeneous to dimmer and segregated. The fluorescence pattern of senescent cells is typical of
late G_1.

Recently, temperature-sensitive (ts) mutants of the SV40
virus have been used as probes applied to senescent cells. We
demonstrated that completely senescent populations of
BrdU-selected WI-38 cells could be made to synthesize cellular
DNA following infection with ts mutants (Gorman and Cristofalo,
1982). This result demonstrated that the cellular machinery
necessary for DNA synthesis (such as polymerases) could be activated given an appropriate signal. At this point the prime can-
didate for the role of signal is the large T antigen, since only
T antigen-positive cells incorporated [^{3}H]TdR. These observations have since been extended (Cristofalo et al., 1983, 1984)
and confirmed (Ide et al., 1983).

Collectively, these data suggest that at least some of the
pathways initiated by mitogen-cell interaction and culminated
some 12-15 hours later with the initiation of DNA synthesis are
blocked in late G_1. However, it is probable that multiple
biochemical pathways lead from mitogen stimulation to DNA synthesis and there is nothing to say that some critical one(s) may not
be blocked in early G_1.

HORMONAL APPROACHES USED TO STUDY THE REGULATION OF CELL
PROLIFERATION

Modulation of proliferative potential has been an approach
taken by several investigators in order to probe the senescence

mechanism. To date, however, once the basic nutritional requirements of the cells have been met there are only two reproducible
ways of extending proliferative capacity of human fibroblasts.
The first is by infection with a transforming virus such as SV40
and the second is by the addition of hydrocortisone (HC) or the
synthetic glucocorticoid dexamethasone (DEX) to the serum-con-
taining culture medium. In 1970, we demonstrated a 40% extension
in the proliferative capacity of WI-38 cells as well as other
fetal lung-derived fibroblasts (Cristofalo, 1970). Rosner and
Cristofalo (1981) have shown that as WI-38 cells senesce they
lose approximately 40% of their specific DEX receptors and, furthermore, that old cells are impaired in their ability to
translocate the temperature-activated, hormone-receptor complex
from the cytoplasm into the nucleus. These data are consistent
with the fact that, although chronic exposure to the glucocorticoid extends the proliferative lifespan of these cells, there
is no rescue effect produced by acute exposure and the cells
eventually become senescent.

     The interpretation of the apparent mode of action of HC or
DEX has been complicated by the work of Didinsky and Rheinwald
(1981). They studied the effects of several factors including
hydrocortisone in cultures that were passaged at low density and
never allowed to reach densities inhibit growth and promote that
cells to enter a quiescent state. Under these conditions the
glucocorticoid had no effect on proliferative lifespan. Although
the two sets of results appear contradictory, we suggested that
WI-38 cells transiently modify the medium from high to low density when subcultivated in the presence of HC or DEX with the result that the saturation density of the mass culture is increased
in a cumulative fashion across the lifespan of the cells
(Cristofalo et al., 1979). This effect appears to be mediated by
the elaboration of a low molecular weight (less than 1000
daltons), heat-stable, protease-resistant molecule (Cristofalo et
al., 1983, 1984). Since Didinsky and Rheinwald (1981) purposely
did not allow their cultures to reach high densities, the effect
was either not apparent or the medium was not modified.

     Studies dealing with the regulation of normal human cell pro-
liferation have been limited by the fact that a background of
unidentified serum mitogens is required to initiate DNA synthesis. The ill-defined nature of serum makes it difficult to study
the regulating processes involved in young cells and their
apparent failure in old cells. Several laboratories have made
important advances in this area by developing serum-free media
that support the proliferation of finite human fibroblast-like
cell lines.

Several years ago, we developed a serum-free medium which
consists of basal medium MCDB-104 supplemented with partially
purified platelet-derived growth factor (PDGF), epidermal growth
factor (EGF), insulin (INS), transferrin (TRS) and DEX (Phillips
and Cristofalo, 1980, 1981). This combination supports the proliferation of WI-38 cells at the same rate and to the same final
plateau density as medium supplemented with 10% fetal bovine
serum. Although these cells were not serially subcultivated
throughout their in vitro lifespan (7 to 10 population doublings
could be achieved), the development of such a five-component,
hormone-growth factor supplement enabled us to begin to examine
the biochemical events associated with the loss of responsiveness
to specific mitogens that characterizes senescent cells.

Ham and co-workers have developed a similar medium that supports the proliferation of another human fetal lung fibroblast-
like cell line (Walthall and Ham, 1981; Bettger et al., 1981).
In addition, Yamane et al. (1981) and Kan and Yamane (1982) have
been successful in serially passaging primary cultures of human
diploid fibroblasts from lung tissue throughout their lifespan in
a modified MEM which includes triiodothyronine, EGF, TRS, INS,
human fibronectin and 5 g/l of bovine serum albumin (BSA). The
lifespan of these cells is the same as in serum-supplemented and
serum-free medium. Although the addition of such a large amount
of BSA detracts from the defined nature of this medium, the
lifespan experiments are clearly impressive. The value of all of
these media lies in their use as tools for studying the regulation of cell proliferation.

Several laboratories have now begun systematic studies of the
responsiveness of young and senescent cells to the specific mitogens in various serum-free media formulations. We have shown
that as cultures of WI-38 cells undergo senescence they become
progressively less responsive to mitogenic stimulation; yet the
concentration of EGF, INS, TRS and DEX that elicited the maximum
proliferative response did not change as a function of age
(Phillips et al., 1984). Similar results for INS have recently
been reported by Chiger and Kaji (1983) with IMR-90 cells. In
the case of PDGF the results have been less clear cut in that
older cells may, in fact, have a shift in their dose-response
curve such that higher concentrations of mitogen are required for
a maximum proliferation response. This finding would be consistent with the data reported by Harley et al. (1981) for the
insulin-like growth factors.

Working with skin fibroblasts from newborns and adults,
Plisko and Gilchrest (1983) have demonstrated a diminished
responsiveness of adult cells to thrombin, INS and EGF alone and

in combination. These results are consistent with the donor age-associated decline in responsiveness of human skin cells to PDGF (Slayback et al., 1977) and also are consistent with the recent report that cells derived from donors of increasing age show a decreasing ability to secrete growth factors such as somatomedin-C (Clemmons, 1983).

Experiments have been designed to probe possible mechanisms which could account for the loss of growth-factor responsiveness with increasing in vitro age. In a study involving EGF, we have found that the binding and processing-degradation systems remained essentially unchanged throughout the lifespan of WI-38 cells (Phillips et al., 1983). The number of specific EGF binding sites per cell increased as the cultures age, although the number of receptors per μm of surface area remained constant. The kinetics of ligand degradation as well as the qualitative and quantitative nature of the degradation products remained essentially unchanged throughout the lifespan. Thus, the failure does not appear to be in the binding domain of the EGF receptor. The EGF receptor, like the receptors for PDGF, INS, somatomedin-C, and the transforming proteins of certain RNA tumor viruses, is a tyrosine-specific protein kinase with autophosphorylating activity. We have demonstrated that EGF receptors isolated by specific antibodies and immunoprecipitation from senescent WI-38 cells have a greatly reduced autocatalytic tyrosine kinase activity, and we have repeated this basic observation with at least four other cell lines (Carlin et al., 1983). This result suggests that tyrosine phosphorylation is essential for cell proliferation, at least in some cells. In support of this idea, Witle et al. (1980) and Rosenberg et al. (1980) have isolated transformation-defective mutants whose transforming proteins lack in vitro kinase activity. Several findings, however, argue that autophosphorylation by tyrosine kinases alone is not sufficient to elicit a proliferative response. The major tyrosine phosphorylation site (tyr-416) of pp60^{src} can be eliminated without altering the ability of the protein to phosphorylate a second internal tyrosine site as well as exogenous substrates, or to mediate cell transformation (Snyder et al. 1983). Divalent monoclonal antibodies specific for the EGF receptor inhibit binding of EGF and enhance autophosphorylation yet promote neither receptor internalization nor DNA synthesis (Schreiber et al., 1983). Phosphorylation of exogenous synthetic substrates by the EGF receptor kinase is not dependent on receptor autophosphorylation, although the two kinase activities most probably utilize a common catalytic site (Cassel et al., 1983). We can therefore speculate that autophosphorylation by growth regulatory proteins confers competence rather than commitment to proliferate.

Several mechanisms can be envisioned to account for the age-dependent diminished autophosphorylation of the EGF receptor of WI-38 cells. The activity of the catalytic site or the availability of internal tyrosine phosphorylation sites may be altered or absent in senescent cells or there may be a conformational change associated with the receptor protein in senescent cells. Whereas it is unlikely that native receptor conformation is preserved in immune complexes, there may be a tightly associated membrane component which is resistant to detergent extraction that either confers an active conformation in vitro or is an essential enzyme cofactor; absence or altered turnover of such an effector molecule might account for diminished receptor autophosphorylation in senescent cells. Alternatively, a tightly bound effector molecule that renders the inherent kinase inactive might be preferentially expressed in senescent cells. Finally, the inherent receptor kinase activity might be inactivated by an endogenous protease; in this case, production of a unique protease, enhanced expression of a constitutively produced protease, or slower regeneration of receptor kinase activity might occur in senescent cells. In any case, this reaction appears to be the first early G_0/G_1 activity that may be blocked in senescent cells. This concept is consistent with a modular G_0/G_1 progression in which multiple parallel pathways are involved from reception of the signal via hormone-receptor interactions to the initiation of DNA synthesis. For the latter to occur, all of the putative pathways would have to be complete.

The EGF receptor system appears to be even more complex than we originally believed, based on the results of a set of closely related experiments (Brooks et al., 1984). When intact plasma membranes were incubated with ^{32}P-ATP, phosphorylated, and EGF receptor solubilized and immunoprecipitated, no difference was observed in total ^{32}P incorporation between young and senescent cells. However, when the EGF receptor was solubilized and immunoprecipitated from plasma membranes and the antibody-receptor complex incubated with ^{32}P-ATP, the autophosphorylating activity of receptors from senescent cells was greatly reduced. The observable differences between these two techniques might be explained by any of several mechanisms. First, the catalytic site or the availability of tyrosine sites might be differentially altered in the senescent EGF receptor during solubilization and immunoprecipitation. Secondly, a cofactor necessary for phosphorylation may be preferentially lost in senescent cells during solubilization and immunoprecipitation. Finally, senescent cells may have increased proteolytic activity that could inactivate the receptor kinase activity upon detergent extraction prior to immunoprecipitation. Alternate interpretations may also be made. For example, we know that at least one other kinase

activity is EGF dependent in these membrane preparations and that
it phosphorylates serine and possibly tyrosine. We are currently
attempting to measure directly the EGF-receptor, tyrosine-
specific autocatlytic activity in young and old plasma membrane
preparations.

It will be of interest to determine whether diminished
autophosphorylating kinase activity is restricted to the EGF
receptors in immune complexes or is also diminished in plasma
membrane preparations, and whether other tyrosine protein kinases
are involved as part of a general phenomenon. In addition, we
are keenly interested in knowing if the senescence of WI-38 cells
is the result of diminished EGF receptor autophosphorylating
kinase activity, or its cause. Regardless, restoration of
inherent tyrosine kinase activity may be one mechanism by which
transformation is achieved in cells otherwise programmed to
senesce.

Of additional interest is the recent report by Grunberger et
al. (1984) which states that mononuclear blood cells from an
insulin-resistant patient have a defect in insulin receptor
phosphorylation when measured in the purified receptor. This
impairment was in spite of the fact that insulin binding was normal. It is interesting to speculate that the failure to
phosphorylate the EGF and the INS receptors may represent regulatory mechanisms normally expressed in aging and inappropriately
expressed in the case of insulin resistance. This study could
also represent specific examples of the modifications of
phosphoprotease and protein kinases with aging that have been
reported by Kahn et al. (1982). These changes may represent an
important regulatory mechanism integrating many physiological
responses to peptide hormones including cell proliferation and
senescence.

SUMMARY

In our view, two major areas of the investigation of the
aging process have been most fruitful over the past few years:
namely, the genetic and hormonal strategies aimed at the
understanding of in vitro cellular senescence. The genetic studies have primarily utilized cell fusion techniques and viral
probes. Along with cell cycle studies involving the induction of
thymidine kinase activity and TTP synthesis, the cell fusion studies are most consistent with a late G_1 block in senescent
cells. This effect would appear to be distinct from the
G_0 arrest of density-inhibited or mitogen-restricted cell populations.

The hormonal studies which have centered on the regulation of cell proliferation have recently focused on peptide hormones. EGF has been of particular interest since it is so well characterized. This receptor system remains largely unchanged throughout the lifespan with the notable exception of the purified receptor-associated, autocatalytic, tyrosine-specific kinase activity, which decreases with age. The functional significance of this decrease in enzyme activity is unknown, although its growth regulatory importance is implicated in several systems, and may well represent a critical early G_0/G_1 event which is absent in senescent cells.

ACKNOWLEDGMENTS

This work was supported by grants AG-00378 and AG-00097 from the National Institutes of Health.

REFERENCES

Bettger, W. J., Boyce, S. T., Walthall, B. J., and Ham, R. G., 1981, Rapid clonal growth and serial passage of human diploid fibroblasts in a lipid-enriched synthetic medium supplemented with epidermal growth factor, insulin and dexamethasone, Proc. Natl. Acad. Sci. USA, 78:5588.

Brooks, K. M., Phillips, P. D., Carlin, C.R., and Cristofalo, V. J., 1984, EGF-dependent phosphorylation of the EGF receptor in young and senescent plasma membranes isolated from WI-38 cells, J. Cell Biol., 99:414a.

Bunn, C. L., and Tarrant, G. M., 1980, Limited lifespan in somatic cell hybrids and hybrids, Exp. Cell Res., 127:385.

Burmer, G. C., Zeigler, C. J., and Norwood, T. H., 1982, Evidence for endogenous polypeptide-mediated inhibition of cell cycle transit in human diploid cells, J. Cell Biol., 94:187.

Carlin, C. R., Phillips, P. D., Knowles, B. B., and Cristofalo, V. J., 1983, Diminished in vitro tyrosine kinase activity of the EGF receptor of senescent human fibroblasts, Nature (London), 306:617.

Cassel, D., Pike, L. J., Grant, G. A., Krebs, E. G., and Glaser, L., 1983, Interaction of epidermal growth factor-dependent protein kinase with endogenous membrane proteins and soluble peptide substrates, J. Biol. Chem., 258:2945.

Chiger, J. L., and Kaji, H., 1983, The influence of insulin in the cell cycle of human aging cells, Exp. Gerontol., 18:375.

Clemmons, D. A., 1983, Age-dependent production of a competence factor by human fibroblasts, J Cell. Physiol., 114:61.

Cristofalo, V. J., 1970, Metabolic aspects of aging in diploid human cells, in: "Aging in Cell and Tissue Culture," pp. 83-119, E. Holeckova and V. J. Cristofalo, eds., Plenum Press, New York.

Cristofalo, V. J., 1973, Cellular senescence: Factors modulating cell proliferation in vitro, INSERM 27:65.

Cristofalo, V. J., Finlay, C. A., Gorman, S. D., and Phillips, P. D., 1983, Modulation of proliferative capacity as a probe of the mechanism of senescence, in: "Modern Aging Research," Vol. 3, pp. 215-232, W. Regelson and F. M. Sintex, eds., Alan R. Liss, Inc., New York.

Cristofalo, V. J., Gorman, S. D., Finlay, C., and Phillips, P. D., 1984, Loss of responsiveness to growth factors in cell senescence, in: "Meadow Brook Conference In Aging: A Biochemical Perspective," pp. 119-141, Academic Press, New York.

Cristofalo, V. J., Wallace, J. M., and Rosner, B. A., 1979, Glucocorticoid enhancement of proliferative activity in WI-38 cells, in: "Hormones and Cell Culture," pp. 875-887, B. Brook, G. H. Sato, and R. Ross, eds., Cold Spring Harbor Laboratory, New York.

Croce, C. M., and Koprowski, H., 1974, Positive control of transformed phenotype in hybrids between SV40-transformed and normal human cells, Science, 184:1288.

Didinsky, J. B., and Rheinwald, J. G., 1981, Failure of hydrocortisone or growth factors to influence the senescence of fibroblasts in a new culture system for assessing replication lifespan, J. Cell. Physiol., 109:171.

Drescher-Lincoln, C. K., and Smith, J. R., 1983, Inhibition of
     DNA synthesis in proliferating human diploid fibroblasts
     by fusion with senescent cytoplasts, Exp. Cell Res., 144:
     455.

Goldstein, S., and Lin, C. C., 1972, Rescue of senescent human
     fibroblasts by hybridization with hamster cells in vitro.
     Exp. Cell Res., 70:436.

Gorman, S. D., and Cristofalo, V. J., 1982, Reinitiation of
     cellular DNA replication in senescent WI-38 cells by
     simian virus 40, J. Cell Biol., 95:21a.

Gorman, S. D., and Cristofalo, V. J., 1984, Evidence that
     senescent WI-38 cells are blocked in late G1, In Vitro,
     20:281.

Grunberger, G., Zick, Y., and Gordon, P., 1984, Defect in
     phosphorylation of insulin receptor in cells from an
     insulin-resistant patient with normal insulin binding,
     Science, 223:932.

Harley, C. B., Goldstein, S., Posner, B. I., and Guyda, H., 1981,
     Decreased sensitivity of old and progeric human fibro-
     blasts to a preparation of factors with insulin-like acti-
     vity, J. Clin. Invest., 68:988.

Ide, T., Tsuji, Y., Ishibashi, S., and Mitsui, Y., 1983,
     Reinitiation of host DNA synthesis in senescent human
     diploid cells by infection with simian virus 40, Exp.
     Cell Res., 143:343.

Kahn, A., Meinhofer, M-C., Guillouzo, A., Cottreau, D., Baffet,
     G., Henry, J., and Dreyfus, J-C., 1982, Modifications of
     phosphoproteins and protein kinases occurring with in
     vitro aging of cultured human cells, Gerontology, 28:360.

Kan, M., and Yamane, I., 1982, In vitro proliferation and
     lifespan of human diploid fibroblasts in serum-free
     BSA-containing medium, J. Cell. Physiol., 111:155.

Muggleton-Harris, A. L., and De Simone, D. W., 1980, Replicative
     potentials of various fusion products between WI-38 and
     SV40 transformed WI-38 cells and their components, Somatic
     Cell Genet., 6:689.

Nette, E. G., Sit, H. L., and King, D. W., 1982, Reactivation of
    DNA synthesis in aging diploid human skin fibroblasts by
    fusion with mouse L karyoplasts, cytoplasts and whole L
    cells, Mech. Ageing Dev., 18:75.

Olashaw, N. E., Kress, E. D., and Cristofalo, V. J., 1983,
    Thymidine triphosphate synthesis in senescent WI-38 cells,
    Exp. Cell Res., 149:547.

Pereira-Smith, O. M., and Smith, J. R., 1981, Expression of SV40
    T antigen in finite lifespan hybrids of normal and
    SV40-transformed fibroblasts, Somatic Cell Genet., 7:411.

Phillips, P. D., and Cristofalo, V. J., 1980, A procedure for the
    serum-free growth of normal human fibroblasts, J. Tissue
    Culture Meth., 6:123.

Phillips, P. D., and Cristofalo, V. J., 1981, Growth regulation
    of WI-38 cells in a serum-free medium, Exp. Cell Res., 134:
    297.

Phillips, P. D., Kuhnle, E., and Cristofalo, V. J., 1983,
    ^{125}I-EGF binding ability is stable throughout the replica-
    tive lifespan of WI-38 cells, J. Cell. Physiol., 114:311.

Phillips, P. D., Kaji, K., and Cristofalo, V. J., 1984,
    Progressive loss of the proliferative response of
    senescing WI-38 cells to platelet-derived growth factor,
    epidermal growth factor, insulin, transferrin and dexa-
    methasone, J. Gerontol., 39:11.

Plisko, A., and Gilchrest, B. A., 1983, Growth factor respon-
    siveness of cultured human fibroblasts declines with age,
    J. Gerontol., 38:513.

Rosenberg, N., Clark, D. R., and Witte, O. N. J., 1980, Abelson
    marine leukemia virus mutants deficient in kinase activity
    and lymphoid cell transformation, J. Virol., 36:766.

Rosner, B. A., and Cristofalo, V. J., 1981, Changes in specific
    dexamethasone binding during aging in WI-38 cells,
    Endocrinology, 108:1965.

Schreiber, A. B., Libermann, T. A., Lax, I., Yarden, Y., and
    Schlessinger, J., 1983, Biological role of epidermal
    growth factor-receptor clustering, J. Biol. Chem., 258:846.

Slayback, J., Cheung, L., and Geyer, R., 1977, Comparative
     effects of human platelet growth factor on the growth and
     morphology of human fetal and adult diploid fibroblasts,
     Exp. Cell Res., 110:462.

Snyder, M. A., Bishop, J. M., Colby, W. W., and Levinson, A. D.,
     1983, Phosphorylation of tyrosine-416 is not required for
     the transforming properties of kinase activity of
     pp60^{v-src}, Cell, 32:891.

Stanbridge, E. J., 1976, Suppression of malignancy in human
     cells, Nature (London), 260:17.

Stein, G. H., and Yanishevsky, R. M., 1981, Quiescent human
     diploid cells can inhibit entry into S phase in replica-
     tive nuclei in heterodikaryons, Proc. Natl. Acad. Sci. USA,
     78:3025.

Stein, G. H., Yanishevsky, R. M., Gordon, L., and Beeson, M.,
     1982, Carcinogen-transformed human cells are inhibited
     from entry into S phase by fusion to senescent cells but
     cells transformed by DNA tumor viruses overcome the inhi-
     bition, Proc. Natl. Acad. Sci. USA, 79:5287.

Stein, G. H., 1983, Human diploid fibroblasts (HDF) can induce
     DNA synthesis in cycling HDF but not in quiescent HDF on
     senescent HDF, Exp. Cell Res., 144:468.

Walthall, B. J., and Ham, R. G., 1981, Multiplication of human
     diploid fibroblasts in a synthetic medium supplemented
     with EGF, insulin, and dexamethasone, Exp. Cell Res.,
     134:303.

Witle, O. N., Goff, S., Rosenberg, N., and Baltimore, D., 1980,
     A transformation-defective mutant of Abelson murine leuke-
     mia virus lacks protein kinase activity, Proc. Natl. Acad.
     Sci. USA, 77:4993.

Yamane, I., Kan, M., Hoshi, H., and Minamoto, Y., 1981, Primary
     culture of human diploid cells and its long-term transfer
     in a serum-free medium, Exp. Cell Res., 134:470.

CHANGES IN GENETIC ORGANIZATION AND EXPRESSION IN AGING CELLS

Samuel Goldstein, Arun Srivastava, Karl T. Riabowol
and Robert J. Shmookler Reis

4301 W. Markham, Departments of Medicine & Biochemistry
University of Arkansas for Medical Sciences and
Veterans Administration Medical Center
Little Rock, Arkansas 72205

INTRODUCTION

In this paper we review our recent studies on the human
fibroblast model of cellular aging, which illustrate how
physiological decline and certain age-dependent diseases may
develop at the cellular level. We will demonstrate that the basis
of these changes may involve a variety of alterations in genetic
structure and expression, and further, that their stochastic nature
probably accounts for the progressive individual variation that
occurs between aging persons and between their component cells.

Three main types of cells can be distinguished by their
replicative capacity in adulthood (Fig. 1):

1. _Continuous Replicators:_ These include gastrointestinal,
hematopoietic, epidermal and spermatogenic cells. Frank
insufficiencies in these systems are unusual in the elderly
although stem cell compartments undergo gradual atrophy while
residual cells show decreased replicative vigor.

2. _Intermittent Replicators:_ These cells normally undergo slow
turnover but appropriate stimuli will evoke a proliferative
response. Damage to the liver, for example, generates a
regenerative burst in surviving hepatocytes. The tissue culture
fibroblast is similiar to its _in vivo_ counterpart in that it
divides infrequently, but following "injury" (in this case,
subculture) it replicates until density-dependent inhibition occurs
in confluent monolayers. Both hepatocytes _in vivo_ and fibroblasts
in vitro show a diminishing capacity for cell division during aging
of the organism.

3. <u>Nonreplicators:</u> These cells are best exemplified by
neurons, and cardiac and skeletal muscle cells, which lose all
replicative capacity before adolescence. Hence, any stimulus for
repair is followed by hypertrophy of surviving cells, or
proliferation of non-specific stromal cells such as the fibroblast.

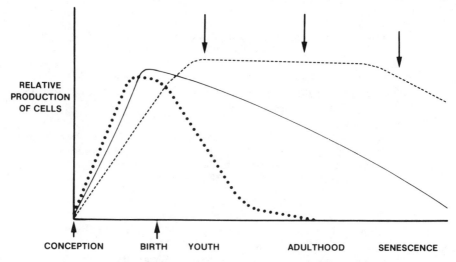

Fig.1.   Cellular replicative capacity during the human lifespan.
         Cells are classified by their replicative capacity during
         adulthood: ---- continous replicators; ⎯⎯ intermittent
         replicators; .... non-replicators; ↑ , specific events
         on a time scale that is otherwise gradual and continuous;
         ↓ , stimuli for cell division. (Reproduced with
         permission from Goldstein, 1971).

    In sum, the clear trend <u>in vivo</u> is toward decreased replicative
capacity with shrinkage of stem cell compartments in all cell
types. However, a paradoxical increase occurs in multifocal
hyperplasias leading progressively to benign and malignant
neoplasms (Martin, 1979). Juxtaposition of these extremes,
replicative senescence and re-emergence, is of great interest in
contemplating mechanisms as discussed below.

THE HUMAN FIBROBLAST MODEL OF CELLULAR AGING

    Hayflick and Moorehead (1961) first documented the limited
replicative lifespan of cultured human fibroblasts, and Hayflick
(1965) then showed that increased donor age was a negative
determinant of replicative capacity. Many studies have
subsequently confirmed and extended these observations by

demonstrating that an inverse correlation exists between the donor age and the cumulative limit of mean population doublings (MPD), a measure of the replicative lifespan (Goldstein et al., 1969; Martin et al., 1970; Schneider & Mitsui, 1976; Goldstein et al., 1978). Furthermore, fibroblasts cultured from patients with the genetically determined disorders of premature aging, progeria and Werner's Syndrome, generally have curtailed replicative lifespans (Martin et al., 1970; Goldstein, 1978; Goldstein et al., 1978; Goldstein et al., 1979). Similar growth deficits have also been demonstrated for skin fibroblasts established from individuals with Down's syndrome and other trisomies, the chromosomal breakage syndromes (inherited as autosomal recessive traits) and also with the diabetic genotype (Goldstein, 1978; Goldstein et al., 1979). In total, it is clear that biological age, the sum of genetic and environmental influences accumulated over the lifespan, rather than chronological age, is paramount in determining the longevity of each person and the replicative capacity of his cultured fibroblasts.

FIBROBLASTS POSSESS A MECHANISM WHICH COUNTS REPLICATIONS TO A LIMIT

Two related questions may be asked about the limited replicative lifespan of the fibroblast. Does it depend on: a) factors unrelated to cell division such as "metabolic time"? Or b) events directly related to cell division, e.g., DNA replication and mitosis?

Experiments on circular outgrowths (Harley & Goldstein, 1978) have confirmed and extended the evidence in favor of a replicative counter in human fibroblasts (Dell'Orco et al., 1973; Goldstein & Singal, 1974). In brief, fibroblasts were inoculated in a small drop into the center of a petri dish and incubated at 37°C. Cells first adhered then proliferated in a circular expansion such that radial growth was linear with time. Autoradiographic studies involving 3H-thymidine incorporation into DNA showed that virtually all DNA replication occurred within a small rim of cells at the circumference of the circular outgrowth. After three or four weeks growth of cells in this outer rim decreased and ultimately ceased due to senescence. The question then was whether the centrally located cells, which were density inhibited, had a greater replicative capacity remaining? Additionally, did cells at intermediate radial positions show a continuous distribution of replicative capacities? Several areas of the circular outgrowth were harvested at different radial positions (Harley & Goldstein, 1978) and subcultured as individual isolates until replicative senescence ensued. The additional number of MPD until senescence was determined for each isolate and the correlation with radial position subjected to regression analysis. The data clearly

indicated that the remaining proliferative capacity decreased
linearly with distance from the center of the outgrowth at a rate
of 1.33 ± 0.14 MPD/mm. With the knowledge that the initial MPD
level of fibroblasts used to initiate the outgrowth was 18 and that
the maximum MPD attainable in replicate cells subcultured in
parallel was 55 we could predict the number of additional MPD
accruing before senescence. This was 37 MPD for the most central
cells (r' < 5mm from the center) and 6 MPD for the most peripheral
cells at r' = 25 mm. The predicted value for the replicative
capacity remaining in cells at a given radius showed a decline of
1.55 MPD/mm, remarkably close to the experimental value of 1.33/mm.

These results confirm and extend the notion that fibroblasts
count the number of replicative events to a uniform maximum limit.
Moreover, fibroblasts in such circular outgrowths exist along a
heterogeneous but ordered scale of MPD. Thus, progressively more
vigorous "stem cells" reside at shorter radial positions and are
available for proliferative bursts. Cells at successively higher
generation levels are more abundant but proceed continuously toward
senescence not only in proliferative capacity but also in other
functions (Harley et al., 1982; Plisko & Gilchrest, 1983; Phillips
et al., 1984). Above all, the model obviates the need to invoke
stem cell immortality. Rather it indicates that proliferative
capacity of cells in specific tissues could easily exceed the
replicative needs over a "normal" lifespan, and yet in some cases
exhaustion could occur focally if not generally.

GENETIC INFORMATION IS LOST DURING CELLULAR AGING

Random elements are clearly involved (Smith & Whitney, 1980;
Shmookler Reis et al., 1980) but a largely deterministic
"programmed" mechanism, perhaps akin to differentiation, now
appears increasingly to be the basis of cellular aging (Cristofalo,
1972; Martin et al., 1974; Goldstein, 1980). If cells were to age
by a mechansim related to differentiation, we asked whether during
replicative senescence alterations occurred in the structure of
nuclear DNA, first in the 20-30% of the genome composed of
repetitive DNA sequences, then in the remainder composed of unique
(protein-coding) sequences (Saunders et al., 1972).

DEPLETION OF THE hRI FAMILY OF TANDEMLY REPEATED DNA SEQUENCES DURING FIBROBLAST AGING

When human fibroblast DNA is purified, cleaved with Eco RI
restriction endonuclease, and electrophoresed on agarose gels, two
bands are displayed at 340 and 680 base pairs (bp). These bands,
representing the human EcoRI (hRI) family of tandem repeats, were
found to be progressively depleted over the replicative lifespan

(Shmookler Reis & Goldstein, 1980). In three cell strains derived
from young normal donors the range of decrease in hRI bands was 7.5
- 23% over 17 to 27 MPD and averaged 0.62% loss per MPD. Similar
results were obtained in these cell strains by another non-
autoradiographic method of ethidium bromide staining. A third
independent method, that of saturation hybridization, revealed an
even more pronounced difference between early and late passage DNA
indicating a 50% loss over 41 MPD in one cell strain (Shmookler
Reis & Goldstein, 1980).

GENERAL LOSS OF REPETITIOUS SEQUENCES DURING CELLULAR AGING

     Kinetic analysis of early and late-passage fibroblast DNA,
(Shmookler Reis & Goldstein, 1980) revealed that those DNA
sequences reassociating most rapidly, at Cot values of 0.05 or less
(implying at least 10^5 copies), were depleted by about 24% at
late-passage, compared to early passage cells (Fig. 2). At Cot
values higher than 1, primarily representing unique sequences,
$Cot_{\frac{1}{2}} \simeq 5000$, reassociation curves converged and could no longer be
distinguished. It is difficult to ascertain the repetition
frequency of the depleted sequences but at low Cot values
significant differences between early and late passage DNA were
reproducible. Other studies (Shmookler Reis & Goldstein, 1982a)
have demonstrated that three other discrete highly repetitive
sequences characterized as bands of 45, 110 and 175 base pairs
generated by the restriction endonuclease Msp I, also diminished in
the same three normal strains of fibroblasts at late passage.

     We carefully considered other explanations for the apparent
loss of highly reiterated DNA sequences during fibroblast aging.
DNA divergence and base modification were ruled out by examining
analysis of cytosine methylation, respectively (Shmookler Reis &
Goldstein, 1980 ; 1982a). A third possiblity, arrest in the
S phase of the cell cycle, would lead to non-replication of the
specific repetitive DNA sequences if they were indeed late
replicating but this mechanism was rendered unlikely by analysis of
published data (Macieira-Coelho et al., 1966; Macieira-Coelho,
1977; Yanishevsky et al., 1974). A fourth possibility, that
chromosomes were lost, either intact or as segments which contain
the specific reiterated sequences, was excluded by karyotypic
analysis using chromosome banding techniques (Shmookler Reis &
Goldstein, 1980). We conclude, therefore, that a fraction of
repeated sequences in late-passage cells have been deleted either
by unequal recombination (Harley et al., 1982) or excision (see
below). However, such DNA rearrangements which lead to the loss of
highly repetitious sequences would be most common among such
sequences but would be difficult to identify individually because
comprises > 3 x 10 copies/haploid genome (Manuelidis & Wu, 1978),
and the Alu repeat family consists of over 5 x 10^5 dispersed

throughout each haploid genome (Schmid & Jelinek, 1982). Thus,
identification of the mechanisms by which DNA is rearranged poses a
formidable problem.

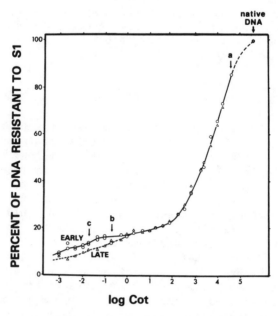

Fig. 2. Reassociation kinetics of ^{14}C-DNA from A2 fibroblasts at
early ○ or late passage △ . Following reassociation
double-stranded DNA duplexes were assayed by their
resistance to S1 nuclease. Arrows at a, b, c indicate
Cots of 40000, 0.2 and 0.02, respectively. "Native DNA"
indicates S1 resistance of sonicated native DNA that was
not denatured and reassociated. (Reproduced with
permission from Shmookler Reis and Goldstein, 1980).

EXTRACHROMOSOMAL CIRCULAR DNAS IN AGING CELLS

We have recently demonstrated that molecules of covalently
closed circular DNA (cccDNA) accumulate in aging cells (Shmookler
Reis et al., 1983). These are clearly not derived from
mitochondrial DNA, itself a cccDNA molecule af 16.5 kb (Shmookler
Reis & Goldstein, 1983). Indeed, the cccDNA population is turning
out to be a heterogeneous population in both size and sequence
(Riabowol et al., 1984 a & b). Our recent studies involve
molecular cloning into the plasmid vector pBR322 of cccDNA
molecules isolated from late-passage fibroblasts and lymphocytes of
elderly persons. Early results indicate substantial representation
of the Alu family as well as KpnI , another family of interspersed

repetitive sequences ($\approx 5 \times 10^4$/haploid genome). Most
interestingly, the coexistence in circular DNA of Alu and Kpn
homologous sequences has been found to be over three times more
frequent than expected from the product of their individual genomic
frequencies. This strongly suggests that juxtaposition of KpnI and
AluI repeats confers on these DNA segments an enhanced propensity
for excision or that extrachromosomal replication once excised.

AMPLIFICATION OF THE C-HA-RAS PROTO-ONCOGENE AND ITS PRODUCTS
DURING FIBROBLAST AGING

While amplification and enhanced expression of cellular
oncogenes are frequently associated with cancers and tumor-derived
cell lines, these genes are likely to play a normal role in
regulating cell growth (Bishop, 1983). The proto-oncogene
c-Ha-ras-1 provides an excellent model for other human
proto-oncogenes in our study (Srivastava et al., 1984) since it
belongs to the well characterized ras gene family, and activated
ras genes have been found in a wide variety of transformed cell
lines, solid tumors and hematopoietic malignancies derived from all
three primary germ layers (Bishop, 1983).

DNA was isolated from seven normal human fibroblast strains
during replicative senescence and restriction fragments hybridizing
to ^{32}P-labeled probe (Shih & Weinberg, 1982) were analyzed on
"Southern blots". In each case the probe detected the predominant
allele of the c-Ha-ras-1 proto-oncogene within a 6.6 kb band
(Srivastava et al., 1984). Strikingly, the intensity of this band
was two-to four-fold greater at late passage than at early passage
in all fibroblast strains examined, indicating that amplification
of the c-Ha-ras-1 proto-oncogene had occurred during protracted
replication. When DNA samples were probed for other genes such as
the alpha subunit of human chorionic gonadotropin (alpha-hCG) and
alpha- and gamma-globins they showed no significant change in
hybridization intensity with increasing passage.

Donor age correlated poorly with Ha-ras gene hybridization
intensity, after allowing for the variable passage level between
cell strains. This is depicted in Fig. 3, where the intensities of
hybridization signals are plotted as a function of passage level.
The straight line describing the direct correlation between
c-Ha-ras-1 hybridization intensity and replicative age in vitro was
highly significant ($r = 0.937$, $p < 10^{-4}$) in contrast to the line
correlating alpha-hCG hybridization signals and replicative age.

When ^{32}P-c-Ha-ras-1 was hybridized to polyadenylated RNA from
fibroblast strains at early and late passage, two major RNA species
were detected, at 5.1 and 1.2 kb. These are presumed to be the
c-Ha-ras-1 initial transcript and mature mRNA respectively, as

reported previously (Parada et al., 1982). Levels of c-Ha-ras-1
mRNA were increased by at least four-fold at late passage, in
proportion to the amplified number of <u>ras</u> genes observed in these
cell strains (Fig. 3). In contrast, mRNA-length transcripts from
the gene encoding, the enzyme hypoxanthine guanine
phosphoribosyltransferase, probed on the same filters, showed no
increase at late passage.

    Normal human fibroblasts contain low levels of a 21 kd protein
(p21 <u>ras</u>) encoded by the c-Ha-ras-1 proto-oncogene (Chang et al.,
1982). When cell proteins were biosynthetically labeled,
immunoprecipitated with a specific monoclonal antibody, and
analyzed by SDS-polyacrylamide gel electrophoresis, we found that
synthesis of p21 protein was augmented at late passage over

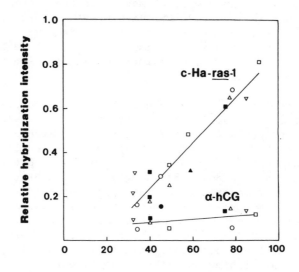

Percent lifespan completed

Fig. 3. Hybridization intensity of human fibroblast DNA to
         c-Ha-ras-1 and alpha-hCG DNA probes correlated to
         percent of maximal fibroblast lifespan completed.
         Autoradiographs were scanned with a microdensito-
         meter and integrated areas under band peaks plotted
         against the percentage of maximal <u>in vitro</u> lifespan
         completed at the time of DNA preparation. Symbols
         represent individual strains (Reproduced with
         permission from Srivastava et al., 1984).

two-fold. This indicates that a passage-dependent enhancement of
p21 <u>ras</u> protein synthesis occurs in these diploid human cells.

GENOMIC PLASTICITY IN HUMAN FIBROBLASTS: IMPLICATIONS FOR
DEVELOPMENT, AGING AND AGE-DEPENDENT DISEASES

The studies reviewed here support the idea of genomic
plasticity in human somatic cells, while also revealing
correlations with cellular aging. Apart from the striking
rearrangements during immunoglublin gene ontogeny (Leder, 1982),
there has been no evidence so far that DNA rearrangements are
involved in other developmental processes. Nonetheless, it is
possible that subtle gene rearrangements occur, leading to
irreversible commitment of somatic cells to a given line of gene
expression with reciprocal loss of totipotent function. Aging of
somatic cells may proceed along similar lines of terminal
differentiation with progressive restriction of options (Goldstein
& Shmookler Reis, 1984). This would best fit a deterministic
molecular mechanism, e.g. a fraction of DNA sequences from the
highly reiterated hRI , AluI ,and KpnI families might be excised
and/or rearranged in the genome. This would lead to progressive
diminution in the functions they subserve, e.g. initiation of DNA
replication for Alu sequences (Schmid & Jelinek, 1982), mitotic
regulation for centromeric arrays such as hRI (Walker, 1971), and
perhaps a protein-coding role for KpnI sequences (Martin et al.,
1984). This could be relevant to the "countdown" toward the
replicative limit of fibroblasts and other continuously or
intermittently mitotic cells in vitro and in vivo. The appearance
of such DNA elements as extrachromosomal circles with the potential
to undergo autonomous replication may enable them to compete for
limiting replicative factors, or ultimately to be re-introduced
into the genome. The latter potential might favor the likelihood
of random, aberrant insertions within a rare cell (rare in
proportion to the vast number of somatic cells) leading to abnormal
DNA replication. Such an occurrence, if combined with the
proliferative impetus generated by amplification and overexpression
of the c-Ha-ras proto-oncogene, could endow the cell with a
selective growth advantage. Such events may indeed predispose to
the focal hyperplasias of aging (Martin, 1979), and trigger
malignant transformation in rare clones within these foci. But
this randomness predicts that variability between tissues and
between persons will increase, thus accounting for the
age-dependent rise in variance for any given physiologic or
pathologic parameter (Kohn, 1971).

Other mechanisms will undoubtedly prove to be involved in
senescence beacuse of the many steps involved in regulating gene
expression (Goldstein & Shmookler Reis, 1984). For example, there
is imperfect transmission of DNA methylation patterns from cell
generation to generation, particularly in the vicinity of unique
genes which code for specific proteins (Shmookler Reis & Goldstein,
1982 a & b), and differing notably from one clonal lineage to
another (Goldstein & Shmookler Reis, in preparation). If gene

methylation is important in repressing genes (Razin & Riggs, 1980) then demethylation may often lead to leaky expression of previously silent genes in individual clones. Studies now underway should yield further insights into the nature of genetic changes during cellular aging and their relationship to differentiation and age-dependent diseases such as cancer.

REFERENCES

Bishop, J. M., 1983, Cellular oncogenes and retrovirus, Ann. Rev. Biochem ., 52:301-354.

Chang, E.H., Furth, M.E., Scolnick, E.M., and Lowry, D.R., 1982, Tumorigenic transformation of mammalian cells induced by a normal human gene homologous to the oncogene of Harvey Murine Sarcoma virus, Nature London, 4: 479-483.

Cristofalo, V., 1972, Animal cell cultures as a model system for the study of aging, Adv. Gerontol. Res ., 4:45-79.

Dell'Orco, R.T., Mertens, J.G. and Kruse, Jr. P.F., 1973, Doubling potential calendar time, and senescence of human dipolid cells in culture, Exp. Cell. Res ., 77:356-360.

Goldstein, S. 1971, The Biology of Aging, N. Engl. J. Med ., 285:1120-1129.

Goldstein, S. 1978, Human genetic disorders which feature accelerated aging, in : "The Genetics of Aging," E.L. Schneider, ed., Plenum Press, New York. pp. 171-224.

Goldstein, S. 1980. Do we differentiate ourselves to death?, Cell ., 20:571-573.

Goldstein, S. and Shmookler Reis, R.J., 1984, Genetic modifications in cellular aging, Mol. Cell. Biochem., 64:15-30.

Goldstein, S., Littlefield, J.W., and Soeldner, J.S., 1969, Diabetes mellitus and aging: Diminished plating efficiency of cultured human fibroblasts, Proc. Natl. Acad. Sci ., 64:155-160.

Goldstein, S., Moerman, E.J., Soeldner, J.S., Gleason, R.E., and Barnett, D.M., 1978, Chronologic and physiologic age affect replicative lifespan of fibroblasts from diabetic, prediabetic and normal donors, Science , 199:781-782.

Goldstein, S., Moerman, E.J., Soeldner, J.S., Gleason, R.E., and Barnett, D.M., 1979, Diabetes mellitus and genetic prediabetes: Decreased replicative capacity of cultured skin fibroblasts, J. Clin. Invest ., 63:358-370.

Goldstein, S. and Singal, D.P., 1974, Senescence of cultured human fibroblasts: mitotic versus metabolic time, Exp. Cell. Res ., 88:359-364.

Harley, C.B. and Goldstein, S., 1978, Cultured human fibroblasts: Distribution of cell generations and a critical limit, J. Cell. Physiol ., 97:509-516.

Harley, C.B., Shmookler Reis, R.J., and Goldstein, S., 1982, Loss of repetitious DNA in proliferating somatic cells may be

due to unequal recombination, J. Theoret. Biol .,
94:1-12.

Hayflick, L., and Moorehead, P.S., 1961, The serial cultivation
of human diploid cell strains, Exp. Cell. Res.,
25:585-621.

Hayflick, L., 1965, The limited in vitro lifetime of human
diploid cell strains, Exp. Cell. Res., 37:614-636.

Kohn, R.R., 1971, Diseases and aging, in: "Principles of
Mammalian Aging" pp. 110-119, Prentice-Hall Inc., New
Jersey.

Leder, P., 1982, The genetics of antibody diversity. Sci. Am.
246:102-115.

Macieira-Coelho, A., Ponten, J., and Philipson, L., 1966, The
division cycle and RNA synthesis in diploid human cells
at different passage levels in vitro, Exp. Cell Res .,
42:673-684.

Macieira-Coelho, A., 1977, Kinetics of the proliferation of human
fibroblasts during their lifespan in vitro, Mech. Ageing
Dev ., 6:341-343.

Manuelidis, L., and Wu, J.C., 1978, Homology between human and
simian repeated DNA, Nature London, 276:92-94.

Martin, G.M., 1979, Proliferative homeostasis and its age-related
aberrations, Mech. Ageing Dev ., 9:385-391.

Martin, G.M., Sprague, C.A., and Epstein, C.J., 1970, Replicative
lifespan of cultivated human cell. Effects of donor's
age, tissue and genotype, Lab. Invest ., 23:86-92.

Martin, G.M., Sprague, C.A., Norwood, T.H., and Pendergrass,
W.R., 1974, Clonal selection, attenuation and
differentiation in an in vitro model of hyperplasia,
Am.J. Path ., 74:137.

Martin, S.L., Voliva, C.F., Burton, F.H., Edgell, M.H., and
Hutchinson, C.A. III., 1984, A large interspersed repeat
found in mouse DNA contains a long open reading frame
that evolves as if it encodes a protein, Proc. Natl.
Acad. Sci ., 81: 2308.

Parada, L.F., Tabin, C.J., Shih, C., and Weinbert, R.A., 1982,
Human EJ bladder carcinoma oncogene is homologic of Harvey
Sarcoma virus RAS gene, Nature London, 297:474-478.

Phillips, P.D., Kaji, K., and Cristofalo, V.J., 1984, Progressive
loss of the proliferative response of senescing WI-38
cells to platelet-derived growth factor, epidermal growth
factor, insulin, transferrin, and Dexamethasone, J.
Gerontol ., 39:11-17.

Plisko, A., and Gilchrest, B.A., 1983, Growth factor
responsiveness of cultured human fibroblasts declines
with age, J. Gerontol ., 35:513-518.

Razin, A., and Riggs, A.D., 1980, DNA methylation and gene
function, Science ., 210:604-610.

Riabowol, K.T., Shmookler Reis, R.J., and Goldstein, S., 1984 a,
Extrachromosomal covalently closed circular DNA of human

diploid fibroblasts: cloning and initial
characterization, Submitted, <u>Mol. and Cell. Biology</u> .

Riabowol, K.T., Goldstein, S., and Shmookler Reis, R.J., 1984 b,
Extrachromosomal nuclear cccDNA clones from human
lymphocytes are homologous to the putatively mobile
HindIII-KpnI repetitive sequence family, 1984 U.C.L.A.
Symposium on Molecular and Cellular Biology, Steamboat
Springs, Colorado, USA., <u>J. Cell. Biochem</u> ., Suppl.
8B:139.

Saunders, G.F., Shigeru, S., Saunders, P.P., Arrighi, F.E., and
Hsu, T.C., 1972, Populations of repeated DNA sequences in
the human genome, <u>J. Mol. Biol</u> ., 63:323-334.

Schmid, C.W., and Jelinek, W.R., 1982, The Alu family of
dispersed repetitive sequences, <u>Science</u> ,
216:1065-1070.

Schneider, E.L., and Mitsui, Y., 1976, The relationship between
in vitro cellular aging and in vivo human age, <u>Proc.
Natl. Acad. Sci</u> ., 73:3584-3588.

Shih, C., and Weinbert, R.A., 1982, Isolation of a transforming
sequence for a human bladder carcinoma line, <u>Cell</u> ,
29:161-169.

Shmookler Reis, R.J., and Goldstein, S., 1980, Loss of reiterated
DNA sequences during serial passages of human diploid
fibroblasts in vitro, <u>Cell</u> , 21:739-749.

Shmookler Reis, R.J., and Goldstein, S., 1982 a, Variability of
DNA methylation patterns during serial passage of human
diploid fibroblasts, <u>Proc. Natl. Acad. Sci</u> ., USA,
79:3949-3953.

Shmookler Reis, R.J., and Goldstein, S., 1982 b, Interclonal
variation in methylation patterns for expressed and
non-expressed genes, <u>Nucleic Acids. Res</u> ., 10:4293-4304.

Shmookler Reis, R.J., and Goldstein, S., 1983, Mitochondrial DNA
in mortal and immortal human cells, <u>J. Biol. Chem</u> .,
258:9078-9085.

Shmookler Reis, R.J., Goldstein, S., and Harley, C.B., 1980, Is
cellular aging a stochastic process? <u>Mech. Ageing Dev</u> .,
13:393-395.

Shmookler Reis, R.J., Lumpkin, C.K., McGill, J.R., Riabowol,
K.T., and Goldstein, S., 1983, Extrachromosomal circular
copies of an Inter-Alu unstable sequence in human DNA are
amplified during in vitro and in vivo ageing, <u>Nature
London,</u> 301:394-398.

Smith, J.R., and Whitney, R.G., 1980, Interclonal variation in
proliferative potential of human diploid fibroblasts:
stochastic mechanism for cellular aging, <u>Science</u> ,
207:82-84.

Srivastava, A., Norris, J.S., Shmookler Reis, R.J., and Goldstein, S., 1984, c-Ha-ras-1 proto-oncogene is amplified
and overexpressed in normal human fibroblasts during replicative senescence in vitro, Submitted <u>J. Biol. Chem.</u>,

Walker, P.M.B., 1971 "Repetitive" DNA in higher organisms, <u>Prog. Biophys. Mol. Biol</u> ., 23:145-190.

Yanishevsky, R., Mendelsohn, M.L., Mayall, B.H., and Cristofalo, V., 1974, Proliferative capacity and DNA content of aging human diploid cells in culture: a cytophotometric and autoradiographic analysis, <u>J. Cell Physiol</u> ., 84:165-170.

THE SIGNIFICANCE OF DNA METHYLATION IN CELLULAR AGING

Robin Holliday

Genetics Division
National Institute for Medical Research
The Ridgeway, Mill Hill
London NW7 1AA, UK

INTRODUCTION

Primary cultures of diploid fibroblasts give rise to populations which have limited growth potential. In the case of human cells, their in vitro life span is usually in the range of 50-70 population doublings (Hayflick, 1965; 1977; Holliday et al., 1977). In spite of strong selective pressure when growth slows down and finally ceases, permanent lines do not emerge from these populations. Diploid rodent cultures have a much shorter in vitro life span, and permanent lines, exemplified by the mouse 3T3 strain, often take over the culture (Todaro and Green, 1963).

It has often been suggested that the limited life span of cultured fibroblasts is due to the accumulation of errors or defects in macromolecules. The first proposal was that genetic defects could often arise in diploid cells without any initial outward effect, but with time multiple mutations or hits would have progressively severe effects on the phenotype of the cells, and lead ultimately to their demise (Hayflick, 1965). However, when this theory is made quantitative on the basis of simple assumptions, it can be shown that it is very hard to reconcile with existing experimental observations. In particular, the recessive mutation or hit rate has to be very high, and the loss of cell viability throughout in vitro growth would have to be much greater than is actually observed (Holliday and Kirkwood, 1981). The second possibility is that errors in protein molecules progressively accumulate during serial subculture of diploid cells (Holliday and Tarrant, 1972; Orgel, 1973). In particular, the possibility exists that a low initial frequency of errors leads by positive feedback, or error propagation, to an ever increasing level of alterations in the primary structure of proteins, which eventually becomes incompatible with further growth (Orgel, 1963; 1970; Kirkwood, 1980). This theory has proved to be much harder to test experimentally than was initially thought and the evidence for and against is conflicting (for recent reviews, see Kirkwood et al., 1984; Holliday, 1984).

A third possibility is that errors arise during cell division in the control of gene expression. Cutler (1982a,b) has discussed this possibility, which he refers to as "dysdifferentiation" associated with aging. Until recently, there were few clues as to the possible molecular basis of the epigenetic control of gene expression in differentiated cells. However, in the last few years evidence has accumulated that the methylation of cytosine in DNA may provide a basis for such controls in higher organisms. This paper assesses the possible significance of defects or errors in the pattern of DNA methylation in bringing about the changes associated with aging in vitro, and also in vivo.

HERITABILITY OF THE PATTERN OF DNA METHYLATION

In higher organisms the major base modification is the methylation of cytosine in CpG doublets. By itself, this obviously provides little specificity in possible interactions between modified or non-modified cytosines in DNA and proteins involved in the regulation of gene expression. The theory that the control of gene activity during development is in part based on DNA methylation, depends on the assumption that specific sequences containing 5-methyl cytosine (5-mC) provide the essential epigenetic information. Thus, only a small subset of all 5-mC may be important for developmental pathways and the control of gene expression, the rest having some other function. It was independently pointed out by Holliday and Pugh (1975) and Riggs (1975) that the theory must have two basic features. Firstly, the pattern of methylation must be changed in given cell lineages by switch mechanisms, based on the transient activities of enzymes, which remove or add methyl groups at specific sequences in DNA. Secondly, the pattern established by such switch mechanisms must often be heritable owing to the existence of a maintenance methylase. Such an enzyme would recognise hemi-methylated DNA at the replication fork and add methyl groups to the nascent strands: it would not recognise non-methylated DNA as a substrate. The spectrum of gene activities in specialised cells is clearly heritable and often very stable. The accurate maintenance of methylated or non-methylated states for controlling sequences adjacent to structural genes could provide a basis for such heritability and stability.

The accumulating evidence that methylation is associated with the control and transcription, X-chromosome inactivation and differentiation, has recently been reviewed by Doerfler (1981; 1983), Riggs and Jones (1984) and Gartler and Riggs (1983). It is clear from many of these experiments that gene activity is associated with hypo-methylation of DNA sequences. In some of the experiments the analogues, 5-azacytidine (azaC) or 5-azadeoxycytidine (azadC), have been used to activate transcriptionally silent genes, or to alter cellular differentiation (Jones and Taylor, 1982). This activity appears to be due to the potent inhibition of DNA methylation during DNA synthesis (Jones and Taylor, 1981; Creusot et al., 1982; Taylor and Jones, 1984). A particularly clear-cut example of the effect of azaC comes from experiments with the gene coding for thymidine kinase (TK). TK^- variants are very stable during normal growth, but can be reverted to TK^+ at frequencies as high as 10% after a single treatment with azaC (Harris, 1982). Such reversions occur only at low frequency after treatment with potent mutagens and it therefore seems very likely that the activation of the TK^- gene is due to the removal of methyl groups. Evidence has been obtained that this is the case for the Herpes TK^- gene integrated into mouse chromosomal DNA when it is activated by azaC (Clough et al., 1982). Although the pattern of DNA methylation is maintained in somatic cells, it appears that embryonic and teratocarcinoma cells are capable of de novo methylation (Jahner et al., 1982; Stewart et al., 1982), that is, they appear to have the ability to methylate regions of DNA which were previously hypo-methylated.

LOSS OF METHYL GROUPS IN DNA

An enzymic mechanism for the maintenance of the pattern of DNA methylation in somatic cells also implies that there is a finite probability that any given methyl group would be lost during cell division. Methyl groups at individual sites could be lost in several ways: i) The maintenance enzyme may be less than 100% efficient. ii) Spontaneous or induced damage to DNA may inhibit its activity (Wilson and Jones, 1983a). iii) Damage to DNA near the replication fork followed by excision repair, would result in the formation of a non-methylated daughter molecule (Holliday, 1979). iv) A single short azaC treatment can result in the permanent loss of DNA methylation, which suggests that the maintenance methylase acts at the replication fork, but not at other times during the cell cycle. It is therefore possible that the enzyme requires a free end of DNA to which it first binds, before acting processively on hemi-methylated sites in newly

synthesised double-stranded DNA. Agents which introduce single-
stranded gaps in DNA, such as x-rays, may have the special
property of inhibiting normal methylation by "titrating out" the
enzyme (see below). v) The methylation of DNA is mediated by S-
adenosyl methionine. Thus, any treatment which inhibits its
formation, such as ethionine, may lead to a loss of methyl
groups.

CELLULAR AGING AND THE LOSS OF METHYLATION

     Wilson and Jones (1983b) measured the levels of 5-mC in the
DNA of diploid mouse, Syrian hamster and human fibroblasts during
serial subculture. They found that there was a progressive
decline in 5-mC which was fastest in mouse cells, intermediate
for hamster and slowest for human cells. This correlates with
the short in vitro life span of mouse cells, the intermediate
life span of hamster cells and the long life span of human cells.
Permanent lines examined, including 3T3 and 10T½, maintained a
constant level of DNA methylation during serial subculture.

     Experiments have been carried out on the human fibroblast
strain MRC-5, on the effect of a single azaC treatment on its
subsequent in vitro life span. The results are clear-cut: a
single pulse treatment has a very significant life-shortening
effect (Fig.1, Table 1). Sequential treatments with lower doses
have an even greater effect in limiting growth potential (Fig.2,
Table 1). Although treatments with azaC initially inhibited
growth, cells usually returned to a cumulative growth rate which
is the same as the control (Fig.1). The final reduction in life
span cannot be explained by the elimination of a major proportion
of cycling cells by azaC. Instead, the results are fully
consistent with the possibility that a significant reduction of
methylation induced by azaC is followed by a further decline in
the absence of the analogue, until the level is reached which is
incompatible with further growth. The results obtained by
Schmookler Reis and Goldstein (1982) on DNA methylation in human
fibroblasts using labelled probes and the restriction enzymes
HpaII and MspI are rather ambiguous. However, in more cases than
not, in vitro aging was associated with the reduction in
methylation.

     It was shown many years ago that the in vitro life span of
human cells was based on the number of cell divisions, rather
than on chronological time (Hayflick, 1965). Also, cells frozen
in liquid nitrogen appear to maintain indefinitely their
population doubling level, that is, their ability to proliferate
for a further given number of doublings remains unchanged. These
observations are compatible with the concept of a "methylation

Table 1. Effect of pulse treatments with azacytidine (azaC) on the life span of MRC-5

	azaC treatment	Passage level	Final life span (Population doublings)	Reduction
Expt. 1.	Control	–	63.2	–
	2 µg/ml	12	42.3	20.9
	5 µg/ml	12	53.5	9.7
Expt. 2.	Control	–	58.3	–
	2 µg/ml	12	48.7	9.6
	5 µg/ml	12	50.6	7.7
	2x1 µg/ml	21,23	46.4	11.9
	3x1 µg/ml	21,23,25	40.6	17.7

For the methods used, see legend to Fig.1.

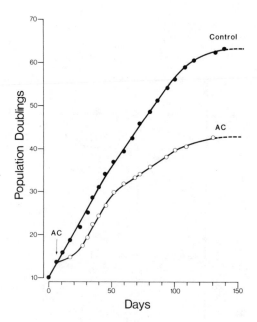

Fig.1.   Cumulative growth curves for foetal lung fibroblast
    strain MRC-5.   The experiment was started with cells defrosted at
    passage 10, which were subsequently sub-cultured in Eagle's
    minimal essential medium (F15, Gibco), supplemented with 10%
    foetal calf serum, 2mM glutamine, antibiotics (100 units
    penicillin and 100µg streptomycin/ml) and 1% non-essential amino
    acids (Gibco), using the method previously described (Holliday et
    al., 1977).   At the time indicated by the arrow, 2µg/ml (8.2µM)
    5-azacytidine was added to one culture (AC) one day after the
    flasks were seeded with trypsinized cells.   Subsequently the
    cells were passaged in normal medium.   Cultures were terminated
    when no cell growth occurred after two to three changes of medium
    at weekly intervals.

clock".   During cell division there is a given probability of
losing methyl groups which is species-specific, and when a given
number have been lost, cell division is no longer possible. The
loss of methylation may be associated with the activation of
genes which are normally silent in fibroblasts, and such
activation may have progressively deleterious effects (see
below).

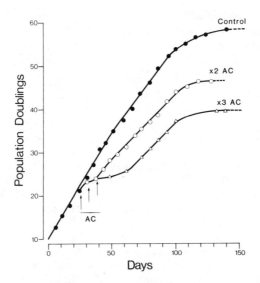

Fig.2. Cumulative growth curves for MRC-5 cells treated with
1μg/ml (4.1μgM) azacytidine (azaC), in 2 or 3 sequential cultures
(x2AC, x3AC). In each case the azaC was added one day after the
cultures were set up with trypsinized cells.

DNA METHYLATION AND AGING <u>IN VIVO</u>

Evidence has been obtained that the inactive X-chromosome in
mammalian cells can be reactivated by azaC or azadC (Mahondas et
al., 1981; Graves, 1982). The possible loss of methylation
during aging immediately suggests an explanation for the very
interesting observations of Cattanach (1974) on X-chromosome
reactivation in mice. It is known that autosomal DNA inserted
into an inactive X-chromosome is often itself inactivated. In
Cattanach's insertional translocation, this inactivation can be
demonstrated, for example, with the tyrosinase wild-type allele,
since it produces an albino phenotype. It is remarkable that as
the animals age, the degree of inactivation declines in the
translocated segment and the animals become progressively more
pigmented. The cells producing colour pigment are continually
dividing, so the finding can be explained if X-chromosome
inactivation and the spreading of inactivation into autosomal DNA
is due to cytosine methylation at particular sites (see Gartler
and Riggs, 1983), and that this methylation declines with age.

More direct evidence comes from the study of intracisternal
A particle sequences in mice by Mays-Hoopes et al (1983). Using
radioactive probes and Msp I and Hpa II digestion of genomic DNA,
they found that the level of methylation decreased about 5-fold
between 6 month and 26 month old animals.

MUTATIONS, EPIMUTATIONS AND AGING

It is important to clearly distinguish the differences
between mutations and epigenetic changes in gene activity. A
mutation is a change in DNA base sequence, whether by base
substitution, insertion or deletion, or re-arrangement.
Alteration in the heritable pattern of DNA methylation involves
no change in base sequence. I propose that such alterations
should be referred to as epimutations, because their phenotypic
effects will be on epigenetic processes, such as the control of
gene expression during development. Epimutations can be induced
by treatments affecting DNA methylation, such as azaC, and often
at very high frequency (Harris, 1982; Clough et al., 1982). I
have also proposed that one of the roles of meiosis in higher
organisms is to remove epigenetic defects as part of a
reprogramming mechanism, and that genetic recombination plays an
essential role in this process (Holliday, 1984).

It has long been known that whole-body X-ray treatment leads
to a reduction in life span (Neary, 1960). The evidence that
this is associated with accelerating aging is compelling (Lindop
and Rotblat, 1960), and the results have often been cited as
support for the somatic mutation theory of aging (Szilard, 1959;
Curtis, 1966; Burnet, 1974). However, there are several reasons
for believing that somatic mutation is not the primary cause of
aging (Maynard Smith, 1959, 1962; Holliday and Kirkwood, 1981),
and it is therefore possible that the effect of X-rays is due to
the introduction of epigenetic defects in somatic cells.
Evidence that X-rays can induce heritable changes at very high
frequency comes from the experiments of Kennedy et al, (1981).
They found that clones arising from irradiated cells were more
often than not predisposed to produce transformed derivatives,
whereas clones from unirradiated cells produced no transformants.
The X-ray treatment used would have introduced several thousand
single-strand breaks per genome, and as previously suggested,
this may inhibit DNA methylase activity and lead to the loss of
5-mc at a significant number of sites.

Epimutations would differ from normal mutations in several
important ways. For instance, they would affect the level of
gene expression, rather than the integrity of coding sequences.
Epimutations leading to the activation of genes would often be

dominant, although the phenotypic effect of producing an
"illegitimate" protein may be much less than the inactivation of
an important gene by mutation. Genes which are inactive in
somatic cells may have a cluster, rather than just one 5-mC in an
adjacent controlling region. If this is so, then the expression
of the phenotypic effect would depend on the sequential loss of
several methyl groups. Therefore there could be silent
epigenetic defects which only produce a deleterious phenotype in
combination with other such defects. The changes associated with
aging do not appear to occur at a steady rate throughout the life
span. Instead, they accumulate more and more rapidly as the end
of the normal life span is reached (Sacher, 1978; Hayflick, 1977;
Holliday, 1984). A multiplicity of phenotypic effects can be
accounted for by a multi-step mechanism, with more than additive
interactions between individual small defects.

TRANSFORMATION OF DIPLOID CELLS TO PERMANENT LINES

        There are striking differences between the frequency of
transformation of human cells and rodent cells. Human cells can
be transformed with difficulty using SV40 virus (Huschtscha and
Holliday, 1983) and there are few, if any, substantiated reports
of transformation by carcinogens. In experiments with SV40, the
first event is the production of cells with many of the
properties of transformation (such as growth in soft agar, loss
of contact-inhibition and an unstable karyotype). However, these
populations invariably enter a "crisis", which may be the same as
senescence of diploid cells, and most frequently the cultures die
out. Occasionally a second event occurs which confers
immortality, and the cells can then be said to be fully
transformed. The situation is quite different in the case of
rodent cells. Immortal cells often arise spontaneously in a
culture of senescent diploid mouse cells, but these retain most
of the properties of diploid cells (Todaro and Green, 1963). A
second event can also occur spontaneously and be induced by
treatment with carcinogens or by transfection with a member of
the ras family on oncogenes (Land et al., 1983; Newbold and
Overall, 1983). The overall frequency of transformation of
cultures in human and rodent cells is vastly different, and this
must also be true of transformation in vivo. This is documented
for man and mouse in Table 2. It is difficult to explain the
differences in transformation between human and mouse cells in
terms of gene mutations, since there is no evidence that mutation
frequencies differ in these species. However, there is evidence
for species differences in the maintenance of methylation (Wilson
and Jones, 1983b), which could also provide a basis for the
difference in the frequency of transformation. It may well be
that cells from large, long-lived species are effectively
buffered against epigenetic changes. This could be accomplished

Table 2. Frequencies of mutation and cellular transformation in cell cultures from mouse and man

	Mouse	Man	Man/mouse
Spontaneous mutations[1]	10^{-6}–10^{-7} (spanning Mouse and Man)		
Spontaneous transformation to permanent lines[2]	10^{-5}–10^{-6}	$<10^{-9}$	
Life span	3 years	90 years	x 30
Weight	20g	65 kg	x 3000
			$x\sim10^{5}$ (product of above ratios)

Assuming tumors arise in 20% of old animals, the probability of in vivo neoplastic transformation per cell is approximately 10^5 times lower in man than mouse, which is similar to the difference seen in vitro.

[1]Based on frequencies of mutants resistant to 6-thioguanine or 8-azaguanine (see, for example, De Mars, 1974; Arlett and Harcourt, 1983, and Cole et al. 1983).

[2]Based on mass cultures of primary diploid fibroblasts. Mouse populations of ~10^6 cells give rise to permanent lines, which subsequently become fully transformed (Todaro and Green, 1963; Barski and Cassingena, 1963). Human cell populations studied in innumerable laboratories have not been reported to transform spontaneously.

in several ways, some of which have been mentioned previously. Perhaps the most likely possibility would be to simply increase the number of methyl groups involved in the control of gene activity. Suppose, for example, that a single 5-mC in a promoter region can prevent transcription, and it can be lost at a frequency of 10^{-3} per cell division, then the existence of two 5-mCs in the same region, either of which can prevent transcription, would ensure that the activation of a gene in question would occur with a frequency of 10^{-6}. This predicts the promoter regions of structural genes would be more heavily methylated in human cells than in rodent cells.

Wilson and Jones (1983b) showed that permanent lines maintain a constant level of methylation, which raises the interesting possibility that they may have acquired de novo methylase activity. Evidence for this comes from further experiments with 10T½ cells (Flatau et al., 1984). Sequential treatments with azadC progressively reduced the overall level of 5-mC from about 3.5% to 0.4%. However, when these cells were passaged in normal medium without further treatment, the level of methylation gradually increased. Other evidence for de novo methylation has been obtained in a T-lymphoid cell line (Gasson et al., 1983). The function of immortalising oncogenes, exemplified by the myc family (Land et al., 1983), may lead to a reactivated de novo methylase, which is usually shut off in somatic cells. This would prevent aging by the progressive loss of DNA methylation.

CONCLUSIONS

At the outset it was mentioned that macromolecular errors could be at the DNA level, in the synthesis of proteins or in the control of gene expression. Any general error of theory of aging must take into account all three possibilities. Two major unsolved questions are, first, the significance, if any, of each type of error in initiating the intrinsic changes which are a prerequisite to the later outward signs of the aging process; and second, how different types of error may interact with each other to produce progressively severe effects on the phenotype.

The possibility that aging may be associated with "dys-differentiation" has previously been discussed, and some evidence for illegitimate transcription in aging tissue has been reported (Ono and Cutler, 1978; Cutler 1982, a,b). A more specific possibility relates to the control of gene expression by DNA methylation. The maintenance of a specific pattern of DNA methylation may be essential for the stability

of the differentiated state in dividing or non-dividing cells. It
follows that changes in methylation, or "epigenetic errors" may
upset the normal control of gene activity and have progressively
severe deleterious effects. There is evidence that methylation
declines during aging, and that single treatments of cultured
human fibroblasts with azaC, which is known to inhibit DNA
methylase, have a strong life shortening effect. The concept of a
methylation clock for the aging of somatic cells, based on the
steady loss of 5-mC, makes many predictions which have yet to be
tested biochemically, or by quantitative studies. The hypothesis
also suggests that transformed cells which grow indefinitely may
have by-passed the clock by the acquisition of de novo methylase
activity.

ACKNOWLEDGEMENTS

     I thank Peter A.Jones and Sebastian Fairweather for
communicating results prior to publication and for helpful
discussion.

REFERENCES

Arlett, C.F., and Harcourt, S.A., 1983. Variation in response to
     mutagens amongst normal and repair defective human cells, in:
     Induced Mutagenesis", p.249, C.W.Lawrence, ed., Plenum Press,
     New York.
Barski, G. and Cassingena, R., 1963, Malignant transformation in
     vitro of cells from C57BL mouse normal pulmonary tissue, J.
     Natl. Cancer Inst., 30:865.
Cattanach, B.M., 1974, Position effect variegation in the mouse,
     Genet. Res. 23:291.
Clough, D.W., Kunkel, L.M. and Davidson, R.L. 1982, 5-Azacytidine-
     induced reactivation of a Herpes simplex thymidine kinase gene,
     Science, 216-70.
Cole, J., Arlett, C.F., Green, M.H.L., Lowe, J. and Muriel, W.,
     1983, A comparison of the agar cloning and microtitration
     techniques for assaying cell survival and mutation frequency
     in L5178Y mouse lymphoma cells. Mutat. res., 111:371.
Creusot, F., Acs, G., and Christman, J.K. 1982, Inhibition of DNA
     methyltransferase and induction of Friend erythroleukaemia cell
     differentiation by 5-azacytidine and 5-aza-2'-deoxycytidine, J.
     Biol. Chem., 257: 2041.
Curtis, H.J., 1966, "Biological Mechanisms of Aging", Springfield,
     Illinois.
Cutler, R.G., 1982a, Longevity is determined by specific genes:
     testing the hypothesis, in "Testing the Theories of Aging",
     p.25, R.C. Adelman and G.S.Roth, eds. CRC Press, Boca Raton,
     Florida.
Cutler, R.G. 1982b, The dysdifferentiative hypothesis of mammalian
     aging and longevity, in "The Aging Brain: Cellular and
     Molecular Mechanisms of Aging in the neurons system", p.1, E.

Giacobini, G.Filogamo, G.Giacobini and A.Vernadakis, eds.,
Raven Press, New York.
DeMars, E., 1974, Resistance of cultured human fibroblasts and other
cells to purine and pyrimidine analogues in relation to
mutagenesis detection, Mutat. Res., 24: 33.
Doerfler, W., 1981, DNA methylation - a regulatory signal in
eukaryotic gene expression, J.Gen.Virol., 57:1.
Doerfler, W., 1983, DNA methylation and gene activity. Ann. Rev.
Biochem., 52:93.
Flatau, E., Gonzales, F.A. Michalowsky, L.A. and Jones, P.A., 1984.
DNA methylation in 5-aza-2'-deoxycytidine resistant variants
of C3H 10T½ C18 cells, Mol. Cell. Biol., 4:2098.
Gartler, S.M. and Riggs, A.D. 1983, Mammalian X-chromosome
inactivation, Ann. Rev. Genet., 17:155.
Gasson, J.C., Ryden, T. and Bourgeois, S., 1983, Role of de novo DNA
methylation in the glucocorticoid resistance of a T-lymphoid
cell line, Nature, 302-621.
Graves, J.A.M., 1982, 5-Azacytidine-induced re-expression of alleles
on the inactive X chromosome in a hybrid mouse cell line, Exptl.
Cell Res., 141:99.
Harris, M., 1982, Induction of thymidine kinase in enzyme-deficient
Chinese hamster cells, Cell, 29:483.
Hayflick, L., 1965, The limited in vitro lifetime of human diploid
cell strains, Exptl. Cell Res., 37:614.
Hayflick, L., 1971, The Cellular basis of human aging, in: "Handbook
of the Biology of Aging," p.159, C.Finch and L.Hayflick, eds.,
Van Norstrand, Reinhold, New York.
Holliday, R., 1979, A new theory of carcinogenesis, Brit. J. Cancer,
40:513.
Holliday, R., 1984, The unsolved problem of cellular ageing, Monogr.
Devel. Biol., 17:60.
Holliday, R., 1984, The biological significance of meiosis, in:
"Controlling Events in Meiosis", C.W.Evans, ed., S.E.B. Symp.
38, Cambridge University Press (in press).
Holliday, R., Huschtscha, L.I., Tarrant, G.M. and Kirkwood, T.B.L.,
1977, Testing the commitment theory of cellular ageing, Science,
198:366.
Holliday, R., and Kirkwood, T.B.L., 1981, Predictions of the somatic
mutation and mortalization theories of cellular ageing are
contrary to experimental observations, J.Theoret. Biol., 93:627.
Holliday, R., and Pugh, J. E., 1975, DNA modification mechanism and
gene activity during development, Science, 187:226.
Huschtscha, L.I., and Holliday, R., 1983, The limited and unlimited
growth of SV40 transformed cells from human diploid MRC-5
fibroblasts, J.Cell Sci., 63:77.
Jahner, D., Stuhlman, H., Stewart, C.H., Haubers, K., Lohler, J.,
Simon, I., and Jaenisch, R., 1982, De novo methylation and
expression of retroviral genomes during mouse embryogenesis,
Nature (Lond.), 298:623.

Jones, P.A. and Taylor, S.M., 1981, Hemimethylated duplex DNAs prepared from 5-azacytidine-treated cells, Nucleic Acids Res., 9:2933.

Jones, P.A. and Taylor, S.M., 1982, Cellular differentiation, cytidine analogues and DNA methylation, Cell, 20:85.

Kennedy, A.R., Fox, M., Murphy, G., and Little, J.B., 1981, Relationship between X-ray exposure and malignant transformation in C3H 10T½ cells, Proc. Nat. Acad. Sci. U.S.A., 77:7262.

Kirkwood, T.B.L., 1980, Error propagation in intracellular information transfer, J.Theoret. Biol., 82:363.

Kirkwood, T.B.L., Rosenberger, R.F., and Holliday, R., 1984, Stability of the cellular translation process, Int. Rev. Cytol., 92:93.

Land, H., Paroda, L.F., and Weinberg, R.A. 1983, Tumorigenic conversion of primary embryo fibroblasts requires at least two co-operating oncogenes, Nature (Lond.), 304:596.

Lindop, P.J., and Rotblat, J., 1961, Shortening of life and causes of death in mice exposed to a single whole body dose of radiation, Nature (Lond.), 189:645.

Mahondas, T., Sparkes, R.S. and Shapiro, L.J., 1981, Reactivation of an inactive human X-chromosome: evidence for X-inactivation by DNA methylation, Science, 211:393.

Maynard Smith, J., 1959, A theory of ageing, Nature (Lond.), 184:959.

Maynard Smith, J., 1962, The causes of ageing. Proc. Roy. Soc. B., 157:115.

Mays-Hoopes, L.L., Brown, A. and Huang, R.C.C., 1983, Methylation and re-arrangement of mouse intracisternal A particle genes during development, aging and myeloma, Mol.Cell.Biol., 3:1371.

Neary, G.J., 1960, Ageing and radiation. Nature (Lond.), 187:10.

Newbold, R.E. and Overell, R.W., 1983, Fibroblast immortality is a prerequisite for transformation by EJc-Ha-ras oncogene, Nature (Lond.), 304:648.

Ono, T. and Cutler, R.C., 1978, Age-dependent relaxation of gene repression: increase of endogenons murine leukemia virus-related and globin-related RNA in brain and livers of mice, Proc. Nat. Acad. Sci. U.S.A., 75:4431.

Orgel, L.E., 1963, The maintenance of the accuracy of protein synthesis and its relevance to ageing. Proc. Nat. Acad. Sci. U.S.A., 49:517.

Orgel, L.E., 1970, The maintenance of the accuracy of protein synthesis and its relevance to ageing; a correction. Proc. Nat. Acad. Sci. U.S.A., 67:1476.

Orgel, L.E., 1973, Ageing of clones of mammalian cells, Nature (Lond.) 243-441.

Riggs, A.D., 1975, X-inactivation, differentiation and DNA methylation Cytogenet. and Cell Genet., 14:9.

Riggs, A.D. and Jones, P.A., 1983, 5-methyl cytosine, gene regulation and cancer, Adv. Cancer Res., 40, 1.

Sacher, G.A., 1978, Evolution of longevity and survival

characteristics in mammals, in "Genetics of ageing," p.151,
E.L. Schneider, ed., Plenum Press, New York.

Schmookler-Reis, R.J. and Goldstein, S., 1982, Variability of DNA
methylation patterns during serial passage of human diploid
fibroblasts, Proc. Nat. Acad. Sci, U.S.A., 79:3949.

Stewart, C.L., Stuhlmann, H., Jahner, D. and Jaenisch, R., 1982,
De novo methylation, expression and infectivity of retroviral
genomes introduced into embryonal carcinoma cells, Proc. Nat.
Acad. Sci., U.S.A., 79:4098.

Szilard, L., 1959, On the nature of the ageing process, Proc. Nat.
Acad. Sci, U.S.A., 45-30.

Taylor, S.M. and Jones, P.A., 1982, Mechanism of action of
eukaryotic DNA methyl transferase: use of 5-azacytidine
containing DNA, J.Mol.Biol., 162:679.

Todaro, G.H. and Green, H., 1963, Quantitative studies of the growth
of mouse embryo cells in culture and their development into
established lines, J.Cell Biol., 17:299.

Wilson, V.L. and Jones, P.A., 1983a, An inhibition of DNA methylation
by chemical in vitro carcinogens, Cell, 32:239.

Wilson, V.L. and Jones, P.A., 1983b, DNA methylation decreases in
aging but not in immortal cells, Science, 220:1055.

DNA MANIPULATING GENES AND THE AGING BRAIN

Chev Kidson, Philip Chen and F. Paula Imray

Queensland Institute of Medical Research
Brisbane 4006, Australia

INTRODUCTION

Although the relative contributions of genetics and environment to aging in biological systems are not known, genes concerned and the possibilities for environmental modification of their expression are likely to be large in number. Inherited polymorphisms at the wide range of gene loci, or acquired mutations at these loci in somatic cell lineages, can have an influence on the aging process of the composite phenotype that constitutes a complex metazoan organism such as man.

Mutations of interest may affect many or a few organ systems or even a single system in a given individual depending on the phenotypic expression of the genes concerned. Thus genetic gerontopathology will include a wide range of phenotypes, with many features having a polygenic basis and a small number appearing to be of monogenic origin. Major mutants may be useful in pin-pointing some genes critical to the aging process but they may give an exaggerated view of the true importance of those genes in normal aging.

Most theories of aging have been concerned directly or indirectly with DNA damage, somatic mutations or combinations thereof, e.g. the error catastrophe theory (Orgel, 1963). There is overlap among these concepts, with considerable evidence occurring in favor of at least some role for accumulation of DNA damage in the aging process (e.g. Gensler and Bernstein, 1981). The report by Hart and Setlow (1974) that UV-induced DNA repair in fibroblasts correlated well with lifespan in seven species of mammals supported the notion that DNA repair capacity is an important determinant -

or correlate - of longevity. However, Kato et al., (1980) did not
find a correlation of DNA excision repair with lifespan in a study
of cells from 34 species in 11 orders of mammals. Similarly, the
report of Price et al., (1971) of accumulation of DNA single
strand breaks in the brain with age has been countered by the
contrary findings of Ono et al., (1976).

Although there is a great deal of seemingly contradictory
evidence, there is a climate of opinion that tends to attribute
considerable weight to the occurrence and cumulative effects of
increasing DNA damage with age (Gensler and Bernstein, 1981). This
idea is attractive, carrying as it does the implication of a
substantial element of stochasticity in the aging of individuals.
However, it is also difficult to escape the compelling holistic
evidence of a major role for genetic programming, for species or
subspecies do indeed tend to have fairly well-defined life-spans,
if environmentally-related events are minimized. There seems to be
no good reason to consider genetic programming and accumulation of
DNA damage as mutually exclusive, indeed, DNA repair capacity may
itself be one of a number of programmed events that set the major
machinery of the biological time clocks. In this context there is
still considerable merit in the evolutionary approach (Medawar,
1952; Williams, 1957), which sees natural selection operating on
genes that are beneficial for youth, even if they are deleterious
in later life, and conceives aging as being controlled at the gene
regulating level (Cutler, 1975).

One of the assumptions that is often made in allotting a key
role to repair of DNA damage in the aging process, is that DNA
repair synthesis has evolved specifically to handle DNA damage. To
an extent this is undoubtedly so. However, the overall mechanisms
of DNA repair, replication and recombination, require overlapping
enzyme systems, such that there can be considerable genetic
interdependence in the broad area of DNA manipulation. This is
nicely exemplified by the pleiotropism of the recA-lexA system of
Escherichia coli (Little and Mount, 1982). Single structural gene
products may subserve multiple functions and control genes may
regulate a range of functions. Thus, measurements of DNA repair
synthesis may be interpreted too narrowly in terms of their
implications for non-replicating versus replicating cell
populations, when the total picture of DNA manipulation capacity
and requirements needs to be considered. It is well known, for
example, that cell survival following exposure to DNA damaging
agents is dependent on the control of DNA replication as well as
repair capacity *per se*. Thus, in ataxia-telangiectasia (A-T)
cells, radiosensitivity is closely associated with their failure to
suppress DNA replication after irradiation, even though their
repair enzymes would otherwise be able to cope (Houldsworth and
Lavin, 1980; Edwards and Taylor, 1980).

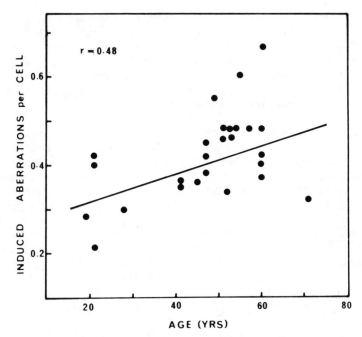

Fig. 1   γ(80 rad)-induced chromosome aberrations in PHA
stimulated lymphocytes versus age of donor

Thus, the relationship of radiosensitivity of lymphocytes to
donor age, for example, (Fig. 1) needs to be interpreted
cautiously, although there is good evidence that mutation frequency
also increases with age (Evans and Vijayalaxmi, 1981). Programming
of cell differentiation and organ system development leads to an
array of cell populations with differing capacities for division
and for manipulation of DNA. T lymphocytes represent one such cell
population, in which lectin stimulation is needed to initiate
replication and cell division for such experiments.

In this context the brain is of particular importance, by
virtue of its cell population diversity and its role in the control
of other systems.

IS THE BRAIN SPECIAL?

When it occurs, brain failure is one of the most debilitating
features of aging in man. The brain is far from uniform and
comprises cell populations with widely differing features. The
mammalian nervous system develops from pluripotent precursor cells
into an array of interacting cell networks with different
specialized functions. In simplified terms there is a genetically
programmed evolution of basic circuitry which is largely completed

during embryonic development. Upon this is superimposed further
extension of circuit construction which occurs postnatally with
learning inputs. The former requires organized patterns of cell
division and migration, whilst the latter is virtually devoid of a
requirement for neuronal multiplication. In the cerebellum the
granule cells continue DNA replication postnatally as they set up
specific ramifications in relation to Purkinje cells.

Special features of the mature mammalian nervous system are
listed in Table 1. Simplistic as this list is, these features
underscore the response of the nervous system, including the brain,
to cellular damage. Extreme redundancy of individual pathways
means that neuronal death may be extensive in a particular circuit
before clinical signs are evident. Neuronal pathway dependence, on
the other hand, means that if one neuron dies, outputs from that
cell to other neurons cease, with death of these secondary neurons
where they are critically dependent on these informational inputs.
The programmed primary circuits are prone to errors in construction
during embryonic development, due to inherited or acquired
mutations or to other damage, while learning-influenced secondary
circuits are subject to a wider set of environmental influences.

Most neurodegenerative diseases of man involve initial death
of a select group of neurons in a particular region, folowed by
dependent pathway degeneration, with the time of clinical
expression depending on circuit redundancy. Thus the causative
events may occur many years before evident clinical disease is
diagnosed and complete degeneration of particular pathways may take
decades.

Table 1.   Special Features of the Mammalian
           Nervous System

NEURONAL PATHWAY REDUNDANCY

NEURONAL PATHWAY DEPENDENCE

PROGRAMMED PRIMARY CIRCUITRY

LEARNING-INFLUENCED SECONDARY CIRCUITS

NON-REPLICATIVE NEURONS

REPLICATIVE GLIAL CELLS

   Replicating and dividing neurons are radiosensitive but become
relatively resistant to ionizing radiation, for example, once cell
division has ceased, whereas many glia retain the capacity to divide
along with radiosensitivity (Kidson, 1979). This picture has been
verified in broad terms experimentally, both in the postnatal
cerebellum and using brain cell cultures. Resistance of neurons to
both UV and γ-radiation increases upon terminal differentiation
(Dambergs and Kidson, 1977). While there is probably a diminution
of DNA repair capacity with terminal differentiation (Kidson 1978,
1979) some repair functions are evidently retained which can cope
with UV (Dambergs and Kidson, 1979) and ionizing radiation (Lett et
al., 1978) damage. The precise capacity of different mature neuron
subsets to repair DNA damage is subject to some controversy
(Glensler and Bernstein, 1981).

   It must be remembered that some groups of neurons are destined
to die as part of the embryonic developmental program, so that
there may be subpopulations with grossly different expression of
repair functions. At the same time this phenomenon of neuronal
death during development reflects the important event of neuronal
competition and selection (Purves, 1980), which occurs in both
peripheral and central nervous systems. While the mechanisms and
criteria for neuronal survival are not known, the process is
fundamental to the structure and function of the brain. If we
assume that this process is, broadly speaking, under control of
genetic systems, some of which relate to the regulation of DNA
manipulation, then programmed neuronal degeneration might become
unbalanced as the result of mutations in such genetic systems.
Conceivable neuronal competition and selection may have mechanistic
parallels with immunocyte subset differentiation, which we know to
depend in part on critical gene rearrangement events involving DNA
recombination (Kidson and Dambergs, 1982).

   The brain - or the nervous system as a whole - does indeed
have special characteristics of relevance to considerations of the
aging process. In man, age-related neuropathology provides a
window on the process, although mechanistic interpretation is at a
somewhat rudimentary stage.

NEURODEGENERATIVE DISEASE

   A remarkable observation has been the range of
neurodegenerative diseases of man that are associated with genetic
susceptibility to DNA damaging agents (Kidson et al., 1983;
Robbins, 1983). We have recorded such an association in a number
of neurodegenerative syndromes (Table 2), while additional ones
have been listed by Robbins (1983). In our experience, in no

Table 2. Neurodegenerative Syndromes Associated With
          Ionizing Radiosensitivity

Ataxia-telangiectasia (A-T)
Huntington's Disease (HD)
Alzheimer's Disease (AD)
Familial Non-specific Dementia (FND)
Amyotrophic Lateral Sclerosis (Guam) (ALS)
Parkinsonism Dementia (Guam) (PD)

---

case is there an absolute association but in all groups the
correlation is impressive. Ionizing radiosensitivity has been
demonstrated variously using PHA-stimulated T lymphocytes, by
clonogenicity or induced chromosome aberrations in B lymphoblastoid
cell lines, or in some cases in cultured fibroblasts. Although the
correlations have been good, these methods are still limiting and
the delineation of sensitivity is a relative judgement.

The prototype of ionizing radiation sensitive
neurodegenerative disease in man is ataxia-telangiectasia.
Although radiosensitivity has become accepted as one of the
criteria of A-T, we and others (unpublished data) have come across
patients with normal cellular radiation sensitivity whose clinical
signs otherwise fit this syndrome. Thus, the precise role of the
radiosensitive phenotype is not certain. Even without taking this
subgroup into account, an impressive feature of this rare autosomal
recessive disorder is the underlying genetic heterogeneity. There
are at least 4 and possibly as many as 9 complementation groups
among cell lines so far analyzed by various methods (Table 3). All
appear to share a defect in control of DNA replication (Houldsworth
and Lavin, 1980; Edwards and Taylor, 1980), while some may exhibit
anomalous DNA repair (Paterson et al., 1982). This heterogeneity
underscores the large number of gene loci that we expect to be
necessary for regulation of DNA manipulation in man (Kidson, 1980).

Whether A-T, like progeria and Werner's syndrome, can be
strictly considered as a disease of premature aging is open to
semantic debate. In terms of progressive loss of the primarily
affected cerebellar neurons, followed by degeneration of dependent
pathways, it fits a loose definition, although some patients can
live for several decades (Sedgwick, 1982) if they survive other
sequelae such as infections and lymphoma. It is useful to keep A-T
under the broad umbrella of aging-related neuropathology, because
its detailed molecular and genetic analysis has indeed begun to
open a window on the process of brain degeneration that we see as
one of the most explosive components of severe aging.

Table 3. Complementation Groups in A-T

GROUP	CELL LINE
A	AT3BI, AT1BE
B	AT2BE
C	AT4BI, AT1PWA
D	AT5BI, AT17BI, AT10S, AT4JTO
?E	AT8BI, AT1ABR
?F	AT14BI
?G	AT3ABR
?H	AT4ABR, AT6ABR, GM717
?I	AT5ABR

The groups E-I are tentative only, pending a complete
matrix analysis of cell lines.

In all the neurodegenerative diseases listed in Table 2, the
pathological process is initiated in a small, select group of
specific neurons, no matter how global the ultimate pathology.
This has been surprisingly and elegantly demonstrated for
Alzheimer's disease (Coyle et al., 1983), where the neurons of the
nucleus basalis of Meynert undergo degeneration. These neurons are
a major source of cholinergic innervation of the cerebral cortex
and related structures and appear to play an important role in
cognitive functions, including memory. Alzheimer's disease and the
continuum through to senile dementia, represents the major syndrome
of brain failure with aging. Thus, these findings represent an
important advance in our understanding of the extreme end of the
spectrum of aging in the human brain.

Most but not all of the small group of sporadic Alzheimer's
(AD) cases we have studied exhibit cellular sensitivity to ionizing
radiation (Kidson et al., 1983). By differential labelling of
parental chromosomes in cell fusion experiments (Chen et al.,
1984), it has been possible to begin unravelling some facets of AD
genetics. Irradiation of heterokaryons between normal and AD cells
show the radiation sensitive AD phenotype to be recessive to the
normal. In contrast, where cells from Huntington's disease (HD)
patients are radiosensitive (Chen et al., 1981), the HD phenotype
is dominant (unpublished data). However, in this same assay, A-T
heterozygotes, which may show a degree of radiosensitivity (Chen et
al., 1978), are recessive to normal cells but show increased
sensitivity in homokaryons that contain two normal alleles (Chen et

al., 1984). AD homokaryons behave similarly and while preliminary cross-hybridization experiments between AD and A-T cells mostly exhibit complementation, in some cases there is an apparent absence of complementation, suggesting a possible relationship between the radiosensitivity genes associated with some AD and A-T mutants. These preliminary studies need to be expanded to a large series but they show promise for the genetic analysis of AD. It is possible that these AD-associated mutants are heterozygotes. Preliminary complementation analysis among AD cell lines suggests that multiple gene loci are involved, as mentioned above for A-T.

INTERPRETATION OF RADIOSENSITIVITY DATA

Although there is a positive association between a number of neurodegenerative diseases and cellular sensitivity to DNA damage, we have not found this to be absolute, even for HD (Chen et al., 1981). Tempting as it is to ponder causal association (Robbins, 1983), we feel this is premature on the basis of present evidence. In the case of HD it should be possible to test for linkage between the chromosome 4 marker (Gusella et al., 1983) and the radiosensitive phenotype, where it occurs. In the case of AD, further cell genetic studies should be helpful, as should extension thereof to familial AD, for the purposes of chromosome mapping and development of gene probes.

The preliminary evidence suggests most of these syndromes will prove to be genetically heterogeneous, each possibly involving a number of gene loci. If indeed solid evidence for causal association between the radiosensitive phenotypes and pathology is forthcoming, then there is a need to consider the mechanistic implications. It is possible that ineffective repair of random DNA damage is a central feature but in our view it is more likely to be of secondary rather than primary importance.

The key feature of each of these neurodegenerative disorders is their initiation in a selective neuron subset, the subsets being different for each syndrome. A-T is clearly a developmental, multisystem disease, with relatively early onset. Given the nature of nervous system organization (Table 1) it is quite conceivable that others in this group are also diseases of development or differentiation - each in a particular neuron population, with extended periods until clinical signs are recognized, dependent on neuronal network redundancy and feedback circuitry. The involvement of genes, whose mutant phenotypes are monitored as radiosensitivity, in DNA recombination operations, for example, could have implications for subtle, specialized differention events (Kidson, 1979; Waldman, 1982). The possibility of selective recombination defects in A-T is being explored in this context (Cox et al., 1984). Whether gene rearrangements, essential for immunocyte differentiation, are necessary for the genesis of neuron subsets is

a matter for conjecture at this time. However, it is clear that if
the radiosensitive phenotypes are indeed causally related to the
differential pathology, the underlying genotypes must exert their
effects in a very selective manner tied to differentiation of
neuronal subsets. Random response to DNA damage would not give
rise to the selective pathology.

There are many other features of Alzheimer's disease that
require explanation. There is good evidence for structural
anomalies in the paired helical filaments that are one of the
hallmarks of the AD brain (Ihara et al., 1983). There is a
continuing debate over the possibility of slow virus involvement
(Prusiner, 1984). There is every chance that we are dealing with
pleiotropic gene functions as occur in A-T.

NEUROPATHOLOGY AND AGING

In the present context we must ask whether neurodegenerative
diseases like AD do indeed provide a window on the normal aging
process in the brain. Certainly Alzheimer's disease, with an
incidence of more than 5 percent among individuals over 65 in some
populations, is a major concomitant of aging in a substantial
number of people. Its importance lies in the possibilities it
opens up for delineation of some gene functions that, when mutant,
give rise to exaggerated, rapid brain failure, a phenomenon that
occurs more slowly, to a lesser degree, in a larger proportion of
the aging human population.

Pursuit of the molecular details of the neurodegeneration-
associated radiosensitivity mutants promises to open up new leads
in this respect. It will be important to consider the spectrum of
activities involved in the genetic control of DNA manipulation
rather than assume that we are dealing simply with repair of DNA
damage. Since neurons are not required to undergo multiplication,
they have a longer time to repair DNA damage than do dividing
cells, where fidelity of DNA replication is a high priority.
Mature neurons are remarkably resistant to DNA damage, at least
that due to ionizing radiation.

The subtleties of nervous system development serve as a
reminder of the possibilities that in broad terms genetic
programming of neuron longevity may be operative. Thus, we can
imagine time-clocks dependent on stochastic operations of neuronal
networks, established on a developmental genetic basis, and
influenced by life-long inputs that govern the evolution,
persistence and desistence of secondary neural nets
interconnecting non-renewable neurons. In this context, aging of
the brain may be seen as programmed genetically but subject to wide
fluctuations in rate and time by multiple, externally generated
events.

REFERENCES

Chen, P., Lavin, M.F., Kidson, C., and Moss, D., 1978,
     Identification of ataxia telangiectasia heterozygotes, a
     cancer prone population, Nature, 274:484-486.
Chen, P., Kidson, C., and Imray, F.P., 1981, Huntington's disease:
     implications of associated cellular radiosensitivity, Clin.
     Genet., 20:331-336.
Chen, P., Imray, F.P., and Kidson, C., 1984, Gene dosage and
     complementation analysis of ataxia-telangiectasia
     lymphoblastoid cell lines assayed by induced chromosome
     aberrations, Mutat. Res., 129:165-172.
Cox, R., Masson, W.K., Debenham, P.G. and Webb, M.B.T., 1984, The
     use of recombinant DNA plasmids for the determination of
     DNA-repair and recombination in cultured mammalian cells,
     Br. J. Cancer, Suppl. VI, 49:67-72.
Coyle, J.T., Price, D.L. and de Long, M.R., 1983, Alzheimer's
     disease: a disorder of cortical cholinergic
     innervation,Science, 219:1184-1190.
Cutler, R.G., 1975, Evolution of human longevity and the genetic
     complexity governing aging rate, Proc. Natl. Acad. Sci. USA,
     72:4664-4668.
Dambergs, R.G., and Kidson, C., 1977, Differential radiosensitivity
     of mouse embryonic neurons and glia in cell culture, J.
     Neuropath. Exp. Neurol., 36:576-585.
Dambergs, R.G., and Kidson, C., 1979, Quantitation of DNA repair in
     brain cell cultures: implications for autoradiographic
     analysis of mixed cell populations, Int. J. Radiat.
     Biol., 36:271-280.
Edwards, M.J., and Taylor, A.M.R., 1980, Unusual levels of ADP-
     ribose and DNA synthesis in ataxia-telangiectasia cells
     following γ-ray irradiation, Nature, 287:745-747.
Evans, H.J., and Vijayalaxmi, 1981, Induction of 8-azaguanine
     resistance and sister chromatid exchange in human
     lymphocytes exposed to mitomycin C and X-rays in vitro,
     Nature, 292:601-605.
Gensler, H.L., and Bernstein, H., 1981, DNA damage as the primary
     cause of aging, Quart. Rev. Biol., 56:279-303.
Gusella, J.F., Wexley, N., Conneally, P.M., Naylor, S.L., Anderson,
     M.A., Tannzi, R.E., Watkins, P.C., Ottina, K., Wallace,
     M.R., Sakaguchi, A.Y., Young, A.B., Shoulson, I., Bonilla,
     E., and Martin, J.B., 1983, A polymorphic DNA marker
     genetically linked to Huntington's disease, Nature, 306:
     234-238.
Hart, R.W., and Setlow, R.B., 1974, Correlation between
     deoxyribonucleic acid excision repair and lifespan in a
     number of mammalian species, Proc. Natl. Acad. Sci. USA,
     71:2169-2173.

Houldsworth, J., and Lavin, M.F., 1980, Effect of ionizing radiation on DNA synthesis in ataxia-telangiectasia cells, Nucleic Acids Res., 8:3709-3720.

Ihora, Y., Abraham, C., and Selkoe, D.J., 1983, Antibodies to paired helical filaments in Alzheimer's disease do not recognize normal brain proteins, Nature, 304:727-730.

Kato, M., Harada, M., Tsuchiya, K., and Moriawaki, K., 1980, Absence of correlation between DNA repair in ultraviolet irradiated mammalian cells and life span of the donor species, Jpn. J. Genet., 55:99-104.

Kidson, C., 1978, DNA repair in differentiation, in: "DNA Repair Mechanisms", pp. 761-768, P.C. Hanawalt, E.C. Friedberg and C.F. Fox, eds., Academic Press, New York.

Kidson, C., 1979, Repair systems and differentation, in: "Radiation Research", pp. 627-631, S. Okada, M. Immamura, T. Terashima and H. Yamaguchi, eds., Toppan, Tokyo.

Kidson, C., 1980, Diseases of DNA repair, Clin. Haematol., 9:141-157.

Kidson, C., and Dambergs, R., 1982, Nervous system development and ataxia-telangiectasia, in: "A Cellular and Molecular link between Cancer, Neuropathology and Immune Deficiency", pp. 373-377, B.A. Bridges and D.G. Harnden, eds., John Wiley and Sons, Chichester.

Kidson, C., Chen, P., Imray, F.P., and Gipps, E., 1983, Nervous system disease associated with dominant cellular radiosensitivity, in: Cellular Responses to DNA Damage", pp. 721-729, E.C. Fiedberg and B.A. Bridges, eds., Alan R. Liss, New York.

Lett, J.T., Keng, P.C., and Sun, C., 1978, Rejoining of DNA strand breaks in nondividing cells irradiated in situ, in: "DNA Repair Mechanisms", pp. 481-484, P.C. Hanawalt, E.C. Friedberg and C.F. Fox, eds., Academic Press, New York.

Little, J.W. and Mount, D.W., 1982, The SOS regulatory system of Escherichia coli, Cell, 29:11-22.

Medawar, P.B., 1952, "An Unsolved Problem in Biology", H.K. Lewis, London.

Ono, T., Okada, S. and Sugahara, T., 1976, Comparative studies of DNA size in various tissues of mice during the aging process, Exp. Gerontol., 11:127-132.

Orgel, L.E., 1963, The maintenance of the accuracy of protein synthesis and its relevance to aging, Proc. Natl. Acad. Sci. USA, 49:517-521.

Paterson, M.C., Smith, P.J., Bech-Hansen, N.T., Smith, B.P., and Middlestadt, M.V., 1982, Anomalous repair in radiogenic DNA damage in skin fibrobalsts from ataxia-telangiectasia patients, in: "Ataxia-telangiectasia - A Cellular and Molecular Link between Cancer, Neuropathology and Immune Deficiency," pp. 271-289, B. A. Bridges and D. G. Harriden, eds., John Wiley and Sons, Chichester.

Price, G.B., Modak, S.P., and Makinodan, T., 1971, Age-associated
     changes in the DNA of mouse tissue, Science, 171:917-920.
Prusiner, S.B., 1984, Some speculations about prions, amyloid and
     Alzheimer's disease, New Engl. J. Med., 310:661-663.
Purves, D., 1980, Neuronal competition, Nature, 287:585-586.
Robbins, J.H., 1983, Hypersensitivity to DNA-damaging agents in
     primary degenerations of excitable tissue, in: "Cellular
     Responses to DNA damage", pp. 671-700, E.C. Friedberg and
     B.A. Bridges, eds., Alan R. Liss, New York.
Sedgwick, R.P., 1982, Neurological abnormalities in ataxia-
     telangiectasia, in: "Ataxia-telangiectasia - A Cellular and
     Molecular Link between Cancer, Neuropathology and Immune
     Deficiency", pp. 23-25, B.A. Bridges and D.G. Harnden, eds.,
     John Wiley and Sons, Chichester.
Waldman, T.A., 1982, Immunological abnormalities in ataxia-
     telangiectasia, in: "Ataxia-telangiectasia - A Cellular and
     Molecular Link between Cancer, Neuropathology and Immune
     Deficiency", pp. 37-51, B.A. Bridges and D.G. Harnden, eds.,
     John Wiley and Sons, Chichester.
Williams, G.C., 1957, Pleiotropy, natural selection and the
     evolution of senescence, Evolution, 11:398.

IN VIVO STUDIES ON DNA REPAIR AND TURNOVER WITH AGE

Takatoshi Ishikawa, Junko Sakurai, and Shozo Takayama

Department of Experimental Pathology
Cancer Institute
Toshima-ku Tokyo 170

SUMMARY

Since the capacity for DNA repair relative to other cellular processes should be an important parameter of mutagenesis, carcinogenesis, and also aging, this capacity should preferably be studied in intact animals. Thus, we developed autoradiographic techniques for measuring DNA repair directly in vivo. By these methods unscheduled DNA synthesis (UDS) was detected quantitatively as silver grains on epithelial cells of mouse skin after treatment with chemical carcinogens or UV irradiation, and on cerebral ganglion cells of aquarium fish after treatment with various chemical carcinogens. Several interesting findings so far obtained are presented.

Possible age-related change in the UDS response was examined by the skin technique with mice of 2 and 18 months old. Similar dose-dependent induction of UDS was observed in mice of both ages after treatment with 4-hydroxyaminoquinoline 1-oxide; their levels of UDS at each dose were not significantly different. The dose-response curves for young and aged animals after UV irradiation showed similar increases to a plateau at low doses, but their responses to high doses were very different: in aged mice the UDS level decreased markedly with increase in the dose, whereas in young mice it remained at the same level. This suggests that in aged animals, high doses of UV irradiation cause deterioration of DNA repair systems, and that aged animals cannot repair extensive DNA damage efficiently.

It is generally thought that DNA has a stable structure and a much slower turnover than other cellular components. Although the effect of DNA repair on DNA turnover may be insignificant,

297

accumulation of repaired DNA in cells should result in detectable
DNA turnover. Therefore, we investigated DNA turnover in post-
mitotic ganglion cells of rat retina. However, careful autoradiographic studies on pairs of eyes showed no detectable DNA turnover
up to nearly their median life span (2 years). This result suggests
that the DNA of post-mitotic cells, which are not replaced throughout
the life span of the animal, is very stable and is possibly protected
in some special way.

IN VIVO STUDIES ON DNA REPAIR

    DNA repair systems are regarded as among the most important in
organisms, and the nature of DNA repair mechanisms and their roles
in carcinogenesis, mutagenesis, aging, etc. have been studied in
various systems (Cleaver, 1978; Howard-Flanders, 1981; Painter,
1975; Setlow, 1978). Relatively little is known about DNA repair
in vivo, because few methods are available for its study.

    DNA strand breakage and rejoining after treatment with agents
that damage DNA have been studied in the liver (Goodman and Potter,
1972; Cox et al., 1973), brain (Wheeler and Lett, 1972; Hadjiolov
and Venkov, 1975), and other organs (Wheeler et al., 1973; Cox and
Irving, 1975; Kanagahngan and Balis, 1975; Koropatnick and Stich,
1976; Petzold and Swenberg, 1978) of intact animals. However, in
this type of study, in which the tissues are treated as a whole
without excluding mesenchymal cells, artifactual DNA breakage tends
to occur. Moreover, the methods involved seem too complicated for
application to a large number of samples. Another approach has been
the direct measurement of specific adducts, such as pyrimidine
dimers in the skin (Bowden et al., 1975; Cooke and Johnson, 1978;
Sutherland et al., 1980) and O^6-alkylguanines in various organs
(Goth and Rajewsky, 1974; Kleihues and Bucheler, 1977; Pegg and
Balog, 1979; Scherer et al., 1977). This method is specific, but
it has the limitation that it cannot give information on the location of DNA repair within the tissues. Another approach is the
autoradiographic procedure. A common method for estimating the
magnitude of DNA repair that is useful for measurement of DNA repair
in individual cells of tissues or organs in vivo is measurement of
incorporation of (methyl-^{3}H)-thymidine (dThd) during repair synthesis and subsequent exposure of the preparation to high resolution
autoradiographic emulsion.

    It had long been thought difficult to demonstrate unscheduled
DNA synthesis (UDS) in vivo. But Epstein et al. (1970; 1978a) demonstrated ultraviolet light (UV)-induced UDS in human and mouse
skin. For this, they injected (methyl-^{3}H)dThd subcutaneously
(s.c.), but they could not demonstrate a dose-dependent response.
As another approach, we reported a procedure for detecting DNA
repair synthesis in vivo in cerebral ganglion cells of aquarium

fishes (Ishikawa et al., 1978a, 1984). For this, the living fish, in which the brain was exposed by operation, were kept in isotonic solution containing a carcinogen and (methyl-^{3}H)dThd. UDS was clearly demonstrated as silver grains on the nuclei of ganglion cells. However, this method is obviously not applicable to mammals. In rodents, unless conditions are adequate, a locally injected aqueous solution of carcinogen seems to be absorbed and to pass into the general circulation very rapidly. Thus, we developed a technique using special forceps for measuring UDS in mouse skin after treatment with various chemical carcinogens (Ishikawa et al., 1982) or UV-irradiation (Kodama et al., 1984). Technically, the main reasons why we could detect UDS in intact animals successfully were that we used (methyl-^{3}H)dThd of high specific activity and our forceps procedure. The (methyl-^{3}H)dThd of high specific activity was effectively incorporated into cellular DNA during the repair process overwhelming the internal thymidine pool.

Induction of UDS in Mouse Skin in vivo

     The techniques used were described in detail in previous papers (Ishikawa et al., 1982; Kodama et al., 1984), and so are described only briefly here (Fig. 1). Female ICR mice (8 weeks old) were used. For carcinogen treatment, animals were anesthetized with sodium pentobarbital and the skin of their back was shaved. Tongue forceps (ring shaped, 20 mm in diameter) were used to clamp off a double fold of the skin. Immediately after clamping off the skin, isotonic Ringer solution containing a carcinogen and (methyl-^{3}H)dThd (100 µCi/ml) was injected s.c. into the clamped-off region. Four carcinogens were used: 4-nitroquinoline 1-oxide (4NQO), 4-hydroxy-aminoquinoline 1-oxide (4HAQO), 1-methyl-1-nitrosourea (MNU) and methylmethanesulphonate (MMS), and each was tested at 4 to 5 doses using 5 animals for each dose. After this treatment the mice were kept at 35°C for 60 minutes, and then the forceps were removed. The animals were killed 3 hours later, and the treated skin was cut out. The skin was fixed and embedded in paraffin. Sections (4-5 µm) were dip covered with NR-M$_2$ emulsion (Konishiroku Photo Co., Tokyo) and exposed for 5 weeks at 4°C. After development, the sections were lightly stained with hematoxylin and eosin.

     The technique used for UV radiation-induced UDS was essentially the same as that used with chemical carcinogens. The skin of the back of mice was shaved with electric clippers and remaining hair was carefully removed with a razor. The skin was exposed to short-wave UV light from a 15-W germicidal lamp (Toshiba GL 15 UV lamp) with predominant emission at 254 nm (dose rate 1.2 J/m^2/s), or UV-AB light from three 20-W sunlamp fluorescent tubes (Toshiba FL 20 S.E. sunlamp) with emission at 270-440 nm and a peak at 312 nm (dose rate 2.2 J/m^2/s). For convenience, we refer to short-wave UV and UV-AB irradiation as 254 nm UV and sunlamp UV irradiation, respectively. Five animals each were exposed to 254 nm UV irradiation or sunlamp

1. Shaving of the back skins of ICR mice (8 week old)

2. UV irradiation

   UV light sources
   a. Short wavelength UV; a 15 W germicidal lamp
      (254 nm as a single sharp peak)

   b. UV–B; three 40 W sunlamps
      (ca. 90% of the energy output in 280–340 nm, peak at 312 nm)

3. Clamping off the skin with tongue forceps
   and injection of (methyl-³H)dThd (50µCi/0.5ml)

4. Treatment at 35ºC for 60 minutes

5. Autoradiography

6. Grain counts on 200 cells

Fig. 1.   Detection of UDS in mouse skin in vivo after UV irradiation.

UV irradiation at 5 to 7 doses. The irradiated region of the skin
was clamped off with forceps. Immediately after clamping off the
region, isotonic Ringer solution (0.5 ml) containing (methyl-³H)dThd
was injected s.c. Autoradiographic procedures were as described
above.

     In carcinogen treated groups, UDS was demonstrated clearly as
silver grains on the nuclei of epithelial cells. The 4 carcinogens
showed similar dose–dependent effects. Dermal fibroblastic cells
also responded to each carcinogen, but the number of grains on them
was significantly fewer than that on epithelial cells in response
to each carcinogen at each dose (Fig. 2). We also demonstrated
dose–dependent UDS in mouse skin after treatment with 254 nm UV and
sunlamp UV irradiation. The dose–dependent curves for 254 nm UV
and sunlamp UV irradiation were similar in shape but differed by one
order of magnitude in energy level; namely, with sunlamp UV irradiation much higher energy was required to induce the same number of
grains on epithelial cells (Fig. 3). This finding is consistent
with previous reports on the dimer yield on irradiation at 313 nm

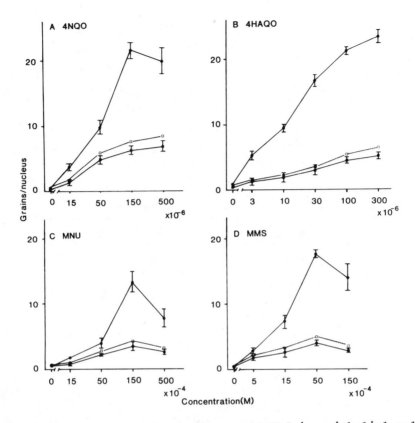

Fig. 2.   Dose response to 4 carcinogens of UDS in epithelial cells
(●) and fibroblastic cells (■) of mouse skin. The number
of grains per nucleus is plotted against the concentration
on a logarithmic scale. Numbers of grains per nucleus are
averages for 5 mice. Bars represent S.D. Corrected values
for fibroblastic cells (□) on the basis of the ratio of the
intensities of S-phase grains (1.2:1). At all doses, the
response of epithelial cells was a significantly (<0.001
or <0.01) stronger than that of fibroblastic cells.
Corrected values were also significant at p<0.001 or p<0.01
except values at 5×10^{-4}M MMS (not significant). Fig.
(Ishikawa et al., 1982) is reproduced with permission of
the publisher.

UV and 265 nm UV (Hariharan and Cerutti, 1977; Rothman and Setlow,
1979). Tests of the validity of these systems showed that the range
of variability was small between animals and even between individual
samples.

DNA repair in epithelial cells was 3- to 5- fold more active

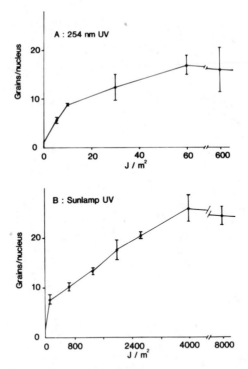

Fig. 3.   Dose response to UV irradiation of UDS in epithelial cells
          of mouse skin exposed to 254 nm UV irradiation (A) and
          sunlamp UV irradiation (B). Numbers of grains per nucleus
          are plotted against the energy dose. Numbers of grains per
          nucleus are averages for 5 mice. Bars represent S.D.
          Fig. (Kodama et al., 1984) is reproduced with permission of
          the publisher.

than in fibroblastic cells, regardless of the dose or type of carcinogen tested. The rate of dThd utilization, estimated from the
intensity of S phase cells, was only slightly different in epithelial cells and fibroblastic cells. The corrected UDS values, judged
by dThd utilization, for epithelial and fibroblastic cells, reflected
DNA repair efficiency in these cells. Even these corrected values
for epithelial and fibroblastic cells showed a highly significant
difference (Fig. 2). We also confirmed that UV-induced DNA repair
was more active in hair follicular epithelial cells than in dermal
fibroblastic cells at the same anatomical level in the skin. In
culture, mouse cells show very low levels of excision repair. It
has been reported that excision repair of pyrimidine dimers does
occur in rodent cells, although at a significantly lower rate than
in human cells (Setlow et al., 1972; Setlow and Regan, 1981).

Peleg et al. (1976) showed that dimer excision in mouse embryo
fibroblasts decreases abruptly during progressive passage of the
cells in culture. In contrast to these previous reports on fibroblastic cells in culture, Bowden et al. (1975) and Cooke and Johnson
(1978) reported that mouse epidermal cells in vivo are capable of
DNA excision repair after UV irradiation, whereas Ley et al. (1977)
reported that mouse epidermal cells have little or no capacity for
excision repair of pyrimidine dimers. Whether this difference reflects differences in mouse strains or in experimental procedures
in not yet clear. On the other hand, Taichman and Setlow (1979)
reported that the extent of UV-induced repair was similar in cultured human epidermal cells and fibroblasts, and we reported that
mouse tracheal epithelial cells and retinal ganglion cells show
active UDS in organ culture (Ishikawa et al., 1980). The above observations suggest that the efficiency of DNA repair depends on both
the cell type and the animal strain.

     The wavelength difference in transmissibility and the protec-
tive role of hair were studied after UV irradiation using this
technique. Autoradiographic results clearly showed that sunlamp UV
irradiation reached deeper sites in the skin than 254 nm UV irradiation. Results also showed that hair served as an effective sunscreen
against UV irradiation, screening about 90% of the UV light energy
from mouse skin.

     In time course studies on UDS at two different UV wavelengths,
similar curves were obtained. At both wavelengths, DNA repair synthesis was induced immediately after irradiation and continued for
48 hours. But at 48 hours after 254 nm UV irradiation, grains on
nuclei had decreased to almost the background level, whereas at 48
hours after sunlamp UV irradiation they were still about 3 times
the background level. A detailed time course study on cultured
human cells was reported by Kantor and Setlow (1981). Our time
course curves were in general similar to their's for cultured human
cells, except for a difference in rate.

Age-related Changes in UDS in Mouse Skin

     Using cultured fibroblasts or lymphocytes from young and aged
donors, many investigators have examined possible age-related differences in DNA repair capability. Most studies on both human and
animal cells have suggested that there is no appreciable age-related
decrease in DNA repair (for reviews see Tice, 1978; Hart et al.,
1979).

     We carried out preliminary studies on possible age-related
changes in the UDS response using a mouse skin system. For this
study, young (2-month-old) and aged (18-month-old) female ICR mice
were used. To compare young and aged animals under as nearly similar
conditions as possible, two matched groups of 3-4 animals each from

young and aged stocks were treated simultaneously with each dose of
a chemical carcinogen or UV irradiation. Animals were treated with
5 doses of the chemical carcinogen 4HAQO (2.5, 7.5, 25, 75, 250 ×
10^{-6}M) or with sunlamp UV irradiation at doses of 260, 660, 1320,
3300 and 5280 J/m². For UV irradiation, animals were shaved with
extreme care under ether anesthesia, and after their recovery from
anesthesia matched groups were placed under sunlamps. To randomize
doses on the back, animals were allowed to move freely in a plastic
cage during irradiation. Immediately after irradiation, animals were
anesthetized with sodium pentobarbital and the irradiated region of
the skin was clamped off with forceps. (Methyl-^{3}H)dThd injection
and autoradiographic procedures were as described above.

In 4HAQO-treated groups similar dose-dependent induction of
UDS was observed in mice of both ages, and the levels of UDS of
young and old animals at each dose were not significantly different.
The dose-response curves for young and aged animals after sunlamp
UV irradiation showed similar increases to a plateau at low doses
(260, 660 and 1320 J/m²), but their responses to high doses (3300
and 5280 J/m²) were very different; in aged mice the UDS level decreased markedly with increase in the dose, whereas in young mice
it remained at the same level. This suggests that in aged animals
high doses of UV irradiation cause deterioration of DNA repair
systems, and that aged animals cannot repair extensive DNA damage
efficiently. This surprising observation raises the question of
whether it is possible to extrapolate experimental results at relatively high dose to the lower levels to which humans are exposed:
a high dose of UV irradiation may fry the skin. Judging from available information, the most carcinogenic rays are in the acute
erythemogenic or sunburn spectrum (Epstein, 1978b). The doses used
in the present experiment were compared with the minimal erythemal
dose (MED) in mouse skin (approximately 500 J/m², unpublished data)
to obtain an estimate of their biological magnitude. No age-
associated differences were observed after exposure to sunlamp UV
irradiation at these doses (0.5 to 2 MED), but significant inhibition of UDS was seen in aged animals after exposure to high UV doses
(6 to 10 MED). Therefore, the doses of UV irradiation used seemed
to be within the biological range of actinic radiation.

The reason why the UDS response decreased at high UV doses in
aged animals is unknown. It could be due to the saturation of
damage to susceptible sites in the DNA strand or an enzymatic reaction in aged cells, or it could be due to another type of damage
altogether. UV irradiation has been shown to inhibit semiconservative DNA synthesis in mammalian cells (Edenberg, 1975), although the
mechanism for this inhibition is not clear. Moreover, we used sunlamp UV because of its higher transmissibility, but since sunlamp UV
irradiation is known to cause other damage to DNA besides pyrimidine
dimer formation (Hariharan and Cerutti, 1977), other types of damage
may be responsible for the inhibition of UDS in aged animals.

No similar inhibition of UDS was observed in groups treated with
4HAQO, although the highest dose used is known to cause necrosis of
the skin (Ishikawa et al., 1982). This difference between results
with the two agents may be explained by differences in the types of
DNA damage or the numbers of lesions induced.

It is unlikely that the observed differences in UDS in young
and aged animals at high doses of UV irradiation were due to differences in their rates of dThd utilization. Their UDS levels
after treatment with 4HAQO and low doses of UV irradiation were
similar, and no age-associated change in the rate of dThd utilization was detected in untreated animals on examination of the intensity of S phase cells (data not shown).

Besides fibroblasts or lymphocytes in culture, postmitotic
ganglion cells in vivo have also been examined for possible decrease
in DNA repair capability with age. Wheeler and Lett (1974) assessed
the capability of cerebellar neurons from beagle dogs of different
ages to repair γ-ray-induced strand breaks by alkaline sucrose
gradient analysis. In addition, Ishikawa et al. (1978a) investigated
the levels of chemical carcinogen-induced UDS in cerebral ganglion
cells of aquarium fish at various ages. These in vivo investigations also showed no age-related change.

Very recently, Plesko and Richardson (1984) observed a significant age-related decline in UV-induced UDS in rat hepatocytes isolated from 6- to 32-month-old rats. Their observations together
with ours suggest that age-related decrease in DNA repair is only
observed in certain types of cells; epithelial cells, such as skin
cells or hepatocytes, seeming to show an age-related change in DNA
repair. Further studies on various cell types are needed to clarify
the association between cellular aging and DNA repair.

IN VIVO STUDIES ON DNA TURNOVER

It is generally assumed that DNA is stable in structure and
that its turnover is much slower than the turnover of other cellular components. Although the effect of DNA repair on DNA turnover may be insignificant, the accumulation of DNA repair synthesis
throughout the life span of an animal should result in detectable
DNA turnover.

Let us consider the effect of exposure to the noon sun in
Texas for one hour every day for 70 years. Such sunlight would
results in approximately 5×10^4 dimers/hour/skin cell (Harm, 1969).
Normal fibroblasts can repair about 8×10^4 dimers/hour/cell (Ahmed
and Setlow, 1978). Assuming that the repair patch is 100 bases
(Cleaver, 1978) and that there are 5600 million nucleotide pairs
in it (McCarthy, 1965), the number of bases excised in 70 years

would be $5 \times 10^4 \times 100 \times 365 \times 70$ (1277.5×10^8). Thus the number of DNA turnovers during this period would be $1277.5 \times 10^8 / 56 \times 10^8 \times 2$ (11.4). Consequently, DNA should have completed 50% turnover by the end of 3 years, the maximum life-span of rats or mice.

There have been a number of studies on DNA turnover in cells (Bendich et al., 1953; Bennett et al., 1960; Devik and Halvorsen, 1963; Pelc, 1963, 1964), but the values for DNA turnover reported are not reliable, because most of these studies were done in the early 1960's when the nature of DNA repair was unknown. Moreover, the values obtained were based on findings in relatively short observation periods and varied in orders of magnitude. Recently, a reliable analysis was carried out by Commerford et al. (1982). They calculated the half-lives of DNA in liver and brain of mice at 318 days and 593 days respectively, based on the rates of loss of tritium from these organs. A drawback of the biochemical approach seems to be that in analysis of turnover by scintillation counting of DNA in whole tissues; it is not possible to distinguish true turnover of cellular DNA from dilution of labeled DNA resulting from cellular turnover of minor cell populations. To overcome this problem, we investigated DNA turnover in post-mitotic photoreceptor cells of rat retina by autoradiography up to nearly their median life-span (the time of 50% survival) (Solleveld et al., 1984); (Ishikawa et al., 1983).

Newborn F344 rats were injected s.c. at intervals of 8 hours with 3 doses of (methyl-^{3}H)dThd (1.5, 3.0 and 6.0 µCi per rat) for 48 hours after birth. The doses and times of injection of thymidine, and the autoradiographic conditions used, were based on the results of preliminary experiments. One eye (the right eye) was removed from all the rats 60 days after birth. The eye was fixed in 10% neutral formalin overnight at 4°C and then cut in half along the optic axis, dehydrated and embedded in paraffin. Usually 2 males and 2 females in each group were killed 180, 365, 540 and 730 days later, and their other eye (left eye) was removed and processed in the same way. Before examination, the paraffin wax was melted and the two eyes from each rat were reembedded in the same paraffin block. Sections containing the pair of retinas were cut at 4-5 µm thickness and mounted on a slide glass. Sections were dip-covered with autoradiographic emulsion and exposed for 4 weeks. All auto-radiographs were processed simultaneously. After development, sections were stained lightly with hematoxylin and eosin.

We confirmed that multiple injections of (methyl-^{3}H)dThd after birth (as described above) were suitable for obtaining a uniform, countable number of silver grains in differentiated retinas at 60 days after birth. Autoradiographs showed that nuclei in the outer nuclear layer had similar, uniform numbers of grains. These nuclei are those of rods and cones, although it is reported that rods pre-dominate in rats (Prince, 1960). Grain counts were made on more

than 500 randomly selected cells from this layer, which was thought
to be the most useful layer for this purpose. Pilot studies indicate that individual variation could be avoided by measuring the
ratios of grains in the two eyes, rather than the absolute grain
counts.

Fig. 4 shows the relative grain ratios of pairs of eyes of
37 rats killed 180, 365, 540 and 730 days after removal of the first
eye; each dot represents the value for one animal, and DNA turnover

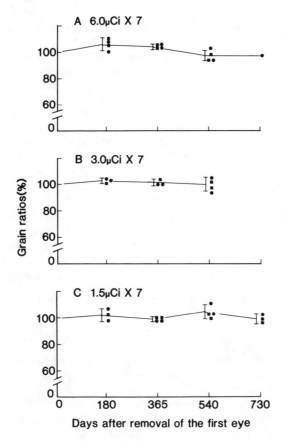

Fig. 4. Grain ratios (second eye/first eye × 100) from 37 rats
         killed 180, 365, 540 and 730 days after removal of the
         first eye (■ males, ● females). Groups A, B and C
         received different doses of (methyl-^{3}H)dThd. Vertical bars
         represent S.D. of means.

is expressed as the grain ratio for the pair of eyes of one animal.
No age-associated decrease was seen in the ratios of the photoreceptor cells in any group up to the end of the experiment. The
average absolute grain count per cell of the first eyes excised on
day 60 were 1.00 ± 0.32, 1.62 ± 0.13 and 2.28 ± 0.14 in the 3 groups
injected with different doses of (methyl-^{3}H)dThd. Judging from
these grain numbers, the levels of tritium incorporated into DNA in
this experiment were low, probably being similar to the level of
UDS in organ culture (Ishikawa et al., 1978b). The data also suggest that DNA damage caused by internal radiation of incorporated
tritium (Cleaver et al., 1972; Pollack et al., 1979) is insignificant due to the levels of tritium used for initial labeling and that
(methyl-^{3}H) at position 5 of the thymine base in DNA is highly resistant to random exchange or enzymatic dimethylation.

    Biochemical and autoradiographic techniques have been used to
detect turnover of DNA. As often pointed out, autoradiographic
methods sometimes give misleading results due to small variations
in thickness of sections and emulsion and in procedures for development. To avoid such errors, we studied pairs of eyes under as
nearly identical conditions as possible. We demonstrated that when
(methyl-^{3}H)dThd was once incorporated into DNA of photoreceptor
cells it remained unchanged for 2 years up to nearly their median
life-span. However, we do not think the present results conflict
with those of Commerford et al. (1982), but rather that the observed
differences reflect differences in the tissues examined. Brain as
a whole is not a post-mitotic organ since even neurons continue to
be produced during adult life (Bayer et al., 1982), whereas photoreceptor cells of adult vertebrates are post-mitotic cells, although
in some teleosts new rods are added to the retina as the eye
increases in size (Johns and Fernald, 1981). Our results also
appear to conflict with the findings that adult retinal ganglion
cells, which have lost the capacity for normal DNA replication, are
still capable of DNA repair in vivo (Wheeler et al., 1973) and in
vitro (Ishikawa et al., 1978b). However, we speculate that special
defensive barriers (Raviola, 1974) have evolved to protect the
retina, as part of the central nervous system, like the brain
against insults of toxic substances including environmental mutagens
(Reese and Karnovsky, 1967). Here, it is interesting to note that
induction of DNA repair in nerve cells has been achieved experimentally by γ-irradiation (Wheeler et al., 1973; Wheeler and Lett,
1972, 1974) or treatment with carcinogens with specific actions on
the nervous system (Goth and Rajewsky, 1974), or by artificial
destruction of these barriers (Ishikawa et al., 1978a, b). Another
possible explanation of why we did not observe DNA turnover in the
retina is that conventional laboratory conditions, such as basal
diet and a low dose of ultraviolet light, are not harmful to DNA
of somatic cells, or harmful at so low a level as to be undetectable
by our methods. These possibilities could be tested by similar
experiments using specific carcinogens of the nervous system that

are known to penetrate the barriers. It is also noteworthy that these photoreceptor cells seem to be very active cells because their outer segments are reported to be renewed about every 10 days (LaVail, 1976; Young, 1971). Therefore, it seems quite possible that the DNA of nerve cells, which is not replaced throughout the lifespan of the animals, is very stable and is possibly protected in some special way.

ACKNOWLEDGEMENTS

This work was supported by Grants-in-Aid for Cancer Research from the Ministry of Education, Science, and Culture and the Ministry of Health and Welfare of Japan. We thank Kiyomi Kohyama and Kayoko Kawana for their assistance in this research and Keiko Isahaya for preparing the manuscript.

REFERENCES

Ahmed, F.E. and Setlow, R.B., 1978, Kinetics of DNA repair in ultraviolet-irradiated and N-acetoxy-2-acetylaminofluorene-treated mammalian cells, Biophys. J., 24:665-675.

Bayer, S.A., Yackel, J.W., and Puri, P.S., 1982, Neurons in the rat dentate gyrus granular layer substantially increase during juvenile and adult life, Science, 216:890-892.

Bendich, A., Russell, P.J.Jr., and Brown, G.B., 1953, On the heterogeneity of the deoxyribonucleic acid, J. Biol. Chem., 203:305-318.

Bennett, L.L.Jr., Simpson, L., and Skipper, H.E., 1960, On the metabolic stability of nucleic acid in mitotically inactive adult tissues labeled during embryonic development, Biochem. Biophys. Acta, 42:237-243.

Bowden, G.T., Trosko, J.E., Shapas, B.G., and Boutwell, R.K., 1975, Excision of pyrimidine dimers from epidermal DNA and non-semiconservative epidermal DNA synthesis following ultra-violet irradiation of mouse skin, Cancer Res., 35:3599-3607.

Cleaver, J.E., Thomas, G.J., and Burki, H.J., 1972, Biological damage from intranuclear tritium: DNA strand breaks and their repair, Science, 117:996-998.

Cleaver, J.E., 1978, DNA repair and its coupling to DNA replication in eukaryotic cells, Biochem. Biophys. Acta, 516:489-516.

Commerford, S.L., 1965, Biological stability of 5-iodo-2'-deoxyuridine labelled with iodine-125 after its incorporation into the deoxyribonucleic acid of the mouse, Nature, 206:949-950.

Commerford, S.L., Carsten, A.L., and Cronkite, E.P., 1982, Histone turnover within nonproliferating cells. Proc. Natl. Acad. Sci. U.S.A., 79:1163-1165.

Cooke, A., and Johnson, B.E., 1978, Dose response, wavelength

dependence, and rate excision of ultraviolet radiation-
induced pyrimidine dimers in mouse skin DNA, Biochem. Biophys.
Acta, 517:24-30.

Cox, R., Damjanov, I., Abanoli, S.E., and Sarma, D.S.R., 1973, A
method for measuring DNA damage and repair in the liver in
vivo, Cancer Res., 33:2114-2121.

Cox, R., and Irving, C.C., 1975, Damage and repair of DNA in various tissues of the rat induced by 4-nitroquinoline 1-oxide,
Cancer Res., 35:1858-1860.

Devik, F., and Halvorsen, K., 1963, Observations by biochemical
analisis and autoradiography on labelled deoxyribonucleic
acid in the normal and regenerating liver of mice., Nature,
197:148-150.

Edenberg, H.J., 1975, Inhibition of DNA synthesis by ultraviolet
light, in:"Molecular Mechanisms for Repair of DNA", P.C.
Hanawalt and R.B. Setlow, eds., Plenum Press, New York, pp.
631-633.

Epstein, J.H., 1978a, Ultraviolet carcinogenesis, in:"Photo-
physiology," Vol. 15, A.C. Giese, ed., Academic Press, New
York, pp. 235-273.

Epstein, J.H., 1978b, Photocarcinogenesis: A review, Natl. Cancer
Inst. Monogr. 50:13-25.

Epstein, J.H., Fukuyama, K., Read, W.B., and Epstein, W.L., 1970,
Defect in DNA synthesis in skin of patients with xeroderma
pigmentosum demonstrated in vivo, Science, 168:1477-1478.

Goodman, J.I., and Potter, V.R., 1972, Evidence for DNA repair
synthesis and turnover in rat liver following ingestion of
3'-methyl-4-dimethylaminoazobenzene, Cancer Res., 32:766-775.

Goth, R., and Rajewsky, M.F., 1974, Persistence of 0-6-ethylguanine
in rat brain DNA: Correlation with nervous system-specific
carcinogenesis by ethylnitrosourea, Proc. Natl. Acad. Sci.
U.S.A., 71:639-643.

Hadjiolov, D., and Venkov, L., 1975, Strand breakage in rat brain
DNA and its repair induced by ethylnitrosourea in vivo,
Z. Krebsforsch., 84:223-225.

Hariharan, P.V., and Cerutti, P.A., 1977, Formation of products of
the 5,6-dihydroxydihydrothymine type by ultraviolet light in
HeLa cells, Biochemistry, 12:2791-2795.

Harm, W., 1969, Biological determination of the germicidal activity
of sunlight, Radiat. Res., 40:63-69.

Hart, R.W., Sacher, G.A., and Hoskins, T.L., 1979, DNA repair in
a short- and a long-lived rodent species, J. Gerontol.,
34:808-817.

Howard-Flanders, P., 1981, Inducible repair of DNA, Sci. Amer.,
245(5):56-64.

Ishikawa, T., Takayama, S., and Kitagawa, T., 1978a, Autoradiographic
demonstration of DNA repair synthesis in ganglion cells of
aquarium fish at various ages in vivo, Virchow Arch. (Cell
Path.), 28:235-242.

Ishikawa, T., Takayama, S., and Kitagawa, T., 1978b, DNA repair

synthesis in rat retinal ganglion cells treated with chemical
carcinogens or ultraviolet light in vitro, with special reference to aging and repair level, J. Natl. Cancer Inst., 61:
1101-1105.

Ishikawa, T., Ide, F., and Takayama, S., 1980, Autoradiographic study
of DNA repair synthesis in vivo and in short-term organ cultures, with special reference to DNA repair levels, aging and
species difference, in:"Genetic and Environmental Factors in
Experimental and Human Cancer.", H.V. Gelboin et al., eds.,
Jap. Sci. Press, Tokyo, pp. 215-229.

Ishikawa, T., Kodama, K., Ide, F., and Takayama, S., 1982, Demonstration of in vivo DNA repair synthesis in mouse skin exposed to
various chemical carcinogens, Cancer Res., 42:5216-5221.

Ishikawa, T., Nakajima, H., Kodama, K., and Takayama, S., 1983, DNA
turnover: Long-term labeling study in ganglion cells, Trans.
Soc. Pathol. Jap., 72:66.

Ishikawa, T., Prince Masahito, and Takayama, S., 1984, Usefulness of
the medaka, Oryzias latipes, as a test animal: DNA repair
processes in medaka exposed to carcinogens, Natl. Cancer Inst.
Monogr., 65:35-43.

Johns, P.R., and Fernald, R.D., 1981, Genesis of rods in teleost
fish retina, Nature, 293:141-142.

Kanagahngan, K., and Balis, M.E., 1975, In vivo repair of rat intestinal DNA damage by alkylating agents, Cancer Res., 36:
2364-2372.

Kantor, G.J., and Setlow, R.B., 1981, Rate and extent of DNA repair
in nondividing human diploid fibroblasts, Cancer Res., 41:
819-825.

Kleihues, P., and Bucheler, J., 1977, Long-term persistence of O^6-
methylguanine in rat brain DNA, Nature, 269:625-626.

Kodama, K., Ishikawa, T., and Takayama, S., 1984, Dose response,
wavelength dependence and time course of ultraviolet
radiation-induced unscheduled DNA synthesis in mouse skin
in vivo, Cancer Res., 44:2150-2154.

Koropatnick, D.J., and Stich, H.F., 1976, DNA fragmentation in mouse
gastric epithelial cells by precarcinogens, ultimate
carcinogens and nitrosation products. An indicator for the
determination of organotrophy and metabolic activation, Int.
J. Cancer, 17:765-772.

LaVail, M.M., 1976, Rod outer segment disk shedding in rat retina:
relationship to cyclic lighting, Science, 194:1071-1073.

Ley, R.D., Sedita, A., Grube, D.D., and Fry, R.J.M., 1977, Induction
and persistence of pyrimidine dimers in the epidermal DNA
of two strain of hairless mice, Cancer Res., 37:3243-3248.

MacCarthy, B.J., 1965, The evolution of base sequences in poly-
nucleotides, Progr. Nucleic Acid Res. Mol. Biol., 4:129-160.

Painter, R.B., 1975, Repair in mammalian cells: Overview, in:
"Molecular Mechanisms for Repair of DNA,"P.C. Hanawalt and
R.B. Setlow, eds., Plenum Press, New York, pp. 595-600.

Pegg, A.E., and Balog, B., 1979, Formation and subsequent excision

of O^6-ethylguanine from DNA of rat liver following administration of diethylnitrosamine, Cancer Res., 39:5003-5009.

Pelc, S.R., 1963, On the question of renewal of differentiated
   cells, Exp. Cell Res., 29:194-198.

Pelc, S.R., 1964, Labelling of DNA and cell division in so called
   non-dividing tissues, J. Cell Biol., 22:21-28.

Peleg, L., Raz, E., and Ben-Ishai, R., 1976, Changing capacity for
   DNA excision repair in mouse embryonic cells in vitro,
   Exp. Cell Res., 104:301-307.

Petzold, G.L., and Swenberg, J.A., 1978, Detection of DNA damage
   induced in vivo following exposure of rat to carcinogens,
   Cancer Res., 38:1589-1594.

Plesko, M.M., and Richardson, A., 1984, Age-related changes in
   unscheduled DNA synthesis by rat hepatocytes, Biochem.
   Biophys. Res. Comm., 118:730-735.

Pollack, A., Bagwell, C.B., and Irvin, G.L.III, 1979, Radiation
   from tritiated thymidine perturbs the cell cycle progression
   of stimulated lymphocytes, Science, 203:1025-1027.

Prince, J.H., 1960, "Comparative Anatomy of the Eye", Charles C.
   Thomas, Springfield, IL.

Raviola, G., 1974, Effects of paracentesis on the blood-aqueous
   barrier: an electron microscope study on Macaca mulatta
   using horseradish peroxidase as a tracer, Invest. Ophthal.,
   13:823-858.

Reese, T.S., and Karnovsky, M.J., 1967, Fine structural localization
   of a blood-brain barrier to exogenous peroxidase, J. Cell
   Biol., 34:207-217.

Rothman, R.H., and Setlow, R.B., 1979, An action spectrum for cell
   killing and pyrimidine dimer formation in Chinese hamster
   V-79 cells, Photochem. Photobiol., 29:57-61.

Scherer, E., Steward, A.P., and Emmelot, P., 1977, Kinetics of
   formation of O^6-ethylguanine in, and its removal from liver
   DNA of rats receiving diethylnitrosamine, Chem. Biol. Interact., 19:1-11.

Setlow, R.B., 1978, Repair deficient human disorders and cancer,
   Nature, 271:713-717.

Setlow, R.B., 1982, DNA repair, aging, and cancer, Natl. Cancer
   Inst. Monogr., 60:249-255.

Setlow, R.B., and Regan, J.D., 1981, Measurement of repair synthesis
   by photolysis of bromouracil, in:"DNA Repair," Vol. 1,
   E.C. Friedberg and P.C. Hanawalt, eds., Marcel Dekker,
   New york, pp. 307-318.

Setlow, R.B., Regan, J.D., and Carrier, W.L., 1972, Different levels
   of excision repair in mammalian cell lines (abstract), 16th
   Ann. Biophysical Society Meeting, Toronto, Canada, February
   1972, pp. 19.

Solleveld, H.A., Haseman, J.K., and McConnell, E.E., 1984, Natural
   history of body weight gain, survival, and neoplasia in the
   F 344 rat, J. Natl. Cancer Inst., 72:929-940.

Sutherland, B.M., Harber, L.C., and Kochever, I.E., 1980, Pyrimidine dimer excision and repair in human skin, Cancer Res., 40: 3181-3185.

Taichman, L.B., and Setlow, R.B., 1979, Repair of ultraviolet light damage to the DNA of cultured human epidermal Keratinocytes and fibroblasts, J. Invest. Dermatol., 73:217-219.

Tice, R.R., 1978, Aging and DNA-repair capability, in:"The Genetics of Aging," E.L. Schneider, ed., Plenum Press, New York, pp. 53-89.

Wheeler, K.T., and Lett, J.T., 1972, Formation and rejoining of DNA strand breaks in irradiated neurons: In vivo, Radiat. Res. 52:59-67.

Wheeler, K.T., and Lett, J.T., 1974, On the possibility that DNA repair is related to age in non-dividing cells, Proc. Natl. Acad. Sci. U.S.A., 71:1862-1865.

Wheeler, K.T., Sheridan, R.E., Pauler, E.L., and Lett, J.T., 1973, In vivo restitution of the DNA structure in gamma irradiated rabbit retinas, Radiat. Res., 53:414-427.

Young, R.W., 1971, The renewal of rod and cone outer segments in the rhesus monkey, J. Cell Biol., 49:303-318.

HYPERSENSITIVITY TO DNA-DAMAGING AGENTS IN ABIOTROPHIES: A NEW EXPLANATION FOR DEGENERATION OF NEURONS, PHOTORECEPTORS, AND MUSCLE IN ALZHEIMER, PARKINSON AND HUNTINGTON DISEASES, RETINITIS PIGMENTOSA, AND DUCHENNE MUSCULAR DYSTROPHY

Jay H. Robbins,[a] Roger A. Brumback,[b] Ronald J. Polinsky,[c] Jonathan D. Wirtschafter,[d] Robert E. Tarone,[e] Dominic A. Scudiero,[f] and Fujio Otsuka[a]

[a]Dermatology Branch
National Cancer Institute
National Institutes of Health
Bethesda, MD

[b]Division of Neuropathology
University of Rochester
   Medical Center
Rochester, NY

[c]Laboratory of Clinical Science
National Institute of Mental
   Health
National Institutes of Health
Bethesda, MD

[d]Department of Ophthalmology
University of Minnesota
   Hospitals
Minneapolis, MN

[e]Biostatistics Branch
National Cancer Institute
National Institutes of Health
Bethesda, MD

[f]Chemical Carcinogenesis
   Program
NCI-Frederick Cancer
   Research Facility
Frederick, MD

INTRODUCTION

Gowers (1902) introduced the term 'abiotrophy' to signify the premature death of neurons and skeletal muscle in primary neuronal degenerations and in muscular dystrophies respectively. Collins (1919) classified retinitis pigmentosa, with its premature degeneration of photoreceptors, as an abiotrophy. Abiotrophies share several characteristics in addition to the primary degeneration of excitable tissue which occurs in the absence of histopathologic evidence of the etiology (Gowers, 1902; Collins, 1919; Blackwood and Corsellis, 1976; Richardson and Adams, 1977). The abiotrophic degenerations: 1) become evident after the excitable tissue has attained a normal, mature development; 2) are relentlessly progressive; 3) selectively affect certain excitable tissues but not others; 4) have either a clear heredi-

tary or a sporadic basis; and 5) may be variable in their clinical and pathological features and often overlap with one another.
Examples of abiotrophies include xeroderma pigmentosum (XP),
ataxia telangiectasia, Cockayne syndrome, Alzheimer disease,
Parkinson disease, Huntington disease, Friedreich ataxia, Duchenne
muscular dystrophy, and retinitis pigmentosa.

The cause of abiotrophies has long been unknown, but it has
recently been suggested that the degeneration of neural, retinal,
and muscle cells may result from the accumulation of damaged DNA
(Robbins, 1983). This DNA-damage hypothesis is based primarily
on information obtained from the study of the rare autosomal
recessive disorder XP, certain forms of which include a primary
neuronal degeneration (De Sanctis and Cacchione, 1932; Yano, 1950;
Robbins et al., 1974; Robbins, 1983). It has been known for
several years that skin fibroblasts from patients with XP do not
repair ultraviolet-radiation (UV)-induced damage in their deoxyribonucleic acid (DNA) (Cleaver, 1968; Robbins et al., 1974;
Kraemer, 1977; Setlow, 1978; Friedberg et al., 1979; Cleaver, 1983).
Since XP patients develop solar damage, pigmentation abnormalities,
and malignancies in skin exposed to sunlight (Robbins et al.,
1974), these findings suggested that the DNA repair defect caused
the clinical abnormalities through somatic mutation resulting
from unrepaired UV-damaged DNA. As reviewed previously (Robbins
et al., 1974; Kraemer, 1977; Setlow, 1978; Friedberg et al.,
1979; Cleaver, 1983), XP fibroblasts have defective DNA nucleotide
excision repair, defective removal of UV-induced pyrimidine
dimers, defective repair of UV-treated viruses and of DNA damage
caused by certain chemical carcinogens, hypersensitivity to the
lethal effects of UV, and abnormally high levels of UV-induced
chromosome aberrations. In addition, XP fibroblasts are more
readily mutated and transformed in vitro by UV and by UV-mimetic
chemicals than are normal fibroblasts (Maher et al., 1982).

The age of occurrence of neurological abnormalities in XP
patients correlates well with the ability of their cultured cells
to survive treatment with UV (Andrews et al., 1976, 1978a). This
correlation led to the theory that efficient DNA repair prevents
premature death of neurons (Andrews et al., 1976, 1978a) and to
the discovery of hypersensitivity to DNA-damaging agents in cells
from patients with diseases characterized by primary degeneration
of neurons, including Huntington disease (Moshell et al., 1980;
Scudiero et al., 1981a; Chen et al., 1981; Bridges, 1981; McGovern
and Webb, 1982; Paterson et al., 1983; Arlett and Priestly, 1984),
Alzheimer disease (Kidson et al., 1983; Robbins et al., 1983a),
Parkinson disease (Robbins et al., 1983a), and Friedreich ataxia
(Chamberlain and Lewis, 1982; Evans et al., 1983). The DNA-damage
hypothesis has recently been extended (Robbins, 1983) to include
other excitable tissues such as skeletal muscle (Moshell et al.,
1980; Tarone et al., 1983, 1984; Robbins et al., 1984) and retinal

photoreceptors (Lytle et al., 1983; Robbins et al., 1984) which undergo a primary degeneration in muscular dystrophy and retinitis pigmentosa, respectively. This paper reviews the accumulating evidence linking these and other abiotrophic disorders to cellular hypersensitivity to DNA-damaging agents.

NEUROLOGICAL ABNORMALITIES, CELLULAR SENSITIVITY, AND DNA-DAMAGE HYPOTHESIS IN XP

The neurological features of XP include microcephaly, progressive mental deterioration, ataxia, choreoathetosis, sensorineural deafness, spasticity, extensor plantar responses, areflexia, and a peripheral neuropathy (Robbins et al., 1974). Neuropathologically (Yano, 1950; Robbins et al., 1974), there is loss of central nervous system neurons, specifically pyramidal cells of the cerebral cortex, Purkinje cells of the cerebellum, neurons of deep nuclei of the basal ganglia and cerebellum, and pigmented neurons of the locus coeruleus and the zona compacta of the substantia nigra [as in Parkinson disease (Blackwood and Corsellis, 1976)]. The spinal cord pathology resembles that of Friedreich ataxia (Yano, 1950; Lewis et al., 1979). The abnormalities in XP result from a primary neuronal degeneration—that is, a premature death of neurons in the absence of histopathological evidence of a specific etiology (Yano, 1950; Robbins et al., 1974; Blackwood and Corsellis, 1976). Clinically, XP patients who develop neurological abnormalities differ only in age of onset and rate of progression of the abnormalities (De Sanctis and Cacchione, 1932; Yano, 1950; Robbins et al., 1974, 1983b).

Complementation studies in XP have been performed by fusion in vitro of a cell line from one patient with that of another. When two cell lines complement each other, there is restoration of host-cell reactivation (Friedberg et al., 1979), resistance to killing by UV (Cleaver, 1982), and removal of dimers (Friedberg et al., 1979) and UV endonuclease-sensitive sites (Friedberg et al., 1979). Different complementation groups probably have different inherited, defective, deoxyribonucleotide sequences involved (Robbins et al., 1974). Members of the same complementation group are likely to have the same sequence defective (Robbins et al., 1974), although they may have different mutations in that sequence (Robbins et al., 1974; Andrews et al., 1978a). Bootsma and associates initially found two complementation groups among a group of XP patients (De Weerd-Kastelein et al., 1972), and the number of complementation groups has since increased to eight (Friedberg et al., 1979; Moshell et al., 1983; Robbins, 1983). A form of XP, the "variant" form, was found with a normal rate of repair of UV-induced DNA damage (Burk et al., 1971; Robbins et al., 1974). Additional variants have been discovered (Friedberg et al., 1979; Cleaver, 1983). The variant cells were shown to have markedly abnormal

post-replication repair, i.e., they cannot normally synthesize
new DNA using their UV-damaged DNA as a template (Lehmann et al.,
1975; Doniger et al., 1980).

Neurological and DNA repair data on patients representing all
known forms of XP are presented in Table 1. Analysis of the abnormalities in unscheduled DNA synthesis, host-cell reactivation,
and post-replication repair values shows no correlation with the
presence or absence of the neurological abnormalities. However,
a correlation has been found between the age of onset of neurological abnormalities and the sensitivity of the cultured fibroblasts to the lethal effects of UV (Table 1, last column; Fig. 1)
(Andrews et al., 1976, 1978a; Robbins, 1978a; Barrett et al., 1981;
Robbins et al., 1983b). Cells from patients without neurological
abnormalities show post-UV survival in the complementation group
C zone or higher (Fig. 1). This region also includes two group A
patients (XP8LO and XP1LO) who had no known neurological abnormalities by 6 and 33 years of age, respectively (Table 1) (Andrews
et al., 1978a). Slightly more sensitive than cells in the group
C zone are cells from patients XP1MI of group C, who had only one
neurological finding of XP (Robbins, 1978a), and cells from patient
XP12BE of group A (Robbins et al., 1974), who developed more
than two neurological abnormalities only after 12 years of age
(Robbins, 1978a; Robbins et al, 1983b). Cells from seven group D
patients and the group G patient, XP2BI, whose neurological abnormalities appeared between 7 and 12 years of age (Robbins et al.,
1974; Andrews et al., 1978a; Keijzer et al., 1979), are even more
sensitive (group D zone) (Andrews et al., 1978a; Barrett et al.,
1981). Cells from five group A patients, who by the age of 7 years
showed numerous neurological abnormalities (Andrews et al., 1978a),
are the most hypersensitive (group A zone) (Andrews et al., 1978a).
The relative post-UV survival of XP lymphoblastoid lines is generally
the same as that of the fibroblast lines (Moshell et al., 1981).

The neuronal DNA-damage theory was developed to account
for the premature death of neurons in XP (Robbins et al., 1974,
1983b, 1984; Andrews et al., 1976, 1978a; Robbins, 1978a, b, 1979,
1983; Lytle et al., 1983). The theory states: 1) the neurological
abnormalities of XP result from premature death of neurons; 2)
the in vitro post-UV colony-forming ability of XP fibroblasts is
determined by their ability to repair a UV type of DNA damage; 3)
the premature death of neurons in vivo results from their inability
to repair a UV type of damage in their DNA; 4) since UV in sunlight
cannot reach the central nervous system, neuronal DNA is damaged
by endogenous, intracellular metabolites and/or by "spontaneous"
physicochemical events; 5) patients with the most defective in
vitro post-UV colony-forming ability have the earliest onset of
neurological abnormalities, because the integrity of their neuronal
DNA is lost at an early age; 6) each of the neurons of a particular
neuron group or system has the same qualitative and quantitative

Table 1.   Neurological and DNA Repair Data on All Known Forms of Xeroderma Pigmentosum

Form of xeroderma pigmentosum	Patients whose lines are used in survival experiments[a]	Xeroderma pigmentosum neurological abnormalities[b]	DNA-repair-dependent tests			Post-UV survival (% of normal D_{001}[f])
			UV-induced unscheduled DNA synthesis (% of normal)[c]	Host-cell reactivation (% of normal)[d]	Post replication repair (impairment)[e]	
Variant	XP4BE XP13BE	None	100	70	Extreme	>70
Group A	XP25RO XP26RO XP6TO XP4LO XPKFSF	<7 yr	0.4-1.3	3.5	Intermediate	18-22
	XP12BE	>12 yr	0.4-1.3	3.5	Intermediate	40
	XP1LO	None by 33 yr	0.4-1.3	6.8	---	53
	XP8LO	None by 6 yr	30	---	---	>70
Group B	XP-CS-1[g]	None; CS type	3-7	11	Intermediate	---
Group C	XP2BE XP9BE XP10BE XP4RO	None	10-20	11-35	Intermediate	>50
	XP1BE XP3BE	None by 30 yr[h]	10-20	11-35	Intermediate	>41
	XP1MI	Microcephaly	13	---	---	38
Group D	XP5BE XP6BE XP2NE XP3NE XP7BE XPKABE XP17BE	7-12 yr	25-50	3.3-3.6	Intermediate	27-32
Group E	XP2RO	None by 34 yr	>40	47	None	>70
Group F	XP230S	None by 41 yr	10	Intermediate	---	>70
Group G	XP2BI	12 yr	2	21	Intermediate	32
Group H	XP-CS-2[i]	None; CS type	30	<11	Intermediate	---

[a]Survival for all but group B and H lines in Fig 2. Complementation group assignments presented or cited in De Weerd-Kastelein et al., 1972; Robbins et al., 1974; Andrews et al., 1978a; Robbins, 1978a; Arase et al., 1979; Keijzer et al., 1979; Barrett et al., 1981; Moshell et al., 1983.
[b]Age of onset and type of neurological abnormalities presented or cited in Robbins et al., 1974; Andrews et al., 1978a; Robbins, 1978a; Arase et al., 1979; Friedberg et al., 1979; Keijzer et al., 1979; Barrett et al., 1981; Moshell et al., 1983; Robbins et al., 1983b.
[c]Data from, or cited in, Robbins et al., 1974; Petinga et al., 1977; Robbins, 1978a; Arase et al., 1979; Friedberg et al., 1979; Keijzer et al., 1979; Barrett et al., 1981; Moshell et al., 1983.
[d]Host-cell reactivation data of UV-irradiated virus presented or cited in Day, 1974; Friedberg et al., 1979; Keijzer et al., 1979; Lytle et al., 1983; group F data from Arase et al., 1979; group H data from Day and Robbins, unpublished.
[e]Data from Lehmann et al., 1975, 1977; Friedberg et al., 1979; Keijzer et al., 1979; Doniger et al., 1980; group H data from Doniger and Robbins, unpublished.
[f]D_{001} is dose (erg/mm^2) of 254-nm UV reducing colony-forming ability to 0.1%; values from Fig. 1.
[g]This patient has both XP and Cockayne syndrome and is patient XP11BE (Robbins et al., 1974).
[h]A few minimal abnormalities were found after 30 yr of age (Robbins et al., 1983b).
[i]This patient has both XP and Cockayne syndrome (Moshell et al., 1983).

spectrum of DNA damage, but neuron groups with different environments and neurotransmitters have different spectra of DNA damage; 7) those groups of neurons with relatively large amounts of the type of DNA damage which is the substrate for the defective DNA repair process accumulate the largest amount of unrepaired DNA and die, thereby accounting for the selective degeneration of certain neuron groups and tracts but not of others; 8) the accumulation of unrepaired DNA damage prevents normal transcription of RNA with resultant inability to synthesize critical enzymes or other molecules necessary for cell survival, and the neurons die prematurely, perhaps in accord with the error catastrophe concept of Orgel (1963).

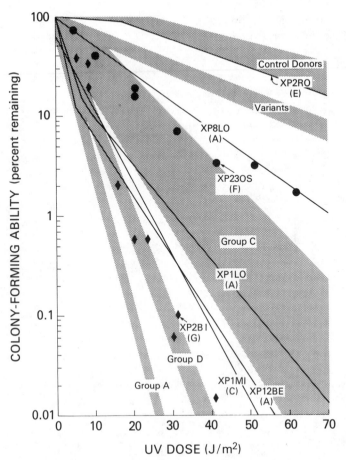

Fig. 1. Survival of xeroderma pigmentosum (XP) fibroblast
         lines of Table 1 after exposure to 254-nm UV. Shaded
         areas represent the range of survival curves of the
         indicated groups. Modified from (Andrews et al., 1976,
         1978a; Robbins et al. 1978a, 1983b; Arase et al., 1979;
         Barrett et al., 1981). Letters in parentheses indicate
         the XP complementation group.

CLINICOPATHOLOGIC AND DNA REPAIR CHARACTERISTICS OF COCKAYNE
SYNDROME

     Schmickel and coworkers (1977) reported that fibroblasts from
patients with the rare autosomal recessive disorder Cockayne syndrome were hypersensitive to the lethal effects of UV. While
Cockayne syndrome cell lines are hypersensitive to UV (Schmickel
et al., 1977; Andrews et al., 1978b; Otsuka et al., 1984) and to

UV-mimetic chemicals (Friedberg et al., 1979), they are not as
sensitive as the group D or most sensitive group C XP lines
(Andrews et al., 1978b; Otsuka et al., 1984). As summarized by
Lytle et al. (1983), Cockayne syndrome cells have normal rates of
UV-induced unscheduled DNA synthesis, normal pyrimidine dimer
excision, normal postreplication repair, defective host-cell reactivation of UV-treated virus (indicating strongly that the cells have
defective repair of damaged DNA), and an abnormally long inhibition
of both DNA and RNA synthesis after exposure to UV. Several
Cockayne syndrome complementation groups have been identified
(Tanaka et al., 1981; Lehmann, 1982). Two patients with both
Cockayne syndrome and XP have been reported (Robbins et al.,
1974; Moshell et al., 1983; Otsuka et al., 1984).

     Relevant clinical signs of Cockayne syndrome include: 1) cu-
taneous sensitivity to sunlight (usually manifested as acute sun
sensitivity but never manifested by sunlight-induced malignancies
or excessive freckling) (Guzzetta, 1972; Brumback et al., 1978;
Otsuka et al., 1984); 2) a primary degeneration of photoreceptor
rods and cones which results in a retinitis pigmentosa; and 3)
relentlessly progressive neurological abnormalities principally
due to demyelination rather than to primary neuronal degeneration.
It has been suggested that there is an accumulation of DNA damage
in the Cockayne syndrome photoreceptors due to defective DNA
repair processes (Lytle et al., 1983; Robbins, 1983). Furthermore, since myelin in the normal central nervous system has
minimal, if any, metabolic turnover (Man et al., 1983), it is
likely that the oligodendroglial cells which produce myelin are
long lived, highly differentiated cells. Consequently, if they
shared the Cockayne syndrome DNA repair defect, oligodendroglia
might be expected to accumulate DNA damage resulting in their
death and demyelination.

CLINICOPATHOLOGIC FEATURES AND CELLULAR SENSITIVITY IN ATAXIA
TELANGIECTASIA

     Ataxia telangiectasia is an autosomal recessive disease with
numerous abnormalities including primary neuronal degeneration
(Sedgwick and Boder, 1972; Blackwood and Corsellis, 1976; Kraemer,
1977; Friedberg et al., 1979; Sedgwick, 1982). The reports of
fatal radiation reactions in ataxia telangiectasia patients
receiving standard doses of radiotherapy for malignancies prompted
Taylor et al. (1975) to study the response of ataxia telangiectasia
fibroblast lines to the lethal effects of ionizing radiation.
They found the ataxia telangiectasia cells to be markedly
hypersensitive to ionizing radiation, a finding confirmed by
many other investigators (Kraemer, 1977; Chen et al., 1978;
Friedberg et al., 1979; Moshell et al., 1980; Scudiero et al.,
1982a; Paterson et al., 1984). Ataxia telangiectasia lines

are also hypersensitive to certain radiomimetic chemicals (Kraemer, 1977; Friedberg et al., 1979; Scudiero, 1980; Teo and Arlett, 1981; Paterson et al., 1984), but have normal sensitivity to 254-nm UV (Friedberg et al., 1979; Moshell et al., 1980; Scudiero, 1980; Scudiero et al., 1982a; Paterson et al., 1984) and normal host-cell reactivation of virus damaged by ionizing radiation (Rainbow, 1981). Some lines are unable to repair certain types of DNA damage induced by ionizing radiation, and some, but not all, lines have abnormally low levels of DNA repair replication induced by ionizing radiation (Paterson et al., 1976). The cells have a prolonged phase of semiconservative DNA synthesis (Murnane and Painter, 1982) and lack the inhibition of semiconservative DNA synthesis which occurs in normal cells after treatment with the X-ray type of DNA-damaging agent (Jaspers and Bootsma, 1982; Jaspers et al., 1982; Murnane and Painter, 1982). However, this DNA synthesis abnormality is not the cause of the radiosensitivity, since delaying DNA synthesis [e.g., by plateau-phase culturing (Cox, 1982) or by aphidicolin treatment (Smith and Paterson, 1983)] does not reduce the hypersensitivity to ionizing radiation. Several investigators have shown that ataxia telangiectasia fibroblasts lack potentially lethal damage repair (Weichselbaum et al., 1978; Cox, 1982; Paterson et al., 1983; Utsumi and Sasaki, 1984).

N-Methyl-N'-nitro-N-nitrosoguanidine (MNNG), a potent alkylating agent, produces numerous types of damage to DNA, including methylation of phosphate groups and all purines and pyrimidines, which ultimately result in DNA strand breakage, cytotoxicity, mutation, and tumor formation (Singer, 1979). Several studies have indicated that mammalian cells respond to alkylating agents in a manner similar to their response to ionizing radiation. Both Scudiero (1980) and Paterson et al. (1984) have found most ataxia telangiectasia fibroblast lines to have less survival, measured as colony-forming ability, than normal cells after treatment with MNNG. However, for unknown reasons, studies by others have failed to demonstrate hypersensitivity of ataxia telangiectasia cells to MNNG (Teo and Arlett, 1981; Jaspers et al., 1982).

Chen and colleagues (1978), using the trypan-blue lymphoblastoid line survival assay of Andrews et al. (1974), showed that the post-X-ray survival not only of ataxia telangiectasia homozygote lines but also of the less sensitive heterozygote lines could be readily distinguished from that of normal lines. Since ataxia telangiectasia heterozygote lines cannot be readily distinguished from normal lines using the typical fibroblast-ionizing-radiation colony-forming ability test (Paterson et al., 1979), the trypan-blue lymphoblastoid line survival test, particularly with survival calculated as the viability ratio (Moshell et al., 1980, 1981; Scudiero et al., 1982a; Robbins et al., 1983a, 1984; Tarone et al., 1984), is the more sensitive test for identifying diseases with small degrees of hypersensitivity to ionizing

radiation. Fig. 2 shows that ataxia telangiectasia homozygote and
heterozygote lymphoblastoid lines are hypersensitive to X rays
but have a normal sensitivity to UV, while XP and Cockayne syndrome
lines, which are hypersensitive to UV, have a normal sensitivity
to X rays. Since all ataxia telangiectasia lines have a similar
degree of hypersensitivity to ionizing radiation (Friedberg et al.,
1979; Paterson et al., 1984) but only some have been shown to have
defective DNA repair processes (Friedberg et al., 1979; Paterson
et al., 1976, 1984), the actual defect in ataxia telangiectasia
cells which accounts for their radiosensitivity is unknown.
Several complementation groups have been demonstrated in ataxia
telangiectasia (Paterson et al., 1976; Murnane and Painter, 1982;
Jaspers and Bootsma, 1982).

CLINICOPATHOLOGIC FEATURES AND CELLULAR SENSITIVITY IN OTHER
PRIMARY NEURONAL DEGENERATIONS

     Huntington disease (Huntington, 1872) is a dominantly inher-
ited, relentlessly progressive primary neuronal degeneration with
reported prevalence in the United States of five cases per 100,000
(Blackwood and Corsellis, 1976).

     Some, but not all, Huntington disease fibroblast lines have
a small hypersensitivity to the lethal effects of ionizing radiation in colony-forming ability studies (Bridges, 1981; Paterson
et al., 1983; Arlett and Priestley, 1984). Fibroblast lines
from some persons at a 50-percent risk for Huntington disease
also had lower than normal colony-forming ability after treatment
with ionizing radiation (Bridges, 1981; Paterson et al., 1983).
In all of these studies the standard fibroblast colony-forming
ability test was used: log-phase fibroblasts were irradiated
with the usual acute dose rate (i.e., >100 rads/min) of ionizing
radiation. However, this standard colony-forming ability test
is known to be inadequate for detecting hypersensitivity in
radiosensitive disorders with a hypersensitivity equal to, or
less than, that of ataxia telangiectasia heterozygotes, as described in detail elsewhere (Scudiero et al., 1982a; Tarone et
al., 1984). Using a colony-forming ability test of Huntington
disease fibroblasts after treatment with the radiomimetic chemical
MNNG, a group of six Huntington disease lines was found to be
significantly hypersensitive to the chemical (Scudiero et al.,
1981a). It is not known why other investigators (Teo and Arlett,
1981) have not found hypersensitivity to MNNG in Huntington
disease lines. A significant hypersensitivity to X rays was found
in a group of four Huntington disease lymphoblastoid lines using
the trypan-blue dye-exclusion test (Moshell et al., 1980). Subsequently, a group of ten Huntington disease lymphoblastoid lines
was shown to be significantly hypersensitive to ionizing radiation
in a colony-forming ability test by Chen et al. (1981). Lympho-

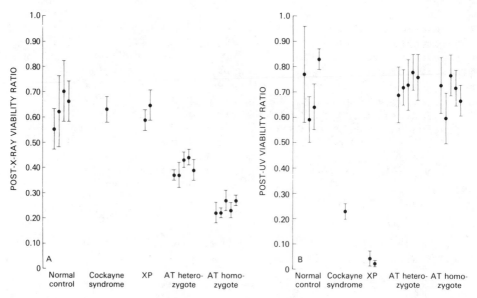

Fig. 2. Survival of normal, Cockayne syndrome, xeroderma
         pigmentosum (XP), ataxia telangiectasia (AT) heterozygote,
         and AT homozygote lymphoblastoid lines after exposure
         to: A) X rays (100 rads) or B) UV (6 J/m^2). Each symbol
         represents the mean viability ratio of the replicate
         experiments performed on a cell line. The error bars
         represent ±2 SEM. The viability ratios were determined
         on the third day after irradiation. Based on values
         presented in Moshell et al., 1980.

blastoid lines from some persons at risk for Huntington disease
were also hypersensitive to ionizing radiation (Moshell et al.,
1980; Chen et al., 1981). Hypersensitivity to the lethal effects
of X rays has been demonstrated with the trypan-blue dye-exclusion
test using peripheral blood lymphocytes from a group of 22 Huntington disease patients (McGovern and Webb, 1982). Huntington disease peripheral blood lymphocytes also have abnormally increased
numbers of X-ray-induced chromosome aberrations (Chen et al.,
1981). When Huntington disease lymphoblastoid cells were fused
in culture to normal lymphoblastoid cells, this hypersensitivity
was transferred to the normal cells, since in the fused cells
both the Huntington disease and the normal chromosomes manifested
abnormally high frequencies of ionizing-radiation-induced chromosomal aberrations (Kidson et al., 1983). Huntington disease
lymphoblastoid lines are abnormally sensitive to the radiomimetic
chemical bleomycin which reduces their viability in the trypan-blue
dye-exclusion test and causes an abnormally high proportion of
cells to be blocked in the G_1 phase of the cell cycle (Imray and
Kidson, 1983).

Alzheimer disease and Parkinson disease are primary neuronal degenerations and are two of the most common neurological disorders of the elderly. Alzheimer disease is a form of progressive irreversible dementia with a prevalence greater than three per 1000 in the United States and a peak incidence in the fifth and sixth decades (Alzheimer, 1907; De Boni and McLachlan, 1980). Most cases are sporadic, but familial cases occur and appear to have autosomal dominant inheritance (Cook and Austin, 1978; Nee et al., 1983). Parkinsonism is a clinical syndrome characterized by resting tremor, rigidity, bradykinesia, postural instability, diminished spontaneous movement, and lack of associated movements. Most cases unassociated with the use of neuroleptic drugs are the result of the idiopathic degenerative Parkinson disease (Parkinson, 1955) which is sporadically acquired and not inherited (DuVoisin, 1984).

Fig. 3A shows the post-X-ray survival of lymphoblastoid lines from three sporadic Alzheimer disease patients, six sporadic Parkinson disease patients, and seven neurologically affected patients with XP, Cockayne syndrome, and XP together with Cockayne syndrome. The Alzheimer and Parkinson disease groups had significantly less post-X-ray survival than the normal control group (P≤0.016), but they had normal survival after treatment with UV (Fig. 3B). The radiosensitivity in serially propagated cells in tissue culture is likely to be the result of a stable genetic defect. Therefore, this defect, which may also result in the premature death of the patients' neurons in vivo, is probably caused by a dominant somatic mutation arising during embryogenesis. Since germ cells are not involved, the genetic defect is not heritable. Radiosensitivity has been reported also in cell lines from patients with the familial form of Alzheimer disease and from patients with the amyotrophic lateral sclerosis-Parkinsonism-dementia syndrome of Guam (Kidson et al., 1983).

Some patients with neurodegenerative disease have a severe primary neuronal degeneration of autonomic neurons. The disorders affecting adults are idiopathic orthostatic hypotension and multiple system atrophy (Shy-Drager syndrome) (Polinsky et al., 1981); the disorder of children is familial dysautonomia (Riley-Day syndrome) (Axelrod, 1979). Idiopathic orthostatic hypotension patients have only autonomic dysfunction, while patients with multiple system atrophy have additional degeneration of central nervous system neurons (Polinsky et al., 1981). Familial dysautonomia is an autosomal recessive disorder involving cell loss in the intermediolateral cell column of the spinal cord (Pearson and Pytel, 1978), sympathetic ganglia (Pearson and Pytel, 1978), and dorsal root ganglia (Pearson et al., 1978). Lymphoblastoid lines from patients with idiopathic orthostatic hypotension (Robbins et al., 1981a), multiple system atrophy (Robbins et al., 1981a), and familial dysautonomia (Robbins et al., 1981b) were found to be hypersensitive to the lethal effects of X rays, and

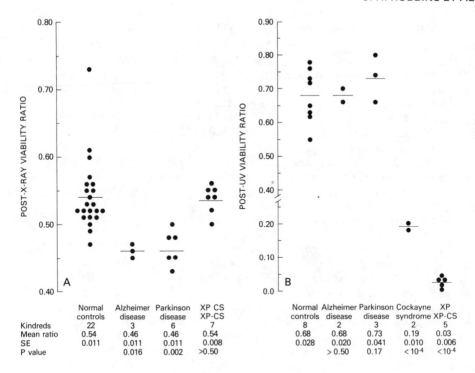

	Normal controls	Alzheimer disease	Parkinson disease	XP CS XP-CS		Normal controls	Alzheimer disease	Parkinson disease	Cockayne syndrome	XP XP-CS
Kindreds	22	3	6	7		8	2	3	2	5
Mean ratio	0.54	0.46	0.46	0.54		0.68	0.68	0.73	0.19	0.03
SE	0.011	0.011	0.011	0.008		0.028	0.020	0.041	0.010	0.006
P value		0.016	0.002	>0.50			> 0.50	0.17	< 10^{-4}	< 10^{-4}

Fig. 3.   Survival of normal, Alzheimer disease, Parkinson disease,
          xeroderma pigmentosum (XP), Cockayne syndrome (CS), and
          xeroderma pigmentosum–Cockayne syndrome (XP-CS) lympho-
          blastoid lines after exposure to: A) X rays (100 rads)
          or B) UV (6 J/mm^2). Each symbol represents the mean
          viability ratio of the replicate experiments performed
          on a cell line. Each horizontal bar represents the
          mean viability ratio for its group. The viability
          ratio was determined on the third day after irradiation.
          Based on values presented in Robbins et al., 1983a.

fibroblast lines from these patients are hypersensitive to the
lethal effects of MNNG (Scudiero et al., 1981a, b).

     Amyotrophic lateral sclerosis is a form of motor neuron dis-
ease affecting both the upper and lower motor neurons (Blackwood
and Corsellis, 1976). This primary neuronal degeneration has a
prevalence of two to seven per 100,000 and an average age of
onset between 50 and 60 years (Brooke, 1977; Walton, 1981). At
least 90% of patients have no family history of the disease and
are apparently sporadic cases (Walton, 1981; Baraitser, 1982).
Proximal spinal muscular atrophy is a hereditary form of motor
neuron disease with degeneration of lower motor neurons in the
anterior horns of the spinal cord and the cranial nerve motor

nuclei (Blackwood and Corsellis, 1976; Walton, 1981).

In accord with the DNA-damage hypothesis (Bradley and Krasin, 1982; Chamberlain and Lewis, 1982; Robbins, 1983; Scudiero et al., 1983), it was expected that amyotrophic lateral sclerosis and spinal muscular atrophy cell lines would be hypersensitive to the X-ray-type of DNA-damaging agent. However, it was found that the mean post-X-ray viability ratio of a group of five amyotrophic lateral sclerosis lymphoblastoid lines was the same as that of the normal group (Robbins, 1983) and that groups of two amyotrophic lateral sclerosis and of five spinal muscular atrophy fibroblast lines had a normal sensitivity to MNNG (Scudiero et al., 1983). Chamberlain and Lewis (1982) showed that a group of eight motor neuron disease fibroblast lines had a normal sensitivity to the lethal effects of ionizing radiation. These results with motor neuron disease lines do not rule out the possibilities that an individual amyotrophic lateral sclerosis (Scudiero et al., 1983) or spinal muscular atrophy (Scudiero et al., 1981b, 1983) line might be hypersensitive to these DNA-damaging agents or that these motor neuron disease lines might be hypersensitive to some other type of DNA-damaging agent.

Friedreich ataxia is a recessively inherited, spinocerebellar, primary neuronal degeneration (Walton, 1981; Baraitser, 1982). Fibroblast lines have hypersensitivity to the lethal effects of ionizing radiation in colony-forming ability tests (Chamberlain and Lewis, 1982), moderately impaired potentially lethal DNA damage repair (Chamberlain and Lewis, 1982), normal inhibition of postirradiation DNA synthesis (Chamberlain et al., 1981), and abnormally increased frequencies of bleomycin-induced chromosomal aberrations (Evans et al., 1983).

CLINICOPATHOLOGIC FEATURES AND CELLULAR SENSITIVITY IN MUSCULAR DYSTROPHIES

Duchenne (X-linked pseudohypertrophic) muscular dystrophy is an inherited muscular dystrophy with a frequency of 13 to 33 per 100,000 live-born males (Rowland and Layzer, 1979). Even though there is laboratory evidence that the disease is present at birth (Rowland and Layzer, 1979), clinical symptomatology rarely appears before the second year of life (Brooke, 1977). In the early stages the muscle biopsy picture of marked muscle fiber degeneration and regeneration and increased endomysial connective tissue, together with values of serum creatine phosphokinase 25 to 200 times the upper limit of normal, is virtually diagnostic of Duchenne muscular dystrophy (Rowland and Layzer, 1979). Differentiating clearly inherited forms of this X-linked disorder from sporadic isolated forms, which may represent new mutations, necessitates identification of the carrier status of the mother. The most useful test for detecting carriers has been serum creatine phosphokinase determination, since two-thirds of obligate carriers will have increased levels (Rowland and Layzer, 1979). Becker muscular dystrophy (Becker variant of X-linked pseudohypertrophic muscular dystrophy) closely resembles Duchenne muscular dystrophy except that the onset of symptoms is usually much later (the mean age of onset is 11 years) and the progression is much slower (Rowland and Layzer, 1979; Baraitser, 1982). Muscle biopsy findings are the same as those found in Duchenne muscular dystrophy, but the changes occur at a much later age.

Myotonic muscular dystrophy (myotonia atrophica, dystrophia myotonica, Steinert disease) is an autosomal, dominantly inherited, multisystem disorder affecting up to 13.5 per 100,000 (Harper, 1979). This disorder has a very wide variability in expression of clinical signs, symptoms, and laboratory values even within the same pedigree, and it is not uncommon to find obligate heterozygotes in the pedigree who have signs of neither myotonia nor dystrophy (Roses et al., 1979). Patients with limb-girdle dystrophy have progressive involvement of proximal musculature, absence of facial involvement, markedly elevated serum creatine phosphokinase levels (20 or more times normal), a muscle biopsy showing nonspecific neuromyopathic changes, and do not fit into other specific syndromes (Brooke, 1977; Walton, 1981).

The post-MNNG survival of muscular dystrophy lines has been compared to that of normal lines. The methods for statistical analysis and the D_{01} values for the 17 normal lines and for the nine muscular dystrophy lines studied were reported previously (Tarone et al., 1983). Five normal lines were studied concurrently with five muscular dystrophy lines. The post-MNNG survival curves of the five normal lines are shown individually in Fig. 4A and as the shaded area of Fig. 4B. Their average D_0 and D_{01} values were, respectively, 2.8 (range: 2.3-3.4) and 16.1 (range: 13.8-18.9). Of the curves of the five muscular dystrophy lines (Fig. 4B), the Becker dystrophy line AG 4035 was the most sensitive; its D_0 of 1.7 and D_{01} of 9.6 were significantly below the corresponding values of each of the normal lines (one-sided P=0.018 and 0.032, respectively). The curve of the Duchenne line RB 4364 was very low in the normal zone. Myotonic dystrophy line RB 5213 had D_0 and D_{01} values of 1.9 and 12.3, respectively, which were lower, but not significantly lower, than those of the lowest normal line. The other two myotonic dystrophy lines had curves in the lower part of the normal zone. These three myotonic dystrophy lines had average D_0 (2.3) and D_{01} (13.5) values which were lower than the corresponding normal values (P=0.14 and 0.042, respectively). When all five of these muscular dystrophy lines were considered as a group, their average D_0 (2.2) and D_{01} (12.8) values were significantly less than those of the five normal lines (P=0.055 and 0.022, respectively).

Eight additional normal lines were studied (Fig. 4C) concurrently with four additional muscular dystrophy lines (Fig. 4D).
Average D_0 and D_{01} values of the normal lines were, respectively,
2.7 (range: 2.1-3.1) and 14.2 (range: 12.3-16.4). The four
muscular dystrophy lines, from donors unrelated to the muscular
dystrophy donors of Fig. 4B, had very low survival curves (Fig.
4D). The average D_0 (2.1) and D_{01} (12.1) values for the Becker and two Duchenne muscular dystrophy lines, considered as
a group of pseudohypertrophic muscular dystrophy lines, were
significantly less than the corresponding averages of the eight
normal lines (P=0.049 and 0.008, respectively). The summary P
values for the D_0 and D_{01} values for these three pseudohypertrophic muscular dystrophy lines and the two in Fig. 4B were 0.08
and 0.011, respectively, indicating that these five lines are
hypersensitive to MNNG. The D_{01} of 9.5 for the limb-girdle dystrophy line was significantly less than that of each of the eight
normal lines (P=0.009). When all four of the muscular dystrophy
lines in Fig. 4D were considered as a group, their average D_0 and
D_{01} values were significantly less than those of the eight normal
lines (P=0.011 and 0.011, respectively). The summary P values
for the mean D_0 and D_{01} values of these four muscular dystrophy
lines and the five in Fig. 4B were 0.009 and 0.004, respectively,
demonstrating that the group of nine muscular dystrophy lines was
significantly hypersensitive to MNNG.

Post-X-ray survival in the trypan-blue dye-exclusion assay of
ten Duchenne muscular dystrophy lymphoblastoid lines (including
three pairs of affected siblings) representing seven kindreds
has been studied (Robbins et al., 1984; Tarone et al., 1984).
The viability ratio of each affected member of a pair from a
kindred was within 2% of the average ratio of the pair. The mean
viability ratio of the seven kindreds was 0.49 which differed
significantly from that of 0.54 of the 26 normal lines (P=0.012).
The Duchenne muscular dystrophy lymphoblastoid lines had a normal
sensitivity to 254-nm UV. Thus, Duchenne muscular dystrophy
is the first of the muscular dystrophies to be shown to have a
hypersensitivity to X rays.

CLINICOPATHOLOGIC FEATURES AND CELLULAR SENSITIVITY IN RETINAL
DYSTROPHIES

Retinitis pigmentosa is the designation for a group of nonin-
flammatory dystrophies (or abiotrophies) of the sensory retina
sometimes associated in specific kindreds with other neurologic
and systemic disorders (McKusick, 1983). In retinitis pigmentosa
the rods undergo degeneration prior to the cones, giving rise to
the symptom of night blindness. Autosomal dominant, autosomal
recessive, and X-linked inheritance have each been reported in
kindreds having retinitis pigmentosa uncomplicated by associated

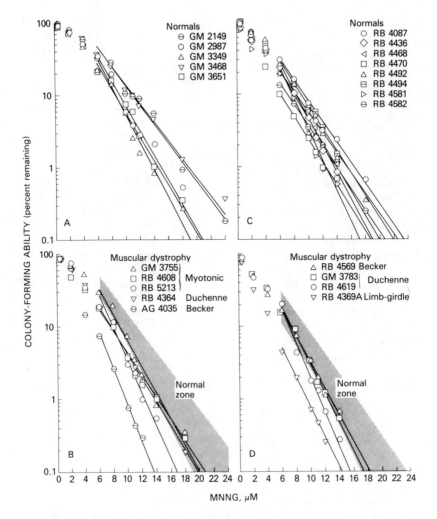

Fig. 4.   Survival of normal and muscular dystrophy fibroblast
          lines after treatment with N-methyl-N'-nitro-N-nitroso-
          guanidine (MNNG).   A and B, series IV; C and D, series
          V.   The shaded normal zones in B and D encompass the
          survival curves of the normal lines of A and C, respec-
          tively.   Each plotted point for a cell line is the
          geometric mean of the colony-forming ability obtained
          at the indicated dose from the replicate experiments
          performed.   The straight line depicting the exponential
          portion of each survival curve corresponds to the D_0
          and D_{01} estimates.

disorders (McKusick, 1983).   The largest proportion of cases in
most series of retinitis pigmentosa is sporadic and assumed to

be recessive, and the inherited and sporadic recessive forms account
for about 84% of cases in the United States.   About 10% are autosomal
dominant and 6% are X-linked.   The estimated incidence of retinitis
pigmentosa is about one per 3,700 (Boughman, et al., 1980).

Usher syndrome (Gorlin et al., 1979; McKusick, 1983) is
a combination of retinitis pigmentosa and sensorineural deafness.   It has an incidence of three per 100,000 persons and is
estimated to account for 3 to 6% of profound childhood deafness
and 50% of deaf-blindness.   Four types have been described, the
first three of which have autosomal recessive inheritance, while
the fourth has X-linked inheritance.   Profound congenital deafness
and onset of retinitis pigmentosa by 10 years of age characterize
type I Usher syndrome which makes up 90% of the total cases.   Type
I patients also have vestibular abnormalities resulting in ataxia.
Type II patients, comprising about 10% of the cases, have moderate
to severe congenital deafness with onset of retinitis pigmentosa
around the beginning of the third decade of life.   Types III and
IV are very rare.   Caution is required in the diagnosis of Usher
syndrome, because a heterogeneous group of conditions may have
similar presentation (Fishman, 1979; Bateman et al., 1980).

Studies have been conducted on the post-X-ray survival of
eight type I and one type II Usher syndrome lymphoblastoid lines
(representing eight kindreds) (Robbins et al., 1984), ten lines
from patients with dominantly inherited retinitis pigmentosa
(representing seven kindreds) (Robbins et al., 1984), and six
lines from patients with presumed recessively inherited retinitis
pigmentosa (representing five kindreds) (Otsuka et al., 1983b).
The Usher syndrome kindreds had a mean post-X-ray viability ratio
of 0.49 which differed significantly from that of 0.54 of the 26
normal lines (P=0.009).   The mean post-X-ray viability ratio of
the dominant retinitis pigmentosa kindreds was 0.55 and did not
differ significantly from that of the normal lines (P=0.28).
The six recessive retinitis pigmentosa lines had a mean post-X-ray
viability ratio of 0.50, which differed significantly from that of
the normal lines (P=0.042) (Otsuka et al., 1983b).   Usher syndrome fibroblast lines were studied (Robbins et al., 1984) after
treatment with X rays or MNNG.   The mean post-X-ray colony-forming
ability of the seven Usher syndrome fibroblast lines studied was
significantly less than that of the normal lines, and the post-
MNNG colony-forming ability of the three Usher syndrome fibroblast
lines tested was significantly less than that of the normal lines.

CLINICOPATHOLOGIC FEATURES AND NORMAL RADIOSENSITIVITY IN A NERVOUS SYSTEM DISORDER WITHOUT PRIMARY DEGENERATION OF EXCITABLE TISSUE

Multiple sclerosis is a demyelinating disease of the central
nervous system in which there are lesions "disseminated in space

and in time," i.e., there are multiple white matter lesions of
different ages in varying areas of the central nervous system
(Vinken and Bruyn, 1970).

Lymphoblastoid lines from five patients with clinically
definite multiple sclerosis (Rose et al., 1976) have been studied
Robbins, 1983). Their mean post-X-ray viability ratio was 0.53,
which was the same as that of the normal group. The one multiple
sclerosis fibroblast line studied had post-MNNG survival well in
the normal zone (Scudiero et al., 1982b). Unlike the demyelinating
disease Cockayne syndrome, which has a relentlessly progressive
course and a primary degeneration of photoreceptors, the pathological
changes in multiple sclerosis are secondary to exacerbating and
remitting demyelination. Thus, unlike the abiotrophic disorders,
multiple sclerosis would not have been expected to be hypersensitive
to DNA-damaging agents. These results are in conflict with those
of Gipps and Kidson (1981), who reported a hypersensitivity to the
lethal effects of ionizing radiation in lymphoblastoid lines from
multiple sclerosis patients. However, Seshadri et al. (1983)
found no hypersensitivity to the lethal effects of ionizing radiation in peripheral blood lymphocytes from multiple sclerosis patients. Vijayalaxmi et al. (1983) and Seshadri et al. (1983) have
found increased numbers of sister chromatid exchanges in phytohem-
agglutinin-stimulated peripheral blood lymphocytes from multiple
sclerosis patients and considered it possible that this increased
incidence of sister chromatid exchanges might be the result of a
viral infection.

HYPERSENSITIVITY TO DNA-DAMAGING AGENTS AS A NEWLY DESCRIBED
CHARACTERISTIC OF ABIOTROPHIC DISORDERS

Degenerations of excitable tissue known to have hypersensensi-
tivity to DNA-damaging agents are listed in Table 2. In XP (Robbins
et al., 1974; Kraemer, 1977; Friedberg et al., 1979; Cleaver,
1983; Robbins, 1983) and Cockayne syndrome (Schmickel et al.,
1977; Andrews et al., 1978; Friedberg et al., 1979; Lehmann, 1982;
Lytle et al., 1983; Robbins, 1983) the hypersensitivity appears to
be due to a defective DNA repair process, while the defect responsible for the ataxia telangiectasia radiosensitivity (Paterson et
al., 1976; Kraemer, 1977; Friedberg et al., 1979; Rainbow, 1981;
Jaspers and Bootsma, 1982; Jaspers et al., 1982; Murnane and
Painter, 1982) and that of the other radiosensitive disorders is
not known. X rays and MNNG are likely to produce their lethal
effects by damaging DNA (Elkind and Whitmore, 1967). Exposure
of cells to either of these agents in vitro results in a myriad
of different types of lesions in DNA (Hutterman et al., 1978;
Singer 1979), some of which are not lethal even if unrepaired;
others are potentially lethal. In normal cells a certain fraction
of these potentially lethal lesions are not repaired. In the

Table 2.   Abiotrophies Tested for Hypersensitivity to the Lethal
Effects of DNA-damaging Agents

Type of degeneration	Type of hypersensitivity[a]	
	X-ray	UV
Primary neuronal		
Xeroderma pigmentosum	–	+
Ataxia telangiectasia	+	–
Huntington disease	+	–
Alzheimer disease	+	–
Down syndrome[b]	+	–
Parkinson disease	+	–
Familial dysautonomia	+	–
Friedreich ataxia	+	nt
Motor neuron disease[c]	–	nt
Muscular dystrophy		
Group of nine lines[d]	+	nt
Duchenne	+	–
Retinal dystrophy		
Cockayne syndrome	–	+
Usher syndrome	+	–

[a]Hypersensitivity of disease groups to 254-nm UV radiation or to
the X-ray-type of DNA-damaging agent (ionizing radiation and/or
MNNG). +, disease group significantly more sensitive than normal
(P≤0.05); –, group not significantly different from normal; nt,
not tested. Most references are cited in text. An individual
cell line in a disease group may occasionally have a different
sensitivity than the group as a whole.

[b]Classified as a primary neuronal degeneration because all Down
syndrome patients by the end of the fourth decade of life develop
the neuropathology of Alzheimer disease (Price et al., 1982).
Down syndrome lymphoblastoid lines are hypersensitive to X rays
(Otsuka et al., 1983a).

[c]Spinal muscular atrophy and amyotrophic lateral sclerosis fibroblast lines (Chamberlain and Lewis, 1982; Scudiero et al., 1983);
amyotrophic lateral sclerosis lymphoblastoid lines (Robbins,
1983).

[d]Group comprised of one limb-girdle, two Becker, three myotonic,
and three Duchenne muscular dystrophy fibroblast lines treated
with MNNG (Tarone et al., 1983).

patients' cells, a slightly higher fraction may not be repaired
due to an inability to repair an infrequent type of normally re-
pairable lesion. Thus, the slight increase in number of unrepaired
lethal lesions remaining in the patients' cells would cause the
small (but statistically significant) hypersensitivity demonstrated
(Figs. 3 and 4). Presumably, greater differences between disease
and normal cells in vitro would be evident if more selective
DNA-damaging agents were used. It should be noted that the
absence of a large hypersensitivity to the pertinent DNA-damaging
agent does not mean that the cell line has no DNA repair defect.
Thus, the lymphoblastoid line tested (Moshell et al., 1981) from
one member of the XP complementation group E kindred which has
proven DNA repair defects (Friedberg et al., 1979), as well as
the fibroblast line (Barrett et al., 1981) from the other member
(line XP2RO of Fig. 1), had post-UV survival in the normal range.

Except in the case of ataxia telangiectasia, the survival
tests used to detect radiosensitivity in cultured cells from
patients with primary degeneration of neurons, muscle, and photoreceptors are currently not sensitive enough for use in either
presymptomatic or prenatal diagnosis. However, more sensitive
tests are likely to be developed by using different experimental
conditions during irradiation (Cox and Masson, 1981; Paterson et
al., 1984) or by using more suitable DNA-damaging chemicals (Shiloh
et al., 1982). Furthermore, abnormal numbers of radiation-induced
chromosome aberrations or sister chromatid exchanges can be
obtained in XP, Cockayne syndrome, and ataxia telangiectasia cells
in vitro (Kraemer, 1977; Friedberg et al., 1979). It is therefore
possible that such increased numbers of cytogenetic abnormalities
will occur in vitro in cells from patients with most of the disorders described above which have the newly defined hypersensitivity to X rays and MNNG. Such induced chromosome abnormalities have already been reported in cultured cells from patients
with Huntington disease (Chen et al., 1981) and Friedreich ataxia
(Evans et al., 1983).

Burnet (1974) suggested that the death of neurons in degenerative diseases of the nervous system, such as Huntington and
Alzheimer diseases, could be caused by a cumulative development
of somatic mutations in accord with the earlier error catastrophe
concept of Orgel (1963). While Burnet's suggestion was based
primarily on the late onset of many of these diseases and on his
concept of the relationship between intrinsic mutagenesis and
aging, defective repair of damaged DNA would be consistent with
his proposal as well as with the neuronal DNA damage theory.

In presenting the neuronal DNA damage theory of XP (Robbins,
1983; Robbins et al., 1984), an explanation for the death of certain neuron groups and the survival of others was proposed. This
proposal could also explain how different DNA repair defects could

produce the different neurodegenerations or the degenerations of
skeletal muscle or photoreceptors (Robbins et al., 1984). The
DNA of postmitotic excitable tissue is constantly being damaged
in vivo by intracellular metabolites, reactive forms of oxygen,
and spontaneous hydrolytic reactions (Lindahl, 1977; Barrows and
Magee, 1982; Setlow, 1982; Alberts et al., 1983). Due to differences in the intracellular or extracellular environments, the
types and quantities of this DNA damage would differ among neuronal
groups and among different excitable tissues (Robbins, 1978a, b,
1983; Lytle, 1983; Robbins et al., 1984). A defect in a DNA
repair process would leave unrepaired only that type of damage
which is normally the substrate for the defective repair process.
Only neuron groups or excitable tissue in which this irrepairable
type of damage represents a relatively large proportion of the
potentially lethal lesions induced would undergo premature death.
Thus, different defects in DNA repair processes would lead to the
degeneration of different neuronal groups or different excitable
tissue (Lytle et al., 1983; Robbins, 1983; Robbins et al., 1984).
In recessively inherited degenerations and dystrophies the defect
is likely to be in DNA repair enzymes or in other enzymes involved
in reactions affecting DNA repair processes; dominantly inherited
and sporadically occurring degenerations and dystrophies are
likely to be due to the production of abnormal proteins involved
with the structure and configuration of DNA and chromatin,
thereby indirectly affecting the enzymatic repair of DNA.

Recognition of the hypersensitivity to DNA-damaging agents in
cultured cells from patients with neurodegeneration, muscular dystrophy, and retinitis pigmentosa may provide an approach not only
for elucidating the molecular basis for the premature death of
excitable tissue in these diseases but also for correcting the
abnormal responses. Complementation studies of XP (De Weerd-
Kastelein et al., 1972; Robbins et al., 1974; Kraemer, 1977;
Friedberg et al., 1979; Cleaver, 1983), Cockayne syndrome (Tanaka
et al., 1981; Lehmann, 1982), and ataxia telangiectasia (Paterson
et al., 1976; Jaspers and Bootsma, 1982; Murnane and Painter, 1982)
have shown that certain defects can be corrected in vitro by
fusing cells from one patient with cells from another patient.
Hopefully, as new and better tests are applied to cultured cells
from patients with the other diseases manifesting hypersensitivity
to DNA-damaging agents, approaches to correct the deficiencies will
be forthcoming. If these diseases are, in fact, caused by the
accumulation of damaged DNA, methods for increasing the efficiency
of the DNA repair processes, or for lessening the amounts of DNA
damage, may provide the basis for developing in vivo therapies
to prevent the premature death of excitable tissue.

REFERENCES

Alberts, B., Bray, D., Lewis, J., Raff, M., Roberts, K., and
    Watson, J. D., 1983, in: "Molecular Biology of the Cell,"
    pp. 216-221, Garland, New York.
Alzheimer, A., 1907, Ueber eine Eigenartige erkrankung der
    Hirnrinde. Allg. Z. Psychiat., 64:146.
Andrews, A. D., Barrett, S. F., and Robbins, J. H., 1976, Relation
    of DNA repair processes to pathological aging of the nervous
    system in xeroderma pigmentosum, Lancet, 1:1318.
Andrews, A. D., Barrett, S. F., and Robbins, J. H., 1978a, Xeroderma
    pigmentosum neurological abnormalities correlate with colony-
    forming ability after ultraviolet radiation, Proc. Natl.
    Acad. Sci. USA, 75:1984.
Andrews, A. D., Barrett, S. F., Yoder, F. W., and Robbins, J. H.,
    1978b, Cockayne's syndrome fibroblasts have increased sen-
    sitivity to ultraviolet light but normal rates of unscheduled
    DNA synthesis, J. Invest. Dermatol., 70:237.
Andrews, A. D., Robbins, J. H., Kraemer, K. H., and Buell, D. N.,
    1974, Xeroderma pigmentosum long-term lymphoid lines with
    increased ultraviolet sensitivity, J. Natl. Cancer Inst.,
    53:691.
Arase, S., Kosuka, T., Tanaka, K., Ikenaga, M., and Takebe, H.,
    1979, A sixth complementation group in xeroderma pigmentosum,
    Mutat. Res., 59:143.
Arlett, C. F., and Priestley, A., 1984, Deficient recovery from
    potentially lethal damage in some γ-irradiated human fibro-
    blast cell strains, Brit. J. Cancer, 49:227.
Axelrod, F. B., 1979, Familial dysautonomia, in: "Genetic Diseases
    Among Ashkenazi Jews," pp. 149-155, R. M. Goodman and
    E. G. Motulsky, eds., Raven Press, New York.
Baraitser, M., 1982, "The Genetics of Neurological Disorders,"
    University Press, Oxford.
Barrett, S. F., Tarone, R. E., Moshell, A. N., Ganges, M. B., and
    Robbins, J.H., 1981, The post-UV colony-forming ability of
    normal fibroblast strains and of the xeroderma pigmentosum
    group G strain, J. Invest. Dermatol., 76:59.
Barrows, L. R., and Magee, P. N., 1982, Nonenzymatic methylation of
    DNA by S-adenosylmethionine in vitro, Carcinogenesis, 3:349.
Bateman, J. B., Reidner, E. D., Levin, I. S., and Maumenee, I. H.,
    1980, Heterogeneity of retinal degeneration and hearing
    impairment syndromes, Am. J. Ophthalmol., 90:755.
Blackwood, W., and Corsellis, J. A. N., 1976, "Greenfield's
    Neuropathology," 3rd ed., Edward Arnold, London.
Boughman, J. A., Conneally, M. P., and Nance, W. E., 1980, Population
    studies in retinitis pigmentosa, Am. J. Hum. Genet., 32:223.
Bradley, W. G., and Krasin, F., 1982, A new hypothesis of the etiol-
    ogy of amyotrophic lateral sclerosis. The DNA hypothesis,
    Arch. Neurol., 32:677.
Bridges, B. A., 1981, Review lecture. Some DNA-repair-deficient

human syndromes and their implications for human health,
  Proc. R. Soc. Lond. Biol., 212:263.
Brooke, M. H., 1977, "A Clinician's View of Neuromuscular Diseases,"
  Williams & Wilkins, Baltimore.
Brumback, R. A., Yoder, F. W., Andrews, A. D., Peck, G. L., and
  Robbins, J. H., 1978, Normal pressure hydrocephalus: recog-
  nition and relationship to neurological abnormalities in
  Cockayne's syndrome, Arch Neurol., 35:337.
Burk, P. G., Lutzner, M. A., Clarke, D. D., and Robbins, J. H.,
  1971, Ultraviolet-stimulated thymidine incorporation in xero-
  derma pigmentosum lymphocytes, J. Lab. Clin. Med., 77:759.
Burnet, M., 1974, "Intrinsic Mutagenesis: a Genetic Approach
  to Aging," John Wiley and Sons, New York.
Chamberlain, S., Cramp, W. A., and Lewis, P. D., 1981, Defects in
  newly synthesized DNA in skin fibroblasts from patients with
  Friedreich's ataxia, Lancet, 1:1165.
Chamberlain, S., and Lewis, P. D., 1982, Studies of cellular hyper-
  sensitivity to ionizing radiation in Friedreich's ataxia, J.
  Neurol. Neurosurg. Psychiat., 45:1136.
Chen, P., Kidson, C., and Imray, F. P., 1981, Huntington's disease:
  implications of associated cellular radiosensitivity, Clin.
  Genet., 20:331.
Chen, P. C., Lavin, M. F., Kidson, C., and Moss. D., 1978,
  Identification of ataxia telangiectasia heterozygotes, a
  cancer-prone population, Nature, 274:484.
Cleaver, J. E., 1968, Defective repair replication of DNA in
  xeroderma pigmentosum, Nature, 218:652.
Cleaver, J. E., 1982, Rapid complementation method for classifying
  excision repair-defective xeroderma pigmentosum cell strains,
  Somatic Cell Genet., 8:801.
Cleaver, J. E., 1983, Xeroderma pigmentosum, in: "The Metabolic
  Basis of Inherited Disease," pp. 1227-1248, 5th ed., J. B.
  Stanbury, J. B. Wyngaarden, D. S., Fredrickson, J. L.
  Goldstein, and H. S. Brown, eds., McGraw-Hill, New York.
Collins, E. T., 1919, IX. Diseases of the retina. 1. Abiotrophy
  of the retinal neuro-epithelium or "retinitis pigmentosa,"
  Trans. Ophthal. Soc. UK, 39:165.
Cook, R. H., and Austin, J. H., 1978, Precautions in familial
  transmissible dementia, Arch. Neurol., 35:697.
Cox, R., 1982, A cellular description of the repair defect in
  ataxia-telangiectasia, in: "Ataxia-telangiectasia--a Cell-
  ular and Molecular Link Between Cancer, Neuropathology,
  and Immune Deficiency," pp. 141-153, B. A. Bridges and D.
  G. Harnden, eds., John Wiley and Sons, New York.
Cox, R., and Masson, W. K., 1981, Radiosensitivity in cultured
  human fibroblasts, Int. J. Radiat. Biol., 38:575.
Day, R. S., 1974, Studies on repair of adenovirus 2 by human
  fibroblasts using normal, xeroderma pigmentosum and xeroderma
  pigmentosum heterozygous strains, Cancer Res., 34:1965.
DeBoni, U., and McLachlan, D. R. C., 1980, Senile dementia and

Alzheimer's disease: a current view, Life Sci., 27:1.

De Sanctis, C., and Cacchione, A., 1932, L'idiozia xerodermica, Rev. Sper. Freniatr., 56:269.

De Weerd-Kastelein, E. A., Keijzer, W., and Bootsma, D., 1972, Genetic heterogeneity of xeroderma pigmentosum demonstrated by somatic cell hybridization, Nature, 238:80.

Doniger, J., Barrett, S. F., and Robbins, J. H., 1980, Human fibroblast strain with normal survival but abnormal post-replication repair after ultraviolet light irradiation, Cancer Res., 40:2736.

DuVoisin, R. C., 1984, Is Parkinson's disease acquired or inherited? Can. J. Neurol. Sci., 11:151.

Elkind, M. M., and Whitmore, G. F., 1967, "The Radiobiology of Cultured Mammalian Cells," Gordon and Breach, New York.

Evans H. J., Vijayalaxmi, Pentland, B., and Newton, M. S., 1983, Mutagen hypersensitivity in Friedreich ataxia, Ann. Hum. Genet., 47:193.

Fishman, G. A., 1979, Usher's syndrome: visual loss and variations in clinical expressivity, Perspect. Ophthalmol., 3:97.

Friedberg, E. C., Ehmann, U. K., and Williams, J. I., 1979, Human diseases with defective DNA repair, in: "Advances in Radiation Biology," pp. 85-174, Vol. 8., J. H. Lett and H. Adler, eds., Academic Press, New York.

Gipps, E., and Kidson, C., 1981, Ionising radiation sensitivity in multiple sclerosis, Lancet, 1:947.

Gorlin, R. J., Tisner, J. T., Feinstein, S., and Duvall, A. J., 1979, Usher's syndrome type III, Arch Otolaryngol., 105:353.

Gowers, W. R., 1902, A lecture on abiotrophy, Lancet, 1:1003.

Guzzetta, F., 1972, Cockayne-Neill-Dingwall syndrome, in: "Neuroret-inal Degenerations," (Handbook of Clinical Neurology. Vol. 13.), pp. 431-440, P. J. Vinken and G. W. Bruyn, eds., North Holland, Amsterdam.

Harper, P. S., 1979, "Myotonic Dystrophy," Saunders, Philadelphia.

Huntington, G., 1872, On chorea, Med. Surg. Reporter, 26:320.

Huttermann, J., Kohnlein, W., and Teoule, R., 1978, "Effects of Ionizing Radiation on DNA," Springer-Verlag, Berlin.

Imray, F. P., and Kidson, C., 1983, Responses of Huntington's disease and ataxia telangiectasia lymphoblastoid cells to bleomycin, Chem. Biol. Interact., 47:325.

Jaspers, N. G. J., and Bootsma, D., 1982, Genetic heterogeneity in ataxia telangiectasia studied by cell fusion, Proc. Natl. Acad. Sci. USA, 79:2641.

Jaspers, N. G. J., de Wit, J., Regulski, M. R., and Bootsma, D., 1982, Abnormal regulation of DNA replication and increased lethality in ataxia telangiectasia cells exposed to carcino-genic agents, Cancer Res., 42:335.

Keijzer, W., Jaspers, N. G. J., Abrahams, P. J., Taylor, A. M. R., Arlett, C. F., Zelle, B., and Takebe, H., 1979, A seventh complementation group in excision-deficient xero-derma pigmentosum, Mutat. Res., 62:183.

Kidson, C., Chen, P., Imray, F. P., and Gipps, E., 1983, Nervous system disease associated with dominant cellular radiosensitivity, in: "Cellular Responses to DNA Damage," pp. 721-729, E. C. Friedberg and B. A. Bridges, eds., Alan R. Liss, New York.

Kraemer, K. H., 1977, Progressive degenerative diseases associated with defective DNA repair, in: "DNA Repair Processes. Cellular Senescence and Somatic Cell Genetics," pp. 37-71, W. W. Nichols and D. G. Murphy, eds., Symposia Specialists, Miami.

Lehmann, A. R., 1982, Three complementation groups in Cockayne syndrome, Mutat. Res., 106:347.

Lehmann, A. R., Kirk-Bell, S., Arlett, C. F., Harcourt, S. A., de Weerd-Kastelein, E. A., Keijzer, W., and Hall-Smith, P., 1977, Repair of ultraviolet light damage in a variety of human fibroblast cell strains, Cancer Res., 37:904.

Lehmann, A. R., Kirk-Bell, S., Arlett, C. F., Paterson, M. C., Lohman, P. H. M., de Weerd-Kastelein, E. A., and Bootsma, D., 1975, Xeroderma pigmentosum cells with normal levels of excision repair have a defect in DNA synthesis after ultraviolet-irradiation, Proc. Natl. Acad. Sci. USA, 72:219.

Lewis, P. D., Corr, J. B., Arlett, C. F., Harcourt, S. A., 1979, Increased sensitivity to gamma irradiation of skin fibroblasts in Friedreich's ataxia, Lancet, 2:474.

Lindahl, T., 1977, DNA repair enzymes acting on spontaneous lesions in DNA, in: "DNA Repair Processes, Cellular Senescence and Somatic Cell Genetics," pp. 225-240, W. W. Nichols and D. G. Murphy, eds., Symposia Specialists, Miami.

Lytle, C. D., Tarone, R. E., Barrett, S. F., Wirtschafter, J. D., Dupuy, J.-M., and Robbins, J. H., 1983, Host cell reactivation by fibroblasts from patients with pigmentary degeneration of the retina, Photochem. Photobiol., 37:503.

Maher, V. M., Rowan, L. A., Silinskas, K. C., Kateley, S. A., and McCormick, J. J., 1982, Frequency of UV-induced neoplastic transformation of diploid human fibroblasts is higher in xeroderma pigmentosum cells than in normal cells, Proc. Natl. Acad. Sci. USA, 79:2613.

Man, E. H., Sandhouse, M. E., Burg, J., and Fisher, G. H., 1983, Accumulation of D-aspartic acid with age in the human brain, Science, 220:1407.

McGovern, D., and Webb, T., 1982, Sensitivity to ionizing radiation of lymphocytes from Huntington's chorea patients compared to controls, J. Med. Genet., 19:168.

McKusick, V. A., 1983, "Mendelian Inheritance in Man, Catalogs of Autosomal Dominant, Autosomal Recessive, and X-linked Phenotypes," 6th ed., Johns Hopkins University Press, Baltimore.

Moshell, A. N., Ganges, M. B., Lutzner, M. A., Coon, H. G., Barrett, S. F., Dupuy, J.-M., and Robbins, J. H., 1983, A new patient with both xeroderma pigmentosum and Cockayne syndrome comprises the new xeroderma pigmentosum complementation group

H, in: "Cellular Responses to DNA Damage," pp. 209-213, E. C.
    Friedberg and B. A. Bridges, eds., Alan R. Liss, New York.
Moshell, A. N., Tarone, R. E., Barrett, S. F., and Robbins, J. H.,
    1980, Radiosensitivity in Huntington's disease: implications
    for pathogenesis and presymptomatic diagnosis, Lancet, 1:9.
Moshell, A. N., Tarone, R. E., Newfield, S. A., Andrews, A. D., and
    Robbins, J. H., 1981, A simple and rapid method for evaluating
    the survival of xeroderma pigmentosum lymphoid lines after
    irradiation with ultraviolet light, In Vitro, 17:299.
Murnane, J. P., and Painter, R. B., 1982, Complementation of the de-
    fects in DNA synthesis in irradiated and unirradiated ataxia
    telangiectasia cells, Proc. Natl. Acad. Sci. USA, 79:1960.
Nee, L. E., Polinsky, R. J., Eldridge, R., Weingartner, H.,
    Smallberg, S., and Ebert, M., 1983, Family with histolog-
    ically confirmed Alzheimer's disease, Arch. Neurol., 40:203.
Orgel, L. E., 1963, The maintenance of the accuracy of protein
    synthesis and its relevance to aging, Proc. Natl. Acad. Sci.
    USA, 49:517.
Otsuka, F., Tarone, R. E., Cayeux, S., and Robbins, J. H., 1984,
    Use of lymphoblastoid cell lines to evaluate the hypersensi-
    tivity to ultraviolet radiation in Cockayne syndrome, J.
    Invest. Dermatol., 82:480.
Otsuka, F., Tarone, R. E., and Robbins, J. H., 1983a, Lymphoblastoid
    lines from Down's syndrome patients are hypersensitive to X
    rays, Clin. Res. 31:658A.
Otsuka, F., Tarone, R. E., Wirtschafter, J. D., and Robbins, J.
    H., 1983b, Lymphoblastoid lines from patients with reces-
    sively inherited retinitis pigmentosa are hypersensitive
    to X rays, Clin. Res., 31:683A.
Parkinson, J., 1955, An essay on the shaking palsy (1817),
    in: "James Parkinson," M. Critchley, ed., Macmillan, London.
Paterson, M. C., Anderson, A. K., Smith, B. P., and Smith, P. H.,
    1979, Enhanced radiosensitivity of cultured fibroblasts from
    ataxia telangiectasia heterozygotes manifested by defective
    colony-forming ability and reduced DNA repair replication
    after hypoxic γ-irradiation, Cancer Res., 39:3725.
Paterson, M. C., Bech-Hansen, N. T., Blattner, W. A., and Fraumeni,
    Jr., J. F., 1983, Survey of human hereditary and familial dis-
    orders for γ-ray response in vitro: occurrence of both cellu-
    lar radiosensitivity and radioresistance in cancer-prone fami-
    lies, in: "Radioprotectors and Anticarcinogens," pp. 615-638,
    O. F. Nygaard and M. G. Simic, eds., Academic Press, New York.
Paterson, M. C., Bech-Hansen, N. T., Smith, P. J., and Mulvihill,
    J. J., 1984, Radiogenic neoplasia, cellular radiosensitivity,
    and faulty DNA repair, in: "Radiation Carcinogenesis: Epidem-
    iology and Biological Significance," pp. 319-336, J. D. Boice,
    Jr., and J. F. Fraumeni, Jr., eds., Raven Press, New York.
Paterson, M. C., Smith, B. P., Lohman, P. H. M., Anderson, A. K.,
    and Fishman, L., 1976, Defective excision repair of γ-ray-
    damaged DNA in human (ataxia telangiectasia) fibroblasts,
    Nature, 260:444.

Pearson J., and Pytel, B. A., 1978, Quantitative studies of sympathetic ganglia and spinal cord intermedio-lateral gray columns in familial dysautonomia, J. Neurol. Sci., 39:47.

Pearson, J., Pytel, B. A., Grover-Johnson, N., Axelrod, R., and Dancis, R., 1978, Quantitative studies of dorsal root ganglia and neuropathologic observations on spinal cords in familial dysautonomia, J. Neurol. Sci., 35:77.

Petinga, R. A., Andrews, A. D., Tarone, R. E., and Robbins, J. H., 1977, Typical xeroderma pigmentosum complementation group A fibroblasts have detectable ultraviolet light-induced unscheduled DNA synthesis, Biochim Biophys Acta., 479:400.

Polinsky, R. J., Kopin, I. J., Ebert, M. H., and Weise, V., 1981, Pharmacologic distinction of different orthostatic hypotension syndromes, Neurology, 31:1.

Price, D. L., Whitehouse, P. J., Struble, R. G., Coyle, J. T., Clark, A. W., DeLong, M. R., Cork, L. C., and Hedreen, H. C., 1982, Alzheimer's disease and Down's syndrome, in: "Alzheimer's Disease, Down's Syndrome, and Aging," pp. 145-164, F. M. Sinex and C. R. Merril, eds., New York Academy of Sciences, New York.

Rainbow, A. J., 1981, Reactivation of viruses, in: "Short-term Tests for Chemical Carcinogens," pp. 20-35, H. F. Stich and R. H. C. San, eds., Springer, New York.

Richardson, Jr., E. P., and Adams, R. D., 1977, Degenerative diseases of the nervous system, in: "Harrison's Principles of Internal Medicine," pp. 1919-1934, 8th ed., G. W. Thorn, R. D. Adams, E. Braunwald, K. J. Isselbacher, and R. G. Petersdorf, eds., McGraw-Hill, New York.

Robbins, J. H., 1978a, The significance of repair of human DNA: evidence from studies of xeroderma pigmentosum, J. Natl. Cancer Inst., 61:645.

Robbins, J. H., 1978b, Workshop summary: xeroderma pigmentosum, in: "DNA Repair Mechanisms," pp. 603-607, P. C. Hanawalt, E. C. Friedberg, and C. F. Fox, eds., Academic Press, New York.

Robbins, J. H., 1983, Hypersensitivity to DNA-damaging agents in primary degenerations of excitable tissue, in: "Cellular Responses to DNA Damage," pp. 671-700, E. C. Friedberg and B. A. Bridges, eds., Alan R. Liss, New York.

Robbins, J. H., Kraemer, K. H., Lutzner, M. L., Festoff, B. W., and Coon, H., 1974, Xeroderma pigmentosum. An inherited disease with sun sensitivity, multiple cutaneous neoplasms, and abnormal DNA repair, Ann. Intern. Med., 80:221.

Robbins, J. H., and Moshell, A. N., 1979, DNA repair processes protect human beings from premature solar skin damage: evidence from studies of xeroderma pigmentosum, J. Invest. Dermatol., 73:103.

Robbins, J. H., Moshell, A. N., Scarpinato, R. G., Polinsky, R. J., Nee, L. E., and Tarone, R. E., 1981a, Hypersensitivity to ionizing radiation in sporadic primary neuronal degenerations, Clin. Res., 29:669A.

Robbins, J. H., Moshell, A. N., Scarpinato, R. G., and Tarone,
    R.E., 1981b, Hypersensitivity to ionizing radiation in
    familial dysautonomia, Clin. Res., 29:669A.
Robbins, J. H., Otsuka, F., Tarone, R. E., Polinsky, R. J.,
    Brumback, R. P., Moshell, A. N., Nee, L. E., Ganges, M. B.,
    and Cayeux, S. J., 1983a, Radiosensitivity in Alzheimer
    disease and Parkinson disease, Lancet, 1:468.
Robbins, J. H., Polinsky, F. J., and Moshell, A. N., 1983b, Evidence
    that lack of deoxyribonucleic acid repair causes death of
    neurons in xeroderma pigmentosum, Ann. Neurol., 13:682.
Robbins, J. H., Scudiero, D. A., Otsuka F, Tarone, R. E., Brumback,
    R. A., Wirtschafter, J. D., Polinsky, R. J., Barrett, S.
    F., Moshell, A. N., Scarpinato, R. G., Ganges, M. B., Nee,
    L. E., Meyer, S. A., and Clatterbuck, B. E., 1984, Hypersen-
    sitivity to DNA-damaging agents in cultured cells from
    patients with Usher's syndrome and Duchenne muscular
    dystrophy, J. Neurol. Neurosurg. Psychiat., 47:391.
Rose, A. G., Ellison, G., Myers, L., and Tourtellotte, W., 1976,
    Criteria for the clinical diagnosis of multiple sclerosis,
    Neurology, 26 (Part 2):20.
Roses, A. D., Harper, P. S., and Bossen, E. H., 1979, Myotonic
    muscular dystrophy, in: "Diseases of Muscle," Part I,
    (Handbook of Clinical Neurology, Vol. 40), pp. 485-532, P.
    J. Vinken, G. W. Bruyn, and S. P. Ringel, eds., Elsevier-
    North Holland Biomedical Press, Amsterdam.
Rowland, L. P., and Layzer, R. B., 1979, X-linked muscular
    dystrophies, in: "Diseases of Muscle," Part I. (Handbook of
    Clinical Neurology, Vol. 40), pp. 349-414, P. J. Vinken, G.
    W. Bruyn, and S. P. Ringel, eds., Elsevier-North Holland
    Biomedical Press, Amsterdam.
Schmickel, R. D., Chu, E. H. Y., Trosko, J. E., and Chang, C. C.,
    1977, Cockayne syndrome: a cellular sensitivity to ultraviolet
    light, Pediatrics, 60:135.
Scudiero, D. A., 1980, Decreased DNA repair synthesis and defective
    colony-forming ability of ataxia telangiectasia fibroblast
    cell strains treated with N-methyl-N'-nitro-N-nitrosoguani-
    dine, Cancer Res., 40:984.
Scudiero, D. A., Brumback, R. A., Clatterbuck, B. E., Tarone,
    R. E., and Robbins, J. H., 1982b, Cells from patients with
    demyelinating diseases are not hypersensitive to N-methyl-
    N'-nitro-N-nitrosoguanidine, Clin. Res., 30:688A.
Scudiero, D. A., Brumback, R. A., Tarone, R. E., Clatterbuck,
    B. E., and Robbins, J. H., 1983, Amyotrophic lateral sclerosis
    and spinal muscular atrophy fibroblasts are not hypersensitive
    to killing by a DNA-damaging agent, Clin. Res., 31:292A.
Scudiero, D. A., Meyer, S. A., Clatterbuck, B. E., Tarone, R. E.,
    and Robbins, J. H., 1981a, Hypersensitivity to N-methyl-N'-ni-
    tro-N-nitrosoguanidine in fibroblasts from patients with Hun-
    tington disease, familial dysautonomia and other primary neu-

ronal degenerations, Proc. Natl. Acad. Sci. USA, 78:6451.

Scudiero, D. A., Moshell, A. N., Scarpinato, R. G., Meyer, S. A., Clatterbuck, B. E., Tarone, R. E., and Robbins, J. H., 1982a, Lymphoblastoid lines and skin fibroblasts from patients with tuberous sclerosis are abnormally sensitive to ionizing radiation and to a radiomimetic chemical, J. Invest. Dermatol., 78:234.

Scudiero, D. A., Polinsky, R. J., Nee, L. E., Meyer, S. A., Clatterbuck, B. E., Tarone, R. E., and Robbins, J. H., 1981b, Cells from patients with sporadic neuronal degenerations are hypersensitive to killing by N-methyl-N'-nitro-N-nitroso-guanidine, Clin. Res., 29:670A.

Sedgwick, R. P., 1982, Neurological abnormalities in ataxia-telangiectasia, in: "Ataxia-telangiectasia--a Cellular and Molecular Link Between Cancer, Neuropathology, and Immune Deficiency," pp. 23-35, B. A. Bridges and D. G. Harnden, eds. John Wiley and Sons, New York.

Sedgwick, R. P., and Boder, E., 1972, Ataxia-telangiectasia, in: "The Phakomatoses," (Handbook of Clinical Neurology, Vol. 14), pp. 267-339, P. J. Vinken and G. W. Bruyn, eds., North Holland, Amsterdam.

Seshadri, R., Sutherland, G. R., Baker, E., Kutlaca, R., Wigmore, D., and Morley, A. A., 1983, SCE, X-radiation sensitivity and mutation rate in multiple sclerosis, Mutat. Res., 110:141.

Setlow, R. B., 1978, Repair deficient human disorders and cancer, Nature, 271:713.

Setlow, R. B., 1982, DNA repair, aging, and cancer, in: "Research Frontiers in Aging and Cancer: International Symposium for the 1980's," pp. 249-255, National Cancer Institute Monograph 60 (NIH Publication No. 82-2436).

Shiloh, Y., Tabor, E., and Becker, Y., 1982, The response of ataxia-telangiectasia homozygous and heterozygous skin fibroblasts to neocarzinostatin, Carcinogenesis, 3:815.

Singer, B., 1979, N-nitroso alkylating agents: formation and persistence of alkyl derivatives in mammalian nucleic acids as contributing factors in carcinogenesis, J. Natl. Cancer Inst., 62:1329.

Smith, P. H., and Paterson, M. C., 1983, Effect of aphidicolin on de novo DNA synthesis, DNA repair and cytotoxicity in γ-irradiated human fibroblasts. Implications for the enhanced radiosensitivity in ataxia telangiectasia, Biochim. Biophys. Acta., 739:17.

Tanaka, K., Kawai, K., Kumahara, Y., Ikenage, M., and Okada Y., 1981, Genetic complementation groups in Cockayne syndrome, Somatic Cell Genet., 7:445.

Tarone, R. E., Otsuka, F., and Robbins, J. H., 1984, A sensitive assay for detecting hypersensitivity to ionizing radiation in lymphoblastoid lines from patients with Duchenne muscular dystrophy and primary neuronal degenerations, J. Neurol. Sci., 65:367.

Tarone, R. E., Scudiero, D. A., and Robbins, J. H., 1983, Statistical
    methods for in vitro cell survival assays, Mutat. Res.,
    111:79.
Taylor, A. M. R., Harnden, D. G., Arlett, C. F., Harcourt, S. A.,
    Lehmann, A. R., Stevens, S., and Bridges, B. A., 1975,
    Ataxia-telangiectasia: human mutation with abnormal radi-
    ation sensitivity, Nature, 258:427.
Teo, I. A., and Arlett, C. F., 1981, The response of a variety of
    human fibroblast cell strains to the lethal effects of
    alkylating agents, Carcinogenesis, 3:33.
Utsumi, H., and Sasaki, M. S., 1984, Deficient repair of potentially
    lethal damage in actively growing ataxia telangiectasia
    cells, Radiat. Res., 97:407.
Vijayalaxmi, Newton, M. S., Steel, C. M., Evans, H. J., and Pent-
    land, B., 1983, Spontaneous and mutagen induced sister
    chromatid exchange in multiple sclerosis, J. Med. Genet.,
    20:372.
Vinken, P. J., and Bruyn, G. W., eds., 1970, "Multiple Sclerosis
    and Other Demyelinating Diseases," (Handbook of Clinical
    Neurology, Vol. 9.), North Holland, Amsterdam.
Walton, J., 1981, "Disorders of Voluntary Muscle," 4th ed.,
    Churchill Livingstone, Edinburgh.
Weichselbaum, R. R., Nove, J., and Little, J. B., 1978, Deficient
    recovery from potentially lethal radiation damage in
    ataxia-telangiectasia and xeroderma pigmentosum, Nature,
    271:261.
Yano, K., 1950, Xeroderma pigmentosa mit Störungen des
    Zentralnervensystems: Eine histopathologische Untersuchung,
    Folia Psychiat. Neurol. Jpn., 4:143.

RELIABILITY THEORETIC METHODS AND AGING: CRITICAL ELEMENTS, HIERARCHIES AND LONGEVITY—INTERPRETING SURVIVAL CURVES

Matthew Witten

Department of Engineering Mathematics and Computer Science
University of Louisville
Louisville, Kentucky 40292 USA

INTRODUCTION

Studying the processes of senescence is, in a sense, equivalent to studying the processes of longevity. In studies of this type we may ask a variety
of questions concerning the longevity of a specified biological organism. For
example, given that a specified organism has survived until time t , what
is the chance that it will survive until time $t + \Delta t$ (where Δt is a small
increment in time)?

One of the most common means for analyzing senescence data lies in the
form of survival curves. In particular, one may plot (a)Percent survivorship
vs. age, (b)Percent original population dying per year vs. age, or (c)Percent
mortality rate per year vs. age. It is well known that each of these curves
has a characteristic form associated with it. Most commonly, biologists plot
percent or fraction survivorship vs. age. That is, one is plotting the number
or fraction of individuals which have survived until a certain chronological
age a . One of the classic survival curves that is manifested in the biological
literature is the Gompertzian survival curve(Gompertz 1825). Strehler(1977)
illustrates the curve for U.S. white males. Johnson and Wood(1982) illustrate
the same curves for various populations of the nematode C. elegans. Smith–
Sonnenborn(1984) illustrates Gompertzian survival for Paramecia, and Hirsch
and Peretz(1984) illustrate it for the marine mollusk Aplysia californica. A

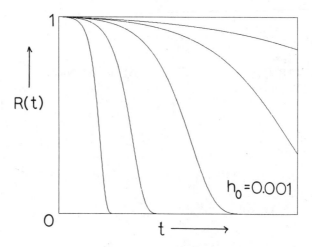

Fig.1.   An illustration of Gompertian curves.

most recent discussion of mortality, which exhibits excellent survival curves, is the paper by Myers and Manton(1984). The general Gompertz equation is given by the following equation:

$$N(t) = N_0 \exp\left[\frac{h_0}{\gamma}(1 - \exp(\gamma t))\right] \tag{1}$$

Fig.1 illustrates equation(1) for the hypothetical values of $h_0 = 0.001$ and $\gamma = 2^{(1-j)}$ where $j = 1, 2, \ldots, 5$. The parameters γ and h_0 are entities who's meaning we will address at a later stage of this paper; when we address the question of the biological interpretation of the Gompertz equation illustrated by equation(1) above. Observe that as γ is decreased, the $N(t)$ curve shows a more gentle and gradual slope; thereby allowing for potentially greater lifespan in the population.

Of great interest is why, given the variety of possible biologically reasonable survival curves, the Gompertz curve manifests itself as the characteristic descriptor of aging organisms. Further, why should it be so uniformly common amoung living systems? It is the purpose of this chapter to address this question; to demonstrate that, under certain reasonable assumptions, the complexity of biological systems requires Gompertzian–like survival. In order to do this, we will need to define certain mathematical concepts which appear in the field of reliability theory.

A BRIEF INTRODUCTION TO RELIABILITY THEORY

Reliability theory appeared as an outgrowth of the need to predict failure in complex engineering structures. That is, when engineering systems became more complex, there came an increased need for effective maintenance and cost evaluation of these same systems. As repeated system failure exacts a price, it soon became clear that it was necessary to understand how systems fail. The outgrowth of these early researches was the field of reliability theory.

When we think of reliability, we think of the chance a component of a system, or the whole system, fails at a given time t . Hence, it is natural to think of the reliability $R(t)$ as a probability. That is, it is the probability that a component or system fails in the time interval $(t, t + \Delta t)$, given that it survives until a time t . The instantaneous failure rate is defined as follows:

$$R(t) = Prob[\![\text{ a component survives until a time} > t]\!] \qquad (2)$$

We denote the system reliability $R_{SYS}(t)$ and we define it in precisely the same manner as we did for the component reliability $R(t)$. Since a component(or system) is either reliable or unreliable, we define the unreliability as $U(t) = 1 - R(t)$.

The biological literature of aging is replete with examples of mortality curves. Hence, let us define the mortality $m(t)$ of a component or of a system.

$$m(t) = Prob[\![\text{ a component will fail at time t}]\!] \qquad (3)$$

We may relate the mortality $m(t)$ to the reliability $R(t)$ as follows. If we choose Δt to be a small time interval, then the probability a component(or system) will fail in $(t, t + \Delta t)$ is given by $m(t)\Delta t$. However, from our definition of the reliability $R(t)$, we see that

$$m(t)\Delta t = R(t) - R(t + \Delta t) \qquad (4)$$

Dividing both sides of equation(4) by Δt and letting Δt go to zero, we obtain

$$m(t) = -\frac{dR(t)}{dt} \qquad (5)$$

It is important to realize that the mortality, as we have defined it, is the apriori probability that a component or system will fail at time t. It is not what biologists normally think of when they speak of mortality.

When a biologist speaks of mortality or mortality rate, he is actually speaking of what we call the instantaneous failure rate or hazard rate. This failure rate is a conditional probability defined as follows:

$$\lambda(t) = \frac{m(t)}{R(t)} \tag{6}$$

Replacing equation(5) in equation(6) we obtain,

$$\lambda(t) = -\frac{1}{R(t)} \cdot \frac{dR(t)}{dt} \tag{7}$$

Observe, however, that we may replace $R(t)$ with $R(t) = N(t)/N_0$ where $N(t)$ is the number of individuals in the population at time t, and N_0 is the initial number of individuals in the population. If we make this replacement, we obtain

$$\lambda(t) = -\frac{1}{N(t)} \cdot \frac{dN(t)}{dt} \tag{8}$$

By means of illustration, let us consider the Gompertz survival function. As given in equation(1), it is easy to show that the mortality $m(t)$ is given by

$$m(t) = -\frac{dR(t)}{dt} = h_0 \exp{(\gamma t)}R(t) \tag{9}$$

Combining equations(1) and (9) in (7) we obtain the instantaneous failure rate $\lambda(t)$ which is given by

$$\lambda(t) = \frac{m(t)}{R(t)} = h_0 \exp{(\gamma t)} \tag{10}$$

Observe, that if we plot the natural logarithm of both sides of equation(10), we would obtain a straight line. A sample of this type of calculation is illustrated, for real data, in Fig.2.

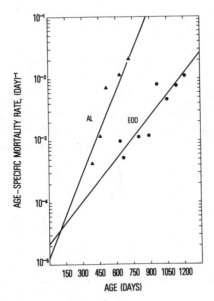

Fig.2.   An illustration of $\lambda(t)$ for realworld data. Courtesy of Ingram
et al.(1982). AL $=$ Ad libitum, EOD $=$ Every other day.

Notice that we may rewrite equation(7) as a differential equation for
the reliability when we are given the instantaneous failure rate $\lambda(t)$. That
is

$$\frac{dR(t)}{dt} = -\lambda(t)R(t) \tag{11}$$

Let us briefly see why equation(11) is of interest.

Equation(11) describes the reliability $R(t)$ for any instantaneous failure
rate $\lambda(t)$ that we might choose to specify. Further, since it is a simple

differential equation, we may solve it very generally to yield the following
equation for $R(t)$

$$R(t) = \exp\left[-\int_0^t \lambda(\tau)d\tau\right] \qquad (12)$$

If we assume that $\lambda(t) = \lambda_0$ where λ_0 is a constant(this is equivalent
to the biological condition that the probability an organism fails in the age
interval $(a, a + \Delta a)$, given that it has survived until age a , is independent
of age), then we obtain the exponential reliability or survival curve

$$R(t) = \exp\left[-\lambda_0 t\right] \qquad (13)$$

If we assume that the instantaneous failure rate is a function of the form
$\lambda(t) = \lambda_1 t + \lambda_0$ (that is, failure is a linear function of time), then we obtain
Gaussian or bell–shaped curves. And, as we have seen in our previous discus-
sion, if we assume an exponential instantaneous failure rate then we arrive at
the Gompertzian survival curve. For further discussion on reliability theoretic
methods, see Witten(1983a,b, 1984).

In the next section, we show how we can apply the concepts of reliability
to two simple networks: (1)A series network and (2)A parallel network. This
will lead us naturally into the application of reliablity methods as applied to
biological systems.

RELIABILITY OF HIERARCHICAL STRUCTURES

In this section we will consider how to apply the basic concepts that we
have just discussed, to the problem of finding the reliability of a series network
and to the problem of finding the reliability of a parallel network. The goal
of this discussion is to begin to understand how the system reliability may be
constructed out of the reliability of its components and an understanding of
how the system might fail (a failure rule). Fig.3 illustrates a hypothetical series
network. Here, we have a series of connected components which are denoted
C_i for the ith component.

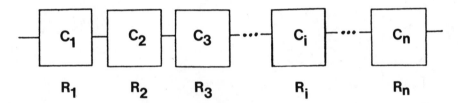

Fig.3.   An illustration of a hypothetical series network.

Assume that we have n of them. The failure rule for a series circuit is simple: The moment one element in the circuit (network, hierarchy) fails, the whole network fails. Hence, the system reliability (probability it survives until a time $>$ t) is given by the system reliability $R_{SYS}(t)$ which must satisfy

$$R_{SYS}(t) = Prob[\![\text{all components } C_i \text{ survive past time t}]\!] \qquad (14)$$

However, the righthand side of equation(14) may be rewritten as follows

$$R_{SYS}(t) = Prob[\![C_1 \text{ and } C_2 \text{ and },\ldots, C_n \text{ survive past time t}]\!] \qquad (15)$$

Observing that the components fail in an independent manner, we may rewrite equation(15) as

$$R_{SYS}(t) = \prod_{i=1}^{n} Prob[\![C_i \text{ survives past time t}]\!] \qquad (16)$$

or, if we simplify our notation, we obtain:

$$R_{SYS}(t) = \prod_{i=1}^{n} R_i(t) = R_1(t)R_2(t)\ldots R_n(t) \qquad (17)$$

where $R_i(t)$ is the reliability of the ith element in the series. If we further assume that the hierarchy is a homogeneous hierarchy (everybody is identical), then equation(17) reduces to the very simple

$$R_{SYS}(t) = [R(t)]^n \qquad (18)$$

where we assume that $R(t)$ is the reliability of the homogeneous element in the series hierarchy. For the purposes of example, let us assume that

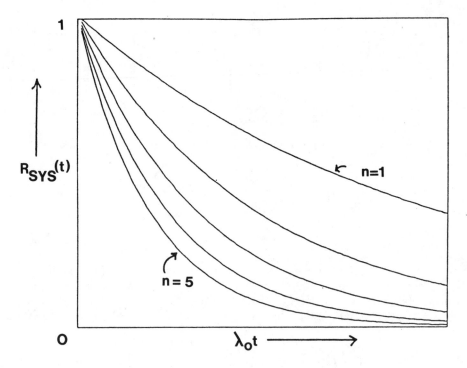

Fig.4.   Sample reliability curves for a series hierarchy.

$R(t) = \exp\left[-\lambda_0 t\right]$. Replacing this into equation(18), we find that the system reliability, for a series structure in which all of the homogeneous elements have exponentially decreasing reliability, is given by

$$R_{SYS}(t) = \exp\left[-n\lambda_0 t\right] \tag{19}$$

Fig.4 illustrates sample curves for equation(19). Notice, in this figure, that increasing the number of elements n in the hierarchy decreases the probability of survival for the hierarchy. This is natural as increasing the number of elements in the hierarchy increases the number of chances that the system can fail; hence decreasing the survival probability.

Let us quickly look at a parallel hierarchy. This is illustrated in Fig.5 . Here, the failure rule is simple: As long as any single element in the hierarchy functions, the whole hierarchy will function. Again, assuming that there are n elements in the structure, we follow the same line of arguments as for the

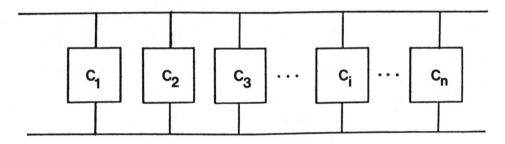

Fig.5.   An illustration of a parallel hierarchy.

series hierarchy, this leads to the following equation for the reliability of a
parallel network

$$R_{SYS}(t) = 1 - \prod_{i=1}^{n} [1 - R_i(t)] \qquad (20a)$$

or, rewriting equation(20a) in an alternate manner, we obtain:

$$R_{SYS}(t) = 1 - (1 - R_1(t))(1 - R_2(t))\ldots(1 - R_n(t)) \qquad (20b)$$

If we have a homogeneous network, equation(20b) simplifies to:

$$R_{SYS}(t) = 1 - [1 - R(t)]^n \qquad (21)$$

where, as before, $R(t)$ is the reliability of the homogeneous element in
the parallel hierarchy. Fig.6 illustrates sample reliability curves for a parallel
network in which each element has an exponential reliability. Notice their
striking similarity to Gompertzian curves.

In the next section, we briefly introduce the concepts of a graph, and
how these give rise to critical elements.

GRAPH THEORY AND CRITICAL ELEMENTS

In Witten(1984a) we discussed the concept of representing the complexity of biological systems in terms of graphs. The essence of this argument
was to reduce the complexity of a biological organism to basic biological functions that were connected to each other in terms of a natural dependency
ordering. We assumed that each biological function was the node of a graph,
and the ordering was in terms of the dependence of each function on another.

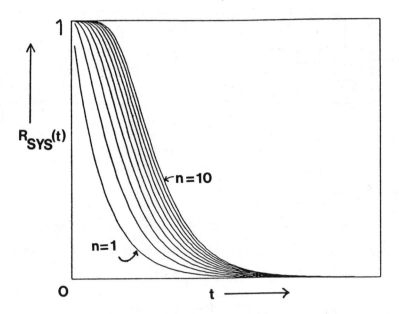

Fig.6.   Reliability curves for a parallel network.

Fig.7 illustrates a hypothetical hierarchy in which each element M_i per-
forms a certain biological function of interest, and each element R_i is its
associated repair function. Notice that, if M_3 were damaged or failing, R_3
could repair it as long as M_1 were functioning correctly. This is because
R_3 needs the output of M_1 in order to function properly. However, if
M_1 were to fail, then M_6 would not function properly (as it depends
upon output from M_1). However, failure of M_6 will cause R_1 to fail;
thereby making it impossible to repair M_1 . Such an element is said to be
non-reestablishable or critical in the hierarchy. In Witten(1984a), we further
proved that every hierarchy of this type must contain at least one critical
component or critical element. A trivial example of such a component, if we
were to look at the human being in terms of its organ structure, would be
the heart. When it fails, the organism "usually" dies.

Suppose we assume that there are n such critical elements in a
biological organism. Further, suppose that the organism fails when all of
the critical elements fail. Further, suppose that the reliability of the critical
elements is given by $R(t)$, then Witten(1984a,b) has shown that the reliability
of the system is obtained by observing that all of the elements must fail in
order for the system to fail. Hence,

$$R_{SYS}(t) = [R(t)]^n$$

which is just our equation for a series hierarchy of n components.

CRITICAL ELEMENTS AND THEIR RELIABILITY

In Witten(1983b) we introduced the concept of how a cell, or other biological entity, might view its functional r(3b) pointed out that biological organisms have a certain role to perform, and they have a certain leeway in which to perform that role. We might say that, if $d(t)$ was an element's deviation from normality at a given time t, then d^* is the critical deviation beyond which the element cannot function; hence it dies.

Before we construct our Gompertzian distribution and obtain an estimate for the critical number of elements in our system, we must first describe the reliability distribution for $R(t)$. We know that the average element in our hierarchy will fail when $d(t) \geq d^*$. Since, as far as we have been able to determine, biological systems have finite lifespan, we will assume that there is a finite time t^* such that $d(t^*) = d^*$. That is, there is a critical time t^* at which the critical deviation d^* is reached. However, most probability distributions assume that any lifespan is possible. Hence, if we are to assume the existence of a finite lifespan, we must truncate our probability distribution so that it is zero beyond the critical time t^*.

Letting T be the random variable describing the time–to–failure of our arbitrary critical element, then the probability it fails before time t is given by

$$Prob[\![T \leq t]\!] = \int_0^t f(\varsigma)d\varsigma \tag{22}$$

where $f(\varsigma)$ is the density function for the probability distribution of interest. One common choice for such a function is the exponential distribution satisfying

$$f(\varsigma) = \lambda_0 \exp[-\lambda_0 \varsigma] \tag{23}$$

Hence

$$Prob[\![T \leq t]\!] = 1 - \exp[-\lambda_0 t] \tag{24}$$

Up to this point, our discussion has assumed that the random variable T could be infinite. As we wish to restrict T, the time–to–failure to the interval $0 \geq T = t \leq t^*$ we truncate the probability as follows

$$Prob[\![T \leq t]\!] = \frac{\int_0^t f(\varsigma)d\varsigma}{\int_0^{t^*} f(\varsigma)d\varsigma} \tag{25}$$

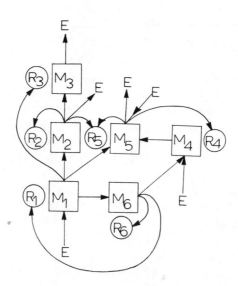

Fig.7.   A hypothetical hierarchy of process and repair elements.

Combining equations(23–25) we obtain,

$$Prob[\![T \leq t]\!] = \frac{1 - \exp[-\lambda_0 t]}{1 - \exp[-\lambda_0 t^*]} \qquad (26)$$

Which represents the truncated time–to–failure probability distribution.

Observe, however, that equation(26) is the unreliability of our system(see Section 2.0 for the definition of unreliability). Hence, the required reliability is

$$R(t) = 1 - Prob[\![T \leq t]\!] \qquad (27)$$

Combining equations(18,26–27), we obtain the following system reliability:

$$R_{SYS}(t) = \left[1 - \frac{1 - \exp[-\lambda_0 t]}{1 - \exp[-\lambda_0 t^*]}\right]^n \qquad (28)$$

Defining κ as

$$\kappa = \frac{1}{1 - \exp\left[-\lambda_0 t^*\right]} \qquad (29)$$

it is possible to show that

$$R_{SYS}(t) \approx \exp\left[-n\kappa(1 - \exp(-\lambda_0 t))\right] \qquad (30)$$

Comparing the parameters in equation(30) with those in the exact Gompertz equation given by equation(1), we have that the critical number n is given by

$$n = -\left(\frac{h_0}{\gamma}\right)\left[1 - \exp(-\gamma t^*)\right] \qquad (31)$$

Thus, knowledge of the parameters h_0, γ, and t^* allows us to calculate the number of critical elements in the hierarchy.

Cutler(1984) calculates a maximum lifespan for humans at 95 years. From Strehler and Mildvan(1960), we find values of $0.0612 \leq \gamma \leq 0.119$ per year and $0.022 \times 10^{-3} \leq h_0 \leq 0.820 \times 10^{-3}$. Combining this data with equation(31), one can show that the critical element number must lie in the range $5 \leq n \leq 15$.

It is important to examine the meaning of these results within the context of survival data of the type usually obtained in longevity studies. Observe that if we compare equations(1) and (30) we see that a change in γ corresponds to a change in λ_0. That is, a statistically significant change in the slope of the population instantaneous failure rate curve implies that the instantaneous failure rate of the average element(organism) in the population has been changed. Or, biologically speaking, if there is a significant change in the slope of the mortality curve(in the biological sense of mortality), then we may say that the biological protocol inducing this change has had an affect upon the individuals in the population. However, a change in h_0 may be interpreted as a population effect; not necessarily changing the instantaneous failure rate of an individual in the population. Thus, the results of Masoro(1984) may now be biologically interpreted. In the cases where Masoro obtains a significantly different mortality curve(slopes are different), we may interpret the diet restriction protocol as having an effect upon the actual individual aging processes. However, in the case where the intersection point h_0 is changed, this represents an overall response by the whole population; possibly shifting the lifespan, but not reflecting an intrinsic change in individual aging mechanisms.

CRITICAL ELEMENTS AND PARAMETER CHANGES

Numerous investigators have demonstrated that a variety of factors can change the shape of the Gompertzian curve. We often hear of "squaring the curve" in discussions of longevity and survival. Clearly, environmental factors can come into play. Cleaner environments, better health facilities, and better medical treatments all play into extending the longevity of the human species. However, more subtle factors can come into play. For example, Smith–Sonnenborn(1984) has demonstrated the ability of electromagnetic waves to extend the lifespan of paramecia.

The literature on diet restriction and its role in influencing aging processes is now well known. Fig.8 illustrates the data of Yu et al.(1982) on longevity. Clearly, we see that lifespan is extended. However, we also see that the character of the Gompertzian curve is changed. This immediately implies that the Gompertzian parameters h_0 and γ are changed. However, if these parameters are changed, and if t^* is changed then, from equation(31) we would expect the number of critical elements to change. Clearly, this is an unreasonable assumption. One would not expect the appearance or disappearance of critical elements to be left to the whimsical nature of the parameters in the Gompertz function. Rather, the implication is that the changing Gompertz parameters are somehow affecting a change in the interaction of the critical elements. If you will remember, our whole analysis was based upon the argument that the critical elements were functioning independently of each other. Clearly this is not a realistic assumption. For example, if the kidneys, or lungs, or liver begin to fail, we might expect to see certain ramifications in other physiological systems. Hence, independently functioning critical elements is a very naive assumption. To more accurately reflect the reality of biological organisms, we must incorporate an interplay(of some type)between the critical elements. We must also incorporate the fact that some systems may have backup or standby replacement systems, redundancy, degraded performance with time, various monitoring strategies as well as a variety of other sophisticated operational schemes. The complexity of these problems will be left for future papers. An extensive discussion of the material of this paper may be found in Witten(1984b).

It is also important to address issues of parameter estimation in survival models. If we are to make conclusions based upon the results of experimental data, we must have accurate methods with which to estimate the parameters in our survival models. Seemingly small errors in the values of our parameters might lead to incorrect results in a statistical analysis, or rejection of an otherwise acceptable hypothesis. In an equally bad outcome, incorrect parameter estimates might cause us to accept a null hypothesis H_0 that there is no biological difference between two slopes when, in point of fact, there actually is a meaningful difference. Thus, not only must we have an accurate method for estimation of our survival model parameters, but we must also have a

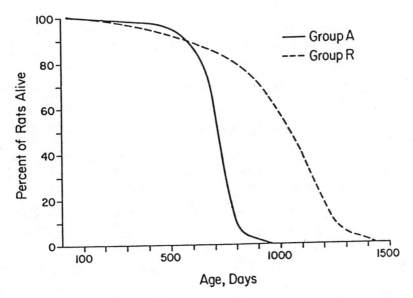

Fig.8.   An illustration of the effects of diet upon survival. Courtesy of Yu
           et al.(1982):A = Ad libitum, R = Restricted.

means to interpret meaningful differences between those parameters. It is the
attempt of this series of papers to address these very issues.

REFERENCES

Cutler, R., 1984, Evolutionary biology of aging and longevity in mammalian
species, in: "Aging And Cell Structure", vol.2, J.E. Johnson, ed., Plenum
Press, New York.

Gompertz, B., 1825, On the nature of the function expressive of the law of
human mortality, Phil. Trans. Roy. Soc.(London), 115:513.

Hirsch, H.R., and Peretz, B., 1984, Survival and aging of a small laboratory
population of marine mollusk, Aplysia californica, Mech. Ageing Dev., 27:43.

Johnson, T.E., and Wood, W.B., 1982, Genetic analysis of lifespan in C.
Elegans, Proc. Nat. Acad. Sci. USA, 79:6603.

Myers, G.C., and Manton, K.G., 1984, Compression of mortality: Myth or reality, J. Gerontol., 24:346.

Smith–Sonnenborn, J., 1984, Programmed increased longevity induced by weak pulsating current in Paramecium, Bioelectrochemistry and Bioenergetics, in press.

Strehler, B.L., and Mildvan, A.S., 1960, General theory of mortality and aging, Science, 132:14.

Strehler, B., 1977, "Time, Cells, And Aging", Academic Press, New York.

Witten, M., 1983a, A reliability theoretic approach to the modeling of cell culture proliferation and senescence: I. Issues of principle, deterministic, and stochastic models, Mech. Ageing Dev., submitted.

Witten, M., 1983b, A return to time, cells, systems, and aging: Rethinking the concept of senescence in mammalian organisms, Mech. Ageing Dev., 21:69.

Witten, M., 1984a, A return to time, cells, systems, and aging: II. Relational and reliability theoretic approaches to the study of senescence in living systems, Mech. Ageing Dev., 27:323.

Witten, M., 1984b, A return to time, cells, systems, and aging: III. Critical elements, Gompertzian dynamics, Mech. Ageing Dev., submitted.

Witten, M., 1985, "Mathematical Gerontology", Johns Hopkins University Press, Baltimore, MD, to appear.

Yu, B.P., Masoro, E.J., Murata, I., Bertrand, H.A., and Lynd, F.T., 1982, Lifespan study of SPF Fischer 344 male rats fed ad libitum or restricted diets: Longevity, growth, lean body mass, and disease, J. Gerontol., 37:130.

THE ODDS ON NORMAL AGING

Lewis Thomas

Departments of Medicine and Pathology
State University of NY at Stony Brook
Stony Brook, NY 11794

In spite of today's ignorance about so many different diseases, including most of the chronic illnesses associated with
aging, there is the most surprising optimism, amounting to something almost like exhilaration, within the community of basic
biomedical researchers. There has never, I think, been a time
quite like the present. Most of the investigators, the young ones
especially, have only a remote idea of the connection of their
work to human disease problems, although they have an awareness
that sooner or later something practical and useful may come from
their research. But this possibility is not the driving force
behind their endeavors. The main impetus is that researchers are
becoming confident about finding out how things work. This is
true for the immunologists threading their way through the unimag-
inably complex network of cells and intercellular messages comprising the human immune system. It is true for the experimental
pathologists and biochemists at work on the components of the
inflammatory reaction and turning up new regulatory cell products
and signalling devices almost every month. The cancer biologists
are totally confident that they are getting close to the molecular
intimacies of cellular transformation, and the virologists are
riding high. Out in the front lines are the molecular biologists
and the geneticists in possession of research techniques that
permit them to ask (and answer) almost any question that pops into
their minds.

The science underlying the aging problem, including the
problem of cancer, relies on basic research for finding out how
things work in a normal cell; but, at the same time, it is a
venture in applied science, for no one doubts that we will not
only be provided with a clear comprehension of how cells age and

361

become cancerous, but we will very likely develop some useful
methods to reverse or control these conditions. Aging research
provides a good example of the way in which biomedical science in
recent years has become an international venture moving back and
forth across national boundaries. If the problems of human aging
and of cancer are solved by one or more of today's research approaches, the ultimate solution cannot be fairly claimed by any
nation or by any particular laboratory or group of laboratories.
The work has reached its present state of high promise as the
result of an intricate network of international collaborators, and
it will have to progress in the same way if it is to be ultimately
successful. To be sure, there will be the usual strident claims
on priority by whomsoever is successful in putting the final piece
of the puzzle in place, but everyone will know, and I hope remember, that the puzzle itself could not have been shaped into being
without the most intense international cooperation over at least
the last 35 years. Crucial bits of information, indispensable for
today's level of incomplete comprehension and even more indispensable for framing the questions that lie ahead, are coming from
laboratories all over the world. The scientists in the field have
been keeping in such close touch with each other that everyone
knows the contents of the latest paper months before its publication. The results of the latest experiment in Edinburgh or Boston
are known to colleagues in Melbourne or Tokyo almost as soon as
completed! The mechanism for the international exchange of scientific information is informal and seemingly casual, resembling
gossip more closely than any other sort of information system,
except that gossip has a reputation of unreliability, and this
scientific exchange is generally solid and undistorted. The
information is not just passed around automatically; it is literally given away, a curious phenomenon in itself, looking something
like altruism in the biological sense of that term. It is intui-
tively recognized by the participant that free exchange of data is
the only way to keep the game going. If one's own new information
is withheld from another laboratory in the interests of secrecy,
the flow of essential information from that laboratory will itself
be stalled, and the whole exchange may slow down and perhaps stop
altogether.

There was not this sense of optimism in cancer research not
very long ago. Around twelve years ago, while I was busy doing
research on various problems of immunity and infection, I could
not have imagined a scientific problem less attractive than the
problem of cancer. I thought of cancer research as an impossible
undertaking, and I had the same hunch about aging: they appeared,
at that time, insoluble. I wondered at the zeal and courage of my
colleagues who were engaged in research in those fields and felt
sorry for their entrapment in a scientific "blind alley." Aging
and cancer then seemed to be not single problems but a hundred
different problems, each requiring its own separate solution, and

all of the questions that arose were not only very hard questions
but had the look of being unanswerable ones. How could anyone
begin to seek answers to questions about a process such as cancer
that seemed to encompass almost every discipline in biomedical
science: virology, immunology, cell biology, and membrane structure and function. Aging as a research problem seemed worse. I
knew that a few people here and there were doing clinical research
and had discovered that a few chemical agents had a modulating
effect in the leukemias of childhood. The chemicals were dangerous and toxic and difficult to handle, and, while the clinicians
were hopeful, as an outsider I was not. If any young post-doctoral student or M.D. had asked me about the advisability of going
into cancer or aging research in the late 1960s, my advice would
have been to stay away and pick a field where things were moving
along nicely, like immunology. Even in the early 1970s when the
National Cancer Program was being put together for the declared
purpose of launching the so-called conquest of cancer, with a
substantial infusion of new funds for the support of cancer research, I and many of my colleagues remained skeptical about the
whole venture. "It is just too early for a crash program," we
said. "Biological science is not ready for this. We do not know
enough." Some of us even said in testimony before various congres-
sional committees that the problem of cancer would not become
approachable for another 50 years. Then, still in the early
1970s, things began to change at a great rate, and they have been
changing with stunning speed ever since, astonishing everyone.
Now, in 1984, work that had been the state-of-the-art just three
or four years ago has already an antique look, and the most tal-
ented of the rising generation of scientists are streaming into
cancer research everywhere. Best of all, they are entering the
field because it is becoming one of the most exciting and enchant-
ing of all problems in biology and alive with possibilities; it is
beginning to look like an approachable problem and even a soluble
one.

What has happened to bring about this change? I suppose
money had something to do with it at the outset, but it was not
primarily responsible. What happened was that basic science did
what basic science tends to do every once in a while; namely, it
produced by luck an overwhelming, totally unplanned-for set of
surprises. There were two outstanding and memorable surprises,
both of which turned out to be indispensable for research not only
on cancer but on a whole range of human diseases, including aging.
The first astonishment was the technology of recombinant DNA,
enabling an investigator to ask almost any question about the
intimate details of a living cell's genes and then to receive
sharp, clear answers. Using these techniques, it soon became
plain that there were cancer genes and also other genes that
restrain the cancer process. Now we have learned how chemical
carcinogens and cancer viruses can change and switch on such

genes. The whole field of specific intracellular systems and
their specific signals and receptors is being transformed by the
new recombinant DNA technologies. The other big development was
the discovery of cell fusion and then the formation of cell fac-
tories for making monoclonal antibodies.

With these tools, it is now possible to identify gene products that are elaborated by cancer cells and other abnormal cells,
and to examine with a high degree of precision and specificity the
changes that take place in the cell membrane when the normal cell
is switched to a cancer cell and probably we soon will discover
why a normal cell becomes an aging cell. The virologists are
having a perpetual field day; the immunologists are ready to claim
the whole problem of cancer as well as aging as their own; and the
biophysicists, the nucleic acid chemists, the geneticists, the
cell biologists are falling all over each other in the race to
final answers. There has never been a period of such high excite-
ment and such exhuberance and confidence in any field in biology.
It begins to resemble what one reads about in the early days in
twentieth century physics, when quantum theory was just beginning
to take shape. Biological science is in the process of upheaval
by what is being discovered about cell biology, and nobody can be
sure what lies ahead beyond the certainty that there will be
brand-new information at the deepest levels and therefore important and useful.

Two aspects of this scientific phenomenon seem to me remarkable in terms of public policy and the implications for the future
of the health sciences. First, no committee anywhere could possibly have predicted any of the events that have taken place. We
are observing basic science at its best, moving along from one
surprise to the next, capitalizing on surprise, following new
facts wherever they seem to lead, taking chances and making guess-
es all the way and driving the problems along toward their ultimate solution; the researchers are not following any rule book or
any long-range plan but playing hunches. The second remarkable
feature is the sheer spread of biomedical territory that is opening up as the work goes along. Cancer itself is turning into a
soluble problem, although I have no way of guessing at the likeli-
est outcome. The answer may lie in gaining control pharmacologi-
cally or immunologically over the switching mechanisms responsible
for the activation and transformation of cells, or it may lie in
the chemical nature and mode of action of protein gene products
coded by oncogenes. On the other hand, a set of signalling events
occurring at the cell surface or within the cell membrane may be
responsible for transforming a normal cell into a neoplastic
cell. The point is that whatever it is, the research technologies
are becoming sufficiently powerful and precise that it is almost
unthinkable that the inner mechanism can long remain hidden. And
at the same time, cell biology advances as a huge new enterprise

in biology, quite independent of the cancer problem. Within a decade, cellular immunology has become one of the most sophisticated of biomedical displines, capable of opening the way into problems of the so-called autoimmune diseases, such as rheumatoid arthritis, diabetes, and multiple sclerosis. A combination of the forces of modern virology and cellular immunology has opened up new approaches to the mechanism of damage to pancreatic islet cells in diabetes and its eventual reversal. Neurobiology has also begun to take off in the last few years. The discovery of the endorphins, followed by a cascade of other internal hormones secreted by brain cells into the brain itself, is turning the central nervous system from an incomprehensible computer-like, hardwired apparatus into a chemically governed system of signals. Experiments with primitive marine organisms are revealing neural mechanisms and structures involved in short-term and long-term memory. Selective enzyme deficiencies have been observed in the brain tissue in patients with Alzheimer's disease, while other forms of senile dementia are known to be caused by a so-called slow virus, the CJ agent.

Aspirin seems to work by inhibiting a chain of enzyme reactions converting arachidonic acid to one or another of the prostaglandins. Components of that same chain are responsible for the stickiness of the blood platelets, which may become lodged against the inner wall of the coronary or cerebral arteries and be responsible for the first stage of coronary or cerebral thrombosis, respectively. Along the way, we may find ourselves with "spinoff" information important in preventing coronary occlusion and stroke. Indeed, it is conceivable that the rather spectacular and unaccountable decrease in the incidence of coronary thrombosis (a twenty percent drop since 1950) may have been due to the introduction of television at that time, for the commercials touting headache remedies probably have raised the national blood level of salicylate and kept them high most of the time! Malignant hypertension has become a treatable disease, although, when I was an intern, it was a sure death sentence. Moreover, new drugs have been deliberately designed for inhibiting particular enzymes that lead to hypertension. Cardiovascular pharmacology is emerging as a field in which the chemists can call the shots in advance of making their chemicals. The whole field of biomedical science is on the move as never before in the history of medicine.

I do not know what will happen over the next twenty years, but my guess is that we are on the verge of discoveries that will match the best achievements in infectious disease a generation ago. As we develop new decisive technologies that are based on a deep understanding of disease mechanisms, my guess is that they will turn out to be relatively inexpensive compared to the kinds of measures that medicine presently is obliged to rely on. A genuine high medical technology will make an enormous difference

to medical practice in the decades ahead, provided that we keep
the basic biomedical sciences going and couple them as congenially
as possible to clinical research. We should not forget how useful
medicine can be when its scientific base is solid and effective.
Fifty years ago, when I was a medical student, the diseases which
ranked as the greatest menaces to human health were, in order of
the degree of fear which they caused: first, tertiary syphilis of
the brain, which filled more asylum beds than schizophrenia;
second, pulmonary tuberculosis, especially in the very young and
the very old, for whom it was a flat death sentence; third, acute
rheumatic fever, which was far and away the commonest cause of
disabling heart disease and early death; and finally, of course,
poliomyelitis. These four diseases were feared by everyone as
cancer is today. Thanks to some excellent basic science and some
exceedingly "classy" clinical research, all four have nearly
vanished as public health problems. The vanishing involved the
expenditure of pennies compared to what we would be spending if
any of the four were still with us. I expect this level of effectiveness in the practice of medicine in the days ahead.

The proceedings of this conference have already made it
abundantly clear that the problem of aging is a proper field for
scientific study and one of the broadest of all fields in human
biology. The array of specific questions to be asked is long and
impressive, and each question is a hard one requiring close and
attentive scrutiny by the best practitioners of basic science and
clinical medicine. And, as the answers come in, there is no doubt
that medicine will be able to devise new technologies for coping
with the things that go wrong in the process of aging. This is an
optimistic appraisal but not overly so, provided we are careful
with that phrase "things that go wrong." There is indeed an
extensive pathology of aging, one thing after another goes wrong,
failure after failure, and the cumulative impact of these failures
is what most people have in mind and fear as the image of aging.
But behind these ailments, often obscured by the individual pathologies, is a quite different phenomenon: normal aging, which is
not a disease at all--but a stage of living that cannot be averted
or bypassed except in one totally unsatisfactory way. Nonetheless, we regard aging these days as a sort of slow death with
everything going wrong.

I would like to separate these two aspects of the problem,
for I think that the former can be approached directly by the
usual methods of science. The list of pathologic events is long
but finite. Away at the top are the disorders of the brain leading to dementia, which is the single most dreaded disease by all
aging people and their families; then there is cancer, of course;
bone weakness; fractures; arthritis; incontinence; muscular wasting; Parkinsonism; eschemic heart disease; prosthetic hypertrophy;
pneumonia; and a generally increased vulnerability to infection.

They represent the discrete, sharply identifiable disease states
that are superimposed on the natural process of aging, each capable of turning a normal stage of life into chronic illness and
incapacity, or into premature death. Medicine and biomedical
science can only attack them one by one, dealing with each by the
established methods of science, which is to say, by relying on the
most detailed and highly reductionist techniques for research. If
we succeed in learning enough of the still obscure facts about
Alzheimer's disease, we will have a chance to turn it around
sooner or later, and, in the best of worlds, to prevent it. But
lacking these facts, we have no way at all to alleviate it or to
help the victims. If the scientists are successful, we can hope
for a time when the burden of individual disease states can be
lifted from the backs of old people, and they are then left to
face nothing but aging itself.

And what then? Will such an achievement remove aging from
our agenda of social concerns if old people do not become ill with
outright diseases right up to the hours of dying? Are their
health and social problems at an end and shall we then give up the
profession of geriatrics and confine our scientific interest to
gerontology? Of course not, but it is likely that there will be
fewer things to worry about for old people than is the case today
and fewer of them coming to the doctor's office for help. Even
so, aging will still be aging, and a strange process posing problems for every human being, and perhaps their approach should
become less reductionist and more general. They may wish to view
the whole person rather than concentrating on the singularities of
individual diseases. The word "holistic" was invented in the
1920s by General Jan Smuts to provide shorthand for the almost
self-evident truth that any living organism, and perhaps any
collection of organisms, is something more than the sum of its
working parts. I wish holism could remain a respectable term for
scientific usage, but, alas, it has fallen in bad company. Science itself is really a holistic enterprise, and no other word
would serve quite as well to describe it. Years ago, the mathema-
tician Poincare wrote, "Science is built up with facts as a house
is with stones, but a collection of facts is no more a science
than a heap of stones is a house." The word is becoming trendy, a
buzzword now, almost lost to science. What is called holistic
thought these days strikes me as more like the transition from a
mind like a steel trap to a mind like steel wool. What is sometimes called holistic medicine these days, if it is anything,
strikes me as an effort to give science the heave-ho out of medicine, and to forget all about the working parts of the body and
get along with any old wild guess about disease. We need another
word, a word to distinguish a system from the components of a
system, and I cannot think of one.

So, at present, we should continue to look at aging from the

point of view of a biomedical scientist, which is the reductionist
approach. In this way, we can construct hypotheses about the
possible mechanisms of such problems as senile dementia and set
about looking for selective enzyme deficiencies or scrapie-like
slow viruses in the brain. Or we can theorize about the failure
of cell-to-cell signals in the cellular immune system of aging
animals and examine closely the vigor of lymphocytes at all stages
of development; in the end, we may find out what goes wrong in an
aging immune system. And perhaps we have within our grasp the
information needed for explaining bone demineralization and resolving the problem, and we can track the neural pathways involved
in incontinence and may learn to do something about that. Given
some luck and a better knowledge of immunology and microbiology,
we ought to be able to solve the problems of rheumatoid arthritis
and osteoarthritis once and for all. We are learning some facts
about nutrition and longevity that we never understood before.
But we will still have people who will grow old before dying, and
medicine will have to learn more about what growing old is like.
The behavioral scientists, the psychiatrists, the psychologists,
the sociologists, the anthropologists and probably the economists,
too, will all have a part in the work that needs doing, obtaining
data, piecing information together, trying to make sense of the
whole out of separate parts of the problem; but their individual
efforts, although useful, may not be enough.

I suggest that we need a reading list for all young investigators and physicians to consult at the outset of planning for
their careers in the scientific study of aging. Young people find
it hard to begin constructing hypotheses without having the ghost
of an idea what it means to be old. To get a glimpse of the
matter, you have to leave science behind for awhile and consult
literature, not "the" literature, as we call our compendiums of
research, just plain old, pure literature. I have a few source-
books in mind. At the top of my list is the novelist, Wallace
Stegner, as good or better a writer as anybody around, who wrote
"The Spectator Bird" in 1976 about a literary man and his wife in
their late sixties and early seventies. To qualify for my list,
you have to be old enough to know what you are writing about, and
Stegner was the right age for his book; his novel should be required reading for any young doctor planning on geriatrics.
Indeed, "The Spectator Bird" is good enough to help educate any
young doctor for any career. Stegner was a friend of Bruce
Bliven, the former editor of "The New Republic," and Bliven is
brought into the novel for a brief episode and provides a wonderful quotation. Somebody asked him, when he had reached the age of
82, what it was like to be an old man. Bliven said, "I don't feel
like an old man; I feel like a young one with something the matter
with him." Number two on my list is Malcolm Cowley and his book
of personal essays called, "The View from Eighty." This book is
better than any textbook on medicine, infinitely more informative

than most monographs and journals on geriatrics. Cowley writes
with all the authority of a man who has reached 80 "on the run"
and is just getting his second wind. He, like Wallace Stegner,
was also attached to Bruce Bliven, and quotes Bliven, who wrote,
"We live by the rules of the elderly. If the toothbrush is wet,
you have cleaned your teeth. If the bedside radio is warm in the
morning, you left it on all night. If you are wearing one brown
and one black shoe, quite possibly, there is a similar pair in the
closet." Bliven goes on, "I stagger when I walk, and small boys
follow me making bets on which way I'll go next. This upsets me;
children should not gamble." Malcolm Cowley writes in good humor,
and most of the people he admires who have reached their eighties
and nineties seem to share this gift, but the humor is not always
as light as it seems. An octogenarian friend of his, a distinguished lawyer, said in a dinner speech, "They tell you that you
lose your mind when you grow older, but what they don't tell you
is that you won't miss it very much." Stegner's central character
in "The Spectator Bird" recounts crankily that among his other
junk mail there was a questionnaire from some research outfit that
was sampling senior citizens and wanted to know intimate things
about his self-esteem. He writes, "The self-esteem of the elderly
declines in this society, which indicates in every possible way
that it does not value the old in the slightest, finds them an
expense and an embarrassment, laughs at their experience, evades
their problems, isolates them in hospitals and sunshine cities,
and generally ignores them, except when soliciting their votes or
whipping off their handbags and Social Security checks." A few
other old people have written seriously about their condition with
insight and wisdom. Florida Scott Maxwell, a successful British
actress, a scholar and always a writer, wrote, "Age puzzles me. I
thought it was a quiet time. My seventies were interesting and
serene, but my eighties are passionate. I grow more intense with
age. To my own surprise, I burst out in hot conviction. I have
to calm down. I am too frail to indulge in moral fervor." Living
alone in a London flat after the departure of her grandchildren
for Australia and nearing her nineties, she wrote, "We who are old
know that age is more than a disability. It is an intense and
varied experience almost beyond our capacity at times but something to be carried high. If it is a long defeat, it is also a
victory, meaningful for the initiates of time if not for those who
have come less far." She also wrote, "When a new disability
arrives, I look about me to see if death has come, and I call
quietly, 'Death, is that you? Are you there?' and so far the
disability has answered, 'Don't be silly. It's me.'"

It is possible to say all sorts of good things about aging
when you are talking about aging free of meddling diseases. It is
an absolutely unique stage of human life--the only stage in which
one has both the freedom and the world's blessing to look back and
contemplate what has happened during one's lifetime instead of

pressing forward to new high deeds. It is one of the three manifestations of human life responsible for passing along our culture from one generation to the next. The other two are, of course, the children who make the language and pass it along and the mothers who see to it that whatever love there is in a society moves into the next generation. The aged, if they are listened to, hand along experience and wisdom, and this transference, in the past, has always been a central fixture in the body of any culture. We do not use this resource well in today's society. We tend always to think of aging as a disability in itself--a sort of long illness without any taxonomic name, a disfigurement of both human form and spirit. Aging is natural, as we say, just as death is natural, but we pay our respects to the one no more cheerfully than to the other. If science could only figure out a way to avoid aging altogether, zipping us all straight from the tennis court to the deathbed at the age of, say, 120, we would probably all vote for that. But even if this could be accomplished by science, which is well beyond my imagining for any future time, society as a whole would take a loss. In my view, human civilization could not exist without an aging generation for its tranquility, and every individual would be deprived of an experience not to be missed in a well-run world. Aging is not universal in nature; it is not even common. Most creatures in the wild die off or are killed off at the first loss of physical or mental power, just as our own Olympic gymnasts lose their powers in their late teens and tennis stars begin to drop off in their twenties, and virtually all of our athletes become old for their professions long before late middle age. Aging, real aging--the continuation of living throughout a long period of senescence--is a human invention and perhaps a relatively recent one at that. Our remotest ancestors probably dealt with their aging relatives much after the fashion of more primitive cultures; that is, by one or another form of euthanasia. It took us a long time and a reasonably workable economy to recognize that healthy, intelligent, old human beings are an asset to the evolution of human culture. It was a good idea, and we should keep hold of it; but if the concept is to retain its earlier meaning, we will have to find better ways to make use of the older minds among us. We need reminders that exceedingly useful pieces of work have been done in the past and are still being done by some extremely able people, sometimes in good health and sometimes in bad. Johann Sebastian Bach was relatively old for the eighteenth century when he died at age 65, but he had just discovered a strange, new kind of music and was working to finish the incorporation of the art of the fugue into an astonishing piece based on the old rules but turning the form of composition into the purest of absolutely pure music. Montaigne was even younger at his death at 59, but that was an old age for the 1500s. He was still revising his essays and making notes for a new addition for which he had chosen the appropriate title, "He Picks Up Strength as He Goes." And in our own time,

Santayana, Russell, Shaw, Yeats, Frost, and Forster--and I could
lengthen the list by the score--were busy thinking and writing
their way into their 70s and 80s and beyond. The great French
poet, Paul Claudel, wrote on his birthday, "Eighty years old. No
eyes left. No ears, no teeth, no legs, no wind, and, when all is
said and done, how astonishingly well one does without them."

Of all the things that can go wrong in aging, the loss of the
mind is far and away the worst and the most feared. And here, I
believe, is the greatest of all opportunities for medical science
in the improvement of the human condition. I think that most
aging people would willingly put up with all the other inconveni-
ences of age, the awkwardnesses, the enfeeblements, even the
assorted pains and aches, in trade for the assurance of hanging
onto their minds. I cannot think of a higher priority for biomedical science today, and I believe that most younger people, now at
no threat from Alzheimer's disease or any other kind of dementia,
would agree with the priority. As matters stand today, with the
recent increased public awareness of this disease, whole families
are beginning to worry about the problem, scrutinizing their
parents and grandparents for any tell-tale sign of mental failure
and wondering whether and when the entire family will topple in
the devastating aftermath of this one disease. We need more and
better research on the aging brain, on the biochemical and structural changes associated with dementia, on strokes and their
prevention, on the slow viruses, and on autoimmune mechanisms. We
need better ways of looking after afflicted patients than have yet
been devised and more improvements in our facilities for institutional and home care and more help for the families. But, most of
all, if we hope to rid ourselves of this disaster, we need research, good, old-fashioned, obsessive, reductionist science.

So I conclude on the same note of qualified optimism with
which I began. If we keep at it, sticking to the facts at our
reductionist best, we should be able to move gerontology onto a
new plane among the biomedical sciences. The odds on success are
very high indeed, provided that international cooperation in basic
biomedical science is sustained and fostered in the years ahead.
The odds on normal aging are already better than ever before in
human history, and with a lot of work and a lot of scientific
luck, the odds can eventually become wholly on our side and medicine will have earned its keep.

DISCUSSION

Question: You believe that old people have got a lot to
offer, and, as biomedical research improves and problems like
Alzheimer's disease are cured, there will be a lot more old people. But that will not help our social problems. How do we get
the old people back into the community?

Thomas: God knows.

Question: You have said that aging is not a disease, but
would you define disease?

Thomas: Aging is both an inevitable and a normal stage of
living for all living things on the planet, and if science pro-
gresses as well as I hope that it will, aging will not be associated with any particular disease state. The only analogy I can
think of that makes any sense to me is contained in Oliver Wendell
Holmes' celebrated poem called, "The Deacon's Masterpiece," about
the famous one-horse shay that was designed and manufactured in
such absolute perfection that it could not have had a disease.
When its time came, it simply fell apart in dust on the road.

Question: You have given us a glowing picture of the way in
which all of this scientific information is shared, yet it seems
to me that there may be a cloud the size of a man's hand, if we
put it biblically, on the horizon. Small companies engaged in
genetic engineering do not seem to me to be devoted to sharing
their kind of information. Would you comment on that?

Thomas: I am worried about the situation, and I think everybody is worried about the effect that biomedical technology (as it
is called in the marketplace) will have on what has up until now
been the almost absolutely free exchange of basic scientific
information. It may be that, if some of the existing arrangements
that have been made between several of the big pharmaceutical and
chemical industries and the universities specifying that secrecy
and withholding of information from publication is against the
rules succeed, it will relieve us of this anxiety. Yet I would
not worry about it unduly, because the secrecy usually involves
pieces of information that I would regard as applied science
rather than new and astonishing pieces of fundamental information.

INTRODUCTORY REMARKS, SESSION VI

Leon Sokoloff

Health Sciences Center
State University of New York at Stony Brook
Stony Brook, NY 11794

A useful distinction has already been made between processes of aging and diseases of aging. The present session is devoted to several diseases of aging that may provide insights into broader mechanisms of aging processes. Three of the papers address the significance of disorders featuring apparently accelerated rates of aging--more particularly Hutchinson-Gilford progeria and Werner's syndrome. The presentations of Dr. Brown and Dr. Salk will inquire into the extent that these rare conditions reflect authentic exaggeration of certain aging events as distinct from only mimicking them. Dr. Gracy will examine the molecular basis for protein errors in progeric fibroblasts and its relevance to aging in normal tissues. The mechanism he proposes--accumulation of deamidated forms through failure of proteolysis--should be juxtaposed to the conformational changes previously suggested by Dr. Rothstein.

I regret that there is insufficient time to consider more systematically recent developments in thinking about Down's syndrome and Alzheimer's disease. The improved prognosis for life in Down's syndrome, that has resulted from modern cardiac surgery and control of infections, has uncovered a consistent pattern of mental deterioration in the fourth decade that resembles senile dementia of the Alzheimer's type clinically and pathologically. As such it represents the most common model of accelerated aging. Furthermore the chromosomal abnormality serves as a handle for identifying gene products that may be involved in the pathogenesis of Alzheimer's disease. Any one interested in this subject is referred to a recent symposium of the New York Academy of Sciences (1982).

Dr. Gorevic's paper will take a different turn. It deals with what is at one time a common but heterogeneous group of diseases

373

and also a special process of protein alteration. Certain varieties of amyloidosis are clearly related to aging while others are not. What they share is precipitation of certain normally soluble proteins--or portions of them--in a particular configuration in various tissues. We have then an additional type of protein abnormality that ramifies widely in diseases of aging as diverse as senile dementia and cardiac amyloidosis.

REFERENCES

Sinex, E.M., Merril, C.R., (eds.) 1982, Alzheimer's Disease, Down's Syndrome, and Aging. Ann. N.Y. Acad. Sci. 396:1-199.

PROGERIA, A MODEL DISEASE FOR THE STUDY OF ACCELERATED AGING

W. Ted Brown, Michael Zebrower, and Fred J. Kieras

New York State Institute for Basic
Research in Developmental Disabilities
1050 Forest Hill Road
Staten Island, NY 10314

INTRODUCTION

The cause of aging is little understood at the present time,
but it does appear to have a strong genetic component. This is
reflected by the wide variation of approximately 50000 fold, in
the maximal lifespan potential (MLP), seen in the various animal
species (Brown, 1979). Among even mammals, approximately a
100-fold variation in MLP is seen. The smokey shrew has a
lifespan of only about one year, while the oldest documented
human died at the age of 118, and second to him the oldest human
lived to 113 (McWhirter, 1984).

An analysis of the degree of genetic complexity underlying
longevity has suggested it may be encoded by a limited number of
genes, perhaps 20-50, which have a major gene effect on aging
(Cutler,1980; Sacher,1980). A useful approach to understanding
the genetic basis of aging may be to study appropriate genetic
mutants which appear to affect that process. Although no
mutations are known to extend the maximal human lifespan, there
are a number which shorten the lifespan. Several genetic
diseases have mutations which appear to accelerate many but not
all features or segments of the aging process. They have been
described as "segmental progeroid" syndromes by Martin (1977).
It is our conviction that diseases can serve as useful models for
the study of aging. Insight into the nature of the basic
mutations in these syndromes may identify genes which play a
major role in aging.

The two genetic diseases which appear to us to show the most striking features suggestive of accelerated aging are the Hutchinson-Gilford Progeria Syndrome (progeria) and the Werner Syndrome (WS, also called progeria of the adult). The basic mutations underlying these two diseases are not known. Recent findings in several laboratories including our own indicate that patients with these two diseases may excrete an excessive amount of the glycosaminoglycan, hyaluronic acid (HA) (Takunaga et al., 1975, 1978, Goto et al., 1978; Brown et al., 1985, Kieras et al., 1985). Cultured cells from patients with these diseases show an excessive amount of HA accumulation (Tajima et al., 1981; Zebrower et al., 1985). Experimentally, excess HA has also been shown to inhibit vascular development, and may act as an anti-angiogenesis factor (Feinberg and Beebe, 1983). These findings raise the possibility that one or several major genes affecting aging may relate to HA metabolism. Understanding the basis and nature of these genetic abnormalities may help to elucidate further the basis of normal aging. In the following, we review clinical aspects, genetic features and laboratory investigations of progeria as a model of accelerated aging.

THE HUTCHINSON-GILFORD PROGERIA SYNDROME

Progeria, illustrated in Fig. 1, is a rare genetic disease with a reported birth incidence of about 1 in 8 million and with striking clinical features that resemble premature aging (Debusk, 1972). Patients with this condition generally appear normal at birth but by about one year of age, severe growth retardation is usually seen. Balding occurs, and loss of eyebrows and eyelashes is common in the first few years of life. Widespread loss of subcutaneous tissue occurs. As a result, the veins over the scalp become prominent. The skin appears old, and pigmented age spots appear. The patients are very short and thin. They average about 40 inches in height, but they usually weigh no more than 25 or 30 pounds even as teenagers. The weight-to-height ratio is thus very low. The voice is thin and high pitched. Sexual maturation usually does not occur. They have a characteristic facial appearance with prominent eyes, a beaked nose, a "plucked-bird" appearance, and facial disproportion resulting from a small jaw and large cranium. The large balding head and small face give them an extremely aged appearance. The bones show distinctive changes, with frequent resorption of the clavicles and replacement by fibrous tissue. Resorption of the terminal finger bones (acroosteolysis), stiffening of finger joints, elbow and knee joint enlargement, coxa valga, and a resulting "horse-riding" stance are all seen. Asceptic necrosis of the head of the femur and hip dislocation are common (Moen, 1982).

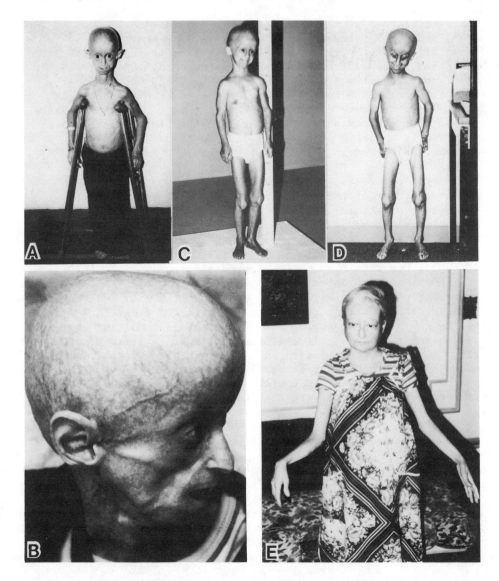

Fig. 1. Progeria and Werner syndrome subjects. A. A 10 yr. old girl
with progeria (TS). By this age she had suffered a stroke and
had bilateral hip dislocations. B. Same subject at the age of 14
yrs. She died of cardiac arrest 4 months later. C. Another 10
yr. old girl with progeria. Note arthritic changes of knees.
She (BS) had developed heart disease by age 13. D. A 13 yr. old
boy with progeria (FM). He died at age 15 of cardiac arrest.
E. A 37 year old woman with Werner syndrome (NV). She had a
history of premature white hair (age 13), cataract extractions
(age 26), bilateral femoral-popliteal bypass surgery (age 31),
diabetes mellitus, and left leg amputation for ulcers.

Progeria subjects have a normal to above-average
intelligence. The median age of death is 12 years. Over 80% of
deaths are due to heart attacks or congestive heart failure.
Widespread atherosclerosis, with interstitial fibrosis of the
heart, is usually seen at postmortem examination (Baker et al.,
1981). Occasionally marked enlargement of the thymus gland is
noted. However, some features often associated with normal aging
such as tumors, cataracts, diabetes, and hyperlipidemia although
occasionally reported (King et al., 1978, Villee and Powers,
1978, Rosenbloom et al., 1983) are not usually present.

Over the past 10 years, we have had the opportunity to
examine 24 cases of progeria. Information on these cases is
summarized in Table 1. Recently we have established an
International Progeria Registry. As of late 1984, the Registry
included 20 living cases: 15 living in the United States, 3 in
Canada, 1 in Holland, and 1 in South Africa. We have had
correspondence regarding three other cases from Russia, China and
Iran, but confirmation that they have true progeria is lacking.
We have helped to organize an annual progeria family conference.
Beginning in the summer of 1981, all interested progeria families
have been brought together for one week. At each meeting there
have been 8 to 14 progeria children and their families present.
This has allowed the children and families to meet each other,
and to share common experiences. Several interested physicians
have been present. Genetic counseling has been given to the
families regarding this rare condition.

A consideration of the mode of inheritance in progeria is
important for genetic counseling and may help to understand the
nature of the underlying mutation. Recessive diseases often
appear to be due to enzymatic deficiencies which lead to
metabolic abnormalities. Dominant diseases often involve
structural proteins. However, they may be due to partial
deficiencies of rate-limiting enzymes (i.e., Porphyria) or
cell-surface receptors (i.e., familial hypercholesterolemia)
where half the normal level of the gene product can lead to a
disease.

Several genetic considerations suggest progeria is most
likely a sporadic dominant mutation. First, high rates of
consanguinity, i.e. first cousin marriages, are expected in rare
recessive diseases. High consanguinity is not seen in progeria.
Debusk (1972) noted that consanguinity was present in only 3 out
of 19 families in which it was specifically discussed. Some of
these cases had come from areas of the world with high background
population levels of consanguinity. It addition, it was not
reported in 41 other families. Thus, 3 of 60 or 5% was the
reported frequency as of 1972. A family history of consanguinity

Table 1.   Summary of 24 cases of progeria.

Case	ID.	Sex.	Age At Exam	Birthdate	Died	Age At Birth (Yr.Mo.) Mother	Father	Age Diff.	Normal Sibs.	Half Sibs.
1	MC	F	27	10/01/55	05/25/85	40.0	45.8	5.8	6	
2	RM	F	15	08/06/66	04/24/83	27	27	0	1	
3	FM	M	13	1966	1981	28	25	-3	2	
4	KC	M	10	1968	--------	24	24	0	2	
5	TS	F	10	02/01/68	09/11/82	25.8	26	0.8	3	
6	AF	F	12	09/12/69	--------	37.4	45.6	8.2	3	
7	AG	F	13	02/20/70	04/01/85	24.5	49.11	25.6	6	7
8	BS	F	10	1970	--------	26	38	12	2	
9	MH	M	11	06/30/72	--------	19	26	7	1	
10	FG	M	11	12/31/72	--------	21.0	27.0	6	1	
11	SK	F	2	06/09/76	--------	33	47	14	1	6
12	RP	M	9	11/26/73	06/20/73	20.0	27.4	7.4	1	
13	JE	M	9	08/16/74	--------	17	17	0	1	
14	PS	M	6	05/10/77	--------	24.0	23.9	-0.3	2	1
15	AK	F	5	06/28/78	--------	29.11	34.10	4.11	1	
16	AB	F	6	09/10/78	--------	16.11	16.9	-0.2	1	
17	LC	M	4	08/20/79	--------	33.0	41.4	8.4	3	
18	AF	F	3	04/18/80	--------	23.0	23.0	0	1	
19	BS	M	3	07/26/80	--------	28.8	28.8	0	1	
20**	C/CR	M/M	2	01/26/81	--------	25.6	26.2	0.8	1	
21	MB	M	2	05/02/82	--------	31.8	39.1	7.5	1	
22	KS	F	1	06/22/82	--------	26.4	28.3	1.11	1	
23	MS	F	1	07/11/82	--------	28.6	25.3	-3.3		1
24	ZW	M	1/2	12/22/83	--------	35.8	40.6	4.10	3	

Total (Average)   (26.9)   (31.4)   (4.5)   45   15

**Twins

was not present in any of the 24 progeria cases that we have examined. Thus, we estimate the frequency of progeria cases born to consanguinious marriages to be less than 3/84, (3.6%). For rare recessive diseases, an estimate of expected frequency of consanguinity can be derived using the Dahlberg formula (Epstein et al., 1966). Assuming a birth incidence of progeria to be 1 per 8 million, and a background population consanguinity frequency of 1%, leads to an estimate of expected consanguinity of 64% in progeria families. Thus, the 3.6% observed consanguinity frequency in progeria is much lower than the high level that would be expected for such a rare recessive disease.

Although the reported incidence of progeria in the United States is about 1 in 8 million births (Debusk, 1972), the true population incidence may be somewhat higher as not all cases are reported. Based on our experience, we estimate that about 50% of all cases in the United States do get reported, which leads to an estimate of 1 in 4 million births. Even if progeria were to have an incidence of 1 in 1 million, this would still lead to a much higher expected consanguinity frequency, 45%, than the low frequency that is seen in progeria families. This lack of consanguinity suggests progeria is unlikely to be a rare recessive.

Secondly, a paternal age effect is seen in progeria which is also observed in some other sporadic dominant type mutations. Jones et al (1975) reported that among 18 progeria cases the fathers were older than expected by an average of 2.56 years when controlled for maternal age, a difference which was highly significant (p = 0.005). In addition to progeria, they reported a paternal age effect in seven other disorders (Basal Cell Nevus Syndrome, Waardenburg Syndrome, Crouzon Syndrome, Cleido-cranial dysostosis, Oculo-dental-digital Syndrome, Treatcher-Collins Syndrome, and multiple exostoses) involving new mutations for which autosomal dominant inheritance had been clearly established and in four disorders (Achondroplasia, Apert Syndrome, Fibrodysplasia ossiicans progressiva, and Marfan Syndrome) in which older paternal age in the setting of new mutation had been previously shown.

We have also observed a paternal age effect in the 24 cases of progeria we have examined (Table 1). The fathers were older than the mothers by an average of 4.5 years which is higher than the expected control value of 2.8 years (Jones et al, 1975). The paternal age effect observed in these 24 cases confirms the previously reported paternal age effect in the 18 earlier cases by Jones et al (1975) and also suggests dominant inheritance. The paternal age effect appears to be due to an excess of a few older fathers which produces a secondary age peak as is illustrated in figure 2. A similar secondary paternal age peak has been reported in new cases of neurofibromatosis, another dominant disease (Riccardi, 1983).

Third, for a recessive condition, the proportion of affected sibs is expected to be 25%. In progeria it is clearly much less than 25%. The majority of cases are sporadic. A case of identical progeria twins with 14 normal sibs was reported (Viegas et al, 1974). Here, 3 or 4 affected sibs would be expected if it was a recessive disease. It is recognized that for new dominant mutations, occasionally the mutation can occur in a germ line leading to somatic mosaicism within the ovary or testes (McKusick, 1982). Several cases could then occur within one family. Probable cases of familial progeria have been reported in only a few instances among more than 100 families and some of these may have been misidentified (Mostafa and Gabr, 1954; Gabr et al., 1960; Rautenstrauch and Snigula, 1977; Franklyn, 1976). Among the 24 cases we have examined (table 1), no family had more than one affected child. There were 45 unaffected sibs. One would expect there to be 11 or 12 of the 45 sibs affected (25%) if a recessive mode of inheritance were to apply to these 24 progeria families.

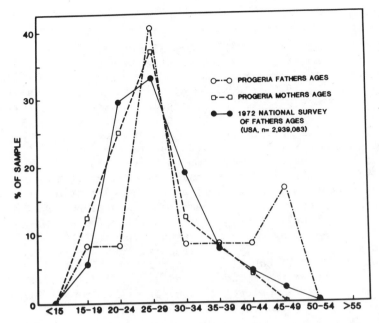

Fig. 2. Paternal age effect in progeria. A secondary age peak for father of 24 cases of progeria is shown. This secondary age peak is not seen in a normal age distribution of fathers, nor in the progeria mothers.

In general, the lack of consanguinity, the paternal age effect, and the lack of affected sibs, argues that progeria is not a rare recessive, but most probably is a sporadic dominant mutation. Progeria was formerly considered to be a recessive disease and was so classified in early editions of McKusick's Catalog of Mendelian Inheritance in Man. Because of a lack of consanguinity, a lack of affected sibs, and a paternal age effect, we suggested progeria should be classified as a sporadic autosomal dominant mutation (Brown and Darlington, 1980). Subsequently, it was moved from the recessive to the dominant section of the catalogue (McKusick, 1982). The possibility of genetic heterogeneity in progeria in which some cases have a similar clinical presentation but with a recessive mode of inheritance seems possible but because of the rarity of the condition, quite unlikely. The majority of cases appear to represent isolated sporadic dominant mutations, although a few may be the result of a germ line mutations. For genetic counseling of families with a progeria child, the recurrence risk can be stated to be very low, but may be on the order of 1 in 500 with each pregnancy.

WERNER SYNDROME

Werner Syndrome (WS) (Fig. 1), also called progeria of the adult, has a number of features which resemble premature aging but in contrast to progeria has an adult age of onset (Epstein et al., 1966; Salk, 1982; Brown, 1984). WS subjects generally appear normal during childhood but cease growth during teenage years. Premature graying and whitening of hair occurs at an early age. Striking features include early cataract formation, skin which appears aged with a sclerodermatous appearance, a high-pitched voice, peripheral musculature atrophy, poor wound-healing, chronic leg and ankle ulcers, hypogonadism, widespread atherosclerosis, soft tissue calcification, osteoporosis, and a high prevalence of diabetes mellitus. About 10% of patients develop neoplasms with a particularly high frequency of sarcomas and meningiomas (German, 1984). The diagnosis of WS is usually made when patients are in their 30´s. They commonly die of complications of atherosclerosis in their 40´s. The mode of inheritance of WS is clearly autosomal recessive. Thus WS and progeria subjects show many similarities but have many differences as well (Brown et al., 1985).

BASIC RESEARCH ON PROGERIA

Laboratory investigations of progeria have involved a search for a genetic marker in an attempt to help define the underlying defect. The cultured lifespan of progeric fibroblasts was initially reported to be very reduced (Goldstein, 1969). Subsequent studies have shown that although difficulties may sometimes occur in the initial establishment of a culture, once established, a normal or only a modest reduction in lifespan is seen (Martin et al., 1970; Goldstein and Moerman, 1975). We have examined the in vitro lifespans of 11 progeria cell cultures, 4 WS cultures, 4 parents of progeria subjects, and 3 control cultures (Fig. 3). The WS cell lines showed extremely rapid senescence with a range of 9-15 maximal population doubling levels. The progeria cell lines had a range from about 20 to 60 population doubling levels. This was reduced by about 1/3 compared to the parent lines and the normal controls. The WS line population doubling levels were greatly reduced. Thus, a markedly reduced in vitro lifespan of progeria cells such as was seen in WS was not present. The modest and variable reduction in lifespan in culture is unlikely to represent a useful marker for the disease.

Goldstein and Moerman (1975) reported finding an increased fraction of abnormally thermolabile enzymes, including glucose-6-phosphate dehydrogenase (G6PD), 6-phosphogluconate dehydrogenase (6PGD), and hypoxanthine phosphoribosyltransferase (HPRT) in progeria fibroblasts. Based in part on the Orgel error-catastrophe hypothesis of aging (1963), it was suggested

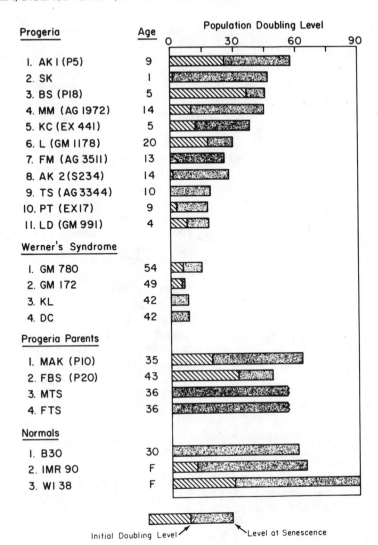

Fig. 3. <u>In vitro</u> cell lifespans of Progeria and Werner syndrome
fibroblasts. Cell cultures were initiated from skin biopsies
(SK, FM, TS, KL, DC, MTS, FTS, B30) or were obtained from other
investigators (AK1, BS, MM, KC, AK2, PT, MAK, FBS), or were
obtained from the Camden Cell Repository (GM1178, GM991, GM780,
GM712, IMR90, WI38). Ages of subjects are indicated (F is
fetal lung). Cultures were split 4:1 or 2:1 once a week which
added 2 and 1 population doubling levels respectively. Where
cells became too sparce to be subcultured in one month, they
were judged senescent. Progeria cells showed a variably modest
reduction. WS cells showed a marked reduction in comparison to
parents and normals.

that diseases resembling premature aging may be the result of widespread errors in protein synthesis (Goldstein and Moerman, 1976). Abnormally high thermolabile enzyme levels in circulating erythrocytes from one progeria patient with intermediate levels in the parents was also reported (Goldstein and Moerman, 1978a,b). It was suggested that this would support autosomal recessive inheritance. Our studies of three progeria patients and their families did not confirm these elevations as no increased erythrocyte thermolabile enzyme elevations were seen (Brown and Darlington, 1980). In our opinion, this lack of confirmation indicates that a defect in protein synthetic fidelity is unlikely to be the basic defect in progeria, and does not support the suggestion of autosomal recessive inheritance. Subsequent work by Wojityk and Goldstein (1980) on cell-free protein synthesis using progeria fibroblast extracts also found no decreased translation ability, which also argues against a generalized defect in progeria protein synthesis.

Abnormal immune function has been postulated as a defect in progeria. Walford suggested that progeria could reflect an abnormality of immune function because of the similarity to experiment graft-versus-host reaction and to runting disease (1970). In support of this concept, Singal and Goldstein (1973) reported that HLA expression on two cultured progeria fibroblast strains was absent. They later reported that there was not an absence, but a greatly reduced concentration of HLA cell-surface molecules (Goldstein et al., 1975; Goldstein and Moerman, 1976). In studies of ten progeria fibroblast strains, we were unable to confirm this reported abnormality. We found no evidence for either qualitative or quantitative abnormalities of HLA expression and no association with HLA type was detected (Brown et al., 1980a). Thymic hormone levels have been reported as age appropriate (Iwata et al., 1981). Thus, no immune abnormalities have been established for progeria.

An abnormality of X-ray DNA-repair capacity in progeria fibroblasts was suggested by Epstein et al. (1973, 1974) who detected decreased single-strand rejoining of gamma-irradiated DNA using alkaline sucrose gradients. The presence of altered DNA-repair capability was not found in another study. Using a somewhat modified method for assay of single-strand rejoining, no differences between one progeric strain and two atypical progeric strains were seen as compared to normals (Regan and Setlow, 1974). Brown et al. (1976, 1977) showed that co-cultivation of two progeric cell strains with normal strains or with each other reversed the single-strand DNA-rejoining defect and suggested that complementation groups for DNA repair might exist in progeria. Weichselbaum et al. (1980) assayed the X-ray sensitivity of various types of human fibroblasts by measuring their ability to form colonies following irradiation. They found two progeric strains with increased sensitivity and three strains with normal sensitivity. These studies suggested some increase in radiosensitivity but left open the possibility that damage to cellular components other than DNA might be responsible. Rainbow and Howes (1977) using a sensitive host-cell-reactivation (HCR) assay of X-irradiated adenovirus reported that two progeric strains showed a deficiency of DNA-repair capacity. Brown et al. (1980b) studied HCR in two other strains and found one strain to show decreased HCR while another showed normal HCR under a variety of cell growth conditions. These results suggest that heterogeneity of DNA-repair capacity exists among progeria fibroblasts. Defective DNA-repair capacity therefore does not appear to be a consistent marker for progeria and it seems unlikely to represent a basic genetic defect.

A few other isolated reports have suggested abnormalities in progeria. Elevated levels of fibroblast tissue factor were reported in both progeria and WS cells (Goldstein and Niewiarowski, 1976). This could reflect variations in culture conditions or growth state of cells unrelated to genotype, such as has been reported for other cell types (Magniord et al., 1977). A normal insulin-binding receptor response, but decreased binding of insulin to non-specific receptors in progeria cells has been reported (Rosenbloom and Goldstein, 1976). The significance of nonspecific receptor binding is unclear.

HYALURONIC ACID (HA) URINARY LEVELS IN PROGERIA AND WS

A potentially unique marker for both progeria and Werner Syndrome appears to be urinary HA excretion. HA excretion has been found to be elevated in these two syndromes and has not been reported to be elevated for any other genetic disease. HA levels in controls are normally considered to represent less than 1% of total GAGs. Elevated HA levels have been reported to vary from 2 to 22% in a series of Japanesse WS subjects (Tokunaga et al., 1975; Goto and Murata, 1978; Maekawa and Hayashibara, 1981; Murata, 1982). In progeria, urinary HA as a percent of total GAGs present was also reported to be elevated to 4.4% in one Japanese subject compared to controls of 0.2 and 0.3% (Tokunaga et al., 1978).

We have determined the total urinary excretion of GAGs and HA in one Werner Syndrome patient, and three progeria patients, one patient with an atypical progeroid syndrome, and a control subject using standard methods for GAG analysis including CPC

precipitation, pronase digestion, TCA treatment, ethanol
precipitation and uronic acid determination before and after
hyaluronidase digestion (Kieras et al., 1985). Normal levels of
total urinary GAGs were observed in all affected individuals and
the control, as shown in Table 2.

Table 2. Urinary Execretion of Hyaluronic Acid (HA) in Progeria
and Werner Syndrome

Sample	Age (yrs)	HA as percent of GAG
Progeria		
1. (PS)	5	10
2. (FC)	12	16
3. (TS)	14	5
WS (NV)	41	14
Control	12	1

HA analyses for the patients and for the control showed that
the Werner Syndrome patient and 3 progeria patients had increased
levels of urinary HA which ranged from a high of 16% to a low of
about 5%. The normal individual and the atypical progeroid
subject showed no significant elevation of HA excretion.
Although it has generally been accepted that urinary HA levels
are normally less than about 1% of GAGs, there is no systematic
study available. We have carried out a preliminary study of six
normal individuals to determine HA excretion as a fdunction of
age. These results are presented in Table 3.

Table 3. Hyaluronic Acid Execretion in Normal Subjects vs Age

Age (yrs)	HA as % of GAGS
2	0.3
12	1.7
22	1.1
30	5.2
41	6.7
65	5.8

Our initial studies have verified that HA content in young
children and adolescents was low but after age 30 there was an
elevation to 5-6%. These results suggest that elevated excretion
of urinary HA may be a normal characteristic of aging which
occurs in these premature aging syndromes at an accelerated rate.

HA AND GAG PRODUCTION IN CULTURED CELLS

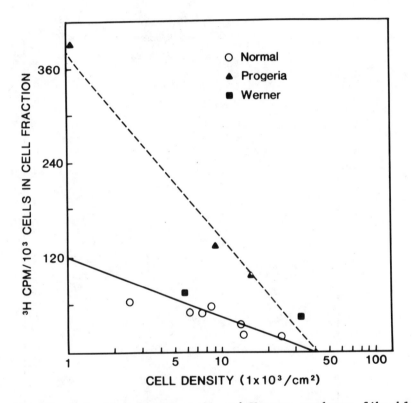

Fig. 4. HA production by Progeria and Werner syndrome fibroblasts
as a function of cell density. HA assayed by ^{3}H-glucosamine
incorporation as described (Zebrower et al., 1984). Three day
cultures. Progeria and Werner Syndrome fibroblasts were obtained from the NIA Aging Cell Repository (AG 1972, AG 3513, AG
4110, AG 5230) or were established from primary biopsies of
Progeria subjects (SK). Control fibroblast lines were established from age matched subjects with developmental disabilities but
without accelerated aging phenotypes. Approximately, a three-
fold excess of HA production was observed in Progeria and Werner
fibroblasts at all cell densities studied.

To determine if the elevated HA excretion seen in progeria
was also reflected in cell culture, we analyzed HA and GAG
production in normal, progeria, and WS fibroblasts (Zebrower et
al., 1984).   HA and GAG production by progeria, WS, and control
cells were assayed by measuring both total glucosamine and
sulfate incorporation into cells and media.   HA production was

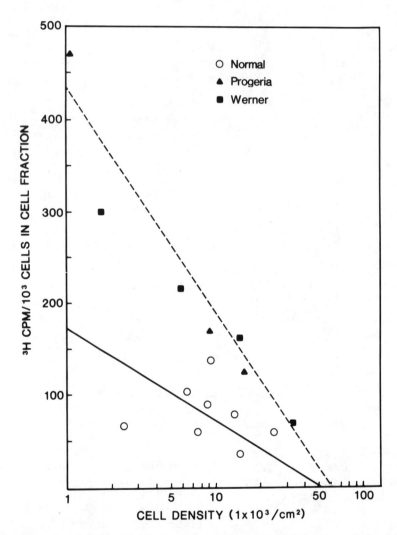

Fig. 5. GAG production by Progeria and Werner Syndrome fibroblasts.
GAG was assayed as described (Zerbrower et al., 1984), following
three day culture of the same cultures in fig. 4. Approximately
a three fold elevation of production was seen at all cell densities examined.

found to be elevated in progeria and Werner Syndrome compared to
normal cultures at all cell densities measured, as shown in Fig.
4. A pronounced difference in total GAG production was also
observed when normal fibroblasts were compared with Werner and
progeria fibroblasts as a function of cell density, as
illustrated in Fig. 5. A similar difference in GAG and HA
excretion into the media was seen in comparing Werner and
progeria to normals as a function of cell density. Non-HA
containing GAGs, as assayed by sulfur incorporation, were also
found to decrease as a function of cell density, and were also
found to be produced in excess in Werner and progeria
fibroblasts.

In order to determine whether the overproduction of GAGs, in
general, and HA, in particular, was related to increased
synthesis or to faulty degradation, cultures from normal, Werner,
and progeria lines were labelled for 4, 8, and 24 hours and then
assayed. There was little comparative difference in either total
tritiated GAGs or HA produced unlike the marked difference that
was seen at 72 hours of cultivation.. This suggests a
degradative pathway abnormality is apparently present since
initial synthesis was relatively unimpaired.

The question of how this defect in GAG metabolism in
progeria and Werner cases is mediated was studied by employing a
complementation assay similar to that used in studies, of Hurler
and Hunter syndromes (Fratantoni et al., 1968a, 1968b). As shown
in Fig. 6, when Werner cultures were fed with conditioned media
from normal lines, tritium incorporation into GAGs in both the
cell and media fractions was decreased. Progeria fibroblasts
were also complemented by Werner media in a similar manner. Less
reduction was observed when progeria cells were cross-fed with
normal media.

FACTORS GOVERNING HA AND GAG PRODUCTION

The relationship governing GAG production in fibroblasts
appears to vary in a complex fashion as a function of age of the
culture, age of the donor from which it was taken, the density of
the culture, and possibly the disease afflicting the donor. The
total production of GAGs and HA in fibroblast cultures has been
found to vary inversely as a function of cell density (Hronowski
and Anastassiades, 1980) regardless of the source of the
fibroblasts. The composition of GAGs though has been found to
change as a function of the population doubling level (PDL) of
the cultures. Schachtschabel and Wever (1981) examined the
synthesis and distribution of GAGs as a function of PDL in human
embryonic fibroblasts. It was observed that GAG synthesis

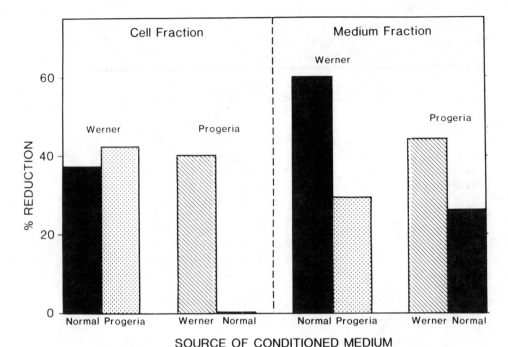

Fig. 6. Complementation of Werner and Progeria lines by conditioned
media. Percent reduction in GAGs produced by cross feeding with
conditioned media was measured by ³H glucosamine incorporation.
The graph shows the varying sources of conditioned media produced differing degrees of reduction of the excess GAGs
produced.

declined only during the last 5 divisions before phaseout. This
decline was accompanied by a decline in HA production both in
absolute and relative quantity in cellular and media fractions.
Production of another GAG, heparan sulfate, was found to increase
continually during the very last population doublings. Vogel et
al., (1981) reported that   HA production was found to increase in
the medium fraction of an old donor relative to a young donor.
Total GAG production appeared greater in the older than the young
donor. One complication in the interperation of all these
studies is that the data were normalized in terms of cell protein
content as measured at the beginning of the labelling period
rather than cell density at the end of the labelling period. As
the growth rates of the lines may be significantly different,
vastly different incorporation rates may be present because of
the relationship between cell density and GAG production. The
underlying biochemical reasons for these changes in GAG
production have not been explained.

Excess HA and GAG production has been reported by Tajima et al. (1981) for one line of WS fibroblasts; however, these workers did not normalize their data to constant cell densities. Fibroblasts from another genetic disease affecting connective tissue, Marfan Syndrome, have been observed to accumulate significantly greater amounts of HA than normal lines (Malaton and Dofman, 1968). This accumulation of HA was found to be related to an overactive synthetase rather than some degradation defect. In a cell-free system, increased rates of synthesis were observed even though the physical properties of the particular enzymes involved did not seem to change (Appel et al., 1979). Production of HA in fibroblasts has been found to be elevated in Osteogenesis Imperfect (Turakainen et al.,1980). This elevation has also been found to be due to an aberrant synthetase as measured in a cell-free system.

HA and GAG production during embryogenesis is believed to play a very important role in morphogenesis. HA production in particular is associated with the formation of the primary mesenchyme and the first cell-free spaces in the rat embryo (Solursh and Moriss, 1977). In chick embryos, a striking correlation between hyaluronate synthesis and cell movement and proliferation is observed as well as between HA degradation and differentiation. For example, in the chick embryo cornea, a close correlation exists between the presence of HA and the period during which corneal mesenchyme migration and proliferation in the hydrated primary stroma occur. Both corneal mesenchyme migration and HA production occur during days 3-9 of development. The removal of HA by hyaluronidase begins on day 10 and corresponds with the cessation of migration and proliferation of the mesenchymal cells as well as their differentiation into corneal keratocytes (Hay, 1980; Toole and Trelstad, 1971; Trelstad et al., 1974; Toole, 1981).

HA appears to act as an anti-angiogenesis factor. During development tissue regions that are high in HA concentration are invariably avascular zones. HA containing implants were shown to cause avascularity when implanted into normal vascular wing mesoderm (Feinberg and Beebe, 1983). HA thus appears to be crutial in the morphogenesis of blood vessels in the embryo and may be expected to play an equally important role as an anti-angiogenesis factor during maturation and aging. Our results in progeria and WS suggest abnormalities of HA excretion on degradation may provide a consistent marker. Mutations of HA metabolism may underlie these diseases and relate to major genes affecting accelerated aging.

CONCLUSIONS

     Progeria is a rare genetic disease with striking features
that resemble accelerated aging. The inheritance pattern,
paternal age effect, and lack of consanguinity argue that it is
due to a sporadic dominant mutation. We have observed elevated
levels of HA excretion in progeria and WS patients. Their
cultured cells also accummulate excessive HA. We hypothesize
that the failure of patients with progeria and WS to thrive may
be due to a lack of vasculogenesis caused by excess HA. Clinical
features which supports this hypothesis include the
sclerodermatous appearance of the skin, decreased number of blood
vessels and increased incidence of death due to cardiovascular
problems found in patients with these disorders. The nature of
such a genetic mutation leading to an increase in HA needs to be
elucidated to understand the cause of progeria. Insight into the
nature of this mutation may help in understanding a gene or genes
with a major effect on aging.

REFERENCES

Appel, A., Horwitz, A., and Dorfman, A., 1979, Cell free
     synthesis of hyaluronic acid in marfan syndrome, J. Biol.
     Chem., 254:12199.
Baker, P.B., Baba, N., and Boesel, C.P., 1981, Cardiovascular
     abnormalities in progeria, Arch. Pathol. Lab. Med., 105: 384.
Brown, W.T., Epstein, J., and Little, J.B., 1976, Progeria cells
     are stimulated to repair DNA by co-cultivation with normal
     cells, Expt. Cell Res., 97:291.
Brown, W.T., Little, J.B., Epstein, J., and Williams, J.R., 1977,
     DNA repair defect in progeria cells, in: "Genetic Effects on
     Aging," D. Bergsma, and D.E. Harrison, eds, Alan R. Liss,
     Inc.,New York, p.417.
Brown, W.T., 1979, Human mutations affecting aging: A review,
     Mech. Ageing Dev., 9:325.
Brown, W., and Darlington, G., 1980a, Thermobile enzymes in
     progeria and Werner syndrome: Evidence contrary to the
     protein error hypothesis, Am. J. Hum. Genet., 32:614.
Brown, W.T., Darlington, G.J., Fotino, M., and Arnold A., 1980b,
     Detection of HLA antigens in progeria syndrome fibroblasts,
     Clin. Genet., 17:213.
Brown, W., Ford, J., and Gershey, E., 1980c, Variation of DNA
     repair capacity in progeria cells unrelated to growth
     conditions, Biochem. Biophys. Res. Commun., 97:247.
Brown, W.T., 1983, Werner's syndrome, in: "Chromosome Mutation
     and Neoplasia," p. 85. German, J., ed, Alan R. Liss, Inc, New
     York.

Brown, W.,and Wisniewski, H., 1983, Genetics of human aging. Rev. Biol. Res. Aging, 1:81.

Brown, W.T., Kieras, F.J., Houck, G.E., Dutkowski, R., and Jenkins, E.C., 1985, A comparison of adult and childhood progerias: Werner syndrome and Hutchinson-Gilford progeria syndrome, in: "Werner's Syndrome and Human Aging," Plenum Press, New York, In press.

Cutler, R., 1980, Evolution of human longevity. Adv. Pathobiol., 7:43.

DeBusk, F., 1972, The Hutchinson-Gilford progeria syndrome, J. Pediatr., 80:697.

Epstein, C., Martin, G., Schultz, A., and Motulsky, A., 1966, Werner's syndrome: A review of its symptomatology, natural history, pathologic features, genetics and relationship to the natural aging process, Medicine, 45:177.

Epstein, J., Williams, J.R., and Little, J.B., 1973, Deficient DNA repair in human progeroid cells, Proc. Natl. Acad. Sci. USA, 70:977.

Epstein, J., Williams, J.R., and Little, J.B., 1974, Rate of DNA repair in progeria and normal fibroblasts, Biochem. Biophys. Res. Commun., 59:850.

Feinberg, R., and Beebe, D., 1983, Hyaluronate in vasculogenesis. Science, 220:1177.

Franklin, P.P., 1976, Progeria in siblings, Clin. Radiol., 27:327.

Fratantoni, J., Hall, C., and Neufeld, E., 1968a, Hurler and Hunter syndromes: Mutual correction of the defect in cultured fibroblasts, Science, 162:570.

Fratantoni, J., Hall, C., and Neufeld, E., 1968b, Hurler and Hunter syndromes: The defect in Hurler and Hunter syndrome II. Deficiency of specific factors involved in mucopolysaccharide degradation, Biochemistry, 64:360.

Fujiwara, Y., Higashikawa, T., and Tatsumi, M., 1977, A retarded rate of DNA replication and normal level of DNA repair in Werner's syndrome fibroblasts in culture, J. Cell. Physiol., 92:365.

Gabr, M., Hashem, N., Hashem, M., Fahni, A., and Satouh, M., 1960, Progeria, a pathologic study, J. Pediatr., 57:70.

German, J., 1983, Patterns of neoplasia associated with the chromosome-breakage syndromes, in: "Chromosome Mutation and Neoplasia," p.97. German, J. ed, Alan R. Liss, Inc., New York.

Goldstein, S., 1969, Lifespan of cultured cells in progeria, Lancet, 1969(i):424.

Goldstein, S., and Moerman, E., 1975, Heat-labile enzymes in skin fibroblasts from subjects with progeria, New Engl. J. Med., 292:1305.

Goldstein, S., Niewiarowski, S., and Sinegal, D.P., 1975, Pathological implications of cell aging in vitro, Fed. Proc. Am. Soc. Exp. Biol., 34:55.

Goldstein, S., and Niewiarowski, S., 1976, Increased procoagulant activity in cultured fibroblasts from progeria and Werner's syndromes of premature aging, Nature (London), 260:711.

Goldstein, S., and Moerman, E., 1976, Defective protein in normal and abnormal fibroblasts during aging in vitro. Interdiscip. Top. Gerontol., 10:24.

Goldstein, S., and Moerman, E.J., 1978a, Heat-labile enzymes in circulating erythrocytes of a progeria family, Am. J. Hum. Genet., 30:167.

Goldstein, S., and Moerman, E.J., 1978b, Unstable enzymes in erythrocytes of a family with the Hutchinson-Gilford progeria syndrome, in: "The Red Cell," Brewer, G.J. ed., Alan R. Liss, Inc., New York, p. 217.

Goto, M., and Murata, K., 1978, Urinary excretion of macromolecular acidic glycosaminoglycans in Werner's syndrome,. Clin. Chim. Acta, 85:101.

Hay, E.D., 1980, Development of the vertebrate cornea, Int. Rev. Cytol., 63:263.

Hronowski L., and Anastassiades, T., 1980, The effect of cell density on net rates of glycosaminoglycan synthesis and secretion by cultured rat fibroblasts, J. Biol. Chem., 255: 10091.

Iwata, T., Incefy, G.S., Cunningham-Rundles, S., Smithwick, E., Geller, N., O'Reilly, R., and Good, R.A., 1981, Circulating thymic hormone activity in patients with primary and secondary immunodeficiency diseases, Am. J. Med., 71:385.

Jones, K., Smith, P., Harvey M., Hall, B., and Quan, L., 1975, Older paternal age and fresh gene mutation: Data on addditional disorders, J. Pediatr., 86:84.

Kieras, F.J., Brown, W.T., Houck, G.E., and Zebrower, M., 1985, Elevation of urinary hyaluronic acid in Werner syndrome and progeria, Life Sciences, Submitted.

King, C.R., Lemmer, J., Campbell, J.R., and Atkins, A.R., 1978, Osteosarcoma in a patient with Hutchinson-Gilford progeria, J. Med. Genet., 15:481.

Maekawa, Y., and Hayashibar, T., 1981, Determination of hyaluronic acid in the urine of a patient with Werner's syndorme, J. Dermatol., 8:467.

Magniord, J.R., Dreyer, B.E., Stemerman, M.B., and Pitlick, F.A., 1977, Tissue factor coagulant activity of cultured human endothelial and smooth muscle cells and fibroblasts, Blood, 50:387.

Martin, G., Sprague, C., and Epstein, C., 1970, Replicative life-span of cultivated human cells: Effects of donor's age, tissue, and genotype, Lab. Invest., 23:86.

Martin, G.M., 1977, Genetic syndromes in man with potential relevance to the pathobiology of aging, Birth Defects Orig. Artic. Ser., 14:5.

Matalon, R., and Dorman, A., 1968, The accumulation of hyaluronic acid in cultured fibroblasts of the Marfan syndrome, Biochem. Biophys. Res. Commun., 32:150.

McKusick, V.A., 1982, "Mendelian Inheritance in Man, Catalogues of Autosomal Dominant, Autosomal Recessive, and X-Linked Phenotypes," 6th ed., Johns Hopkins University Press, Baltimore.

McWhirter, Norris, 1984, Authenticated national longevity records, in: "Guinness 1984 Book of World Records," p. 18, Bantam Books, New York, p.18.

Moen, C., 1982, Orthopaedic aspects of progeria, J. Bone Joint Surg., 64A:542.

Mostafa, A.H., and Gabr, M., 1954, Hereditary progeria with follow-up of two affected sisters, Arch. Pediat., 71:163.

Murata, K., 1982, Urinary acidic glycosaminoglycans in Werner's syndrome, Experientia, 38:313.

Orgel, L.E., 1963, The maintenance of the accuracy of protein synthesis and its relevance to aging, Proc. Natl. Acad. Sci. USA, 49:517.

Orkin, R., and Toole, B., 1980, Isolation and characterization of hyaluronidase from cultures of chick embryo and muscle-derived fibroblasts, J. Biol. Chem., 255:1036.

Regan, J.D., and Setlow, R.B., 1974, DNA repair in human progeroid cells, Biochem. Biophys. Res. Commun., 59:858.

Rainbow, A. and Howes, M., 1977, Decreased repair of gamma ray damaged DNA in progeria, Biochem. Biophys. Res. Commun., 74:714.

Rautenstrauch, T., Snigula, F., Kreig, T., Gay, and Muller, P., 1977, Progeria: A cell culture study and clinical report of familial incidence, Euro. J. Pediatr., 124:101.

Riccardi, V.M., 1983, Neurofibromatosis, in: "Principles and Practice of Medical Genetics," p.314, A. Emery, and D. Rimoin, eds, Churchill Livingstone, New York.

Rosenbloom, A.L., and Goldstein, S., 1976, Insulin binding to cultured human fibroblasts increases with normal and precocious aging, Science, 19:412.

Rosenbloom, A.L., Kappy, M.S., DeBusk, F.L., Francis, G.L., Philpot, T.J., and Maclaren, N.K., 1983, Progeria: Insulin resistance and hyperglycemia, J. Pediatr., 102:400.

Sacher, G., 1980, Mammalian life histories: Their evolution and molecular-genetic mechanisms, Adv. Pathobiol., 7:21.

Salk, D., 1982, Werner's syndrome: A review of recent research with an analysis of connective tissue metabolism, growth control of cultured cells, and chromosomal aberrations, Hum. Genet., 62:1.

Schachtschabel, D., and Wever J., 1978, Age-related decline in the synthesis of glycosaminoglycans by cultured human fibroblasts, Mech. Ageing Dev., 8:257.

Singal, D.P., and Goldstein, S., 1973, Absence of detectable HL-A antigens on cultured fibroblasts in progeria, J. Clin. Invest., 52:2259.

Solursh, M., and Moriss, G., 1977, Glycosaminoglycan synthesis in rat embryos during the foundation of the primary mesenchyme and neural folds, Dev. Biol., 57:75.

Tajima, T., Watanabe, T., Iijima, K., Ohshika, Y. and Yamaguchi,
    H., 1981, The increase of glycosaminoglycans synthesis and
    accumulation on the cell surface of cultured skin fibroblasts
    in Werner's syndrome, Exper. Pathol., 20:221.
Takaeuchi, F., Hanaoka, F., Goto M., Akaoka, I., Hori, T., Yamada
    M., and Miyamoto, T., 1982, Altered frequency of initiation
    sites of DNA replication in Werner's syndrome cells, Human
    Genet., 60:365.
Takunaga, M., Futami, T., Wakamatsu, E., Endo, M., and Yosizawa,
    Z., 1975, Werner's syndrome as "Hyaluronuria." Clin. Chim.
    Acta, 62:89.
Takunaga, M., Wakamatsu, E., Soto, K., Satake, S., Aoyama, K.,
    Saito, K., Sugawara, M., and Yosizawa, Z., 1978, Hyaluronuria
    in a case of progeria (Hutchinson-Gilford syndrome), J. Am.
    Geriatr. Soc., 26:296.
Toole, B., and Trelstad, R., 1971, Hyalruonate production and
    removal during corneal development in the chick, Dev. Biol.,
    26:28.
Toole, B., 1981, Glycosaminoglycans in Morphogenesis, in: "Cell
    Biology of Extracellular Matrix," p. 259, E. Hay, ed.,Plenum
    Press, New York.
Trelstad, R., Hayashi, K., and Toole, B., 1974, Epithelial
    collagens and glycosaminoglycans in the embryonic cornea, J.
    Cell Biol., 62:815.
Turakainen, H., Larjava, H., Saarni, H., and Penttinen, R., 1980,
    Synthesis of hyaluronic acid and collagen in skin fibroblasts
    cultured from patients with Osteogenesis Imperfecta, Biochim.
    Biophys. Acta, 628:388.
Turakainen, H., 1983, Altered glycosaminoglycan production in
    cultured osteogenesis imperfecta cultured fibroblasts,
    Biochem. J., 213:171.
Viegus, J., Souza, P.L.R., and Salzanio, F.M., Progeria in twins,
    J. Med. Genet., 11:384.
Villee, D.B., and Powers, M.L., 1978, Progeria: A model for the
    study of aging, in: "Senile Dementia: A Biomedical
    Approach," p. 259, K. Nandy, ed, Elsevier Biomedical Press, New York.
Vogel, K., Kendall, V., and Sapien, R., 1981, Glycosaminoglycan
    synthesis and composition in human fibroblasts during in vitro
    cellular aging (IMR-90), J. Cell. Physiol., 107:271.
Walford, R.L., 1970, Antibody diversity, histocompatibility
    systems, disease states, and aging, Lancet, 1970(ii):1226.
Weichselbaum, R.R., Nove, J., and Little, J.B., 1980, X-ray
    sensitivity of fifty-three human fibroblast cell strains from
    patients with characterized genetic disorders, Cancer Res.,
    40:920.
Wojtyk, R., and Goldstein, S., 1980, Fidelity of protein
    synthesis does not decline during aging of cultured human
    fibroblasts, J. Cell. Physiol., 103:299.
Zebrower, M., Kieras, F.J., and Brown, W.T., 1985,
    Glycosaminoglycan and hyaluronic acid elevation in genetic
    aging syndromes, Am. J. Hum. Genet. 36:84S.

AMYLOID, IMMUNOPATHOLOGY AND AGING

Peter D. Gorevic,* Jules Elias and Nancy Peress

Departments of Medicine* and Pathology, State University of New York, Stony Brook, New York 11794

INTRODUCTION

Recent advances in our understanding of the biochemistry and pathogenesis of the amyloid diseases have begun to provide information regarding the age-related amyloidoses in humans. Monospecific antisera to fibril subunit proteins are being used for the immunohistological typing of different forms of amyloid. This review will summarize current information relating amyloid to aging, particularly in regard to the pathoanatomic triad of islet cell hyalinization of the pancreas (type II diabetes mellitus), senile cardiac amyloidosis, and plaques/congophilic angiopathy in brain (senile dementia/Alzheimers disease).

PATHOGENIC FACTORS

Amyloid deposits are homogeneous, hyaline and extracellular bodies, with specific tinctorial properties, most notably metachromasia and birefringence after staining with alkaline congo red. Electron microscopy reveals that they are composed primarily of unbranching 100-150°A fibrils. Fibrils form in tissue due to polymerization of low molecular weight subunit proteins that can be isolated under dissociating conditions. The consequences of amyloid deposition depend on the organ system involved, the size of the deposits, and their location. Since the early pathologic descriptions of Virchow, it has been recognized that systemic amyloidoses may be associated with striking congophilic angiopathy, with vessel wall involvement characteristically contiguous to early tissue deposits. The latter, in turn, appears to reflect the origin of some of these subunit proteins from the blood. In spite of ultrastructural and tinctorial homogeneity, however, amyloid fibrils

397

associated with different underlying diseases may, in fact, be composed of distinct chemical types of subunit protein. Pathogenic
factors identified to date include the presence of variant or abnormal precursor molecules, structural "amyloidogenicity" (often
associated with a beta pleated sheet configuration), polymorphism
and proteolysis of subunit proteins. Levels at which genetic factors may be operative include abnormal synthesis or translation of
amyloid-related proteins, or faulty degradation of precursors or
fibrils (Thomas 1975; Glenner, 1980; Gorevic et al., 1982).

A nomenclature for the classification of the major types of
systemic amyloidosis has been developed based on structural studies
of fibril subunit proteins (Cohen and Wegelius, 1980)(Table 1).
These include so-called "primary" and myeloma-associated amyloidosis, in which fibrils are composed of intact immunoglobulin light
chains and/or fragments of light chain (AL), "secondary" amyloidosis
and amyloidosis associated with familial meditteranean fever (FMF),
and the prealbumin-related amyloidoses. All types of amyloid also
contain a second, less prominent, structural component, designated
the P, or "pentagonal" component because of its "doughnut" configuration in cross section as seen electron microscopically in extracted material (Pepys and Baltz, 1983). The biologic significance of P-component for the pathogenesis of amyloidosis is not
clear. This nomenclature includes the designation "AS" to be used
for senile amyloid subunit proteins, further modified by a letter
to denote the major organ system involvement, and subscript numbers
for different amyloid fibril proteins identified in the same organ.
Thus, amyloid fibril proteins isolated from senile brain will be
designated ASb_1, ASb_2 etc. as they are characterized biochemically
and/or immunohistologically.

AGE-RELATED AMYLOID IN OTHER SPECIES

Spontaneous amyloidosis occurs in a wide variety of mammalian
species (Walford, 1967; Rigdon, 1974). However, most forms of age-
related amyloid in animals so far characterized biochemically have
proven to be similar to human secondary (AA) amyloid (Gorevic et al,
1977; Westermark et al., 1979). Here the apparent relation to age
may simply reflect duration of exposure to causative factor(s),
often a chronic inflammatory stimulus, such as chronic granulomatous disease in monkeys. Studies in the duck (Rigdon, 1974) and
mouse (Thung, 1957) have shown that genetic differences may pro-
foundly influence the rate of development of spontaneous amyloidosis in these species.

Amyloid developing in the "senescence-accelerated mouse" (SAM)
(Takeda et al., 1981), as well as the SJL (Scheinberg et al., 1976)
and Low-Leukocyte Count (LLC) (Chai, 1976) strains of mice does not
appear to be AA in nature biochemically and/or immunohistologically.
The fibril subunit proteins obtained in each of these strains have

Table 1. Nomenclature and Classification of Amyloid

Structural Component		Fibril-Subunit Protein	Amyloid-Related Serum Protein
Amyloid Fibril	Primary (1°) Myeloma-Associated	AL	SAL
	Secondary (2°) Familial Meditteranean Fever (FMF)	AA	SAA_1, $_2$, etc.
	FAP Syndromes	AF $(P,J,etc)^a$	PA
	SCA	ASc^o	
	Medullary Carcinoma of the Thyroid	AE_+	Thyrocalcitonin
P-Component	All Types	AP =	SAP

AL - Immunoglobulin light chain-derived; AA - Amyloid A protein; Pa-Prealbumin (transthyretin); $SAA_{1,2}$ etc. - SAA isotypes; AP = SAP serum and tissue forms of P-component appear to be identical to each other; AE - Endocrine organ-related.

[a] Familial amyloid subunit protein has been designated AF, with subscript referring to specific kindred (e.g. Portuguese, Japanese) Not all forms of FAP have been shown to be Pa.

[b] ASc refers to subunit proteins occurring in Senile Cardiac Amyloidosis. So-called Isolated Atrial Amyloidosis (IAA) has been shown to be immunohistolocially and clinically distinct from the diffuse ventricular form (SCA) (Cornwell and Westermark, 1980) and may be found eventually to contain other classes of subunit proteins. The two types of senile cardiac amyloid subunit have been designated ASc_1 and ASc_2 (Cohen and Wegelius, 1980).

different amino acid compositions from murine AA protein. In the case of the SAM and LLC mouse strains they also do not react with standard immunoglobulin light chain determinants (Matsumura et al., 1982). The SAM strain has been advanced as a model for accelerated

senescence based on the fact that amyloid deposition occurs following normal development, involves articular structures and interver-
tebral discs (Shimizu et al., 1981) in addition to a number of
other organ systems, and is accompanied by other signs of premature
aging such as cataracts, loss of hair and skin glossiness (Takeda
et al., 1981). The relavence of this animal model to human aging
awaits further characterization of the subunit protein and its
putative serum precursor.

SENILE AMYLOIDOSIS IN HUMANS

Age-related amyloidosis in humans tends to occur in certain
organ systems as distinct pathologic entities (Wright et al., 1969),
most notably the pancreas (Opie, 1901), heart (Soyka, 1876), lungs
(Smith, et al., 1979), brain (Divry, 1934), aorta (Cornwell, et al.,
1982), seminal vesicles (Pitkanen, et al., 1983) and osteoarticular
structures (Ladefoged and Christensen, 1980). Although the incidence of amyloid in each increases with age, there is only a poor
correlation between organ systems in any individual, perhaps suggesting different pathogenic factors for each entity. Consequently,
it may be more correct to classify some of the "senile" amyloidoses
as localized or organ-specific (Glenner, 1980) rather than systemic
and to stress the importance of ground substance or local metabolic
factors in explaining selective deposition in certain organs. Pancreatic amyloid tends to occur earlier with a much flatter age-
related incidence than brain, heart or aorta; there is also considerable sampling variation when different series are compared (Wright,
1969).

Originally, it was considered that secondary (AA) amyloidosis
may relate to aging. However, older reports of increased levels
of serum amyloid A (SAA) protein, a major acute phase reactant, in
the blood of old people (Rosenthal and Franklin, 1975) independent
of any disease processes present, have not been substantiated in
more recent studies (Hijman and Sipe, 1979).

ISLET CELL HYALINIZATION

Postmortem studies have shown that the major correlate of
islet cell amyloid is a history of diabetes mellitus and, although
deposition also occurs in older nondiabetic persons, the relation
to aging may be more apparent than real (Maloy, et al., 1981).
Pancreatic amyloid deposits primarily involve individual islets,
often in a spotty distribution (Fig. 1), more so the head than the
tail of the organ and rarely extend to surrounding exocrine tissue
or blood vessels. The degree of islet amyloidosis appears to
correlate somewhat with the clinical severity of antecedent diabetes. It thus appears that amyloid deposition in this setting
is a concomitant, but unlikely to be a cause of, clinical diabetes.

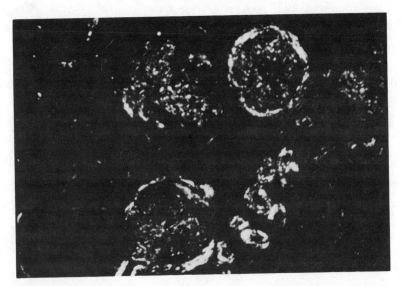

Fig. 1. Amyloid deposits in pancreatic islets; congo red stain viewed by polarizing microscopy (x 75).

Histochemical features of this form of senile amyloidosis, including absence of tryptophan in deposits, has suggested similarity to what Pearse has termed "Apudamyloid" (Pearse, et al., 1972), localized forms occurring in association with tumors such as medullary carcinoma of the thyroid (Westermark et al., 1977). Amyloid associated with the latter has been shown to contain thyrocalcitonin by sequence analysis (Sletten et al., 1976) and immunohistology (Table 1). By analogy, several investigators have suggested that islet cell amyloid may prove to be composed of prohormones of insulin or glucagon. Although this has yet to be substantiated by direct amino acid sequence analysis of isolated fibril subunit protein, reactivity with an antiserum to insulin B chain was shown in a recent study, both by binding to purified

fractionated fibrils and immunohistochemically in tissue section
(Westermark and Wilander, 1983).

SENILE CARDIAC AMYLOIDOSIS

Three forms of cardiovascular age-related amyloid have been
distinguished, including Isolated Atrial Amyloidosis (IAA, localized), Diffuse Ventricular Senile Cardiac Amyloidosis (SCA, generalized) (Cornwell and Westermark, 1980), and a third form involving the aorta (Cornwell et al., 1982). Each type occurs with a
distinct incidence and immunohistology. Cardiac amyloidosis may
be present in up to 50% persons over age 65 in postmortem series
and is more commonly restricted to the atria (left > right) than
the ventricles, with earliest deposits forming on the subendocar-
dial surface (Wright and Calkins, 1975). Many cases are asympto-
matic in life and only discovered postmortem (Fig. 2). SCA may
also be associated with the finding of small deposits of amyloid in
the lung, involving primarily blood vessels and/or alveolar septa
(Smith et al., 1979).

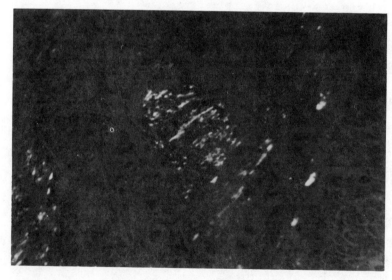

Fig. 2.   Nodular amyloid deposit in left ventricle found inciden-
          tially at post mortem; congo red stain viewed by polariz-
          ing microscopy (x 250).

Two groups of researchers have isolated SCA amyloid fibrils
and characterized the subunit protein as being thyroxine-binding
prealbumin (transthyretin) (Sletten et al.,1980; Cornwell et al.,
1987; Gorevic et al., Submitted). The same serum protein has also
been identified biochemically in fibrils isolated from at least
five different kindred affected by Familial Amyloidotic Polyneuropathy (FAP). Amino acid sequence studies of these proteins has
shown some to be mutant or variant molecules from the sequence of
normal pooled plasma prealbumin (Pras et al., 1981; Saraiva et al.,
1984). The FAP syndromes are distinct from SCA, however, in that
they occur in younger individuals, are inherited in an autosomal
dominant fashion and, whereas the amyloid is often widespread,
there is a distinct predilection for deposition in the peripheral
nervous system. In both SCA and some FAP syndromes, the existence
of prealbumin in tissue deposits can be demonstrated by immunoperoxidase staining of formalin-fixed material (Fig. 3).

SENILE PATHOLOGY IN BRAIN

Glenner has termed Alzheimers disease "the commonest form of
amyloidosis" (Glenner, 1983) because of its prevalence and the age-
related increased incidence of the characteristic pathologic lesions
in the aging brain (Peress et al., 1973). The neurofibrillary
tangle, neuritic plaque core and amyloid deposits in vessel walls
(Kidd, 1964; Terry et al., 1964) are all congophilic, but none are
unique to senility and each occurs in other disease entities (Table
2). The structural components of senile pathology in brain may
also be discordant in individual cases; thus, striking fibrillary
pathology may be found in some instances of Alzheimers Disease, in
spite of the presence of few senile plaques, and vice versa. Such
observations suggest that the development of each lesion may be
due to distinct pathogenic factors. Identical pathology to Alzheimers disease also occurs in high frequency in adult Down's syndrome, making this disease an important model in which to study the
clinical correlates of senile pathology in brain (Epstein, 1983).

Changes in the neuronal perikaryon include neurofibrillary
(Alzheimer, 1906) and granulovacuolar (Simchowicz, 1911) degenera-
tion, affecting up to 40% of the neurons in the hippocampal cortex.
The ultrastructural correlate of the Neurofibrillary Tangle (NFT),
seen both in tissue section (Kidd, 1964; Terry et al., 1964;
Yagashia et al., 1981) and in purified material (Iqbal et al., 1975;
Wisniewski et al., 1983), is the "Paired Helical Filament" (PHF) or
"Twisted Tangle", which is both argyrophilic and binds congo red.
PHF are composed of 90-120 A^O filaments with an 80 nm periodicity;
recent electron microscopic studies of purified material have in-

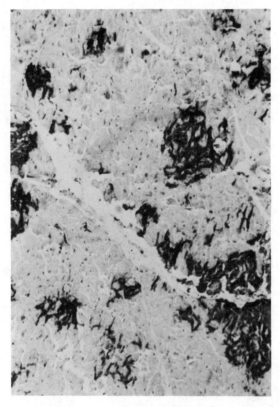

Fig. 3.   Immunoperoxidase stain of cardiac muscle from a case of
          diffuse ventricular "senile" cardiac amyloidosis (SCA),
          developed with an antiserum to prealbumin 1:200 dilution,
          showing masses of amyloid around muscle fibers (x 125).

dicated that each filament may be composed in turn of four proto-
filaments (Wisniewski et al., 1983).

Enriched preparations of NFT have been obtained by utilizing the
insolubility of these structures in urea, SDS, reducing agents,
guanidine and acid/alkali (Selkoe et al., 1982). Purified NFT are
remarkably resistant to all proteinases and yet appear to be predominantly protein, yielding a reproducible amino acid composition
on acid hydrolysis (Selkoe et al., 1982; Pons-Estel et al., Submitted). Iqbal et al (19) have reported that NFT repeatedly extracted
in 10% SDS, 10% beta-mercaptoethanol, followed by serial sonication
and sucrose gradient centrifugation have low molecular weight peptides in the range of 45,000-55,000 daltons which appear to be inherent antigens that can be visualized on SDS gels (Iqbal et al.,
1984). Purified NFT have been used to raise antisera (Ihara et al.,
1983; Grundke-Iqbal et al., 1984) which recognize tangles in tissue
section, both in affected neurons (Fig. 4a) and in dystrophic neu-
rites of senile plaques (Fig. 4b). Ihara et al have reported that
polyclonal anti-NFT does not react with normal brain proteins or
recognize low molecular weight proteins on immunoblots of purified
NFT or brain homogenates run onto SDS gels (Ihara et al., 1983). A
series of monoclonal antibodies to NFT have also been recently developed (Wang et al., 1984; Selkoe et al., 1984), some of which
appear to be useful immunohistological reagents for the definition
of neurofibrillary degeneration in tissue section.

In spite of the above findings, the issue of shared antigeni-
city between NFT and normal brain antigenic determinants is still
unsettled. Grundke-Iqbal et al (Grundke-Iqbal et al., 1979) have
reported that antisera raised to microtubule-enriched preparations
of normal brain cross-react with NFT, and that on the basis of cross
absorption studies the shared antigen is neither tubulin or neurofilament protein. Several investigators have found some antineuro-
filament antisera to react with NFT in tissue section, though not
with NFT isolated in SDS/mercaptoethanol or Tris/saline (Dahl et al.,
1982; Anderton et al., 1982; Gambetti et al., 1983). Anti-NFT,
however, do not react with purified neurofilament proteins. Possible
explanations for these cross reactivities include a deformation in
vivo of normal neurofilament ultrastructure (Schlaepfer, 1978) to
produce NFT, or the close association of altered neurofilaments
with NFT structure that is somehow lost during extraction.

SENILE PLAQUE CORE

Structurally, the senile plaque is the most unique form of
amyloid in aging, and potentially the most difficult to isolate to
homogeneity because of its close association with other fibrillary
structures, including the NFT (Fig. 4b) (Narang, 1980). In aging
brains, plaques are found primarily in the hippocampus whereas in
Alzheimers disease they are widely distributed throughout the cortex.

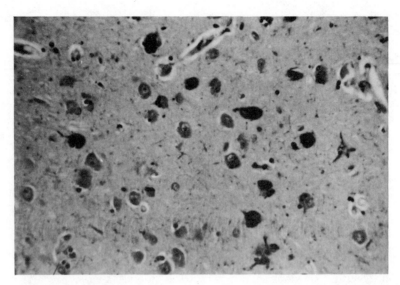

Fig. 4a. Immunoperoxidase stain of hippocampal cortex from a case
          of Alzheimers disease, developed with a polyclonal anti-
          serum to NFT, 1:250 dilution, showing numerous neurons
          with intracellular neurofibrillary pathology (x 250).

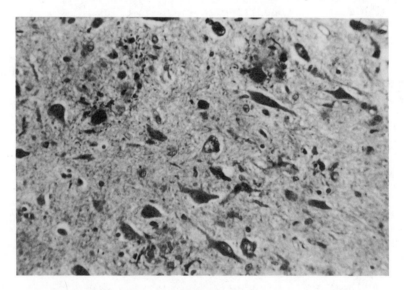

Fig. 4b. High power view of a field of hippocampal cortex con-
          taining several mature senile plaques, stained with anti-
          NFT showing neurofibrillary degeneration of neuritic end
          processes, but no staining of the amyloid plaque core (x
          500). Courtesy Drs. B. Pons-Estel, F. Goni and B. Frangione,
          NYU Medical Center.

Correlates of the density of senile plaques include the degree of
neuronal cell loss, deficiency of choline acetyl transferase and
intellectual impairment.

Early anatomic studies noted the contiguity of plaques to small
blood vessels, many of which were found to have amyloid in their
walls (Scholz, 1938; Vander Horst et al., 1960). A major unresolved
controversy is whether contiguous congophilic angiopathy reflects
the fact that the core originates from the blood like other forms
of systemic amyloidosis, or whether it is laid down due to modification of locally synthesized protein in a fibrillar configuration
(Wisniewski and Terry, 1973). Histochemically, the senile plaque
core also resembles Apudamyloid (Powers and Spicer, 1977) in lacking tryptophan and being permanganate-resistant (Wright et al., 1977).
Various claims have been made for specific immunoreactivity of core
protein in tissue section, including the demonstration of immunoglobulin determinants by electron microscopy (Ishii and Haga, 1976),
staining of plaque amyloid and congophilic angiopathy by antibodies
to neurofilament triplet proteins (Powers et al., 1981), and the
presence of prealbumin in neuritic plaque, NFT and angiopathy by
immunoperoxidase staining (Shirahama et al., 1982). Of the three
however, only congophilic angiopathy was found to stain positively
for P-component (Westermark et al., 1982). A consistent finding
so far is that anti-NFT does not cross react with plaque core
(Fig. 4b).

Allsop et al (68) recently published amino acid compositions
of senile plaque core preparations isolated from cases of senile
dementia by serial sieving of brain homogenates, followed by sucrose
gradient centrifugation under nondissociating conditions (contamin-
ating neuronal cell nuclei and cell bodies were lysed by treatment
of the preparations with subtilisin). Purified plaque core protein
was found to share with NFT the properties of insolubility in SDS
and urea, as well as resistance to proteolysis. The amino acid
composition obtained differed from that of known AL, AA and Pa-
related proteins, suggesting the presence of a unique subunit protein.

Although the exact nature of the plaque core protein remains
unknown, some interest has centered on the Prion (Proteinaceous
Infectious Particle) as a factor in its genesis, or as an actual
constituent of the plaque itself (Prusiner, 1984). Amyloid plaques
histologically identical to those seen in senile dementia may occur
in the subacute spongioform encephalopathies, including Kuru and
Creutzfeldt-Jakob Disease (sporadic and familial) in humans (Masters
et al., 1981), as well as naturally occurring or induced scrapie
in animals (Bruce and Fraser, 1975). In mice, the density and
distribution of plaques vary with the route of infection and the
genotype of the host (Bruce et al., 1976; Bruce and Fraser, 1981).
Prusiner et al have isolated the scrapie agent to homogeneity in

a hamster model and shown that it copurifies with rod-like structures that bind congo red and are birefringent (Prusiner et al.,
1983). These rods appear to be composed exclusively of a subunit
glycoprotein, designated PrP, which has a molecular weight of 27-
30,000 daltons and is also resistant to proteolysis (Prusiner et al.,
1984). Anti-PrP stains amyloid plaques in the infected hamster
brain and can be used to demonstrate the agent immunohistologically
during the preclinical period of scrapie infection (Bendheim et al.,
1984).

     In spite of pathologic similarities, the relationship of
Alzheimer Disease to the transmissible spongioform encephalopathies
remains unclear. The latter are associated with the presence of a
third type of filamentous structure, designated Scrapie-Associated
Fibrils (SAF), which can be identified ultrastructurally (Merz et al.,
1981) in homogenized brain fractionated on discontinuous sucrose
gradients. SAF are distinct from amyloid fibrils or NFT in having
a diameter of 11-14 nm, consisting of 2-4 twisted filaments with
a 40-90 nm periodicity. One group has reported the presence in
SAF preparations of a subunit protein with a molecular weight of
26,000 (Diringer et al., 1983). Although SAF could be demonstrated
in Kuru, Creutzfeldt-Jakob Disease and Scrapie-infected animals,
they were not observed in Alzheimers Disease or other conditions in
humans associated with neurofibrillary degeneration (Merz et al.,
1984) (Table 2).

CEREBRAL AMYLOID ANGIOPATHY

     Congophilic angiopathy in brain primarily affects medium-
sized and small arteries of the leptomeninges and superficial cerebral cortex, with a predilection for the temporal and occipital
lobes but generally spares the white matter, basal ganglia, cerebellum and brainstem (Okazaki et al., 1979). It is usually not
associated with systemic amyloidosis (including the FAP syndromes),
cardiac or pancreatic amyloid of aging, or cerebral or visceral
arteriosclerosis. Cerebrovascular amyloidosis may occur in several
forms. It may be associated with plaques and tangles in Alzheimers
disease (Mandybur, 1975) and adult Down's syndrome, or present as
recurrent intracranial hemorrhages in younger individuals unaffected
by hypertension, diabetes or arteriosclerosis, either in the sporadic
or familial forms (Gudmundsson et al., 1972). Cerebrovascular
amyloidosis has been reported to be present in as many as 90% of
cases of Alzheimers disease (Glenner et al., 1981).

     Amyloid fibrils have been isolated from dissected leptomeningeal
vessels obtained postmortem from cases of a large Icelandic kindred
affected by angiopathy, and from the brains of individuals with
Alzheimers disease and Down's syndrome with senile dementia found
to have prominent vascular involvement at autopsy. Subunit proteins
obtained under dissociating conditions from Icelanders with amyloid

Table 2. Congophilic Structures in Alzheimers Disease

A. Neurofibrillary Degeneration

> ? Unique Protein
> ? Deformation of Neurofilamentous Structure
> ? Other Shared Antigens (e.g. Microtubule-Associated
>   Antigens)

Found In (Wisniewski et al., 1979)   Experimental

Aging Brain   Aluminum Intoxication
Presenile/Senile Dementia   Spindle Inhibitors
Down's Syndrome
Dementia Pugilistica
Guam-Parkinson Dementia Complex
(including unaffected Guamanians)
Postencephalitic Parkinsonism
Amyotrophic Lateral Sclerosis
Steele-Richardson-Olszewski Syndrome

B. Senile Plaques

> ? Prion
> ? Modification of Neurofibrillary Tangle Protein(s)
> ? Modification of Other Proteins (e.g. Neurohormones)

Found In   Experimental

Aging Brain   Scrapie
Alzheimers Disease   Aging Brain (Horses,
Down's Syndrome   Dogs, Monkey)
Kuru   Wasting Disease of
Creutzfeldt-Jakob Disease   Mule Deer
Gerstman-Straussler Syndrome

C. Cerebrovascular Amyloid

> ? Beta Protein (Alzheimers Disease/Adult Downs Syndrome)
> ? Gamma Trace Protein (Familial Angiopathy)
Age-Associated
Sporadic
Hereditary
Alzheimers Disease
Adult Down's Syndrome (Trisomy 21)

angiopathy were found to have sequence homology to gamma trace
(Cohen et al., 1983), a protein initially identified in normal
cerebrospinal fluid and urine of patients in renal failure, which
also appears to be selectively present in certain neuronal cell
populations by immunohistology (Grubb and Lofberg, 1982). Amino
acid sequence analysis of vascular amyloid fibrils from cases of
Alzheimer's disease and Down's syndrome have disclosed a novel
"beta" protein (beta pleated sheet by x-ray diffraction) with no
sequence homology to any known brain or serum protein (Glenner and
Wong, 1984; Glenner and Wong, 1984).

IMMUNOPATHOLOGY OF THE AMYLOID DISEASES

All the senile amyloidoses are distinct from the AA form of
systemic amyloid on the basis of permanganate resistance (Table
3) and lack of reactivity with antisera to AA protein. The isolated atrial form of cardiac, as well as islet cell and plaque
core amyloids share with the Apudamyloids a lack of tryptophan
(Pearse et al., 1972), assessed histologically by the p-dimethyla-
minobenzaldehydenitrate method. However, this observation will
need to be corroborated by detailed amino acid compositions of
purified subunit proteins. It is of interest, nevertheless, that
plaque core and congophilic angiopathy in brain differ histochemically in regard to tryptophan reactivity, providing additional evidence that they may be biochemically different pathologic entities.
All forms of senile amyloid excepting the plaque core (Powers et al.,
1981), appear to contain P-component, which has been demonstrated
immunohistologically or by direct extraction (Westermark et al.,
1975) (Table 3). It should also be noted that in blood vessels
AP reactivity may be difficult to interpret, as this protein has
been shown to be a component of elastic fiber microfibrils in various
normal tissues (Cornwell et al., 1982; Breathnach et al., 1981).

The utility of immunohistochemical methods for the typing of
the systemic amyloid in tissue has been established recently
(Fujihara et al., 1980; Shirahama et al., 1981). Monospecific
antisera to AA protein, P-component, prealbumin, thyrocalcitonin
and, in some instances, light chain determinants, have increased
the specificity and accuracy of the immunodiagnosis of the amyloid
diseases. Recent studies in our laboratory have shown that the
specificity of reactions with monospecific antisera in tissue section
can be corroborated in immunoblots of small frozen biopsy specimens
solubilized in dissociating buffers and run onto two-dimensional
gels (Turner et al., 1983). To a great extent such approaches
circumvent artefacts or inconsistencies of staining due to non-
specific absorption of proteins onto amyloid deposits. Although
the immunopathologic differentiation of the senile amyloidoses is
still in its infancy, it may be anticipated that monoclonal or
polyclonal antisera to core and beta proteins, PrP or SAF antigenic
determinants, variant prealbumin molecules or fragments, or extracted

islet cell fibril fractions will further refine our ability to
distinguish between the various forms age-related amyloid in humans.

Table 3. Histochemistry of the "Senile" Amyloidoses in Humans

| | Cardiac | | Pancreas | Brain | Aorta |
	SCA	IAA			
Congo Red Bire-fringence	+	+	+	+	+
Fibrils (EM)	+	+	+	+	+
Tryptophan-Con-taining*	+	-	-	Plaques - Vessels +	+
Permanganate Re-sistant(Narang, 1980)	Yes	Yes	Yes	Yes	Yes
P-Component	+	+	+	Plaques - Vessels +	?+

* Lacking in amyloid of polypeptide-producing tumors of endocrine
  tissue (Pearse et al., 1972).

+ Background immunofluorescence due to reactivity of antiserum
  with aortic tissue (Cornwell et al., 1982).

AMYLOID AND AGING

     Some amyloid-related proteins may prove to be biochemical
markers for either the aging process, or for specific diseases
associated with aging. Isolation and characterization of fibril
subunit proteins in some instances has led to the identification
of cross-reactive serum proteins, the development of sensitive
quantitative assays and the characterization of abnormal polymorphs
or mutant molecules which appear to be more susceptible to polymerization, proteolysis and, perhaps in some instances, cross
linking. Information regarding the biological functions of many
of these proteins is still rudimentary. It is of interest, however,
that some, such as prealbumin and gammatrace share sequence homo-
logies to various peptidergic gastroenteropancreatic neuroendocrine
hormones (Grubb and Lofberg, 1982; Jurnvall et al., 1981), and
others (prealbumin, SAA) have been found to have immunoregulatory

properties in vitro (Burton et al., 1978). Deposition of these proteins in tissue is an important pathologic correlate of the functional decline of specific organ systems in humans. It is not clear,
however, whether this process is a result of somatic mutation, is
genetically determined but expressed late in life, or is the result
of errors in translation, transcription, processing or degradation,
perhaps related to abnormalities of specific enzyme or scavenger
systems. Ultimately, these alternatives will require further biochemical characterization of the heterogeneous forms of amyloidosis
in aging, cloning of the genes responsible for the production of
these proteins, and the study of their elaboration in various amyloid
diseases and in older persons in whom senile pathology is either
clearly demonstrable or apparently lacking.

Work supported by NIH grants AGO1973, GM 31866 and the HOR
Foundation. The authors gratefully acknowledge the secretarial
help of Mrs. Karen Abramowski, and the technical support of Ms.
Eleanor Boss.

REFERENCES

Allsop, D., Landon, M., Kidd, M., 1983, The isolation and amino
    acid composition of senile plaque core protein, Brain Res.,
    259:340.
Anderton, B. H., Breinburg, M. J., Downes, P. J., Green, B. E.,
    Tomlinson, B. E., Ulrich, J., Wood, J. N., 1982, Monoclonal
    antibodies show that neurofibrillary tangles and neurofilaments
    share antigenic determinants, Nature, 298:84.
Bendheim, P. D., Barry, R. A., Dearmond, S. J., Stites, D. P.,
    Prusiner, S. B., 1984, Antibodies to a scrapie prion protein,
    Nature, 310:418.
Breathnach, S. M., Melrose, S. M., Bhogal, B., De Beer, F. C., Dyck,
    R. F., Tenent, G., Black, M. M., Pepys, M. B., 1981, Amyloid
    P-Component is located on elastic fibre microfibrils in normal
    human tissue, Nature, 293:652.
Bruce, M. E., Dickinson, A. G., Fraser, H., 1976, Cerebral amyloid-
    osis in scrapie in the mouse: Effect of agent strain and mouse
    genotype, Neuropathol. Appl. Neurobiol., 2:471.
Bruce, M. E., Fraser, H., 1975, Amyloid plaques in the brains of
    mice infected with scrapie: morphological variation and stain-
    ing properties, Neuropathol. Appl. Neurobiol.,1:189.
Bruce, M. E., Fraser, H., 1981, Effect of route of infection on the
    frequency and distribution of amyloid plaques in scrapie mice.
    Neuropathol. Appl. Neurobiol., 7:289.
Burton, P., Iden, S., Mitchell, K., White, A., 1978, Thymic hormone-
    like restoration by human prealbumin of azathioprine sensitivity
    of spleen cells from thymectomized mice, Proc. Natl. Sci.,
    75:823.

Chai, C. K., 1976, Reticular cell hyperplasia and amyloidosis in a line of mice with low leukocyte counts, Amer. J. Pathol., 85:49.

Cohen, A. S., Wegelius, O., 1980, Classification of amyloid, Arth. Rheum., 23:644.

Cohen, D. H., Feiner, H., Jensson, O., Frangione, B., 1983, Amyloid fibril in hereditary cerebral hemorrhage with amyloidosis is related to the gastroenteropancreatic neuroendocrine protein, gamma trace, J. Exp. Med., 158:623.

Cornwell, III, G. G., Westermark, P., 1980, Senile amyloidosis: A protean manifestation of the aging process, J. Clin. Path. 33:1146.

Cornwell, III, G. G., Westermark, P., Murdoch, W., Pitkanen, P., 1982, Senile aortic amyloid. A third distinctive type of age-related cardiovascular amyloid, Amer. J. Pathol., 108:135.

Cornwell, III, G. G., Westermark, P., Natvig, J. B., Murdoch, W., 1987, Senile cardiac amyloid: evidence that fibrils contain a protein immunologically related to prealbumin, Immunol. 44:447.

Dahl, D., Selkoe, D. J., Pero, R., Bignami, A., 1982, Immunostaining of neurofibrillary tangles in Alzheimers senile dementia with a neurofilament antiserum, J. Neurol. Sci., 1:113.

Diringer, H., Gelderblom, H., Hilmert, H., Ozel, M., Edelbluth, C., 1983, Scrapie infectivity fibrils and low molecular weight protein, Nature, 306:476.

Divry, P., 1934, De La Nature De L'Alteration Fibrillaire D'Alzheimer, J. Belge De Neurologie Et De Psych., 34:197.

Epstein, C. J., "Downs syndrome and Alzheimers disease: implications and approaches" Biological Aspects of Alzheimers Disease, R. Katzman, ed. Banbury Report 15, Cold Spring Harbor Laboratory; 1983, p. 169-182.

Fujihara, S., Balow, J. E., Costa, J. C., Glenner, G. G., 1980, Identification and classification of amyloid in formalin-fixed, paraffin-embedded tissue sections by the unlabeled immunoper-oxidase method, Lab. Invest., 43:358.

Gambetti, P., Autilo-Gambetti, L., Perry, G., Shecket, G., Crane, R. C., 1983, Antibodies to neurofibrillary tangles of Alzheimers disease raised from human and animal neurofilament proteins, Lab. Invest., 49:430.

Glenner, G. G., 1980, Amyloid deposits and amyloidosis, New Eng. J. Med., 302:1283, 1333.

Glenner, G. G., 1983, Alzheimers disease. The commonest form of amyloidosis, Arch. Pathol. Lab. Med., 107:281.

Glenner, G. G. Henry, J. H., Fujihara, S., 1981, Congophilic angio-pathy in the pathogenesis of Alzheimers degeneration, Ann. Pathol., 1:120.

Glenner, G. G., Wong, C. W., 1984, Alzheimers disease: initial report of the purification and characterization of a novel cerebrovascular amyloid protein, Biochem. Biophys. Res. Commun., 120:885.

Glenner, G. G., Wong, C. W., 1984, Alzheimers disease and Downs
    syndrome: Sharing of a unique cerebrovascular amyloid fibril
    protein, Biochem. Biophys. Res. Commun., 122:1131.
Gorevic, P. D., Cleveland, A. B., Franklin, E. C., 1982, The
    biologic significance of amyloid, Ann. N.Y. Acad. Sci., 289:
    380.
Gorevic, P. D., Cleveland, A. B., Pras, M., Wright, J. R., Prelli,
    R., Frangione, B., "Senile" cardiac amyloidosis: Biochemical
    studies and immunohistological identity with heredofamilial
    neuropathic amyloid due to tissue deposition of prealbumin,
    Submitted for Publication.
Gorevic, P. D., Greenwald, M., Frangione, B., Pras, M., Franklin,
    E. C., 1977, The amino acid sequence of duck amyloid A (AA)
    protein, J. Immunol, 118:1113.
Grubb, A., Lofberg, H., 1982, Human γ trace, a basic microprotein:
    amino acid sequence and presence in the adenohypophysis,
    Proc. Natl. Acad. Sci., 79:3024.
Grundke-Iqbal, I., Iqbal, K., Tung, Y. C., Wisniewski, H. M.,
    1984, Alzheimers paired helical filaments: immunochemical
    identification of polypeptides, Acta Neuropathol. (Berl.),
    62:259.
Grundke-Iqbal, I., Johnson, A. B., Wisniwski, H. M., Terry, R. D.,
    1979, Evidence that Alzheimer neurofibrillary tangles origi-
    nate from neurotubules, Lancet, 1:578.
Gudmundsson, G., Hallgrimsson, J., Jonasson, T. A., Bjarnason, O.,
    1972, Hereditary cerebral hemorrhage with amyloidosis, Brain,
    95:387.
Hijman, S. W., Sipe, J. D., 1979, Levels of serum amyloid A protein
    (SAA) in normal persons of different age groups, Clin Exp
    Immunol. 35:96.
Ihara, Y., Abraham, C., Selkoe, D. J., 1983, Antibodies to paired
    helical filaments in alzheimers disease do not recognize
    normal brain proteins, Nature,
Iqbal, K., Wisniewski, H. M., Grundke-Iqbal, I., Korthals, J. K.,
    Terry, R. D., 1975, Chemical pathology of neurofibrils.
    Neurofibrillary tangles of Alzheimers presenile senile
    dementia, J. Histochem. Cytochem., 23:563.
Iqbal, K., Zaidi, T., Thompson, C.H., Merz, P.A., Wisniewski, H. M.,
    1984, Alzheimers paired helical filaments: Bulk isolation,
    solubility and protein composition, Acta Neuropathol (Berl.),
    62:167.
Ishii, T., Haga, S., 1976, Immuno-electron microscopic localization
    of immunoglobulins in amyloid fibrils of senile plaques,
    Acta. Neuropathol.(Berl.), 36:243.
Jurnvall, H., Carlstrom, A., Pettersson, T., Jacobsson, B., Persson,
    M., Mutt, V., 1981, Structural homologies between prealbumin,
    gastrointestinal prohormones and other proteins, Nature
    291:261.
Kidd, M., 1964, Alzheimers Disease - an electron microscopical
    study, Brain, 87:307.

Ladefoged, C., Christensen, H. B., 1980, Congophilic substance with
    green dichoism in hip joints in autopsy material, Acta. Pathol.
    Microbiol. Immunol. Scand. (A), 88:55.
Maloy, A. L., Longnecker, D. S., Greenberg, E. R., 1981, The re-
    lation of islet amyloid to the clinical type of diabetes,
    Human Pathol., 12:917.
Mandybur, T. I., 1975, The incidence of cerebral amyloid angio-
    pathy in Alzheimers disease, Neurology, 25:120.
Masters, C. L., Gajdusek, D. C., Gibbs, Jr., C. J., 1981, Creutzfeldt-
    Jakob disease virus-isolations from the Gerstmann-Straussler
    syndrome, Brain, 104:559.
Matsumura, A., Higuchi, K., Shimizu, K., Hosokawa, M., Hashimoto, K.,
    Yasuhira, K., Takeda, T., 1982, A novel amyloid fibril protein
    isolated from senescence-accelerated mice, Lab Invest, 47:270.
Merz, P. A., Rohwer, R. G., Kascsak, R., Wisniewski, H. M.,
    Somerville, R. A., Gibbs, Jr., C. J., Gajdusek, D. C., 1984,
    Infection-specific particle from the unconventional slow virus
    diseases, Science, 225:437.
Merz, P. A., Somerville, R. A., Wisniewski, H. M., Iqbal, K., 1981,
    Abnormal fibrils from scrapie-infected brain, Acta. Neuropathol.
    (Berl.), 54:63.
Narang, K., 1980, High resolution electron microscopic analysis of
    the amyloid fibril in Alzheimers disease, J. Neuropathol.
    Exp. Neurol., 39:621.
Okazaki, H., Reagan, T. J., Campbell, R. J., 1979, Clinico-pathologic
    studies of primary cerebral amyloid angiopathy, Mayo Clinic
    Proc., 54:22.
Opie, E. L., 1901, The relation of diabetes mellitus to lesions of
    the pancreas. Hyaline degeneration of the islets of Langer-
    hans, J. Exp. Med., 5:527.
Pearse, A. G. E., Ewen, S. W. B., Polak, J. M., 1972, The genesis
    of Apudamyloid in endocrine polypeptide tumors: histochemical
    distinction from immuno amyloid, Virchows Arch. Abt., B 10:92.
Pepys, M. B., Baltz, M. L., 1983, Actue phase proteins with special
    reference to C-reactive protein and related proteins (pentraxins)
    and serum amyloid A protein, Adv. Immunol., 34:141.
Peress, N. S., Kane, W. C., Aronson, S. M., 1973, "Central nervous
    system findings in a tenth decade autopsy population" Progr.
    Brain Res., Neurobiological Aspects of Maturation and Aging,
    Vol. 40, p. 473, Elsevier.
Pitkanen, P., Westermark, P., Cornwell, G. G. III, Murdoch, W., 1983,
    Amyloid of the seminal vesicles: A distinctive and common
    localized form of senile amyloidosis. Amer. J. Pathol. 110:64.
Pons-Estel, B., Goni, F., Alvarez, F., Gorevic, P. D., Frangione, B.
    Isolation and partial characterization of Alzheimers neurofibril-
    lary tangles, Submitted for Publication.
Powers, J. M., Schlaepfer, W. W., Willingham, M. C., Hall, B. J.,
    1981, An immunoperoxidase study of senile cerebral amyloidosis
    with pathogenetic considerations. J. Neuropathol. Exp. Neurol.
    40:592.

Pras, M., Franklin, E. C., Prelli, F., Frangione, B., 1981, A variant of prealbumin from amyloid fibrils in familial poly-neuropathy of Jewish origin, J. Exp. Med., 154:989.

Prusiner, S. B., 1984, Some speculations about prions, amyloid and Alzheimers disease, New Eng. J. Med., 310:661.

Prusiner, S. B., Groth, D. F., Bolton, D. C., Kent, S. B., Hood, L. E., 1984, Purification and structural studies of a major scrapie prion protein, Cell, 38:127.

Prusiner, S. B., McKinley, M. P., Bowman, K. A., Bolton, D. C., Bendheim, P. E., Groth, D. F., Glenner, G. G., 1983, Scrapie prions aggregate to form amyloid-like birefringent rods, Cell, 35:349.

Rigdon, R. H., 1974, Occurrence and association of amyloid with dis-eases in birds and mammals including man: a review, Tex. Rev. Biol. Med., 32:667.

Rosenthal, C. J., Franklin, E. C., 1975, Variation with age and disease of an amyloid A protein-related serum component, J. Clin. Invest., 55:746.

Saraiva, M. J. M., Birken, S., Costa, P. P., Goodman, D. S., 1984, Amyloid fibril protein in familial amyloidotic polyneuropathy, portuguese type, J. Clin. Invest, 74:104.

Scheinberg, M. A., Cathcart, E. S., Eastcott, J. W., Skinner, M., Benson, M., Shirahama, T., Bennett, M., 1976, The SJL/J mouse: A new model for spontaneous age-associated amyloidosis. I. Morphologic and immunochemical aspects, Lab. Invest., 35:47.

Schlaepfer, W. W., 1978, Deformation of isolated neurofilaments and the pathogenesis of neurofibrillary pathology, J. Neuropathol. Exp. Neurol., 38:244.

Scholz, W., 1938, Studien zur pathologie der hirngefaesse II. Die drusige entartung der hirnarterieren and kapillieren ceine form senile gefaesser-krankung, Z. Ges. Neurol. Psych., 162:694.

Selkoe, D. J., Abraham, C., Rasool, C. G., McCluskey, A., Duffy, L. K., Monoclonal antibodies to Alzheimer paire helical fila-ments produced by rat-mouse hybridomas (Abstr), Amer. Assoc. Neuropathologists, June 14-17, 1984.

Selkoe, D. J., Ihara, Y., Salazar, F. J., 1982, Alzheimers disease: Insolubility of partially purified paired helical filaments in sodium dodecyl sulfate and urea, Science, 215:1243.

Sletten, K., Westermark, P., Natvig, J. B., 1976, Characterization of amyloid fibril protein from medullary carcinoma of the thyroid, J. Exp. Med., 143:993.

Sletten, K., Westermark, P., Natvig, J. B., 1980, Senile cardiac amyloid is related to prealbumin, Scand. J. Immunol., 12:503.

Smith, R. R. L., Hutchins, G. M., Moore, G. W., Humphrey, R. L., 1979, Type and distribution of pulmonary parenchymal and vascular amyloid, Amer. J. Med., 66:96.

Shimizu, K., Kasai, R., Yamamuro, T., Hosokawa, M., Takeshita, S., Takeda, T., 1981, Amyloid deposition in the articular structures of SKR senescent mice, Arth. Rheum., 24:1540.

Shirahama, T., Skinner, M., Cohen, A. S., 1981, Immunocytochemical
    identification of amyloid in formalin-fixed sections. Histo-
    chemistry, 72:161.
Shirahama, T., Skinner, M., Westermark, P., Rubinow, A., Cohen, A.
    S., Brun, A., Kemper, T. L., 1982, Senile cerebral amyloid.
    Prealbumin as a common constituent in the neuritic plaque, in
    the neurofibrillary tangle, and in the microangiopathi lesion,
    Amer. J. Pathol., 107:41.
Soyka, J., 1876, Ueber amyloide degeneration. Prager Med. Schnschr.,
    1:165.
Takeda, T., Hosokawa, M., Takeshita, S., Irino, M., Higuchi, K.,
    Matsushita, T., Tomita, Y., Yasuhira, K., Hamamoto, H., Shimizu,
    K., Ishii, M., Yamamuro, T., 1981, A new murine model of
    accelerated senescence, Mech. Ageing Devel., 17:183.
Terry, R. D., Gonatas, N. K., Weiss, M., 1964, Ultrastructural
    studies in Alzheimers presenile dementia, Amer. J. Pathol.,
    44:269.
Thomas, P. K., 1975, Genetic factors in amyloidosis, J. Med. Genet.,
    12:317.
Thung, P. J., 1957, The relation between amyloid and aging in com-
    parative pathology, Gerontologia, 1:235.
Turner, W. J., Cleveland, A. B., Gorevic, P. D., 1983, A novel
    method for the typing of amyloid in small biopsy specimens:
    western blot analysis of two dimensional gels, Clin. Res.,
    31:355A.
Vander Horst, L., Stam, F. C., Wigboldus, J. M., 1960, Amyloidosis
    in senile and presenile involutional processes of the central
    nervous system, J. Neuromental Dis., 130:578.
Walford, R. L., 1967, The general immunology of aging, Adv. Geront.
    Res., 2:159.
Wang, G. P., Grundke-Iqbal, I., Kasesak, R. J., Iqbal, K., Wisniewski,
    H. M., 1984, Alzheimer neurofibrillary tangles: Monoclonal
    antibodies to inherent antigen (s), Acta Neuropathol (Berl),
    62:268.
Westermark, P., Grimelius, C. L., Polak, J. M., Larsson, L. T.,
    Van Noorden, S., Wilander, S., Pearse, A. G. E., 1977, Amyloid
    in polypeptide hormone-producing tumors, Lab Invest., 37:212.
Westermark, P., Shirahama, T., Skinner, M., Brun, A., Cameron, R.,
    Cohen, A. S., 1982, Immunohistochemical evidence for the lack
    of amyloid P component in some intracerebral amyloids, Lab
    Invest, 46:457.
Westermark, P., Skinner, M., Cohen, A. S., 1975, The P-component
    of amyloid of human islets of langerhans, Scand. J. Immunol.,
    4:95.
Westermark, P., Sletten, K., Naeser, P., Natvig, J. B., 1979,
    Characterization of amyloid of aging obese-hyperglycemic mice
    and their lean littermates, Scand. J. Immunol., 9:193.
Westermark, P., Wilander, E., 1983 , Islet amyloid in type 2 (non-
    insulin-dependent) diabetes is realted to insulin, Diabetologia,
    24:342.

Wisniewski, H. M., Merz, G. S., Merz, P. A., Huang, Y. W. Iqbal, K.,
    1983, Morphology and biochemistry of neuronal paired helical
    filaments and amyloid fibers in humans and animals, Prog.
    Neuropath., 5:145.
Wisniewski, H. M., Terry, R. D., 1973, Reexamination of the patho-
    genesis of the senile plaque, Progr. Neuropathol., 2:1.
Wisniewski, K., Jervis, G. A., Moretz, R. C., Wisniewski, H. M.,
    1979, Alzheimer neurofibrillary tangles in diseases other than
    senile and presenile dementia, Ann. Neurol., 5:288.
Wright, J. R., Calkins, E., 1975, Amyloid in the aged heart; frequency
    and clinical significance, J. Amer. Ger. Soc., 23;97.
Wright, J. R., Calkins, E., Breen, W. J., Stolte, G., Shultz, R. T.,
    1969, Relationship of amyloid to aging. Review of the liter-
    ature and systematic study of 83 patients derived from a general
    hospital population, Medicine, 48:39.
Wright, J. R., Calkins, E., Humphrey, R. L., 1977, Potassium permang-
    anate reaction in amyloidosis: A histologic method to assist
    in differentiating forms of this disease, Lab. Invest., 36:274.
Yagashia, S., Itoh, Y., Nav., W., Amano, N., 1981, Reappraisal of
    the fine structure of Alzheimers neurofibrillary tangles,
    Acta Neuropathol., 54:239.

<u>IN VITRO</u> STUDIES OF WERNER SYNDROME CELLS: ABERRANT

GROWTH AND CHROMOSOME BEHAVIOR

Darrell Salk

Departments of Pathology and Pediatrics
University of Washington
Seattle, Washington

WERNER SYNDROME

When he was a medical student in the ophthalmology clinic at Kiel University, Otto Werner (1904) described four siblings who had "scleroderma in association with cataracts." Although he felt that there was no "evidence for a degenerative condition" in the family, the pedigree is classical for an autosomal recessive condition. Thannhauser (1945) reviewed published cases, listed twelve characteristics of the syndrome, including the tendency to occur in siblings, and pointed out that the skin changes were not true scleroderma. The modern era of Werner syndrome research was ushered in by the publication of Epstein et al. (1966), in which 125 cases were reviewed and the natural history, pathologic changes, and genetics of the condition were defined.

Although sometimes referred to as "progeria of the adult", Werner syndrome is more properly described as a caricature of normal aging rather than a process of rapid, premature aging. There are many clinical features similar to those observed in normal elderly patients, but there are important distinctions as well (Table 1). An understanding of the (presumably) single molecular defect that can lead to multiple progeroid features may shed light on the basic biology of the aging process or on the development of specific geriatric disorders such as diabetes, atherosclerosis, osteoporosis, and the development of neoplasia. Since 1966, many studies have been

Table 1.   Principal Differences Between Werner Syndrome and Normal
           Aging.

	Werner syndrome	Aging
Inheritance:	Autosomal recessive	Universal; multifactorial
Short stature:	Primary	Acquired
Laryngeal abnormalities:	Common	Uncommon
Cataracts:	Juvenile	Senile
Soft tissue calcifications:	Common	Uncommon
Osteoporosis:	Peripheral (limbs)	Central (spine)
Hypertension:	Uncommon	Common
Neoplasia:	Many sarcomas, meningiomas	Mostly carcinomas
Central nervous system:	No changes	Senile changes
Hyaluronic aciduria:	Present	Absent

pursued in an attempt to identify the underlying molecular defect in
this condition (for reviews, see Salk, 1982; Salk et al., 1984).   In
this chapter I will summarize some of the studies of growth and
chromosome behavior of Werner syndrome cultured skin fibroblasts and
lymphoblastoid cell lines.

CELL GROWTH

    Cultured skin fibroblast-like (FL) cells from patients with
Werner syndrome grow poorly: reduced growth potential has been
reported by more than 11 laboratories for cultures from more than 26
patients, using many different tissue culture media.   It is not yet
known whether this poor growth is a primary or a secondary

manifestation of the basic molecular defect, nor is the relationship clear between reduced growth of cultured skin fibroblasts and the other manifestations of Werner syndrome in vitro and in vivo. This characteristic also makes it difficult to obtain sufficient growth for clonal studies or for biochemical studies that require a large number of cells.

We previously studied the growth of 20 independently derived skin FL cell strains from three patients with Werner syndrome in comparison with the growth of ten FL cell strains from non-Werner patients (Salk et al., 1981b). Population growth rates and total replicative lifespans of Werner syndrome strains averaged 55 percent and 27 percent, respectively, of the growth rates and lifespans of non-Werner strains. In the first few passages, four Werner syndrome cultures had population growth rates in the low normal range, but the longest-lived Werner syndrome strain had only 75 percent of the total replicative lifespan of the shortest lived normal strain.

Exponential growth rates, cloning efficiencies, and saturation densities of Werner syndrome FL cell strains were also reduced, whereas cell attachment was normal. Viable cells, identified by dye exclusion, were maintained in postreplicative Werner syndrome and control cultures for periods of at least ten months: there was no evidence of accelerated postreplicative senescence or cell death of Werner syndrome FL cells. Co-cultivation of Werner syndrome and normal strains did not influence population growth rates of either strain. Two proliferating hybrid clones were obtained from fusions of normal and Werner syndrome FL cells, and these hybrids displayed the reduced growth potential typical of Werner syndrome FL cells.

Recently, results suggest that the poor growth of Werner syndrome cells is not limited to cultured skin fibroblasts. Epstein-Barr (EB) virus-transformed lymphoblastoid cells are generally considered to be continuously propagating cell lines with an indefinite in vitro lifespan, but two such cultures derived from patients with Werner syndrome grew poorly and ceased replicating while we were maintaining them for cytogenetic studies. We subsequently repeated the observation by using cryogenically preserved cells from these two cultures and by using a third cell line derived from another Werner patient. Although an established line derived from a non-Werner patient grew continuously in the laboratory at the same time, all Werner lymphoblastoid cell lines died out and had markedly reduced growth rates (Table 2). One cell line derived from the brother of a Werner patient also ceased replicating, although its growth rate appeared to be normal.

Table 2. Growth of EB Virus Transformed Lymphoblastoid Cell
          Lines. All Cultures Except for the Normal
          Established Line Ceased Replication After the Number
          of Doublings and Number of Days Indicated.

	Population doublings per day	Cumulative population doublings	Cumulative days in culture
Normal	0.72	180+	256+
Werner syndrome brother	0.64	158	254
Werner syndrome patients			
(DC)	--	--	66
(KL)	0.44	54	106
(TB)	0.44	88	193

These studies have been extended to include eight newly
transformed lymphoblastoid cell lines from Werner patients, four
from normal persons, and one well-established line from a normal
person. Preliminary results indicate that, with one exception, the
Werner syndrome cultures have reduced growth rates (approximately
74% of normal) and cease replicating. One of the newly transformed
normal lines has also ceased replicating after continuous
propagation although, like the cell line from the brother of a
Werner patient, it had a normal growth rate, achieved many more
cumulative population doublings, and survived in culture far longer
than any of the Werner cultures.

CYTOGENETICS

Cultured skin fibroblast-like (FL) cells from patients with
Werner syndrome display frequent pseudodiploidy involving multiple,
variable structural chromosome rearrangements that are clonal

(Salk et al., 1981a). This cytogenetic abnormality, which has been
called variegated translocation mosaicism (VTM), has also been
observed in peripheral blood lymphocytes (Scappaticci et al., 1982).
In the studies of FL cells, ninety-two percent of 1,538 metaphases
from 29 independent FL cell strains from five patients with Werner
syndrome demonstrated multiple, variable, stable chromosome
rearrangements. In contrast, only eight (8.4 percent) of 95 non-
Werner FL cell cultures demonstrated VTM: seven with low-grade VTM
(approximately five percent of 300 metaphases) and one with VTM
affecting 90 to 100 percent of metaphases. Unlike the cytogenetic
abnormalities observed in the terminal stages of normal FL cell
cultures, VTM occurred throughout the lifespan of Werner syndrome
cultures.

       Individual chromosomes are affected approximately in proportion
to their length, but within chromosomes there is a nonrandom
distribution of rearrangement sites: four chromosomal sites (1q12,
1q44, 5q12, and 6cen), representing only 3% of the identifiable
breakpoints in 1134 banded metaphases, accounted for 13% of all
definable rearrangements. The frequency distribution of
rearrangement sites is consistent with a model of specific
chromosomal hotspots overlying a Poisson-distributed background of
random rearrangement events. The chromosomal hotspots are not
reminiscent of those for nonrandom structural chromosome changes
that are spontaneous, radiation-induced, or chemical-induced.

       Werner syndrome may be classified as a chromosome instability
syndrome because it is autosomal recessive, displays chromosome
instability, and is associated with an increased incidence of
neoplasia. Chromosome breakage and unstable rearrangements are the
most obvious cytogenetic manifestations in the the other chromosome
instability syndromes in humans (Bloom syndrome, Fanconi anemia,
ataxia telangiectasia, xeroderma pigmentosum), but stable structural
chromosome rearrangements are also seen with some frequency (Hoehn
and Salk, 1984). The fact that chromatid aberrations, unstable
rearrangements, and chromatid exchange figures appear to be uncommon
in Werner syndrome suggests that the initial structural change in
VTM occurs during the G0/G1- or early S-phase of the cell cycle,
and/or that the de novo formation of aberrant chromosomes is a
rather infrequent event.

       Several observations have suggested that at least some of the
chromosome aberrations in Werner syndrome occur in vitro, but the
studies have not been conclusive. We tested for the frequency of de
novo chromosomal rearrangements in FL cells in vitro by preparing

multiple skin explants from one patient with Werner syndrome and studying the cytogenetics of colonies derived from single cells. We analyzed a total of thirty-one colonies derived from dilute platings of six independent primary cultures. Within each colony all of the metaphases had the same basic cytogenetic description. We observed fourteen instances of cells within a colony showing a new structural rearrangement in addition to the basic clonal karyotype: a number of these variants were chromosome breaks or deletions for which an exchange of material could not be documented. Twelve cells were single instances of different rearrangements and two cells in one colony showed identical new rearrangements, thereby fitting the definition of a de novo cytogenetic clone. In view of the variety and number of structural rearrangements observed in Werner syndrome FL cell cultures, these results demonstrate remarkable stability in vitro: 90% of 139 metaphases displayed only the basic karyotype characteristic of a given colony.

Two cytogenetically identical clones appeared in more than one dilute-plated culture. These two cultures were independently derived from separate explants. Considering the stability we observed in vitro and the rarity of identical rearrangements in our previous studies, it appears that multiple cells with these two chromosome markers were already present in the piece of skin from which the explants were prepared. This observation indicates that chromosome rearrangements can occur in dermal cells in vivo in patients with Werner syndrome.

Chromosome breakage and the formation of unstable aberrations have not been striking findings in Werner syndrome cultures when control cultures have not been simultaneously analyzed (Salk et al., 1981a; Schonberg et al., 1984). However, both Nordenson (1977) and Scappaticci et al. (1982) reported an increase in breakage in Werner syndrome cells compared with normal controls (Table 3). We have also analyzed both FL cells and peripheral blood lymphocytes from two Werner syndrome patients and controls, and consistently found a slight increase (2.6- to 4.6-fold) in the amount of gaps, breaks, and unstable chromosome aberrations in the Werner syndrome cells. We did not see a significant difference between the amount of chromatid and chromosome lesions. The amount of breakage reported by Nordenson seems much greater, but the increase she observed was not as large as that for her patients with Fanconi anemia.

These recent results indicate that the chromosome instability associated with Werner syndrome is not limited to stable chromosome rearrangements in cultured FL cells. Aberrations are observed in

Table 3.   Unstable Structural Chromosome Lesions in Werner Syndrome.

Study	Cell type*	Type† and no. of subjects	No. of cells	Aberration frequency	Relative rates
Nordenson	PBL	WS - 4	650	.136	19
(1977)		Nl - 3	300	.007	1
Scappaticci	PBL	WS - 6	900	.140	4
et al.		Hz - 4	400	.040	1
(1982)		Nl - 6	600	.040	1
Scappaticci	FL	WS - 5	58	.260	2.6
et al.		Nl- 5	130	.100	1
(1982)					

* PBL: peripheral blood lymphocytes; FL: cultured skin fibroblast-
  like cells. WS: Werner syndrome; Hz: obligate Werner syndrome
† WS: Werner syndrome; Hz: obligate Werner syndrome heterozygote;
  Nl: normal control.

hematopoetic cells, apparently occur in vivo, and there is an
elevated level of chromosomal breakage, albeit much less than that
observed in the classical chromosome instability syndromes.

REFERENCES

Epstein, C. J., Martin, G. M., Schultz, A. L., and Motulsky, A. G.,
      1966, Werner's syndrome: A review of its symptomatology,
      natural history, pathologic features, genetics and relationship
      to the natural aging process, Medicine, 45:177.
Hoehn, H., and Salk, D., 1984, Clonal analysis of Bloom syndrome
      fibroblasts. II. Frequency and distribution of stable
      rearrangements, Cancer Genet. Cytogenet., 11:405.
Nordenson, I., 1977, Chromosome breaks in Werner's syndrome and
      their prevention in vitro by radical-scavenging enzymes,
      Hereditas, 87:151.

Salk, D., 1982, Werner syndrome: A review of recent research with
    an analysis of connective tissue metabolism, growth control of
    cultured cells, and chromosomal aberrations, Hum. Genet., 62:1.
Salk, D., Au, K., Hoehn, H., and Martin, G. M., 1981a, Cytogenetics of
    Werner syndrome cultured skin fibroblasts: Variegated
    translocation mosaicism, Cytogenet. Cell Genet., 30:92.
Salk, D., Bryant, E., Hoehn, H., and Martin, G. M., 1981b, Systematic
    growth studies, cocultivation, and cell hybridization studies
    of Werner syndrome cultured skin fibroblasts, Hum. Genet.,
    58:310.
Salk, D., Fujiwara, Y., and Martin, G. M., 1984, "Werner Syndrome and
    Aging," Plenum Press, N.Y., in press.
Scappaticci, S., Cerimele, D., and Fraccaro, M., 1982, Clonal
    structural chromosomal rearrangements in primary fibroblast
    cultures and in lymphocytes of patients with Werner's syndrome,
    Hum. Genet., 62:16.
Schonberg, S., Niermeijer, M. F., Bootsma, D., Henderson, E., and
    German, J., 1984, Werner's syndrome: Proliferation in vitro
    of clones of cells bearing chromosome translocations, Am. J.
    Hum. Genet., 36:387.
Thannhauser, S. J., 1945, Werner's syndrome (progeria of the
    adult) and Rothmund's syndrome: Two types of closely related
    heredo-familial atrophic dermatosis with juvenile cataracts and
    endocrine features. A critical study with five new cases,
    Ann. Intern. Med., 23:559.
Werner, O., 1904, Ueber Kataract in Verbindung mit Skelrodermie
    (doctoral dissertation, Kiel University). Schmidt and Klaunig,
    Kiel. (English translation by H. Hoehn, in: "Werner Syndrome
    and Aging," Salk, D., Fujiwara, Y., and Martin, G. M., eds.,
    Plenum Press, N.Y., in press.).

MOLECULAR BASIS OF THE ACCUMULATION OF ABNORMAL PROTEINS IN PROGERIA AND AGING FIBROBLASTS

Robert W. Gracy, M.L. Chapman, J.K. Cini, M. Jahani, T.O. Tollefsbol and K.Ü. Yüksel

Department of Biochemistry, North Texas State University and Texas College of Osteopathic Medicine
Fort Worth, TX 76107

INTRODUCTION

The use of fibroblasts as in vitro models for the study of cellular and molecular changes which accompany aging was recognized almost twenty-five years ago. Fibroblasts exhibit a finite replicative capacity which is related to the age of the donor and the expected longevity of the species (Hayflick, 1965). In addition, fibroblasts from individuals with premature aging diseases such as progeria and Werner's syndrome, exhibit decreased in vitro replicative capacities (Goldstein, 1969; Tollefsbol et al., 1982; Martin et al., 1970). These observations have been interpreted as an indication of a biological barrier or clock for the survival of the cells.

The accumulation of abnormal or modified proteins in aging cells including fibroblasts is also well documented and has been reviewed elsewhere (Gracy, 1983; Gafni and Noy, 1984; Dreyfus et al., 1978). Toward the end of the replicative lifespan fibroblasts accumulate large amounts of "defective" enzymes. Similarly, fibroblasts from individuals with premature aging syndromes also appear to accumulate these "abnormal" enzymes to a greater than normal extent. The accumulation of defective enzymes during aging has been thought to result in a diminished ability of cells to respond to environmental stresses, compromising their functional capacity and leading to senescence and death of the organism. Whether the accumulation of defective enzymes is a cause or effect of aging is not known, but if the mechanism(s) for the accumulation of these abnormal enzymes was understood, a much better picture of the aging process might be possible. Orgel (1963) originally proposed that alterations in transcription and/or translation could lead to the accumulation of

427

defective enzymes with age. Holliday and Tarrant (1972) proposed that the increase in labile forms of enzymes in progeria and Werner's cells might be due to a breakdown in the fidelity of protein synthesis resulting in the incorrect incorporation of amino acids into polypeptide chains. However, evidence exists against this hypothesis, and the fidelity of protein synthesis does not appear to decline during aging of cultured human fibroblasts or in cells from premature aging diseases (Harley et al., 1980; Wojtyk and Goldberg, 1980). In addition, evidence against the involvement of protein synthetic errors has arisen from studies on labile glucose 6-phosphate dehydrogenase in erythrocytes from progeric individuals (Goldstein and Moerman, 1978). Alternatively, the accumulation of unstable enzymes with age may be due to increased incidence of post-synthetic modifications and/or a decrease in the normal processes of degradation of proteins.

The accumulation of abnormal enzymes has often been assessed by determining the kinetics of heat inactivation. Many examples have been reported from aging fibroblasts and premature aging syndromes (Holliday and Tarrant, 1972; Goldstein and Moerman, 1978; Tollefsbol et al., 1982; Holliday et al., 1974; Goldstein and Moerman, 1975). The use of unstable enzymes as a measure of senescence is not without problems (Brown and Darlington, 1980; Pendergrass et al., 1976). The direct examination of the structures of senescent enzymes clearly provides a more direct method for assessing the mechanisms whereby "abnormal" enzymes accumulate during aging. Two primary problems exist in the elucidation of the molecular basis of these abnormal enzymes. First, most data suggest that the "defective" enzymes are very similar to their respective "young" counterparts, thus requiring very detailed structural analysis to identify the specific changes. Secondly, the amount of "defective" enzyme, in most cases, is extremely limited thereby requiring ultra-sensitive methods of protein structural analyses. The present report examines the details of one such enzyme, triosephosphate isomerase (EC 5.3.1.1) in several cellular aging model systems. Secondly, correlations are made with other "senescent" enzymes for which less detailed structural information is presently available.

ACCUMULATION OF LABILE ENZYMES IN AGING CELLS

Table I summarizes observations from several laboratories regarding the accumulation of labile enzymes in aging fibroblasts. Only a small percentage of labile enzymes is observed in fibroblasts from young donors at early in vitro passages. The percentage is markedly increased in cells from old donors, cells from young donors after extensive population doublings, as well as in fibroblasts from individuals with progeria or Werner's syndrome.

Triosephosphate isomerase (TPI) exhibits several acidic (negatively charged) isozymes which accumulate in aging cells.

Table 1. Accumulation of Labile Enzymes in Aging Human Fibroblasts

Enzyme[a]	Conditions	Labile Enzyme (%)	References
TPI	Young donors–early passage	0–3	(Tollefsbol et
	Old donors–early passage	9–10	al., 1982; Tol-
	Young donors–late passage	10–15	lefsbol and Gracy,
	Progeria donors–early passage	41–50	1983)
	Werner's donors–early passage	20–42	
G6PD	Young donors–early passage	0–5	(Hayflick, 1965;
	Young donors–late passage	15–18	Holliday et al.,
	Progeria donors–early passage	12–22	1974; Goldstein
	Werner's donors–early passage	14–28	and Moerman, 1975)
6PGD	Young donors–early passage	0–5	(Holliday et al.,
	Young donors–late passage	15–18	1974; Goldstein
	Progeria donors–early passage	10–25	and Moerman, 1975;
	Werner's donors–early passage	14–24	Goldstein, 1979)
HGPRT	Young donors–early passage	7–12	(Goldstein and
	Young donors–late passage	21–26	Moerman, 1975;
	Progeria donors–early passage	21–31	Goldstein, 1979)
	Werner's donors–early passage	36–50	

[a]Abbreviations:

TPI: Triosephosphate isomerase (EC 5.3.1.1)
G6PD: Glucose 6-phosphate dehydrogenase (EC 1.1.1.49)
6PGD: 6-phosphogluconate dehydrogenase (EC 1.1.1.43)
HGPRT: Hypoxanthine guanine phosphoribosyl transferase (EC 2.4.2.8)

These acidic isozymes are more labile and accumulate in fibroblasts from aged donors, fibroblasts aged _in vitro_, fibroblasts from progeria and Werner's syndrome (Gracy, 1983; Tollefsbol et al., 1982; Tollefsbol and Gracy, 1983), as well as in several other aging systems. For example, these acidic-labile isozymes accumulate in old erythrocytes (Turner et al., 1975) and as shown in Fig. 1, in the oldest nonproliferating cells in the nucleus of the eye lens. Thus, since these aging isozymes of TPI accumulate in several different aging systems, it was felt that TPI might provide a potential marker for assessing age-related alterations of proteins.

After isolating the normal and senescent isozymes of TPI (Yuan

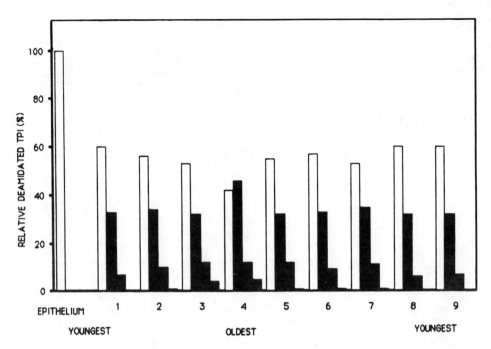

Fig 1. Relative distribution of TPI-isozymes in the eye lens.
Bovine lens was sectioned from the epithelial layers
(youngest cells) through the nucleus (oldest cells).
Sections 0 and 9 represent the youngest cells while
sections 4 and 5 represent the oldest cells. The relative distribution of the TPI-isozymes was measured by
electrophoresis and a specific TPI activity stain (Turner
et al., 1975). The open bars represent the nondeamidated
isozyme while the black bars show the amounts of the
deamidated isozymes.

et al., 1981) we proceeded to examine the primary structure of the
enzyme and its isozymes. Using high-sensitivity microsequencing
methods (Lu and Gracy, 1984) it was possible to obtain the entire
sequence of human triosephosphate isomerase (Lu et al., 1984) which
is shown in Fig. 2. The only differences between the enzyme found
in young cells and that accumulating in old cells are the result of
two specific deamidations. In the young form of the enzyme asparagine residues occupy positions 15 and 71 while these are deamidated
to aspartic acids in the senescent forms of the enzyme. These
specific deamidations account for the acidic, labile isozymes which
accumulate in all of the aging systems thus far studied. After
completion of the sequence of human TPI it was found to be 85%
homologous with the enzyme from chicken (Furth et al., 1974), for

```
        10        15     20              30
A P S R K F F V G G N W K M Ⓝ G R K K N L G E L I S T L Q G A K V


        40              50              60
P A D T E V V C I G P T A Y L D F A R Q K L D Q K I A A G A Q N C

                                    \ |
    70 71              80              90
Y K V T Ⓝ G A F T G E I S P G M I K D C G A T W V V L G H S E R R


100            110              120            130
H V F G E S D E L I G Q K V A H A L N E G L G V I A C I G E K L D E


        140            150              160
R E A G I T E K V V F E Q T K V I A D D V K D W S K V V L A Y E N


    170            180              190
V W A I G T G K T A T P Q Q A E E V H E K L R G W L K S N V S D A


200            210              220            230
V A Q Q T R I I Y G G S V T G A T C K E L A S Q P D V D G F I V G


    240
G A S L K P E F V D L I N A K Q
```

Fig. 2. Amino acid sequence of human triosephosphate isomerase.
The entire sequence of the enzyme is shown using the
standard single letter abbreviations. The two points
of deamidation Asn 15 and Asn 71 are indicated as the
circled residues.

which high-resolution x-ray crystallographic data was available
(Banner et al., 1975). Thus, it was possible to construct a three-
dimensional model of the enzyme, and it became clear that the two
deamidating residues on each subunit of the dimeric enzyme are in
juxtaposition in the contact sites between the two subunits (Fig. 3).

Thus, the deamidation of Asn 15 and 71 causes the two subunits
to more readily dissociate and unfold. The sequential deamidation
of Asn 15 and 71 accounts for the appearance of four more acidic
labile forms of the enzyme. In normal young cells TPI is synthesized
with asparagines in positions 15 and 71. These residues deamidate
under physiological conditions (Yuan et al., 1981) leading to the
dissociation, unfolding and ultimate proteolytic catabolism of the

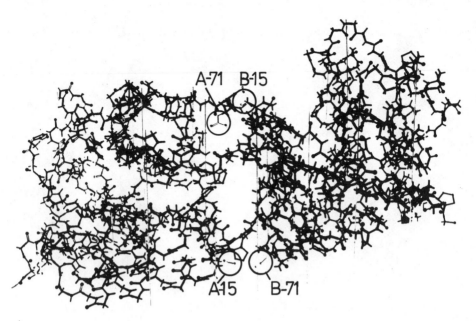

Fig. 3. Model of structure of human triosephosphate isomerase.
The dimeric enzyme is shown with the subunit on the left
arbitrarily designated as "A" and the subunit on the right
designated as "B". The positions of asparagines 15 and
71 on each subunit are indicated and are seen to be in
juxtaposition in the subunit-subunit contact sites.
(Figure reprinted from Yuan et al., 1981, with permission
of the publisher).

enzyme. It is interesting that only these two asparagines deamidate
under physiological conditions. Human TPI contains eight asparagine
and twelve glutamine residues per subunit, but only Asn 15 and Asn
71 undergo this spontaneous deamidation. The amino acid sequences
around these Asn residues are remarkably similar.

$$- Lys^{13} - Met - Asn - Gly^{16} -$$

$$-Lys^{68} - Val - Thr - Asn - Gly^{72} -$$

No other asparagines or glutamines in the enzyme reside in similar
sequences and no other asparagines or glutamines deamidate.

Based on the above observations a model has been proposed
(Fig. 4) to explain the accumulation of the deamidated forms of TPI
in aging cells. In young and old cells TPI is synthesized with

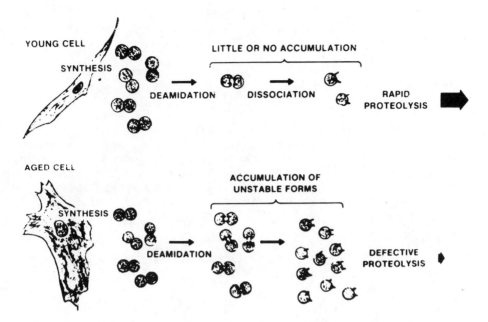

Fig. 4.   Proposed mechanism for the accumulation of deamidated TPI
          in aging cells and cells from premature aging syndromes.
          (Figure from Tollefsbol and Gracy, 1983, reprinted with
          permission of the publisher).

asparagines in positions 15 and 71. However, these residues deamidate as the first step in the normal catabolism of the enzyme. The
deamidations lead to subunit dissociation, unfolding, and proteolysis. In young cells this is a steady state process and thus the
deamidated forms do not accumulate and are found in only trace
amounts (Table 1). In contrast, in aging cells a defect at the level
of proteolysis could cause the accumulation of these deamidated
forms.

    If, indeed, the accumulation of the deamidated forms of TPI
is due to a defect in protein turnover and the accumulation of intermediates of the catabolism of this enzyme, then studies designed to
stimulate or inhibit proteolysis and protein turnover could provide
important information. When protein turnover in fibroblasts was
stimulated by starvation, the levels of deamidated TPI markedly
decreased Table 2).

On the other hand, if pre-starved fibroblasts were treated with insulin to inhibit proteolysis, a significant increase in the levels of the deamidated forms of TPI was found (Fig. 5).

The mechanism(s) of proteolysis and the regulation of protein turnover are still not well understood. However, labeling studies have clearly documented an overall decrease in protein turnover in aging cells and in aging animals (Millward et al., 1975; Goldstein et al., 1976; Schimke and Bradley, 1975). Examination of the levels of several proteolytic enzymes in fibroblasts revealed lower levels in cells from fibroblasts from premature aging syndromes (Tollefsbol and Gracy, 1983). An extensive examination of the levels of cathepsin B in several aging systems also indicates that the proteolytic capacity may be depressed in old and premature aging cells (Fig. 6).

Table 2.   Effects of Serum Deprivation on Levels of Deamidated TPI[a]

Conditions	Deamidated TPI (%)
Fibroblasts fed	23.5
Fibroblasts starved 48 hr	14.5
Fibroblasts starved 96 hr	12.0
Fibroblasts starved 240 hr	2.5

[a]Human skin fibroblasts were grown first in complete media. The cultures were then rinsed with PBS and fresh media with and without fetal bovine serum was added. Levels of deamidated enzyme in fed control cultures and in starved cultures (2-10 days) were measured.

DISCUSSION

The deamidated forms of TPI in aging cells are only one example of the accumulation of post-synthetically modified proteins in senescence. Many cases of deamidated proteins have been observed which may also accumulate during aging. Van Klee et al. (1975) showed that α-crystallin undergoes spontaneous deamidations with age in the nucleus of the eye lens, and the deamidation appears to be the first step in catabolism of the protein. Horecker and coworkers (1969, 1970) showed an age-dependent deamidation of an asparagine

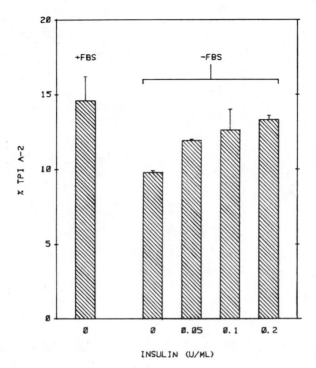

Fig. 5.   Effect of insulin on the deamidation of human TPI. Fibro-
           blasts were grown in the presence of fetal bovine serum
           (+FBS) or starved of FBS for 72 hours (-FBS). The starved
           cells were grown in the presence of the indicated concen-
           trations of insulin for 24 hours, harvested and assayed by
           electrophoresis for TPI A-2.

in aldolase, and the in vitro half-life of deamidation is essentially
the same as the in vivo half-life of the enzyme (Midelfort and
Mehler, 1972). Ribonuclease-A undergoes a specific, spontaneous
deamidation, which results in a structure more easily unfolded
that alters the proteolytic susceptibility of the enzyme (Das and
Vithayathil, 1978; Manjula et al., 1977). Multiple electrophoretic
forms of aspartate amino transferase also appear to be due to
spontaneous deamidations, which may be the first step in the
catabolism of the enzyme (John and Jones, 1974; Williams and John,
1979). Other specific examples of deamidation in normal human
tissues include cytochrome c (Flatmark and Sletten, 1968) salivary
amylases (Lorentz, 1979), carbonic anhydrase (Funakoshi and Deutsch,
1969 and 1971), nucleoside phosphorylase (Turner et al., 1975), and
human growth hormone (Lewis et al., 1981). In addition, there are
general observations that are also consistent with the accumulation
of deamidated enzymes with age. For example, in Drosophilia homogenates, the levels of glutamic acid were observed to increase with

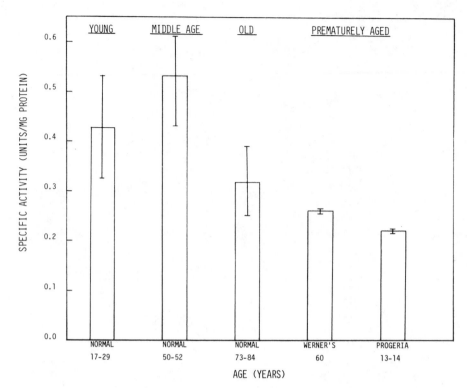

Fig. 6. Activity of cathepsin B in aging fibroblasts. Human
         fibroblasts from donors of the indicated age groups,
         all at early in vitro passage were assayed for levels
         of cathepsin B. The data are expressed as units of
         enzyme per mg of protein. The bars indicate one stand-
         ard deviation.

age with a simultaneous decrease in glutamine levels (Robinson,
1979). Pushkina (1979) reported the increased content of aspartic
acid and decreased asparagine in rat brain, liver, and heart of
old animals.

     Clearly, there are many other types of covalent and noncovalent
modified proteins which accumulate in aging cells, including changes
which may result from differences in the state of oxidation.
Stadtman and coworkers (1984) have demonstrated the specific
oxidation of glutamine synthetase and suggested oxidative forms
which may also accumulate in progeria fibroblasts (Levine, 1984).
Similarly, Gafni and Noy (1984) suggest the accumulation of "aged"
glyceraldehyde 3-phosphate dehydrogenase is due to controlled oxidation of cys-149 followed by an irreversible conformational change
in the enzyme. Other types of covalent modifications such as glycosylation (Ulrich et al., 1984), racemization (Helfman et al., 1977),

phosphorylation (Cristofalo et al., 1984), and perhaps ADP-ribo-
sylation may "prepare" enzymes for catabolism. Rothstein and
coworkers (1980) have shown that non-covalent conformational changes
also occur which normally result in unfolding and catabolism of the
protein.

In each of these cases it appears that the period of time in
which the modified proteins exist in young cells is substantially
shorter than in aging cells or cells from individuals with premature
aging diseases. The studies reported here in which acceleration of
proteolysis by starvation results in a lowering of the levels of
deamidated TPI are strikingly similar to studies in animals by
Wulf and Cutler (1975), who measured the levels of labile G6PD in
different mouse tissues of different age groups. They observed
the accumulation of unstable G6PD in all tissues of the aging
animal, but the levels of the unstable enzymes markedly decreased
upon stimulation of protein turnover by starvation.

The decreased levels of the proteolytic enzymes reported in
our present study in senescent or premature aging fibroblasts also
have interesting corroborative studies in whole animals. It is well
established that as animals grow older there is a decrease in rates
of cardiac proteolysis (Crie et al., 1979). Goldstein et al. (1976)
used pulse chase radiolabelling studies with normal, aging, progeria,
and Werner's fibroblasts and concluded that aged cells have a reduced proteolytic capacity. Recently, Wiederanders and Oelke (1984)
reported that inactive cathepsin D accumulates in senescent rats.

It should also be pointed out that there are cases in which
there is little or no evidence for the accumulation of a modified
form of a particular enzyme during the aging process. Houben et
al., (1980) suggested that while most cytoplasmic enzymes accumulate
in modified forms, this is not the case for compartmentalized
mitochondrial or lysosomal enzymes. It is also likely that the
levels of critical metabolites such as glutathione and NAD may be
markedly altered in aging cells and thereby contribute to such
modifications. Goldstein et al. (1982) have measured energy
metabolism in human fibroblasts during in vitro aging and concluded
old and progeria cells exhibit a rise in energy demand and/or
inefficiency of oxidative phosphorylation. We have observed changes
in energy charge in young versus aging cells (Chapman et al., 1981),
and have demonstrated major differences in the ability of old cells
to synthesize NAD (Chapman et al., 1983). The levels of such
components as NAD not only could effect overall metabolic fluxes
but redox levels may be directly linked to the protein turnover
system (Tischler and Fagan, 1982).

What are the possible consequences of slowed protein turnover
in aging cells? In some cases fully inactive enzymes accumulate,
measurable with immunological methods. In other cases enzymes of

altered (usually decreased) stability accumulate. The stability, activity, and turnover of enzymes appear to be regulated by a complex set of cellular conditions including the concentrations of coenzymes and substrates. The primary change during aging which ultimately leads to the accumulation of these defective enzymes remains unknown. However, there is growing evidence that post-synthetically modified proteins accumulate in aging cells in many different models. Future studies should provide significant information on the accumulation of "abnormal" proteins in aging, and also provide a better understanding of the normal processes of protein turnover and its regulation.

ACKNOWLEDGEMENTS

This work supported in part by research grants from the National Institutes of Health (AGO1274, AM14638) and the R.A. Welch Foundation (B-502). The authors acknowledge the expert technical assistance of Drs. B. Oray, P.M. Yuan and J.M. Talent and C.E. Wheeler.

REFERENCES

Banner, D.W., Bloomer, A.C., Petsko, G.A., Phillips, D.C., Pogson, C.J., Wilson, I.A., Corran, P.H., Furth, A.J., Milman, J.D., Offord, R.E., Priddle, J.D. and Waley, S.G., 1975, Structure of chicken muscle triosephosphate isomerase at 2.5 A° resolution using amino acid sequence data, Nature, London, 255:609.

Bong-Whan, A., Oliver, C.N., and Stadtman, E.R., 1984, Oxidative inactivation of enzymes during aging, Fed. Proc., 43:2021.

Brown, W.T. and Darlington, G.J., 1980, Thermolabile enzymes in progeria and Werner's syndrome: Evidence to the contrary of the protein error hypothesis, Am. J. Human Genet., 32:614.

Chapman, M. L., Zaun, M. R. and Gracy, R. W., 1981, Effects of age on energy status and redox state of lymphocytes during blastogenesis, Biochem. Biophys. Res. Commun., 98:303.

Chapman, M.L., Zaun, M.R. and Gracy, R.W., 1983, Changes in NAD levels in human lymphocytes and fibroblasts during aging and in premature aging syndromes, Mech. Ageing Develop., 21:157.

Crie, J.S., Griffin, E.E. and Wildenthal, K., 1979, Age-related alterations in cardiac protein turnover, J. Mol. Cell. Cardiol., 11 Sup 1:16.

Cristofalo, V.J., Phillips, P.D., Carlin, C.R. and Knowles, B.B.,

1984, Altered phosphorylation of the EGF receptor in cellular senescence, FASEB Meetings, June.

Das, M.K. and Vithayathil, P.J., 1978, Proteolytic susceptibility and methionine modification of monodeamidated ribonuclease-A, Int. J. Peptide Res., 12:242.

Dreyfus, J.C., Kahn, A. and Shapira, F., 1978, Post-translational modification of enzymes, Curr. Top. Cell. Reg., 14:243.

Flatmark, T. and Sletten, K., 1968, Multiple forms of cytochrome c in the rat, J. Biol. Chem., 243:1623.

Funakoshi, S. and Deutsch, H.F., 1969, Human carbonic anhydrase II. Some physiochemical properties of native isozymes and similar isozymes generated in vitro, J. Biol. Chem., 244:3438.

Funakoshi, S. and Deutsch, H.F., 1971, Human carbonic anhydrase VI. Levels of isozymes in old and young erythrocytes and in various tissues, J. Biol. Chem., 246:1088.

Furth, A.J., Milman, J.D., Priddle, J.D. and Offord, R.E., 1974, Studies on the subunit structure and amino acid sequence of triosephosphate isomerase from chicken heart muscle, Biochem. J., 139:11.

Gafni, A. and Noy, N., 1984, Age-related effects in enzyme catalysis, Mol. Cell. Biochem., 59:113.

Garland, D., Stadtman, E.R. and Kinoshita, J., 1984, Oxidative modification of human lens, Fed. Proc., 43:2021.

Goldstein, S., 1969, Life-span of cultured cells in progeria, Lancet, 1:424.

Goldstein, S. and Moerman, E.J., 1975, Heat-labile enzymes from skin fibroblasts from subjects with progeria, New Eng. J. Med., 292:1305.

Goldstein, S., Stotland, D. and Cordeiro, R.A.J., 1976, Decreased proteolysis and increased amino acid efflux in aging human fibroblasts, Mech. Ageing Develop., 5:221.

Goldstein, S. and Moerman, E.J., 1978, Heat-labile enzymes in circulating erythrocytes of a progeria family, Am. J. Genet., 30:167.

Goldstein, S., 1979, Studies on age-related diseases in cultured skin fibroblasts, J. Invest. Dermatol., 73:19.

Goldstein, S., Ballantyne, S.R., Robson, A.L. and Moerman, E.J., 1982, Energy metabolism in cultured human fibroblasts during aging in vitro, J. Cell. Physiol., 112:419.

Gracy, R.W., 1983, Epigenetic formation of isozymes: The effect of aging, in: "Isozymes Current Topics in Biological and Medical Research," M. Rattazzi, J.C. Scandalios and G. Whitt, eds., Alan R. Liss, Inc., New York, pp 178-201.

Hayflick, L., 1965, The limited in vitro lifetime of human diploid cell strains, Exp. Cell. Res., 37:614.

Harley, D.B., Pollard, J.W., Chamberlain, J.W., Stanners, C.P. and Goldstein, S., 1980, Protein synthetic errors do not increase during aging of cultured human fibroblasts, Proc. Natl. Acad. Sci. USA, 77:1885.

Helfman, P.M., Bada, J.L. and Shou, M.Y., 1977, Consideration on the role of aspartic acid racemization in the aging process, Gerontology, 23:419.

Holliday, R. and Tarrant, G.M., 1972, Altered enzymes in aging human fibroblasts, Nature, London, 238:26.

Holliday, R., Porterfield, J.S. and Gibbs, D.D., 1974, Premature aging and occurance of altered enzyme in Werner's syndrome fibroblasts, Nature, London, 248:762.

Houben, A., Houbion, A. and Remacle, J., 1980, Lysosomal and mitochondrial heat labile enzymes in Werner's syndrome fibroblasts, Exp. Geront., 15:629.

John, A.R. and Jones, R.E., 1974, The nature of the multiple form of cytoplasmic aspartate aminotransferase from pig and sheep heart, Biochem. J., 141:401.

Koida, M., Lai, C.Y. and Horecker, B.L., 1969, Subunit structure of rabbit muscle aldolase: Extent of homology of the $\alpha\beta$ subunits and age-dependent changes in their ratio, Arch. Biochem. Biophys., 134:623.

Lai, C.Y., Chen, C. and Horecker, B.L., 1970, Primary structure of two COOH-terminal hexapeptides from rabbit muscle aldolase: a difference in the structure of $\alpha\beta$ subunits, Biochem. Biophys. Res. Commun., 40:461.

Levine, R.L., 1984, Oxidative modification of glutamine synthetase: Sequence of the modified peptide, Fed. Proc., 43:2021.

Lewis, U.J., Singh, R.N.P., Bonewald, L.F. and Seavey, B.K., 1981,

Altered proteolytic cleavage of human growth hormone as a result of deamidation, J. Biol. Chem., 256:11645.

Lorentz, K., 1979, Salivary isoamylases: deamidation products of amylase, Clin. Chem. Acta., 93:161.

Lu, H.S. and Gracy, R.W., 1984, Solid-phase protein and peptide sequencing using either 4-N,N-dimethylaminoazobenzene 4'-isothiocyanate or phenylisothiocyanate, Arch. Biochem. Biophys., in press.

Lu, H.S., Yuan, P.M. and Gracy, R.W., 1984, The primary structure of human triosephosphate isomerase, J. Biol. Chem., in press.

Manjula, B.N., Acharya, A.S. and Vithayathil, P.J., 1977, Subtilisin modification of monodeamidated ribonuclease-A, Biochem. J., 165:337.

Martin, G.M., Sprague, D.A. and Epstein, E.J., 1970, Replicative lifespan of cultivated human cells: Effects of donor's age, tissue, and genotype, Lab. Invest., 23:86.

Midelfort, D.F. and Mehler, A.H., 1972, Deamidation in vivo of an asparagine residue of rabbit muscle aldolase, Proc. Natl. Acad. Sci. USA, 69:1816.

Millward, D.J., Garlick, P.J., Stewart, R.J.C., Nnanyleugo, D.O., and Waterlow, J.C., 1975, Skeletal-muscle growth and protein turnover, Biochem. J., 150:235.

Orgel, L.E., 1963, The maintenance of the accuracy of protein synthesis and its relevance, Proc. Natl. Acad. Sci. USA, 49:517.

Pendergrass, W.R., Martin, G.M. and Bornstein, P., 1976, Evidence contrary to the protein error hypothesis for in vitro senescence, J. Cell. Physiol., 87:3.

Pushkina, N.V., 1979, Amidirorannost' belkor aristarenii oranizma, Ukr. Biokim. Zh., 51:680.

Robinson, A.B., 1979, Molecular clocks, molecular profiles and optimum diets, three approaches to the problem of aging, Mech. Ageing Dev., 9:225.

Schimke, R.T. and Bradley, M.O., 1975, Properties of protein turnover in animal cells and a possible role for turnover in "quality" control of proteins, in: "Proteases and Biological Control," E. Reich, D.B. Rifkin and E. Shaw, eds., Cold Spring Harbor Laboratory, New York, pp 515-530.

Sharma, H.K. and Rothstein, M., 1980, Altered enolase in aged
     Turbatrix aceti results from conformational changes in the
     enzyme, Proc. Natl. Acad. Sci. USA, 77:5865.

Tischler, M.E. and Fagan, J.M., 1982, Relationship of the reduction-
     oxidation state to protein degradation in skeletal and atrial
     muscle, Arch. Biochem. Biophys., 217:191.

Tollefsbol, T.O., Zaun, M.R. and Gracy, R.W., 1982, Increased
     lability of triosephosphate isomerase in progeria and Werner's
     syndrome of fibroblasts, Mech. Ageing Dev., 20:93.

Tollefsbol, T.O. and Gracy, R.W., 1983, Premature aging diseases:
     Cellular and molecular changes, BioScience, 33:634.

Turner, B.M., Fisher, R.A. and Harris, H., 1975, Post-translational
     alterations of human erythrocyte enzymes, in: "Isozymes,"
     V. I, C.L. Market, ed., Academic Press, New York, pp 781-795.

Ulrich, P., Ponger, S., Bencsath, A. and Cerami, A., 1984, Aging of
     proteins. The Furoyl Furanyl Imidazole Crosslink as a key
     advanced glycosylation event, Fed. Proc., 43:1671.

Van Klee, F.S.M., DeJong, W.W. and Hoenders, H.J., 1975, Stepwise
     degradations and deamidation of the eye lens protein α-
     crystallin in aging, Nature, London, 258:264.

Wiederanders, B. and Oelke, B., 1984, Accumulation of inactive
     cathepsin D in old rats, Mech. Ageing Dev., 24:265.

Williams, J.A. and John, A.R., 1979, Generation of aspartate amino
     transferase multiple forms by deamidation, Biochem. J.,
     177:121.

Wojtyk, R.I. and Goldstein, S., 1980, Fidelity of protein synthesis
     does not decline during aging of cultured human fibroblasts,
     J. Cell. Physiol., 103:299.

Wulf, J.H. and Cutler, R.G., 1975, Altered protein hypothesis of
     mammalian aging process. I. Thermal stability of glucose
     6-phosphate dehydrogenase in C57BL16J mouse tissue, Exp.
     Gerontol., 10:1.

Yuan, P.M., Talent, J.M. and Gracy, R.W., 1981, A tentative eluci-
     dation of the sequence of human triosephosphate isomerase by
     homology peptide mapping, Biochim. Biophys, Acta., 671:211.

Yuan, P.M., Talent, J.M. and Gracy, R.W., 1981, Molecular basis for
     the accumulation of acidic isozymes of triosephosphate
     isomerase on aging, Mech. Ageing Dev., 17:151.

SUMMARIES AND FUTURE DIRECTIONS IN AGING RESEARCH

Ronald W. Hart and Angelo Turturro

National Center for Toxicological Research
Jefferson, Arkansas 72079

This meeting has been very interesting, and has demonstrated, among other things, that the quality of research in gerontology has definitely improved. It is making much more use of modern methods and concepts in biology (especially molecular biology) as well as increasing its sophistication in asking more detailed questions. The naive approaches of finding "panaceas" and simplistic explanations are slowly giving way to an appreciation for the biological complexity of organisms and the complexity of understanding the phenomenon of aging.

Also derived from this meeting was the observation that a synthesis is starting to emerge on what questions are useful in considering the molecular aspects of aging. An important part of this synthesis is the goal of explaining observed organismic effects, such as the effects of diet restriction, on molecular grounds.

Some of the topics presented have been of special interest from the standpoint of molecular biology and aging.

Considering a molecular parameter, DNA repair, Ishikawa made an interesting attempt to measure in vivo repair and produced some provocative results, however, lack of quantitation of effective dose and thymidine specific activity suggests that additional work needs to be done, especially if the results are going to be interpreted quantitatively. Also, if the author is going to suggest that his observations are relative to in vivo aging, the rodents used will have to be older than 18 months.

From a more mechanistic standpoint, Williams approached the
question of DNA structure and its relevance to aging, and in so
doing made a number of important observations. The role of X-rays
in sensitizing DNA to the mutagenizing effects of psolaren–UVA
treatment may be important in a clinical context, as well as lead to
speculations on cooperative effects on DNA structure. The observed
effect of temperature indicated that the process was mediated by an
energy-requiring process, while the effect of novobiocin (a topiso-
merase inhibitor) suggested that the effect was mediated at the
level of DNA structure. Although a great deal more work has to be
done, the suggestion that the relationship between DNA structure and
aging is important relative to gene expression seems to be gaining.

Holliday addressed the question of changes in gene expression
from a different standpoint, DNA methylation. While not a new concept, the idea of hypomethylation in senescent cultures (perhaps relating to differentiation) suggests genes are turned on compared to
younger cultures. Support for this view came from Goldstein, who
showed that similar cells had an increased expression of oncogene
ras, its RNA and the oncogene product. Cutler has suggested the
importance of gene derepression in vivo, from very diverse lines of
evidence. These studies as a whole are important and should be
expanded to in vivo model systems, especially those involving calor-
ically restricted animals.

Finally, Schwartz discussed DHEA and its analogues relative to
its mechanism of action. Once believed to act via an effect on
glucose-6-phosphate dehydrogenase (and, through this effect on the
pentose shunt and NADPH production), it now appears that its effects
may be modulated by other routes, e.g., an effect on fatty acyl
dehydrogenase. Alternatively, the overall effect can be thought of
as an anti-promoter, which, though some effect on a growth factor
(perhaps insulin-like peptides), could result in genetic stabiliza-
tion, counteracting some of the derepression seen in aging.

On the other hand, the other major possibility in changes in
gene expression, a lack of expression, was supported by the work of
Rothstein and Gracy, who showed exciting data suggesting that some
proteins demonstrate conformational changes as a function of age.
An important mechanism for this effect appears to be a decline in
protein turnover. This slowdown, in Gracy's system, seems to result
in a deamidation and, eventually a loss in activity. The importance
of cellular environment was shown by Rothstein, by the observation
concerning the influence of hepatectomy, and the resultant change
from the "new" proteins that are produced to the "old" pattern that
eventually emerges. From a general standpoint, this is consistent
with the work of Strehler that there is a loss of rRNA with age as
an ultimate result of transposition.

The two views can be reconciled in a number of aspects if one believes that expression of inappropriate proteins will cause the slowing of turnover of appropriate ones, however, this area requires more hard data. The focusing of attention on gene expression is of major importance and investigations in organismic systems will be useful.

Future Directions—

A number of paths presently appear to be opening up.

1) Expansion of the use of onc gene probes as markers for gene expression, repression, derepression. These markers are relatively well characterized, and the exploration of their function is proceeding rapidly. This information, and the observation that most of the onc genes seems to be involved in growth control (a homeostatic function which is effected in aging) seem to indicate that this approach will be very productive.

2) Cell cultures as good models for differentiation. Increased emphasis will have to be placed on post-mitotic cells, either directly, in culture, or by using Phase III cells as a model for them.

3) The expansion of data on longevity assurance mechanisms. This appears to be a necessary step to allow the understanding of organismic phenomena in mechanistic terms. Similar approaches are developing in understanding carcinogenesis, and aging research can profit from this example. A corollary of this is bridging the work seen in culture systems to in vivo, especially in regards to the only treatment known to extend in vivo maximum lifespan, caloric restriction.

Summary—

Significant advances are occurring in the understanding of cellular and organismic biology, mostly as a result of the intensive effort made to understand cancer. The quality of aging research is slowly starting to reflect these advances, the result being some of the synthesis which has been observed at this meeting. Future research will more aggressively pursue these advances and exploit them to understand the most complicated of biological phenomena, aging.

FUTURE DIRECTIONS IN AGING RESEARCH

Leonard Hayflick

Center for Gerontological Studies
University of Florida 3357 GPA
Gainesville, Florida 32611

INTRODUCTION

The research results presented at this conference underscore my belief that biogerontology is maturing rapidly as a science. It is only within the last decade that research in this field has moved from descriptive studies to those in which age changes are examined at the cellular and molecular level.

This dramatic change is the best evidence that the ultimate causes of aging are believed by most investigators to occur in individual cells and in the molecules that compose them. The belief has diminished that the basic causes of aging might be found in the intracellular matrix or confined to whole organs or tissues. Research in biogerontology at the cellular and molecular level is now the mainstream of interest, reflecting a general belief that molecular changes are the fundamental causes of aging. Although this is probably true, it is important to recognize that studies at the molecular level are rational only if they are based on an age-related marker that is recognized at the cell, organ, or whole animal level. I point out what may be self evident, because there is a danger that emphasis on the molecular biology of aging should not be so great as to preclude the probability that discoveries of important age-related phenomena still remain to be made at higher levels of organization. Biogerontology is the youngest science. Surely there must be important biological phenomena at levels of organization greater than the molecule that have not yet been described and without which studies at the molecular level will be constrained. For those who may be new to biogerontology and who may be attracted to it, I urge you to consider the probability that many fundamental macro-molecular phenomena remain to

447

be discovered. It is on these anticipated discoveries that future studies at the molecular level will surely be dependent.

I would also urge those who may be new to this field to recognize that, like other broad disciplines, major observations are likely to come from unexpected findings in other fields. Since the study of age changes covers virtually every facet of biology, it is imperative that we remain alert to developments in all fields of biology. Indeed the array of papers on so many diverse subjects presented at this symposium is good evidence for this belief.

I do not believe that it would serve any useful purpose to summarize each paper presented at this symposium. What might be useful, however, is to direct my attention to the other assignment given to me, namely, to speculate on the future directions in aging research.

CYTOGERONTOLOGY

In the area of the cell biology of aging, or cytogerontology, I expect to find the continued exploitation of the phenomenon of the finite lifetime of cultured normal human and animal cells in the study of aging at the cellular level (Hayflick and Moorhead, 1961; Hayflick, 1965). This system, frequently referred to as a model system, in the judgement of many, has now graduated from a model system to being a direct expression of aging at the cellular level with no further qualification. Research results from liter- ally hundreds of laboratories over the past twenty years have persuaded many investigators to believe that the behavior of normal cells in culture is no longer a model for aging; it is aging.

The main observations that have persuaded so many people to this point of view are the following:

1. There is an inverse relationship between donor age and population doubling potential, first demonstrated by us and later confirmed and greatly extended by others. This inverse relationship occurs in normal human cells derived from lung (Hayflick, 1965), skin (Martin et al., 1970; Schneider and Mitsui, 1976; Goldstein et al., 1978; Vracko and McFarland, 1980), liver (LeGuilly et al., 1973), arterial smooth muscle (Bierman, 1978; Grunewald et al., 1983) lens cells (Tassin et al., 1979) and T-lymphocytes (Walford et al., 1981).

2. More than 60 increments and 50 decrements have been shown to occur in cultured human fibroblasts as they age in culture (reviewed by Hayflick, 1980a). These include changes

in lipid content and synthesis; carbohydrate utilization; protein content, synthesis and breakdown; RNA and DNA content, synthesis and turnover; enzyme activity and synthesis; cell cycle kinetics; morphology, ultrastructure and cell architecture; and incorporation and stimulation.

Many of the changes that herald the loss of replicative capacity and function of cultured normal cells (Phase III) are identical to changes recognized as characteristic of aging in intact humans and animals. These findings substantiate our contention that the finite capacity for replication by cultured normal cells may not, per se, be as important in understanding in vivo aging as the plethora of biochemical, physiological, and morphological changes that precede it (Hayflick, 1977, 1979, 1980a, 1980b, 1980c).

It is important to note that contrary to the misconception that fibroblast behavior may be unrelated to age changes because they are not functional cells is this catalogue of 110 functional properties that do change as fibroblasts age in culture. One change, collagen production (Houck et al., 1971), is a specialized physiological function of fibroblasts.

3.   The in vivo counterpart of in vitro experiments where normal cells are, respectively, transplanted and sub-cultivated show identical results. That is, normal cells have a finite capacity to replicate under both conditions. These in vivo results effectively make untenable the suggestion that in vitro conditions are likely to be found which permit the unlimited replication of normal cells. Even when normal cells are transplanted in vivo, where ideal conditions would be expected to occur, the Phase III phenomenon is expressed (Hayflick, 1977, 1980a).

4.   Normal human cells that are frozen at particular population doubling levels are capable of "remembering" that doubling level and, when thawed, resume doublings until the maximum number is reached (Hayflick and Moorhead, 1961; Hayflick, 1965). Ampules of one normal human diploid cell strain developed by us in 1962 (WI-38) have been frozen for 23 years, and the cells still accurately retain their memory of the population doubling level at which they were frozen. This is the longest period of time that living normal human cells have ever been frozen (Hayflick, 1984b).

5.   There is increasingly compelling evidence for the notion that there may be a direct relationship between species lifespan and population doubling potential. Comparison of the published results from 10 species suggest that the

population doubling potential of cultured normal fibroblasts decreases as a function of lifespan (Hayflick, 1980a; Rohme, 1981).

6.   The latent period, that is the time necessary for cell migration over a unit distance from cultured tissue explants, increases as a function of donor age (reviewed by Hayflick, 1977).

7.   The population doubling potential of cultured normal human fibroblasts is significantly diminished from that of age-matched controls when cells are grown from patients with progeria, Werner's Syndrome and Cockayne's Syndrome.   These conditions are believed to typify accelerated aging (reviewed in Hayflick, 1977).

8.   One of the major theories of aging involves decreased, or less efficient, mechanisms for repair of DNA damage as a function of age.   In 1974, Hart and Setlow made the important observation that cultured skin fibroblasts from long-lived species have a greater capacity to repair UV-induced damage than do cells from shorter-lived species.   Later, they showed that the average amount of unscheduled DNA synthesis decreases as cultured human cells approach Phase III (reviewed in Hayflick, 1980a, 1980c).

THE FUTURE OF CYTOGERONTOLOGY

The concept seems to be emerging in cytogerontology that normal cells contain a molecular chronometer capable of counting functional events; included in the broad category of functional events is cell division.   I expect that within the next decade the intimate details of this molecular clock will be revealed.   The revelations will come about by continued exploitation of cell fusion and cell enucleation techniques.   They will be expanded to include isolation and insertion of specific chromosomes and the exploitation of recombinant DNA techniques.

Our group and others have established that the master chronometer is in the nucleus.   Dr. James Smith and others have made the important finding that the senescent phenotype is dominant over the immortal phenotype and that the low finite proliferative potential of old human diploid fibroblasts is dominant over the high finite proliferative potential of young fibroblasts.   In addition, hybrids of two different immortal cell lines sometimes yield hybrids with limited proliferative potential.   It seems probable that two separate steps under genetic control may determine mortality or immortality.   These findings may be intertwined with the two step initiation and promotion theory in carcinogenesis by which cell immortality may be conferred. Studies on the myc gene suggest that it has a role in conferring immortality on the cells in which it is expressed.

Dr. Vincent Cristofalo and his colleagues made the interesting observation of diminished tyrosine kinase activity of the pidermal growth factor receptor in cultured senescent human fibroblasts. Many oncogenes have been shown to code for proteins with tyrosine kinase activity. Dr. Robin Holliday's findings that cell senescence is associated with progressive loss of 5-methyl cytosine may fit into this equation since immortal cells are postulated to have acquired the ability for de novo methylase activity. Oncogene expression may be associated with this acquisition.

The powerful techniques of recombinant DNA technology are now being applied to cultured normal cells in an effort to understand the putative chronometer. Drs. Samuel Goldstein and Robert Shmookler-Reis and their colleagues have used the inter-alu DNA sequence to investigate DNA changes with age. This sequence, which is repeated about fifty times in the human genome, has no known function. These workers found significant amplification of these genes in senescent human fibroblasts and in lymphocytes from older human donors. These amplified genes are found in circular copies extrachromosomally.

Recombinant DNA technology may identify genes responsible for important age-related disease. These genetic markers may be heritable differences in DNA base sequences. Using restriction fragment length polymorphism that displays close genetic linkage to the gene for Huntington's Disease in two families, the chromosomal location of the gene has been found. Similar technologies may allow demonstration of the chromosomal location of putative genes involved, for example, in familial Alzheimer's Disease. Identification may lead in turn to isolation and cloning of the gene and characterization of the gene product.

THE GENOME AS THE BASIS FOR AGING

I would like to conclude my remarks by summarizing (1) why there is widespread belief that the cell genome is the major determinant of age changes and (2) the prevailing theories that are based on this supposition. No formal discussion of theories of aging has been given at this conference and I believe that those who are new to this field would benefit from a brief sketch of the better known hypotheses.

A variety of age-related biological phenomena appear to be orchestrated by events that occur in the genetic apparatus. Many

of these phenomena are so profound that, when taken together,they
provide the factual underpinning for several genetically based
theories of the cause of age-related changes in cell metabolism
and function. Some of these phemonena are:

1.   The life spans of animal species are remarkably constant
and species-specific. For example, a fruit-fly lives about
one month, a mouse about three years, and a human no more
than about 115 years.

2.   In humans, for example, the mean difference in longevity
between fraternal twins was found to be twice as great as
that in identical twins (Kallman and Jarvik, 1959). The
ancestors of centenarians and nonagenarians have significantly greater longevity when compared with a series of
ancestors of individuals not having great longevity (Pearl,
1934).

3.   In many animal species the female is more longevous than
the male, but this is by no means true for all animal species
(Comfort, 1979).

4.   In the past decade, it has become apparent that some
single gene changes result in accelerated aging in humans, as
in the case of Progeria and Werner's Syndrome. On the other
hand, Down's Syndrome is characterized by trisomy. In each
of these conditions several age-related phenomena appear to
be accelerated. Polygenic changes are also thought to
influence the rate and characteristics of age changes in
normal individuals.

5.   Genotoxic effects, that is the effect of mutagens (e.g.
radiation) on longevity, are thought to result from effects
on the cell genome.

6.   A direct correlation has been reported to occur between
the efficiency of certain kinds of DNA repair processes and
species longevity. Longer lived species have more efficient
DNA repair capabilities (Hart and Setlow, 1974).

7.   Heterosis, or hybrid vigor, occurs when members of two
different inbred strains are mated. They produce F_1 hybrids
having greater longevity than either parental strain. A
phenomenon known as the Lansing effect suggests that in some
animals, including humans, the progeny of older mothers have
a shorter life expectation and that this effect may extend
through several generations (Strehler, 1977; Comfort, 1979).

8.   In a study of inbred mouse strains, Goodrick (1975)
estimated that half of the variance associated with longevity
was due to genetic factors.

These observations have persuaded many biogerontologists to believe that the genetic apparatus plays the central role in causing age changes. It is important, however, to emphasize that contrary opinions prevail. Some of the non-genetic factors that may produce age changes include passive stochastic processes such as the accumulation of damage or errors in important macromolecules (Hayflick, 1984a).

GENOME-BASED THEORIES OF BIOLOGICAL AGING

The Somatic Mutation Theory

The somatic mutation theory of aging enjoyed its greatest popularity in the late 1950s and early 1960s as a derivative of burgeoning developments in the field of radiobiology. The central concept is that the accumulation of a sufficient level of mutations in somatic cells will produce physiological decrements characteristic of aging. If mutations are the fundamental cause of age changes, they must occur randomly in time and location (Maynard-Smith, 1962). Early champions of this idea were Szilard (1959) and Failla (1958, 1960). Failla postulated dominant mutations as causes of aging. However, Szilard argued that aging was due to genes ("targets") being "hit" or "struck," producing a mutational event which, unlike Failla, he regarded as recessive. Thus, a pair of homologous genes must be hit at a particular rate and in a sufficient number of cells in order to achieve phenotypic expression.

Maynard-Smith (1962) pointed out that if Szilard was correct, inbred animals, homologous at most gene loci, would display the maximum species life span since homozygous faults would be lethal and heterozygous faults would be few or nonexistent. Yet, in mice and _Drosophila_, inbreeding reduces life span. Furthermore, Szilard's hypothesis would predict that diploid organisms would live longer than their haploid counterparts who contain only one chromosome set. In the hymenopteran wasp, _Habrobracon_, haploid and diploid males have identical life spans. Haploid males are more sensitive to ionizing radiation than are diploid male wasps, yet irradiation shortens the life span of diploids far more than that of haploids. These observations are inconsistent with the mutation theory. Although reduced life spans do occur in irradiated animals, extended life spans have also been observed (Sacher, 1963; Lamb, 1964). Also, irradiated old animals should show accelerated age changes, as should animals treated with mutagenic agents, but they do not (Alexander, 1969).

Curtis and Miller (1971), the last major advocates of the

somatic mutation theory, based their conclusions on the frequency of abnormalities observed in the chromosomes of dividing cells in the livers of old mice. They found a higher frequency of abnormalities in the cells of a short-lived strain when compared with those found in long-lived strains of mice. They made similar observations in guinea pigs and dogs. Nevertheless, other comparisons between short- and long-lived strains and of hybrids between the two were inconsistent with these findings. Neutron irradiation of dividing cells yielded aberrations in up to 90 percent of the cells, yet life span was unaffected (Curtis and Miller, 1971).

In the past decade, few significant studies have been conducted on the role of somatic mutations in aging. In spite of the contrary evidence cited above, there is an expectation that the critical experiments should be redesigned using the technology of modern molecular biology.

The Error Theory

This theory, to some extent derivative of the somatic mutation theory, was first postulated by Medvedev (reviewed in Medvedev, 1972), elaborated by Orgel (1963), and received experimental support principally from Holliday and Tarrant (1972).

Repeated DNA nucleotide sequences in the genome of eukaryotic organisms may be (1) a reserve of information for evolutionary change, (2) a means of increasing functional expression, and (3) a reserve mechanism for protecting vital information from random errors that may occur in functioning DNA sequences. Medvedev proposed that the loss of unique, nonrepeated DNA sequences could produce age decrements and that selected reiterated sequences may be an evolved means for delaying the inevitability of the event by providing redundancy necessary for the maintenance of vital information. Cutler (1974) has provided equivocal experimental evidence for Medvedev's view.

Derivative of error accumulation in reiterated DNA sequences is the notion of Orgel (1963) in which he postulates the occurrence of inaccuracies in protein synthesis as the essential source of age-associated decrements in cell function. This hypothesis resulted in a flurry of experiments designed to learn whether an incorrect amino acid incorporated in a protein molecule could accelerate aging phenomena, or whether misspecified proteins accumulated in old cells. Errors in enzyme molecules that processed information-containing molecules were thought to be the most important potential sources of significant damage. A misspecified enzyme could produce a cascade of faulty molecules with presumably profound effects called an "error catastrophe." Holliday and Tarrant (1972) claimed to have obtained evidence for the error catastrophe theory, but many other studies have provided no evidence for its support. The idea is now in general disfavor, despite the fact that altered proteins are frequently found in the cells of old organisms.

A correlate of error accumulation as a cause of age changes is the effectiveness of those systems that repair genome damage. Hart and Setlow (1974) obtained evidence from the cultured cells of several different species that the efficiency of repair of ultraviolet damage to DNA was directly correlated to species' life span. Again, contrary evidence has also been reported, and the original finding currently is being reassessed.

The Program Theory of Aging

Adherents of this theory, unlike advocates of such stochastically based theories as error accumulation, believe that a purposeful sequence of events is written into the genome that leads to age changes, much as similar instructions written into the genetic message lead to the orderly expression of developmental sequences.

The conceptual simplicity of this idea is part of its attractiveness, but attempts to test it experimentally have met with little success. Our finding (Hayflick and Moorhead, 1961) that cultured normal human and animal cells have a finite ability to replicate and function has provided good evidence in support of the theory, but so does the fact that aging occurs naturally in intact animals. Programming assumes an orderly sequence of events with which few would disagree, but it does not provide mechanistic details. On the other hand, it has been effectively argued that although events occurring from conception to the full expression of adulthood may be programmed, subsequent events characterized as aging may not be purposely determined by the genome. That is, age changes may be produced by a kind of free-wheeling independent continuation of the inertia produced by previously determined developmental events. Therefore, function declines or terminates in a more or less random fashion like the eventual demise of a new automobile that is poorly repaired or maintained.

To complete the analogy, the manufacture of an automobile, like the growth of an individual animal, is predicated on the presence of accurate blueprints and their proper execution. What happens after the automobile is built or after the individual reaches sexual maturation is not governed by blueprints but occurs randomly and inevitably. Which system fails first and leads to the demise of the automobile or the individual is, therefore, a random process with, nevertheless, a narrowly expressed "mean time to failure." This would be characteristic of the specific brand of automobile or particular animal species. Regarded in these terms, aging in its extreme manifestations occurs only in humans or in protected species such as domestic or zoo animals. The survival of a species does not depend on its members surviving much beyond the age of sexual maturation. From the standpoint of evolution, there is no survival value for our species to have a life expectation much beyond the reproductive years.

In terms of modern physics, a genetic program should succumb to the second law of thermodynamics which states that a closed system tends to a state of equilibrium or of maximum entropy in which nothing more happens. That is, ordered systems tend to move to greater disorder. The initially well organized genetic program, by increasing entropy, thus becomes disordered, producing those changes recognized as aging. In this way our mortality may be decreed by the second law of thermodynamics. Although this may be a tenable hypothesis as it pertains to somatic cells or to individual members of a species, it seems to fly in the face of the enormous amount of evidence for biological evolution that superficially appears to be in conflict with the second law. Moreover, it seems to be in conflict with the apparent immortality of the germ plasm and certain immortal, abnormal, cancer cell populations.

Medawar (1957) has argued persuasively that the presence of deleterious genes in a species might be thwarted by a selection process that would postpone their manifestations, if it could not eliminate them. This strategy would result in the piling up of deleterious genes in the postreproductive period when their expression would do less harm. A variation on this theme is expressed by Williams (1957) who postulates that there are pleiotropic genes having both favorable and unfavorable actions. If the favorable gene expression is increased in fecundity, that gene might be selected even though it might express a deleterious action later in life. Deleterious age changes then would be the penalty paid by individuals for the expression of beneficial genes early in life. An accumulation of such late-acting genes in various organ systems would behave like late-programmed events and give rise to the entire constellation of age changes.

Sacher is critical of the program theory of aging for what he believes to be errors in logic (Sacher, 1968, 1982). He illustrates his point by comparing the life histories of annual plants and mammals. Annual plants are semelparous; that is, they are characterized by a single reproductive effort, completed at the end of the life span and frequently not until somatic cell death. The final step of the reproductive process, seed dispersal, depends on the death of the plant, and this requires that senescence be closely integrated with prior stages. The stages are known to be under the specific control of hormones and end with formation of specific hydrolytic enzymes. Sacher restricts programmed aging to cases such as this, where there is specific control of onset either by internal or external signals, presence of a specific enzyme mechanism, and finally, a functional role for senescence and/or death in a specific temporal relationship with other life processes. The rapid aging and death of the Pacific salmon after spawning is a good example of this event occurring in animals.

Mammals, on the other hand, are examples of iteroparous reproduction where reproductive success depends on producing a number of litters over an extended reproductive span. Sacher argues that this offers no functional role for senescence and death. On the contrary, he maintains that this would place a premium on the maintenance of physiological vigor and survival. Long life in mammals, therefore, is the result of selection for an extended period of assured physiological performance. A great whale that lives 30 times longer than a mouse has a million times more cells at risk for age changes. Nevertheless, a comparable whale cell is orders of magnitude more stable than a mouse cell. "It would be expected," says Sacher, "that the selective process acts on mechanisms for increasing the stability of the organism at all levels, from the molecular to the systemic." Sacher emphasizes the more evolutionary logical role of genetic systems that maintain life rather than suppositions that these systems might program age changes. Until it can be shown that evolution selects for greater longevity, at least in mammals, the study of life maintenance systems or "longevity assurance genes" may be more productive than the current emphasis on a search for the causes of age-associated physiological decrements (Sacher 1982, 1968).

The postulated longevity-assurance genes may be simply sets of genes that have evolved to express themselves at later times during the development of an animal in order to increase its survivability. These genes would not per se be directly involved with aging, but by their later expression would serve to delay age changes. Aging then would be a secondary manifestation of earlier occurring developmental events. For example, natural selection in a species may favor individuals capable of reaching sexual maturity at a later time in order to provide better opportunities for survival of progeny. A secondary effect of this, and not directly selected for, would be a concomitant postponement of age-dependent changes.

REFERENCES

Alexander, P., 1969, The relationship between aging and cancer: Somatic mutations or breakdown of host defence mechanisms, Bull. Schweiz. Akad. Med. Wiss., 24:258.

Bierman, E.L., 1978, The effect of donor age on the in vitro
    lifespan of cultured human arterial smooth-muscle cells, In
    Vitro, 14:951.

Comfort, A., 1979, The Biology of Senescence, Churchill Living-
    stone, London.

Curtis, J.H., and Miller, K., 1971, Chromosome aberrations in
    liver cells of guinea pigs, J. Gerontol., 26:292.

Cutler, R., 1974, Redundancy of information content in the genome
    of mammalian species as a protective mechanism determining
    aging rate, Mech. Ageing Dev., 2:381.

Failla, G., 1958, The aging process and carcinogenesis, Ann. NY
    Acad. Sci., 71:1124.

Failla, G., 1960, The aging process and somatic mutations, in:
    The Biology of Aging, page 170, B.L. Strehler, ed., American
    Institute of Biological Sciences, Washington.

Goldstein, S., Moerman, E.J., Soeldner, J.S., Gleason, R.E., and
    Barnett, D.M., 1978, Chronological and physiological age
    effect replicative lifespan of fibroblasts from diabetics,
    prediabetics, and normal donors, Science, 199:781.

Goodrick, C.L., 1975, Life-span and inheritance of longevity of
    inbred mice, J. Gerontol., 30:247.

Grunewald, J., Mey, J., Schonleben, W., Hauss, J., and Hauss,
    W.H., 1983, Cultivated human arterial smooth muscle cells:
    The effect of donor age, blood pressure, diabetes and smoking
    on in vitro growth, Path. Biol., 31:819.

Hart, R.W., and Setlow, R.B., 1974, Correlation between deoxy-
    ribonucleic acid excision repair and life-span in a number of
    mammalian species, Proc. Natl. Acad. Sci. USA, 71:2169.

Hayflick, L., 1965, The limited in vitro lifetime of human diploid
    cells strains, Exp. Cell Res., 37:614.

Hayflick, L., 1977, The cellular basis for biological aging, in:
    Handbook of the Biology of Aging, page 159, C. Finch, and L.
    Hayflick, eds., Van Nostrand Reinhold, New York.

Hayflick, L., 1979, Progress in cytogerontology: Special volume on
    research frontiers in biological ageing research, Mech.
    Ageing Dev.; 9:393.

Hayflick, L., 1980a, Cell aging, in: Annual Review of Gerontology and Geriatrics, page 26, C. Eisdorfer, ed., Springer, New York.

Hayflick, L., 1980b, The cell biology of human aging. Scientific American, 242 (1):58.

Hayflick, L., 1980c, Recent advances in the cell biology of aging, Mech. Ageing Dev., 14:59.

Hayflick, L. 1984a, Theories of biological aging, in: Principles of Geriatric Medicine, page 9, R. Andres, E.L. Bierman, and W. Hazzard, eds., McGraw Hill, New York.

Hayflick, L., 1984b, The coming of age of WI-38, in: Advances in Cell Culture, page 303, K. Maramorosch, ed., Vol 3, Academic Press, New York.

Hayflick, L., and Moorhead, P.S., 1961, The serial cultivation of human diploid cell strains, Exp. Cell Res., 25:585.

Holliday, R., and Tarrant, G.M., 1972, Altered enzymes in aging human fibroblasts, Nature, 238:26, London.

Houck, J.C., Sharma, V.K., and Hayflick, L., 1971, Functional failures of cultured human diploid fibroblasts after contin- ued population doublings, Proc. Soc. Exp. Biol. Med., 137: 331.

Kallman, E.J., and Jarvik, L.F., 1959, Individual differences in constitution and genetic background, in: Handbook of Aging in the Individual, page 216, J.E. Birren, ed., University of Chicago, Chicago.

Lamb, M.J., 1964, The effects of radiation on the longevity of the female Drosophila subobscura, J. Insect Physiol., 10:487.

LeGuilly, Y., Simon, M., Lenoir, P., and Bourel, M., 1973, Long-term culture of human adult liver cells: Morphological changes related to in vitro senescence and effect of donor's age on growth potential, Gerontologia, 19:303.

Martin, G.M., Sprague, C.A., and Epstein, C.J., 1970, Replicative lifespan of cultivated human cells: Effect of donor's age, tissue and genotype, Lab. Invest., 23:86.

Maynard-Smith, J., 1962, The causes of aging, Proc. Royal Soc. Lond. B., 157:115.

Medawar, P.B., 1957, The Uniqueness of the Individual, Methuen, London.

Medvedev, Zh.A., 1972, Repetition of molecular-genetic information as a possible factor in evolutionary changes of life span, Exp. Gerontol., 7:227.

Orgel, L.D., 1963, The maintenance of the accuracy of protein synthesis and its relevance to aging, Proc. Natl. Acad. Sci. USA, 49:517.

Pearl, R., and Pearl, R.deW., 1934, The Ancestry of the Long-Lived, Milford, London.

Rohme, D., 1981, Evidence for a relationship between longevity of mammalian species and life spans of normal fibroblasts in vitro and erythrocytes in vivo, Proc. Natl. Acad. Sci. USA, 78:5009.

Sacher, G.A., 1963, Effects of X-rays on the survival of Drosophila imagoes, Physiol. Zool., 36:295.

Sacher, G.A., 1968, Molecular versus systemic theories on the genesis of ageing, Exp. Gerontol., 3:265.

Sacher, G.A., 1982, Evolutionary theory in gerontology, Perspect. Biol. Med., 25(3):339.

Schneider, E.L., and Mitsui,Y., 1976, The relationship between in vitro cellular aging and in vivo human aging, Proc. Natl. Acad. Sci. USA, 73:3584.

Szilard, L., 1959, On the nature of the aging process, Proc. Natl. Acad. Sci. USA, 45:30.

Strehler, B.L., 1977, Time, Cells and Aging, Academic, New York.

Tassin, J., Malaise, E., and Courtois, Y., 1979, Human lens cells have an in vitro proliferative capacity inversely proportional to the donor age, Exp. Cell Res., 123:388.

Vracko, R., and McFarland, B.M., 1980, Lifespan of diabetic and non-diabetic fibroblasts in vitro, Exp. Cell. Res., 129:345.

Walford, R.L., Jawaid, S.Q., and Naeim, F., 1981, Evidence for in vitro senescence of T-lymphocytes cultured from normal human peripheral blood, Age, 4:67.

Williams, G.C., 1957, Pleiotrophy, natural selection, and the evolution of senescence, Evolution, 11:398.

FUTURE DIRECTIONS IN AGING RESEARCH

J. Edwin Seegmiller

Institute for Research on Aging
University of California San Diego
La Jolla, California 72079

During the past three days we have seen the latest results of laboratory investigations on a wide range of disciplines that have in common the expansion of our understanding of the aging process. It has been a most stimulating experience for all of us to see the development of the new technologies that are now being applied to this area of research that has largely been ignored in the past. This meeting has provided new evidence of valid approaches that can be used to dissect the biochemical, genetic and molecular basis of the phenomena associated with differences in the aging process.

In the course of our future planning I feel it is important that we separate the normal aging process from the pathology associated with advancing years. Most provocative is the work of Dr. Edward LaKatta at the Geriatric Center in Baltimore, reported by Dr. Schneider in his opening address, showing the maintenance of essentially normal heart function for much longer time than was previously reported if the individuals with heart pathology were removed from the series. It suggests we should take a second look at the "normal" changes of function of other organs with aging and the possible role of unrecognized pathology in the progressive decrement in function that has been identified in the past. The mere fact that a given change such as osteoarthritis is seen in by far the majority of individuals with advancing years does not automatically make it a "normal" part of the aging process, for we all have seen individuals who escape this type of pathology.

Until fairly recently most of the research devoted to aging was still devoted to the first stage of any science, that of description--in this case of phenomenon associated with the aging process. The work of Dr. Sohal on house flies shows a correlation between the metabolic rate and survival, while that of Dr. Flemming shows objective evidence of changes in the appearance of mitochondria with aging of Drosophila. The large number of well-characterized mutants of this species holds forth the possibility of gaining further insight into the nature of mitochondrial deterioration by taking advantage of these mutant strains for some possible additional clues as to the nature of the process. It also suggests the possibility of examining the mitochondria in Dr. Sohal's house flies by similar methods. Dr. Cutler's work on the possible role of oxygen radical scavenging systems as determinants of the maximum lifespan of various species is also very provocative. It will be important, of course, for us to keep in mind that all species may not have the same rate-limiting processes determining their lifespan; different scavenging systems may therefore have difference degrees of importance in other species because of the presence of varying rate-limiting processes. The remarkable effects of dehydroepiandrosterone reported by Dr. Schwartz in preventing a great many of the degenerative disorders associated with aging in certain genetically susceptible strains of rodents is most impressive, and suggests the posibility of a common shared mechanism for the development of the various degenerative diseases. The mechanisms responsible for this effect, when eventually found, could very well provide insight into important elements in development of this pathology as well as of the process.

The increase in 5'-nucleotidase in cultured human cells during senescence reported by Dr. Sun has a counterpart, to some extent, in vivo. The very low activities of this enzyme in peripheral blood lymphocytes at birth appears to be a marker of the immaturity of these cells. Concurrent with their maturation the activity of this enzyme rises markedly and remains elevated until about the fifth decade of life after which it shows a progressive decline with advancing age in both B and T cells (Boss et al., 1980).

The extension of lifespan and avoidance of degenerative diseases of older age in rodents by caloric restriction is a most fascinating phenomena brought up-to-date in Dr. Masoro's report. The possibility needs to be evaluated of its being mediated by the normal accumulation of deaminated or other post-translationally modified proteins with age as a result of decreased proteolysis reported by Dr. Gracy. An attractive hypothesis is that the increase in proteolytic enzyme activity that he notes with starvation may also occur with caloric restriction, and result in an increased destruction of accumulated proteins in the cells of the longer living rodents. It is obvious that posttranslational changes in proteins result from many different processes including oxidative attack, possibly from free radicals, glycosylation as well as spontaneous instability of certain amino acid groups within the proteins.

Along this line we need also in the future to take advantage of the natural experiments in the human populations that are within our midst. In particular, the substantial decrease in mortality from cardiovascular disease and malignancies seen among members of the Mormon church (Lyon et al., 1980) and among the Seventh Day Adventists should be examined in greater detail for identification of the specific dietary and lifestyle variations that protect them from these degenerative diseases of aging.

The observations of Dr. Robbins relating certain degenerative diseases of the central nervous system with abnormalities in DNA repair processes is a most fascinating area that deserves much more detailed investigation.

I am sure we all feel most heartened by the substantial progress that has been made in the very recent past and reported here at these meetings during these past three days. I am confident that each of us have been able to identify new areas in their own research that might well tie into observations of other investigators.

REFERENCES

Boss, G. R., Thompson, L. F., Spiegelberg, H. L., Pichler, W. J., and Seegmiller, J. E., 1980, Age dependency of lymphocyte ecto-5'-nucleotidase activity, J. Immunol., 125:679.

Lyon, J. L., Gardner, J. W., and West, D. W., 1980, Cancer risk and life-style; Cancer among Mormons from 1967-1975, in: Banbury Report 4. Cancer Incidence in Defined Populations, Cold Spring Harbor Lab., 3:28.

PARTICIPANTS

AKESSON, Bengt
Dept. of Psychiatry and
  Neurochemistry
St. Jorgen's Hospital
S-422 03 Hisings Backa
Sweden

ALOYO, Vincent J.
Center on Aging
U. of Kentucky Med. Center
311 Sanders Brown Bldg.
Lexington, KY 40536

BAN, Sadayuki
Biology Dept.
Brookhaven National Lab.
Upton, NY 11973

BERGTOLD, David S.
Dept. of Radiology
  and Radiation Biology
Colorado State U.
Fort Collins, CO 80523

BIRNBAUM, Jay
Consumers Prod. Res. Div.
American Cyanamid Co.
Wayne, NJ 07470

BLACKETT, Anthony D.
Molecular Neurobiology Lab.
Dept. of Opthalmic Optics
U. of Manchester
Institute of Science and
  Technology
Jackson's Mill-P.O. Box 88
Manchester M60 1QD, UK

BROWN, Sally
Dept. of Neurology
U. of Rochester
Box 673
601 Elmwood Ave.
Rochester, NY 14642

BROWN, W. Ted
Dept. of Human Genetics
N.Y. State Institute for
  Basic Research in
  Developmental Disabilities
1050 Forest Hill Road
Staten Island, NY 10314

CASTANEDA, Mario
Inst. de Investigaciones
  Biomedicas
Universidad Nacional
  Autonoma de Mexico
Apart. Postal 70228
04510 Mexico D.F. Mexico

CHOU, Ta-Ching
Dept. of Physiology and
  Biophysics
524 Burrill Hall
U. of Illinois
407 Goodwin Avenue
Urbana, IL 61801

CIOCA, Gheorghe
Estée Lauder, Inc.
125 Pinelawn Road
Melville, NY 11746

COHEN, Craig J.
Dept. of Medicine
Louisiana State U.
  Medical Center
1542 Tulane Avenue
New Orleans, LA 70112

COMFORT, Alex
The Windmill House
The Hill
Granbrook, Kent
TN17 3All, UK

465

COPPARD, Nick
 Dept. of Biostructural
  Chemistry
 Kenish Institute
 Lengelandsgade 140
 DK-8000 Aarhus C, Denmark
CRISTOFALO, Vincent J.
 The Wistar Institute
 3601 Spruce Street
 Philadelphia, PA 19104
CUTLER, Richard G.
 Key Medical Center
 Natl. Institute on Aging
 Baltimore, MD 21224

DEHAAN, Robert
 Dept. of Human Sciences
 Lincoln U.
 University, PA 19352
DELIHAS, Neva
 Biology Dept.
 Brookhaven National Lab.
 Upton, NY 11973
DELL'ORCO, Robert
 The Noble Foundation
 P.O. Box 2180
 2510 Highway 70 East
 Ardmore, OK 73402
DE PUGH, Robert
 Delta Research Lab.
 400 Admiral Boulevard
 Kansas City, MO 64106
DUNCAN, Michael
 Noble Foundation
 P.O. Box 2180
 2510 Highway 70 East
 Ardmore, OK 73402

FLEMING, James E.
 Linus Pauling Institute of
  Science and Medicine
 440 Page Mill Road
 Palo Alto, CA 94306
FLORES, Sonia C.
 Dept. of Biochemistry
 U. of South Alabama
 2170 MSB
 Mobile, AL 36688

FORD, John
 Actagen, Inc.
 4 Westchester Plaza
 Elmsford, NY 10523

GAMBLE, David A.
 Cornell Medical Center
 New York Hospital
 1300 York Avenue
 New York, NY 10022
GOLDSTEIN, Samuel
 Dept. of Medicine and
  Biochemistry
 U. of Arkansas for
  Medical Science
 Mail Slot 604
 4301 West Markham
 Little Rock, AR 72205
GOREVIC, Peter
 Dept. of Medicine and
  Pathology
 Health Sciences Center
 State U. of New York
 Stony Brook, NY 11794
GRACY, Robert W.
 Dept. of Biochemistry
 Texas College of
  Osteopathic Medicine
 Camp Bowie at Montgomery
 Fort Worth, TX 76107
GRAUERHOLZ, John
 Fusion Energy Foundation
 Fifth Floor
 304 West 58 Street
 New York, NY 10019
GRIST, Eleanor
 Biology Dept.
 Brookhaven National Lab.
 Upton, NY 11973
GURAL, Paul D.
 Estée Lauder, Inc.
 125 Pinelawn Road
 Melville, NY 11746

HART, Ronald W.
 National Center for
  Toxicological Research
 (HFT-1)
 Jefferson, AR 72079

HAYFLICK, Leonard
 Center for Gerontological
   Studies - 3357 GPA
 U. of Florida
 Gainesville, FL   32611
HIRSCH, Betsy
 Dept. of Genetics and Cell
   Biology
 Dight Institute
 U. of Minnesota
 Minneapolis, MN   55455
HOFFMANN-GABEL, Barbara
 Medical Dept.
 Brookhaven National Lab..
 Upton, NY   11973
HOLEHAN, Anne M.
 Wolfson Institute
 U. of Hull
 Hull, HU6 7RX, UK
HOLLIDAY, Robin
 National Institute for
   Medical Research
 The Ridgeway
 Mill Hill
 London NW7 1AA, UK
HUGHES, Donald H.
 Proctor and Gamble Co.
 Ivorydale Technical Center
 Cincinnati, OH   45217

ISHIKAWA, Takatoshi
 Dept. of Experimental
   Pathology
 Cancer Institute, 1-37-1
 Kami-Ikebukuro, Toshima-ku
 Tokyo 170, Japan

JENKINS, Stephen W.
 Southwest Michigan Health
   Care Association
 3140 S. Lakeshore Drive
 St. Joseph, MI   49085

KELLEY, Robert O.
 Dept. of Anatomy
 School of Medicine
 U. of New Mexico
 Albuquerque, NM   87131

KENT, Barbara
 Dept. of Geriatrics
 Mt. Sinai Medical Center
 One Gustave Levy Place
 New York, NY   10029
KIDSON, Chev
 Queensland Institute of
   Medical Research
 Bramston Terrace, Herston,
 Brisbane, Queensland, 4006
 Australia
KOSIK, Kenneth S.
 Mailman Research Center
 McLean Hospital
 Harvard Medical School
 Belmont, MA   02178

LIPMAN, Jack
 Dept. of Pathology
 Basic Health Sciences
 State U. of New York
 Stony Brook, NY   11794
LITTLE, Brian
 Dept. of Pathology
 University Hospital
 State U. of New York
 Stony Brook, NY   11794
LUKACOVIC, Michael F.
 Proctor and Gamble Co.
 11520 Reed Hartman Highway
 Cincinnati, OH   45241

MAKINODAN, Takashi
 Geriatric Research Educa-
   tion and Clinical Center
 VA Wadsworth Medical Center
 Wilshire and Sautelle Blvds.
 Los Angeles, CA   90073
MASORO, Edward
 Dept. of Physiology
 U. of Texas Health
   Science Center
 7703 Floyd Curl Drive
 San Antonio, TX   78284
McDOWELL, Kathi
 Biology Dept.
 Brooklyn College
 City U. of New York
 Brooklyn, NY   11210

MERRY, Brian J.
Wolfson Institute
U. of Hull
Hull HU6 7RX, UK
MILLIS, Albert
Biology Dept.
State U. of New York
Albany, NY 12222
MUKHERJEE, Asit B.
Dept. of Biological Sciences
Fordham U.
Bronx, NY 10458
MUNRO, Hamish N.
Human Nutrition Research
  Center on Aging
U.S. Dept. of Agriculture
711 Washington St.
Boston, MA 02111

NARYSHKIN, Sonya
The Wistar Institute
36th Street at Spruce
Philadelphia, PA 19104

PAVLOVA, Maria
Medical Dept.
Brookhaven National Lab.
Upton, NY 11973
PELLE, Edward
Estée Lauder, Inc.
125 Pinelawn Road
Melville, NY 11746
PELLICCIONE, Nicholas
Estée Lauder, Inc.
125 Pinelawn Road
Melville, NY 11746
PENNA, Fred
Estée Lauder, Inc.
125 Pinelawn Road
Melville, NY 11746
PERESS, Nancy
Dept. of Pathology
University Hospital
State U. of New York
Stony Brook, NY 11794

ROBBINS, Jay H.
National Cancer Institute
Natl. Institutes of Health
Building 10, Rm. 12N258
Bethesda, MD 20205
RODRIGUEZ, Lewis V.
Dept. of Pathology
M.D. Anderson Hospital and
  Tumor Institute
Box 85, 6723 Bertner Avenue
Houston, TX 77030
ROSENHEIMER, Julie L.
Dept. of Physiology
U. of Wisconsin
1300 University Avenue
Madison, WI 53706
ROTHCHILD, Henry
Dept. of Medicine
Louisiana State U. Medical Center
1542 Tulane Avenue
New Orleans, LA 70112
ROTHSTEIN, Morton
Dept. of Biological Sciences
State U. of New York
Buffalo, NY 14260
RUDENKO, Larisa
Biology Dept.
Brookhaven National Lab.
Upton, NY 11973
RYBICKA, Krystyna
Dept. of Applied Sciences
Brookhaven National Lab.
Upton, NY 11973

SACCOMANNO, Colette F.
Dept. of Biological Sciences
Fordham U.
Bronx, NY 10458
SALADINO, Charles F.
Dept. of Medicine
Nassau County Medical Center
East Meadow, NY 11554
SALK, Darrell
Dept. of Pathology, SM-30
U. of Washington
Seattle, WA 98195
SALLIN, Craig
Vita Formularies
710 SE 17th St.
Fort Lauderdale, FL 33316

SCHLITZ, John
 Consumers Prod. Res. Div.
 American Cyanamid Co.
 Wayne, NJ 07470
SCHNEIDER, Edward L.
 Natl. Institute on Aging
 Natl. Institutes of Health
 Building 31
 9000 Rockville Pike
 Bethesda, MD 20205
SCHWARTZ, Arthur G.
 Dept. of Microbiology
 Fels Research Institute
 Temple U. School of
   Medicine
 Philadelphia, PA 19140
SEEGMILLER, J. Edwin
 Dept. of Medicine
 M-0131
 U. of California
   at San Diego
 La Jolla, CA 92093
SETLOW, Richard B.
 Biology Dept.
 Brookhaven National Lab.
 Upton, NY 11973
SINGH, Narendra P.
 Ohio State University
 Home: P.O. Box 1560
 Medical Lake, WA 99022
SMITH, James R.
 Dept. of Virology and
   Epidemiology
 Baylor University
 College of Medicine
 Houston, TX 77030
SOHAL, Raj S.
 Dept. of Biology
 Southern Methodist U.
 Dallas, TX 75275
SOKOLOFF, Leon
 Basic Health Sciences
 State U. of New York
 Stony Brook, NY 11794
STEPHENS, Ralph E.
 Medical Complex
 M368
 Starling Loving Hall
 Ohio State U.
 Columbus, OH 43210-1240

STOUT, Daniel L.
 U. of Texas System
   Cancer Center
 M.D. Anderson Hospital
 6723 Bertner Avenue
 Houston, TX 77030
STREHLER, Bernard
 Dept. of Molecular Biology
 U. of Southern California
 Los Angeles, CA 90089
SUN, Alexander S.
 Dept. of Neoplastic Diseases
 Mount Sinai Medical Center
 One Gustave Levy Place
 New York, NY 10029
SUTHERLAND, Betsy M.
 Biology Dept.
 Brookhaven National Lab.
 Upton, NY 11973

THOMAS, Lewis
 Dept. of Pathology
 Basic Health Sciences
 State U. of New York
 Stony Brook, NY 11794
TICE, Raymond R.
 Medical Dept.
 Brookhaven National Lab.
 Upton, NY 11973
TOTTER, John R.
 Institute for Energy Analysis
 Oak Ridge Associated
   Universities
 P.O. Box 117
 Oak Ridge, TN 37831-0117
TURTURRO, Angelo
 National Center for
   Toxicological Research
 (HFT-1)
 Jefferson, AR 72079

UITTERLINDEN, Andre G.
 Institute for Experimental
   Gerontology
 TNO, P.O. Box 5815
 Rijswijk 2280 HV
 The Netherlands

UNGER, Phyllis
  Estee Lauder, Inc.
  125 Pinelawn Road
  Melville, NY 11746

WANG, Ju-Jun
  Biology Dept.
  Brookhaven National Lab.
  Upton, NY 11973
WARNER, Huber R.
  Natl. Institute on Aging
  Natl. Institutes of Health
  Building 31
  Room 5C19
  Bethesda, MD 20205
WILLIAMS, Jerry R.
  Radiobiology Lab.
  Johns Hopkins Oncology
    Center
  600 N. Wolfe Street
  Baltimore, MD 21205
WITTEN, Matthew
  Mathematics Dept.
  Illinois Institute of
    Technology
  Chicago, IL 60616

WOODHEAD, Avril D.
  Biology Dept.
  Brookhaven National Lab.
  Upton, NY 11973

YANNUZZI, Rose M.
  Clinical Dept.
  Avon Products, Inc.
  Division Street
  Suffern, NY 10901
YUNIS, Edmond J.
  Division of Immunogenetics
  Dana-Farber Cancer Institute
  44 Binney Street
  Boston, MA 02115

ZEBROWER, Michael
  N. Y. State Institute for
    Basic Research in
    Developmental Disabilities
  1050 Forest Hill Road
  Staten Island, NY 10314